VIRGIL
AENEID I-VI

VIRGIL

AENEID
BOOKS I-VI

Edited with Introduction
and Notes by
R. DERYCK WILLIAMS

Bristol Classical Press

Cover illustration: Mercury warns Aeneas to leave Carthage,
engraving by P. Fourdrinier from *The Works of Virgil*
by John Dryden (1748).

First published by Macmillan Education Ltd in 1972

This edition published in 1996 by
Bristol Classical Press
an imprint of
Gerald Duckworth & Co. Ltd
The Old Piano Factory
48 Hoxton Square, London N1 6PB

A catalogue record for this book is available
from the British Library

ISBN 1-85399-496-0

Printed in Great Britain by
Booksprint, Bristol

Contents

Contents

Preface

No commentary on the whole *Aeneid* (except Mackail's highly selective commentary, 1930) has appeared in English since T. E. Page's exemplary edition of 1894–1900. Page was one of the most perceptive commentators Virgil has ever had, a man almost always in tune with the poet (except for his Victorian views on *Aeneid* 4), and familiar with him not through card-indexes but through constant reading of Latin literature. In seventy years our approaches to poetry have changed and our knowledge of the ancient world has been enlarged in many ways, and the times call for a new commentary in a more modern idiom.

The present edition is intended to be suitable for the upper forms of schools and for universities, and I hope that it will also be useful for more advanced scholars. It is designed on a scale which requires brevity and immediate relevance to the text; the fuller type of exposition to be found in the Clarendon Press editions of individual books is therefore precluded, but I have always tried to be concise rather than omissive. I have not hesitated to explain relatively simple questions of diction, metre, and construction, but I have aimed above all to interpret the poetic methods and intentions of the *Aeneid*, and to explain not only what Virgil says but how he says it and why he says it in the particular way which he chooses. I have quite frequently quoted imitations and similarities of diction from English poets, especially from Spenser and Milton, because this can illuminate the literary impact of the Virgilian passage.

I have established a new text, and in the Introduction I

have listed its points of difference from Sir Roger Mynors's recent Oxford Text (1969), and from its predecessor (Hirtzel, 1900). I have discussed all such instances, and others where there is any significant doubt about the text, in the note on the passage in question. I have not thought it necessary to include an *apparatus criticus*, as the salient features of the evidence which have led me to adopt a particular reading are outlined in the notes, and fuller details are easily available for those who require them in the apparatus of Mynors or Hirtzel (or Sabbadini or Goelzer and Durand — see Bibliography).

I have refrained from overloading the commentary with the names of scholars who have helped me towards my interpretations, but I am of course enormously indebted, directly or indirectly, to an almost countless number of Virgilian commentators and critics, of whom I mention here Servius, Heyne, Conington, Henry, Page, Lejay, Mackail, Conway, Austin. I owe a very special debt to T. R. Glover, who taught me in my undergraduate years to begin to appreciate the poetry of Virgil.

I am most grateful for help in the preparation of my commentary to Mr. P. T. Eden, Professor E. Laughton, Mr. A. G. Lee, Mr. F. Robertson, Professor W. J. N. Rudd; I am particularly indebted to Mr. E. L. Harrison, who has read and improved the first draft of the whole of the work. Finally I gratefully acknowledge the kind permission of the Delegates of the Clarendon Press for me to use in an abridged form the material of my commentaries on *Aeneid* 5 and *Aeneid* 3, published by the Clarendon Press in 1960 and 1962 respectively.

Reading, February 1971

R. D. WILLIAMS

Introduction

VIRGIL's *Aeneid* has been for two thousand years the most widely read and studied and imitated[1] of all the poetry of antiquity. In Roman times Virgil was universally regarded as the greatest Roman poet, who portrayed the Roman character and claims to world-empire in language refined to the ultimate of perfection. During the Middle Ages he was admired for the same reasons and also as a precursor of Christianity (e.g. in Dante), and a prophet of magical powers. In the Renaissance he was a model for Spenser and Milton, and during this period and later was venerated for his ethical teaching and as the classical exemplar of perfect artistic form. He was beloved by the nineteenth century for his pathos and sympathy, as the poet of the 'tears in things'. In the twentieth we respond especially to his exploration of contrasting attitudes and ideals, his juxtaposition of public and private aspiration, of divine and human causation in men's affairs — and of course, as every reader with enough Latin always has responded, to his mastery of diction and word-music, the 'sweetness of the sound' of his hexameters.

[1] For Virgil's influence see especially D. Comparetti, *Vergil in the Middle Ages*, trans. Benecke, 1895; D. P. Harding, *The Club of Hercules*, Urbana, 1962 (about Virgil and Milton); R. D. Williams, *Changing Attitudes to Virgil* (*Dryden to Tennyson*) in *Virgil* (*Studies in Latin Literature and its influence*), ed. D. R. Dudley, London, 1969, pp. 119–38 (with bibliography given there).

1 *LIFE AND WORKS OF VIRGIL*[1]

PUBLIUS VERGILIUS[2] Maro was born on October 15th 70 B.C., of peasant stock, at a village called Andes near Mantua, in Northern Italy in the area of the River Po. Here he spent his childhood on his father's farm, living a countryman's life and learning to love the beauties of the north Italian landscape. He was educated at Cremona, Milan and then at Rome; we know that for a time he studied with the Epicurean Siro. During his youth he had met some of the men who were destined to play prominent parts in public life, and through his poetry he met more (Pollio, Gallus, Varus, Octavian himself); he became an important member of the literary court circle under Maecenas, and though he himself took no part in military or political life, he was on close terms with those who did, and was thus in constant touch with national problems and aspirations.

His earliest poems[3] were the *Eclogues*, a collection of ten

---

[1] The main ancient sources (apart from the poems themselves) are to be found in the lives by Servius and by Aelius Donatus (the latter sometimes attributed to Suetonius); these are published in the *O.C.T. Vitae Vergilianae Antiquae* (ed. C. Hardie, 1954). See also Mackail's *Aeneid*, Intro. pp. xxiiif., W. F. Jackson Knight, *Roman Vergil*[2] chap. ii, and the introduction to E. de Saint-Denis' Budé *Eclogues* (1942).

[2] Strictly his name in English should be spelled Vergil, but the spelling Virgil has been traditional for so long that it seems inappropriate to abandon it.

[3] There exist a number of minor poems attributed to Virgil, collected under the title of the *Appendix Vergiliana*. Very few of these are likely to be genuine works of Virgil.

pastoral poems written during the period 42–37 B.C., and
published in 37 B.C. From the first and ninth of these it
seems that he was involved in the confiscation of property
in the Mantua area during the resettlement of the veterans
of the civil wars; at all events he did not return to live in the
north, but spent the rest of his life in Campania, at Nola or
Naples. Here from 37–30 B.C. he composed the *Georgics*, a
poetic account (dedicated to Maecenas) of Italian farming
which bears full witness to his personal knowledge of the
countryside, its crops, its animals, its farmers, and of his
deep love for rural Italy, as well as of his mastery of the
Latin hexameter.

During all this time Virgil had been preparing[1] himself
to undertake an epic poem, the peak of literary aspiration,
and in 30 B.C. he began to compose the *Aeneid*, a poem to
express Rome's national greatness and destiny by means of
the story of her legendary origins. By 19 B.C. the *Aeneid* was
virtually complete,[2] but Virgil decided to give it a further
three years' revision, and set out on a voyage to Greece to
give himself local colour for the parts he meant to modify.
Early in his travels he fell ill of a fever, and was forced to
return to Italy; he died at Brundisium within a few days of
landing. He left instructions that the *Aeneid* should be burnt,
but Augustus countermanded them and had the poem
published posthumously.

[1] See *Ecl.* 6.3–5, *Geo.* 3.16f.; Servius tells us of a project to
write on the Alban kings, and Donatus that Virgil began a Roman
theme but finding his material uncongenial resumed pastoral
poetry.

[2] It has some fifty incomplete lines and some stop-gap passages,
and clearly was undergoing continuous revision and rewriting,
but it is in no real sense unfinished.

2 VIRGIL AND AUGUSTUS

WHEN Virgil was born, Cisalpine Gaul (the name of the area of northern Italy around the river Po) was not yet part of Roman Italy. Parts of the province did not gain Roman citizenship until 49 B.C., and it was not finally incorporated into Italy until 42 B.C. Catullus too was born in this area, and it is possible that the deeply-felt and 'romantic' sensitivity which the two poets have in common is partly due to their environment. During Virgil's early manhood Italy was ravaged by the civil wars between Caesar and Pompey, and subsequently by those between Antony and Octavian on the one side and Brutus and Cassius on the other; finally there was the conflict between Antony and Octavian (the future emperor Augustus).[1] When Augustus finally defeated Antony and Cleopatra at the battle of Actium in 31 B.C., Virgil and his contemporaries had indeed experienced so much of the suffering involved in civil war that their intense longing for peace and stability is easily understood.[2] This was what it seemed that Augustus could offer;[3] with the restoration of morality and religion[4] the new Golden Age of the *pax Romana* could be inaugurated. In the public sector optimism prevailed and hopes were high; Virgil's personal friends included many who had a large part to play in directing events — what wonder that he was

[1] For a vivid account of this period see R. Syme, *The Roman Revolution*, Oxford, 1939.

[2] Cf. *Ecl.* 4, *Geo.* 1.498f., Hor. *Epod.* 7 and 16.

[3] Cf. Prop. 4.6.37 *mundi servator*.

[4] See Livy 3.20.5, Hor. *Odes* 3.6.1 f. for the disaster brought by neglecting religion.

inspired to portray the hopes of peace and concord at last after seemingly endless discord? When we are told, as we often have been since antiquity in one form of phraseology or another, that Augustus 'imposed' upon Virgil the composition of his epic, we may reply that this is true to approximately the same extent as that Virgil imposed upon Augustus the political, social and religious reforms which he inaugurated. The truth is that there were very many people at this time, including Virgil and Augustus, who felt that only by a return to the religion and patriotic virtues of the past could Rome recapture her true identity. The emperor embodied these ideas in political and administrative procedures, and the poet embodied them in the *Aeneid*.

3 THE LEGEND OF AENEAS

IT IS POSSIBLE to isolate a number of reasons for Virgil's choice of the Aeneas legend as his subject for an epic poem. It satisfied his first requirement, which was that the theme should be national (in a way that Valerius Flaccus' *Argonautica* or Statius' *Thebaid* could not be), and yet it avoided the inflexibility of a historical subject (like Lucan's *Pharsalia* or Silius' *Punica*) or annalistic treatment (like Ennius' *Annales*). By using the legendary story of the very first settlement in Italy which led ultimately to the foundation of Rome, Virgil could constantly relate distant events to his own time, partly by adumbration of Roman *mores* in the character of Aeneas, and of Roman customs and festivals in describing their origins (the method of aetiology), and partly by prophecies, visions and imaginary pictures of future events (as on Aeneas' shield). In particular he could glorify the origins of Rome by relating them to an antique past, and especially magnify the Julian *gens* of Augustus. At the same time his subject was contemporary with the *Iliad* and the *Odyssey*, and could contain elements from the fabulous and distant world of the *Odyssey* (as in Book 3), as well as specific retelling of the Homeric stories (as of *Odyssey* 5–8 in *Aeneid* 1 and *Iliad* 22 in *Aeneid* 12).

The legend itself[1] was of great antiquity in Virgil's time, but it was also very flexible and varied (like our own King Arthur legend before Malory). Strong traces of a Trojan foundation in the west are found from the sixth century onwards, and by the third century the story of the Trojan foundation of Rome was strongly established, for example in Timaeus, Lycophron and Naevius. A comparison with the beginning of Livy 1 and with the first book of Dionysius of Halicarnassus shows the very large extent to which Virgil could vary the legend to achieve his own poetic purposes — the story of Aeneas and Dido for example (though probably already in Naevius' epic poem) played no part comparable with that which Virgil has given it; the second visit to Sicily (and the consequent funeral celebrations for Anchises) was Virgil's own; and the arrangement of the relationship between Latinus, Turnus, Mezentius, Evander was very different in other versions than Virgil's. The legend then was important, well-known, national, but of such a kind that Virgil could re-arrange its episodes and universalise it in his own special poetic way.

[1] See my Oxford edition of *Aeneid* 3, pp. 7 f.

4 *SOURCES OF THE* AENEID

WE HAVE seen that a primary source for the composition of the *Aeneid* was Virgil's enthusiasm for Rome and her future destiny; an equally important source was the literature of the past, especially the spell which the poems of Homer[1] had cast upon Virgil. Here was a Greek panorama of the human experience which Virgil could try to rival for the Romans; here was a framework into which he could set his own thoughts. The *Iliad* and the *Odyssey* offered a method of presenting heroic behaviour which Virgil could adapt to a more complex society. He could use the structure, the episodes, the divine machinery, the similes, the very phraseology, in order to create something quite new in ethos and tone, something that would be as relevant to the Roman world as Homer was to the Greeks. By taking the Aeneas legend as the subject for his national poem he could not only adumbrate Roman values and ways of life through the story of the first founder of the Roman people, but he could also keep the closest possible link with Homer's world; for Aeneas was a contemporary of Achilles and Odysseus, a member of the heroic age who has to step out into a new civilisation, and from being the last Trojan become the first Roman.

Homer was by far the most important literary influence on Virgil, but there were others of great importance. The tragedies of fifth-century Athens deeply influenced

[1] See Brooks Otis, *Virgil* (passim); W. S. Anderson, *T.A.Ph.A.*, 1957, pp. 17f.; R. D. Williams, *Phoenix*, 1963, pp. 266f. The parallel passages have been tabulated in full by G. N. Knauer, *Die Aeneis und Homer*, Göttingen 1964.

Virgil's account of the fall of Troy, and especially of the fate of Dido and of Turnus. Apollonius of Rhodes had shown how a love-motif, sensitively and intensely presented as in lyric or elegy, could be incorporated into epic, and Virgil's fourth *Aeneid* owes (for all its differences) a good deal to him. Of the Romans Ennius had adapted the Greek hexameter to the Latin language and portrayed the character of early Rome in many a memorable passage, and Virgil frequently echoes his phrases. Lucretius had shown how the hexameter could be used majestically and with vivid imagery. Catullus in his sixty-fourth poem used a delicate and sensitive rhythm to convey the pathos of desertion, and is recalled often in the fourth *Aeneid*, and elsewhere in passages of special tenderness. Virgil is unique in his ability to appreciate and recreate moods of contrasting and indeed contradictory kinds: Ennius and Catullus were poles apart, yet Virgil could respond to what each was seeking to portray. The *Aeneid* is a poem founded firmly on the real life of Augustan Rome, yet it seeks enlightenment for its deepest problems from literature of every kind. It is indeed a brilliant personal synthesis of the human situation as it had been seen through many different eyes.

5 *SYNOPSIS OF THE* AENEID

THE *Aeneid* tells the story of how Aeneas escaped from Troy when it was destroyed by the Greeks, and under a divine mission sailed west to found a new city which Fate had decreed should rule the world.

Book I. The poem begins as the Trojans, after seven years of wanderings, are leaving Sicily for Italy, the place of their promised city. But Juno arouses a storm and they are driven off course to Carthage. Here they are hospitably welcomed by the queen Dido. Through the scheming of Venus Dido falls in love with Aeneas and at a banquet asks to hear the story of his wanderings.

Books 2 and 3. These books are a flash-back in which Aeneas tells to Dido the story of his fortunes prior to the action of Book 1. The second book is intense and tragic, concerned with the events of one single night, the night of Troy's destruction. The third book is slow-moving, conveying the weary endurance of years of voyaging to reach the 'ever-receding shores' of Italy.

Book 4. The story of the love of Dido and Aeneas is continued. Jupiter sends Mercury to order Aeneas to leave Carthage in order to fulfil his divine mission to found Rome, and he immediately realises that he must sacrifice his personal love for Dido to his national and religious duty. He attempts to explain to Dido why he has to leave her, but she accepts no explanation and, as the Trojans depart, in frenzy and despair she kills herself.

Book 5. The Trojans return to Sicily and celebrate funeral games for Aeneas' father Anchises who had died there a year earlier. Juno causes the Trojan women to set fire to the ships, but the fire is quenched by Jupiter. On the last stage of the journey the helmsman Palinurus is swept overboard by the god Sleep.

Book 6. The Trojans reach Italy at Cumae, and Aeneas descends with the Sibyl to the underworld in order to consult the ghost of his father Anchises. The future heroes of

Roman history pass in a pageant before him, and he returns to the upper world strengthened in resolution.

Book 7. The Trojans reach the Tiber, and are hospitably welcomed by King Latinus, who recognises that Aeneas is the stranger referred to in an oracle as the destined husband of his daughter Lavinia. She is already betrothed to Turnus the Rutulian, and Juno again intervenes to ensure that Turnus will fight the Trojans. War breaks out, and the book ends with a catalogue of the Italian forces assisting Turnus.

Book 8. Aeneas visits Evander, an Arcadian living at Pallanteum on the site of Rome, to seek help. Evander sends his son Pallas at the head of a contingent of Arcadians. Venus has a new shield made for her son Aeneas, and the book ends with a description of the pictures from Roman history depicted on the shield — a reminder before the full-scale outbreak of hostilities of why Aeneas has to fight this war against Turnus, and what depends on it.

Book 9. In the absence of Aeneas Turnus the Rutulian achieves great deeds. The sally from the Trojan camp by Nisus and Euryalus ends in their death, and Turnus breaks into the Trojan camp, but in his pride and self-confidence fails to open the gates for his forces to join him, and escapes by jumping into the Tiber.

Book 10. Aeneas returns with Pallas and the fighting continues. Turnus seeks out Pallas and kills him, arrogantly boasting over him and stripping off his sword-belt. Aeneas in violent anger and guilt rages over the battlefield, and kills many of his opponents, including Lausus, young son of Mezentius, and Mezentius himself.

Book 11. The funeral for Pallas is described; a truce is made for burial of the dead, but shortly the fighting is resumed, and the heroic deeds and death of the Italian warrior-maiden Camilla are described.

Book 12. A single combat is arranged between Turnus and Aeneas; but the truce is broken and Aeneas is wounded. The scene shifts to Olympus where the discord is settled on the divine plane when Juno accepts defeat on condition that the Italians shall be the dominant partners in the Trojan–Italian stock from which the Romans will be born. Aeneas pursues Turnus as Achilles had pursued Hector, and wounds him. Turnus begs for mercy, but Aeneas, seeing the sword-belt of Pallas on Turnus' shoulder, kills him in vengeance.

The subsequent events, between the death of Turnus at the end of the *Aeneid* (twelfth century B.C.) and the foundation of Rome itself (eighth century B.C.), are foretold in Jupiter's prophecy (*Aen.* 1.266 f.). Aeneas founds Lavinium; after three years his son Ascanius succeeds him and rules for thirty years in Lavinium before transferring the settlement to Alba Longa. Here the Alban kings (*Aen.* 6.760 f.) rule for 300 years until Romulus, grandson of Numitor, founds Rome (traditional date 753 B.C.).

6 STRUCTURE AND THEMES[1]

THE STRUCTURE of the *Aeneid* is elaborately organised, as is essential for an epic poem (in the words of Dr. Johnson

[1] See the introductory note to the commentary on each book for a brief literary analysis of the individual books.

'whoever purposes, as it is expressed in Milton, "to build the lofty rhyme" must first acquaint himself with the law of poetic architecture, and take care that his edifice be solid as well as beautiful'). The *Aeneid* may be viewed as two halves, an Odyssean and an Iliadic half; equally it may be viewed as three thirds, the tragedy of Dido, the Roman centre, the tragedy of Turnus. Individual books act as blocks to give symmetry or contrast: thus the third and fifth books are relatively calm and unemotional, serving to vary the intensity of the second, fourth, and sixth books. Again, there are balances between the two halves — the seventh book reiterates the hostility of Juno which motivates the action of the first book; the eighth book gives the first glimpse of Rome as the second book had given the last glimpse of Troy; the tenth book has in the death of Pallas something of the intense feeling of tragedy which colours the whole fourth book. The death of Turnus at the end of Book 12 recalls the sense of bewilderment caused by the prophecy of Marcellus' death at the end of Book 6. This description of structural organisation could be prolonged, but we must always remind ourselves that in a poem the structure is a servant of the themes.

The themes of the *Aeneid* are perhaps best considered as the exploration of various tensions. Here I shall present three.[1] Firstly there is a powerful tension between the primary subject of the poem, Rome's greatness, and the pathos of human suffering which exists in spite of, or even because of, Rome's greatness. The element of pathos is so obvious to all readers of Virgil, and has been so strongly stressed in the last hundred years of Virgilian criticism, that

[1] For a fuller account see my article in *Antichthon*, 1967, pp. 29f.

it is necessary to emphasise the other polarity, the optimistic note of Rome's greatness. The poem is first and foremost about Rome's mission, about the restoration of the Golden Age which can be achieved under Augustus. This was what the ancient critics thought the poem was about, and so did the English eighteenth century,[1] and they were not wrong. Consider the proud certainty of Jupiter's prophecy to Venus in Book 1 (278–9, 291): 'To these I set no bounds in space or time — I have given them rule without end' . . . 'Then shall the rough generations be softened into peace. . .'. Or the pageant of Roman heroes in Book 6, ending with Anchises' claim (851–3) that the Romans will rule the peoples with their government, give them peace and civilisation, spare the conquered and suppress the arrogant. Consider the description of Aeneas' shield in Book 8 (626f.), where the concepts of military success leading to a settled and religious way of life are powerfully conveyed; or the final promise of Jupiter to Juno in Book 12 (834f.) that the Romans, inheriting the qualities of the Italians, will surpass all others in *pietas* (devotion to the gods and service to men). There should not be, indeed cannot be, any doubt that Virgil's public voice was sincerely optimistic.

But side by side with his public voice is the private voice, expressing deep concern for the lonely individual who does not fit into these cosmic schemes. The fulfilment of the Roman mission requires the sacrifice of Dido and the

---

[1] For Servius the poem's intention was 'to imitate Homer and praise Augustus through his ancestors'. Dryden says 'he concluded it to be in the interest of his country to be so governed; to infuse an aweful respect into the people towards such a prince; by that respect to confirm their obedience to him, and by that obedience to make them happy. This was the moral of his divine poem.'

destruction of Turnus and countless other warriors; it seems
to require in Aeneas himself a rejection of love (for Dido)
and mercy (for Turnus). It involves the opposition of Juno
and all the suffering which she can cause — 'why do the
heavenly powers feel such anger?' (*Aen.* 1.11). We may call
this private voice a Catullan voice, set in tension with the
strong vigorous attitude of an Ennius or a Livy. The conflict
involves Virgil in a question which permits of no clear
answer, and it could be (though this is pure conjecture) that
his failure to find an answer, his failure to justify Rome on
all counts, led to his dying wish that the poem should be
burned. In two ways he approximates to an answer: the
first is that 'it was so great a task to found the Roman race'
(*Aen.* 1.33), and only through great suffering can greatness
be achieved; and the second is that (as we see in Book 6)
in some way imperfectly understood, indeed only faintly
glimpsed, the life to come may set aright and compensate
the seemingly senseless suffering of this world. But when all
is said Virgil has no real answer. It is a measure of his
greatness as a poet that he has posed and explored the
question in so many of its aspects, always honestly and without pretence or specious simplification.

The second tension is that between the Homeric world to
which Aeneas belongs and the Roman world which he has
to inaugurate. The poem operates on a double time-scale:
Aeneas belongs to the heroic age, yet he also has to be a
proto-Augustan. Virgil's problem is to depict a new kind
of hero, a hero for an age no longer 'heroic'. Patently the
qualities of Achilles will not exactly fit the first founder of
Rome; some no doubt will (bravery, resolution and so on),
but others not (like impetuosity, proud self-confidence,
concern for self). Aeneas has to find out which of his heroic

qualities to preserve and which to jettison, and it is because he is trying to find out that he does not 'cut a figure' as Achilles does. There is something splendid and larger than life about the man who, like Achilles, always knows what is expected and required of him and acts accordingly; there is something much more human in the man who ponders, worries, negotiates — but such a man does not perhaps command our envy or our wonder in the same way. This is one reason why the character of Aeneas has been frequently criticised[1] (i.e. because he is insufficiently 'heroic'), and why Turnus (an entirely 'heroic' character) has seemed to many more convincing. And there is a further aspect of this criticism: Aeneas is by no means entirely successful in realising this new concept of heroism. Basically this is a social type of heroism, concerned with the group rather than the individual (how much we admire Odysseus, man of many resources, for getting safely back to Ithaca — but he did not succeed in bringing any of his comrades safely back with him). It is based on *pietas*, an attitude of responsibility towards gods and men, an attitude which may involve the subjugation of individual passions (like the desire for glorious death at Troy, or the love of Dido) to the demands of duty. In the outcome Aeneas is not totally able or even totally willing to achieve this degree of self-denial; he forgets his mission in order to stay with Dido until Jupiter intervenes, and he is sometimes overcome by elements of irrational passion (*furor*) within himself or as manifested by others. On the battlefield he tries for the most part to behave humanely, and there is a real contrast between him (as he

[1] Another reason, discussed later in this section, is that his relationship with the gods makes him seem to some to be lacking in free-will.

fights only because war is forced upon him) and Turnus, the warrior of heroic type (who fights because he enjoys it and is good at it). But on three occasions at least Aeneas becomes exactly like Turnus — after the death of Pallas (10.510f.), after he has himself been wounded (12.441f.), and at the very end of the poem. Here, when Turnus begs for mercy, we expect Aeneas to grant it; but he sees the belt of Pallas on Turnus' shoulder and in a fit of fury and a lust for vengeance he kills him. If we remember the circumstances of the death of Pallas (10.441f.), we easily understand why Aeneas feels himself justified — but the fact remains that at the last moment Aeneas is no different from the old heroic type he is supposed to be superseding. Nothing could have been easier for Virgil than to avoid this dilemma — instead of being wounded in battle Turnus could have been killed — but he wanted his readers to be involved in the dilemma. How righteous is righteous anger? Are we glad that Aeneas yields to it?

The third tension is between the world of men and the world of gods. Virgil inherited from Homer the supernatural machinery of Olympian deities, and in certain ways uses it as Homer had done, for example to initiate action on the human plane, and to diversify the familiar human scene with glimpses of an imagined world. This visual aspect of another world beyond the clouds is one that figures very largely in the *Aeneid*; the sheer pictorial beauty of shapes which the human eye cannot see forms a great part of Virgil's imagery. Think of Juno, proud queen of heaven, stately and forbidding; of Neptune with his trident and retinue of sea-deities calming the storm; of Iris descending on the path of the rainbow; of Mercury with his winged sandals and his wand winging his way to Mt. Atlas; of Jupiter with his serene nod of supreme authority — this is the material of mythological painting on canvas which Virgil seeks to capture in words.

But there is one special respect in which Virgil's concept of supernatural powers differed from Homer's, and this is the idea that fate and Jupiter are working out their far-reaching purpose for the benefit of mankind. Aeneas is *fato profugus* (*Aen.* 1.2). It is a concept greatly influenced by Roman Stoicism, and it introduces a theme of human endeavour to achieve what the gods wish, a theme dominant throughout Aeneas' actions. Aeneas accepts a divine mission, and to the extent of his human ability devotes himself to it. Often it seems that the task is too great for his human frailty, but in moments of despair and crisis he receives help and strength from the supernatural world which enable him to continue. This does not mean that he is without free-will; it means that Virgil is exploring the meaning of his profound conviction that man does not live in this world alone. In the memorable words of Cicero, as he expounds the Stoic attitude (*Tusc.* 1.118): *Non enim temere nec fortuito sati et creati sumus, sed profecto fuit quaedam vis quae generi consuleret humano* . . . 'For we were not born and brought into this world blindly or by chance, but there existed surely a power to look after mortal men . . .' For Virgil as for Cicero there existed a divine power which guided and directed those capable of receiving its instructions; the character of Aeneas is to be interpreted in the light of his Stoic endeavours, often imperfectly realised, to understand and to follow the will of this divine power.

7. *VIRGIL'S HEXAMETER*

THE METRICAL movement[1] of Virgil's hexameter, the
sheer word-music, has always been acclaimed even by those
who would deny him much else,[2] and Virgil's achievement
is very justly summarised in Tennyson's famous line 'Wielder
of the stateliest measure ever moulded by the lips of man'.
Here attention may be drawn to three aspects of Virgil's
mastery.

First of all, Virgil more than any other Latin poet was
able to exploit the possibility of interplay between sentence
endings and line endings. In his predecessors generally
speaking the line was the sentence unit; it had been relatively rare for a sentence to end elsewhere than at a line
ending. Virgil in the Latin hexameter, like Milton in
English blank verse, made new use of the kinds of emphasis
available through run-on words, mid-line pauses, staccato
short sentences. The result of this is not only an extra force
in particular places, but an enormous increase in the variety
of narrative movement, so that the hexameter can retain
the reader's attention (as it could not have if used as in
Catullus 64) over thousands of lines.[3]

Secondly Virgil achieved the variety he needed by the
continued use, but within strict control, of metrical ab-

[1] For methods of scansion see Huxley's edition of *Georgics* 1 and
4 (London, 1963) and Maguinness' edition of *Aeneid* 12 (London,
1953). For aesthetic appreciation see also L. P. Wilkinson,
Golden Latin Artistry, Cambridge, 1963.

[2] Cf. Coleridge's famous question: 'If you take from Virgil his
diction and metre, what do you leave him'?

[3] For illustrations see the indexes to my Oxford editions of
Aeneid 3 and 5 under the heading of 'metre'.

normalities and licences used by his predecessors. He occupies a middle place between the freedom or mannerisms of Ennius, Lucretius, Catullus and the disappearance of almost all irregularities in Ovid and afterwards. Earlier poetry is recalled by monosyllabic endings, lengthening in arsis, hypermetric elisions, hiatus, spondaic fifth feet, unusual caesurae; but these features are employed rarely, and often with deliberate effect. Examples may be studied by use of the index under the heading 'metre'.

Thirdly Virgil understood and exploited more than any other Latin poet the two rhythms which were inherent in his metre ever since Ennius had employed the quantitative hexameter (taken from the Greeks) for the more strongly stressed Latin language. The result of this was to impose on the normal stress pronunciation of Latin an artificial scheme of scansion according to long and short syllables; and the effect was to make possible at every point coincidence or conflict of these two rhythms.[1] The quantitative pattern called for a metrical ictus, or beat, at the beginning of each foot of the hexameter; the natural stress accent[2] on each word could occur in the same place as the ictus or not, according to choice. Clearly the interplay of these rhythms can be used for aesthetic effects of various kinds: in Virgil's

spargens | umida | mella so|porife|rumque pa|paver (4.486)

[1] On this see especially W. F. Jackson Knight, *Accentual Symmetry in Vergil* (Oxford, 1939), and *Roman Vergil,*[2] pp. 292f., as well as Wilkinson (cited above).

[2] The rules for the Latin stress accent are very easy, being almost exactly the same as English: thus if the last syllable but one is long it takes the stress (*amóris, condúntur*), otherwise the stress is on the last syllable but two (*cármina, carmínibus*).

the total coincidence of the two rhythms gives a peaceful and drowsy line, while in

$$\bar{-} \acute{a}\text{ppa}|\text{rent } \bar{\text{ra}}|\acute{\text{ri}} \ \bar{\text{nan}}|\bar{\text{tes in}} \ | \ \acute{\text{gur}}\text{gite} | \acute{\text{vas}}\text{to} \bar{-} \quad (\text{1.118})$$

the conflict in the first four feet (especially with the spondaic movement) gives a feeling of struggle. These are extreme examples; Virgil's mastery is to be seen in the controlled use of these two rhythms throughout his poem, and it is this interplay of ictus and accent (or, as it equally is, of word pattern within the metrical structure) which perhaps more than any other single feature makes 'the stateliest measure'.

Using these technical devices, and many others (like the interplay of spondees and dactyls, the subtle music of alliteration and assonance, the variation of the Catullan patterned line for description with vigorous and fast-moving rhythms for narrative) Virgil was able to an extraordinary degree to make the sound suit the sense. The boxing-match in Book 5 is violent and excessive in metrical rhythm as well as in meaning; the last speech of Dido to Aeneas is vehement in movement as well as diction; the scene as Aeneas enters the underworld is ghostly in sound as well as sense. In the last analysis it is the range of metrical movement, as it is the range of mood and emotion, which triumphantly sustains the epic theme.

8 THE MANUSCRIPTS OF THE AENEID AND THE ANCIENT COMMENTATORS

THE TEXT of Virgil has been preserved far better than that of any other Latin poet. We possess manuscripts in capital letters from the fourth and fifth century, as well as many citations in ancient authors such as Seneca, Quintilian, Aulus Gellius and the invaluable commentary of Servius (c. A.D. 400). Ninth-century MSS (the date of our earliest testimony for very many authors) abound for Virgil, and the recent collation of a dozen of these by Mynors for his Oxford Text (1969) has served to confirm the enormous reliability of our capital MSS. In most cases of doubt about the text in Virgil the choice is between variants already existing by the fifth century; the number of places in which our fifth century testimony has to be rejected is very small indeed.

The following are the chief MSS:

M (*Mediceus*), fifth century, complete for the *Aeneid*.

P (*Palatinus*), fourth or fifth century, containing about nine-tenths of the *Aeneid*.

R (*Romanus*), fifth century, containing about four-fifths of the *Aeneid*, less reliable than *M* and *P*.

(The missing portions of *P* and *R* can be restored with fair confidence by ninth century MSS which are closely related to them: γ (*Gudianus*) for *P*, and *a* (*Bernensis*) for *R*).

In addition there are four other much more fragmentary capital MSS:

F (*Vaticanus*), fourth century, with illustrations, containing about a fifth of the *Aeneid*.

V (*Veronensis*), fifth century, containing about an eighth of the *Aeneid*.

G (*Sangallensis*), fifth century, only small fragments.

A (*Augusteus*), fragments of the *Georgics*, and four lines of the *Aeneid* (now lost, but known from a transcription).

The commentary of Servius (edited Thilo and Hagen, 1878–1902, and *edit. Harvard.* 1946–65 for *Aen.* i–v) is of the utmost importance in establishing the text as well as explaining it. The commentary exists in two versions, a shorter and a longer (called Servius *auct.* or Servius *Dan.*); the relationship between these two has not yet been established, and I have not differentiated between them in this edition. One of the outstanding merits of the commentary from the point of view of Virgil's text is the preservation of the views and readings of earlier grammarians like Probus, Asper, Aelius Donatus.

The *Saturnalia* of Macrobius (*c.* A.D. 400) contains very large numbers of citations from Virgil, and is of value (though less so than Servius) for the text as well as for its explanation.

The commentary of Tiberius Claudius Donatus (*c.* A.D. 400) is of far less value, concerned as it is with paraphrase rather than explanation, and with verbose expositions of the moral significance of the *Aeneid*.

9 *DIFFERENCES OF TEXT*

LIST OF differences of text between this edition and those of Hirtzel (O.C.T., 1900) and Mynors (O.C.T., 1969) (omitting minor points of orthography and punctuation and the following misprints in Mynors — 2.326 *omnis*, 4.91–2 *tara . . . calibus*, 5.146 *immisis*, 6.581 *flumine*).

Aen.	Williams	Hirtzel	Mynors
1.1a–d	om.	habet	om.
1.2	Laviniaque	Lavinaque	Laviniaque
1.193	humo	humi	humi
1.224	despiciens	dispiciens	despiciens
1.343	agri	agri	auri
1.374	componat	componet	componet

1.427	theatri	theatris	theatris
1.429	alta	alta	apta
1.455	inter	intra	inter
1.599	exhaustis	exhaustis	exhaustos
1.604	iustitiae	iustitia	iustitiae
1.708	pictis.	pictis.	pictis
2.37	subiectisve	subiectisque	subiectisque
2.114	scitantem	scitatum	scitatum
2.349	audendi	audendi	audentem
2.392	Androgeo	Androgeo	Androgei
2.433	vices Danaum	vices, Danaum	vices, Danaum
2.567–88	*habet*	*habet*	*secludit*
2.569	clara	clara	claram
2.572	Danaum poenam	poenas Danaum	Danaum poenam
2.584	nec habet	nec habet	habet haec
2.587	flammae	flammae	†famam
2.616	nimbo	limbo	nimbo
2.691	augurium	augurium	auxilium
2.727	ex agmine	ex agmine	examine
2.739	lassa	lassa	lapsa
2.778	hinc comitem asportare	hinc comitem asportare	comitem hinc portare
3.125–6	Naxon, Olearon, Paron	-um, -um, -um	-on, -on, -on
3.127	concita	consita	concita
3.360	tripoda ac Clarii	tripodas, Clarii	tripodas Clarii et
3.416	ferunt; cum	ferunt, cum	ferunt, cum
3.465	ac secto	sectoque	ac secto
3.535	dimittunt	dimittunt	demittunt
3.673	intremuere	contremuere	intremuere
3.684	Scyllam atque Charybdim	S. atque C.	Scyllamque Charybdinque
3.685	inter, utramque	inter utramque	inter, utrimque
3.686	teneant	teneant	teneam
4.25	adigat	abigat	adigat
4.54	incensum	impenso	impenso
4.427	cineres	cineres	cinerem

4.540	ratibusve	ratibusque	ratibusve
4.559	iuventa	iuventae	iuventa
4.573	'praecipites vigilate	praecipitis: 'vigilate	praecipitis: 'vigilate
4.593	diripientque	deripientque	diripientque
4.614	haeret,	haeret:	haeret,
4.641	celerabat	celebrabat	celebrabat
4.646	rogos	gradus	rogos
5.29	demittere	demittere	dimittere
5.112	talenta	talentum	talenta
5.162	cursum	gressum	cursum
5.238	porriciam	proiciam	proiciam
5.279	nixantem	nexantem	nexantem
5.317	signant	signant.	signant,
5.326	ambiguumve	ambiguumque	ambiguumque
5.349	pueri,	pueri	pueri
5.486	ponit	dicit	dicit
5.505	timuitque	timuitque	micuitque
5.512	atra	alta	atra
5.520	contorsit	contorsit	contendit
5.551	discedere	discedere	decedere
5.649	quis	quis	qui
5.768	nomen	numen	numen
5.776	porricit	proicit	proicit
5.777–8	778 *post* 777	778 *post* 777	777 *post* 778
5.825	tenent	tenent	tenet
5.851	caelo	caelo	caeli
6.122	totiens —	totiens.	totiens.
6.122	Thesea magnum	Thesea, magnum	Thesea, magnum
6.141	quis	qui	quis
6.177	sepulcri	sepulcro	sepulcro (?)
6.193	agnovit	agnoscit	agnovit
6.203	gemina	geminae	gemina
6.255	lumina	lumina	limina
6.383	terrae	terra	terra
6.427	flentes in	flentes, in	flentes, in
6.433	consilium	concilium	consilium
6.438	tristique . . . unda	tristisque . . . undae	tristisque . . . undae

6.475	concussus	concussus	percussus
6.495	vidit	vidit	videt et
6.505	Rhoeteo	Rhoeteo	Rhoeteo in
6.524	amovet	amovet	emovet
5.561	plangor ad auras	clangor ad auris	plangor ad auras
6.586	flammas	flammam	flammas
6.602	quos	quo *post lacunam*	quos
6.609	aut	aut	et
6.658	lauris	lauri	lauris
6.664	aliquos	alios	aliquos
6.724	terras	terram	terras
6.731	noxia corpora	corpora noxia	noxia corpora
6.742–3	igni. quisque	igni — quisque	igni (quisque
6.744	tenemus donec	tenemus — donec	tenemus), donec
6.827	prementur	premuntur	prementur
6.852	pacique	pacisque	pacique
6.882–3	rumpas! tu	rumpas, tu	rumpas, tu
6.900	litore	litore	limite

10 *BIBLIOGRAPHY*

(THE ENTRIES are listed in chronological order. For fuller information see *Greece and Rome, New Surveys in the Classics No. 1: Virgil* by R. D. Williams, 1967).

(a) *Texts*

Ribbeck (1859–68); Hirtzel (O.C.T., 1900); Goelzer and Durand (Budé, 1925–36); Janell (Teubner, 1930); Sabbadini (Rome, 1930), reprinted with minor alterations by Castiglioni (Corpus Paravianum, 1945–52); Mynors (O.C.T., 1969).

(b) *Commentaries*

Servius (ed. Thilo and Hagen, 1878–1902 and *edit. Harvard.*, *Aen.* i–v, 1946–65); Heyne-Wagner (fourth ed.

1830-41); James Henry, *Aeneidea* (1873-92); Conington–Nettleship–Haverfield (1858-98); T. E. Page (1894-1900); Plessis–Lejay (1919); J. W. Mackail (*Aeneid* with full Intro. and very brief commentary, 1930). *Separate books:* Conway, *Aen.* i (1935); Austin, *Aen.* ii (1964); Williams, *Aen.* iii (1962); Austin, *Aen.* iv (1955); Pease, *Aen.* iv (1935); Williams, *Aen.* v (1960); Norden, *Aen.* vi (third ed. 1926); Butler, *Aen.* vi (1920); Fletcher, *Aen.* vi (1941); Maguinness, *Aen.* xii (1953).

(c) *Translations*

Dryden (1697), Mackail (1908), Fairclough (Loeb, second ed. 1934-5), Day Lewis (1952), Jackson Knight (1955).

(d) *Literary criticism, etc.*

C. A. Sainte-Beuve, *Étude sur Virgile* (Paris, 1857).

W. Y. Sellar, *The Roman Poets of the Augustan Age: Virgil* (Oxford, 1877; third ed. 1897).

R. Heinze, *Virgils epische Technik* (Leipzig, 1903; third ed. 1915).

T. R. Glover, Virgil (London, 1904; seventh ed. 1942).

C. Bailey, *Religion in Virgil* (Oxford, 1935).

W. F. Jackson Knight, *Roman Vergil* (London, 1944; second ed. 1966).

T. S. Eliot, *What is a Classic?* (London, 1945).

C. M. Bowra, *From Virgil to Milton* (London, 1945).

V. Pöschl, *Die Dichtkünst Virgils: Bild und Symbol in der Aeneis* (Innsbruck, 1950, trans. Seligson, Michigan, 1962).

J. Perret, *Virgile, l'homme et l'oeuvre* (Paris, 1952; second ed. 1965).

Brooks Otis, *Virgil: a Study in Civilized Poetry* (Oxford, 1963).

L. P. Wilkinson, *Golden Latin Artistry* (Cambridge, 1963).

A. Parry, *The Two voices of Virgil's Aeneid* (*Arion* ii, 1963, pp. 66 f.).

M. C. J. Putnam, *The Poetry of the Aeneid* (Harvard, 1965).

Steele Commager (ed.), *Twentieth Century Views: Virgil* (New Jersey, 1966).

F. Klinger, *Virgil: Bucolica, Georgica, Aeneis* (Zürich, 1967).

R. D. Williams, *Virgil* (*Greece and Rome, New Surveys in the Classics No. 1, Oxford, 1967*).

K. Quinn, *Virgil's Aeneid; a Critical Description* (London, 1968).

W. S. Anderson, *The Art of the Aeneid* (New Jersey, 1969).

D. R. Dudley (ed.), 'Virgil' (*Studies in Latin Literature and its influence*, London, 1969).

W. A. Camps. *An introduction to Virgil's Aeneid* (Cambridge, 1969).

BOOK 1

Arma virumque cano, Troiae qui primus ab oris
Italiam fato profugus Laviniaque venit
litora, multum ille et terris iactatus et alto
vi superum, saevae memorem Iunonis ob iram,
multa quoque et bello passus, dum conderet urbem   5
inferretque deos Latio; genus unde Latinum
Albanique patres atque altae moenia Romae.
   Musa, mihi causas memora, quo numine laeso
quidve dolens regina deum tot volvere casus
insignem pietate virum, tot adire labores   10
impulerit. tantaene animis caelestibus irae?
   Urbs antiqua fuit (Tyrii tenuere coloni)
Karthago, Italiam contra Tiberinaque longe
ostia, dives opum studiisque asperrima belli,
quam Iuno fertur terris magis omnibus unam   15
posthabita coluisse Samo: hic illius arma,
hic currus fuit; hoc regnum dea gentibus esse,
si qua fata sinant, iam tum tenditque fovetque.
progeniem sed enim Troiano a sanguine duci
audierat Tyrias olim quae verteret arces;   20
hinc populum late regem belloque superbum
venturum excidio Libyae; sic volvere Parcas.
id metuens veterisque memor Saturnia belli,
prima quod ad Troiam pro caris gesserat Argis
(necdum etiam causae irarum saevique dolores   25
exciderant animo; manet alta mente repostum

iudicium Paridis spretaeque iniuria formae
et genus invisum et rapti Ganymedis honores) —
his accensa super iactatos aequore toto
Troas, reliquias Danaum atque immitis Achilli,   30
arcebat longe Latio, multosque per annos
errabant acti fatis maria omnia circum.
tantae molis erat Romanam condere gentem.

    Vix e conspectu Siculae telluris in altum
vela dabant laeti et spumas salis aere ruebant,   35
cum Iuno aeternum servans sub pectore vulnus
haec secum: 'mene incepto desistere victam
nec posse Italia Teucrorum avertere regem?
quippe vetor fatis. Pallasne exurere classem
Argivum atque ipsos potuit summergere ponto   40
unius ob noxam et furias Aiacis Oilei?
ipsa Iovis rapidum iaculata e nubibus ignem
disiecitque rates evertitque aequora ventis,
illum exspirantem transfixo pectore flammas
turbine corripuit scopuloque infixit acuto;   45
ast ego, quae divum incedo regina Iovisque
et soror et coniunx, una cum gente tot annos
bella gero. et quisquam numen Iunonis adorat
praeterea aut supplex aris imponet honorem?'

    Talia flammato secum dea corde volutans   50
nimborum in patriam, loca feta furentibus Austris,
Aeoliam venit. hic vasto rex Aeolus antro
luctantis ventos tempestatesque sonoras
imperio premit ac vinclis et carcere frenat.
illi indignantes magno cum murmure montis   55
circum claustra fremunt; celsa sedet Aeolus arce
sceptra tenens mollitque animos et temperat iras;
ni faciat, maria ac terras caelumque profundum

quippe ferant rapidi secum verrantque per auras.
sed pater omnipotens speluncis abdidit atris   60
hoc metuens molemque et montis insuper altos
imposuit, regemque dedit qui foedere certo
et premere et laxas sciret dare iussus habenas.
ad quem tum Iuno supplex his vocibus usa est: 64
   'Aeole, namque tibi divum pater atque hominum rex
et mulcere dedit fluctus et tollere vento,
gens inimica mihi Tyrrhenum navigat aequor
Ilium in Italiam portans victosque penatis:
incute vim ventis summersasque obrue puppis,
aut age diversos et disice corpora ponto.   70
sunt mihi bis septem praestanti corpore Nymphae,
quarum quae forma pulcherrima Deiopea,
conubio iungam stabili propriamque dicabo,
omnis ut tecum meritis pro talibus annos
exigat et pulchra faciat te prole parentem.'   75
   Aeolus haec contra: 'tuus, o regina, quid optes
explorare labor; mihi iussa capessere fas est.
tu mihi quodcumque hoc regni, tu sceptra Iovemque
concilias, tu das epulis accumbere divum
nimborumque facis tempestatumque potentem.'   80
   Haec ubi dicta, cavum conversa cuspide montem
impulit in latus; ac venti velut agmine facto,
qua data porta, ruunt et terras turbine perflant.
incubuere mari totumque a sedibus imis
una Eurusque Notusque ruunt creberque procellis   85
Africus, et vastos volvunt ad litora fluctus;
insequitur clamorque virum stridorque rudentum.
eripiunt subito nubes caelumque diemque
Teucrorum ex oculis; ponto nox incubat atra.
intonuere poli et crebris micat ignibus aether   90

praesentemque viris intentant omnia mortem.
extemplo Aeneae solvuntur frigore membra;
ingemit et duplicis tendens ad sidera palmas
talia voce refert: 'o terque quaterque beati,
quis ante ora patrum Troiae sub moenibus altis   95
contigit oppetere! o Danaum fortissime gentis
Tydide! mene Iliacis occumbere campis
non potuisse tuaque animam hanc effundere dextra,
saevus ubi Aeacidae telo iacet Hector, ubi ingens
Sarpedon, ubi tot Simois correpta sub undis   100
scuta virum galeasque et fortia corpora volvit!'
    Talia iactanti stridens Aquilone procella
velum adversa ferit, fluctusque ad sidera tollit.
franguntur remi, tum prora avertit et undis
dat latus, insequitur cumulo praeruptus aquae mons.   105
hi summo in fluctu pendent; his unda dehiscens
terram inter fluctus aperit, furit aestus harenis.
tris Notus abreptas in saxa latentia torquet
(saxa vocant Itali mediis quae in fluctibus Aras,
dorsum immane mari summo), tris Eurus ab alto   110
in brevia et syrtis urget, miserabile visu,
inliditque vadis atque aggere cingit harenae.
unam, quae Lycios fidumque vehebat Oronten,
ipsius ante oculos ingens a vertice pontus
in puppim ferit; excutitur pronusque magister   115
volvitur in caput, ast illam ter fluctus ibidem
torquet agens circum et rapidus vorat aequore vertex.
apparent rari nantes in gurgite vasto,
arma virum tabulaeque et Troia gaza per undas.
iam validam Ilionei navem, iam fortis Achatae,   120
et qua vectus Abas, et qua grandaevus Aletes,
vicit hiems; laxis laterum compagibus omnes

accipiunt inimicum imbrem rimisque fatiscunt.
  Interea magno misceri murmure pontum
emissamque hiemem sensit Neptunus et imis   125
stagna refusa vadis, graviter commotus; et alto
prospiciens summa placidum caput extulit unda.
disiectam Aeneae toto videt aequore classem,
fluctibus oppressos Troas caelique ruina;
nec latuere doli fratrem Iunonis et irae.   130
Eurum ad se Zephyrumque vocat, dehinc talia fatur:
  'Tantane vos generis tenuit fiducia vestri?
iam caelum terramque meo sine numine, venti,
miscere et tantas audetis tollere moles?
quos ego — sed motos praestat componere fluctus;   135
post mihi non simili poena commissa luetis.
maturate fugam regique haec dicite vestro:
non illi imperium pelagi saevumque tridentem,
sed mihi sorte datum. tenet ille immania saxa,
vestras, Eure, domos; illa se iactet in aula   140
Aeolus et clauso ventorum carcere regnet.'
  Sic ait et dicto citius tumida aequora placat
collectasque fugat nubes solemque reducit.
Cymothoe simul et Triton adnixus acuto
detrudunt navis scopulo; levat ipse tridenti   145
et vastas aperit syrtis et temperat aequor
atque rotis summas levibus perlabitur undas.
ac veluti magno in populo cum saepe coorta est
seditio saevitque animis ignobile vulgus,
iamque faces et saxa volant, furor arma ministrat; 150
tum, pietate gravem ac meritis si forte virum quem
conspexere, silent arrectisque auribus astant;
ille regit dictis animos et pectora mulcet:
sic cunctus pelagi cecidit fragor, aequora postquam

prospiciens genitor caeloque invectus aperto 155
flectit equos curruque volans dat lora secundo.

Defessi Aeneadae quae proxima litora cursu
contendunt petere, et Libyae vertuntur ad oras.
est in secessu longo locus: insula portum
efficit obiectu laterum, quibus omnis ab alto 160
frangitur inque sinus scindit sese unda reductos.
hinc atque hinc vastae rupes geminique minantur
in caelum scopuli, quorum sub vertice late
aequora tuta silent; tum silvis scaena coruscis
desuper, horrentique atrum nemus imminet umbra. 165
fronte sub adversa scopulis pendentibus antrum,
intus aquae dulces vivoque sedilia saxo,
Nympharum domus. hic fessas non vincula navis
ulla tenent, unco non alligat ancora morsu.
huc septem Aeneas collectis navibus omni 170
ex numero subit; ac magno telluris amore
egressi optata potiuntur Troes harena
et sale tabentis artus in litore ponunt.
ac primum silici scintillam excudit Achates
suscepitque ignem foliis atque arida circum 175
nutrimenta dedit rapuitque in fomite flammam.
tum Cererem corruptam undis Cerealiaque arma
expediunt fessi rerum, frugesque receptas
et torrere parant flammis et frangere saxo.

Aeneas scopulum interea conscendit, et omnem 180
prospectum late pelago petit, Anthea si quem
iactatum vento videat Phrygiasque biremis
aut Capyn aut celsis in puppibus arma Caici.
navem in conspectu nullam, tris litore cervos
prospicit errantis; hos tota armenta sequuntur 185
a tergo et longum per vallis pascitur agmen.

constitit hic arcumque manu celerisque sagittas
corripuit, fidus quae tela gerebat Achates,
ductoresque ipsos primum capita alta ferentis
cornibus arboreis sternit, tum vulgus et omnem   190
miscet agens telis nemora inter frondea turbam;
nec prius absistit quam septem ingentia victor
corpora fundat humo et numerum cum navibus aequet.
hinc portum petit et socios partitur in omnis.
vina bonus quae deinde cadis onerarat Acestes   195
litore Trinacrio dederatque abeuntibus heros
dividit, et dictis maerentia pectora mulcet:
    'O socii (neque enim ignari sumus ante malorum),
o passi graviora, dabit deus his quoque finem.
vos et Scyllaeam rabiem penitusque sonantis   200
accestis scopulos, vos et Cyclopia saxa
experti: revocate animos maestumque timorem
mittite; forsan et haec olim meminisse iuvabit.
per varios casus, per tot discrimina rerum
tendimus in Latium, sedes ubi fata quietas   205
ostendunt; illic fas regna resurgere Troiae.
durate, et vosmet rebus servate secundis.'
    Talia voce refert curisque ingentibus aeger
spem vultu simulat, premit altum corde dolorem.
illi se praedae accingunt dapibusque futuris: 210
tergora diripiunt costis et viscera nudant;
pars in frusta secant veribusque trementia figunt,
litore aëna locant alii flammasque ministrant.
tum victu revocant viris, fusique per herbam
implentur veteris Bacchi pinguisque ferinae.   215
postquam exempta fames epulis mensaeque remotae,
amissos longo socios sermone requirunt,
spemque metumque inter dubii, seu vivere credant

sive extrema pati nec iam exaudire vocatos.
praecipue pius Aeneas nunc acris Oronti, 220
nunc Amyci casum gemit et crudelia secum
fata Lyci fortemque Gyan fortemque Cloanthum.
Et iam finis erat, cum Iuppiter aethere summo
despiciens mare velivolum terrasque iacentis
litoraque et latos populos, sic vertice caeli 225
constitit et Libyae defixit lumina regnis.
atque illum talis iactantem pectore curas
tristior et lacrimis oculos suffusa nitentis
adloquitur Venus: 'o qui res hominumque deumque
aeternis regis imperiis et fulmine terres, 230
quid meus Aeneas in te committere tantum,
quid Troes potuere, quibus tot funera passis
cunctus ob Italiam terrarum clauditur orbis?
certe hinc Romanos olim volventibus annis,
hinc fore ductores, revocato a sanguine Teucri, 235
qui mare, qui terras omnis dicione tenerent,
pollicitus. quae te, genitor, sententia vertit?
hoc equidem occasum Troiae tristisque ruinas
solabar fatis contraria fata rependens;
nunc eadem fortuna viros tot casibus actos 240
insequitur. quem das finem, rex magne, laborum?
Antenor potuit mediis elapsus Achivis
Illyricos penetrare sinus atque intima tutus
regna Liburnorum et fontem superare Timavi,
unde per ora novem vasto cum murmure montis 245
it mare proruptum et pelago premit arva sonanti.
hic tamen ille urbem Patavi sedesque locavit
Teucrorum et genti nomen dedit armaque fixit
Troia, nunc placida compostus pace quiescit:
nos, tua progenies, caeli quibus adnuis arcem, 250

navibus (infandum!) amissis unius ob iram
prodimur atque Italis longe disiungimur oris.
hic pietatis honos? sic nos in sceptra reponis?'
  Olli subridens hominum sator atque deorum
vultu, quo caelum tempestatesque serenat,   255
oscula libavit natae, dehinc talia fatur:
'parce metu, Cytherea, manent immota tuorum
fata tibi; cernes urbem et promissa Lavini
moenia sublimemque feres ad sidera caeli
magnanimum Aenean; neque me sententia vertit.   260
hic tibi (fabor enim, quando haec te cura remordet,
longius, et volvens fatorum arcana movebo)
bellum ingens geret Italia populosque ferocis
contundet moresque viris et moenia ponet,
tertia dum Latio regnantem viderit aestas,   265
ternaque transierint Rutulis hiberna subactis.
at puer Ascanius, cui nunc cognomen Iulo
additur (Ilus erat, dum res stetit Ilia regno),
triginta magnos volvendis mensibus orbis
imperio explebit, regnumque ab sede Lavini   270
transferet, et Longam multa vi muniet Albam.
hic iam ter centum totos regnabitur annos
gente sub Hectorea, donec regina sacerdos
Marte gravis geminam partu dabit Ilia prolem.
inde lupae fulvo nutricis tegmine laetus   275
Romulus excipiet gentem et Mavortia condet
moenia Romanosque suo de nomine dicet.
his ego nec metas rerum nec tempora pono:
imperium sine fine dedi. quin aspera Iuno,
quae mare nunc terrasque metu caelumque fatigat,   280
consilia in melius referet, mecumque fovebit
Romanos, rerum dominos gentemque togatam.

sic placitum.   veniet lustris labentibus aetas
cum domus Assaraci Pthiam clarasque Mycenas
servitio premet ac victis dominabitur Argis.   285
nascetur pulchra Troianus origine Caesar,
imperium Oceano, famam qui terminet astris,
Iulius, a magno demissum nomen Iulo.
hunc tu olim caelo spoliis Orientis onustum
accipies secura; vocabitur hic quoque votis.   290
aspera tum positis mitescent saecula bellis:
cana Fides et Vesta, Remo cum fratre Quirinus
iura dabunt; dirae ferro et compagibus artis
claudentur Belli portae; Furor impius intus
saeva sedens super arma et centum vinctus aënis   295
post tergum nodis fremet horridus ore cruento.'
     Haec ait et Maia genitum demittit ab alto,
ut terrae utque novae pateant Karthaginis arces
hospitio Teucris, ne fati nescia Dido
finibus arceret.   volat ille per aëra magnum   300
remigio alarum ac Libyae citus astitit oris.
et iam iussa facit, ponuntque ferocia Poeni
corda volente deo; in primis regina quietum
accipit in Teucros animum mentemque benignam.
     At pius Aeneas per noctem plurima volvens,   305
ut primum lux alma data est, exire locosque
explorare novos, quas vento accesserit oras,
qui teneant (nam inculta videt), hominesne feraene,
quaerere constituit sociisque exacta referre.
classem in convexo nemorum sub rupe cavata   310
arboribus clausam circum atque horrentibus umbris
occulit; ipse uno graditur comitatus Achate
bina manu lato crispans hastilia ferro.
cui mater media sese tulit obvia silva

virginis os habitumque gerens et virginis arma   315
Spartanae, vel qualis equos Threissa fatigat
Harpalyce volucremque fuga praevertitur Hebrum.
namque umeris de more habilem suspenderat arcum
venatrix dederatque comam diffundere ventis,
nuda genu nodoque sinus collecta fluentis.   320
ac prior 'heus', inquit, 'iuvenes, monstrate, mearum
vidistis si quam hic errantem forte sororum
succinctam pharetra et maculosae tegmine lyncis,
aut spumantis apri cursum clamore prementem.'

  Sic Venus, et Veneris contra sic filius orsus: 325
'nulla tuarum audita mihi neque visa sororum,
o quam te memorem, virgo? namque haud tibi vultus
mortalis, nec vox hominem sonat; o, dea certe
(an Phoebi soror? an Nympharum sanguinis una?),
sis felix nostrumque leves, quaecumque, laborem   330
et quo sub caelo tandem, quibus orbis in oris
iactemur doceas; ignari hominumque locorumque
erramus vento huc vastis et fluctibus acti.
multa tibi ante aras nostra cadet hostia dextra.'

  Tum Venus: 'haud equidem tali me dignor honore;   335
virginibus Tyriis mos est gestare pharetram
purpureoque alte suras vincire coturno.
Punica regna vides, Tyrios et Agenoris urbem;
sed fines Libyci, genus intractabile bello.
imperium Dido Tyria regit urbe profecta,   340
germanum fugiens. longa est iniuria, longae
ambages; sed summa sequar fastigia rerum.
huic coniunx Sychaeus erat, ditissimus agri
Phoenicum, et magno miserae dilectus amore,
cui pater intactam dederat primisque iugarat   345
ominibus. sed regna Tyri germanus habebat

Pygmalion, scelere ante alios immanior omnis.
quos inter medius venit furor. ille Sychaeum
impius ante aras atque auri caecus amore
clam ferro incautum superat, securus amorum   350
germanae; factumque diu celavit et aegram
multa malus simulans vana spe lusit amantem.
ipsa sed in somnis inhumati venit imago
coniugis ora modis attollens pallida miris;
crudelis aras traiectaque pectora ferro   355
nudavit, caecumque domus scelus omne retexit.
tum celerare fugam patriaque excedere suadet
auxiliumque viae veteres tellure recludit
thesauros, ignotum argenti pondus et auri.
his commota fugam Dido sociosque parabat.   360
conveniunt quibus aut odium crudele tyranni
aut metus acer erat; navis, quae forte paratae,
corripiunt onerantque auro. portantur avari
Pygmalionis opes pelago; dux femina facti.
devenere locos ubi nunc ingentia cernes   365
moenia surgentemque novae Karthaginis arcem,
mercatique solum, facti de nomine Byrsam,
taurino quantum possent circumdare tergo.
sed vos qui tandem? quibus aut venistis ab oris?
quove tenetis iter?' quaerenti talibus ille   370
suspirans imoque trahens a pectore vocem:
   'O dea, si prima repetens ab origine pergam
et vacet annalis nostrorum audire laborum,
ante diem clauso componat Vesper Olympo.
nos Troia antiqua, si vestras forte per auris   375
Troiae nomen iit, diversa per aequora vectos
forte sua Libycis tempestas appulit oris.
sum pius Aeneas, raptos qui ex hoste penatis

classe veho mecum, fama super aethera notus;
Italiam quaero patriam, et genus ab Iove summo.   380
bis denis Phrygium conscendi navibus aequor,
matre dea monstrante viam data fata secutus;
vix septem convulsae undis Euroque supersunt.
ipse ignotus, egens, Libyae deserta peragro,
Europa atque Asia pulsus.' nec plura querentem   385
passa Venus medio sic interfata dolore est:
    'Quisquis es, haud, credo, invisus caelestibus auras
vitalis carpis, Tyriam qui adveneris urbem.
perge modo atque hinc te reginae ad limina perfer.
namque tibi reduces socios classemque relatam   390
nuntio et in tutum versis Aquilonibus actam,
ni frustra augurium vani docuere parentes.
aspice bis senos laetantis agmine cycnos,
aetheria quos lapsa plaga Iovis ales aperto
turbabat caelo; nunc terras ordine longo   395
aut capere aut captas iam despectare videntur:
ut reduces illi ludunt stridentibus alis
et coetu cinxere polum cantusque dedere,
haud aliter puppesque tuae pubesque tuorum
aut portum tenet aut pleno subit ostia velo.   400
perge modo et, qua te ducit via, derige gressum.'
    Dixit et avertens rosea cervice refulsit,
ambrosiaeque comae divinum vertice odorem
spiravere; pedes vestis defluxit ad imos,
et vera incessu patuit dea. ille ubi matrem   405
agnovit tali fugientem est voce secutus:
'quid natum totiens, crudelis tu quoque, falsis
ludis imaginibus? cur dextrae iungere dextram
non datur ac veras audire et reddere voces?'
talibus incusat gressumque ad moenia tendit.   410

at Venus obscuro gradientis aëre saepsit,
et multo nebulae circum dea fudit amictu,
cernere ne quis eos neu quis contingere posset
molirive moram aut veniendi poscere causas.
ipsa Paphum sublimis abit sedesque revisit   415
laeta suas, ubi templum illi, centumque Sabaeo
ture calent arae sertisque recentibus halant.

Corripuere viam interea, qua semita monstrat.
iamque ascendebant collem, qui plurimus urbi
imminet adversasque aspectat desuper arces.   420
miratur molem Aeneas, magalia quondam,
miratur portas strepitumque et strata viarum.
instant ardentes Tyrii: pars ducere muros
molirique arcem et manibus subvolvere saxa,
pars optare locum tecto et concludere sulco;   425
iura magistratusque legunt sanctumque senatum.
hic portus alii effodiunt; hic alta theatri
fundamenta locant alii, immanisque columnas
rupibus excidunt, scaenis decora alta futuris.
qualis apes aestate nova per florea rura   430
exercet sub sole labor, cum gentis adultos
educunt fetus, aut cum liquentia mella
stipant et dulci distendunt nectare cellas,
aut onera accipiunt venientum, aut agmine facto
ignavum fucos pecus a praesepibus arcent;   435
fervet opus redolentque thymo fragrantia mella.
'o fortunati, quorum iam moenia surgunt!'
Aeneas ait et fastigia suspicit urbis.
infert se saeptus nebula (mirabile dictu)
per medios, miscetque viris neque cernitur ulli.   440

Lucus in urbe fuit media, laetissimus umbrae,
quo primum iactati undis et turbine Poeni

effodere loco signum, quod regia Iuno
monstrarat, caput acris equi; sic nam fore bello
egregiam et facilem victu per saecula gentem.   445
hic templum Iunoni ingens Sidonia Dido
condebat, donis opulentum et numine divae,
aerea cui gradibus surgebant limina nexaeque
aere trabes, foribus cardo stridebat aënis.
hoc primum in luco nova res oblata timorem   450
leniit, hic primum Aeneas sperare salutem
ausus et adflictis melius confidere rebus.
namque sub ingenti lustrat dum singula templo
reginam opperiens, dum quae fortuna sit urbi
artificumque manus inter se operumque laborem   455
miratur, videt Iliacas ex ordine pugnas
bellaque iam fama totum vulgata per orbem,
Atridas Priamumque et saevum ambobus Achillem.
constitit et lacrimans 'quis iam locus' inquit 'Achate,
quae regio in terris nostri non plena laboris?   460
en Priamus. sunt hic etiam sua praemia laudi,
sunt lacrimae rerum et mentem mortalia tangunt.
solve metus; feret haec aliquam tibi fama salutem.'
sic ait atque animum pictura pascit inani
multa gemens, largoque umectat flumine vultum.   465
namque videbat uti bellantes Pergama circum
hac fugerent Grai, premeret Troiana iuventus,
hac Phryges, instaret curru cristatus Achilles.
nec procul hinc Rhesi niveis tentoria velis
agnoscit lacrimans, primo quae prodita somno   470
Tydides multa vastabat caede cruentus,
ardentisque avertit equos in castra prius quam
pabula gustassent Troiae Xanthumque bibissent.
parte alia fugiens amissis Troilus armis,

infelix puer atque impar congressus Achilli, 475
fertur equis curruque haeret resupinus inani,
lora tenens tamen; huic cervixque comaeque trahuntur
per terram, et versa pulvis inscribitur hasta.
interea ad templum non aequae Palladis ibant
crinibus Iliades passis peplumque ferebant 480
suppliciter, tristes et tunsae pectora palmis;
diva solo fixos oculos aversa tenebat.
ter circum Iliacos raptaverat Hectora muros
exanimumque auro corpus vendebat Achilles.
tum vero ingentem gemitum dat pectore ab imo, 485
ut spolia, ut currus, utque ipsum corpus amici
tendentemque manus Priamum conspexit inermis.
se quoque principibus permixtum agnovit Achivis,
Eoasque acies et nigri Memnonis arma.
ducit Amazonidum lunatis agmina peltis 490
Penthesilea furens mediisque in milibus ardet
aurea subnectens exsertae cingula mammae
bellatrix, audetque viris concurrere virgo.
    Haec dum Dardanio Aeneae miranda videntur,
dum stupet obtutuque haeret defixus in uno, 495
regina ad templum, forma pulcherrima Dido,
incessit magna iuvenum stipante caterva.
qualis in Eurotae ripis aut per iuga Cynthi
exercet Diana choros, quam mille secutae
hinc atque hinc glomerantur Oreades; illa pharetram 500
fert umero gradiensque deas supereminet omnis
(Latonae tacitum pertemptant gaudia pectus):
talis erat Dido, talem se laeta ferebat
per medios instans operi regnisque futuris.
tum foribus divae, media testudine templi, 505
saepta armis solioque alte subnixa resedit.

iura dabat legesque viris, operumque laborem
partibus aequabat iustis aut sorte trahebat:
cum subito Aeneas concursu accedere magno
Anthea Sergestumque videt fortemque Cloanthum   510
Teucrorumque alios, ater quos aequore turbo
dispulerat penitusque alias avexerat oras.
obstipuit simul ipse, simul percussus Achates
laetitiaque metuque; avidi coniungere dextras
ardebant, sed res animos incognita turbat.   515
dissimulant et nube cava speculantur amicti
quae fortuna viris, classem quo litore linquant,
quid veniant; cunctis nam lecti navibus ibant
orantes veniam et templum clamore petebant.

    Postquam introgressi et coram data copia fandi,   520
maximus Ilioneus placido sic pectore coepit:
'o regina, novam cui condere Iuppiter urbem
iustitiaque dedit gentis frenare superbas,
Troes te miseri, ventis maria omnia vecti,
oramus: prohibe infandos a navibus ignis,   525
parce pio generi et propius res aspice nostras.
non nos aut ferro Libycos populare penatis
venimus, aut raptas ad litora vertere praedas;
non ea vis animo nec tanta superbia victis.
est locus, Hesperiam Grai cognomine dicunt,   530
terra antiqua, potens armis atque ubere glaebae;
Oenotri coluere viri; nunc fama minores
Italiam dixisse ducis de nomine gentem.
hic cursus fuit,
cum subito adsurgens fluctu nimbosus Orion   535
in vada caeca tulit penitusque procacibus Austris
perque undas superante salo perque invia saxa
dispulit; huc pauci vestris adnavimus oris.

quod genus hoc hominum? quaeve hunc tam barbara morem
permittit patria? hospitio prohibemur harenae;   540
bella cient primaque vetant consistere terra.
si genus humanum et mortalia temnitis arma,
at sperate deos memores fandi atque nefandi.
rex erat Aeneas nobis, quo iustior alter
nec pietate fuit, nec bello maior et armis.   545
quem si fata virum servant, si vescitur aura
aetheria neque adhuc crudelibus occubat umbris,
non metus, officio nec te certasse priorem
paeniteat: sunt et Siculis regionibus urbes
armaque, Troianoque a sanguine clarus Acestes.   550
quassatam ventis liceat subducere classem
et silvis aptare trabes et stringere remos,
si datur Italiam sociis et rege recepto
tendere, ut Italiam laeti Latiumque petamus;
sin absumpta salus, et te, pater optime Teucrum,   555
pontus habet Libyae nec spes iam restat Iuli,
at freta Sicaniae saltem sedesque paratas,
unde huc advecti, regemque petamus Acesten.'
talibus Ilioneus; cuncti simul ore fremebant
Dardanidae.   560
    Tum breviter Dido vultum demissa profatur:
'solvite corde metum, Teucri, secludite curas.
res dura et regni novitas me talia cogunt
moliri et late finis custode tueri.
quis genus Aeneadum, quis Troiae nesciat urbem,   565
virtutesque virosque aut tanti incendia belli?
non obtunsa adeo gestamus pectora Poeni,
nec tam aversus equos Tyria Sol iungit ab urbe.
seu vos Hesperiam magnam Saturniaque arva
sive Erycis finis regemque optatis Acesten,   570

auxilio tutos dimittam opibusque iuvabo.
vultis et his mecum pariter considere regnis?
urbem quam statuo, vestra est; subducite navis;
Tros Tyriusque mihi nullo discrimine agetur.
atque utinam rex ipse noto compulsus eodem   575
adforet Aeneas! equidem per litora certos
dimittam et Libyae lustrare extrema iubebo,
si quibus eiectus silvis aut urbibus errat.'

   His animum arrecti dictis et fortis Achates
et pater Aeneas iamdudum erumpere nubem   580
ardebant. prior Aenean compellat Achates:
'nate dea, quae nunc animo sententia surgit?
omnia tuta vides, classem sociosque receptos.
unus abest, medio in fluctu quem vidimus ipsi
summersum; dictis respondent cetera matris'.   585
vix ea fatus erat cum circumfusa repente
scindit se nubes et in aethera purgat apertum.
restitit Aeneas claraque in luce refulsit
os umerosque deo similis; namque ipsa decoram
caesariem nato genetrix lumenque iuventae   590
purpureum et laetos oculis adflarat honores:
quale manus addunt ebori decus, aut ubi flavo
argentum Pariusve lapis circumdatur auro.
tum sic reginam adloquitur cunctisque repente
improvisus ait: 'coram, quem quaeritis, adsum,   595
Troius Aeneas, Libycis ereptus ab undis.
o sola infandos Troiae miserata labores,
quae nos, reliquias Danaum, terraeque marisque
omnibus exhaustis iam casibus, omnium egenos,
urbe, domo socias, grates persolvere dignas   600
non opis est nostrae, Dido, nec quidquid ubique est
gentis Dardaniae, magnum quae sparsa per orbem.

di tibi, si qua pios respectant numina, si quid
usquam iustitiae est, et mens sibi conscia recti
praemia digna ferant.   quae te tam laeta tulerunt   605
saecula? qui tanti talem genuere parentes?
in freta dum fluvii current, dum montibus umbrae
lustrabunt convexa, polus dum sidera pascet,
semper honos nomenque tuum laudesque manebunt,
quae me cumque vocant terrae.'   sic fatus amicum   610
Ilionea petit dextra laevaque Serestum,
post alios, fortemque Gyan fortemque Cloanthum.

   Obstipuit primo aspectu Sidonia Dido,
casu deinde viri tanto, et sic ore locuta est:
'quis te, nate dea, per tanta pericula casus   615
insequitur? quae vis immanibus applicat oris?
tune ille Aeneas quem Dardanio Anchisae
alma Venus Phrygii genuit Simoentis ad undam?
atque equidem Teucrum memini Sidona venire
finibus expulsum patriis, nova regna petentem   620
auxilio Beli; genitor tum Belus opimam
vastabat Cyprum et victor dicione tenebat.
tempore iam ex illo casus mihi cognitus urbis
Troianae nomenque tuum regesque Pelasgi.
ipse hostis Teucros insigni laude ferebat   625
seque ortum antiqua Teucrorum a stirpe volebat.
quare agite, o tectis, iuvenes, succedite nostris.
me quoque per multos similis fortuna labores
iactatam hac demum voluit consistere terra.
non ignara mali miseris succurrere disco.'   630
sic memorat; simul Aenean in regia ducit
tecta, simul divum templis indicit honorem.
nec minus interea sociis ad litora mittit
viginti tauros, magnorum horrentia centum

terga suum, pinguis centum cum matribus agnos,   635
munera laetitiamque dii.
at domus interior regali splendida luxu
instruitur, mediisque parant convivia tectis:
arte laboratae vestes ostroque superbo,
ingens argentum mensis, caelataque in auro   640
fortia facta patrum, series longissima rerum
per tot ducta viros antiqua ab origine gentis.

  Aeneas (neque enim patrius consistere mentem
passus amor) rapidum ad navis praemittit Achaten,
Ascanio ferat haec ipsumque ad moenia ducat;   645
omnis in Ascanio cari stat cura parentis.
munera praeterea Iliacis erepta ruinis
ferre iubet, pallam signis auroque rigentem
et circumtextum croceo velamen acantho,
ornatus Argivae Helenae, quos illa Mycenis,   650
Pergama cum peteret inconcessosque hymenaeos,
extulerat, matris Ledae mirabile donum;
praeterea sceptrum, Ilione quod gesserat olim,
maxima natarum Priami, colloque monile
bacatum, et duplicem gemmis auroque coronam.   655
haec celerans iter ad navis tendebat Achates.

  At Cytherea novas artis, nova pectore versat
consilia, ut faciem mutatus et ora Cupido
pro dulci Ascanio veniat, donisque furentem
incendat reginam atque ossibus implicet ignem.   660
quippe domum timet ambiguam Tyriosque bilinguis,
urit atrox Iuno et sub noctem cura recursat.
ergo his aligerum dictis adfatur Amorem:
'nate, meae vires, mea magna potentia, solus,
nate, patris summi qui tela Typhoëa temnis,   665
ad te confugio et supplex tua numina posco.

frater ut Aeneas pelago tuus omnia circum
litora iactetur odiis Iunonis acerbae,
nota tibi, et nostro doluisti saepe dolore.
nunc Phoenissa tenet Dido blandisque moratur   670
vocibus, et vereor quo se Iunonia vertant
hospitia: haud tanto cessabit cardine rerum.
quocirca capere ante dolis et cingere flamma
reginam meditor, ne quo se numine mutet,
sed magno Aeneae mecum teneatur amore.   675
qua facere id possis nostram nunc accipe mentem:
regius accitu cari genitoris ad urbem
Sidoniam puer ire parat, mea maxima cura,
dona ferens pelago et flammis restantia Troiae;
hunc ego sopitum somno super alta Cythera   680
aut super Idalium sacrata sede recondam,
ne qua scire dolos mediusve occurrere possit.
tu faciem illius noctem non amplius unam
falle dolo et notos pueri puer indue vultus,
ut, cum te gremio accipiet laetissima Dido   685
regalis inter mensas laticemque Lyaeum,
cum dabit amplexus atque oscula dulcia figet,
occultum inspires ignem fallasque veneno.'
paret Amor dictis carae genetricis, et alas
exuit et gressu gaudens incedit Iuli.   690
at Venus Ascanio placidam per membra quietem
inrigat, et fotum gremio dea tollit in altos
Idaliae lucos, ubi mollis amaracus illum
floribus et dulci aspirans complectitur umbra.

  Iamque ibat dicto parens et dona Cupido   695
regia portabat Tyriis duce laetus Achate.
cum venit, aulaeis iam se regina superbis
aurea composuit sponda mediamque locavit;

iam pater Aeneas et iam Troiana iuventus
conveniunt, stratoque super discumbitur ostro.   700
dant manibus famuli lymphas Cereremque canistris
expediunt tonsisque ferunt mantelia villis.
quinquaginta intus famulae, quibus ordine longam
cura penum struere et flammis adolere penatis;
centum aliae totidemque pares aetate ministri,   705
qui dapibus mensas onerent et pocula ponant.
nec non et Tyrii per limina laeta frequentes
convenere, toris iussi discumbere pictis.
mirantur dona Aeneae, mirantur Iulum,
flagrantisque dei vultus simulataque verba,   710
pallamque et pictum croceo velamen acantho.
praecipue infelix, pesti devota futurae,
expleri mentem nequit ardescitque tuendo
Phoenissa, et pariter puero donisque movetur.
ille ubi complexu Aeneae colloque pependit   715
et magnum falsi implevit genitoris amorem,
reginam petit. haec oculis, haec pectore toto
haeret et interdum gremio fovet inscia Dido
insidat quantus miserae deus. at memor ille
matris Acidaliae paulatim abolere Sychaeum   720
incipit et vivo temptat praevertere amore
iam pridem resides animos desuetaque corda.
    Postquam prima quies epulis mensaeque remotae,
crateras magnos statuunt et vina coronant.
fit strepitus tectis vocemque per ampla volutant   725
atria; dependent lychni laquearibus aureis
incensi et noctem flammis funalia vincunt.
hic regina gravem gemmis auroque poposcit
implevitque mero pateram, quam Belus et omnes
a Belo soliti; tum facta silentia tectis: 730

'Iuppiter, hospitibus nam te dare iura loquuntur,
hunc laetum Tyriisque diem Troiaque profectis
esse velis, nostrosque huius meminisse minores.
adsit laetitiae Bacchus dator et bona Iuno;
et vos o coetum, Tyrii, celebrate faventes.'   735
dixit et in mensam laticum libavit honorem
primaque, libato, summo tenus attigit ore;
tum Bitiae dedit increpitans; ille impiger hausit
spumantem pateram et pleno se proluit auro;
post alii proceres. cithara crinitus Iopas   740
personat aurata, docuit quem maximus Atlas.
hic canit errantem lunam solisque labores,
unde hominum genus et pecudes, unde imber et ignes,
Arcturum pluviasque Hyadas geminosque Triones;
quid tantum Oceano properent se tingere soles   745
hiberni, vel quae tardis mora noctibus obstet.
ingeminant plausu Tyrii, Troesque sequuntur.
nec non et vario noctem sermone trahebat
infelix Dido longumque bibebat amorem,
multa super Priamo rogitans, super Hectore multa;   750
nunc quibus Aurorae venisset filius armis,
nunc quales Diomedis equi, nunc quantus Achilles.
'immo age et a prima dic, hospes, origine nobis
insidias' inquit 'Danaum casusque tuorum
erroresque tuos; nam te iam septima portat   755
omnibus errantem terris et fluctibus aestas.'

BOOK 2

Conticuere omnes intentique ora tenebant.
inde toro pater Aeneas sic orsus ab alto:
'infandum, regina, iubes renovare dolorem,
Troianas ut opes et lamentabile regnum
eruerint Danai, quaeque ipse miserrima vidi   5
et quorum pars magna fui. quis talia fando
Myrmidonum Dolopumve aut duri miles Ulixi
temperet a lacrimis? et iam nox umida caelo
praecipitat suadentque cadentia sidera somnos.
sed si tantus amor casus cognoscere nostros   10
et breviter Troiae supremum audire laborem,
quamquam animus meminisse horret luctuque refugit,
incipiam. fracti bello fatisque repulsi
ductores Danaum tot iam labentibus annis
instar montis equum divina Palladis arte   15
aedificant, sectaque intexunt abiete costas;
votum pro reditu simulant; ea fama vagatur.
huc delecta virum sortiti corpora furtim
includunt caeco lateri penitusque cavernas
ingentis uterumque armato milite complent.   20
    Est in conspectu Tenedos, notissima fama
insula, dives opum Priami dum regna manebant,
nunc tantum sinus et statio male fida carinis:
huc se provecti deserto in litore condunt.
nos abiisse rati et vento petiisse Mycenas.   25
ergo omnis longo solvit se Teucria luctu:

panduntur portae, iuvat ire et Dorica castra
desertosque videre locos litusque relictum:
hic Dolopum manus, hic saevus tendebat Achilles;
classibus hic locus, hic acie certare solebant.   30
pars stupet innuptae donum exitiale Minervae
et molem mirantur equi; primusque Thymoetes
duci intra muros hortatur et arce locari,
sive dolo seu iam Troiae sic fata ferebant.
at Capys, et quorum melior sententia menti,   35
aut pelago Danaum insidias suspectaque dona
praecipitare iubent subiectisve urere flammis,
aut terebrare cavas uteri et temptare latebras.
scinditur incertum studia in contraria vulgus.

   Primus ibi ante omnis magna comitante caterva   40
Laocoon ardens summa decurrit ab arce,
et procul 'o miseri, quae tanta insania, cives?
creditis avectos hostis? aut ulla putatis
dona carere dolis Danaum? sic notus Ulixes?
aut hoc inclusi ligno occultantur Achivi,   45
aut haec in nostros fabricata est machina muros,
inspectura domos venturaque desuper urbi,
aut aliquis latet error; equo ne credite, Teucri.
quidquid id est, timeo Danaos et dona ferentis.'
sic fatus validis ingentem viribus hastam   50
in latus inque feri curvam compagibus alvum
contorsit. stetit illa tremens, uteroque recusso
insonuere cavae gemitumque dedere cavernae.
et, si fata deum, si mens non laeva fuisset,
impulerat ferro Argolicas foedare latebras,   55
Troiaque nunc staret, Priamique arx alta maneres.

   Ecce, manus iuvenem interea post terga revinctum
pastores magno ad regem clamore trahebant

Dardanidae, qui se ignotum venientibus ultro,
hoc ipsum ut strueret Troiamque aperiret Achivis,   60
obtulerat, fidens animi atque in utrumque paratus,
seu versare dolos seu certae occumbere morti.
undique visendi studio Troiana iuventus
circumfusa ruit certantque inludere capto.
accipe nunc Danaum insidias et crimine ab uno   65
disce omnis.
namque ut conspectu in medio turbatus, inermis,
constitit atque oculis Phrygia agmina circumspexit,
'heu, quae me tellus' inquit 'quae me aequora possunt
accipere? aut quid iam misero mihi denique restat,   70
cui neque apud Danaos usquam locus, et super ipsi
Dardanidae infensi poenas cum sanguine poscunt?'
quo gemitu conversi animi compressus et omnis
impetus. hortamur fari quo sanguine cretus,
quidve ferat; memoret quae sit fiducia capto.   75
[ille haec deposita tandem formidine fatur:]
    'Cuncta equidem tibi, rex, fuerit quodcumque, fatebor
vera,' inquit; 'neque me Argolica de gente negabo.
hoc primum; nec, si miserum Fortuna Sinonem
finxit, vanum etiam mendacemque improba finget.   80
fando aliquod si forte tuas pervenit ad auris
Belidae nomen Palamedis et incluta fama
gloria, quem falsa sub proditione Pelasgi
insontem infando indicio, quia bella vetabat,
demisere neci, nunc cassum lumine lugent: 85
illi me comitem et consanguinitate propinquum
pauper in arma pater primis huc misit ab annis.
dum stabat regno incolumis regumque vigebat
conciliis, et nos aliquod nomenque decusque
gessimus. invidia postquam pellacis Ulixi   90

(haud ignota loquor) superis concessit ab oris,
adflictus vitam in tenebris luctuque trahebam
et çasum insontis mecum indignabar amici.
nec tacui demens et me, fors si qua tulisset,
si patrios umquam remeassem victor ad Argos,   95
promisi ultorem et verbis odia aspera movi.
hinc mihi prima mali labes, hinc semper Ulixes
criminibus terrere novis, hinc spargere voces
in vulgum ambiguas et quaerere conscius arma.
nec requievit enim donec Calchante ministro —   100
sed quid ego haec autem nequiquam ingrata revolvo,
quidve moror? si omnis uno ordine habetis Achivos,
idque audire sat est, iamdudum sumite poenas:
hoc Ithacus velit et magno mercentur Atridae.'

    Tum vero ardemus scitari et quaerere causas,   105
ignari scelerum tantorum artisque Pelasgae.
prosequitur pavitans et ficto pectore fatur:

    'Saepe fugam Danai Troia cupiere relicta
moliri et longo fessi discedere bello;
fecissentque utinam! saepe illos aspera ponti   110
interclusit hiems et terruit Auster euntis.
praecipue cum iam hic trabibus contextus acernis
staret equus, toto sonuerunt aethere nimbi.
suspensi Eurypylum scitantem oracula Phoebi
mittimus, isque adytis haec tristia dicta reportat: 115
"sanguine placastis ventos et virgine caesa,
cum primum Iliacas, Danai, venistis ad oras:
sanguine quaerendi reditus animaque litandum
Argolica." vulgi quae vox ut venit ad auris,
obstipuere animi gelidusque per ima cucurrit   120
ossa tremor, cui fata parent, quem poscat Apollo.
hic Ithacus vatem magno Calchanta tumultu

protrahit in medios; quae sint ea numina divum
flagitat. et mihi iam multi crudele canebant
artificis scelus, et taciti ventura videbant.   125
bis quinos silet ille dies tectusque recusat
prodere voce sua quemquam aut opponere morti.
vix tandem, magnis Ithaci clamoribus actus,
composito rumpit vocem et me destinat arae.
adsensere omnes et, quae sibi quisque timebat,   130
unius in miseri exitium conversa tulere.
iamque dies infanda aderat; mihi sacra parari
et salsae fruges et circum tempora vittae.
eripui, fateor, leto me et vincula rupi,
limosoque lacu per noctem obscurus in ulva   135
delitui dum vela darent, si forte dedissent.
nec mihi iam patriam antiquam spes ulla videndi
nec dulcis natos exoptatumque parentem,
quos illi fors et poenas ob nostra reposcent
effugia, et culpam hanc miserorum morte piabunt.   140
quod te per superos et conscia numina veri,
per si qua est quae restet adhuc mortalibus usquam
intemerata fides, oro, miserere laborum
tantorum, miserere animi non digna ferentis.'

His lacrimis vitam damus et miserescimus ultro.   145
ipse viro primus manicas atque arta levari
vincla iubet Priamus dictisque ita fatur amicis:
'quisquis es, amissos hinc iam obliviscere Graios;
noster eris. mihique haec edissere vera roganti:
quo molem hanc immanis equi statuere? quis auctor? 150
quidve petunt? quae religio? aut quae machina belli?'
dixerat. ille dolis instructus et arte Pelasga
sustulit exutas vinclis ad sidera palmas:
'vos, aeterni ignes, et non violabile vestrum

testor numen,' ait, 'vos arae ensesque nefandi,   155
quos fugi, vittaeque deum, quas hostia gessi:
fas mihi Graiorum sacrata resolvere iura,
fas odisse viros atque omnia ferre sub auras,
si qua tegunt; teneor patriae nec legibus ullis.
tu modo promissis maneas servataque serves   160
Troia fidem, si vera feram, si magna rependam.
omnis spes Danaum et coepti fiducia belli
Palladis auxiliis semper stetit. impius ex quo
Tydides sed enim scelerumque inventor Ulixes,
fatale adgressi sacrato avellere templo   165
Palladium caesis summae custodibus arcis,
corripuere sacram effigiem manibusque cruentis
virgineas ausi divae contingere vittas,
ex illo fluere ac retro sublapsa referri
spes Danaum, fractae vires, aversa deae mens.   170
nec dubiis ea signa dedit Tritonia monstris.
vix positum castris simulacrum: arsere coruscae
luminibus flammae arrectis, salsusque per artus
sudor iit, terque ipsa solo (mirabile dictu)
emicuit parmamque ferens hastamque trementem.   175
extemplo temptanda fuga canit aequora Calchas,
nec posse Argolicis exscindi Pergama telis
omina ni repetant Argis numenque reducant
quod pelago et curvis secum avexere carinis.
et nunc quod patrias vento petiere Mycenas,   180
arma deosque parant comites pelagoque remenso
improvisi aderunt; ita digerit omina Calchas.
hanc pro Palladio moniti, pro numine laeso
effigiem statuere, nefas quae triste piaret.
hanc tamen immensam Calchas attollere molem   185
roboribus textis caeloque educere iussit,

ne recipi portis aut duci in moenia posset,
neu populum antiqua sub religione tueri.
nam si vestra manus violasset dona Minervae,
tum magnum exitium (quod di prius omen in ipsum   190
convertant!) Priami imperio Phrygibusque futurum;
sin manibus vestris vestram ascendisset in urbem,
ultro Asiam magno Pelopea ad moenia bello
venturam, et nostros ea fata manere nepotes.'

  Talibus insidiis periurique arte Sinonis   195
credita res, captique dolis lacrimisque coactis
quos neque Tydides nec Larisaeus Achilles,
non anni domuere decem, non mille carinae.

  Hic aliud maius miseris multoque tremendum
obicitur magis atque improvida pectora turbat.   200
Laocoon, ductus Neptuno sorte sacerdos,
sollemnis taurum ingentem mactabat ad aras.
ecce autem gemini a Tenedo tranquilla per alta
(horresco referens) immensis orbibus angues
incumbunt pelago pariterque ad litora tendunt;   205
pectora quorum inter fluctus arrecta iubaeque
sanguineae superant undas, pars cetera pontum
pone legit sinuatque immensa volumine terga.
fit sonitus spumante salo; iamque arva tenebant
ardentisque oculos suffecti sanguine et igni   210
sibila lambebant linguis vibrantibus ora.
diffugimus visu exsangues. illi agmine certo
Laocoonta petunt; et primum parva duorum
corpora natorum serpens amplexus uterque
implicat et miseros morsu depascitur artus;   215
post ipsum auxilio subeuntem ac tela ferentem
corripiunt spirisque ligant ingentibus; et iam
bis medium amplexi, bis collo squamea circum

terga dati superant capite et cervicibus altis.
ille simul manibus tendit divellere nodos   220
perfusus sanie vittas atroque veneno,
clamores simul horrendos ad sidera tollit:
qualis mugitus, fugit cum saucius aram
taurus et incertam excussit cervice securim.
at gemini lapsu delubra ad summa dracones   225
effugiunt saevaeque petunt Tritonidis arcem,
sub pedibusque deae clipeique sub orbe teguntur.
tum vero tremefacta novus per pectora cunctis
insinuat pavor, et scelus expendisse merentem
Laocoonta ferunt, sacrum qui cuspide robur   230
laeserit et tergo sceleratam intorserit hastam.
ducendum ad sedes simulacrum orandaque divae
numina conclamant.
dividimus muros et moenia pandimus urbis.
accingunt omnes operi pedibusque rotarum   235
subiciunt lapsus, et stuppea vincula collo
intendunt: scandit fatalis machina muros
feta armis.   pueri circum innuptaeque puellae
sacra canunt funemque manu contingere gaudent;
illa subit mediaeque minans inlabitur urbi.   240
o patria, o divum domus Ilium et incluta bello
moenia Dardanidum! quater ipso in limine portae
substitit atque utero sonitum quater arma dedere;
instamus tamen immemores caecique furore
et monstrum infelix sacrata sistimus arce.   245
tunc etiam fatis aperit Cassandra futuris
ora dei iussu non umquam credita Teucris.
nos delubra deum miseri, quibus ultimus esset
ille dies, festa velamus fronde per urbem.

   Vertitur interea caelum et ruit Oceano nox   250

involvens umbra magna terramque polumque
Myrmidonumque dolos; fusi per moenia Teucri
conticuere; sopor fessos complectitur artus.
et iam Argiva phalanx instructis navibus ibat
a Tenedo tacitae per amica silentia lunae   255
litora nota petens, flammas cum regia puppis
extulerat, fatisque deum defensus iniquis
inclusos utero Danaos et pinea furtim
laxat claustra Sinon. illos patefactus ad auras
reddit equus, laetique cavo se robore promunt   260
Thessandrus Sthenelusque duces et dirus Ulixes,
demissum lapsi per funem, Acamasque Thoasque
Pelidesque Neoptolemus primusque Machaon
et Menelaus et ipse doli fabricator Epeos.
invadunt urbem somno vinoque sepultam;   265
caeduntur vigiles, portisque patentibus omnis
accipiunt socios atque agmina conscia iungunt.
    Tempus erat quo prima quies mortalibus aegris
incipit et dono divum gratissima serpit.
in somnis, ecce, ante oculos maestissimus Hector   270
visus adesse mihi largosque effundere fletus,
raptatus bigis ut quondam, aterque cruento
pulvere perque pedes traiectus lora tumentis.
ei mihi, qualis erat, quantum mutatus ab illo
Hectore qui redit exuvias indutus Achilli   275
vel Danaum Phrygios iaculatus puppibus ignis!
squalentem barbam et concretos sanguine crinis
vulneraque illa gerens, quae circum plurima muros
accepit patrios. ultro flens ipse videbar
compellare virum et maestas expromere voces: 280
'o lux Dardaniae, spes o fidissima Teucrum,
quae tantae tenuere morae? quibus Hector ab oris

exspectate venis? ut te post multa tuorum
funera, post varios hominumque urbisque labores
defessi aspicimus! quae causa indigna serenos   285
foedavit vultus? aut cur haec vulnera cerno?'
ille nihil, nec me quaerentem vana moratur,
sed graviter gemitus imo de pectore ducens,
'heu fuge, nate dea, teque his' ait 'eripe flammis.
hostis habet muros; ruit alto a culmine Troia.   290
sat patriae Priamoque datum: si Pergama dextra
defendi possent, etiam hac defensa fuissent.
sacra suosque tibi commendat Troia penatis;
hos cape fatorum comites, his moenia quaere
magna pererrato statues quae denique ponto.'   295
sic ait et manibus vittas Vestamque potentem
aeternumque adytis effert penetralibus ignem.

  Diverso interea miscentur moenia luctu,
et magis atque magis, quamquam secreta parentis
Anchisae domus arboribusque obtecta recessit,   300
clarescunt sonitus armorumque ingruit horror.
excutior somno et summi fastigia tecti
ascensu supero atque arrectis auribus asto:
in segetem veluti cum flamma furentibus Austris
incidit, aut rapidus montano flumine torrens   305
sternit agros, sternit sata laeta boumque labores
praecipitisque trahit silvas; stupet inscius alto
accipiens sonitum saxi de vertice pastor.
tum vero manifesta fides, Danaumque patescunt
insidiae. iam Deiphobi dedit ampla ruinam   310
Volcano superante domus, iam proximus ardet
Ucalegon; Sigea igni freta lata relucent.
exoritur clamorque virum clangorque tubarum.
arma amens capio; nec sat rationis in armis,

sed glomerare manum bello et concurrere in arcem   315
cum sociis ardent animi; furor iraque mentem
praecipitat, pulchrumque mori succurrit in armis.
  Ecce autem telis Panthus elapsus Achivum,
Panthus Othryades, arcis Phoebique sacerdos,
sacra manu victosque deos parvumque nepotem   320
ipse trahit cursuque amens ad limina tendit.
'quo res summa loco, Panthu? quam prendimus arcem?'
vix ea fatus eram gemitu cum talia reddit:
'venit summa dies et ineluctabile tempus
Dardaniae. fuimus Troes, fuit Ilium et ingens   325
gloria Teucrorum; ferus omnia Iuppiter Argos
transtulit; incensa Danai dominantur in urbe.
arduus armatos mediis in moenibus astans
fundit equus victorque Sinon incendia miscet
insultans. portis alii bipatentibus adsunt,   330
milia quot magnis umquam venere Mycenis;
obsedere alii telis angusta viarum
oppositis; stat ferri acies mucrone corusco
stricta, parata neci; vix primi proelia temptant
portarum vigiles et caeco Marte resistunt.'   335
talibus Othryadae dictis et numine divum
in flammas et in arma feror, quo tristis Erinys,
quo fremitus vocat et sublatus ad aethera clamor.
addunt se socios Rhipeus et maximus armis
Epytus, oblati per lunam, Hypanisque Dymasque   340
et lateri adglomerant nostro, iuvenisque Coroebus
Mygdonides — illis ad Troiam forte diebus
venerat insano Cassandrae incensus amore
et gener auxilium Priamo Phrygibusque ferebat,
infelix qui non sponsae praecepta furentis   345
audierit!

quos ubi confertos audere in proelia vidi,
incipio super his: 'iuvenes, fortissima frustra
pectora, si vobis audendi extrema cupido
certa sequi, quae sit rebus fortuna videtis: 350
excessere omnes adytis arisque relictis
di quibus imperium hoc steterat; succurritis urbi
incensae; moriamur et in media arma ruamus.
una salus victis nullam sperare salutem.'
sic animis iuvenum furor additus. inde, lupi ceu   355
raptores atra in nebula, quos improba ventris
exegit caecos rabies catulique relicti
faucibus exspectant siccis, per tela, per hostis
vadimus haud dubiam in mortem mediaeque tenemus
urbis iter; nox atra cava circumvolat umbra.   360
quis cladem illius noctis, quis funera fando
explicet aut possit lacrimis aequare labores?
urbs antiqua ruit multos dominata per annos;
plurima perque vias sternuntur inertia passim
corpora perque domos et religiosa deorum   365
limina. nec soli poenas dant sanguine Teucri;
quondam etiam victis redit in praecordia virtus
victoresque cadunt Danai. crudelis ubique
luctus, ubique pavor et plurima mortis imago.

   Primus se Danaum magna comitante caterva   370
Androgeos offert nobis, socia agmina credens
inscius, atque ultro verbis compellat amicis:
'festinate, viri! nam quae tam sera moratur
segnities? alii rapiunt incensa feruntque
Pergama: vos celsis nunc primum a navibus itis?'   375
dixit, et extemplo (neque enim responsa dabantur
fida satis) sensit medios delapsus in hostis.
obstipuit retroque pedem cum voce repressit.

improvisum aspris veluti qui sentibus anguem
pressit humi nitens trepidusque repente refugit   380
attollentem iras et caerula colla tumentem,
haud secus Androgeos visu tremefactus abibat.
inruimus densis et circumfundimur armis,
ignarosque loci passim et formidine captos
sternimus; aspirat primo Fortuna labori.   385
atque hic successu exsultans animisque Coroebus
'o socii, qua prima' inquit 'Fortuna salutis
monstrat iter, quaque ostendit se dextra, sequamur:
mutemus clipeos Danaumque insignia nobis
aptemus.   dolus an virtus, quis in hoste requirat?   390
arma dabunt ipsi.' sic fatus deinde comantem
Androgeo galeam clipeique insigne decorum
induitur laterique Argivum accommodat ensem.
hoc Rhipeus, hoc ipse Dymas omnisque iuventus
laeta facit: spoliis se quisque recentibus armat.   395
vadimus immixti Danais haud numine nostro
multaque per caecam congressi proelia noctem
conserimus, multos Danaum demittimus Orco.
diffugiunt alii ad navis et litora cursu
fida petunt; pars ingentem formidine turpi   400
scandunt rursus equum et nota conduntur in alvo.
   Heu nihil invitis fas quemquam fidere divis!
ecce trahebatur passis Priameia virgo
crinibus a templo Cassandra adytisque Minervae
ad caelum tendens ardentia lumina frustra,   405
lumina, nam teneras arcebant vincula palmas.
non tulit hanc speciem furiata mente Coroebus
et sese medium iniecit periturus in agmen.
consequimur cuncti et densis incurrimus armis.
hic primum ex alto delubri culmine telis   410

nostrorum obruimur oriturque miserrima caedes
armorum facie et Graiarum errore iubarum.
tum Danai gemitu atque ereptae virginis ira
undique collecti invadunt, acerrimus Aiax
et gemini Atridae Dolopumque exercitus omnis;   415
adversi rupto ceu quondam turbine venti
confligunt, Zephyrusque Notusque et laetus Eois
Eurus equis; stridunt silvae saevitque tridenti
spumeus atque imo Nereus ciet aequora fundo.
illi etiam, si quos obscura nocte per umbram   420
fudimus insidiis totaque agitavimus urbe,
apparent; primi clipeos mentitaque tela
agnoscunt atque ora sono discordia signant.
ilicet obruimur numero, primusque Coroebus
Penelei dextra divae armipotentis ad aram   425
procumbit; cadit et Rhipeus, iustissimus unus
qui fuit in Teucris et servantissimus aequi
(dis aliter visum); pereunt Hypanisque Dymasque
confixi a sociis; nec te tua plurima, Panthu,
labentem pietas nec Apollinis infula texit.   430
Iliaci cineres et flamma extrema meorum,
testor, in occasu vestro nec tela nec ullas
vitavisse vices Danaum, et, si fata fuissent
ut caderem, meruisse manu. divellimur inde,
Iphitus et Pelias mecum (quorum Iphitus aevo   435
iam gravior, Pelias et vulnere tardus Ulixi),
protinus ad sedes Priami clamore vocati.
hic vero ingentem pugnam ceu cetera nusquam
bella forent, nulli tota morerentur in urbe,
sic Martem indomitum Danaosque ad tecta ruentis   440
cernimus obsessumque acta testudine limen.
haerent parietibus scalae postisque sub ipsos

nituntur gradibus clipeosque ad tela sinistris
protecti obiciunt, prensant fastigia dextris.
Dardanidae contra turris ac tota domorum   445
culmina convellunt; his se, quando ultima cernunt,
extrema iam in morte parant defendere telis,
auratasque trabes, veterum decora alta parentum,
devolvunt; alii strictis mucronibus imas
obsedere fores, has servant agmine denso.   450
instaurati animi regis succurrere tectis
auxilioque levare viros vimque addere victis.

    Limen erat caecaeque fores et pervius usus
tectorum inter se Priami, postesque relicti
a tergo, infelix qua se, dum regna manebant,   455
saepius Andromache ferre incomitata solebat
ad soceros et avo puerum Astyanacta trahebat.
evado ad summi fastigia culminis, unde
tela manu miseri iactabant inrita Teucri.
turrim in praecipiti stantem summisque sub astra   460
eductam tectis, unde omnis Troia videri
et Danaum solitae naves et Achaica castra,
adgressi ferro circum, qua summa labantis
iuncturas tabulata dabant, convellimus altis
sedibus impulimusque; ea lapsa repente ruinam   465
cum sonitu trahit et Danaum super agmina late
incidit. ast alii subeunt, nec saxa nec ullum
telorum interea cessat genus.

    Vestibulum ante ipsum primoque in limine Pyrrhus
exsultat telis et luce coruscus aëna;   470
qualis ubi in lucem coluber mala gramina pastus,
frigida sub terra tumidum quem bruma tegebat,
nunc, positis novus exuviis nitidusque iuventa,
lubrica convolvit sublato pectore terga

arduus ad solem, et linguis micat ore trisulcis.   475
una ingens Periphas et equorum agitator Achillis,
armiger Automedon, una omnis Scyria pubes
succedunt tecto et flammas ad culmina iactant.
ipse inter primos correpta dura bipenni
limina perrumpit postisque a cardine vellit   480
aeratos; iamque excisa trabe firma cavavit
robora et ingentem lato dedit ore fenestram.
apparet domus intus et atria longa patescunt;
apparent Priami et veterum penetralia regum,
armatosque vident stantis in limine primo.   485
at domus interior gemitu miseroque tumultu
miscetur, penitusque cavae plangoribus aedes
femineis ululant; ferit aurea sidera clamor.
tum pavidae tectis matres ingentibus errant
amplexaeque tenent postis atque oscula figunt.   490
instat vi patria Pyrrhus; nec claustra nec ipsi
custodes sufferre valent; labat ariete crebro
ianua, et emoti procumbunt cardine postes.
fit via vi; rumpunt aditus primosque trucidant
immissi Danai et late loca milite complent.   495
non sic, aggeribus ruptis cum spumeus amnis
exiit oppositasque evicit gurgite moles,
fertur in arva furens cumulo camposque per omnis
cum stabulis armenta trahit. vidi ipse furentem
caede Neoptolemum geminosque in limine Atridas,   500
vidi Hecubam centumque nurus Priamumque per aras
sanguine foedantem quos ipse sacraverat ignis.
quinquaginta illi thalami, spes ampla nepotum,
barbarico postes auro spoliisque superbi
procubuere; tenent Danai qua deficit ignis.   505
    Forsitan et Priami fuerint quae fata requiras.

urbis uti captae casum convulsaque vidit
limina tectorum et medium in penetralibus hostem,
arma diu senior desueta trementibus aevo
circumdat nequiquam umeris et inutile ferrum   510
cingitur, ac densos fertur moriturus in hostis.
aedibus in mediis nudoque sub aetheris axe
ingens ara fuit iuxtaque veterrima laurus
incumbens arae atque umbra complexa penatis.
hic Hecuba et natae nequiquam altaria circum,   515
praecipites atra ceu tempestate columbae,
condensae et divum amplexae simulacra sedebant.
ipsum autem sumptis Priamum iuvenalibus armis
ut vidit, 'quae mens tam dira, miserrime coniunx,
impulit his cingi telis? aut quo ruis?' inquit.   520
'non tali auxilio nec defensoribus istis
tempus eget; non, si ipse meus nunc adforet Hector.
huc tandem concede; haec ara tuebitur omnis,
aut moriere simul.' sic ore effata recepit
ad sese et sacra longaevum in sede locavit.   525
   Ecce autem elapsus Pyrrhi de caede Polites,
unus natorum Priami, per tela, per hostis
porticibus longis fugit et vacua atria lustrat
saucius. illum ardens infesto vulnere Pyrrhus
insequitur, iam iamque manu tenet et premit hasta.   530
ut tandem ante oculos evasit et ora parentum,
concidit ac multo vitam cum sanguine fudit.
hic Priamus, quamquam in media iam morte tenetur,
non tamen abstinuit nec voci iraeque pepercit:
'at tibi pro scelere,' exclamat, 'pro talibus ausis   535
di, si qua est caelo pietas quae talia curet,
persolvant grates dignas et praemia reddant
debita, qui nati coram me cernere letum

fecisti et patrios foedasti funere vultus.
at non ille, satum quo te mentiris, Achilles   540
talis in hoste fuit Priamo; sed iura fidemque
supplicis erubuit corpusque exsangue sepulcro
reddidit Hectoreum meque in mea regna remisit.'
sic fatus senior telumque imbelle sine ictu
coniecit, rauco quod protinus aere repulsum,   545
et summo clipei nequiquam umbone pependit.
cui Pyrrhus: 'referes ergo haec et nuntius ibis
Pelidae genitori. illi mea tristia facta
degeneremque Neoptolemum narrare memento.
nunc morere.' hoc dicens altaria ad ipsa trementem   550
traxit et in multo lapsantem sanguine nati,
implicuitque comam laeva, dextraque coruscum
extulit ac lateri capulo tenus abdidit ensem.
haec finis Priami fatorum, hic exitus illum
sorte tulit Troiam incensam et prolapsa videntem   555
Pergama, tot quondam populis terrisque superbum
regnatorem Asiae. iacet ingens litore truncus,
avulsumque umeris caput et sine nomine corpus.

    At me tum primum saevus circumstetit horror.
obstipui; subiit cari genitoris imago,   560
ut regem aequaevum crudeli vulnere vidi
vitam exhalantem; subiit deserta Creusa
et direpta domus et parvi casus Iuli.
respicio et quae sit me circum copia lustro.
deseruere omnes defessi, et corpora saltu   565
ad terram misere aut ignibus aegra dedere.

    Iamque adeo super unus eram, cum limina Vestae
servantem et tacitam secreta in sede latentem
Tyndarida aspicio; dant clara incendia lucem
erranti passimque oculos per cuncta ferenti.   570

illa sibi infestos eversa ob Pergama Teucros
et Danaum poenam et deserti coniugis iras
praemetuens, Troiae et patriae communis Erinys,
abdiderat sese atque aris invisa sedebat.
exarsere ignes animo; subit ira cadentem   575
ulcisci patriam et sceleratas sumere poenas.
'scilicet haec Spartam incolumis patriasque Mycenas
aspiciet, partoque ibit regina triumpho,
coniugiumque domumque patris natosque videbit
Iliadum turba et Phrygiis comitata ministris?   580
occiderit ferro Priamus? Troia arserit igni?
Dardanium totiens sudarit sanguine litus?
non ita. namque etsi nullum memorabile nomen
feminea in poena est nec habet victoria laudem,
exstinxisse nefas tamen et sumpsisse merentis   585
laudabor poenas, animumque explesse iuvabit
ultricis flammae et cineres satiasse meorum.'
talia iactabam et furiata mente ferebar,
cum mihi se, non ante oculis tam clara, videndam
obtulit et pura per noctem in luce refulsit   590
alma parens, confessa deam qualisque videri
caelicolis et quanta solet, dextraque prehensum
continuit roseoque haec insuper addidit ore:
'nate, quis indomitas tantus dolor excitat iras?
quid furis aut quonam nostri tibi cura recessit?   595
non prius aspicies ubi fessum aetate parentem
liqueris Anchisen, superet coniunxne Creusa
Ascaniusque puer? quos omnis undique Graiae
circum errant acies et, ni mea cura resistat,
iam flammae tulerint inimicus et hauserit ensis.   600
non tibi Tyndaridis facies invisa Lacaenae
culpatusve Paris, divum inclementia, divum,

has evertit opes sternitque a culmine Troiam.
aspice (namque omnem, quae nunc obducta tuenti
mortalis hebetat visus tibi et umida circum   605
caligat, nubem eripiam; tu ne qua parentis
iussa time neu praeceptis parere recusa):
hic, ubi disiectas moles avulsaque saxis
saxa vides, mixtoque undantem pulvere fumum,
Neptunus muros magnoque emota tridenti   610
fundamenta quatit totamque a sedibus urbem
eruit. hic Iuno Scaeas saevissima portas
prima tenet sociumque furens a navibus agmen
ferro accincta vocat.
iam summas arces Tritonia, respice, Pallas   615
insedit nimbo effulgens et Gorgone saeva.
ipse pater Danais animos virisque secundas
sufficit, ipse deos in Dardana suscitat arma.
eripe, nate, fugam finemque impone labori.
nusquam abero et tutum patrio te limine sistam.'   620
dixerat et spissis noctis se condidit umbris.
apparent dirae facies inimicaque Troiae
numina magna deum.

Tum vero omne mihi visum considere in ignis
Ilium et ex imo verti Neptunia Troia;   625
ac veluti summis antiquam in montibus ornum
cum ferro accisam crebrisque bipennibus instant
eruere agricolae certatim; illa usque minatur
et tremefacta comam concusso vertice nutat,
vulneribus donec paulatim evicta supremum   630
congemuit traxitque iugis avulsa ruinam.
descendo ac ducente deo flammam inter et hostis
expedior: dant tela locum flammaeque recedunt.

Atque ubi iam patriae perventum ad limina sedis

antiquasque domos, genitor, quem tollere in altos   635
optabam primum montis primumque petebam,
abnegat excisa vitam producere Troia
exsiliumque pati. 'vos o, quibus integer aevi
sanguis,' ait, 'solidaeque suo stant robore vires,
vos agitate fugam.   640
me si caelicolae voluissent ducere vitam,
has mihi servassent sedes. satis una superque
vidimus excidia et captae superavimus urbi.
sic o sic positum adfati discedite corpus.
ipse manu mortem inveniam; miserebitur hostis   645
exuviasque petet. facilis iactura sepulcri.
iam pridem invisus divis et inutilis annos
demoror, ex quo me divum pater atque hominum rex
fulminis adflavit ventis et contigit igni.'
    Talia perstabat memorans fixusque manebat.   650
nos contra effusi lacrimis coniunxque Creusa
Ascaniusque omnisque domus, ne vertere secum
cuncta pater fatoque urgenti incumbere vellet.
abnegat inceptoque et sedibus haeret in isdem.
rursus in arma feror mortemque miserrimus opto.   655
nam quod consilium aut quae iam fortuna dabatur?
'mene efferre pedem, genitor, te posse relicto
sperasti tantumque nefas patrio excidit ore?
si nihil ex tanta superis placet urbe relinqui,
et sedet hoc animo perituraeque addere Troiae   660
teque tuosque iuvat, patet isti ianua leto,
iamque aderit multo Priami de sanguine Pyrrhus,
natum ante ora patris, patrem qui obtruncat ad aras.
hoc erat, alma parens, quod me per tela, per ignis
eripis, ut mediis hostem in penetralibus utque   665
Ascanium patremque meum iuxtaque Creusam

alterum in alterius mactatos sanguine cernam?
arma, viri, ferte arma; vocat lux ultima victos.
reddite me Danais; sinite instaurata revisam
proelia. numquam omnes hodie moriemur inulti.'   670
   Hinc ferro accingor rursus clipeoque sinistram
insertabam aptans meque extra tecta ferebam.
ecce autem complexa pedes in limine coniunx
haerebat, parvumque patri tendebat Iulum:
'si periturus abis, et nos rape in omnia tecum;   675
sin aliquam expertus sumptis spem ponis in armis,
hanc primum tutare domum. cui parvus Iulus,
cui pater et coniunx quondam tua dicta relinquor?'
   Talia vociferans gemitu tectum omne replebat,
cum subitum dictuque oritur mirabile monstrum.   680
namque manus inter maestorumque ora parentum
ecce levis summo de vertice visus Iuli
fundere lumen apex, tactuque innoxia mollis
lambere flamma comas et circum tempora pasci.
nos pavidi trepidare metu crinemque flagrantem   685
excutere et sanctos restinguere fontibus ignis.
at pater Anchises oculos ad sidera laetus
extulit et caelo palmas cum voce tetendit:
'Iuppiter omnipotens, precibus si flecteris ullis,
aspice nos, hoc tantum, et si pietate meremur,   690
da deinde augurium, pater, atque haec omina firma.'
   Vix ea fatus erat senior, subitoque fragore
intonuit laevum, et de caelo lapsa per umbras
stella facem ducens multa cum luce cucurrit.
illam summa super labentem culmina tecti   695
cernimus Idaea claram se condere silva
signantemque vias; tum longo limite sulcus
dat lucem et late circum loca sulphure fumant.

hic vero victus genitor se tollit ad auras
adfaturque deos et sanctum sidus adorat.   700
'iam iam nulla mora est; sequor et qua ducitis adsum,
di patrii; servate domum, servate nepotem.
vestrum hoc augurium, vestroque in numine Troia est.
cedo equidem nec, nate, tibi comes ire recuso.'
dixerat ille, et iam per moenia clarior ignis   705
auditur, propiusque aestus incendia volvunt.
'ergo age, care pater, cervici imponere nostrae;
ipse subibo umeris nec me labor iste gravabit;
quo res cumque cadent, unum et commune periclum,
una salus ambobus erit.   mihi parvus Iulus   710
sit comes, et longe servet vestigia coniunx.
vos, famuli, quae dicam animis advertite vestris.
est urbe egressis tumulus templumque vetustum
desertae Cereris, iuxtaque antiqua cupressus
religione patrum multos servata per annos;   715
hanc ex diverso sedem veniemus in unam.
tu, genitor, cape sacra manu patriosque penatis;
me bello e tanto digressum et caede recenti
attrectare nefas, donec me flumine vivo
abluero.'   720
haec fatus latos umeros subiectaque colla
veste super fulvique insternor pelle leonis,
succedoque oneri; dextrae se parvus Iulus
implicuit sequiturque patrem non passibus aequis;
pone subit coniunx.   ferimur per opaca locorum,   725
et me, quem dudum non ulla iniecta movebant
tela neque adverso glomerati ex agmine Grai,
nunc omnes terrent aurae, sonus excitat omnis
suspensum et pariter comitique onerique timentem.
    Iamque propinquabam portis omnemque videbar   730

evasisse viam, subito cum creber ad auris
visus adesse pedum sonitus, genitorque per umbram
prospiciens 'nate' exclamat 'fuge, nate; propinquant.
ardentis clipeos atque aera micantia cerno.'
hic mihi nescio quod trepido male numen amicum   735
confusam eripuit mentem. namque avia cursu
dum sequor et nota excedo regione viarum,
heu misero coniunx fatone erepta Creusa
substitit, erravitne via seu lassa resedit,
incertum; nec post oculis est reddita nostris.   740
nec prius amissam respexi animumve reflexi
quam tumulum antiquae Cereris sedemque sacratam
venimus: hic demum collectis omnibus una
defuit, et comites natumque virumque fefellit.
quem non incusavi amens hominumque deorumque,   745
aut quid in eversa vidi crudelius urbe?
Ascanium Anchisenque patrem Teucrosque penatis
commendo sociis et curva valle recondo;
ipse urbem repeto et cingor fulgentibus armis.
stat casus renovare omnis omnemque reverti   750
per Troiam et rursus caput obiectare periclis.
principio muros obscuraque limina portae,
qua gressum extuleram, repeto et vestigia retro
observata sequor per noctem et lumine lustro:
horror ubique animo, simul ipsa silentia terrent.   755
inde domum, si forte pedem, si forte tulisset,
me refero: inruerant Danai et tectum omne tenebant.
ilicet ignis edax summa ad fastigia vento
volvitur; exsuperant flammae, furit aestus ad auras.
procedo et Priami sedes arcemque reviso: 760
et iam porticibus vacuis Iunonis asylo
custodes lecti Phoenix et dirus Ulixes

praedam adservabant. huc undique Troia gaza
incensis erepta adytis, mensaeque deorum
crateresque auro solidi, captivaque vestis   765
congeritur. pueri et pavidae longo ordine matres
stant circum.
ausus quin etiam voces iactare per umbram
implevi clamore vias, maestusque Creusam
nequiquam ingeminans iterumque iterumque vocavi.   770
quaerenti et tectis urbis sine fine ruenti
infelix simulacrum atque ipsius umbra Creusae
visa mihi ante oculos et nota maior imago.
obstipui, steteruntque comae et vox faucibus haesit.
tum sic adfari et curas his demere dictis: 775
'quid tantum insano iuvat indulgere dolori,
o dulcis coniunx? non haec sine numine divum
eveniunt; nec te hinc comitem asportare Creusam
fas aut ille sinit superi regnator Olympi.
longa tibi exsilia et vastum maris aequor arandum,   780
et terram Hesperiam venies, ubi Lydius arva
inter opima virum leni fluit agmine Thybris.
illic res laetae regnumque et regia coniunx
parta tibi; lacrimas dilectae pelle Creusae.
non ego Myrmidonum sedes Dolopumve superbas   785
aspiciam aut Grais servitum matribus ibo,
Dardanis et divae Veneris nurus;
sed me magna deum genetrix his detinet oris.
iamque vale et nati serva communis amorem.'
haec ubi dicta dedit, lacrimantem et multa volentem   790
dicere deseruit, tenuisque recessit in auras.
ter conatus ibi collo dare bracchia circum;
ter frustra comprensa manus effugit imago,
par levibus ventis volucrique simillima somno.

sic demum socios consumpta nocte reviso.   795
    Atque hic ingentem comitum adfluxisse novorum
invenio admirans numerum, matresque virosque,
collectam exsilio pubem, miserabile vulgus.
undique convenere animis opibusque parati
in quascumque velim pelago deducere terras.   800
iamque iugis summae surgebat Lucifer Idae
ducebatque diem, Danaique obsessa tenebant
limina portarum, nec spes opis ulla dabatur.
cessi et sublato montis genitore petivi.

BOOK 3

Postquam res Asiae Priamique evertere gentem
immeritam visum superis, ceciditque superbum
Ilium et omnis humo fumat Neptunia Troia,
diversa exsilia et desertas quaerere terras
auguriis agimur divum, classemque sub ipsa   5
Antandro et Phrygiae molimur montibus Idae,
incerti quo fata ferant, ubi sistere detur,
contrahimusque viros. vix prima inceperat aestas
et pater Anchises dare fatis vela iubebat,
litora cum patriae lacrimans portusque relinquo   10
et campos ubi Troia fuit. feror exsul in altum
cum sociis natoque penatibus et magnis dis.
  Terra procul vastis colitur Mavortia campis
(Thraces arant) acri quondam regnata Lycurgo,
hospitium antiquum Troiae sociique penates   15
dum fortuna fuit. feror huc et litore curvo
moenia prima loco fatis ingressus iniquis
Aeneadasque meo nomen de nomine fingo.
  Sacra Dionaeae matri divisque ferebam
auspicibus coeptorum operum, superoque nitentem   20
caelicolum regi mactabam in litore taurum.
forte fuit iuxta tumulus, quo cornea summo
virgulta et densis hastilibus horrida myrtus.
accessi viridemque ab humo convellere silvam
conatus, ramis tegerem ut frondentibus aras,   25
horrendum et dictu video mirabile monstrum.

nam quae prima solo ruptis radicibus arbos
vellitur, huic atro liquuntur sanguine guttae
et terram tabo maculant. mihi frigidus horror
membra quatit gelidusque coit formidine sanguis.   30
rursus et alterius lentum convellere vimen
insequor et causas penitus temptare latentis;
ater et alterius sequitur de cortice sanguis.
multa movens animo Nymphas venerabar agrestis
Gradivumque patrem, Geticis qui praesidet arvis,   35
rite secundarent visus omenque levarent.
tertia sed postquam maiore hastilia nisu
adgredior genibusque adversae obluctor harenae
(eloquar an sileam?) gemitus lacrimabilis imo
auditur tumulo et vox reddita fertur ad auris: 40
'quid miserum, Aenea, laceras? iam parce sepulto,
parce pias scelerare manus. non me tibi Troia
externum tulit aut cruor hic de stipite manat.
heu fuge crudelis terras, fuge litus avarum:
nam Polydorus ego. hic confixum ferrea texit   45
telorum seges et iaculis increvit acutis.'
tum vero ancipiti mentem formidine pressus
obstipui steteruntque comae et vox faucibus haesit.
    Hunc Polydorum auri quondam cum pondere magno
infelix Priamus furtim mandarat alendum   50
Threicio regi, cum iam diffideret armis
Dardaniae cingique urbem obsidione videret.
ille, ut opes fractae Teucrum et Fortuna recessit,
res Agamemnonias victriciaque arma secutus
fas omne abrumpit: Polydorum obtruncat, et auro   55
vi potitur. quid non mortalia pectora cogis,
auri sacra fames! postquam pavor ossa reliquit,
delectos populi ad proceres primumque parentem

monstra deum refero, et quae sit sententia posco.
omnibus idem animus, scelerata excedere terra,   60
linqui pollutum hospitium et dare classibus Austros.
ergo instauramus Polydoro funus, et ingens
aggeritur tumulo tellus; stant manibus arae,
caeruleis maestae vittis atraque cupresso,
et circum Iliades crinem de more solutae;   65
inferimus tepido spumantia cymbia lacte
sanguinis et sacri pateras, animamque sepulcro
condimus et magna supremum voce ciemus.
   Inde ubi prima fides pelago, placataque venti
dant maria et lenis crepitans vocat Auster in altum,   70
deducunt socii navis et litora complent.
provehimur portu terraeque urbesque recedunt.
sacra mari colitur medio gratissima tellus
Nereidum matri et Neptuno Aegaeo,
quam pius arquitenens oras et litora circum   75
errantem Mycono e celsa Gyaroque revinxit,
immotamque coli dedit et contemnere ventos.
huc feror, haec fessos tuto placidissima portu
accipit; egressi veneramur Apollinis urbem.
rex Anius, rex idem hominum Phoebique sacerdos,   80
vittis et sacra redimitus tempora lauro
occurrit; veterem Anchisen agnovit amicum.
iungimus hospitio dextras et tecta subimus.
   Templa dei saxo venerabar structa vetusto:
'da propriam, Thymbraee, domum; da moenia fessis   85
et genus et mansuram urbem; serva altera Troiae
Pergama, reliquias Danaum atque immitis Achilli.
quem sequimur? quove ire iubes? ubi ponere sedes?
da, pater, augurium atque animis inlabere nostris.'
vix ea fatus eram: tremere omnia visa repente,   90

liminaque laurusque dei, totusque moveri
mons circum et mugire adytis cortina reclusis.
summissi petimus terram et vox fertur ad auris:
'Dardanidae duri, quae vos a stirpe parentum
prima tulit tellus, eadem vos ubere laeto   95
accipiet reduces. antiquam exquirite matrem.
hic domus Aeneae cunctis dominabitur oris
et nati natorum et qui nascentur ab illis.'
haec Phoebus; mixtoque ingens exorta tumultu
laetitia, et cuncti quae sint ea moenia quaerunt,   100
quo Phoebus vocet errantis iubeatque reverti.
tum genitor veterum volvens monimenta virorum
'audite, o proceres,' ait 'et spes discite vestras.
Creta Iovis magni medio iacet insula ponto,
mons Idaeus ubi et gentis cunabula nostrae.   105
. centum urbes habitant magnas, uberrima regna,
maximus unde pater, si rite audita recordor,
Teucrus Rhoeteas primum est advectus in oras,
optavitque locum regno. nondum Ilium et arces
Pergameae steterant; habitabant vallibus imis.   110
hinc mater cultrix Cybeli Corybantiaque aera
Idaeumque nemus, hinc fida silentia sacris,
et iuncti currum dominae subiere leones.
ergo agite et divum ducunt qua iussa sequamur:
placemus ventos et Cnosia regna petamus.   115
nec longo distant cursu: modo Iuppiter adsit,
tertia lux classem Cretaeis sistet in oris.'
sic fatus meritos aris mactavit honores,
taurum Neptuno, taurum tibi, pulcher Apollo,
nigram Hiemi pecudem, Zephyris felicibus albam.   120
    Fama volat pulsum regnis cessisse paternis
Idomenea ducem, desertaque litora Cretae,

hoste vacare domum sedesque astare relictas.
linquimus Ortygiae portus pelagoque volamus
bacchatamque iugis Naxon viridemque Donusam,   125
Olearon niveamque Paron sparsasque per aequor
Cycladas, et crebris legimus freta concita terris.
nauticus exoritur vario certamine clamor:
hortantur socii Cretam proavosque petamus.
prosequitur surgens a puppi ventus euntis,   130
et tandem antiquis Curetum adlabimur oris.
ergo avidus muros optatae molior urbis
Pergameamque voco, et laetam cognomine gentem
hortor amare focos arcemque attollere tectis.

Iamque fere sicco subductae litore puppes;   135
conubiis arvisque novis operata iuventus;
iura domosque dabam; subito cum tabida membris
corrupto caeli tractu miserandaque venit
arboribusque satisque lues et letifer annus.
linquebant dulcis animas aut aegra trahebant   140
corpora; tum sterilis exurere Sirius agros,
arebant herbae et victum seges aegra negabat.
rursus ad oraclum Ortygiae Phoebumque remenso
hortatur pater ire mari veniamque precari,
quam fessis finem rebus ferat, unde laborum   145
temptare auxilium iubeat, quo vertere cursus.

Nox erat et terris animalia somnus habebat:
effigies sacrae divum Phrygiique Penates,
quos mecum ab Troia mediisque ex ignibus urbis
extuleram, visi ante oculos astare iacentis   150
in somnis multo manifesti lumine, qua se
plena per insertas fundebat luna fenestras;
tum sic adfari et curas his demere dictis:
'quod tibi delato Ortygiam dicturus Apollo est,

hic canit et tua nos en ultro ad limina mittit.   155
nos te Dardania incensa tuaque arma secuti,
nos tumidum sub te permensi classibus aequor,
idem venturos tollemus in astra nepotes
imperiumque urbi dabimus. tu moenia magnis
magna para longumque fugae ne linque laborem.   160
mutandae sedes. non haec tibi litora suasit
Delius aut Cretae iussit considere Apollo.
est locus, Hesperiam Grai cognomine dicunt,
terra antiqua, potens armis atque ubere glaebae;
Oenotri coluere viri; nunc fama minores   165
Italiam dixisse ducis de nomine gentem:
hae nobis propriae sedes, hinc Dardanus ortus
Iasiusque pater, genus a quo principe nostrum.
surge age et haec laetus longaevo dicta parenti
haud dubitanda refer: Corythum terrasque requirat   170
Ausonias; Dictaea negat tibi Iuppiter arva.'
talibus attonitus visis et voce deorum
(nec sopor illud erat, sed coram agnoscere vultus
velatasque comas praesentiaque ora videbar;
tum gelidus toto manabat corpore sudor)   175
corripio e stratis corpus tendoque supinas
ad caelum cum voce manus et munera libo
intemerata focis. perfecto laetus honore
Anchisen facio certum remque ordine pando.
agnovit prolem ambiguam geminosque parentis,   180
seque novo veterum deceptum errore locorum.
tum memorat: 'nate, Iliacis exercite fatis,
sola mihi talis casus Cassandra canebat.
nunc repeto haec generi portendere debita nostro
et saepe Hesperiam, saepe Itala regna vocare.   185
sed quis ad Hesperiae venturos litora Teucros

crederet? aut quem tum vates Cassandra moveret?
cedamus Phoebo et moniti meliora sequamur.'
sic ait, et cuncti dicto paremus ovantes.
hanc quoque deserimus sedem paucisque relictis   190
vela damus vastumque cava trabe currimus aequor.

   Postquam altum tenuere rates nec iam amplius ullae
apparent terrae, caelum undique et undique pontus,
tum mihi caeruleus supra caput astitit imber
noctem hiememque ferens, et inhorruit unda tenebris.   195
continuo venti volvunt mare magnaque surgunt
aequora, dispersi iactamur gurgite vasto;
involvere diem nimbi et nox umida caelum
abstulit, ingeminant abruptis nubibus ignes.
excutimur cursu et caecis erramus in undis.   200
ipse diem noctemque negat discernere caelo
nec meminisse viae media Palinurus in unda.
tris adeo incertos caeca caligine soles
erramus pelago, totidem sine sidere noctes.
quarto terra die primum se attollere tandem   205
visa, aperire procul montis ac volvere fumum.
vela cadunt, remis insurgimus; haud mora, nautae
adnixi torquent spumas et caerula verrunt.
servatum ex undis Strophadum me litora primum
excipiunt. Strophades Graio stant nomine dictae   210
insulae Ionio in magno, quas dira Celaeno
Harpyiaeque colunt aliae, Phineia postquam
clausa domus mensasque metu liquere priores.
tristius haud illis monstrum, nec saevior ulla
pestis et ira deum Stygiis sese extulit undis.   215
virginei volucrum vultus, foedissima ventris
proluvies uncaeque manus et pallida semper
ora fame.

huc ubi delati portus intravimus, ecce
laeta boum passim campis armenta videmus   220
caprigenumque pecus nullo custode per herbas.
inruimus ferro et divos ipsumque vocamus
in partem praedamque Iovem; tum litore curvo
exstruimusque toros dapibusque epulamur opimis.
at subitae horrifico lapsu de montibus adsunt   225
Harpyiae et magnis quatiunt clangoribus alas,
diripiuntque dapes contactuque omnia foedant
immundo; tum vox taetrum dira inter odorem.
rursum in secessu longo sub rupe cavata
[arboribus clausam circum atque horrentibus umbris]   230
instruimus mensas arisque reponimus ignem;
rursum ex diverso caeli caecisque latebris
turba sonans praedam pedibus circumvolat uncis,
polluit ore dapes. sociis tunc arma capessant
edico, et dira bellum cum gente gerendum.   235
hand secus ac iussi faciunt tectosque per herbam
disponunt ensis et scuta latentia condunt.
ergo ubi delapsae sonitum per curva dedere
litora, dat signum specula Misenus ab alta
aere cavo. invadunt socii et nova proelia temptant,   240
obscenas pelagi ferro foedare volucris.
sed neque vim plumis ullam nec vulnera tergo
accipiunt, celerique fuga sub sidera lapsae
semesam praedam et vestigia foeda relinquunt.
una in praecelsa consedit rupe Celaeno,   245
infelix vates, rumpitque hanc pectore vocem:
'bellum etiam pro caede boum stratisque iuvencis,
Laomedontiadae, bellumne inferre paratis
et patrio Harpyias insontis pellere regno?
accipite ergo animis atque haec mea figite dicta,   250

quae Phoebo pater omnipotens, mihi Phoebus Apollo
praedixit, vobis Furiarum ego maxima pando.
Italiam cursu petitis ventisque vocatis:
ibitis Italiam portusque intrare licebit.
sed non ante datam cingetis moenibus urbem   255
quam vos dira fames nostraeque iniuria caedis
ambesas subigat malis absumere mensas.'
dixit, et in silvam pennis ablata refugit.
at sociis subita gelidus formidine sanguis
deriguit: cecidere animi, nec iam amplius armis,   260
sed votis precibusque iubent exposcere pacem,
sive deae seu sint dirae obscenaeque volucres.
et pater Anchises passis de litore palmis
numina magna vocat meritosque indicit honores:
'di, prohibete minas; di, talem avertite casum   265
et placidi servate pios.' tum litore funem
deripere excussosque iubet laxare rudentis.
tendunt vela Noti: fugimus spumantibus undis
qua cursum ventusque gubernatorque vocabat.
iam medio apparet fluctu nemorosa Zacynthos   270
Dulichiumque Sameque et Neritos ardua saxis.
effugimus scopulos Ithacae, Laertia regna,
et terram altricem saevi exsecramur Ulixi.
mox et Leucatae nimbosa cacumina montis
et formidatus nautis aperitur Apollo.   275
hunc petimus fessi et parvae succedimus urbi;
ancora de prora iacitur, stant litore puppes.

   Ergo insperata tandem tellure potiti
lustramurque Iovi votisque incendimus aras,
Actiaque Iliacis celebramus litora ludis.   280
exercent patrias oleo labente palaestras
nudati socii: iuvat evasisse tot urbes

Argolicas mediosque fugam tenuisse per hostis.
interea magnum sol circumvolvitur annum
et glacialis hiems Aquilonibus asperat undas;   285
aere cavo clipeum, magni gestamen Abantis,
postibus adversis figo et rem carmine signo:
AENEAS HAEC DE DANAIS VICTORIBVS ARMA.
linquere tum portus iubeo et considere transtris.
certatim socii feriunt mare et aequora verrunt.   290
protinus aërias Phaeacum abscondimus arces
litoraque Epiri legimus portuque subimus
Chaonio et celsam Buthroti accedimus urbem.

Hic incredibilis rerum fama occupat auris,
Priamiden Helenum Graias regnare per urbis   295
coniugio Aeacidae Pyrrhi sceptrisque potitum,
et patrio Andromachen iterum cessisse marito.
obstipui, miroque incensum pectus amore
compellare virum et casus cognoscere tantos.
progredior portu classis et litora linquens,   300
sollemnis cum forte dapes et tristia dona
ante urbem in luco falsi Simoentis ad undam
libabat cineri Andromache manisque vocabat
Hectoreum ad tumulum, viridi quem caespite inanem
et geminas, causam lacrimis, sacraverat aras.   305
ut me conspexit venientem et Troia circum
arma amens vidit, magnis exterrita monstris
deriguit visu in medio, calor ossa reliquit;
labitur et longo vix tandem tempore fatur:
'verane te facies, verus mihi nuntius adfers,   310
nate dea? vivisne? aut, si lux alma recessit,
Hector ubi est?' dixit, lacrimasque effudit et omnem
implevit clamore locum. vix pauca furenti
subicio et raris turbatus vocibus hisco:

'vivo equidem vitamque extrema per omnia duco;   315
ne dubita, nam vera vides.
heu! quis te casus deiectam coniuge tanto
excipit, aut quae digna satis fortuna revisit,
Hectoris Andromache? Pyrrhin conubia servas?'
deiecit vultum et demissa voce locuta est: 320
'o felix una ante alias Priameia virgo,
hostilem ad tumulum Troiae sub moenibus altis
iussa mori, quae sortitus non pertulit ullos
nec victoris heri tetigit captiva cubile!
nos patria incensa diversa per aequora vectae   325
stirpis Achilleae fastus iuvenemque superbum
servitio enixae tulimus; qui deinde secutus
Ledaeam Hermionen Lacedaemoniosque hymenaeos
me famulo famulamque Heleno transmisit habendam.
ast illum ereptae magno flammatus amore   330
coniugis et scelerum furiis agitatus Orestes
excipit incautum patriasque obtruncat ad aras.
morte Neoptolemi regnorum reddita cessit
pars Heleno, qui Chaonios cognomine campos
Chaoniamque omnem Troiano a Chaone dixit,   335
Pergamaque Iliacamque iugis hanc addidit arcem.
sed tibi qui cursum venti, quae fata dedere?
aut quisnam ignarum nostris deus appulit oris?
quid puer Ascanius? superatne et vescitur aura?
quem tibi iam Troia —   340
ecqua tamen puero est amissae cura parentis?
ecquid in antiquam virtutem animosque virilis
et pater Aeneas et avunculus excitat Hector?'
talia fundebat lacrimans longosque ciebat
incassum fletus, cum sese a moenibus heros   345
Priamides multis Helenus comitantibus adfert,

agnoscitque suos laetusque ad limina ducit,
et multum lacrimas verba inter singula fundit.
procedo et parvam Troiam simulataque magnis
Pergama et arentem Xanthi cognomine rivum   350
agnosco, Scaeaeque amplector limina portae.
nec non et Teucri socia simul urbe fruuntur.
illos porticibus rex accipiebat in amplis:
aulai medio libabant pocula Bacchi
impositis auro dapibus, paterasque tenebant.   355

  Iamque dies alterque dies processit, et aurae
vela vocant tumidoque inflatur carbasus austro:
his vatem adgredior dictis ac talia quaeso:
'Troiugena, interpres divum, qui numina Phoebi,
qui tripoda ac Clarii laurus, qui sidera sentis   360
et volucrum linguas et praepetis omina pennae,
fare age (namque omnis cursum mihi prospera dixit
religio, et cuncti suaserunt numine divi
Italiam petere et terras temptare repostas;
sola novum dictuque nefas Harpyia Celaeno   365
prodigium canit et tristis denuntiat iras
obscenamque famem) quae prima pericula vito?
quidve sequens tantos possim superare labores?'
hic Helenus caesis primum de more iuvencis
exorat pacem divum vittasque resolvit   370
sacrati capitis, meque ad tua limina, Phoebe,
ipse manu multo suspensum numine ducit,
atque haec deinde canit divino ex ore sacerdos:

  'Nate dea (nam te maioribus ire per altum
auspiciis manifesta fides, sic fata deum rex   375
sortitur volvitque vices, is vertitur ordo),
pauca tibi e multis, quo tutior hospita lustres
aequora et Ausonio possis considere portu,

expediam dictis: prohibent nam cetera Parcae
scire Helenum farique vetat Saturnia Iuno.   380
principio Italiam, quam tu iam rere propinquam
vicinosque, ignare, paras invadere portus,
longa procul longis via dividit invia terris.
ante et Trinacria lentandus remus in unda
et salis Ausonii lustrandum navibus aequor   385
infernique lacus Aeaeaeque insula Circae,
quam tuta possis urbem componere terra.
signa tibi dicam, tu condita mente teneto:
cum tibi sollicito secreti ad fluminis undam
litoreis ingens inventa sub ilicibus sus   390
triginta capitum fetus enixa iacebit,
alba solo recubans, albi circum ubera nati,
is locus urbis erit, requies ea certa laborum.
nec tu mensarum morsus horresce futuros:
fata viam invenient aderitque vocatus Apollo.   395
has autem terras Italique hanc litoris oram,
proxima quae nostri perfunditur aequoris aestu,
effuge; cuncta malis habitantur moenia Grais.
hic et Narycii posuerunt moenia Locri,
et Sallentinos obsedit milite campos   400
Lyctius Idomeneus; hic illa ducis Meliboei
parva Philoctetae subnixa Petelia muro.
quin ubi transmissae steterint trans aequora classes
et positis aris iam vota in litore solves,
purpureo velare comas adopertus amictu,   405
ne qua inter sanctos ignis in honore deorum
hostilis facies occurrat et omina turbet.
hunc socii morem sacrorum, hunc ipse teneto;
hac casti maneant in religione nepotes.
ast ubi digressum Siculae te admoverit orae   410

ventus, et angusti rarescent claustra Pelori,
laeva tibi tellus et longo laeva petantur
aequora circuitu; dextrum fuge litus et undas.
haec loca vi quondam et vasta convulsa ruina
(tantum aevi longinqua valet mutare vetustas)   415
dissiluisse ferunt; cum protinus utraque tellus
una foret, venit medio vi pontus et undis
Hesperium Siculo latus abscidit, arvaque et urbes
litore diductas angusto interluit aestu.
dextrum Scylla latus, laevum implacata Charybdis   420
obsidet, atque imo barathri ter gurgite vastos
sorbet in abruptum fluctus rursusque sub auras
erigit alternos, et sidera verberat unda.
at Scyllam caecis cohibet spelunca latebris
ora exsertantem et navis in saxa trahentem.   425
prima hominis facies et pulchro pectore virgo
pube tenus, postrema immani corpore pistrix
delphinum caudas utero commissa luporum.
praestat Trinacrii metas lustrare Pachyni
cessantem, longos et circumflectere cursus,   430
quam semel informem vasto vidisse sub antro
Scyllam et caeruleis canibus resonantia saxa.
praeterea, si qua est Heleno prudentia vati,
si qua fides, animum si veris implet Apollo,
unum illud tibi, nate dea, proque omnibus unum   435
praedicam et repetens iterumque iterumque monebo,
Iunonis magnae primum prece numen adora,
Iunoni cane vota libens dominamque potentem
supplicibus supera donis: sic denique victor
Trinacria finis Italos mittere relicta.   440
huc ubi delatus Cumaeam accesseris urbem
divinosque lacus et Averna sonantia silvis,

insanam vatem aspicies, quae rupe sub ima
fata canit foliisque notas et nomina mandat.
quaecumque in foliis descripsit carmina virgo   445
digerit in numerum atque antro seclusa relinquit:
illa manent immota locis neque ab ordine cedunt.
verum eadem, verso tenuis cum cardine ventus
impulit et teneras turbavit ianua frondes,
numquam deinde cavo volitantia prendere saxo   450
nec revocare situs aut iungere carmina curat.
inconsulti abeunt sedemque odere Sibyllae.
hic tibi ne qua morae fuerint dispendia tanti,
quamvis increpitent socii et vi cursus in altum
vela vocet, possisque sinus implere secundos,   455
quin adeas vatem precibusque oracula poscas
ipsa canat vocemque volens atque ora resolvat.
illa tibi Italiae populos venturaque bella
et quo quemque modo fugiasque ferasque laborem
expediet, cursusque dabit venerata secundos.   460
haec sunt quae nostra liceat te voce moneri.
vade age et ingentem factis fer ad aethera Troiam.'
    Quae postquam vates sic ore effatus amico est,
dona dehinc auro gravia ac secto elephanto
imperat ad navis ferri, stipatque carinis   465
ingens argentum Dodonaeosque lebetas,
loricam consertam hamis auroque trilicem,
et conum insignis galeae cristasque comantis,
arma Neoptolemi. sunt et sua dona parenti.
addit equos, additque duces,   470
remigium supplet, socios simul instruit armis.
    Interea classem velis aptare iubebat
Anchises, fieret vento mora ne qua ferenti.
quem Phoebi interpres multo compellat honore:

'coniugio, Anchisa, Veneris dignate superbo,   475
cura deum, bis Pergameis erepte ruinis,
ecce tibi Ausoniae tellus: hanc arripe velis.
et tamen hanc pelago praeterlabare necesse est:
Ausoniae pars illa procul quam pandit Apollo.
vade,' ait 'o felix nati pietate. quid ultra   480
provehor et fando surgentis demoror Austros?'
nec minus Andromache digressu maesta supremo
fert picturatas auri subtemine vestis
et Phrygiam Ascanio chlamydem (nec cedit honore)
textilibusque onerat donis, ac talia fatur   485
'accipe et haec, manuum tibi quae monimenta mearum
sint, puer, et longum Andromachae testentur amorem,
coniugis Hectoreae. cape dona extrema tuorum,
o mihi sola mei super Astyanactis imago.
sic oculos, sic ille manus, sic ora ferebat;   490
et nunc aequali tecum pubesceret aevo.'
hos ego digrediens lacrimis adfabar obortis:
'vivite felices, quibus est fortuna peracta
iam sua: nos alia ex aliis in fata vocamur.
vobis parta quies: nullum maris aequor arandum,   495
arva neque Ausoniae semper cedentia retro
quaerenda. effigiem Xanthi Troiamque videtis
quam vestrae fecere manus, melioribus, opto,
auspiciis, et quae fuerit minus obvia Grais.
si quando Thybrim vicinaque Thybridis arva   500
intraro gentique meae data moenia cernam,
cognatas urbes olim populosque propinquos,
Epiro Hesperiam (quibus idem Dardanus auctor
atque idem casus), unam faciemus utramque
Troiam animis: maneat nostros ea cura nepotes.'   505
   Provehimur pelago vicina Ceraunia iuxta,

unde iter Italiam cursusque brevissimus undis.
sol ruit interea et montes umbrantur opaci.
sternimur optatae gremio telluris ad undam
sortiti remos passimque in litore sicco   510
corpora curamus; fessos sopor inrigat artus.
necdum orbem medium Nox Horis acta subibat:
haud segnis strato surgit Palinurus et omnis
explorat ventos atque auribus aëra captat;
sidera cuncta notat tacito labentia caelo,   515
Arcturum pluviasque Hyadas geminosque Triones,
armatumque auro circumspicit Oriona.
postquam cuncta videt caelo constare sereno,
dat clarum e puppi signum: nos castra movemus
temptamusque viam et velorum pandimus alas.   520
  Iamque rubescebat stellis Aurora fugatis
cum procul obscuros collis humilemque videmus
Italiam.   Italiam primus conclamat Achates,
Italiam laeto socii clamore salutant.
tum pater Anchises magnum cratera corona   525
induit implevitque mero, divosque vocavit
stans celsa in puppi:
'di maris et terrae tempestatumque potentes,
ferte viam vento facilem et spirate secundi.'
crebrescunt optatae aurae portusque patescit   530
iam propior, templumque apparet in arce Minervae.
vela legunt socii et proras ad litora torquent.
portus ab euroo fluctu curvatus in arcum,
obiectae salsa spumant aspergine cautes,
ipse latet: gemino dimittunt bracchia muro   535
turriti scopuli refugitque ab litore templum.
quattuor hic, primum omen, equos in gramine vidi
tondentis campum late, candore nivali.

et pater Anchises 'bellum, o terra hospita, portas:
bello armantur equi, bellum haec armenta minantur.   540
sed tamen idem olim curru succedere sueti
quadripedes et frena iugo concordia ferre:
spes et pacis' ait.   tum numina sancta precamur
Palladis armisonae, quae prima accepit ovantis,
et capita ante aras Phrygio velamur amictu,   545
praeceptisque Heleni, dederat quae maxima, rite
Iunoni Argivae iussos adolemus honores.

   Haud mora, continuo perfectis ordine votis
cornua velatarum obvertimus antemnarum,
Graiugenumque domos suspectaque linquimus arva.   550
hinc sinus Herculei (si vera est fama) Tarenti
cernitur, attollit se diva Lacinia contra,
Caulonisque arces et navifragum Scylaceum.
tum procul e fluctu Trinacria cernitur Aetna,
et gemitum ingentem pelagi pulsataque saxa   555
audimus longe fractasque ad litora voces,
exsultantque vada atque aestu miscentur harenae.
et pater Anchises 'nimirum hic illa Charybdis:
hos Helenus scopulos, haec saxa horrenda canebat.
eripite, o socii, pariterque insurgite remis.'   560
haud minus ac iussi faciunt, primusque rudentem
contorsit laevas proram Palinurus ad undas;
laevam cuncta cohors remis ventisque petivit.
tollimur in caelum curvato gurgite, et idem
subducta ad manis imos desedimus unda.   565
ter scopuli clamorem inter cava saxa dedere,
ter spumam elisam et rorantia vidimus astra.
interea fessos ventus cum sole reliquit,
ignarique viae Cyclopum adlabimur oris.

   Portus ab accessu ventorum immotus et ingens   570

ipse: sed horrificis iuxta tonat Aetna ruinis,
interdumque atram prorumpit ad aethera nubem
turbine fumantem piceo et candente favilla,
attollitque globos flammarum et sidera lambit,
interdum scopulos avulsaque viscera montis   575
erigit eructans, liquefactaque saxa sub auras
cum gemitu glomerat fundoque exaestuat imo.
fama est Enceladi semustum fulmine corpus
urgeri mole hac, ingentemque insuper Aetnam
impositam ruptis flammam exspirare caminis,   580
et fessum quotiens mutet latus, intremere omnem
murmure Trinacriam et caelum subtexere fumo.
noctem illam tecti silvis immania monstra
perferimus, nec quae sonitum det causa videmus.
nam neque erant astrorum ignes nec lucidus aethra   585
siderea polus, obscuro sed nubila caelo,
et lunam in nimbo nox intempesta tenebat.

  Postera iamque dies primo surgebat Eoo
umentemque Aurora polo dimoverat umbram,
cum subito e silvis macie confecta suprema   590
ignoti nova forma viri miserandaque cultu
procedit supplexque manus ad litora tendit.
respicimus. dira inluvies immissaque barba,
consertum tegimen spinis: at cetera Graius,
et quondam patriis ad Troiam missus in armis.   595
isque ubi Dardanios habitus et Troia vidit
arma procul, paulum aspectu conterritus haesit
continuitque gradum; mox sese ad litora praeceps
cum fletu precibusque tulit: 'per sidera testor,
per superos atque hoc caeli spirabile lumen,   600
tollite me, Teucri; quascumque abducite terras:
hoc sat. erit scio me Danais e classibus unum

et bello Iliacos fateor petiisse penatis.
pro quo, si sceleris tanta est iniuria nostri,
spargite me in fluctus vastoque immergite ponto;   605
si pereo, hominum manibus periisse iuvabit.'
dixerat et genua amplexus genibusque volutans
haerebat.   qui sit fari, quo sanguine cretus,
hortamur, quae deinde agitet fortuna fateri.
ipse pater dextram Anchises haud multa moratus   610
dat iuveni atque animum praesenti pignore firmat.
ille haec deposita tandem formidine fatur:
'sum patria ex Ithaca, comes infelicis Ulixi,
nomine Achaemenides, Troiam genitore Adamasto
paupere (mansissetque utinam fortuna!) profectus.   615
hic me, dum trepidi crudelia limina linquunt,
immemores socii vasto Cyclopis in antro
deseruere.   domus sanie dapibusque cruentis,
intus opaca, ingens.   ipse arduus, altaque pulsat
sidera (di talem terris avertite pestem!)   620
nec visu facilis nec dictu adfabilis ulli;
visceribus miserorum et sanguine vescitur atro.
vidi egomet duo de numero cum corpora nostro
prensa manu magna medio resupinus in antro
frangeret ad saxum, sanieque aspersa natarent   625
limina; vidi atro cum membra fluentia tabo
manderet et tepidi tremerent sub dentibus artus —
haud impune quidem, nec talia passus Ulixes
oblitusve sui est Ithacus discrimine tanto.
nam simul expletus dapibus vinoque sepultus   630
cervicem inflexam posuit, iacuitque per antrum
immensus saniem eructans et frusta cruento
per somnum commixta mero, nos magna precati
numina sortitique vices una undique circum

fundimur, et telo lumen terebramus acuto   635
ingens quod torva solum sub fronte latebat,
Argolici clipei aut Phoebeae lampadis instar,
et tandem laeti sociorum ulciscimur umbras.
sed fugite, o miseri, fugite atque ab litore funem
rumpite.   640
nam qualis quantusque cavo Polyphemus in antro
lanigeras claudit pecudes atque ubera pressat,
centum alii curva haec habitant ad litora vulgo
infandi Cyclopes et altis montibus errant.
tertia iam lunae se cornua lumine complent   645
cum vitam in silvis inter deserta ferarum
lustra domosque traho, vastosque ab rupe Cyclopas
prospicio sonitumque pedum vocemque tremesco.
victum infelicem, bacas lapidosaque corna,
dant rami, et vulsis pascunt radicibus herbae.   650
omnia conlustrans hanc primum ad litora classem
conspexi venientem. huic me, quaecumque fuisset,
addixi: satis est gentem effugisse nefandam.
vos animam hanc potius quocumque absumite leto.'

    Vix ea fatus erat summo cum monte videmus   655
ipsum inter pecudes vasta se mole moventem
pastorem Polyphemum et litora nota petentem,
monstrum horrendum, informe, ingens, cui lumen ademptum.
trunca manum pinus regit et vestigia firmat;
lanigerae comitantur óves; ea sola voluptas   660
solamenque mali.
postquam altos tetigit fluctus et ad aequora venit,
luminis effossi fluidum lavit inde cruorem
dentibus infrendens gemitu, graditurque per aequor
iam medium, necdum fluctus latera ardua tinxit.   665
nos procul inde fugam trepidi celerare recepto

supplice sic merito tacitique incidere funem,
vertimus et proni certantibus aequora remis.
sensit, et ad sonitum vocis vestigia torsit.
verum ubi nulla datur dextra adfectare potestas   670
nec potis Ionios fluctus aequare sequendo,
clamorem immensum tollit, quo pontus et omnes
intremuere undae, penitusque exterrita tellus
Italiae curvisque immugiit Aetna cavernis.
at genus e silvis Cyclopum et montibus altis   675
excitum ruit ad portus et litora complent.
cernimus astantis nequiquam lumine torvo
Aetnaeos fratres caelo capita alta ferentis,
concilium horrendum: quales cum vertice celso
aëriae quercus aut coniferae cyparissi   680
constiterunt, silva alta Iovis lucusve Dianae.
praecipitis metus acer agit quocumque rudentis
excutere et ventis intendere vela secundis.
contra iussa monent Heleni, Scyllam atque Charybdim
inter, utramque viam leti discrimine parvo,   685
ni teneant cursus; certum est dare lintea retro.
ecce autem Boreas angusta ab sede Pelori
missus adest: vivo praetervehor ostia saxo
Pantagiae Megarosque sinus Thapsumque iacentem.
talia monstrabat relegens errata retrorsus   690
litora Achaemenides, comes infelicis Ulixi.

    Sicanio praetenta sinu iacet insula contra
Plemyrium undosum; nomen dixere priores
Ortygiam. Alpheum fama est huc Elidis amnem
occultas egisse vias subter mare, qui nunc   695
ore, Arethusa, tuo Siculis confunditur undis.
iussi numina magna loci veneramur, et inde
exsupero praepingue solum stagnantis Helori.

hinc altas cautes proiectaque saxa Pachyni
radimus, et fatis numquam concessa moveri　　700
apparet Camerina procul campique Geloi,
immanisque Gela fluvii cognomine dicta.
arduus inde Acragas ostentat maxima longe
moenia, magnanimum quondam generator equorum;
teque datis linquo ventis, palmosa Selinus,　　705
et vada dura lego saxis Lilybeia caecis.
hinc Drepani me portus et inlaetabilis ora
accipit.　hic pelagi tot tempestatibus actus
heu, genitorem, omnis curae casusque levamen,
amitto Anchisen.　hic me, pater optime, fessum　　710
deseris, heu, tantis nequiquam erepte periclis!
nec vates Helenus, cum multa horrenda moneret,
hos mihi praedixit luctus, non dira Celaeno.
hic labor extremus, longarum haec meta viarum;
hinc me digressum vestris deus appulit oris.'　　715
　　Sic pater Aeneas intentis omnibus unus
fata renarrabat divum cursusque docebat.
conticuit tandem factoque hic fine quievit.

BOOK 4

At regina gravi iamdudum saucia cura
vulnus alit venis et caeco carpitur igni.
multa viri virtus animo multusque recursat
gentis honos; haerent infixi pectore vultus
verbaque, nec placidam membris dat cura quietem.   5
postera Phoebea lustrabat lampade terras
umentemque Aurora polo dimoverat umbram,
cum sic unanimam adloquitur male sana sororem:
'Anna soror, quae me suspensam insomnia terrent!
quis novus hic nostris successit sedibus hospes,   10
quem sese ore ferens, quam forti pectore et armis!
credo equidem, nec vana fides, genus esse deorum.
degeneres animos timor arguit.   heu, quibus ille
iactatus fatis! quae bella exhausta canebat!
si mihi non animo fixum immotumque sederet   15
ne cui me vinclo vellem sociare iugali,
postquam primus amor deceptam morte fefellit;
si non pertaesum thalami taedaeque fuisset,
huic uni forsan potui succumbere culpae.
Anna, fatebor enim, miseri post fata Sychaei   20
coniugis et sparsos fraterna caede penatis
solus hic inflexit sensus animumque labantem
impulit.   agnosco veteris vestigia flammae.
sed mihi vel tellus optem prius ima dehiscat
vel pater omnipotens adigat me fulmine ad umbras,   25
pallentis umbras Erebo noctemque profundam,

ante, pudor, quam te violo aut tua iura resolvo.
ille meos, primus qui me sibi iunxit, amores
abstulit; ille habeat secum servetque sepulcro.'
sic effata sinum lacrimis implevit obortis.   30

   Anna refert: 'o luce magis dilecta sorori,
solane perpetua maerens carpere iuventa
nec dulcis natos Veneris nec praemia noris?
id cinerem aut manis credis curare sepultos?
esto, aegram nulli quondam flexere mariti,   35
non Libyae, non ante Tyro; despectus Iarbas
ductoresque alii, quos Africa terra triumphis
dives alit: placitone etiam pugnabis amori?
nec venit in mentem quorum consederis arvis?
hinc Gaetulae urbes, genus insuperabile bello,   40
· et Numidae infreni cingunt et inhospita Syrtis;
hinc deserta siti regio lateque furentes
Barcaei. quid bella Tyro surgentia dicam
germanique minas?
dis equidem auspicibus reor et Iunone secunda   45
hunc cursum Iliacas vento tenuisse carinas.
quam tu urbem, soror, hanc cernes, quae surgere regna
coniugio tali! Teucrum comitantibus armis
Punica se quantis attollet gloria rebus!
tu modo posce deos veniam, sacrisque litatis   50
indulge hospitio causasque innecte morandi,
dum pelago desaevit hiems et aquosus Orion,
quassataeque rates, dum non tractabile caelum.'
his dictis incensum animum flammavit amore
spemque dedit dubiae menti solvitque pudorem.   55

   Principio delubra adeunt pacemque per aras
exquirunt; mactant lectas de more bidentis
legiferae Cereri Phoeboque patrique Lyaeo,

Iunoni ante omnis, cui vincla iugalia curae.
ipsa tenens dextra pateram pulcherrima Dido 60
candentis vaccae media inter cornua fundit,
aut ante ora deum pinguis spatiatur ad aras,
instauratque diem donis, pecudumque reclusis
pectoribus inhians spirantia consulit exta.
heu, vatum ignarae mentes! quid vota furentem, 65
quid delubra iuvant? est mollis flamma medullas
interea et tacitum vivit sub pectore vulnus.
uritur infelix Dido totaque vagatur
urbe furens, qualis coniecta cerva sagitta,
quam procul incautam nemora inter Cresia fixit 70
pastor agens telis liquitque volatile ferrum
nescius: illa fuga silvas saltusque peragrat
Dictaeos; haeret lateri letalis harundo.
nunc media Aenean secum per moenia ducit
Sidoniasque ostentat opes urbemque paratam, 75
incipit effari mediaque in voce resistit;
nunc eadem labente die convivia quaerit,
Iliacosque iterum demens audire labores
exposcit pendetque iterum narrantis ab ore.
post ubi digressi, lumenque obscura vicissim 80
luna premit suadentque cadentia sidera somnos,
sola domo maeret vacua stratisque relictis
incubat. illum absens absentem auditque videtque,
aut gremio Ascanium genitoris imagine capta
detinet, infandum si fallere possit amorem. 85
non coeptae adsurgunt turres, non arma iuventus
exercet portusve aut propugnacula bello
tuta parant: pendent opera interrupta minaeque
murorum ingentes aequataque machina caelo.
   Quam simul ac tali persensit peste teneri 90

cara Iovis coniunx nec famam obstare furori,
talibus adgreditur Venerem Saturnia dictis:
'egregiam vero laudem et spolia ampla refertis
tuque puerque tuus, magnum et memorabile numen,
una dolo divum si femina victa duorum est.   95
nec me adeo fallit veritam te moenia nostra
suspectas habuisse domos Karthaginis altae.
sed quis erit modus, aut quo nunc certamine tanto?
quin potius pacem aeternam pactosque hymenaeos
exercemus? habes tota quod mente petisti: 100
ardet amans Dido traxitque per ossa furorem.
communem hunc ergo populum paribusque regamus
auspiciis; liceat Phrygio servire marito
dotalisque tuae Tyrios permittere dextrae.'

Olli (sensit enim simulata mente locutam,   105
quo regnum Italiae Libycas averteret oras)
sic contra est ingressa Venus: 'quis talia demens
abnuat aut tecum malit contendere bello —
si modo quod memoras factum fortuna sequatur?
sed fatis incerta feror, si Iuppiter unam   110
esse velit Tyriis urbem Troiaque profectis,
miscerive probet populos aut foedera iungi.
tu coniunx, tibi fas animum temptare precando.
perge, sequar.' tum sic excepit regia Iuno:
'mecum erit iste labor. nunc qua ratione quod instat 115
confieri possit, paucis (adverte) docebo.
venatum Aeneas unaque miserrima Dido
in nemus ire parant, ubi primos crastinus ortus
extulerit Titan radiisque retexerit orbem.
his ego nigrantem commixta grandine nimbum,   120
dum trepidant alae saltusque indagine cingunt,
desuper infundam et tonitru caelum omne ciebo.

diffugient comites et nocte tegentur opaca:
speluncam Dido dux et Troianus eandem
devenient. adero et, tua si mihi certa voluntas,   125
conubio iungam stabili propriamque dicabo.
hic hymenaeus erit.' non adversata petenti
adnuit atque dolis risit Cytherea repertis.

  Oceanum interea surgens Aurora reliquit.
it portis iubare exorto delecta iuventus,   130
retia rara, plagae, lato venabula ferro,
Massylique ruunt equites et odora canum vis.
reginam thalamo cunctantem ad limina primi
Poenorum exspectant, ostroque insignis et auro
stat sonipes ac frena ferox spumantia mandit.   135
tandem progreditur magna stipante caterva
Sidoniam picto chlamydem circumdata limbo;
cui pharetra ex auro, crines nodantur in aurum,
aurea purpuream subnectit fibula vestem.
nec non et Phrygii comites et laetus Iulus   140
incedunt. ipse ante alios pulcherrimus omnis
infert se socium Aeneas atque agmina iungit.
qualis ubi hibernam Lyciam Xanthique fluenta
deserit ac Delum maternam invisit Apollo
instauratque choros, mixtique altaria circum   145
Cretesque Dryopesque fremunt pictique Agathyrsi:
ipse iugis Cynthi graditur mollique fluentem
fronde premit crinem fingens atque implicat auro,
tela sonant umeris: haud illo segnior ibat
Aeneas, tantum egregio decus enitet ore.   150
postquam altos ventum in montis atque invia lustra,
ecce ferae saxi deiectae vertice caprae
decurrere iugis; alia de parte patentis
transmittunt cursu campos atque agmina cervi

pulverulenta fuga glomerant montisque relinquunt.   155
at puer Ascanius mediis in vallibus acri
gaudet equo iamque hos cursu, iam praeterit illos,
spumantemque dari pecora inter inertia votis
optat aprum, aut fulvum descendere monte leonem.

  Interea magno misceri murmure caelum   160
incipit, insequitur commixta grandine nimbus,
et Tyrii comites passim et Troiana iuventus
Dardaniusque nepos Veneris diversa per agros
tecta metu petiere; ruunt de montibus amnes.
speluncam Dido dux et Troianus eandem   165
deveniunt. prima et Tellus et pronuba Iuno
dant signum; fulsere ignes et conscius aether
conubiis, summoque ulularunt vertice Nymphae.
ille dies primus leti primusque malorum
causa fuit; neque enim specie famave movetur   170
nec iam furtivum Dido meditatur amorem:
coniugium vocat, hoc praetexit nomine culpam.

  Extemplo Libyae magnas it Fama per urbes,
Fama, malum qua non aliud velocius ullum:
mobilitate viget virisque adquirit eundo,   175
parva metu primo, mox sese attollit in auras
ingrediturque solo et caput inter nubila condit.
illam Terra parens ira inritata deorum
extremam, ut perhibent, Coeo Enceladoque sororem
progenuit pedibus celerem et pernicibus alis,   180
monstrum horrendum, ingens, cui quot sunt corpore plumae,
tot vigiles oculi subter (mirabile dictu),
tot linguae, totidem ora sonant, tot subrigit auris.
nocte volat caeli medio terraeque per umbram
stridens, nec dulci declinat lumina somno;   185
luce sedet custos aut summi culmine tecti

turribus aut altis, et magnas territat urbes,
tam ficti pravique tenax quam nuntia veri.
haec tum multiplici populos sermone replebat
gaudens, et pariter facta atque infecta canebat: 190
venisse Aenean Troiano sanguine cretum,
cui se pulchra viro dignetur iungere Dido;
nunc hiemem inter se luxu, quam longa, fovere
regnorum immemores turpique cupidine captos.
haec passim dea foeda virum diffundit in ora.   195
protinus ad regem cursus detorquet Iarban
incenditque animum dictis atque aggerat iras.

      Hic Hammone satus rapta Garamantide nympha
templa Iovi centum latis immania regnis,
centum aras posuit vigilemque sacraverat ignem,   200
excubias divum aeternas, pecudumque cruore
pingue solum et variis florentia limina sertis.
isque amens animi et rumore accensus amaro
dicitur ante aras media inter numina divum
multa Iovem manibus supplex orasse supinis: 205
'Iuppiter omnipotens, cui nunc Maurusia pictis
gens epulata toris Lenaeum libat honorem,
aspicis haec? an te, genitor, cum fulmina torques
nequiquam horremus, caecique in nubibus ignes
terrificant animos et inania murmura miscent?   210
femina, quae nostris errans in finibus urbem
exiguam pretio posuit, cui litus arandum
cuique loci leges dedimus, conubia nostra
reppulit ac dominum Aenean in regna recepit.
et nunc ille Paris cum semiviro comitatu,   215
Maeonia mentum mitra crinemque madentem
subnexus, rapto potitur: nos munera templis
quippe tuis ferimus famamque fovemus inanem.'

Talibus orantem dictis arasque tenentem
audiit Omnipotens, oculosque ad moenia torsit   220
regia et oblitos famae melioris amantis.
tum sic Mercurium adloquitur ac talia mandat:
'vade age, nate, voca Zephyros et labere pennis
Dardaniumque ducem, Tyria Karthagine qui nunc
exspectat fatisque datas non respicit urbes,   225
adloquere et celeris defer mea dicta per auras.
non illum nobis genetrix pulcherrima talem
promisit Graiumque ideo bis vindicat armis;
sed fore qui gravidam imperiis belloque frementem
Italiam regeret, genus alto a sanguine Teucri   230
proderet, ac totum sub leges mitteret orbem.
si nulla accendit tantarum gloria rerum
nec super ipse sua molitur laude laborem,
Ascanione pater Romanas invidet arces?
quid struit? aut qua spe inimica in gente moratur   235
nec prolem Ausoniam et Lavinia respicit arva?
naviget! haec summa est, hic nostri nuntius esto.'
   Dixerat. ille patris magni parcre parabat
imperio; et primum pedibus talaria nectit
aurea, quae sublimem alis sive aequora supra   240
seu terram rapido pariter cum flamine portant.
tum virgam capit: hac animas ille evocat Orco
pallentis, alias sub Tartara tristia mittit,
dat somnos adimitque, et lumina morte resignat.
illa fretus agit ventos et turbida tranat   245
nubila. iamque volans apicem et latera ardua cernit
Atlantis duri caelum qui vertice fulcit,
Atlantis, cinctum adsidue cui nubibus atris
piniferum caput et vento pulsatur et imbri,
nix umeros infusa tegit, tum flumina mento   250

praecipitant senis, et glacie riget horrida barba.
hic primum paribus nitens Cyllenius alis
constitit; hinc toto praeceps se corpore ad undas
misit avi similis, quae circum litora, circum
piscosos scopulos humilis volat aequora iuxta.   255
haud aliter terras inter caelumque volabat
litus harenosum ad Libyae, ventosque secabat
materno veniens ab avo Cyllenia proles.
ut primum alatis tetigit magalia plantis,
Aenean fundantem arces ac tecta novantem   260
conspicit. atque illi stellatus iaspide fulva
ensis erat Tyrioque ardebat murice laena
demissa ex umeris, dives quae munera Dido
fecerat, et tenui telas discreverat auro.
continuo invadit: 'tu nunc Karthaginis altae   265
fundamenta locas pulchramque uxorius urbem
exstruis, heu regni rerumque oblite tuarum?
ipse deum tibi me claro demittit Olympo
regnator, caelum et terras qui numine torquet;
ipse haec ferre iubet celeris mandata per auras: 270
quid struis? aut qua spe Libycis teris otia terris?
si te nulla movet tantarum gloria rerum
[nec super ipse tua moliris laude laborem,]
Ascanium surgentem et spes heredis Iuli
respice, cui regnum Italiae Romanaque tellus   275
debetur.' tali Cyllenius ore locutus
mortalis visus medio sermone reliquit
et procul in tenuem ex oculis evanuit auram.

   At vero Aeneas aspectu obmutuit amens,
arrectaeque horrore comae et vox faucibus haesit.   280
ardet abire fuga dulcisque relinquere terras,
attonitus tanto monitu imperioque deorum.

heu quid agat? quo nunc reginam ambire furentem
audeat adfatu? quae prima exordia sumat?
atque animum nunc huc celerem nunc dividit illuc   285
in partisque rapit varias perque omnia versat.
haec alternanti potior sententia visa est:
Mnesthea Sergestumque vocat fortemque Serestum,
classem aptent taciti sociosque ad litora cogant,
arma parent et quae rebus sit causa novandis   290
dissimulent; sese interea, quando optima Dido
nesciat et tantos rumpi non speret amores,
temptaturum aditus et quae mollissima fandi
tempora, quis rebus dexter modus. ocius omnes
imperio laeti parent et iussa facessunt.   295
    At regina dolos (quis fallere possit amantem?)
praesensit, motusque excepit prima futuros
omnia tuta timens. eadem impia Fama furenti
detulit armari classem cursumque parari.
saevit inops animi totamque incensa per urbem   300
bacchatur, qualis commotis excita sacris
Thyias, ubi audito stimulant trieterica Baccho
orgia nocturnusque vocat clamore Cithaeron.
tandem his Aenean compellat vocibus ultro:
'dissimulare etiam sperasti, perfide, tantum   305
posse nefas tacitusque mea decedere terra?
nec te noster amor nec te data dextera quondam
nec moritura tenet crudeli funere Dido?
quin etiam hiberno moliris sidere classem
et mediis properas Aquilonibus ire per altum,   310
crudelis? quid, si non arva aliena domosque
ignotas peteres, et Troia antiqua maneret,
Troia per undosum peteretur classibus aequor?
mene fugis? per ego has lacrimas dextramque tuam te

(quando aliud mihi iam miserae nihil ipsa reliqui),   315
per conubia nostra, per inceptos hymenaeos,
si bene quid de te merui, fuit aut tibi quicquam
dulce meum, miserere domus labentis et istam,
oro, si quis adhuc precibus locus, exue mentem.
te propter Libycae gentes Nomadumque tyranni   320
odere, infensi Tyrii; te propter eundem
exstinctus pudor et, qua sola sidera adibam,
fama prior. cui me moribundam deseris, — hospes
(hoc solum nomen quoniam de coniuge restat)?
quid moror? an mea Pygmalion dum moenia frater   325
destruat aut captam ducat Gaetulus Iarbas?
saltem si qua mihi de te suscepta fuisset
ante fugam suboles, si quis mihi parvulus aula
luderet Aeneas, qui te tamen ore referret,
non equidem omnino capta ac deserta viderer.'   330
   Dixerat. ille Iovis monitis immota tenebat
lumina et obnixus curam sub corde premebat.
tandem pauca refert: 'ego te, quae plurima fando
enumerare vales, numquam, regina, negabo
promeritam, nec me meminisse pigebit Elissae   335
dum memor ipse mei, dum spiritus hos regit artus.
pro re pauca loquar. neque ego hanc abscondere furto
speravi (ne finge) fugam, nec coniugis umquam
praetendi taedas aut haec in foedera veni.
me si fata meis paterentur ducere vitam   340
auspiciis et sponte mea componere curas,
urbem Troianam primum dulcisque meorum
reliquias colerem, Priami tecta alta manerent,
et recidiva manu posuissem Pergama victis.
sed nunc Italiam magnam Gryneus Apollo,   345
Italiam Lyciae iussere capessere sortes;

hic amor, haec patria est. si te Karthaginis arces
Phoenissam Libycaeque aspectus detinet urbis,
quae tandem Ausonia Teucros considere terra
invidia est? et nos fas extera quaerere regna.   350
me patris Anchisae, quotiens umentibus umbris
nox operit terras, quotiens astra ignea surgunt,
admonet in somnis et turbida terret imago;
me puer Ascanius capitisque iniuria cari,
quem regno Hesperiae fraudo et fatalibus arvis.   355
nunc etiam interpres divum Iove missus ab ipso
(testor utrumque caput) celeris mandata per auras
detulit: ipse deum manifesto in lumine vidi
intrantem muros vocemque his auribus hausi.
desine meque tuis incendere teque querelis;   360
Italiam non sponte sequor.'
  Talia dicentem iamdudum aversa tuetur
huc illuc volvens oculos totumque pererrat
luminibus tacitis et sic accensa profatur:
'nec tibi diva parens generis nec Dardanus auctor,   365
perfide, sed duris genuit te cautibus horrens
Caucasus Hyrcanaeque admorunt ubera tigres.
nam quid dissimulo aut quae me ad maiora reservo?
num fletu ingemuit nostro? num lumina flexit?
num lacrimas victus dedit aut miseratus amantem est? 370
quae quibus anteferam? iam iam nec maxima Iuno
nec Saturnius haec oculis pater aspicit aequis.
nusquam tuta fides. eiectum litore, egentem
excepi et regni demens in parte locavi.
amissam classem, socios a morte reduxi   375
(heu furiis incensa feror!): nunc augur Apollo,
nunc Lyciae sortes, nunc et Iove missus ab ipso
interpres divum fert horrida iussa per auras.

scilicet is superis labor est, ea cura quietos
sollicitat. neque te teneo neque dicta refello: 380
i, sequere Italiam ventis, pete regna per undas.
spero equidem mediis, si quid pia numina possunt,
supplicia hausurum scopulis et nomine Dido
saepe vocaturum. sequar atris ignibus absens
et, cum frigida mors anima seduxerit artus,   385
omnibus umbra locis adero. dabis, improbe, poenas.
audiam et haec manis veniet mihi fama sub imos.'
his medium dictis sermonem abrumpit et auras
aegra fugit seque ex oculis avertit et aufert,
linquens multa metu cunctantem et multa parantem   390
dicere. suscipiunt famulae conlapsaque membra
marmoreo referunt thalamo stratisque reponunt.

  At pius Aeneas, quamquam lenire dolentem
solando cupit et dictis avertere curas,
multa gemens magnoque animum labefactus amore   395
iussa tamen divum exsequitur classemque revisit.
tum vero Teucri incumbunt et litore celsas
deducunt toto navis. natat uncta carina,
frondentisque ferunt remos et robora silvis
infabricata fugae studio.   400
migrantis cernas totaque ex urbe ruentis:
ac velut ingentem formicae farris acervum
cum populant hiemis memores tectoque reponunt,
it nigrum campis agmen praedamque per herbas
convectant calle angusto; pars grandia trudunt   405
obnixae frumenta umeris, pars agmina cogunt
castigantque moras, opere omnis semita fervet.
quis tibi tum, Dido, cernenti talia sensus,
quosve dabas gemitus, cum litora fervere late
prospiceres arce ex summa, totumque videres   410

misceri ante oculos tantis clamoribus aequor!
improbe Amor, quid non mortalia pectora cogis!
ire iterum in lacrimas, iterum temptare precando
cogitur et supplex animos summittere amori,
ne quid inexpertum frustra moritura relinquat.   415
   'Anna, vides toto properari litore circum:
undique convenere; vocat iam carbasus auras,
puppibus et laeti nautae imposuere coronas.
hunc ego si potui tantum sperare dolorem,
et perferre, soror, potero. miserae hoc tamen unum   420
exsequere, Anna, mihi; solam nam perfidus ille
te colere, arcanos etiam tibi credere sensus;
sola viri mollis aditus et tempora noras:
i, soror, atque hostem supplex adfare superbum:
non ego cum Danais Troianam exscindere gentem   425
Aulide iuravi classemve ad Pergama misi,
nec patris Anchisae cineres manisve revelli:
cur mea dicta negat duras demittere in auris?
quo ruit? extremum hoc miserae det munus amanti:
exspectet facilemque fugam ventosque ferentis.   430
non iam coniugium antiquum, quod prodidit, oro,
nec pulchro ut Latio careat regnumque relinquat:
tempus inane peto, requiem spatiumque furori,
dum mea me victam doceat fortuna dolere.
extremam hanc oro veniam (miserere sororis),   435
quam mihi cum dederit cumulatam morte remittam.'
   Talibus orabat, talisque miserrima fletus
fertque refertque soror. sed nullis ille movetur
fletibus, aut voces ullas tractabilis audit;
fata obstant placidasque viri deus obstruit auris.   440
ac velut annoso validam cum robore quercum
Alpini Boreae nunc hinc nunc flatibus illinc

eruere inter se certant; it stridor, et altae
consternunt terram concusso stipite frondes;
ipsa haeret scopulis et quantum vertice ad auras   445
aetherias, tantum radice in Tartara tendit:
haud secus adsiduis hinc atque hinc vocibus heros
tunditur, et magno persentit pectore curas;
mens immota manet, lacrimae volvuntur inanes.

Tum vero infelix fatis exterrita Dido   450
mortem orat; taedet caeli convexa tueri.
quo magis inceptum peragat lucemque relinquat,
vidit, turicremis cum dona imponeret aris,
(horrendum dictu) latices nigrescere sacros
fusaque in obscenum se vertere vina cruorem.   455
hoc visum nulli, non ipsi effata sorori.
praeterea fuit in tectis de marmore templum
coniugis antiqui, miro quod honore colebat,
velleribus niveis et festa fronde revinctum:
hinc exaudiri voces et verba vocantis   460
visa viri, nox cum terras obscura teneret,
solaque culminibus ferali carmine bubo
saepe queri et longas in fletum ducere voces;
multaque praeterea vatum praedicta priorum
terribili monitu horrificant. agit ipse furentem   465
in somnis ferus Aeneas, semperque relinqui
sola sibi, semper longam incomitata videtur
ire viam et Tyrios deserta quaerere terra,
Eumenidum veluti demens videt agmina Pentheus
et solem geminum et duplices se ostendere Thebas,   470
aut Agamemnonius scaenis agitatus Orestes,
armatam facibus matrem et serpentibus atris
cum fugit ultricesque sedent in limine Dirae.

Ergo ubi concepit furias evicta dolore

decrevitque mori, tempus secum ipsa modumque 475
exigit, et maestam dictis adgressa sororem
consilium vultu tegit ac spem fronte serenat:
'inveni, germana, viam (gratare sorori)
quae mihi reddat eum vel eo me solvat amantem.
Oceani finem iuxta solemque cadentem 480
ultimus Aethiopum locus est, ubi maximus Atlas
axem umero torquet stellis ardentibus aptum:
hinc mihi Massylae gentis monstrata sacerdos,
Hesperidum templi custos, epulasque draconi
quae dabat et sacros servabat in arbore ramos, 485
spargens umida mella soporiferumque papaver.
haec se carminibus promittit solvere mentes
quas velit, ast aliis duras immittere curas,
sistere aquam fluviis et vertere sidera retro,
nocturnosque movet manis: mugire videbis 490
sub pedibus terram et descendere montibus ornos.
testor, cara, deos et te, germana, tuumque
dulce caput, magicas invitam accingier artis.
tu secreta pyram tecto interiore sub auras
erige, et arma viri thalamo quae fixa reliquit 495
impius exuviasque omnis lectumque iugalem,
quo perii, super imponas: abolere nefandi
cuncta viri monimenta iuvat monstratque sacerdos.'
haec effata silet, pallor simul occupat ora.
non tamen Anna novis praetexere funera sacris 500
germanam credit, nec tantos mente furores
concipit aut graviora timet quam morte Sychaei.
ergo iussa parat.
　　At regina pyra penetrali in sede sub auras
erecta ingenti taedis atque ilice secta, 505
intenditque locum sertis et fronde coronat

funerea; super exuvias ensemque relictum
effigiemque toro locat haud ignara futuri.
stant arae circum et crinis effusa sacerdos
ter centum tonat ore deos, Erebumque Chaosque   510
tergeminamque Hecaten, tria virginis ora Dianae.
sparserat et latices simulatos fontis Averni,
falcibus et messae ad lunam quaeruntur aënis
pubentes herbae nigri cum lacte veneni;
quaeritur et nascentis equi de fronte revulsus   515
et matri praereptus amor.
ipsa mola manibusque piis altaria iuxta
unum exuta pedem vinclis, in veste recincta,
testatur moritura deos et conscia fati
sidera; tum, si quod non aequo foedere amantis   520
curae numen habet iustumque memorque, precatur.

  Nox erat et placidum carpebant fessa soporem
corpora per terras, silvaeque et saeva quierant
aequora, cum medio volvuntur sidera lapsu,
cum tacet omnis ager, pecudes pictaeque volucres,   525
quaeque lacus late liquidos quaeque aspera dumis
rura tenent, somno positae sub nocte silenti.
[lenibant curas et corda oblita laborum.]
at non infelix animi Phoenissa, neque umquam
solvitur in somnos oculisve aut pectore noctem   530
accipit: ingeminant curae rursusque resurgens
saevit amor magnoque irarum fluctuat aestu.
sic adeo insistit secumque ita corde volutat:
'en, quid ago? rursusne procos inrisa priores
experiar, Nomadumque petam conubia supplex,   535
quos ego sim totiens iam dedignata maritos?
Iliacas igitur classis atque ultima Teucrum
iussa sequar? quiane auxilio iuvat ante levatos

et bene apud memores veteris stat gratia facti?
quis me autem, fac velle, sinet ratibusve superbis   540
invisam accipiet? nescis heu, perdita, necdum
Laomedonteae sentis periuria gentis?
quid tum? sola fuga nautas comitabor ovantis?
an Tyriis omnique manu stipata meorum
inferar et, quos Sidonia vix urbe revelli,   545
rursus agam pelago et ventis dare vela iubebo?
quin morere ut merita es, ferroque averte dolorem.
tu lacrimis evicta meis, tu prima furentem
his, germana, malis oneras atque obicis hosti.
non licuit thalami expertem sine crimine vitam   550
degere more ferae, talis nec tangere curas;
non servata fides cineri promissa Sychaeo.'
  Tantos illa suo rumpebat pectore questus:
Aeneas celsa in puppi iam certus eundi
carpebat somnos rebus iam rite paratis.   555
huic se forma dei vultu redeuntis eodem
obtulit in somnis rursusque ita visa monere est,
omnia Mercurio similis, vocemque coloremque
et crinis flavos et membra decora iuventa:
'nate dea, potes hoc sub casu ducere somnos,   560
nec quae te circum stent deinde pericula cernis,
demens, nec Zephyros audis spirare secundos?
illa dolos dirumque nefas in pectore versat
certa mori, variosque irarum concitat aestus.
non fugis hinc praeceps, dum praecipitare potestas?   565
iam mare turbari trabibus saevasque videbis
conlucere faces, iam fervere litora flammis,
si te his attigerit terris Aurora morantem.
heia age, rumpe moras. varium et mutabile semper
femina.' sic fatus nocti se immiscuit atrae.   570

Tum vero Aeneas subitis exterritus umbris
corripit e somno corpus sociosque fatigat:
'praecipites vigilate, viri, et considite transtris;
solvite vela citi.   deus aethere missus ab alto
festinare fugam tortosque incidere funis					575
ecce iterum instimulat.   sequimur te, sancte deorum,
quisquis es, imperioque iterum paremus ovantes.
adsis o placidusque iuves et sidera caelo
dextra feras.'   dixit vaginaque eripit ensem
fulmineum strictoque ferit retinacula ferro.					580
idem omnis simul ardor habet, rapiuntque ruuntque;
litora deseruere, latet sub classibus aequor,
adnixi torquent spumas et caerula verrunt.

Et iam prima novo spargebat lumine terras
Tithoni croceum linquens Aurora cubile.					585
regina e speculis ut primam albescere lucem
vidit et aequatis classem procedere velis,
litoraque et vacuos sensit sine remige portus,
terque quaterque manu pectus percussa decorum
flaventisque abscissa comas 'pro Iuppiter! ibit					590
hic,' ait 'et nostris inluserit advena regnis?
non arma expedient totaque ex urbe sequentur,
diripientque rates alii navalibus? ite,
ferte citi flammas, date tela, impellite remos!
quid loquor? aut ubi sum? quae mentem insania mutat? 595
infelix Dido, nunc te facta impia tangunt?
tum decuit, cum sceptra dabas.   en dextra fidesque,
quem secum patrios aiunt portare penatis,
quem subiisse umeris confectum aetate parentem!
non potui abreptum divellere corpus et undis					600
spargere? non socios, non ipsum absumere ferro
Ascanium patriisque epulandum ponere mensis?

verum anceps pugnae fuerat fortuna. fuisset:
quem metui moritura? faces in castra tulissem
implessemque foros flammis natumque patremque   605
cum genere exstinxem, memet super ipsa dedissem.
Sol, qui terrarum flammis opera omnia lustras,
tuque harum interpres curarum et conscia Iuno,
nocturnisque Hecate triviis ululata per urbes
et Dirae ultrices et di morientis Elissae,   610
accipite haec, meritumque malis advertite numen
et nostras audite preces. si tangere portus
infandum caput ac terris adnare necesse est,
et sic fata Iovis poscunt, hic terminus haeret,
at bello audacis populi vexatus et armis,   615
finibus extorris, complexu avulsus Iuli
auxilium imploret videatque indigna suorum
funera; nec, cum se sub leges pacis iniquae
tradiderit, regno aut optata luce fruatur,
sed cadat ante diem mediaque inhumatus harena.   620
haec precor, hanc vocem extremam cum sanguine fundo.
tum vos, o Tyrii, stirpem et genus omne futurum
exercete odiis, cinerique haec mittite nostro
munera. nullus amor populis nec foedera sunto.
exoriare aliquis nostris ex ossibus ultor   625
qui face Dardanios ferroque sequare colonos,
nunc, olim, quocumque dabunt se tempore vires.
litora litoribus contraria, fluctibus undas
imprecor, arma armis: pugnent ipsique nepotesque.'
  Haec ait, et partis animum versabat in omnis,   630
invisam quaerens quam primum abrumpere lucem.
tum breviter Barcen nutricem adfata Sychaei,
namque suam patria antiqua cinis ater habebat:
'Annam, cara mihi nutrix, huc siste sororem:

dic corpus properet fluviali spargere lympha,   635
et pecudes secum et monstrata piacula ducat.
sic veniat, tuque ipsa pia tege tempora vitta.
sacra Iovi Stygio, quae rite incepta paravi,
perficere est animus finemque imponere curis
Dardaniique rogum capitis permittere flammae.'   640
sic ait.   illa gradum studio celerabat anili.
at trepida et coeptis immanibus effera Dido
sanguineam volvens aciem, maculisque trementis
interfusa genas et pallida morte futura,
interiora domus inrumpit limina et altos   645
conscendit furibunda rogos ensemque recludit
Dardanium, non hos quaesitum munus in usus.
hic, postquam Iliacas vestis notumque cubile
conspexit, paulum lacrimis et mente morata
incubuitque toro dixitque novissima verba: 650
'dulces exuviae, dum fata deusque sinebat,
accipite hanc animam meque his exsolvite curis.
vixi et quem dederat cursum Fortuna peregi,
et nunc magna mei sub terras ibit imago.
urbem praeclaram statui, mea moenia vidi,   655
ulta virum poenas inimico a fratre recepi,
felix, heu nimium felix, si litora tantum
numquam Dardaniae tetigissent nostra carinae.'
dixit, et os impressa toro 'moriemur inultae,
sed moriamur' ait.   'sic, sic iuvat ire sub umbras.   660
hauriat hunc oculis ignem crudelis ab alto
Dardanus, et nostrae secum ferat omina mortis.'

  Dixerat, atque illam media inter talia ferro
conlapsam aspiciunt comites, ensemque cruore
spumantem sparsasque manus.   it clamor ad alta   665
atria: concussam bacchatur Fama per urbem.

lamentis gemituque et femineo ululatu
tecta fremunt, resonat magnis plangoribus aether,
non aliter quam si immissis ruat hostibus omnis
Karthago aut antiqua Tyros, flammaeque furentes   670
culmina perque hominum volvantur perque deorum.
audiit exanimis trepidoque exterrita cursu
unguibus ora soror foedans et pectora pugnis
per medios ruit, ac morientem nomine clamat:
'hoc illud, germana, fuit? me fraude petebas?   675
hoc rogus iste mihi, hoc ignes araeque parabant?
quid primum deserta querar? comitemne sororem
sprevisti moriens? eadem me ad fata vocasses;
idem ambas ferro dolor atque eadem hora tulisset.
his etiam struxi manibus patriosque vocavi   680
voce deos, sic te ut posita, crudelis, abessem?
exstinxti te meque, soror, populumque patresque
Sidonios urbemque tuam.   date vulnera lymphis
abluam et, extremus si quis super halitus errat,
ore legam.'   sic fata gradus evaserat altos,   685
semianimemque sinu germanam amplexa fovebat
cum gemitu atque atros siccabat veste cruores.
illa gravis oculos conata attollere rursus
deficit; infixum stridit sub pectore vulnus.
ter sese attollens cubitoque adnixa levavit,   690
ter revoluta toro est oculisque errantibus alto
quaesivit caelo lucem ingemuitque reperta.

    Tum Iuno omnipotens longum miserata dolorem
difficilisque obitus Irim demisit Olympo
quae luctantem animam nexosque resolveret artus.   695
nam quia nec fato merita nec morte peribat,
sed misera ante diem subitoque accensa furore,
nondum illi flavum Proserpina vertice crinem

abstulerat Stygioque caput damnaverat Orco.
ergo Iris croceis per caelum roscida pennis   700
mille trahens varios adverso sole colores
devolat et supra caput astitit. 'hunc ego Diti
sacrum iussa fero teque isto corpore solvo.'
sic ait et dextra crinem secat; omnis et una
dilapsus calor atque in ventos vita recessit.   705

BOOK 5

Interea medium Aeneas iam classe tenebat
certus iter fluctusque atros Aquilone secabat
moenia respiciens, quae iam infelicis Elissae
conlucent flammis. quae tantum accenderit ignem
causa latet; duri magno sed amore dolores   5
polluto, notumque furens quid femina possit,
triste per augurium Teucrorum pectora ducunt.
ut pelagus tenuere rates nec iam amplius ulla
occurrit tellus, maria undique et undique caelum,
olli caeruleus supra caput astitit imber   10
noctem hiememque ferens et inhorruit unda tenebris.
ipse gubernator puppi Palinurus ab alta:
'heu quianam tanti cinxerunt aethera nimbi?
quidve, pater Neptune, paras?' sic deinde locutus
colligere arma iubet validisque incumbere remis,   15
obliquatque sinus in ventum ac talia fatur:
'magnanime Aenea, non, si mihi Iuppiter auctor
spondeat, hoc sperem Italiam contingere caelo.
mutati transversa fremunt et vespere ab atro
consurgunt venti, atque in nubem cogitur aër.   20
nec nos obniti contra nec tendere tantum
sufficimus. superat quoniam Fortuna, sequamur,
quoque vocat vertamus iter. nec litora longe
fida reor fraterna Erycis portusque Sicanos,
si modo rite memor servata remetior astra.'   25
tum pius Aeneas: 'equidem sic poscere ventos

iamdudum et frustra cerno te tendere contra.
flecte viam velis. an sit mihi gratior ulla,
quove magis fessas optem demittere navis,
quam quae Dardanium tellus mihi servat Acesten   30
et patris Anchisae gremio complectitur ossa?'
haec ubi dicta, petunt portus et vela secundi
intendunt Zephyri; fertur cita gurgite classis,
et tandem laeti notae advertuntur harenae.

At procul ex celso miratus vertice montis   35
adventum sociasque rates occurrit Acestes,
horridus in iaculis et pelle Libystidis ursae,
Troia Criniso conceptum flumine mater
quem genuit. veterum non immemor ille parentum
gratatur reduces et gaza laetus agresti   40
excipit, ac fessos opibus solatur amicis.

Postera cum primo stellas Oriente fugarat
clara dies, socios in coetum litore ab omni
advocat Aeneas tumulique ex aggere fatur:
'Dardanidae magni, genus alto a sanguine divum,   45
annuus exactis completur mensibus orbis,
ex quo reliquias divinique ossa parentis
condidimus terra maestasque sacravimus aras;
iamque dies, nisi fallor, adest, quem semper acerbum,
semper honoratum (sic di voluistis) habebo.   50
hunc ego Gaetulis agerem si Syrtibus exsul,
Argolicove mari deprensus et urbe Mycenae,
annua vota tamen sollemnisque ordine pompas
exsequerer strueremque suis altaria donis.
nunc ultro ad cineres ipsius et ossa parentis,   55
haud equidem sine mente reor sine numine divum,
adsumus et portus delati intramus amicos.
ergo agite et laetum cuncti celebremus honorem:

poscamus ventos, atque haec me sacra quotannis
urbe velit posita templis sibi ferre dicatis.   60
bina boum vobis Troia generatus Acestes
dat numero capita in navis; adhibete penatis
et patrios epulis et quos colit hospes Acestes.
praeterea, si nona diem mortalibus almum
Aurora extulerit radiisque retexerit orbem,   65
prima citae Teucris ponam certamina classis;
quique pedum cursu valet, et qui viribus audax
aut iaculo incedit melior levibusque sagittis,
seu crudo fidit pugnam committere caestu,
cuncti adsint meritaeque exspectent praemia palmae.   70
ore favete omnes et cingite tempora ramis.'
    Sic fatus velat materna tempora myrto.
hoc Helymus facit, hoc aevi maturus Acestes,
hoc puer Ascanius, sequitur quos cetera pubes.
ille e concilio multis cum milibus ibat   75
ad tumulum magna medius comitante caterva.
hic duo rite mero libans carchesia Baccho
fundit humi, duo lacte novo, duo sanguine sacro,
purpureosque iacit flores ac talia fatur:
'salve, sancte parens, iterum salvete, recepti   80
nequiquam cineres animaeque umbraeque paternae.
non licuit finis Italos fataliaque arva
nec tecum Ausonium, quicumque est, quaerere Thybrim.'
dixerat haec, adytis cum lubricus anguis ab imis
septem ingens gyros, septena volumina traxit   85
amplexus placide tumulum lapsusque per aras,
caeruleae cui terga notae maculosus et auro
squamam incendebat fulgor, ceu nubibus arcus
mille iacit varios adverso sole colores.
obstipuit visu Aeneas. ille agmine longo   90

tandem inter pateras et levia pocula serpens
libavitque dapes rursusque innoxius imo
successit tumulo et depasta altaria liquit.
hoc magis inceptos genitori instaurat honores,
incertus geniumne loci famulumne parentis   95
esse putet; caedit binas de more bidentis
totque sues, totidem nigrantis terga iuvencos,
vinaque fundebat pateris animamque vocabat
Anchisae magni manisque Acheronte remissos.
nec non et socii, quae cuique est copia, laeti   100
dona ferunt, onerant aras mactantque iuvencos;
ordine aëna locant alii fusique per herbam
subiciunt veribus prunas et viscera torrent.

    Exspectata dies aderat nonamque serena
Auroram Phaethontis equi iam luce vehebant,   105
famaque finitimos et clari nomen Acestae
excierat: laeto complerant litora coetu
visuri Aeneadas, pars et certare parati.
munera principio ante oculos circoque locantur
in medio, sacri tripodes viridesque coronae   110
et palmae pretium victoribus, armaque et ostro
perfusae vestes, argenti aurique talenta;
et tuba commissos medio canit aggere ludos.

    Prima pares ineunt gravibus certamina remis
quattuor ex omni delectae classe carinae.   115
velocem Mnestheus agit acri remige Pristim,
mox Italus Mnestheus, genus a quo nomine Memmi,
ingentemque Gyas ingenti mole Chimaeram,
urbis opus, triplici pubes quam Dardana versu
impellunt, terno consurgunt ordine remi;   120
Sergestusque, domus tenet a quo Sergia nomen,
Centauro invehitur magna, Scyllaque Cloanthus

caerulea, genus unde tibi, Romane Cluenti.
Est procul in pelago saxum spumantia contra
litora, quod tumidis summersum tunditur olim   125
fluctibus, hiberni condunt ubi sidera Cauri;
tranquillo silet immotaque attollitur unda
campus et apricis statio gratissima mergis.
hic viridem Aeneas frondenti ex ilice metam
constituit signum nautis pater, unde reverti   130
scirent et longos ubi circumflectere cursus.
tum loca sorte legunt ipsique in puppibus auro
ductores longe effulgent ostroque decori;
cetera populea velatur fronde iuventus
nudatosque umeros oleo perfusa nitescit.   135
considunt transtris, intentaque bracchia remis;
intenti exspectant signum, exsultantiaque haurit
corda pavor pulsans laudumque arrecta cupido.
inde ubi clara dedit sonitum tuba, finibus omnes,
haud mora, prosiluere suis; ferit aethera clamor   140
nauticus, adductis spumant freta versa lacertis.
infindunt pariter sulcos, totumque dehiscit
convulsum remis rostrisque tridentibus aequor.
non tam praecipites biiugo certamine campum
corripuere ruuntque effusi carcere currus,   145
nec sic immissis aurigae undantia lora
concussere iugis pronique in verbera pendent.
tum plausu fremituque virum studiisque faventum
consonat omne nemus, vocemque inclusa volutant
litora, pulsati colles clamore resultant.   150
Effugit ante alios primisque elabitur undis
turbam inter fremitumque Gyas; quem deinde Cloanthus
consequitur, melior remis, sed pondere pinus
tarda tenet. post hos aequo discrimine Pristis

Centaurusque locum tendunt superare priorem;   155
et nunc Pristis habet, nunc victam praeterit ingens
Centaurus, nunc una ambae iunctisque feruntur
frontibus et longa sulcant vada salsa carina.
iamque propinquabant scopulo metamque tenebant
cum princeps medioque Gyas in gurgite victor   160
rectorem navis compellat voce Menoeten:
'quo tantum mihi dexter abis? huc derige cursum;
litus ama et laeva stringat sine palmula cautes;
altum alii teneant.' dixit; sed caeca Menoetes
saxa timens proram pelagi detorquet ad undas.   165
'quo diversus abis?' iterum 'pete saxa, Menoete!'
cum clamore Gyas revocabat, et ecce Cloanthum
respicit instantem tergo et propiora tenentem.
ille inter navemque Gyae scopulosque sonantis
radit iter laevum interior subitoque priorem   170
praeterit et metis tenet aequora tuta relictis.
tum vero exarsit iuveni dolor ossibus ingens
nec lacrimis caruere genae, segnemque Menoeten
oblitus decorisque sui sociumque salutis
in mare praecipitem puppi deturbat ab alta;   175
ipse gubernaclo rector subit, ipse magister
hortaturque viros clavumque ad litora torquet.
at gravis ut fundo vix tandem redditus imo est
iam senior madidaque fluens in veste Menoetes
summa petit scopuli siccaque in rupe resedit.   180
illum et labentem Teucri et risere natantem
et salsos rident revomentem pectore fluctus.

Hic laeta extremis spes est accensa duobus,
Sergesto Mnestheique, Gyan superare morantem.
Sergestus capit ante locum scopuloque propinquat,   185
nec tota tamen ille prior praeeunte carina;

parte prior, partim rostro premit aemula Pristis.
at media socios incedens nave per ipsos
hortatur Mnestheus: 'nunc, nunc insurgite remis,
Hectorei socii, Troiae quos sorte suprema   190
delegi comites; nunc illas promite viris,
nunc animos, quibus in Gaetulis Syrtibus usi
Ionioque mari Maleaeque sequacibus undis.
non iam prima peto Mnestheus neque vincere certo
(quamquam o!—sed superent quibus hoc, Neptune, dedisti);
extremos pudeat rediisse: hoc vincite, cives,   196
et prohibete nefas.' olli certamine summo
procumbunt: vastis tremit ictibus aerea puppis
subtrahiturque solum, tum creber anhelitus artus
aridaque ora quatit, sudor fluit undique rivis.   200
attulit ipse viris optatum casus honorem:
namque furens animi dum proram ad saxa suburget
interior spatioque subit Sergestus iniquo,
infelix saxis in procurrentibus haesit.
concussae cautes et acuto in murice remi   205
obnixi crepuere inlisaque prora pependit.
consurgunt nautae et magno clamore morantur
ferratasque trudes et acuta cuspide contos
expediunt fractosque legunt in gurgite remos.
at laetus Mnestheus successuque acrior ipso   210
agmine remorum celeri ventisque vocatis
prona petit maria et pelago decurrit aperto.
qualis spelunca subito commota columba,
cui domus et dulces latebroso in pumice nidi,
fertur in arva volans plausumque exterrita pennis   215
dat tecto ingentem, mox aëre lapsa quieto
radit iter liquidum celeris neque commovet alas:
sic Mnestheus, sic ipsa fuga secat ultima Pristis

aequora, sic illam fert impetus ipse volantem.
et primum in scopulo luctantem deserit alto   220
Sergestum brevibusque vadis frustraque vocantem
auxilia et fractis discentem currere remis.
inde Gyan ipsamque ingenti mole Chimaeram
consequitur; cedit, quoniam spoliata magistro est.
solus iamque ipso superest in fine Cloanthus,   225
quem petit et summis adnixus viribus urget.

Tum vero ingeminat clamor cunctique sequentem
instigant studiis, resonatque fragoribus aether.
hi proprium decus et partum indignantur honorem
ni teneant, vitamque volunt pro laude pacisci;   230
hos successus alit: possunt, quia posse videntur.
et fors aequatis cepissent praemia rostris,
ni palmas ponto tendens utrasque Cloanthus
fudissetque preces divosque in vota vocasset:
'di, quibus imperium est pelagi, quorum aequora curro, 235
vobis laetus ego hoc candentem in litore taurum
constituam ante aras voti reus, extaque salsos
porriciam in fluctus et vina liquentia fundam.'
dixit, eumque imis sub fluctibus audiit omnis
Nereidum Phorcique chorus Panopeaque virgo,   240
et pater ipse manu magna Portunus euntem
impulit: illa noto citius volucrique sagitta
ad terram fugit et portu se condidit alto.

Tum satus Anchisa cunctis ex more vocatis
victorem magna praeconis voce Cloanthum   245
declarat viridique advelat tempora lauro,
muneraque in navis ternos optare iuvencos
vinaque et argenti magnum dat ferre talentum.
ipsis praecipuos ductoribus addit honores:
victori chlamydem auratam, quam plurima circum   250

purpura maeandro duplici Meliboea cucurrit,
intextusque puer frondosa regius Ida
velocis iaculo cervos cursuque fatigat
acer, anhelanti similis, quem praepes ab Ida
sublimem pedibus rapuit Iovis armiger uncis: 255
longaevi palmas nequiquam ad sidera tendunt
custodes, saevitque canum latratus in auras.
at qui deinde locum tenuit virtute secundum,
levibus huic hamis consertam auroque trilicem
loricam, quam Demoleo detraxerat ipse   260
victor apud rapidum Simoenta sub Ilio alto,
donat habere, viro decus et tutamen in armis.
vix illam famuli Phegeus Sagarisque ferebant
multiplicem conixi umeris; indutus at olim
Demoleos cursu palantis Troas agebat.   265
tertia dona facit geminos ex aere lebetas
cymbiaque argento perfecta atque aspera signis.
iamque adeo donati omnes opibusque superbi
puniceis ibant evincti tempora taenis,
cum saevo e scopulo multa vix arte revulsus   270
amissis remis atque ordine debilis uno
inrisam sine honore ratem Sergestus agebat.
qualis saepe viae deprensus in aggere serpens,
aerea quem obliquum rota transiit aut gravis ictu
seminecem liquit saxo lacerumque viator;   275
nequiquam longos fugiens dat corpore tortus
parte ferox ardensque oculis et sibila colla
arduus attollens; pars vulnere clauda retentat
nixantem nodis seque in sua membra plicantem:
tali remigio navis se tarda movebat;   280
vela facit tamen et velis subit ostia plenis.
Sergestum Aeneas promisso munere donat

servatam ob navem laetus sociosque reductos.
olli serva datur operum haud ignara Minervae,
Cressa genus, Pholoe, geminique sub ubere nati.   285

    Hoc pius Aeneas misso certamine tendit
gramineum in campum, quem collibus undique curvis
cingebant silvae, mediaque in valle theatri
circus erat; quo se multis cum milibus heros
consessu medium tulit exstructoque resedit.   290
hic, qui forte velint rapido contendere cursu,
invitat pretiis animos, et praemia ponit.
undique conveniunt Teucri mixtique Sicani,
Nisus et Euryalus primi,
Euryalus forma insignis viridique iuventa,   295
Nisus amore pio pueri; quos deinde secutus
regius egregia Priami de stirpe Diores;
hunc Salius simul et Patron, quorum alter Acarnan,
alter ab Arcadio Tegeaeae sanguine gentis:
tum duo Trinacrii iuvenes, Helymus Panopesque,   300
adsueti silvis, comites senioris Acestae;
multi praeterea, quos fama obscura recondit.
Aeneas quibus in mediis sic deinde locutus:
'accipite haec animis laetasque advertite mentes.
nemo ex hoc numero mihi non donatus abibit.   305
Cnosia bina dabo levato lucida ferro
spicula caelatamque argento ferre bipennem;
omnibus hic erit unus honos. tres praemia primi
accipient flavaque caput nectentur oliva.
primus equum phaleris insignem victor habeto;   310
alter Amazoniam pharetram plenamque sagittis
Threiciis, lato quam circum amplectitur auro
balteus et tereti subnectit fibula gemma;
tertius Argolica hac galea contentus abito.'

Haec ubi dicta, locum capiunt signoque repente   315
corripiunt spatia audito limenque relinquunt,
effusi nimbo similes. simul ultima signant
primus abit longeque ante omnia corpora Nisus
emicat et ventis et fulminis ocior alis;
proximus huic, longo sed proximus intervallo,   320
insequitur Salius; spatio post deinde relicto
tertius Euryalus;
Euryalumque Helymus sequitur; quo deinde sub ipso
ecce volat calcemque terit iam calce Diores
incumbens umero, spatia et si plura supersint   325
transeat elapsus prior ambiguumve relinquat.
iamque fere spatio extremo fessique sub ipsam
finem adventabant, levi cum sanguine Nisus
labitur infelix, caesis ut forte iuvencis
fusus humum viridisque super madefecerat herbas.   330
hic iuvenis iam victor ovans vestigia presso
haud tenuit titubata solo, sed pronus in ipso
concidit immundoque fimo sacroque cruore.
non tamen Euryali, non ille oblitus amorum:
nam sese opposuit Salio per lubrica surgens,   335
ille autem spissa iacuit revolutus harena;
emicat Euryalus et munere victor amici
prima tenet, plausuque volat fremituque secundo.
post Helymus subit et nun tertia palma Diores.
hic totum caveae consessum ingentis et ora   340
prima patrum magnis Salius clamoribus implet,
ereptumque dolo reddi sibi poscit honorem.
tutatur favor Euryalum lacrimaeque decorae,
gratior et pulchro veniens in corpore virtus.
adiuvat et magna proclamat voce Diores,   345
qui subiit palmae frustraque ad praemia venit

ultima, si primi Salio reddentur honores.
tum pater Aeneas 'vestra' inquit 'munera vobis
certa manent, pueri, et palmam movet ordine nemo;
me liceat casus miserari insontis amici.'   350
sic fatus tergum Gaetuli immane leonis
dat Salio villis onerosum atque unguibus aureis.
hic Nisus 'si tanta' inquit 'sunt praemia victis,
et te lapsorum miseret, quae munera Niso
digna dabis, primam merui qui laude coronam   355
ni me, quae Salium, fortuna inimica tulisset?'
et simul his dictis faciem ostentabat et udo
turpia membra fimo.   risit pater optimus olli
et clipeum efferri iussit, Didymaonis artes,
Neptuni sacro Danais de poste refixum.   360
hoc iuvenem egregium praestanti munere donat.
   Post, ubi confecti cursus et dona peregit:
'nunc, si cui virtus animusque in pectore praesens,
adsit et evinctis attollat bracchia palmis.'
sic ait, et geminum pugnae proponit honorem,   365
victori velatum auro vittisque iuvencum,
ensem atque insignem galeam solacia victo.
nec mora; continuo vastis cum viribus effert
ora Dares magnoque virum se murmure tollit,
solus qui Paridem solitus contendere contra,   370
idemque ad tumulum quo maximus occubat Hector
victorem Buten immani corpore, qui se
Bebrycia veniens Amyci de gente ferebat,
perculit et fulva moribundum extendit harena.
talis prima Dares caput altum in proelia tollit,   375
ostenditque umeros latos alternaque iactat
bracchia protendens et verberat ictibus auras.
quaeritur huic alius; nec quisquam ex agmine tanto

audet adire virum manibusque inducere caestus.
ergo alacris cunctosque putans excedere palma   380
Aeneae stetit ante pedes, nec plura moratus
tum laeva taurum cornu tenet atque ita fatur:
'nate dea, si nemo audet se credere pugnae,
quae finis standi? quo me decet usque teneri?
ducere dona iube.' cuncti simul ore fremebant   385
Dardanidae reddique viro promissa iubebant.
    Hic gravis Entellum dictis castigat Acestes,
proximus ut viridante toro consederat herbae:
'Entelle, heroum quondam fortissime frustra,
tantane tam patiens nullo certamine tolli   390
dona sines? ubi nunc nobis deus ille, magister
nequiquam memoratus, Eryx? ubi fama per omnem
Trinacriam et spolia illa tuis pendentia tectis?'
ille sub haec: 'non laudis amor nec gloria cessit
pulsa metu; sed enim gelidus tardante senecta   395
sanguis hebet, frigentque effetae in corpore vires.
si mihi quae quondam fuerat quaque improbus iste
exsultat fidens, si nunc foret illa iuventas,
haud equidem pretio inductus pulchroque iuvenco
venissem, nec dona moror.' sic deinde locutus   400
in medium geminos immani pondere caestus
proiecit, quibus acer Eryx in proelia suetus
ferre manum duroque intendere bracchia tergo.
obstipuere animi: tantorum ingentia septem
terga boum plumbo insuto ferroque rigebant.   405
ante omnis stupet ipse Dares longeque recusat,
magnanimusque Anchisiades et pondus et ipsa
huc illuc vinclorum immensa volumina versat.
tum senior talis referebat pectore voces:
'quid, si quis caestus ipsius et Herculis arma   410

vidisset tristemque hoc ipso in litore pugnam?
haec germanus Eryx quondam tuus arma gerebat
(sanguine cernis adhuc sparsoque infecta cerebro),
his magnum Alciden contra stetit, his ego suetus,
dum melior viris sanguis dabat, aemula necdum   415
temporibus geminis canebat sparsa senectus.
sed si nostra Dares haec Troius arma recusat
idque pio sedet Aeneae, probat auctor Acestes,
aequemus pugnas. Erycis tibi terga remitto
(solve metus), et tu Troianos exue caestus.'   420
haec fatus duplicem ex umeris reiecit amictum
et magnos membrorum artus, magna ossa lacertosque
exuit atque ingens media consistit harena.
tum satus Anchisa caestus pater extulit aequos
et paribus palmas amborum innexuit armis.   425
constitit in digitos extemplo arrectus uterque
bracchiaque ad superas interritus extulit auras.
abduxere retro longe capita ardua ab ictu
immiscentque manus manibus pugnamque lacessunt,
ille pedum melior motu fretusque iuventa,   430
hic membris et mole valens; sed tarda trementi
genua labant, vastos quatit aeger anhelitus artus.
multa viri nequiquam inter se vulnera iactant,
multa cavo lateri ingeminant et pectore vastos
dant sonitus, erratque auris et tempora circum   435
crebra manus, duro crepitant sub vulnere malae.
stat gravis Entellus nisuque immotus eodem
corpore tela modo atque oculis vigilantibus exit.
ille, velut celsam oppugnat qui molibus urbem
aut montana sedet circum castella sub armis,   440
nunc hos, nunc illos aditus, omnemque pererrat
arte locum et variis adsultibus inritus urget.

ostendit dextram insurgens Entellus et alte
extulit; ille ictum venientem a vertice velox
praevidit celerique elapsus corpore cessit;   445
Entellus viris in ventum effudit et ultro
ipse gravis graviterque ad terram pondere vasto
concidit, ut quondam cava concidit aut Erymantho
aut Ida in magna radicibus eruta pinus.
consurgunt studiis Teucri et Trinacria pubes;   450
it clamor caelo primusque accurrit Acestes
aequaevumque ab humo miserans attollit amicum.
at non tardatus casu neque territus heros
acrior ad pugnam redit ac vim suscitat ira;
tum pudor incendit viris et conscia virtus,   455
praecipitemque Daren ardens agit aequore toto
nunc dextra ingeminans ictus, nunc ille sinistra.
nec mora nec requies: quam multa grandine nimbi
culminibus crepitant, sic densis ictibus heros
creber utraque manu pulsat versatque Dareta.   460
    Tum pater Aeneas procedere longius iras
et saevire animis Entellum haud passus acerbis,
sed finem imposuit pugnae fessumque Dareta
eripuit mulcens dictis ac talia fatur:
'infelix, quae tanta animum dementia cepit?   465
non viris alias conversaque numina sentis?
cede deo.' dixitque et proelia voce diremit.
ast illum fidi aequales genua aegra trahentem
iactantemque utroque caput crassumque cruorem
ore eiectantem mixtosque in sanguine dentes   470
ducunt ad navis; galeamque ensemque vocati
accipiunt, palmam Entello taurumque relinquunt.
hic victor superans animis tauroque superbus
'nate dea, vosque haec' inquit 'cognoscite, Teucri,

et mihi quae fuerint iuvenali in corpore vires   475
et qua servetis revocatum a morte Dareta.'
dixit, et adversi contra stetit ora iuvenci
qui donum astabat pugnae, durosque reducta
libravit dextra media inter cornua caestus
arduus, effractoque inlisit in ossa cerebro: 480
sternitur exanimisque tremens procumbit humi bos.
ille super talis effundit pectore voces:
'hanc tibi, Eryx, meliorem animam pro morte Daretis
persolvo; hic victor caestus artemque repono.'

  Protinus Aeneas celeri certare sagitta   485
invitat qui forte velint et praemia ponit,
ingentique manu malum de nave Seresti
erigit et volucrem traiecto in fune columbam,
quo tendant ferrum, malo suspendit ab alto.
convenere viri deiectamque aerea sortem   490
accepit galea; et primus clamore secundo
Hyrtacidae ante omnis exit locus Hippocoontis;
quem modo navali Mnestheus certamine victor
consequitur, viridi Mnestheus evinctus oliva.
tertius Eurytion, tuus, o clarissime, frater,   495
Pandare, qui quondam iussus confundere foedus
in medios telum torsisti primus Achivos.
extremus galeaque ima subsedit Acestes,
ausus et ipse manu iuvenum temptare laborem.
tum validis flexos incurvant viribus arcus   500
pro se quisque viri et depromunt tela pharetris,
primaque per caelum nervo stridente sagitta
Hyrtacidae iuvenis volucris diverberat auras,
et venit adversique infigitur arbore mali.
intremuit malus timuitque exterrita pennis   505
ales, et ingenti sonuerunt omnia plausu.

post acer Mnestheus adducto constitit arcu
alta petens, pariterque oculos telumque tetendit.
ast ipsam miserandus avem contingere ferro
non valuit; nodos et vincula linea rupit   510
quis innexa pedem malo pendebat ab alto;
illa Notos atque atra volans in nubila fugit.
tum rapidus, iamdudum arcu contenta parato
tela tenens, fratrem Eurytion in vota vocavit,
iam vacuo laetam caelo speculatus et alis   515
plaudentem nigra figit sub nube columbam.
decidit exanimis vitamque reliquit in astris
aetheriis fixamque refert delapsa sagittam.
    Amissa solus palma superabat Acestes,
qui tamen aërias telum contorsit in auras   520
ostentans artemque pater arcumque sonantem.
hic oculis subitum obicitur magnoque futurum
augurio monstrum; docuit post exitus ingens
seraque terrifici cecinerunt omina vates.
namque volans liquidis in nubibus arsit harundo   525
signavitque viam flammis tenuisque recessit
consumpta in ventos, caelo ceu saepe refixa
transcurrunt crinemque volantia sidera ducunt.
attonitis haesere animis superosque precati
Trinacrii Teucrique viri, nec maximus omen   530
abnuit Aeneas, sed laetum amplexus Acesten
muneribus cumulat magnis ac talia fatur:
'sume pater; nam te voluit rex magnus Olympi
talibus auspiciis exsortem ducere honores.
ipsius Anchisae longaevi hoc munus habebis,   535
cratera impressum signis, quem Thracius olim
Anchisae genitori in magno munere Cisseus
ferre sui dederat monimentum et pignus amoris.'

sic fatus cingit viridanti tempora lauro
et primum ante omnis victorem appellat Acesten.   540
nec bonus Eurytion praelato invidit honori,
quamvis solus avem caelo deiecit ab alto.
proximus ingreditur donis qui vincula rupit,
extremus volucri qui fixit harundine malum.

At pater Aeneas nondum certamine misso   545
custodem ad sese comitemque impubis Iuli
Epytiden vocat, et fidam sic fatur ad aurem:
'vade age et Ascanio, si iam puerile paratum
agmen habet secum cursusque instruxit equorum,
ducat avo turmas et sese ostendat in armis   550
dic' ait.   ipse omnem longo discedere circo
infusum populum et campos iubet esse patentis.
incedunt pueri pariterque ante ora parentum
frenatis lucent in equis, quos omnis euntis
Trinacriae mirata fremit Troiaeque iuventus.   555
omnibus in morem tonsa coma pressa corona;
cornea bina ferunt praefixa hastilia ferro,
pars levis umero pharetras;   it pectore summo
flexilis obtorti per collum circulus auri.
tres equitum numero turmae ternique vagantur   560
ductores;   pueri bis seni quemque secuti
agmine partito fulgent paribusque magistris.
una acies iuvenum, ducit quam parvus ovantem
nomen avi referens Priamus, tua clara, Polite,
progenies, auctura Italos;   quem Thracius albis   565
portat equus bicolor maculis, vestigia primi
alba pedis frontemque ostentans arduus albam.
alter Atys, genus unde Atii duxere Latini,
parvus Atys pueroque puer dilectus Iulo.
extremus formaque ante omnis pulcher Iulus   570

Sidonio est invectus equo, quem candida Dido
esse sui dederat monimentum et pignus amoris.
cetera Trinacriis pubes senioris Acestae
fertur equis.
excipiunt plausu pavidos gaudentque tuentes   575
Dardanidae, veterumque agnoscunt ora parentum.
postquam omnem laeti consessum oculosque suorum
lustravere in equis, signum clamore paratis
Epytides longe dedit insonuitque flagello.
olli discurrere pares atque agmina terni   580
diductis solvere choris, rursusque vocati
convertere vias infestaque tela tulere.
inde alios ineunt cursus aliosque recursus
adversi spatiis, alternosque orbibus orbis
impediunt pugnaeque cient simulacra sub armis;   585
et nunc terga fuga nudant, nunc spicula vertunt
infensi, facta pariter nunc pace feruntur.
ut quondam Creta fertur Labyrinthus in alta
parietibus textum caecis iter ancipitemque
mille viis habuisse dolum, qua signa sequendi   590
frangeret indeprensus et inremeabilis error:
haud alio Teucrum nati vestigia cursu
impediunt texuntque fugas et proelia ludo,
delphinum similes qui per maria umida nando
Carpathium Libycumque secant [luduntque per undas]. 595
hunc morem cursus atque haec certamina primus
Ascanius, Longam muris cum cingeret Albam,
rettulit et priscos docuit celebrare Latinos,
quo puer ipse modo, secum quo Troia pubes;
Albani docuere suos; hinc maxima porro   600
accepit Roma et patrium servavit honorem;
Troiaque nunc pueri, Troianum dicitur agmen.

hac celebrata tenus sancto certamina patri.

Hinc primum Fortuna fidem mutata novavit.
dum variis tumulo referunt sollemnia ludis,   605
Irim de caelo misit Saturnia Iuno
Iliacam ad classem ventosque aspirat eunti,
multa movens necdum antiquum saturata dolorem.
illa viam celerans per mille coloribus arcum
nulli visa cito decurrit tramite virgo.   610
conspicit ingentem concursum et litora lustrat
desertosque videt portus classemque relictam.
at procul in sola secretae Troades acta
amissum Anchisen flebant, cunctaeque profundum
pontum aspectabant flentes. heu tot vada fessis   615
et tantum superesse maris, vox omnibus una:
urbem orant, taedet pelagi perferre laborem.
ergo inter medias sese haud ignara nocendi
conicit et faciemque deae vestemque reponit;
fit Beroe, Tmarii coniunx longaeva Dorycli,   620
cui genus et quondam nomen natique fuissent,
ac sic Dardanidum mediam se matribus infert.
'o miserae, quas non manus' inquit 'Achaica bello
traxerit ad letum patriae sub moenibus! o gens
infelix, cui te exitio Fortuna reservat?   625
septima post Troiae excidium iam vertitur aestas,
cum freta, cum terras omnis, tot inhospita saxa
sideraque emensae ferimur, dum per mare magnum
Italiam sequimur fugientem et volvimur undis.
hic Erycis fines fraterni atque hospes Acestes: 630
quis prohibet muros iacere et dare civibus urbem?
o patria et rapti nequiquam ex hoste penates,
nullane iam Troiae dicentur moenia? nusquam
Hectoreos amnis, Xanthum et Simoenta, videbo?

quin agite et mecum infaustas exurite puppis.   635
nam mihi Cassandrae per somnum vatis imago
ardentis dare visa faces: "hic quaerite Troiam;
hic domus est" inquit "vobis." iam tempus agi res,
nec tantis mora prodigiis. en quattuor arae
Neptuno; deus ipse faces animumque ministrat.'   640
haec memorans prima infensum vi corripit ignem
sublataque procul dextra conixa coruscat
et iacit. arrectae mentes stupefactaque corda
Iliadum. hic una e multis, quae maxima natu,
Pyrgo, tot Priami natorum regia nutrix: 645
'non Beroe vobis, non haec Rhoeteia, matres,
est Dorycli coniunx; divini signa decoris
ardentisque notate oculos, qui spiritus illi,
quis vultus vocisque sonus vel gressus eunti.
ipsa egomet dudum Beroen digressa reliqui   650
aegram, indignantem tali quod sola careret
munere nec meritos Anchisae inferret honores.'
haec effata.
at matres primo ancipites oculisque malignis
ambiguae spectare rates miserum inter amorem   655
praesentis terrae fatisque vocantia regna,
cum dea se paribus per caelum sustulit alis
ingentemque fuga secuit sub nubibus arcum.
tum vero attonitae monstris actaeque furore
conclamant, rapiuntque focis penetralibus ignem,   660
pars spoliant aras, frondem ac virgulta facesque
coniciunt. furit immissis Volcanus habenis
transtra per et remos et pictas abiete puppis.
    Nuntius Anchisae ad tumulum cuneosque theatri
incensas perfert navis Eumelus, et ipsi   665
respiciunt atram in nimbo volitare favillam.

primus et Ascanius, cursus ut laetus equestris
ducebat, sic acer equo turbata petivit
castra, nec exanimes possunt retinere magistri.
'quis furor iste novus? quo nunc, quo tenditis,' inquit, 670
'heu miserae cives? non hostem inimicaque castra
Argivum, vestras spes uritis. en, ego vester
Ascanius!' — galeam ante pedes proiecit inanem,
qua ludo indutus belli simulacra ciebat.
accelerat simul Aeneas, simul agmina Teucrum.   675
ast illae diversa metu per litora passim
diffugiunt, silvasque et sicubi concava furtim
saxa petunt; piget incepti lucisque, suosque
mutatae agnoscunt excussaque pectore Iuno est.

   Sed non idcirco flamma atque incendia viris   680
indomitas posuere; udo sub robore vivit
stuppa vomens tardum fumum, lentusque carinas
est vapor et toto descendit corpore pestis,
nec vires heroum infusaque flumina prosunt.
tum pius Aeneas umeris abscindere vestem   685
auxilioque vocare deos et tendere palmas:
'Iuppiter omnipotens, si nondum exosus ad unum
Troianos, si quid pietas antiqua labores
respicit humanos, da flammam evadere classi
nunc, pater, et tenuis Teucrum res eripe leto.   690
vel tu, quod superest, infesto fulmine morti,
si mereor, demitte tuaque hic obrue dextra.'
vix haec ediderat cum effusis imbribus atra
tempestas sine more furit tonitruque tremescunt
ardua terrarum et campi; ruit aethere toto   695
turbidus imber aqua densisque nigerrimus Austris,
implenturque super puppes, semusta madescunt
robora, restinctus donec vapor omnis et omnes

quattuor amissis servatae a peste carinae.

  At pater Aeneas casu concussus acerbo   700
nunc huc ingentis, nunc illuc pectore curas
mutabat versans, Siculisne resideret arvis
oblitus fatorum, Italasne capesseret oras.
tum senior Nautes, unum Tritonia Pallas
quem docuit multaque insignem reddidit arte   705
(haec responsa dabat, vel quae portenderet ira
magna deum vel quae fatorum posceret ordo) —
isque his Aenean solatus vocibus infit:
'nate dea, quo fata trahunt retrahuntque sequamur;
quidquid erit, superanda omnis fortuna ferendo est.   710
est tibi Dardanius divinae stirpis Acestes:
hunc cape consiliis socium et coniunge volentem;
huic trade amissis superant qui navibus et quos
pertaesum magni incepti rerumque tuarum est;
longaevosque senes ac fessas aequore matres   715
et quidquid tecum invalidum metuensque pericli est
delige, et his habeant terris sine moenia fessi;
urbem appellabunt permisso nomine Acestam.'
  Talibus incensus dictis senioris amici
tum vero in curas animo diducitur omnis.   720
et Nox atra polum bigis subvecta tenebat;
visa dehinc caelo facies delapsa parentis
Anchisae subito talis effundere voces:
'nate, mihi vita quondam, dum vita manebat,
care magis, nate, Iliacis exercite fatis,   725
imperio Iovis huc venio, qui classibus ignem
depulit, et caelo tandem miseratus ab alto est.
consiliis pare quae nunc pulcherrima Nautes
dat senior; lectos iuvenes, fortissima corda,
defer in Italiam. gens dura atque aspera cultu   730

debellanda tibi Latio est. Ditis tamen ante
infernas accede domos et Averna per alta
congressus pete, nate, meos. non me impia namque
Tartara habent, tristes umbrae, sed amoena piorum
concilia Elysiumque colo. huc casta Sibylla   735
nigrarum multo pecudum te sanguine ducet.
tum genus omne tuum et quae dentur moenia disces.
iamque vale; torquet medios Nox umida cursus
et me saevus equis Oriens adflavit anhelis.'
dixerat et tenuis fugit ceu fumus in auras.   740
Aeneas 'quo deinde ruis? quo proripis?' inquit,
'quem fugis? aut quis te nostris complexibus arcet?'
haec memorans cinerem et sopitos suscitat ignis,
Pergameumque Larem et canae penetralia Vestae
farre pio et plena supplex veneratur acerra.   745
   Extemplo socios primumque accersit Acesten
et Iovis imperium et cari praecepta parentis
edocet et quae nunc animo sententia constet.
haud mora consiliis, nec iussa recusat Acestes.
transcribunt urbi matres populumque volentem   750
deponunt, animos nil magnae laudis egentis.
ipsi transtra novant flammisque ambesa reponunt
robora navigiis, aptant remosque rudentisque,
exigui numero, sed bello vivida virtus.
interea Aeneas urbem designat aratro   755
sortiturque domos; hoc Ilium et haec loca Troiam
esse iubet. gaudet regno Troianus Acestes
indicitque forum et patribus dat iura vocatis.
tum vicina astris Erycino in vertice sedes
fundatur Veneri Idaliae, tumuloque sacerdos   760
ac lucus late sacer additur Anchiseo.
   Iamque dies epulata novem gens omnis, et aris

factus honos: placidi straverunt aequora venti
creber et aspirans rursus vocat Auster in altum.
exoritur procurva ingens per litora fletus;   765
complexi inter se noctemque diemque morantur.
ipsae iam matres, ipsi, quibus aspera quondam
visa maris facies et non tolerabile nomen,
ire volunt omnemque fugae perferre laborem.
quos bonus Aeneas dictis solatur amicis   770
et consanguineo lacrimans commendat Acestae.
tris Eryci vitulos et Tempestatibus agnam
caedere deinde iubet solvique ex ordine funem.
ipse caput tonsae foliis evinctus olivae
stans procul in prora pateram tenet, extaque salsos   775
porricit in fluctus ac vina liquentia fundit.
prosequitur surgens a puppi ventus euntis;
certatim socii feriunt mare et aequora verrunt.
   At Venus interea Neptunum exercita curis
adloquitur talisque effundit pectore questus: 780
'Iunonis gravis ira neque exsaturabile pectus
cogunt me, Neptune, preces descendere in omnis;
quam nec longa dies pietas nec mitigat ulla,
nec Iovis imperio fatisque infracta quiescit.
non media de gente Phrygum exedisse nefandis   785
urbem odiis satis est nec poenam traxe per omnem
reliquias Troiae: cineres atque ossa peremptae
insequitur. causas tanti sciat illa furoris.
ipse mihi nuper Libycis tu testis in undis
quam molem subito excierit: maria omnia caelo   790
miscuit Aeoliis nequiquam freta procellis,
in regnis hoc ausa tuis.
per scelus ecce etiam Troianis matribus actis
exussit foede puppis et classe subegit

amissa socios ignotae linquere terrae.   795
quod superest, oro, liceat dare tuta per undas
vela tibi, liceat Laurentem attingere Thybrim,
si concessa peto, si dant ea moenia Parcae.'
tum Saturnius haec domitor maris edidit alti:
'fas omne est, Cytherea, meis te fidere regnis,   800
unde genus ducis. merui quoque; saepe furores
compressi et rabiem tantam caelique marisque.
nec minor in terris, Xanthum Simoentaque testor,
Aeneae mihi cura tui. cum Troia Achilles
exanimata sequens impingeret agmina muris,   805
milia multa daret leto, gemerentque repleti
amnes nec reperire viam atque evolvere posset
in mare se Xanthus, Pelidae tunc ego forti
congressum Aenean nec dis nec viribus aequis
nube cava rapui, cuperem cum vertere ab imo   810
structa meis manibus periurae moenia Troiae.
nunc quoque mens eadem perstat mihi; pelle timores.
tutus, quos optas, portus accedet Averni.
unus erit tantum amissum quem gurgite quaeres;
unum pro multis dabitur caput.'   815
his ubi laeta deae permulsit pectora dictis,
iungit equos auro genitor, spumantiaque addit
frena feris manibusque omnis effundit habenas.
caeruleo per summa levis volat aequora curru;
subsidunt undae tumidumque sub axe tonanti   820
sternitur aequor aquis, fugiunt vasto aethere nimbi.
tum variae comitum facies, immania cete,
et senior Glauci chorus Inousque Palaemon
Tritonesque citi Phorcique exercitus omnis;
laeva tenent Thetis et Melite Panopeaque virgo,   825
Nisaee Spioque Thaliaque Cymodoceque.

Hic patris Aeneae suspensam blanda vicissim
gaudia pertemptant mentem; iubet ocius omnis
attolli malos, intendi bracchia velis.
una omnes fecere pedem pariterque sinistros,   830
nunc dextros solvere sinus; una ardua torquent
cornua detorquentque; ferunt sua flamina classem.
princeps ante omnis densum Palinurus agebat
agmen; ad hunc alii cursum contendere iussi.
iamque fere mediam caeli Nox umida metam   835
contigerat, placida laxabant membra quiete
sub remis fusi per dura sedilia nautae,
cum levis aetheriis delapsus Somnus ab astris
aëra dimovit tenebrosum et dispulit umbras,
te, Palinure, petens, tibi somnia tristia portans   840
insonti; puppique deus consedit in alta
Phorbanti similis funditque has ore loquelas:
'Iaside Palinure, ferunt ipsa aequora classem,
aequatae spirant aurae, datur hora quieti.
pone caput fessosque oculos furare labori.   845
ipse ego paulisper pro te tua munera inibo.'
cui vix attollens Palinurus lumina fatur:
'mene salis placidi vultum fluctusque quietos
ignorare iubes? mene huic confidere monstro?
Aenean credam (quid enim?) fallacibus auris   850
et caelo, totiens deceptus fraude sereni?'
talia dicta dabat, clavumque adfixus et haerens
nusquam amittebat oculosque sub astra tenebat.
ecce deus ramum Lethaeo rore madentem
vique soporatum Stygia super utraque quassat   855
tempora, cunctantique natantia lumina solvit.
vix primos inopina quies laxaverat artus,
et super incumbens cum puppis parte revulsa

cumque gubernaclo liquidas proiecit in undas
praecipitem ac socios nequiquam saepe vocantem;   860
ipse volans tenuis se sustulit ales ad auras.
currit iter tutum non setius aequore classis
promissisque patris Neptuni interrita fertur.
iamque adeo scopulos Sirenum advecta subibat,
difficilis quondam multorumque ossibus albos   865
(tum rauca adsiduo longe sale saxa sonabant),
cum pater amisso fluitantem errare magistro
sensit, et ipse ratem nocturnis rexit in undis
multa gemens casuque animum concussus amici:
'o nimium caelo et pelago confise sereno,   870
nudus in ignota, Palinure, iacebis harena.'

BOOK 6

Sic fatur lacrimans, classique immittit habenas
et tandem Euboicis Cumarum adlabitur oris.
obvertunt pelago proras; tum dente tenaci
ancora fundabat navis et litora curvae
praetexunt puppes. iuvenum manus emicat ardens   5
litus in Hesperium; quaerit pars semina flammae
abstrusa in venis silicis, pars densa ferarum
tecta rapit silvas inventaque flumina monstrat.
at pius Aeneas arces quibus altus Apollo
praesidet horrendaeque procul secreta Sibyllae,   10
antrum immane, petit, magnam cui mentem animumque
Delius inspirat vates aperitque futura.
iam subeunt Triviae lucos atque aurea tecta.

Daedalus, ut fama est, fugiens Minoia regna
praepetibus pennis ausus se credere caelo   15
insuetum per iter gelidas enavit ad Arctos,
Chalcidicaque levis tandem super astitit arce.
redditus his primum terris tibi, Phoebe, sacravit
remigium alarum posuitque immania templa.
in foribus letum Androgeo; tum pendere poenas   20
Cecropidae iussi (miserum!) septena quotannis
corpora natorum; stat ductis sortibus urna.
contra elata mari respondet Cnosia tellus:
hic crudelis amor tauri suppostaque furto
Pasiphae mixtumque genus prolesque biformis   25
Minotaurus inest, Veneris monimenta nefandae;

hic labor ille domus et inextricabilis error;
magnum reginae sed enim miseratus amorem
Daedalus ipse dolos tecti ambagesque resolvit,
caeca regens filo vestigia. tu quoque magnam   30
partem opere in tanto, sineret dolor, Icare, haberes.
bis conatus erat casus effingere in auro,
bis patriae cecidere manus. quin protinus omnia
perlegerent oculis, ni iam praemissus Achates
adforet atque una Phoebi Triviaeque sacerdos,   35
Deiphobe Glauci, fatur quae talia regi:
'non hoc ista sibi tempus spectacula poscit;
nunc grege de intacto septem mactare iuvencos
praestiterit, totidem lectas de more bidentis.'
talibus adfata Aenean (nec sacra morantur   40
iussa viri) Teucros vocat alta in templa sacerdos.
   Excisum Euboicae latus ingens rupis in antrum,
quo lati ducunt aditus centum, ostia centum,
unde ruunt totidem voces, responsa Sibyllae.
ventum erat ad limen, cum virgo 'poscere fata   45
tempus' ait; 'deus ecce deus!' cui talia fanti
ante fores subito non vultus, non color unus,
non comptae mansere comae; sed pectus anhelum,
et rabie fera corda tument, maiorque videri
nec mortale sonans, adflata est numine quando   50
iam propiore dei. 'cessas in vota precesque,
Tros' ait 'Aenea? cessas? neque enim ante dehiscent
attonitae magna ora domus.' et talia fata
conticuit. gelidus Teucris per dura cucurrit
ossa tremor, funditque preces rex pectore ab imo: 55
'Phoebe, gravis Troiae semper miserate labores,
Dardana qui Paridis derexti tela manusque
corpus in Aeacidae, magnas obeuntia terras

tot maria intravi duce te penitusque repostas
Massylum gentis praetentaque Syrtibus arva: 60
iam tandem Italiae fugientis prendimus oras,
hac Troiana tenus fuerit fortuna secuta.
vos quoque Pergameae iam fas est parcere genti,
dique deaeque omnes, quibus obstitit Ilium et ingens
gloria Dardaniae. tuque, o sanctissima vates,   65
praescia venturi, da (non indebita posco
regna meis fatis) Latio considere Teucros
errantisque deos agitataque numina Troiae.
tum Phoebo et Triviae solido de marmore templum
instituam festosque dies de nomine Phoebi.   70
te quoque magna manent regnis penetralia nostris:
hic ego namque tuas sortis arcanaque fata
dicta meae genti ponam, lectosque sacrabo,
alma, viros. foliis tantum ne carmina manda,
ne turbata volent rapidis ludibria ventis: 75
ipsa canas oro.' finem dedit ore loquendi.
   At Phoebi nondum patiens immanis in antro
bacchatur vates, magnum si pectore possit
excussisse deum; tanto magis ille fatigat
os rabidum, fera corda domans, fingitque premendo.   80
ostia iamque domus patuere ingentia centum
sponte sua vatisque ferunt responsa per auras:
'o tandem magnis pelagi defuncte periclis
(sed terrae graviora manent), in regna Lavini
Dardanidae venient (mitte hanc de pectore curam),   85
sed non et venisse volent. bella, horrida bella,
et Thybrim multo spumantem sanguine cerno.
non Simois tibi nec Xanthus nec Dorica castra
defuerint; alius Latio iam partus Achilles,
natus et ipse dea; nec Teucris addita Iuno   90

usquam aberit, cum tu supplex in rebus egenis
quas gentis Italum aut quas non oraveris urbes!
causa mali tanti coniunx iterum hospita Teucris
externique iterum thalami.
tu ne cede malis, sed contra audentior ito   95
qua tua te fortuna sinet.   via prima salutis,
quod minime reris, Graia pandetur ab urbe.'
　　Talibus ex adyto dictis Cumaea Sibylla
horrendas canit ambages antroque remugit,
obscuris vera involvens: ea frena furenti   100
concutit et stimulos sub pectore vertit Apollo.
ut primum cessit furor et rabida ora quierunt,
incipit Aeneas heros: 'non ulla laborum,
o virgo, nova mi facies inopinave surgit;
omnia praecepi atque animo mecum ante peregi.   105
unum oro: quando hic inferni ianua regis
dicitur et tenebrosa palus Acheronte refuso,
ire ad conspectum cari genitoris et ora
contingat; doceas iter et sacra ostia pandas.
illum ego per flammas et mille sequentia tela   110
eripui his umeris medioque ex hoste recepi;
ille meum comitatus iter maria omnia mecum
atque omnis pelagique minas caelique ferebat,
invalidus, viris ultra sortemque senectae.
quin, ut te supplex peterem et tua limina adirem,   115
idem orans mandata dabat.   natique patrisque,
alma, precor, miserere, potes namque omnia, nec te
nequiquam lucis Hecate praefecit Avernis:
si potuit manis accersere coniugis Orpheus
Threicia fretus cithara fidibusque canoris,   120
si fratrem Pollux alterna morte redemit
itque reditque viam totiens — quid Thesea magnum,

quid memorem Alciden? et mi genus ab Iove summo.'
    Talibus orabat dictis arasque tenebat,
cum sic orsa loqui vates: 'sate sanguine divum,   125
Tros Anchisiade, facilis descensus Averno:
noctes atque dies patet atri ianua Ditis;
sed revocare gradum superasque evadere ad auras,
hoc opus, hic labor est. pauci, quos aequus amavit
Iuppiter aut ardens evexit ad aethera virtus,   130
dis geniti potuere. tenent media omnia silvae,
Cocytusque sinu labens circumvenit atro.
quod si tantus amor menti, si tanta cupido est
bis Stygios innare lacus, bis nigra videre
Tartara, et insano iuvat indulgere labori,   135
accipe quae peragenda prius. latet arbore opaca
aureus et foliis et lento vimine ramus,
Iunoni infernae dictus sacer; hunc tegit omnis
lucus et obscuris claudunt convallibus umbrae.
sed non ante datur telluris operta subire   140
auricomos quam quis decerpserit arbore fetus.
hoc sibi pulchra suum ferri Proserpina munus
instituit. primo avulso non deficit alter
aureus, et simili frondescit virga metallo.
ergo alte vestiga oculis et rite repertum   145
carpe manu; namque ipse volens facilisque sequetur,
si te fata vocant; aliter non viribus ullis
vincere nec duro poteris convellere ferro.
praeterea iacet exanimum tibi corpus amici
(heu nescis) totamque incestat funere classem,   150
dum consulta petis nostroque in limine pendes.
sedibus hunc refer ante suis et conde sepulcro.
duc nigras pecudes; ea prima piacula sunto.
sic demum lucos Stygis et regna invia vivis

aspicies.' dixit, pressoque obmutuit ore.   155
   Aeneas maesto defixus lumina vultu
ingreditur linquens antrum, caecosque volutat
eventus animo secum. cui fidus Achates
it comes et paribus curis vestigia figit.
multa inter sese vario sermone serebant,   160
quem socium exanimum vates, quod corpus humandum
diceret. atque illi Misenum in litore sicco,
ut venere, vident indigna morte peremptum,
Misenum Aeoliden, quo non praestantior alter
aere ciere viros Martemque accendere cantu.   165
Hectoris hic magni fuerat comes, Hectora circum
et lituo pugnas insignis obibat et hasta.
postquam illum vita victor spoliavit Achilles,
Dardanio Aeneae sese fortissimus heros
addiderat socium, non inferiora secutus.   170
sed tum, forte cava dum personat aequora concha,
demens, et cantu vocat in certamina divos,
aemulus exceptum Triton, si credere dignum est,
inter saxa virum spumosa immerserat unda.
ergo omnes magno circum clamore fremebant,   175
praecipue pius Aeneas. tum iussa Sibyllae,
haud mora, festinant flentes aramque sepulcri
congerere arboribus caeloque educere certant.
itur in antiquam silvam, stabula alta ferarum;
procumbunt piceae, sonat icta securibus ilex   180
fraxineaeque trabes cuneis et fissile robur
scinditur, advolvunt ingentis montibus ornos.
   Nec non Aeneas opera inter talia primus
hortatur socios paribusque accingitur armis.
atque haec ipse suo tristi cum corde volutat   185
aspectans silvam immensam, et sic forte precatur:

'si nunc se nobis ille aureus arbore ramus
ostendat nemore in tanto! quando omnia vere
heu nimium de te vates, Misene, locuta est.'
vix ea fatus erat geminae cum forte columbae   190
ipsa sub ora viri caelo venere volantes,
et viridi sedere solo. tum maximus heros
maternas agnovit avis laetusque precatur:
'este duces, o, si qua via est, cursumque per auras
derigite in lucos ubi pinguem dives opacat   195
ramus humum. tuque, o, dubiis ne defice rebus,
diva parens.' sic effatus vestigia pressit
observans quae signa ferant, quo tendere pergant.
pascentes illae tantum prodire volando
quantum acie possent oculi servare sequentum.   200
inde ubi venere ad fauces grave olentis Averni,
tollunt se celeres liquidumque per aëra lapsae
sedibus optatis gemina super arbore sidunt,
discolor unde auri per ramos aura refulsit.
quale solet silvis brumali frigore viscum   205
fronde virere nova, quod non sua seminat arbos,
et croceo fetu teretis circumdare truncos,
talis erat species auri frondentis opaca
ilice, sic leni crepitabat brattea vento.
corripit Aeneas extemplo avidusque refringit   210
cunctantem, et vatis portat sub tecta Sibyllae.
    Nec minus interea Misenum in litore Teucri
flebant et cineri ingrato suprema ferebant.
principio pinguem taedis et robore secto
ingentem struxere pyram, cui frondibus atris   215
intexunt latera et feralis ante cupressos
constituunt, decorantque super fulgentibus armis.
pars calidos latices et aëna undantia flammis

expediunt, corpusque lavant frigentis et unguunt.
fit gemitus.   tum membra toro defleta reponunt   220
purpureasque super vestis, velamina nota,
coniciunt.   pars ingenti subiere feretro,
triste ministerium, et subiectam more parentum
aversi tenuere facem.   congesta cremantur
turea dona, dapes, fuso crateres olivo.   225
postquam conlapsi cineres et flamma quievit,
reliquias vino et bibulam lavere favillam,
ossaque lecta cado texit Corynaeus aëno.
idem ter socios pura circumtulit unda
spargens rore levi et ramo felicis olivae,   230
lustravitque viros dixitque novissima verba.
at pius Aeneas ingenti mole sepulcrum
imponit suaque arma viro remumque tubamque
monte sub aërio, qui nunc Misenus ab illo
dicitur aeternumque tenet per saecula nomen.   235
   His actis propere exsequitur praecepta Sibyllae.
spelunca alta fuit vastoque immanis hiatu,
scrupea, tuta lacu nigro nemorumque tenebris,
quam super haud ullae poterant impune volantes
tendere iter pennis: talis sese halitus atris   240
faucibus effundens supera ad convexa ferebat.
[unde locum Grai dixerunt nomine Aornum.]
quattuor hic primum nigrantis terga iuvencos
constituit frontique invergit vina sacerdos,
et summas carpens media inter cornua saetas   245
ignibus imponit sacris, libamina prima,
voce vocans Hecaten caeloque Ereboque potentem.
supponunt alii cultros tepidumque cruorem
suscipiunt pateris.   ipse atri velleris agnam
Aeneas matri Eumenidum magnaeque sorori   250

ense ferit, sterilemque tibi, Proserpina, vaccam.
tum Stygio regi nocturnas incohat aras
et solida imponit taurorum viscera flammis,
pingue super oleum fundens ardentibus extis.
ecce autem primi sub lumina solis et ortus   255
sub pedibus mugire solum et iuga coepta moveri
silvarum, visaeque canes ululare per umbram
adventante dea. 'procul, o procul este, profani,'
conclamat vates, 'totoque absistite luco;
tuque invade viam vaginaque eripe ferrum: 260
nunc animis opus, Aenea, nunc pectore firmo.'
tantum effata furens antro se immisit aperto;
ille ducem haud timidis vadentem passibus aequat.

   Di, quibus imperium est animarum, umbraeque silentes
et Chaos et Phlegethon, loca nocte tacentia late,   265
sit mihi fas audita loqui, sit numine vestro
pandere res alta terra et caligine mersas.

   Ibant obscuri sola sub nocte per umbram
perque domos Ditis vacuas et inania regna:
quale per incertam lunam sub luce maligna   270
est iter in silvis, ubi caelum condidit umbra
Iuppiter, et rebus nox abstulit atra colorem.
vestibulum ante ipsum primis in faucibus Orci
Luctus et ultrices posuere cubilia Curae,
pallentesque habitant Morbi tristisque Senectus,   275
et Metus et malesuada Fames ac turpis Egestas,
terribiles visu formae, Letumque Labosque;
tum consanguineus Leti Sopor et mala mentis
Gaudia, mortiferumque adverso in limine Bellum,
ferreique Eumenidum thalami et Discordia demens   280
vipereum crinem vittis innexa cruentis.

   In medio ramos annosaque bracchia pandit

ulmus opaca, ingens, quam sedem Somnia vulgo
vana tenere ferunt, foliisque sub omnibus haerent.
multaque praeterea variarum monstra ferarum,   285
Centauri in foribus stabulant Scyllaeque biformes
et centumgeminus Briareus ac belua Lernae
horrendum stridens, flammisque armata Chimaera,
Gorgones Harpyiaeque et forma tricorporis umbrae.
corripit hic subita trepidus formidine ferrum   290
Aeneas strictamque aciem venientibus offert,
et ni docta comes tenuis sine corpore vitas
admoneat volitare cava sub imagine formae,
inruat et frustra ferro diverberet umbras.

    Hinc via Tartarei quae fert Acherontis ad undas.   295
turbidus hic caeno vastaque voragine gurges
aestuat atque omnem Cocyto eructat harenam.
portitor has horrendus aquas et flumina servat
terribili squalore Charon, cui plurima mento
canities inculta iacet, stant lumina flamma,   300
sordidus ex umeris nodo dependet amictus.
ipse ratem conto subigit velisque ministrat
et ferruginea subvectat corpora cumba,
iam senior, sed cruda deo viridisque senectus.
huc omnis turba ad ripas effusa ruebat,   305
matres atque viri defunctaque corpora vita
magnanimum heroum, pueri innuptaeque puellae,
impositique rogis iuvenes ante ora parentum:
quam multa in silvis autumni frigore primo
lapsa cadunt folia, aut ad terram gurgite ab alto   310
quam multae glomerantur aves, ubi frigidus annus
trans pontum fugat et terris immittit apricis.
stabant orantes primi transmittere cursum,
tendebantque manus ripae ulterioris amore.

navita sed tristis nunc hos nunc accipit illos,   315
ast alios longe summotos arcet harena.
Aeneas miratus enim motusque tumultu
'dic' ait, 'o virgo, quid vult concursus ad amnem?
quidve petunt animae? vel quo discrimine ripas
hae linquunt, illae remis vada livida verrunt?'   320
olli sic breviter fata est longaeva sacerdos:
'Anchisa generate, deum certissima proles,
Cocyti stagna alta vides Stygiamque paludem,
di cuius iurare timent et fallere numen.
haec omnis, quam cernis, inops inhumataque turba est; 325
portitor ille Charon; hi, quos vehit unda, sepulti.
nec ripas datur horrendas et rauca fluenta
transportare prius quam sedibus ossa quierunt.
centum errant annos volitantque haec litora circum;
tum demum admissi stagna exoptata revisunt.'   330
constitit Anchisa satus et vestigia pressit
multa putans sortemque animo miseratus iniquam.
cernit ibi maestos et mortis honore carentis
Leucaspim et Lyciae ductorem classis Oronten,
quos simul a Troia ventosa per aequora vectos   335
obruit Auster, aqua involvens navemque virosque.
    Ecce gubernator sese Palinurus agebat,
qui Libyco nuper cursu, dum sidera servat,
exciderat puppi mediis effusus in undis.
hunc ubi vix multa maestum cognovit in umbra,   340
sic prior adloquitur: 'quis te, Palinure, deorum
eripuit nobis medioque sub aequore mersit?
dic age. namque mihi, fallax haud ante repertus,
hoc uno responso animum delusit Apollo,
qui fore te ponto incolumem finisque canebat   345
venturum Ausonios. en haec promissa fides est?'

ille autem: 'neque te Phoebi cortina fefellit,
dux Anchisiade, nec me deus aequore mersit.
namque gubernaclum multa vi forte revulsum,
cui datus haerebam custos cursusque regebam,   350
praecipitans traxi mecum. maria aspera iuro
non ullum pro me tantum cepisse timorem,
quam tua ne spoliata armis, excussa magistro,
deficeret tantis navis surgentibus undis.
tris Notus hibernas immensa per aequora noctes   355
vexit me violentus aqua; vix lumine quarto
prospexi Italiam summa sublimis ab unda.
paulatim adnabam terrae; iam tuta tenebam,
ni gens crudelis madida cum veste gravatum
prensantemque uncis manibus capita aspera montis   360
ferro invasisset praedamque ignara putasset.
nunc me fluctus habet versantque in litore venti.
quod te per caeli iucundum lumen et auras,
per genitorem oro, per spes surgentis Iuli,
eripe me his, invicte, malis: aut tu mihi terram   365
inice, namque potes, portusque require Velinos;
aut tu, si qua via est, si quam tibi diva creatrix
ostendit (neque enim, credo, sine numine divum
flumina tanta paras Stygiamque innare paludem),
da dextram misero et tecum me tolle per undas,   370
sedibus ut saltem placidis in morte quiescam.'
talia fatus erat coepit cum talia vates:
'unde haec, o Palinure, tibi tam dira cupido?
tu Stygias inhumatus aquas amnemque severum
Eumenidum aspicies, ripamve iniussus adibis?   375
desine fata deum flecti sperare precando.
sed cape dicta memor, duri solacia casus.
nam tua finitimi, longe lateque per urbes

prodigiis acti caelestibus, ossa piabunt
et statuent tumulum et tumulo sollemnia mittent,   380
aeternumque locus Palinuri nomen habebit.'
his dictis curae emotae pulsusque parumper
corde dolor tristi; gaudet cognomine terrae.
   Ergo iter inceptum peragunt fluvioque propinquant.
navita quos iam inde ut Stygia prospexit ab unda   385
per tacitum nemus ire pedemque advertere ripae,
sic prior adgreditur dictis atque increpat ultro:
'quisquis es, armatus qui nostra ad flumina tendis,
fare age quid venias iam istinc, et comprime gressum.
umbrarum hic locus est, somni noctisque soporae: 390
corpora viva nefas Stygia vectare carina.
nec vero Alciden me sum laetatus euntem
accepisse lacu, nec Thesea Pirithoumque,
dis quamquam geniti atque invicti viribus essent.
Tartareum ille manu custodem in vincla petivit   395
ipsius a solio regis traxitque trementem;
hi dominam Ditis thalamo deducere adorti.'
quae contra breviter fata est Amphrysia vates:
'nullae hic insidiae tales (absiste moveri),
nec vim tela ferunt; licet ingens ianitor antro   400
aeternum latrans exsanguis terreat umbras,
casta licet patrui servet Proserpina limen.
Troius Aeneas, pietate insignis et armis,
ad genitorem imas Erebi descendit ad umbras.
si te nulla movet tantae pietatis imago,   405
at ramum hunc' (aperit ramum qui veste latebat)
'agnoscas.' tumida ex ira tum corda residunt;
nec plura his. ille admirans venerabile donum
fatalis virgae longo post tempore visum
caeruleam advertit puppim ripaeque propinquat.   410

inde alias animas, quae per iuga longa sedebant,
deturbat laxatque foros; simul accipit alveo
ingentem Aenean. gemuit sub pondere cumba
sutilis et multam accepit rimosa paludem.
tandem trans fluvium incolumis vatemque virumque   415
informi limo glaucaque exponit in ulva.

　　Cerberus haec ingens latratu regna trifauci
personat adverso recubans immanis in antro.
cui vates horrere videns iam colla colubris
melle soporatam et medicatis frugibus offam   420
obicit. ille fame rabida tria guttura pandens
corripit obiectam, atque immania terga resolvit
fusus humi totoque ingens extenditur antro.
occupat Aeneas aditum custode sepulto
evaditque celer ripam inremeabilis undae.   425

　　Continuo auditae voces vagitus et ingens
infantumque animae flentes in limine primo,
quos dulcis vitae exsortis et ab ubere raptos
abstulit atra dies et funere mersit acerbo.
hos iuxta falso damnati crimine mortis.   430
nec vero hae sine sorte datae, sine iudice, sedes:
quaesitor Minos urnam movet; ille silentum
consiliumque vocat vitasque et crimina discit.
proxima deinde tenent maesti loca, qui sibi letum
insontes peperere manu lucemque perosi   435
proiecere animas. quam vellent aethere in alto
nunc et pauperiem et duros perferre labores!
fas obstat, tristique palus inamabilis unda
alligat et novies Styx interfusa coercet.
nec procul hinc partem fusi monstrantur in omnem   440
Lugentes Campi; sic illos nomine dicunt.
hic quos durus amor crudeli tabe peredit

secreti celant calles et myrtea circum
silva tegit; curae non ipsa in morte relinquunt.
his Phaedram Procrimque locis maestamque Eriphylen   445
crudelis nati monstrantem vulnera cernit,
Euadnenque et Pasiphaen; his Laodamia
it comes et iuvenis quondam, nunc femina, Caeneus
rursus et in veterem fato revoluta figuram.
inter quas Phoenissa recens a vulnere Dido   450
errabat silva in magna; quam Troius heros
ut primum iuxta stetit agnovitque per umbras
obscuram, qualem primo qui surgere mense
aut videt aut vidisse putat per nubila lunam,
demisit lacrimas dulcique adfatus amore est: 455
'infelix Dido, verus mihi nuntius ergo
venerat exstinctam ferroque extrema secutam?
funeris heu tibi causa fui? per sidera iuro,
per superos et si qua fides tellure sub ima est,
invitus, regina, tuo de litore cessi.   460
sed me iussa deum, quae nunc has ire per umbras,
per loca senta situ cogunt noctemque profundam,
imperiis egere suis; nec credere quivi
hunc tantum tibi me discessu ferre dolorem.
siste gradum teque aspectu ne subtrahe nostro.   465
quem fugis? extremum fato quod te adloquor hoc est.'
talibus Aeneas ardentem et torva tuentem
lenibat dictis animum lacrimasque ciebat.
illa solo fixos oculos aversa tenebat
nec magis incepto vultum sermone movetur   470
quam si dura silex aut stet Marpesia cautes.
tandem corripuit sese atque inimica refugit
in nemus umbriferum, coniunx ubi pristinus illi
respondet curis aequatque Sychaeus amorem.

nec minus Aeneas casu concussus iniquo   475
prosequitur lacrimis longe et miseratur euntem.
    Inde datum molitur iter. iamque arva tenebant
ultima, quae bello clari secreta frequentant.
hic illi occurrit Tydeus, hic inclutus armis
Parthenopaeus et Adrasti pallentis imago,   480
hic multum fleti ad superos belloque caduci
Dardanidae, quos ille omnis longo ordine cernens
ingemuit, Glaucumque Medontaque Thersilochumque,
tris Antenoridas Cererique sacrum Polyboeten,
Idaeumque etiam currus, etiam arma tenentem.   485
circumstant animae dextra laevaque frequentes;
nec vidisse semel satis est: iuvat usque morari
et conferre gradum et veniendi discere causas.
at Danaum proceres Agamemnoniaeque phalanges
ut videre virum fulgentiaque arma per umbras,   490
ingenti trepidare metu; pars vertere terga,
ceu quondam petiere rates, pars tollere vocem
exiguam: inceptus clamor frustratur hiantis.
    Atque hic Priamiden laniatum corpore toto
Deiphobum vidit, lacerum crudeliter ora,   495
ora manusque ambas, populataque tempora raptis
auribus et truncas inhonesto vulnere naris.
vix adeo agnovit pavitantem ac dira tegentem
supplicia, et notis compellat vocibus ultro:
'Deiphobe armipotens, genus alto a sanguine Teucri,   500
quis tam crudelis optavit sumere poenas?
cui tantum de te licuit? mihi fama suprema
nocte tulit fessum vasta te caede Pelasgum
procubuisse super confusae stragis acervum.
tunc egomet tumulum Rhoeteo litore inanem   505
constitui et magna manis ter voce vocavi.

nomen et arma locum servant; te, amice, nequivi
conspicere et patria decedens ponere terra.'
ad quae Priamides: 'nihil o tibi, amice, relictum;
omnia Deiphobo solvisti et funeris umbris.   510
sed me fata mea et scelus exitiale Lacaenae
his mersere malis; illa haec monimenta reliquit.
namque ut supremam falsa inter gaudia noctem
egerimus, nosti: et nimium meminisse necesse est.
cum fatalis equus saltu super ardua venit   515
Pergama et armatum peditem gravis attulit alvo,
illa chorum simulans euhantis orgia circum
ducebat Phrygias; flammam media ipsa tenebat
ingentem et summa Danaos ex arce vocabat.
tum me confectum curis somnoque gravatum   520
infelix habuit thalamus, pressitque iacentem
dulcis et alta quies placidaeque simillima morti.
egregia interea coniunx arma omnia tectis
amovet — et fidum capiti subduxerat ensem —;
intra tecta vocat Menelaum et limina pandit,   525
scilicet id magnum sperans fore munus amanti,
et famam exstingui veterum sic posse malorum.
quid moror? inrumpunt thalamo, comes additus una
hortator scelerum Aeolides. di, talia Grais
instaurate, pio si poenas ore reposco.   530
sed te qui vivum casus age fare vicissim
attulerint. pelagine venis erroribus actus
an monitu divum? an quae te fortuna fatigat,
ut tristis sine sole domos, loca turbida, adires?'
    Hac vice sermonum roseis Aurora quadrigis   535
iam medium aetherio cursu traiecerat axem;
et fors omne datum traherent per talia tempus,
sed comes admonuit breviterque adfata Sibylla est:

'nox ruit, Aenea; nos flendo ducimus horas.
hic locus est, partis ubi se via findit in ambas: 540
dextera quae Ditis magni sub moenia tendit,
hac iter Elysium nobis; at laeva malorum
exercet poenas et ad impia Tartara mittit.'
Deiphobus contra: 'ne saevi, magna sacerdos;
discedam, explebo numerum reddarque tenebris.   545
i decus, i, nostrum; melioribus utere fatis.'
tantum effatus, et in verbo vestigia torsit.

Respicit Aeneas subito et sub rupe sinistra
moenia lata videt triplici circumdata muro,
quae rapidus flammis ambit torrentibus amnis,   550
Tartareus Phlegethon, torquetque sonantia saxa.
porta adversa ingens solidoque adamante columnae,
vis ut nulla virum, non ipsi exscindere bello
caelicolae valeant; stat ferrea turris ad auras,
Tisiphoneque sedens palla succincta cruenta   555
vestibulum exsomnis servat noctesque diesque.
hinc exaudiri gemitus et saeva sonare
verbera, tum stridor ferri tractaeque catenae.
constitit Aeneas strepitumque exterritus hausit.
'quae scelerum facies? o virgo, effare; quibusve   560
urgentur poenis? quis tantus plangor ad auras?'
tum vates sic orsa loqui: 'dux inclute Teucrum,
nulli fas casto sceleratum insistere limen;
sed me cum lucis Hecate praefecit Avernis,
ipsa deum poenas docuit perque omnia duxit.   565
Cnosius haec Rhadamanthus habet durissima regna
castigatque auditque dolos subigitque fateri
quae quis apud superos furto laetatus inani
distulit in seram commissa piacula mortem.
continuo sontis ultrix accincta flagello   570

Tisiphone quatit insultans, torvosque sinistra
intentans anguis vocat agmina saeva sororum.
tum demum horrisono stridentes cardine sacrae
panduntur portae. cernis custodia qualis
vestibulo sedeat, facies quae limina servet?   575
quinquaginta atris immanis hiatibus Hydra
saevior intus habet sedem.   tum Tartarus ipse
bis patet in praeceps tantum tenditque sub umbras
quantus ad aetherium caeli suspectus Olympum.
hic genus antiquum Terrae, Titania pubes,   580
fulmine deiecti fundo volvuntur in imo.
hic et Aloidas geminos immania vidi
corpora, qui manibus magnum rescindere caelum
adgressi superisque Iovem detrudere regnis.
vidi et crudelis dantem Salmonea poenas,   585
dum flammas Iovis et sonitus imitatur Olympi.
quattuor hic invectus equis et lampada quassans
per Graium populos mediaeque per Elidis urbem
ibat ovans, divumque sibi poscebat honorem,
demens, qui nimbos et non imitabile fulmen   590
aere et cornipedum pulsu simularet equorum.
at pater omnipotens densa inter nubila telum
contorsit, non ille faces nec fumea taedis
lumina, praecipitemque immani turbine adegit.
nec non et Tityon, Terrae omniparentis alumnum,   595
cernere erat, per tota novem cui iugera corpus
porrigitur, rostroque immanis vultur obunco
immortale iecur tondens fecundaque poenis
viscera rimaturque epulis habitatque sub alto
pectore, nec fibris requies datur ulla renatis.   600
quid memorem Lapithas, Ixiona Pirithoumque?
quos super atra silex iam iam lapsura cadentique

imminet adsimilis; lucent genialibus altis
aurea fulcra toris, epulaeque ante ora paratae
regifico luxu; Furiarum maxima iuxta   605
accubat et manibus prohibet contingere mensas,
exsurgitque facem attollens atque intonat ore.
hic, quibus invisi fratres, dum vita manebat,
pulsatusve parens aut fraus innexa clienti,
aut qui divitiis soli incubuere repertis   610
nec partem posuere suis (quae maxima turba est),
quique ob adulterium caesi, quique arma secuti
impia nec veriti dominorum fallere dextras,
inclusi poenam exspectant.   ne quaere doceri
quam poenam, aut quae forma viros fortunave mersit. 615
saxum ingens volvunt alii, radiisque rotarum
districti pendent; sedet aeternumque sedebit
infelix Theseus, Phlegyasque miserrimus omnis
admonet et magna testatur voce per umbras:
"discite iustitiam moniti et non temnere divos."   620
vendidit hic auro patriam dominumque potentem
imposuit; fixit leges pretio atque refixit;
hic thalamum invasit natae vetitosque hymenaeos:
ausi omnes immane nefas ausoque potiti.
non, mihi si linguae centum sint oraque centum,   625
ferrea vox, omnis scelerum comprendere formas,
omnia poenarum percurrere nomina possim.'
     Haec ubi dicta dedit Phoebi longaeva sacerdos,
'sed iam age, carpe viam et susceptum perfice munus;
acceleremus' ait; 'Cyclopum educta caminis   630
moenia conspicio atque adverso fornice portas,
haec ubi nos praecepta iubent deponere dona.'
dixerat et pariter gressi per opaca viarum
corripiunt spatium medium foribusque propinquant.

occupat Aeneas aditum corpusque recenti   635
spargit aqua ramumque adverso in limine figit.
  His demum exactis, perfecto munere divae,
devenere locos laetos et amoena virecta
fortunatorum nemorum sedesque beatas.
largior hic campos aether et lumine vestit   640
purpureo, solemque suum, sua sidera norunt.
pars in gramineis exercent membra palaestris,
contendunt ludo et fulva luctantur harena;
pars pedibus plaudunt choreas et carmina dicunt.
nec non Threicius longa cum veste sacerdos   645
obloquitur numeris septem discrimina vocum,
iamque eadem digitis, iam pectine pulsat eburno.
hic genus antiquum Teucri, pulcherrima proles,
magnanimi heroes, nati melioribus annis,
Ilusque Assaracusque et Troiae Dardanus auctor.   650
arma procul currusque virum miratur inanis.
stant terra defixae hastae passimque soluti
per campum pascuntur equi. quae gratia currum
armorumque fuit vivis, quae cura nitentis
pascere equos, eadem sequitur tellure repostos.   655
conspicit, ecce, alios dextra laevaque per herbam
vescentis laetumque choro paeana canentis
inter odoratum lauris nemus, unde superne
plurimus Eridani per silvam volvitur amnis.
hic manus ob patriam pugnando vulnera passi,   660
quique sacerdotes casti, dum vita manebat,
quique pii vates et Phoebo digna locuti,
inventas aut qui vitam excoluere per artis,
quique sui memores aliquos fecere merendo:
omnibus his nivea cinguntur tempora vitta.   665
quos circumfusos sic est adfata Sibylla,

Musaeum ante omnis (medium nam plurima turba
hunc habet atque umeris exstantem suspicit altis):
'dicite, felices animae, tuque, optime vates,
quae regio Anchisen, quis habet locus? illius ergo   670
venimus et magnos Erebi tranavimus amnis.'
atque huic responsum paucis ita reddidit heros:
'nulli certa domus; lucis habitamus opacis,
riparumque toros et prata recentia rivis
incolimus. sed vos, si fert ita corde voluntas,   675
hoc superate iugum, et facili iam tramite sistam.'
dixit, et ante tulit gressum camposque nitentis
desuper ostentat; dehinc summa cacumina linquunt.

   At pater Anchises penitus convalle virenti
inclusas animas superumque ad lumen ituras   680
lustrabat studio recolens, omnemque suorum
forte recensebat numerum, carosque nepotes
fataque fortunasque virum moresque manusque.
isque ubi tendentem adversum per gramina vidit
Aenean, alacris palmas utrasque tetendit,   685
effusaeque genis lacrimae et vox excidit ore:
'venisti tandem, tuaque exspectata parenti
vicit iter durum pietas? datur ora tueri,
nate, tua et notas audire et reddere voces?
sic equidem ducebam animo rebarque futurum   690
tempora dinumerans, nec me mea cura fefellit.
quas ego te terras et quanta per aequora vectum
accipio! quantis iactatum, nate, periclis!
quam metui ne quid Libyae tibi regna nocerent!'
ille autem: 'tua me, genitor, tua tristis imago   695
saepius occurrens haec limina tendere adegit;
stant sale Tyrrheno classes. da iungere dextram,
da, genitor, teque amplexu ne subtrahe nostro.'

sic memorans largo fletu simul ora rigabat.
ter conatus ibi collo dare bracchia circum;   700
ter frustra comprensa manus effugit imago,
par levibus ventis volucrique simillima somno.
   Interea videt Aeneas in valle reducta
seclusum nemus et virgulta sonantia silvae,
Lethaeumque domos placidas qui praenatat amnem.   705
hunc circum innumerae gentes populique volabant:
ac velut in pratis ubi apes aestate serena
floribus insidunt variis et candida circum
lilia funduntur, strepit omnis murmure campus.
horrescit visu subito causasque requirit   710
inscius Aeneas, quae sint ea flumina porro,
quive viri tanto complerint agmine ripas.
tum pater Anchises: 'animae, quibus altera fato
corpora debentur, Lethaei ad fluminis undam
securos latices et longa oblivia potant.   715
has equidem memorare tibi atque ostendere coram,
iampridem hanc prolem cupio enumerare meorum,
quo magis Italia mecum laetere reperta.'
'o pater, anne aliquas ad caelum hinc ire putandum est
sublimis animas iterumque ad tarda reverti   720
corpora? quae lucis miseris tam dira cupido?'
'dicam equidem nec te suspensum, nate, tenebo'
suscipit Anchises atque ordine singula pandit.
   'Principio caelum ac terras camposque liquentis
lucentemque globum lunae Titaniaque astra   725
spiritus intus alit, totamque infusa per artus
mens agitat molem et magno se corpore miscet.
inde hominum pecudumque genus vitaeque volantum
et quae marmoreo fert monstra sub aequore pontus.
igneus est ollis vigor et caelestis origo   730

seminibus, quantum non noxia corpora tardant
terrenique hebetant artus moribundaque membra.
hinc metuunt cupiuntque, dolent gaudentque, neque auras
dispiciunt clausae tenebris et carcere caeco.
quin et supremo cum lumine vita reliquit,   735
non tamen omne malum miseris nec funditus omnes
corporeae excedunt pestes, penitusque necesse est
multa diu concreta modis inolescere miris.
ergo exercentur poenis veterumque malorum
supplicia expendunt: aliae panduntur inanes   740
suspensae ad ventos, aliis sub gurgite vasto
infectum eluitur scelus aut exuritur igni.
quisque suos patimur manis. exinde per amplum
mittimur Elysium et pauci laeta arva tenemus
donec longa dies perfecto temporis orbe   745
concretam exemit labem, purumque relinquit
aetherium sensum atque aurai simplicis ignem.
has omnis, ubi mille rotam volvere per annos,
Lethaeum ad fluvium deus evocat agmine magno,
scilicet immemores supera ut convexa revisant   750
rursus, et incipiant in corpora velle reverti.'

   Dixerat Anchises natumque unaque Sibyllam
conventus trahit in medios turbamque sonantem,
et tumulum capit unde omnis longo ordine posset
adversos legere et venientum discere vultus.   755
   'Nunc age, Dardaniam prolem quae deinde sequatur
gloria, qui maneant Itala de gente nepotes,
inlustris animas nostrumque in nomen ituras,
expediam dictis, et te tua fata docebo.
ille, vides, pura iuvenis qui nititur hasta,   760
proxima sorte tenet lucis loca, primus ad auras
aetherias Italo commixtus sanguine surget,

Silvius, Albanum nomen, tua postuma proles,
quem tibi longaevo serum Lavinia coniunx
educet silvis regem regumque parentem,   765
unde genus Longa nostrum dominabitur Alba.
proximus ille Procas, Troianae gloria gentis,
et Capys et Numitor et qui nomine reddet
Silvius Aeneas, pariter pietate vel armis
egregius, si umquam regnandam acceperit Albam.   770
qui iuvenes! quantas ostentant, aspice, viris
atque umbrata gerunt civili tempora quercu!
hi tibi Nomentum et Gabios urbemque Fidenam,
hi Collatinas imponent montibus arces,
Pometios Castrumque Inui Bolamque Coramque.   775
haec tum nomina erunt, nunc sunt sine nomine terrae.
quin et avo comitem sese Mavortius addet
Romulus, Assaraci quem sanguinis Ilia mater
educet. viden, ut geminae stant vertice cristae
et pater ipse suo superum iam signat honore?   780
en huius, nate, auspiciis illa incluta Roma
imperium terris, animos aequabit Olympo,
septemque una sibi muro circumdabit arces,
felix prole virum: qualis Berecyntia mater
invehitur curru Phrygias turrita per urbes   785
laeta deum partu, centum complexa nepotes,
omnis caelicolas, omnis supera alta tenentis.
huc geminas nunc flecte acies, hanc aspice gentem
Romanosque tuos. hic Caesar et omnis Iuli
progenies magnum caeli ventura sub axem.   790
hic vir, hic est, tibi quem promitti saepius audis,
Augustus Caesar, divi genus, aurea condet
saecula qui rursus Latio regnata per arva
Saturno quondam, super et Garamantas et Indos

proferet imperium; iacet extra sidera tellus,   795
extra anni solisque vias, ubi caelifer Atlas
axem umero torquet stellis ardentibus aptum.
huius in adventum iam nunc et Caspia regna
responsis horrent divum et Maeotia tellus,
et septemgemini turbant trepida ostia Nili.   800
nec vero Alcides tantum telluris obivit,
fixerit aeripedem cervam licet, aut Erymanthi
pacarit nemora et Lernam tremefecerit arcu;
nec qui pampineis victor iuga flectit habenis
Liber, agens celso Nysae de vertice tigris.   805
et dubitamus adhuc virtutem extendere factis,
aut metus Ausonia prohibet consistere terra?
quis procul ille autem ramis insignis olivae
sacra ferens? nosco crinis incanaque menta
regis Romani primam qui legibus urbem   810
fundabit, Curibus parvis et paupere terra
missus in imperium magnum. cui deinde subibit
otia qui rumpet patriae residesque movebit
Tullus in arma viros et iam desueta triumphis
agmina. quem iuxta sequitur iactantior Ancus   815
nunc quoque iam nimium gaudens popularibus auris.
vis et Tarquinios reges animamque superbam
ultoris Bruti, fascisque videre receptos?
consulis imperium hic primus saevasque securis
accipiet, natosque pater nova bella moventis   820
ad poenam pulchra pro libertate vocabit,
infelix, utcumque ferent ea facta minores;
vincet amor patriae laudumque immensa cupido.
quin Decios Drusosque procul saevumque securi
aspice Torquatum et referentem signa Camillum.   825
illae autem paribus quas fulgere cernis in armis,

concordes animae nunc et dum nocte prementur,
heu quantum inter se bellum, si lumina vitae
attigerint, quantas acies stragemque ciebunt,
aggeribus socer Alpinis atque arce Monoeci   830
descendens, gener adversis instructus Eois!
ne, pueri, ne tanta animis adsuescite bella
neu patriae validas in viscera vertite viris;
tuque prior, tu parce, genus qui ducis Olympo,
proice tela manu, sanguis meus! —   835
ille triumphata Capitolia ad alta Corintho
victor aget currum caesis insignis Achivis.
eruet ille Argos Agamemnoniasque Mycenas
ipsumque Aeaciden, genus armipotentis Achilli,
ultus avos Troiae templa et temerata Minervae.   840
quis te, magne Cato, tacitum aut te, Cosse, relinquat?
quis Gracchi genus aut geminos, duo fulmina belli,
Scipiadas, cladem Libyae, parvoque potentem
Fabricium vel te sulco, Serrane, serentem?
quo fessum rapitis, Fabii? tu Maximus ille es,   845
unus qui nobis cunctando restituis rem.
excudent alii spirantia mollius aera
(credo equidem), vivos ducent de marmore vultus,
orabunt causas melius, caelique meatus
describent radio et surgentia sidera dicent: 850
tu regere imperio populos, Romane, memento
(hae tibi erunt artes), pacique imponere morem,
parcere subiectis et debellare superbos.'
   Sic pater Anchises, atque haec mirantibus addit:
'aspice, ut insignis spoliis Marcellus opimis   855
ingreditur victorque viros supereminet omnis.
hic rem Romanam magno turbante tumultu
sistet eques, sternet Poenos Gallumque rebellem,

tertiaque arma patri suspendet capta Quirino.'
atque hic Aeneas (una namque ire videbat   860
egregium forma iuvenem et fulgentibus armis,
sed frons laeta parum et deiecto lumina vultu)
'quis, pater, ille, virum qui sic comitatur euntem?
filius, anne aliquis magna de stirpe nepotum?
qui strepitus circa comitum! quantum instar in ipso!   865
sed nox atra caput tristi circumvolat umbra.'
tum pater Anchises lacrimis ingressus obortis:
'o nate, ingentem luctum ne quaere tuorum;
ostendent terris hunc tantum fata nec ultra
esse sinent.   nimium vobis Romana propago   870
visa potens, superi, propria haec si dona fuissent.
quantos ille virum magnam Mavortis ad urbem
campus aget gemitus! vel quae, Tiberine, videbis
funera, cum tumulum praeterlabere recentem!
nec puer Iliaca quisquam de gente Latinos   875
in tantum spe tollet avos, nec Romula quondam
ullo se tantum tellus iactabit alumno.
heu pietas, heu prisca fides invictaque bello
dextera! non illi se quisquam impune tulisset
obvius armato, seu cum pedes iret in hostem   880
seu spumantis equi foderet calcaribus armos.
heu, miserande puer, si qua fata aspera rumpas!
tu Marcellus eris.   manibus date lilia plenis
purpureos spargam flores animamque nepotis
his saltem accumulem donis, et fungar inani   885
munere.'   sic tota passim regione vagantur
aëris in campis latis atque omnia lustrant.
quae postquam Anchises natum per singula duxit
incenditque animum famae venientis amore,
exim bella viro memorat quae deinde gerenda,   890

Laurentisque docet populos urbemque Latini,
et quo quemque modo fugiatque feratque laborem.

    Sunt geminae Somni portae, quarum altera fertur
cornea, qua veris facilis datur exitus umbris,
altera candenti perfecta nitens elephanto,   895
sed falsa ad caelum mittunt insomnia manes.
his ibi tum natum Anchises unaque Sibyllam
prosequitur dictis portaque emittit eburna.
ille viam secat ad navis sociosque revisit.

    Tum se ad Caietae recto fert litore portum.   900
ancora de prora iacitur; stant litore puppes.

COMMENTARY

AENEID 1

Introductory note

The first book of the *Aeneid* presents in a variety of ways many aspects of the main subject matter of the whole poem, its tensions, its problems, its methods of expression, its levels of meaning. Virgil's relationship with Homer is put before us at the very beginning of the poem (see note on 1 f.), and is particularly evident throughout this book: more than three-quarters of the material corresponds closely with the episode and incident of *Odyssey* 5–8, with occasional elements from elsewhere in the *Odyssey* (see my article in *Phoenix*, 1963, pp. 267f.). The only parts without an Odyssean parallel are those concerned with the gods (12–33, 257–96, 657–94). Virgil invites us to see in Aeneas a new Odysseus, often in similar situations, but in vital ways profoundly different. Odysseus was trying to get back home to Ithaca to resume the life he had left; Aeneas had to leave behind his old way of life and found a new type of civilisation which would lead eventually to the world-rule of the Roman Empire. Virgil explores to what extent such a man would have the same qualities as the heroic Odysseus, and to what extent different qualities.

The non-Odyssean element in the book, that which is special to Aeneas and Rome, is the note of mission, of fate, of the will of Jupiter for the world. This is introduced in the second line (*fato profugus*), is implicit throughout Aeneas' endeavours to struggle onwards to his destined goal (summarised in line 33), and is sonorously and serenely expressed by Jupiter to Venus (see note on 223f.). It is a mission to bring peace and civilisation to all men, and the nobility of its concept never quite fades from Virgil's mind even when he explores the unhappiness and disaster attendant upon it in the story of Aeneas and the history of Rome.

In tension with the will of Jupiter is the hostility of Juno; this is set before us in the prologue before the action starts (12f.), and linked with her support for Carthage. As well as this historical element of opposition, she represents more generally the forces of hostile circumstance, the 'slings and arrows of outrageous fortune' which seem to prevent human achievement even when it is deserved and in accordance with the will of providence. Throughout the poem Juno tries to prevent Aeneas from achieving what he is called on to achieve, and when at the end of Book 12 she is reconciled she has already caused such suffering as to justify Virgil's question (line 11) *tantaene animis caelestibus irae?*

The character of Aeneas is outlined (see note on 81 f., 305 f.); in the invocation he is spoken of as *insignem pietate virum*, and we see in him an honest and honourable endeavour to shoulder his immense social, religious, and military obligations. But he is a new type of hero, an 'unheroic' type. His strength is limited, his resolution sometimes frail; he gropes his way forward through darkness and uncertainty. We are never sure, as the poem develops, whether he will succeed.

The mythology and pictorial symbolism in which Virgil delighted is greatly to the fore in this book (see note on 34 f.). First Juno, then Aeolus, then Neptune — these are all visualised and described in the strange and romantic colours of another world of existence from our own. They play their part in the intellectual development of the poem; they can be rationalised, and seen to portray aspects of the cosmic scene. But the reader of Virgil is not justified in letting their symbolic value replace the visual beauty and terror of these preternatural shapes from a world of poetic imagination.

Finally Book 1 begins the story of Dido (see note on 494 f.). There is a most marked contrast with the tragic tones of Book 4 as we hear from Venus the impressive description of her bravery, meet her administering her city, a queenly figure whose beauty is enhanced by her qualities of leadership, listen to her greeting Aeneas and promising help. Only at the end of the book, when Venus and Cupid scheme to entrap her, do we become aware of the first undertones of disaster.

1–33. *Virgil's statement of the theme of the poem is followed by the invocation to the Muse and by the mention of Carthage, Juno's beloved city. In her fear for Carthage and her hatred of the Trojans she has for*

*long years kept the Trojans away from their promised home in Latium. So
great a task it was to found the Roman race.*

1 f. In the opening sections Virgil places before us many of the
leading themes of the poem. That the *Aeneid* is to be a Roman
continuation of Homer's *Iliad* and *Odyssey* is already suggested in the
opening words *arma* (*Iliad*) *virumque* (*Odyssey*); the Roman element
follows immediately (*fato profugus, dum conderet urbem*); and the
movement of the poem from Troy to Rome, from Homer's heroic
age to Virgil's Augustan Age, is anticipated in the structure of the
long relative clause beginning with *Troiae* and ending with *Romae*.

The nature of the Roman mission decreed by fate is partly
defined in the phrases *dum conderet urbem* and *inferretque deos Latio*.
Aeneas has to found a new city to replace burnt Troy, a city rich
in men to establish and spread a new civilisation; and he has to
do it with proper reverence and respect for the gods. This concept
of Rome's destiny is finely summed up in Horace (*Odes* 3.6.5)
dis te minorem quod geris, imperas.

Another major theme is the hostility of Juno, mentioned in
line 4 as the reason for Aeneas' long sufferings, and presented in
the invocation as the major problem of the poem. Aeneas is
characterised as accepting his social and religious responsibilities
(*insignem pietate virum*) and yet a victim of Juno's persecution.
Two reasons are given for this persecution: first Juno's support
for Carthage (see note on 15–16), Rome's great rival for Mediterranean supremacy (this is a constant undertone in the story of
Dido); and second her mythological hostility to the Trojans
because of the judgment of Paris, and her jealousy of Ganymede.
To these explicit statements we may add a symbolic interpretation
of Juno; that she represents the forces of hostile circumstances
(like the storm she causes) which involve apparently inexplicable
suffering and disaster. Thus paradoxically the project which fate
directs is almost impossibly difficult to fulfil: *tantae molis erat
Romanam condere gentem.*

1. The following four lines are quoted by Donatus and Servius
as having been removed from the beginning of the *Aeneid* by
Varius and Tucca, the posthumous editors of the poem:

> Ille ego, qui quondam gracili modulatus avena
> carmen, et egressus silvis vicina coegi

> ut quamvis avido parerent arva colono,
> gratum opus agricolis, at nunc horrentia Martis
> arma virumque cano . . .

'I am he who once tuned my song on a slender pipe, and then leaving the woods made the nearby fields obey the husbandman however greedy, a work to win favour with farmers; but now I sing of the bristling arms of Mars and the man . . .'

These lines refer autobiographically to the *Eclogues* and the *Georgics*. They are not in any of the major MSS, and it is certain that they should be omitted. Probably they were written long after Virgil by some proud owner of a text of the *Aeneid*; just possibly Virgil himself wrote them, but if so decided against using them. That the Romans thought the poem began with the words *arma virumque* is explicitly attested as early as Ovid (*Trist.* 2.534), and frequently afterwards. The matter is discussed in full by R. G. Austin, *C.Q.* 1968, 107 f.

arma virumque: the first word, indicating war as the subject matter of the poem, challenges a comparison with Homer's *Iliad*; the second challenges comparison with the *Odyssey*, of which the opening words are ἄνδρα μοι ἔννεπε, Μοῦσα. . . . 'Sing, Muse, of the man who. . .'. Throughout the *Aeneid* Virgil sets his Roman theme in tension with the heroic world of Homer; Aeneas has to leave the one world and enter the other.

2. Italiam: accusative of motion towards (like *litora*), quite common in Virgil without the preposition which prose would require (cf. 512). The first vowel is long (*contra naturam*, says Servius); in the adjective *Italus* it is short or long according to the requirement of scansion. Similarly the quantity of the *a* of *Lavinius, Lavinium, Lavinia* varies; see note on 258.

fato profugus: here Virgil indicates the difference between Aeneas and Odysseus. Odysseus, the resourceful individual, overcomes temptation and danger in order to return to his old life in Ithaca; Aeneas on the other hand has a mission laid upon him by fate, to found a new city in a place he will be shown, and to establish a new way of life which the gods plan for the civilised world.

Laviniaque: this is the adjective of Lavinium, the name of

Aeneas' first settlement in Latium. The second *i* is treated as a consonant, see note on 2.16. Some MSS have *Lavinaque* (cf. Prop. 2.34.64), but cf. *Aen.* 4.236.

3. 'much harassed indeed both on land and sea'; the phrase is in apposition to the subject of the relative clause, and *ille* reiterates the subject (like ὅ γε in Hom. *Od.* 1.4). Servius comments that *ille* is redundant, and gives us a choice between metrical necessity or a certain impressiveness; cf. 5.457.

4. **superum**: this genitive form is an archaism, used by Virgil with a limited number of words (*deum, divum, virum, socium,* and often proper names, *Danaum, Argivum, Pelasgum,* etc.).

The opposition of Juno is emphasised very strongly indeed in the opening section; cf. lines 9f., 15f., 36f., and see note on 1f.

5. This phrase refers particularly to the second half of the *Aeneid*; line 3 referred mainly to the first half.

dum conderet: 'until he could establish'; the use of the subjunctive indicates the purpose of his endurance, cf. *Aen.* 10.800.

6. **inferretque deos Latio**: the shade of Hector had entrusted the Penates of Troy to Aeneas, and it was a major feature of his mission that he had to establish a continuity of religious worship between Troy and Rome. Ovid coins the splendid adjective *penatiger* for Aeneas.

Latio: dative of motion towards, very common in Virgil with compound verbs, cf. 377, 616.

7. **Albanique patres**: after the death of Aeneas his son Ascanius moved the new settlement from Lavinium to Alba Longa where his people remained for 300 years (lines 267f. — cf. the Alban kings in 6.760f.), until Romulus founded Rome.

altae moenia Romae: the rhythm (a single word filling the fourth foot) is not very common in Virgil (e.g. in line 1 he does not write *qui Troiae*), and is employed mainly for special effect, particularly to round off a paragraph, as here. This is one of the features discussed by W. F. J. Knight, *Accentual Symmetry in Vergil,* Oxford, 1939.

8–11. Notice that in his invocation Virgil asks the Muse not for the story (as Homer does) but for the reasons behind the story, particularly the reasons why the powers of heaven allow or cause such suffering as is involved in the story of Aeneas, especially when he is *insignis pietate*.

8. **quo numine laeso**: 'through what slight to her divinity'. The phrase is terse: as a direct question it would be *quod numen laesum est?*, 'what aspect of her divinity was harmed?' It is also possible, as Servius says, that *quo* is ablative of manner, corresponding to *in quo, in qua causa*. Compare the phrase lèse-majesté.

10. **insignem pietate virum**: the quality of *pietas*, which gives Aeneas his epithet of *pius*, indicates that he accepted the responsibilities put upon him by his position as destined leader of his men and saviour of Troy's religion, as well as the ordinary social responsibilities towards family and friends.

11. **tantaene ... irae?**: 'can there be such anger in the hearts of gods?'; in Milton's words (*P.L.* 6.788) 'In heav'nly Spirits could such perverseness dwell?' This is the question which the *Aeneid* explores, 'to justify the ways of God to men'; Virgil unlike Milton finds only groping and imperfect answers.

13. Notice the juxtaposition of *Karthago* and *Italiam*: the thought of the Punic Wars would for a Roman reader underlie the whole section about Carthage. The legend of the foundation of Carthage by Dido fleeing from Tyre does not occur in prose versions of the Aeneas story; see note on 297f.

13–14. **Italiam ... ostia**: 'facing Italy and the mouth of the Tiber far off'. *Contra* governs *Italiam* as well as *ostia*: this postposition of disyllabic prepositions is common in Virgil; cf. 32. Carthage is 'facing' in the sense that there is open sea between Carthage and Ostia, with Sicily to the east and Sardinia to the west of the direct line.

14. **opum**: a Greek genitive, variously called 'respect' or 'sphere in which', whose Latin use is extended by Virgil and Horace; cf. 343, 441, and 2.22.

15–16. 'and it is said that Juno loved this land uniquely beyond all others; even Samos came second'. Samos, a feminine word, was an island in the Aegean which had a famous temple to Juno, the Heraeum; cf. Herod. 3.60, Cic. *Verr.* 2.4.71, Ov. *Met.* 8.220–1. Juno's special association with Carthage was due to her identification with the goddess Tanit, the supreme Carthaginian deity.

16. **Samo: hic**: notice the hiatus at the caesura, cf. *Aen.* 5.735.

18. **tenditque fovetque**: 'intends and nurtures' Carthage to be capital of the peoples. The two disparate verbs coalesce in

sense to govern an accusative and infinitive construction, as after some phrase like *propter intentum amorem studet*.

19. **sed enim**: 'but indeed', the archaic force of *enim*, cf. *Aen.* 2.164, 5.395.

duci: 'was being established', a vivid use of the present referring to the future, suggesting that the Roman mission was sure to be fulfilled.

20. **olim**: 'one day', cf. 203, 234, 289. The reference here to the Punic wars of the third and second centuries B.C. is very clear.

22. **excidio**: equivalent to *ad excidium*, a rather extended use of the dative of purpose; cf. 299.

sic volvere Parcas: 'thus the Fates ordained'. The three Parcae were Clotho, Lachesis and Atropos; the image in *volvere* is from spinning, or perhaps from unrolling a volume.

23. **Saturnia**: a constant epithet of Juno, daughter of Saturnus.

24. This line refers to the Trojan war in which Juno had earlier (*prima*) opposed the Trojans on behalf of the Greeks: she is Argive Hera in Homer (*Il.* 4.8). *Argi* is the form Virgil uses for the town Argos. It is possible that *prima* here suggests that Juno was the foremost supporter of the Greeks, but see Conway's note ad loc.

26. **alta mente repostum**: 'stored deep in her heart'; *repostum* is a contracted form (syncope) for *repositum*.

27. **spretaeque iniuria formae**: 'the wrong done to her in the slighting of her beauty'; *spretae formae* is a genitive of definition, indicating the nature of the wrong. Paris, appointed to judge a beauty contest between Juno, Minerva and Venus, awarded the prize of a golden apple to Venus. This element of mythology, along with Juno's jealousy of Ganymede (mentioned in the next line) may seem a less serious reason for her hostility than her support of Carthage; but the importance of mythology in the *Aeneid* should not be underestimated (see note on 34 f.).

28. **genus invisum**: Juno hated the Trojan race as a whole because it was descended from Dardanus, a son of Jupiter by Electra.

rapti Ganymedis honores: 'the privileges of stolen Ganymede'. Jupiter, enamoured of the beauty of the Trojan prince

Ganymede, caused him to be snatched up from earth by an eagle to be his cup-bearer in heaven; cf. *Aen.* 5.252 f.

29. **super**: best taken with *his*, 'angered over this' (cf. *Geo.* 4.559), rather than adverbial, 'angered by this as well'.

30. **reliquias Danaum**: 'remnants left by the Greeks', cf. line 598, 3.87. The Greeks are very frequently called *Danai*, from Danaus the founder of Argos. The first syllable of *reliquias* is scanned long; cf. *rēligio*. According to Servius Virgil spelled the word with double *l*, but the main MSS give only a single *l*.

Achilli: fifth declension form of the genitive; cf. 220 and 207.

33. 'A matter of such toil was it to found the Roman race'; *molis* is genitive of description used predicatively. The line is tremendously emphatic, separated and isolated as it is at the end of the preliminary section, and it summarises the theme of the *Aeneid*. Donatus drily comments: 'magna enim sine magno labore condi non possunt'.

34–80. *As the Trojans are sailing from Sicily on the last stage of their voyage to Italy Juno intervenes to stop them. She goes to Aeolus, king of the winds, and urges him to stir up a storm and wreck the Trojans. He agrees to do so.*

34 f. The theme of Juno's hostility which has dominated the introductory section of the poem continues as the major feature in the beginning of the narrative. The storm symbolises her opposition as she uses the powers of nature to frustrate the Trojan destiny; in Book 7 she reiterates her intense enmity, this time using the fiends from Hell as her instrument.

The planning of the storm is presented in rich mythology, coloured with all the available beauty, majesty, and terror of Greco-Roman myth. This supernatural atmosphere is deliberately sought throughout the *Aeneid*; the gods and demi-gods, nymphs and preternatural beings, play a large part in Virgil's poetic imagination, and must not be rationalised away. They certainly sometimes symbolise ideas, intellectual concepts, but they also exist in their own right, vivid visual creatures of another kind of existence, visions of a world transcending the mortal condition of the human scene. Virgil tries to make a synthesis of the real and the visionary; the storm here, for instance, begins with mythology (Juno and Aeolus), becomes a naturalistic description of a hyperbolical kind (great waves and sand-banks), and ends again with mythology (Neptune and his retinue calming the waves).

As the narrative begins, it is immediately evident that Virgil is following the events of *Odyssey* 5, where we first meet Odysseus on the island of Calypso. As Odysseus sets out on his raft, Poseidon angrily soliloquises and raises a storm, as Juno does here; the cave of Aeolus switches to *Odyssey* 10, and with the storm and the reactions of Aeneas we return to *Odyssey* 5. On this see the introduction to this book.

34. Virgil begins his narrative not at the beginning of Aeneas' voyage, but when it seems near its end (cf. Hor. *A.P.* 148, where Homer is commended for similarly plunging *in medias res*). In this way the prominence already given to Juno in the prologue can be emphasised by her immediate appearance in the narrative; and the visit to Carthage and Dido is made imminent. The events which occurred before the point at which Virgil's narrative starts are told by Aeneas to Dido in Books 2 and 3.

vix e conspectu: these words go together; the Trojans were hardly out of sight of Sicily (round which they had sailed on the last stage of their journey to Italy).

35. spumas salis aere ruebant: 'were churning the foam of the salt sea with their bronze-beaked ships'; for *aere* cf. *Aen.* 10. 214 and 223 *aeratae . . . prorae*, for *ruere* cf. 85. The phrase is a good example of how Latin 'poetic diction' differed from prose; both *sal* and *aes* here are instances of metonymy, and this use of *ruere* (a favourite word of Virgil) is not found in prose.

36f. Compare Hom. *Od.* 5.284f., where Poseidon angrily soliloquises and raises a storm to wreck Odysseus.

36–7. cum . . . secum: supply a verb like *loquitur* or *volutat* (50); cf. 76. The 'inverted' *cum* construction is very frequent in Virgil; it makes the sentence virtually two sentences ('they were sailing along . . . and then all of a sudden . . .'), and it is one of the ways in which Virgil avoids the subordination characteristic of Latin prose style. *Cum* with the pluperfect subjunctive, which would be found several times on almost any page of Caesar or Livy, does not occur in the *Aeneid* at all.

36. servans sub pectore: 'nursing deep in her heart'.

37. mene . . . victam: 'am I, defeated, giving up my plans?' The construction is akin to the accusative and infinitive of exclamation: some phrase like 'who could believe that. . . ?' is understood to govern the oratio obliqua. The enclitic *-ne* makes the phrase into a rhetorical question; cf. 97f.

38. **Italia**: like *incepto* in the previous line, this is ablative of separation; in prose *desistere* can take this ablative without a preposition, but *avertere* would require a preposition. Case-usages which dispense with a preposition are characteristic of poetic style; cf. lines 2 and 6.

Teucrorum: the Trojans are frequently called *Teucri* or *Dardanidae*. According to one version of the legend Teucer was succeeded by Dardanus as king of Troy, and according to another Dardanus was the original founder; see note on 3.167–8.

39. **quippe vetor fatis**: 'but of course I am prevented by the fates', an ironical use of *quippe*, cf. *Aen.* 4.218. Juno is aware (cf. 18) that the fates are against her: nevertheless she has power to scheme against them and even to delay them. For all the dominance of the idea of fate in the *Aeneid*, Virgil is very far from being a fatalist; it needs the efforts of men to bring to fruition the intention of fate, and there are supernatural powers working both for and against fate.

41. 'because of the frenzied crime of a single man, Ajax son of Oileus'. Ajax is so called to differentiate him from the more famous Ajax, son of Telamon. The word scans Oῑlḗi, with synizesis (slurring) of the *e* with the *i*; cf. *Ilionei* (120). The story is that Pallas Athena was angered because Ajax had violated Cassandra in her temple (cf. 2.403f., 6.840), and took vengeance upon him and his companions as well by setting the Greek fleet on fire with a thunderbolt and sinking it in a storm as it was returning home near Euboea (cf. Eur. *Tro.* 77f., Ov. *Met.* 13.410f., and for a somewhat different version Hom. *Od.* 4.499f.).

42. **ipsa**: i.e. Athena was allowed to use the thunderbolt herself (cf. Aesch. *Eum.* 827, Eur. *Tro.* 80); Juno has to work through the help of Aeolus.

43. **-que . . . -que**: 'both . . . and', a feature of epic style not found in normal prose usage.

44–5. 'and as Ajax's breath turned to fire from his pierced lungs she snatched him up in a whirlwind and impaled him on a jagged cliff'; cf. Milton *P.L.* 2.180–2 'caught in a fierie Tempest shall be hurld / each on his rock transfixt, the sport and prey / of racking

whirlwinds'. Note how the spondees of line 44 give way in 45 to
the dactylic movement of Athena's action.

46. **ast**: an archaic form of *at*, used by Virgil a score of
times.

divum: this genitive form is also an archaism, see note on 4.

incedo: this word contributes much to the majesty of the line:
Servius says *proprie est nobilium personarum*. Cf. Shakespeare,
Tempest 4.1.101–2 'Great Juno comes; I know her by her gait',
and lines 405, 497.

47. **et soror et coniunx**: Juno and Jupiter were children of
Saturnus, cf. Hes. *Theog.* 454f.

48. **quisquam**: this pronoun, which is used in negative
sentences, emphasises the negative answer expected to the
rhetorical question.

48–9. **adorat . . . imponet**: the first verb is a vivid use of the
present for the future to express indignation (made clear by
praeterea = *postea*, cf. *Geo.* 4.502); in the second clause Juno uses
the expected future. Some minor MSS have changed to *imponit*
to make the balance which Virgil wants to avoid.

49. **honorem**: 'offerings', a frequent use, cf. line 632.

50. **flammato . . . corde**: 'in burning anger'. The Romans
were very fond of metaphors from fire (cf. *accensa*, 29).

51. 'the land of the storm-clouds, a place teeming with raging
winds': *Austris* (south winds) is used for the winds in general,
especially in their stormier aspects.

52f. King Aeolus in Homer (*Od.* 10.1f.) ruled the floating
island of Aeolia, home of the winds (identified with the blustery
and volcanic Lipari islands, between Italy and Sicily). He is a
very minor deity in Virgil, much dependent on Juno (76f.).
Virgil has used his gusty island as a subject for fine mythological
imagery of a highly pictorial kind, in which the descriptive words
are reinforced with strong metrical effects: the slow spondees of
the long words in 53, as the winds groan and struggle, are released
by the two quick dactyls of *imperio premit*; the very marked
alliteration in the spondaic movement of 55–6 (*i, m, c*); the
dactyls of the imagined escape (first halves of 58–59); the final
reassertion of the alliteration of *m* in 61.

54. **vinclis et carcere**: hendiadys, 'within the confines of their
cell'; with the metaphor *frenat* (taken up again in 63) *carcere*

perhaps has an overtone of its meaning of the starting-barriers on a race-course.

55f. Cf. Lucr. 6.189f., especially 197 (of winds imprisoned in a thunder-cloud) *magno indignantur murmure clausi*. Servius rightly says that *montis* should be taken with *murmure*, not with *claustra*; cf. 245.

57. **animos**: 'passions', perhaps with some play on the Greek word for wind, ἄνεμος, connected etymologically with *animus*.

59. Cf. Lucr. 1.277f.; *verrere*, 'sweep', is transitive.

61. **molemque et montis ... altos**: an oft-quoted example of hendiadys — 'massive high mountains'.

62. **foedere certo**: 'under fixed rules', imposed by Jupiter; cf. *iussus* in the next line.

63. 'who would know how to hold tight the reins and how to let them go slack when instructed to do so'. *Sciret* is final subjunctive; its use with the infinitive in the sense of 'know how to . . .' is regular in prose. *Laxas dare* is equivalent to *laxare*; see Conway ad loc. for Virgil's fondness for periphrases with *dare*.

65. **namque**: the ellipse (I speak to you, for to you . . .) is not uncommon in apostrophe, cf. lines 198 and 731, and Hom. *Il.* 7.328.

divum pater atque hominum rex: the phrase is from Ennius (*Ann.* 175), and with its monosyllabic ending has an archaic and formulaic sound.

66. **mulcere dedit**: the infinitive in this sense is poetic, not uncommon in Virgil; cf. 79, 319, 523, and my note on 5.247–8 (Oxford edition). Compare also 357, 527–8. The line is based on Hom. *Od.* 10.21–2.

67. **Tyrrhenum navigat aequor**: i.e. the sea nearest to Rome; Juno means they are nearly there. *Aequor* is accusative of extent of space, common after words of travelling; cf. 524.

68. **victosque penatis**: see note on 6.

69. 'strike violence into your winds: overwhelm and sink their ships'. The first phrase is very powerful ('goad them to fury'); cf. Enn. *Ann.* 512 *dictis Romanis incutit iram*.

70. **disice**: compounds of *iacio* are normally spelled without the consonantal *i*, but it is pronounced and affects the scansion.

71f. The bribe is reminiscent of Hom. *Il.* 14.267f., where Hera offers to the God Sleep one of her Graces in marriage. The

mythological account of the storm is here given a touch of the
baroque, in the Ovidian manner. Servius is concerned about the
morality of the passage, as Aeolus was married; he offers four
different defences, of which perhaps the nicest is *quod ex priore
coniuge improbos filios Aeolus habuerit.*

72. **Deiopea**: she is one of Cyrene's attendants in *Geo.* 4.343;
the polysyllabic ending is not uncommon with proper names. The
word is in the nominative because it is in the relative clause
grammatically; cf. 573.

73. This line is again used by Juno, goddess of marriage, in
4.126, where she suggests that she will give Dido in marriage to
Aeneas.

conubio: the scansion of this word varies, *cōnŭbĭă* in the plural,
but here *cōnūbĭo* (rather than *cōnūbjo*); see Austin on *Aen.* 4.126.

propriamque dicabo: formulaic words: 'I will pronounce
her your own.'

76f. Aeolus' reply is formal and deferential — it is yours to
consider what you desire and mine to take your orders. Servius
explains that Juno in her capacity of queen of the air (*physica
allegoria*) has special power over Aeolus.

78. **quodcumque hoc regni**: 'all this my little kingdom', cf.
Lucr. 2.16 *hoc aevi quodcumque est* ('all this our little life').

79. **concilias**: the verb is here used with two different
constructions, first with two impersonal objects (= 'procure') and
then with a personal object (= 'make favourable'). Translate:
'it is you, none other, who give me all this my little kingdom, my
power, Jupiter's favour'.

das ... accumbere: see note on 66.

80. **nimborumque ... potentem**: the genitive with *potens* is
common in Livy and the poets, cf. *Aen.* 3.528.

*81–123. Aeolus causes the storm to begin; Aeneas is panic-stricken,
and prays for death. The ships are buffeted, and that of Orontes sinks.*

81f. Virgil here very closely follows the description of the
storm in *Odyssey* 5, colouring it with the hyperbole of Roman
rhetoric and the clashing and sonorous word-music of his
hexameter. As a piece of verbal painting it far surpasses the more
extravagant storm scenes of later Roman poets (Ovid, *Tr.* 1.2,
Met. 11.474f., Lucan 5.597f., Stat. *Th.* 5.361f., Val. Fl. 1.608f.).

The first appearance of Aeneas in the poem is also modelled on *Odyssey* 5; his reactions to the storm and his speech are like those of Odysseus. Two points are important here: one is that Aeneas has much in common with Odysseus initially, but he must learn during the rest of the poem to leave the heroic world behind and enter a Roman world; and the second is that Virgil wishes to show us at the outset Aeneas' human frailty. Though he has fate to support him, he must himself by his own endeavours achieve his mission (this paradox is absolutely central to the significance of the *Aeneid*), and his strength is hardly sufficient for the difficulty of the task. As Conway says: 'It is a mistake to suppose that Virgil meant to portray Aeneas as faultless.' It is because of his human faults and failings that his achievements compel our interest. Aeneas has often been criticised as a puppet, a paragon, an abstraction, all of which he patently is not; he could much more justly be criticised as insufficiently sublime and virtuous, too human, too weak. But Virgil's conception of the human situation was such that for him true heroism did not lie in grandiose and supremely self-confident attitudes, but in the uncertain and wavering quest for what seemed right.

The sound effects are very marked in this passage: there is alliteration of *c*, then *v*, then *t*, and the rhythm of the beginning of 82 (with diaeresis after each of the first two feet) is unusual in Virgil and compels the attention; cf. 116, and Ennius *Ann.* 551–2 *nam me gravis impetus Orci | percutit in latus.*

81–2. 'he reversed his spear and struck it against the side of the hollow mountain', thus causing the *claustra* to open up.

82. **velut agmine facto**: 'as if in armed array', cf. *Geo.* 4.167 (of a swarm of bees).

84. **incubuere mari**: 'now they have swooped down on the ocean'; for this use of the 'instantaneous' perfect cf. line 90, and *Geo.* 1.330f. Cf. Tennyson's phrase (of the winds) 'leaning upon the ridged sea'. Henry draws attention to the energy depicted by the four verbs *incubuere, insequitur, eripiunt, intonuere,* each containing an intensive particle, beginning a line, and preceding its subject.

85–6. These lines are taken from Homer's storm in *Odyssey* 5 (295f.) σὺν δ' Εὖρός τε Νότος τ' ἔπεσον, Ζέφυρός τε δυσαής, | καὶ Βορέης αἰθρηγενέτης, μέγα κῦμα κυλίνδων.

85. ruunt: transitive, 'upheave the whole ocean', a favourite word of Virgil's, both transitively (cf. 35) and intransitively (83).

86. Africus: the south-west wind, cf. Hor. *Odes* 1.1.15.

88–9. Again from *Odyssey* 5 (293–4) σὺν δὲ νεφέεσσι κάλυψε / γαῖαν ὁμοῦ καὶ πόντον. ὀρώρει δ' οὐρανόθεν νύξ. Cf. also *Aen.* 3. 198f.

89. incubat: 'broods over', cf. *Geo.* 2.507.

91. 'the whole scene threatens them with instant death': a magnificently sonorous line, where the solemn alliteration of *n* and *m* is strengthened by the slow spondees and the coincidence of accent and ictus in the fourth foot for the first time since line 83. Compare Cat. 64.187 *omnia sunt deserta, ostentant omnia letum*. On *viris* (meaning little more than *eis*) Mackail has a good note.

92. 'Immediately Aeneas' limbs were numbed in cold fear'; again Virgil follows *Odyssey* 5 (297) καὶ τότ' 'Οδυσσῆος λύτο γούνατα καὶ φίλον ἦτορ. This is Aeneas' first appearance in the poem, and his reactions indicate his human frailty; the hero of the *Aeneid* is not sublimely strong or possessed of super-human resolution. His task often seems too heavy for him, but although he sometimes despairs he does not give up.

93. duplicis: a formal way of saying 'both', appropriate in the formal situation of prayer.

94f. Aeneas' first words are taken from *Odyssey* 5.306f. τρὶς μάκαρες Δαναοὶ καὶ τετράκις οἳ τότ' ὄλοντο. . . . Aeneas' behaviour in Book 2 shows this desire for the heroic death, but in the rest of the poem he has to learn that his life is not his to throw away, but that it must be used in the service of his mission.

95–6. quis . . . contigit oppetere: 'those whose fortune it was to die'; *quis* is a less common alternative form for *quibus*; *oppetere mortem* is a normal prose usage, and *oppetere* is used absolutely in this sense by the poets and in post-Augustan prose.

97. Tydide: Greek vocative — long *e* — of the patronymic *Tydides*, son of Tydeus (Diomedes). Aeneas was almost killed in single combat against him (*Il.* 5.297f.).

97–8. mene . . . occumbere . . . non potuisse: 'why could I not have fallen?', the same construction as in 37.

99. 'where fierce Hector lies low beneath the spear of Aeacides'. *Saevus* seems at first a strange adjective for Aeneas to apply to Hector, but its point here is that for all Hector's fierceness in war he was killed when Aeneas was not. Aeacides refers to Achilles, son of Peleus, son of Aeacus. *Telo iacet* is elliptical, equivalent in sense to *telo necatus iacet*; Aeneas sees the past flash before his eyes.

100. **Sarpedon**: though Zeus wished to save him (*Aen.* 10.470f.), he was killed by Patroclus (*Il.* 16.638f.).

100–1. 'where Simois has seized and sweeps beneath its waters the shields and helmets and brave bodies of so many warriors'. Cf. Hom. *Il.* 12.22f., and for the phraseology cf. *Aen.* 8.538f. Simois and Xanthus (also called Scamander) were the rivers of Troy; cf. 473, 618. Notice the fourth foot rhythm for the paragraph ending; see note on 7.

102–3. 'As he wildly spoke these words, a howling northerly storm struck full against the sails'; *iactanti* ('for him speaking') is a kind of ethic dative, in the loosest possible grammatical relationship with the sentence, cf. *Aen.* 2.713; *iactare* (often used with words like *minas*) suggests wildness, cf. *Aen.* 2.588, 768.

104. **prora avertit**: *avertit* is intransitive, cf. 402. Failure to see this has led the chief MSS to read *proram*, but to supply *procella* as the subject is intolerably harsh.

105. 'a sheer massive mountain of water came on them'; for *cumulo*, ablative of manner, literally 'in a mass', cf. *Aen.* 2.498. The rhythm is deliberately dislocated by the monosyllabic ending; see my note on 5.481 (Oxford edition). Day Lewis renders the effect with 'a precipice of sea hung'.

106–7. 'Some hang on the wave's crest; some see the billow ebb back and reveal the sea-bed between the waves; the wild water is aswirl with sand.' The high rhetorical and hyperbolical style reaches its acme here, but even in a grandiose passage of this kind Virgil (unlike Ovid, *Tr.* 1.2 or Lucan, 5.597f.), prefers to stop short of the grotesque. *Hi* and *his* refer to men still on board their ships.

108. **tris**: alternative accusative form of *tres*, understand *naves*.

109. Suspicion has been cast on this line as an interpolation, but the MSS have it and Quintilian (8.2.14) quotes it (as well he might) as an example of unnatural word order — the prose order would be *saxa quae in mediis fluctibus (latentia) Itali Aras vocant*. The reference evidently is to rocks sometimes visible 'as a huge ridge on the sea's surface' and at other times hidden (cf. *Aen.* 5.125f.).

111. **in brevia et syrtis**: 'into the shallows and the sandbanks'; *brevia* is like the Greek τὰ βραχέα, *syrtis* has particular application to the famous Syrtes off the coast of Africa (4.41).

112. This is a splendid final picture of their fate, static after wild movement, again with the special rhythmic effect in the fourth foot, see note on 7.

114. **ipsius**: i.e. Aeneas.

a vertice: 'from high above', cf. *Geo.* 2.310, *Aen.* 5.444, and *Od.* 5.313 κατ' ἄκρης.

115f. 'the helmsman was hurled out, and fell head-first down into the sea; while the wave whirled the ship and turned it round three times where it was, and the devouring eddy swallowed it in the ocean'. From 6.334 it seems that Orontes' helmsman was called Leucaspis. Notice the metrical effect of *volvitur in caput*; cf. 82. Ribbeck emended *illam* to *aliam* to account for the twenty ships (only 19 are accounted for in the text); it is worth reading Henry's vigorous denunciation of this emendation (*Aeneidea*, i.xxf.).

118. 'Here and there men appear, swimming in the expanse of ocean'; a very remarkable line of spondaic movement (following the dactyls of 117), with word accent clashing with ictus.

119. Supply *apparent* again: 'and the heroes' armour is seen, and planks, and Troy's treasure in the ocean'. The adjective *Troius* is a dactyl, the noun *Troia* (95) a trochee.

120. For the scansion of *Ilionei* see note on 41; Ilioneus is Aeneas' spokesman at 521f. and 7.212f.; Achates is Aeneas' right-hand man (e.g. 312), a very colourless figure. Abas and Aletes in the next line are less important.

122–3. 'through the weakened fastenings of their hulls they all take in the deadly water, and gape at the seams'; for *imber*, often used in this sense by Lucretius, Servius quotes Ennius (*Ann.* 497–8) *ratibusque fremebat / imber Neptuni.*

124–56. *Neptune intervenes, angrily rebukes the winds, and calms the storm.*

124. **misceri**: a favourite word with Virgil to denote turmoil, often (as here) used with alliteration of *m* in adjacent words; cf. 4.160.

125–6. **et imis stagna refusa vadis**: 'and that the still waters were upheaved from the sea's bottom'; *stagna* refers to the water at the bottom of the ocean which even if comparatively shallow (*vadis*) would still normally be calm.

126–7. **alto prospiciens**: 'gazing out over the deep', for the ablative cf. 181.

127. **placidum caput**: although Neptune is very angry (*graviter commotus*) at this interference in his kingdom, the god's countenance is always serene.

129. **caelique ruina**: 'the falling heavens', a rhetorically exaggerated phrase comparable with *Geo.* 1.324 *ruit arduus aether*.

130. Juno was daughter of Saturnus (23); his three sons (Jupiter, Neptune, Pluto) divided the world between them by lot; cf. 139, and Hom. *Il.* 15.187f.

131. **dehinc**: sometimes an iambus in Virgil, sometimes (as here and in 256) a single syllable.

132. **generis . . . fiducia**: 'confidence in your ancestry'; according to Hesiod (*Theog.* 378f.) the winds were born of the Titan Astraeus and the goddess Eos.

133. **numine**: 'divine authority', cf. line 8.

134. **moles**: 'confusion', cf. *Aen.* 5.790, where Venus uses the word to refer to this storm.

135. **quos ego**: these two pronouns, with the sentence left incomplete (aposiopesis), show the power of an inflected language to convey meaning by case endings. This picture of Neptune calming the storm has often been a subject for painters, and is sometimes known as the *Quos ego* scene.

136. 'Later, I promise you, you will pay for what you have done with a very different punishment', i.e. not just words. This seems more natural than to take *non simili* as meaning that the punishment will more than fit the crime.

140. **vestras, Eure, domos**: he speaks to them all (*vestras*), but particularises one of them in the vocative; cf. *Aen.* 9.525.

140–1. Notice the emphasis on the first words in the clauses, *illa* and *clauso*; the jussive subjunctives are limited by the condition imposed by these first words. Day Lewis renders the contemptuous tone with: 'Let Aeolus be king of that castle.'

143. **collectas**: 'gathered'.

144f. The description of the nymph Cymothoe ('wave-runner'), the sea-god Triton, and Neptune himself with his trident rescuing the ships is extremely pictorial; cf. Hom. *Il.* 13.23f., and *Aen.* 5.819f.

148 f. This first simile in the poem is extremely striking because it illustrates the world of nature from the world of human behaviour. Much more often similes operate the other way round: cf. Hom. *Il.* 2.144 f. where the assembly is moved like the waves of the sea or the corn in a windy field; Cicero often speaks of the storms and waves of political life, and cf. Scipio's words in Livy 28.27.11. Like a number of Virgilian similes, this one contains elements which link up not only with the immediate context, but with wide aspects of the narrative as a whole: the word *furor* (150) is the element in human behaviour which seems to be responsible for folly and sin (cf. 294), while the quality of *pietas* (151) is that through which Aeneas seeks to inaugurate a better world order; moreover the control exercised by the wise and responsible statesman depicted here (*regit*, 153) anticipates in miniature the mission of Rome, *regere imperio populos* (see Otis, *Virgil*, pp. 221 f., 229, and Pöschl, *The Art of Vergil*, pp. 20 f.). The violence and storms of passion are more easily calmed here by Neptune than in the *Aeneid* by Aeneas or in Virgil's world by the Romans.

148. **ac veluti ... cum saepe**: 'just as often happens when in a crowded assembly ...'; the misplacement of *saepe* seems to be idiomatic, cf. Lucr. 3.913, *Aen.* 5.273, 527. Some take *magno in populo* to mean 'in a great nation', but this seems less likely.

150. **furor arma ministrat**: cf. Milton *P.L.* 6.635 'Rage prompted them at length, and found them arms.'

151 f. 'then if it happens that they look upon someone respected for his public devotion and services, they fall silent, and stand still listening intently...'. For *si ... virum quem* cf. 181; with an enclitic the monosyllabic ending to the hexameter is hardly felt. It is suggested that Virgil may have had Cato in mind; cf. Plut. *Cat. Min.* 44.3–4.

156. 'and flying onwards gave free rein to his willing chariot'; *curru* is dative, cf. 257, 476.

157–222. *The Trojans land in Africa after the storm. Aeneas reconnoitres, and shoots seven stags. He heartens his men and they feast, saddened by the apparent loss of thirteen of their twenty ships.*

157. **Aeneadae**: the followers of Aeneas, the proto-Romans; cf. Lucr. 1.1 *Aeneadum genetrix* (of Venus, Aeneas' mother). The

people are called after their leader; Conway compares *Thesidae*
(Athenians) in *Geo.* 2.383.

159f. This imaginary description of a harbour is based on
Homer's description of the harbour of Ithaca (*Od.* 13.96f.); all
its parts occur there except the island. It is a full-scale rhetorical
description (ecphrasis), with *est . . . locus* picked up by *huc* (170);
cf. 441f., and Austin on *Aen.* 4.480f., 483.

159–161. 'an island makes a harbour with the barrier of its
edges, for all the waves from the open sea break on it and part
into receding ripples'. The meaning of the last phrase (which
occurs also in *Geo.* 4.420) is not certain, but the version given
seems better than the alternative — 'part into the sheltered
creeks'.

162f. Cf. the harbour of Castrum Minervae in 3.535f. *gemino
dimittunt bracchia muro | turriti scopuli.*

162. **minantur**: Servius says *eminent*, and compares 4.88–9
minaeque | murorum ingentes; he adds *ita est ut quae eminent minari
videantur.*

164f. 'then there is a background of waving trees above, and a
dark wood looming high with its sinister shadows': *tum* means
further backwards and upwards as you look from the harbour;
scaena (*Geo.* 3.24) is the back-drop which closes in the whole
picture (429). Cf. Milton, *P.L.* 4.137f.

166. **fronte sub adversa**: i.e. at the head of the bay, facing
the entrance with its island, and flanked by the cliffs and woods
just described.

167. **vivoque sedilia saxo**: 'seats in the natural rock', cf. Ov.
Met. 5.317. This cave of the Nymphs is based on Hom. *Od.*
12.317f. as well as 13.103f.

168–9. The diction is very far indeed from that of prose; the
'weary' ships, the anchor with its 'hooked bite' (cf. *Aen.* 6.3f.
dente tenaci | ancora).

170. **septem**: he had twenty (line 381) to start with.

172. **Troes**: Greek nominative plural with short final syllable,
cf. 468, 500.

173. **sale tabentis**: 'drenched with salt water'.

174. **silici**: ablative, cf. *capiti*, 7.668. For the sense cf. 6.6f.

175–6. 'and caught the fire in leaves and put dry kindling
around, and got a flame going in brushwood'. For *rapere* of things

catching fire cf. Ov. *Met.* 3.374, Lucan 3.684; Virgil has here varied the construction to mean that Achates 'caught' the flame in the brushwood. There seems no parallel for the suggestion that *rapuit* here means 'fanned'.

177. **Cererem**: 'corn', metonymy of the goddess for her attribute; cf. 701, and *Bacchus* in 215.

Cerealiaque arma: i.e. grinding mills, kneading troughs, etc.

178. **rerum**: cf. 12.589 *trepidi rerum*, Hor. *Odes* 2.6.7 *lasso maris*; it is a Greek genitive of cause (origin), 'wearied from. . .'.

181. **pelago**: 'over the sea', cf. 126.

181–2. **Anthea si quem . . . videat**: 'if he could see some sign of Antheus'; the condition is of the '*si forte*' type, meaning 'in the hope that', cf. 578 and 2.136. *Anthea* is Greek accusative; *quem* (=*aliquem*) is here used strangely, but cf. 2.81–2 *aliquod . . . nomen Palamedis*, 'any mention of the name of Palamedes', and Ov. *Met.* 9.8–9 *nomine si qua suo fando pervenit ad aures | Deianira tuas*, *Met.* 15.497 *aliquem Hippolytum*. It is not unlike the colloquial use of *nullus*: *nullum Anthea vidit* would be 'he saw no sign of Antheus'.

183. **arma**: i.e. armour displayed on the ship's prow, cf. *Aen.* 10.80.

184f. The episode of the shooting of the stags is based on *Od.* 10.158f. (cf. perhaps also 9.154f.), where Odysseus shoots a stag and takes it back to his comrades in the ship. The passage is presented in accordance with the heroic tradition, but is not one of Virgil's most successful adaptations of Homer.

189–90. **capita . . . arboreis**: 'as they held their heads high with their branching antlers'; for *arboreis* cf. *Ecl.* 7.30 *ramosa . . . cornua cervi*.

190–1. **vulgus et omnem . . . turbam**: 'the rest of them, the whole crowd', cf. Enn. *Frag. Inc.* 15 *avium vulgus*, Lucr. 2.921 *praeter vulgum turbamque animantum*, *Geo.* 3.469.

191. **miscet**: 'threw into confusion', cf. 124.

192. **victor**: 'triumphantly', continuing the military phrases of the previous line, but rather over-emphatic.

193. **fundat**: the subjunctive is used to express purpose, cf. 473.

humo: 'to the ground', cf. *Geo.* 2.460, *Aen.* 9.214. It is however very possible that Servius and some inferior MSS are right with *humi*.

195. **deinde**: Virgil is fond of postponing *deinde*; see Conway's note, and cf. *Aen.* 3.609. This is however his most striking example of the usage, and it gives a curiously dislocated effect.

Acestes: the Sicilian king from whom the Trojans had just come, and whom they revisit in Book 5; Segesta was called after him.

196. **Trinacrio**: Sicily was called Trinacria from its triangular shape, see note on 3.384.

heros: this word should certainly be taken with Acestes, subject of *dederat*, not with Aeneas, subject of *dividit*. It means in heroic (i.e. generous, chivalrous) fashion; for its position cf. *dea* in 412.

198f. Aeneas' speech is based on that of Odysseus in Hom. *Od.* 12.208f. Macrobius regards Aeneas' speech as *locupletior* than Odysseus'; and Conway draws attention to the emphasis in Homer on Odysseus' own prowess, in Virgil on Aeneas' trust in the gods and in his men's courage.

198. Cf. Hom. *Od.* 12.208 Ὦ φίλοι, οὐ γάρ πώ τι κακῶν ἀδαήμονές εἰμεν. For *enim* see note on 65; *ante* goes with *sumus*, 'we have not before now been unacquainted with suffering', rather than with *malorum* in the Greek sense of τῶν πρὶν κακῶν.

199. **o passi graviora**: Cf. Hom. *Od.* 20.18 τέτλαθι δή, κραδίη. καὶ κύντερον ἄλλο ποτ' ἔτλης, and Hor. *Odes* 1.7.30–1 *o fortes peioraque passi | mecum saepe viri.*

200–1. In *Aen.* 3.420f. Helenus describes to the Trojans the danger of Scylla and Charybdis, and warns them to keep away; in 3.558f. their escape from this peril is described. *Rabiem* probably refers especially to the dogs associated with Scylla (Lucr. 5.892 *rabidis canibus succincta*, of Scylla); so does *penitusque sonantis scopulos*, cf. 3.432 *caeruleis canibus resonantia saxa*. Immediately after their escape from Scylla (3.569f.) the Trojans come to Etna and the home of the Cyclops, where they land and narrowly escape from Polyphemus and his fellows. These two incidents are among the most marked similarities with the *Odyssey*; cf. *Od.* 12.73f. and 222f., *Od.* 9.106f.

200. **penitusque**: probably with *sonantis*, 'sounding deep within', (cf. *Aen.* 6.59) rather than with *accestis*, 'approached right up to'.

201. **accestis**: syncope for *accessistis*, a mark of archaising style; cf. *Aen.* 4.606.

203. Again this recalls Odysseus' speech in *Od.* 12 (212) καί που
τῶνδε μνήσεσθαι ὀίω. Virgil emphasises the idea of pleasure in
looking back at dangers overcome. *Olim* means 'one day', cf. 20,
234, 289; *forsan* with the indicative is common in poetry.

206. **fas**: the laws of heaven permit it, as Aeneas had learned
from oracles during his journey (e.g. 3.94f., 154f., 376f.). These
had told him of Italy, of Cumae, and of a river past Circe's isle
where he would find rest from his toils; the actual word *Latium*
had not been used, but no reader of Virgil need feel any great
disquiet on that account.

208-9. It is typical of Virgil's method of character-drawing
for him to comment as narrator on the events or statements of the
story; cf. for example 4.331-2 (*curam* . . . *premebat*), 4.393f. Line
209 is imitated by Dryden, *Annus Mirabilis* 73 'His face spake hope,
while deep his sorrows flow'.

210f. This elaborate description of the preparation for a feast
is very much in the Homeric style; cf. *Il.* 1.459f.

215. 'they take their fill of old wine and rich venison'; the
genitive is less common than the ablative after *implentur*, and helps
to emphasise the Greek tone of the passage. For *Bacchus* (wine) cf.
Ceres (corn) in 177.

216-17. This is imitated from Hom. *Od.* 12.308-9, except for
mensaeque remotae, which refers to the Roman custom at the conclusion of a meal (cf. 723).

217. **requirunt**: like *desiderant*, 'they lament the loss of'; cf.
quaerere in *Aen.* 5.814.

218. 'Hovering between hope and fear, not knowing whether
to believe that they still live. . .'. *Dubii* governs both *inter* and the
seu . . . *sive* clauses; for *seu* in an indirect question cf. *Aen.* 2.739.

219. **nec iam exaudire vocatos**: 'can no longer hear when
called', a reference to the Roman custom of *conclamatio* at death,
the calling by name before hope is finally abandoned.

220. **pius**: here with reference to his responsibility as leader,
see note on 10.

Oronti: fifth declension form, see note on 30.

222. Gyas and Cloanthus are two of the competitors in the boat
race in Book 5.

223-96. *Venus complains to Jupiter that the promise of Aeneas'
destiny is not being fulfilled. He replies that it will be fulfilled, and*

*outlines the glory awaiting the Roman people and their mission to civilise
the world.*

223f. The scene in heaven is based to begin with on the
complaints by Thetis to Zeus in Hom. *Il.* 1.495f., and of Athena
to Zeus in *Od.* 5.5f. But it differs entirely from Homer in the
emphasis laid both by Venus and by Jupiter on the mission of the
storm-tossed hero in the context of world-history. Venus knows
that world empire has been promised (234f.), and Jupiter
majestically confirms it, elaborating in serene tones the radiantly
optimistic picture of the new Golden Age. We have been invited
so far in this book to think of Aeneas as a second Odysseus; now
we are shown how he is to be different. Odysseus succeeds as a
brilliantly resourceful individual; Aeneas must succeed as the
leader of his people.

The prophecy of Jupiter outlines the Roman mission, first
conquest and then civilisation and peace; and it gives an impetus
to the poem which lifts it on to a level above the individual actions
of the human characters. It shines through the dark places, and
provides a partial answer to the problems of human suffering
with which the *Aeneid* is so preoccupied. Without it the events of
(say) Book 4 or Book 12 would seem like the senseless suffering
of a blind world; with it there is a reason for the suffering, even
if it does not satisfy us. The world order, which seems here so
desirable, cannot be achieved without suffering and sacrifice, and
as the poem explores these sacrifices, the reader must remember
why they have to be made. We must not be unmindful of Jupiter's
speech when Aeneas has to face the problems which it involves.

223. **Et iam finis erat**: 'and now all was ended', a curious
transition, vaguely and majestically suggesting that when the
mortals had fallen to sleep the king of the gods disposes the
affairs with which they had exhausted themselves.

224. 'looking down on the sail-winged sea and the outspread
lands'; *velivolus* is a most vivid epithet, used by Ennius and
Lucretius to describe ships. See note on 3.544.

225. **sic**: used somewhat redundantly (cf. the Greek οὕτως),
here to emphasise the picture of Jupiter looking down over all the
peoples and while thus occupied (*sicut erat*) suddenly stopping and
fixing his eyes on Libya; cf. *Aen.* 7.668.

227. **talis**: i.e. the thoughts caused by what he saw there.

228. tristior: the comparative signifies 'unusually sad', not with her usual serenity.

oculos suffusa nitentis: 'her bright eyes brimming', the retained accusative construction of which Virgil is fond, based partly on imitation of the Greek middle voice, and partly on the Greek accusative of respect (see note on 320); cf. 481, 561, 579, 658, 713, *Aen.* 12.64f. *lacrimis . . . perfusa genas*, and my note on *Aen.* 5.135 (Oxford edition).

231. meus: used emotionally, a mother speaking of her son; cf. *Aen.* 2.522.

232-3. 'that when they have suffered such great losses the whole expanse of the world is closed to them because of Italy', i.e. to prevent their reaching Italy, Juno persecutes them wherever they are.

234. hinc: 'from them'; cf. line 6.

235. revocato a sanguine Teucri: 'from the restored line of Teucer', restored after the destruction of Troy; for the Trojan king Teucer see note on 38.

237. pollicitus: understand *es*; cf. 202 *experti* (*estis*), 5.687.

quae . . . vertit: 'what thought has changed your mind?', a variation on the commoner phrase *cur sententiam mutavisti*?

238-9. hoc . . . solabar: 'with this I consoled myself for . . .'; this use of *solari* is not uncommon in Virgil, cf. *Geo.* 1.293, *Aen.* 9.489.

239. fatis . . . rependens: 'balancing one fate against another (its opposite)'; according to Servius the metaphor is financial. For the phraseology cf. *Aen.* 7.293f. *fatis contraria nostris | fata Phrygum*.

242f. The story of Antenor (an important Trojan in Homer, e.g. *Il.* 7.347f.) is told in Livy 1.1; he led a party of Trojans to the area of Venice, and called the place Troia — thus he would pass Liburnia and Illyricum (near the head of the Adriatic on the east side) and the river Timavus, right at the head, to reach Patavium, modern Padua near Venice, on the west side. *Penetrare intima regna* merely means that he sailed past this remote northern area of the Adriatic (Livy 1.1 *intimum Adriatici maris sinum*); there is no reason to think that he travelled overland into the hinterland.

244. superare: a nautical term, according to Servius; cf. *Aen.* 3.698, Livy 31.22 *superare Sunium*.

245–6. The intention of Venus is to build up a formidable picture of the difficulties which Antenor was allowed to overcome; the floods of the Timavus are not strictly relevant to people sailing past by sea. *Mare* and *pelago* are used hyperbolically of the river's flood; for *proruptum* 'bursting forth' cf. *Aen.* 7.459, Lucr. 6.436. Henry has a long geographical note on the peculiarities of the Timavus.

248. **armaque fixit**: cf. *Aen.* 3.287; the armour would be hung up and dedicated in a temple.

249. 'now settled in quiet rest he is at peace'; this does not mean that he is dead, but that all his difficulties are over; cf. Enn. *Ann.* 375 *nunc senio confectus quiescit* and for *compositus* Ov. *Am.* 1.4.53. Venus' point is that Antenor has achieved peace after the successful foundation of his city, in contrast with Aeneas whose frustrations and perils seem to know no end.

250. Venus identifies herself with Aeneas; for *adnuis* cf. *Aen.* 12.187. Aeneas, like Romulus, was supposed to have become a god after death.

253. 'Is this the reward for devotion? Is this how you restore us to empire?' Venus' first question recalls the invocation to the poem (10–11), and summarises the nature of the problem which Virgil explores. Cf. Milton, *P.L.* 11.452 'Is Pietie thus and pure Devotion paid?'

254. **olli**: archaic for *illi*, quite frequent in Virgil as in Ennius.

255–6. 'with the countenance (i.e. expression) with which he makes the heavens and the changing skies turn sunny he lightly kissed his daughter's lips'; cf. Enn. *Ann.* 457–8 *Iuppiter hic risit, tempestatesque serenae / riserunt omnes risu Iovis omnipotentis*, where *tempestates* means weather rather than storms.

257. **parce metu**: 'spare your fear', i.e. cease to be afraid; cf. *Aen.* 2.534 *nec voci iraeque pepercit. Metu* is dative, cf. 156.

Cytherea: a frequent epithet of Venus, from the seat of her worship in Cythera (680), an island just south of Greece.

258. **tibi**: ethic dative, cf. 463, and note on 102–3.

Lavini: Aeneas' first settlement, see note on 2. Notice the variation of scansion from *Laviniaque* in line 2; cf. *Italia* and *Italus* (2, 109), *Sychaeus* (343, 348), *Sidonius* (446, 678), *Eous* (489, 2.417), *Diana* (499, 3.681), *Orion* (535, 3.517), *Sicania* and *Sicanos* (557, 5.24). For a full discussion see my note on 5.571 (Oxford edition).

262. **volvens ... movebo**: 'I will unroll and bring to light the secrets of the book of fate'; *volvens* is a metaphor from unrolling a book, cf. 22; for *movebo* cf. Hor. *Odes* 3.7.20.

263-4. Jupiter states the two elements in Aeneas' mission; first to conquer, and then to civilise (for *mores* cf. *Aen.* 6.852 *pacique imponere morem*). Compare 4.230f. *Italiam regeret ... ac totum sub leges mitteret orbem. Moenia* suggests the settled life of city-dwellers.

265-6. These lines refer obliquely to the death (or disappearance from the earth) of Aeneas, three years after the end of the action in the *Aeneid*. The word *hiberna* is generally taken to mean that the Trojans remained in their camp for these three years; but it is more likely to be a Virgilian variation for *hiemes*.

267-8. Virgil uses the Roman form Iulus nearly as often as the Greek name Ascanius for Aeneas' son. The etymological connexion with Ilium (Troy) is taken a stage further in line 288 to connect with the Julian gens. Both Julius Caesar and Augustus were interested in emphasising the alleged Trojan origins of their family; cf. Hor. *Sat.* 2.5.62f. For Virgil's fondness for etymology of this kind cf. 5.117f., 7.706f., and see my note on 5.117f. (Oxford edition).

267. **Iulo**: the dative agreeing with *cui* is a more common idiom than the nominative in apposition with the subject.

269. 'thirty great cycles as the months roll by'. The chronology is three years of rule for Aeneas, thirty for Iulus in Lavinium and Alba Longa, three hundred for his successors in Alba Longa; thus the gap in time (between the fall of Troy early in the twelfth century and the foundation of Rome in the middle of the eighth) is roughly filled up.

volvendis: the gerundive supplies the place of the present participle passive, cf. *Aen.* 9.7, Enn. *Ann.* 531 *clamor ... volvendus*, Lucr. 5.1276 *volvenda aetas*.

271. Some of the kings of Alba Longa are described in the pageant of Roman heroes in 6.760f.

272. **ter centum totos ... annos**: 'full 300 years'.

273. **gente sub Hectorea**: there is strong emotional significance in this reference to Troy's great champion who did not survive Troy; cf. 5.190, 12.440.

273-7. This is the most famous part of the Roman legend: the name Ilia, alternative for Rhea Silvia, the mother by Mars of Romulus and Remus, has obvious connexions with Troy (Ilium).

275. The picture of the she-wolf suckling the twins Romulus and Remus (when they were washed ashore after having been set adrift on the Tiber by the wicked Amulius; Livy 1.3.10f.) was a most familiar aspect of Roman legendary history; Virgil makes it the first picture on Aeneas' shield (8.630f.). Propertius (4.10.20) describes Romulus as wearing a wolf-skin helmet.

276. **Mavortia**: an older form of *Martia* (Mavors = Mars), cf. *Aen.* 3.13.

278–9. 'For them I set no bounds in space or time: I have given them rule without end'. These are sonorous and unforgettable phrases: the proud certainty of Roman imperial rule must have had a profound patriotic impact on Virgil's readers.

279. **quin**: 'indeed', like the fuller form *quin etiam*, cf. *Aen.* 6.115.

280. **metu ... fatigat**: 'is harassing and alarming' (cf. *Aen.* 11.401) rather than 'is harassing because alarmed'.

281. **consilia in melius referet**: cf. *Aen.* 12.807f., Hor. *Odes* 3.3.17f.

282. **rerum dominos gentemque togatam**: 'lords of the world, a people wearing the toga'; i.e. warriors first, and then men of peace, the *toga* being the garment of civilian wear — cf. Cicero's famous phrase *cedant arma togae*.

284. **Assaracus**: grandfather of Anchises, cf. *Aen.* 6.650.

284–5. The reference to the defeat of Greece (it became a Roman province in the second century B.C.) is expressed in terms appropriate to the time of the Trojan war (cf. 6.836f.). Pthia was the home of Achilles, Mycenae of Agamemnon; Argos as well as being a generic term for Greece was specifically the home of Diomedes.

286. **Caesar**: it is much disputed whether this is Julius Caesar or Augustus. Servius gives the former, and Conway argues strongly for this view. But it seems to me that the context, with its tremendous build-up leading to this final tableau, must refer not to any precursor of the restored Golden Age, but to the man thought actually to have restored it (6.791 f.). Two other arguments seem to have overpowering weight in favour of Augustus: (i) the word Caesar elsewhere in the poem is used of Augustus,

and on the one occasion when Julius Caesar is certainly referred to (6.834 f.) it is in a context of sorrow; (ii) the references to the spoils of the east (the battle of Actium, 8.678 f., see next note) is more appropriate to Augustus than to Julius Caesar, and the references to the closing of the gates of war (closed by Augustus in 29 B.C. and again in 25 B.C.) and to the end of civil war (lines 292, 294) must refer to Augustus. With Servius' interpretation the word *tum* has to take us from Julius Caesar to Augustus.

289. **spoliis Orientis**: cf. *Aen.* 8.687–8 (of Antony at Actium) *Aegyptum virisque Orientis et ultima secum | Bactra vehit, Geo.* 2.171 f., 4.560 f.

290. Notice the unusual rhythm, with no strong caesura in the third or fourth foot. *Secura* means 'anxious no more'; Juno will no longer be in opposition.

hic quoque: as well as Aeneas. The poets were ready to promise deification to Augustus (*Geo.* 1.24 f., Hor. *Odes* 3.3.11 f., 3.5.2 f.); Julius had already been deified.

291 f. This is the fullest expression of that vision which is only gradually revealed to Aeneas in the course of the poem; it is this same vision, however dimly seen, which enables him to continue onwards through suffering and discouragement, weariness and disaster towards his ultimate goal. See note on 223 f.

292. **cana Fides et Vesta**: *fides* was a word very highly valued indeed in the Roman moral scheme; Livy tells (1.21.4) that Numa established the worship and the first temple of Fides; cf. Hor. *Carm. Saec.* 57. She is called *cana* because she is one of the original old-fashioned virtues of the *mos maiorum* (cf. *cana Vesta*, 5.744). Similarly Vesta, goddess of the hearth, often associated with the Lares and Penates, personifies traditional family ties (*Geo.* 1.498).

Remo cum fratre Quirinus: Quirinus is also used of Romulus in *Aen.* 6.859. The killing of Remus by Romulus is used as a symbol of the beginning of civil war in Rome; cf. Hor. *Epod.* 7, esp. 17 f., a tremendous protest against the folly of civil war (cf. also *Epod.* 16, *Geo.* 1.498 f.).

294. The gates of war were in Janus' temple; there is a full description of them in *Aen.* 7.607 f. Cf. Enn. *Ann.* 266–7 *postquam Discordia taetra | Belli ferratos postes portasque refregit.* They were closed in 29 B.C. (for the first time since 235), and again in 25 B.C.

Furor impius: here is personified the quality of mad strife seen especially in civil war, in which *pietas* was especially profaned (Hor. *Epod.* 16.9). For the importance of the concepts *furor* and *pietas* in the *Aeneid* see note on 148f. The picture of *Furor impius* is said by Servius to be based on a painting (by Apelles, Pliny *N.H.* 35.93) which Augustus placed in his own forum; certainly it has a most powerful visual impact. Cf. Spenser *F.Q.*, 2.4.15 (Guyon taming Furor).

296. Notice the effect of a single word filling the fourth foot to round off a paragraph; cr. 7 and 101.

297–304. *Jupiter sends Mercury to tell Dido to receive the Trojans hospitably.*

297f. The visit of Aeneas to Carthage and his meeting with Dido was not in the prose version of the legend (as told by Dionysius, for instance); it was ruled out by chronological considerations, as Carthage was certainly not founded until three or four centuries later than the times of Aeneas. There are various traces of early versions of a Dido story without Aeneas, and there is some reason to think that Naevius in his *Bellum Punicum* (late third century B.C.) first brought them together (see Pease's introduction to Book 4). But it is certain that the scope and extent of the Aeneas-Dido story is Virgil's own.

297. **Maia genitum**: Mercury was the son of Maia, daughter of Atlas, cf. *Aen.* 4.258.

298. **novae ... Karthaginis**: (see also 366) according to Servius the word Carthage in Punic meant *Nova Civitas*, so that Virgil here is using *novus* to point to the etymology; see note on 267–8.

299. **fati nescia**: Dido was of course ignorant of the fates. This phrase does not mean that she was told of them (indeed when she was told in Book 4 she was completely unconvinced), but that Jupiter took action to aid the progress of the fates. Page has an interesting note on fate and free-will.

300. **arceret**: the different sequence from *pateant* indicates that while the former clause gives Jupiter's instructions the latter is added as an explanation of this action.

aëra: a few Greek third-declension nouns have their Latin accusative in *-a*, e.g., *aethera, cratera, aegida, lampada*, and a number of proper names.

301. **remigio alarum**: 'on the oarage of his wings', i.e. with wings for oars, cf. *Aen.* 6.19. The metaphor occurs in Aeschylus (*Agam.* 52), and was used by Lucretius (6.743). Cf. Milton, *P.L.* 7.438 f. 'The swan with arched neck / between her white wings mantling proudly, rows / her state with oarie feet.'

305–417. *Aeneas meets his mother Venus, disguised as a huntress. She tells him the history of Dido and Carthage, and when she asks him for his story, he complains bitterly of his ill fortune. She replies that his companions will return safely, and disappears after hiding him and Achates in a cloud.*

305 f. The narrative here, quite often based on *Odyssey* 6 and 7, is very fast-moving and filled with event and fact; it is in marked contrast with the slow and sonorous movement of the previous eighty lines. In it we hear the story of Dido, recounted by Venus in a way which immediately elicits sympathy and admiration (see note on 364). Her fortunes have been in many ways similar to those of Aeneas, with the one great difference that she has already founded her city.

In Aeneas' reply to Venus' questions (372 f.) we see the effects upon him of the strain of seven years wandering and danger. He is angry and resentful at this latest misfortune, and Virgil shows that it is only by a narrow margin that he has been able so far to conquer his anxieties and human frailties, and to continue on with his mission. He is not yet (or ever) the stern, hard, self-sufficient man held out by the Stoics as their ideal (see note on 384–5); we are partly prepared for, and ready to understand, the failure in self-discipline and devotion to duty which leads him to stay on in Carthage long after he should have renewed his pursuit of the ever-receding shores of Italy, and produces a situation of tragedy for which he must bear much of the blame.

305. **pius Aeneas**: see note on 220. Here the nature of his responsibility is stressed by the description of his sleeplessness. Servius says 'decet enim pro cunctis regem esse sollicitum'.

306 f. The construction is *constituit exire locosque explorare novos, quaerere quas oras accesserit. . . .*

308. **videt**: the last syllable is lengthened in arsis, i.e. by the ictus (beat) at the beginning of the foot, cf. 478, 651, 668. See Austin's note on *Aen.* 4.64.

309. **exacta**: 'what he had achieved' (cf. *Aen.* 6.637), here with the sense of 'what he had found out' (as in Hor. *Sat.* 2.4.36).

310. **convexo**: 'arch'; this adjective used in the neuter as a noun is much more common in the plural (e.g. *Aen.* 4.451).

313. 'grasping two broad-bladed spears that quivered in his hand': *crispans* does not mean 'brandishing' here or in 12.165, where this line occurs again.

314 f. Virgil is following Homer *Od.* 7.19 f., where the disguised Athena meets Odysseus (cf. also *Od.* 13.221 f.); he conflates this episode with parts of the story of Nausicaa and Odysseus in *Odyssey* 6.

316 f. Spartan maidens were well-known for their physical toughness in hunting and the like; Harpalyce from Thrace devoted herself to the wild life of the woods (like Virgil's Camilla).

316. **fatigat**: 'outlasts', wearies them out by racing them.

317. **praevertitur**: 'outstrips'. Elsewhere Virgil uses the active form (7.807, 12.345); here the object is governed by the prepositional force of *prae-*.

Hebrum: a river in Thrace. The emendation *Eurum* (the east wind) has found some support, but all the MSS and Servius attest *Hebrum*, and so does Silius (2.73 f.).

318. **de more**: 'in the proper style', explained by *venatrix*.

habilem: 'ready', i.e. of suitable size and well-adjusted, cf. *Aen.* 9.305.

319. For this use of *dederat* see note on 66.

320. **nuda genu**: Greek accusative of respect, found once in Lucretius (3.489), common in Virgil especially with parts of the body; cf. 589 and 5.97 *nigrantis terga iuvencos* with my note there (Oxford edition). See also note on 228.

nodoque sinus collecta fluentis: 'with her flowing garments secured by a knot', literally 'having secured the flowing folds of her garments'; for the retained accusative see on 228, and cf. Ov. *Fast.* 1.407 *illa super suras tunicam collecta.* . . .

321–2. **monstrate . . . vidistis si quam**: 'if you have seen any . . . show me where'; *si* here introduces a true condition, not an indirect question.

322–4. **errantem . . . aut . . . prementem**: 'roaming around . . . or chasing'. Some commentators have found difficulty with *aut* (and have therefore suggested that it might link *lyncis* with *apri*), but the two proper activities of a huntsman are *either* roaming around in search of prey (Servius for *errantem* rightly says *investigantem*) *or* chasing it.

328. **hominem sonat**: 'sound mortal', an extended use of the adverbial or cognate accusative (*humanum sonat*): cf. Pers. 3.21 *sonat vitium* ('rings false'). Compare Spenser *F.Q.* 2.3.33 'O Goddesse (for such I thee take to bee) / For neither doth thy face terrestrial shew, / Nor voyce sound mortall . . .'

329. The sister of Phoebus is Diana the huntress; if not Diana, Aeneas says, then surely one of her Nymphs (Oreades, 500). So spoke Odysseus to Nausicaa, *Od.* 6.149 f.

330. **quaecumque**: in apposition with the subject: 'lighten our suffering, whoever you are'.

332. There are two unusual elisions in this line — the long final vowel of *ignari* before the short first syllable of *hominumque*; and the hypermetric elision of *locorumque* before *erramus* in the next line (cf. 448 and my note on *Aen.* 5.422 (Oxford edition)). The effect here is to suggest the catch in his voice as he speaks these words of despair (cf. the effect of indignation in 4.629).

334. **multa . . . hostia**: 'many a victim'; for the singular cf. Hor. *Odes* 1.5.1 *multa . . . rosa*, *Geo.* 1.187.

336. **virginibus Tyriis**: by implication Venus suggests that she is one.

337. Cf. *Ecl.* 7.32 (of Diana) *puniceo stabis suras evincta coturno*; evidently the type of *coturnus* (a high boot secured with bands) worn by hunters was brightly coloured.

338. **Agenor**: one of Dido's ancestors in Tyre.

339. **sed fines Libyci**: 'but the territory around is Libyan' (i.e. the hinterland of Carthage, in contrast to the city and the area immediately around it) — cf. 367 f., 563 f.

340. **imperium Dido . . . regit**: 'Dido is in command'; for the cognate accusative cf. Ov. *Pont.* 3.3.61. Servius tells us that Elissa was Dido's original Phoenician name (Virgil uses it in the oblique cases), but that she was called Dido (=*virago*, 'Heroine') after she had killed herself rather than break her vows by marrying an African suitor (this is the early form of her story before it was linked, perhaps by Naevius, with the Aeneas legend; see note on 297 f.).

341-2. 'It is a long story of crime, a long involved story, but I will go through the main outlines of the events.' *Fastigia* is a rare variant for *capita*.

343. **Sychaeus**: Servius says his Punic name was Sicarbas; in Virgil's Latinised form the quantity of the *y* varies, cf. 348. See note on 258.

ditissimus agri: for the genitive see on 14; there seems no need for the emendation *auri*.

344. **miserae dilectus**: cf. *Aen.* 4.31 *dilecta sorori*.

345-6. **primisque ... ominibus**: 'and had joined her to him in this her first marriage ceremony'; *primis* repeats the idea of *intactam*.

347. **Pygmalion**: the other Pygmalion, who fell in love with the statue he had made, was also of the royal house of Tyre.

349. **impius**: mainly with reference to the religious crime (*ante aras*), but also including the family crime of killing his brother-in-law.

350-1. **securus amorum germanae**: 'caring nothing for his sister's love', cf. *Aen.* 7.304 and (a little differently) 10.326. The plural *amores* in the sense 'love' (cf. *Aen.* 4.28, 5.334) occurs in prose as well as poetry.

351-2. 'wickedly making up many false stories he deceived the distraught bride with vain hope'.

354. 'lifting his face to look at her, strangely pale'; cf. Lucr. 1.123 *simulacra modis pallentia miris*, a phrase used by Virgil in *Geo.* 1.477.

356. **nudavit ... retexit**: *nudavit* is probably visual (he brought before her eyes in her dream) and *retexit* oral (revealed by telling her).

domus: 'of the family', cf. *Aen.* 3.97.

357. **celerare**: the infinitive with *suadere* is common in Virgil, cf. 3.363 and note on 527-8; so with *hortari* (2.33), *imperare* (7.36), and *instimulare* (4.576).

358. **auxiliumque viae**: in apposition to *thesauros*, 'to help the voyage'.

tellure recludit: in her dream Dido sees Sychaeus 'unearthing' the treasure for her; cf. *Geo.* 2.423.

360 f. The narrative, which has been fast-moving throughout, moves to its climax at great speed, with short sentences and many main verbs. This kind of writing affords a marked contrast with

the descriptive and reflective tone with which Virgil is often specially associated, and it is his command of variety in narrative movement which maintains the impetus of the *Aeneid* through its twelve books. Contrast poem 64 of Catullus.

361. **odium crudele tyranni**: i.e. *odium crudelis tyranni*, says Servius (transferred epithet). This is partly true, but a transferred epithet should also make sense before it is transferred (see Conway ad loc.); so here they felt cruel hatred of a tyrant, the cruelty of the tyrant made their reaction cruel.

362-4. Servius suggests that there are here traces of a story according to which Pygmalion had ships ready laden with gold to go trading for corn, and Dido's party seized these ships.

364. **dux femina facti**: the character of Dido as shown in the rest of Book 1 was in every way equal to facing danger and assuming responsibility. Her ability to establish her city and administer it causes the Trojans to admire and envy her. Thus her abdication of her queenly responsibilities and qualities in Book 4 is all the more tragic.

367. **mercatique**: supply *sunt*; the omission of the verb 'to be' is not very common where, as here, the effect is to suggest a subordinate clause.

Byrsa: this is the Greek word for a bull's hide; the legend is that the hide was cut into one very long thin strip. The story perhaps arose from the fact that Byrsa was according to Strabo the Carthaginian word for their citadel.

370. **talibus**: supply *verbis*, cf. 410, 559.

373. **vacet**: 'if you had time'.

374. 'Before I could finish, the evening star would close up Olympus and lay the day to rest.' *Ante* is adverbial (=*antea*); for *diem . . . componat* cf. 135, *Geo.* 4.189, *Ecl.* 9.52 *cantando . . . condere soles*; *clauso . . . Olympo* refers to the gates of heaven (*Geo.* 3.261). I have with some doubt preferred *componat* to *componet*; the major MSS are divided, and as the tendency would be for scribes to regularise the condition, most editors adopt *componet*, quoting Hor. *Odes* 3.3.7-8. But there a special rhetorical effect is achieved by the irregularity; here there would be nothing but a feeling of awkwardness.

375-6. Notice the irony, reinforced by repetition — from Troy, if you happen ever to have heard of it, Troy it's called.

377. **forte sua**: 'by its caprice'.

378. **sum pius Aeneas**: much indignant ink has been spilled on this phrase. It is based on Odysseus' introduction of himself, *Od.* 9.19–20 εἴμ' Ὀδυσεὺς Λαερτιάδης, ὃς πᾶσι δόλοισιν / ἀνθρώποισι μέλω, καί μευ κλέος οὐρανὸν ἵκει ('I am Odysseus son of Laertes who am known among all men for my subtle resources, and my fame reaches the heavens.') The second half of line 379 is a translation of the Homer passage. Exception is taken to Aeneas' use of the epithet *pius* of himself, but it seems to me that it is used here with tremendous power, implying 'and is this what I get for it?' (*hic pietatis honos?* as Venus had said to Jupiter, 253). This is in tone with the rest of what Aeneas says, as he lists the reasons why he might expect fate to deal less unkindly with him, and launches into bitter complaints about what has happened to him and his people. Henry has a superbly vigorous note on the passage, beginning "Charles James Fox, in a letter to his friend Trotter, having first observed: 'Though the detached parts of the *Aeneid* appear to me to be equal to anything, the story and characters appear more faulty every time I read it. My chief objection (I mean that to the character of Aeneas) is of course not so much felt in the first three books; but afterwards he is always either insipid or odious; sometimes excites interest against him, and never for him;' adds in a postscript and by way of example: "Even in the first book Aeneas says: *sum pius Aeneas...*" and inquires "Can you bear this?". Trotter's answer not having come down to us, I beg leave to answer for him, Yes; why not? Why not as well as any other announcement of a person's real name, rank, dignity, and quality? Why not as well as ... etc. etc." Servius puts it more briefly: *non est hoc loco arrogantia, sed indicium.*

penatis: see note on 6.

380. **patriam**: the meaning is 'to be my fatherland' rather than 'which is already my fatherland', with reference to Dardanus' origins there (cf. 3.167 f.).

'and my ancestry comes from Jupiter the highest'; Aeneas says this again in 6.123. The phrase comes in abruptly here, but perhaps intentionally so, to express Aeneas' angry indignation. Most commentators take *genus* as a second object for *quaero* — 'I seek Italy and a posterity descended from Jupiter'.

381. **conscendi ... aequor**: *conscendere* (*navem* or *in navem*) is

the regular term for 'to embark'; here the normal phrase is given an unexpected construction with the object *aequor*, adding the notion of going up from the shore to the sea; cf. *deferri* (e.g. 5.57) for sailing into harbour.

382. **matre dea**: perhaps with a touch of rebuke; the irony of the situation is exploited. For Venus' help at Troy cf. 2.619 f.; it has often been remarked that Apollo, not Venus, looks after Aeneas in Book 3. Servius gets round this difficulty by quoting Varro to the effect that Venus' star guided him to Latium (cf. 2.801 f.).

384-5. Aeneas' last words are a fine climax to his protests (again echoing what Venus herself had said to Jupiter, 233), and the word *querentem* summarises the content of his speech. He is very far from being the perfect Stoic; see C. M. Bowra, *Greece and Rome* 1933-4, pp. 8 f., and M. W. Edwards, *Phoenix* 1960, pp. 151 f.

387. **quisquis es**: a cruel touch of irony, as Venus affects not to be aware of the names Troy or Aeneas.

387 f. Cf. *Od.* 6.240 f. where Nausicaa says to her maidens that she thinks Odysseus has come to Phaeacia in accordance with the will of the gods.

388. **qui adveneris**: causal subjunctive, implying that the Tyrians will receive him kindly.

391. **versis Aquilonibus**: 'by a shift of the wind'.

392. 'unless my parents have deceived me and taught me augury without any success'.

393. For a similar omen cf. *Aen.* 12.247 f., where an eagle (*fulvus Iovis ales*) seizes a swan but is forced to relinquish its prey by the other swans. Here the twelve swans correspond to Aeneas' twelve lost ships (the thirteenth, that of Orontes, is known to be sunk). The swans are particularly appropriate for this omen, because they were sacred to Venus.

395-6. 'now they can be seen in long line either settling on the ground or looking down where others have settled'; this is the best sense that can be made from *captas*, rather better than 'looking down on where they have decided to settle'. Another possibility is that the swans have been scattered out to sea, and now they are either reaching the shore, or have reached it and are looking down at it for a place to settle. Ribbeck's conjecture *capsos* (a very rare word meaning an enclosure for animals) is one of the most ingenious and most unlikely in the long history of emendation.

398. 'and have circled the sky in formation, and have given song', i.e. they seem to fill the sky because they are flying low and close together, as opposed to the scattered specks when the eagle was chasing them. The perfect tenses in this line convey single actions compared with the longer lasting *ludunt* in the previous line.

400. **portum tenet**: 'has reached harbour', to correspond with *capere*, as *subit* corresponds with *despectare*. Mackail's explanation of *tenet* ('is making for') destroys this correspondence, and would be unnatural Latin.

402 f. 'as she turned away a radiance shone from her rosy-flushed neck, and her immortal locks breathed from her head a perfume divine; her garments were unloosed to cover her feet, and as she went her true divinity was clear to see'. For *avertens* cf. 104; for line 403 cf. Hom. *Il.* 1.529; *defluxit* refers to the unloosing of the knot which had tied up her clothes when she was a huntress; for *incessu* cf. line 46 and for *vera patuit dea* cf. *Aen.* 2.591 *confessa deam*. The hiatus after *dea* (405) is of a kind not found elsewhere in the *Aeneid*; it serves to emphasise the word *dea* and the long pause after the brilliant description of her.

407 f. The pathos of these lines is very marked, and we are reminded that after the death of Anchises Aeneas has no family comfort; he cannot even embrace his goddess mother, and his son is too young yet to help. In *crudelis tu quoque* he summarises his despair.

410. Notice the typically Virgilian co-ordination of two short clauses: in English we should say 'With these words of protest he turned. . .'.

411 f. In Hom. *Od.* 7.14 f. (and 13.189 f.) Odysseus is concealed in a cloud by Athena; the tmesis of *circumfudit* is perhaps suggested by *Od.* 13.189 περὶ γὰρ θεὸς ἠέρα χεῦε; for the position of *dea* cf. 692.

414. **molirive moram**: 'engineer delay', cf. *Geo.* 1.271; *moliri* has here the idea of creating an obstacle as well as making with effort (424). It is a very favourite word with Virgil.

415. **Paphum**: seat of her worship in Cyprus, cf. *Aen.* 10.51.

416–17. **Sabaeo ture**: from Arabia, cf. *Geo.* 1.57.

418–493. Aeneas and Achates marvel at the size and activity of the newly established town of Carthage. They come to the temple of Juno, where they see on the walls pictures of events in the Trojan war; Aeneas is heartened by this, and studies them one after the other, reminding himself of the triumphs and disasters of the war.

418 f. This is a quiet piece of narrative, leading up to the appearance of Dido, and sketching in the background to the Trojans' voyage by means of the pictures on Juno's temple. It is based on events in *Odyssey* 7 and 8; Aeneas marvels at Carthage as Odysseus had at Phaeacia (7.43 f.); the splendour of the temple of Juno is described in terms which recall Alcinous' palace (7.84 f.); the pictures of past events, and Aeneas' tears at recalling them, are reminiscent of Demodocus' song of the Trojan war and Odysseus' tears (8.73 f., 86).

The description of the pictures is a fully developed ecphrasis. This term is used for two kinds of descriptive passage, firstly that of natural scenery (like the harbour, lines 159 f., where see note); and secondly that of works of art, like Achilles' shield in Homer (*Il.* 18.478 f.), imitated by Virgil in *Aen.* 8.625 f., or the carved cup in Theoc. 1.27 f., or the coverlet in Catullus 64.50 f. Compare the pictures on Apollo's temple in *Aen.* 6.20 f., and see my note on *Aen.* 5.254 f. (Oxford edition). Cf. Chaucer, *House of Fame* 119 f., and *Knight's Tale* 1060 f.; Shakespeare, *Rape of Lucrece*, 1366 f.

The pictures here are evidently paintings on the walls of the temple (anachronistic for the heroic age). They are arranged in pairs: (i) the Greeks flee, the Trojans flee; (ii) death of Rhesus, death of Troilus; (iii) supplication by the Trojan women, supplication by Priam; (iv) Memnon's Eastern armies, Penthesilea's Amazons. Aeneas himself is depicted between the third and fourth pairs of pictures, and throughout Virgil shows us these pictures through the eye of the beholder. The descriptive passage is made integral with the poem because of the insight which it gives us into how Aeneas has been affected by these events of his past history — *quaeque ipse miserrima vidi / et quorum pars magna fui,* 2.5–6 — and how he is still affected now; we understand better what he and his friends have suffered; we are given a preview of the tragic descriptions of Book 2. We are shown the ruthless cruelty of the Greek invaders, particularly of Achilles, and the unfolding of the doom of Troy: the oracles about Rhesus and

Troilus (see notes on 469 f., 474 f.), the hostility of Pallas, the death of their champion Hector. For further discussion see my article in *C.Q.* 1960, pp. 145 f.

418. corripuere viam: 'they hastened along their way', a poetic use of the verb, cf. *Geo.* 3.104, *Aen.* 5.145, 316, 6.634. *Rapidus* is related to *rapere*.

419–20. qui plurimus urbi imminet: 'which looms large over the city'; for *plurimus* cf. *Geo.* 3.52, *Aen.* 6.659.

421. magalia: 'huts', a Carthaginian word.

422. strata viarum: 'the paved streets'; the phrase is from Lucretius (1.315, 4.415). For the poetic use of neuter adjectives followed by a genitive see my note on 5.695 (Oxford edition). Compare especially *Aen.* 2.332, 6.633.

423. instant: 'press on', understand *operi*.

ducere: historic infinitive, like the four following verbs; this seems better than punctuating so that the infinitives depend on *instant* (as in *Aen.* 2.627). *Ducere* is normal Latin for building walls or long structures (Livy 7.23.5).

424. molirique: 'toil at', cf. *Aen.* 3.6, 132.

subvolvere: 'roll up'; the word is found only here.

425. tecto: 'for a building' cf. *Aen.* 3.109 *optavitque locum regno*.

et concludere sulco: 'enclosing it with a furrow', a reference to the Roman method of marking out the site for the walls of a city (*Aen.* 5.755), transferred here to the site of a building.

427–8. alta theatri fundamenta locant alii: the MSS vary between *alta* and *lata*, *theatri* and *theatris* (Servius attests the singular) and *locant* and *petunt*.

429. alta: Mynors prints Bentley's conjecture *apta*, to avoid the repetition with 427, but the Romans were less sensitive to this kind of repetition than we are; see my note on 5.254 (Oxford edition).

430 f. The simile is based on phrases and whole lines used in *Geo.* 4.162–9. Virgil has bee similes again in 6.707 f., 12.587 f. Cf. Hom. *Il.* 2.87 f., Milton, *P.L.* 1.768 f.

430–1. qualis . . . labor: 'like the busy activity which seizes the bees. . .'.

431–2. gentis . . . fetus: 'pour forth their populous youth about the hive' (Milton, *P.L.* 1.770).

433. 'and fill to bursting the honey-comb cells with the sweet nectar', a variation of the previous phrase.

435. **ignavum fucos pecus**: 'the drones, an idle tribe'; for the word order (with *fucos* in apposition between the noun and its adjective) cf. *Ecl.* 1.57 *raucae tua cura palumbes*; *Geo.* 4.246 *dirum tineae genus*.

436. **fervet opus**: cf. *Aen.* 4.407 (of ants) *opere omnis semita fervet*.

437. This line summarises Aeneas' frustrated longing during seven years of wandering to begin to build his city; cf. his words to Helenus in 3.493 f.

438. **suspicit**: 'looks up at', having presumably now come down from the hill.

440. **miscetque viris**: it is better to supply *se* from the previous line than to regard *miscet* as intransitive (cf. 104).

ulli: the dative of the agent is used much more freely in poetry than prose; cf. (e.g.) 326, 344, 494.

441. **laetissimus umbrae**: 'very rich in shade'; most MSS have *umbra*, but *umbrae* is attested by Probus, and Servius quotes Sallust *frugum pabulique laetus ager*. For the genitive cf. 14 and 343.

443. **signum**: Servius tells the story that when Dido and her followers fled from Tyre they received an oracle from Juno, as a result of which they dug in the ground on the selected site for their new city. They found an ox's head, but as this indicated servitude, they moved to another site and this time found a horse's head, token of victory in war as well as of peaceful prosperity (*facilem victu*); cf. *Aen.* 3.539 f. The coins of Carthage often showed a horse's head. Conington points out that the horse's head was to the Carthaginians what the white sow was to Aeneas.

444-5. **sic nam fore ... gentem**: the oratio obliqua reports Juno's oracle.

445. **facilem victu**: 'prosperous in their way of life', an unusual phrase extended from the more natural usage of *Geo.* 2.460 *fundit humo facilem victum iustissima tellus*. These two Carthaginian attributes, military power and wealth, were coupled in the first mention of Carthage (14).

446. **Sidonia**: this epithet is used several times of Dido (Virgil uses Tyre and Sidon interchangeably); the quantity of the *o* is sometimes long, sometimes short (678): see note on 258.

447. **donis ... divae**: 'rich with offerings and the presence of the goddess'; the zeugma is striking, although *numen* no doubt implies a statue.

448. 'Its bronze threshold towered high above the steps'; this use of *surgere* is mainly poetic, cf. *Geo.* 3.29, *Aen.* 10.476.

nexaeque: hypermetric elision, see note on 332.

448–9. **nexaeque aere trabes**: Servius reported an alternative *nixaeque* ('the beams rested on bronze', cf. Hom. *Od.* 7.89), but we get a better meaning with the MSS reading *nexaeque*: 'the beams (which form the frame for the door) are bound in with bronze' — i.e. the wooden framework of the door is joined together and decorated with bronze.

449. **stridebat**: a normal word for a heavy door on its hinges (*Aen.* 6.573, 7.613).

450–1. Notice the very powerful repetition of *hoc primum* . . *hic primum*; Virgil sets the scene for his description of the pictures (and for Aeneas' subsequent stay in Carthage) with great emphasis.

450. **nova res oblata**: 'a strange sight that met his eyes'.

timorem: Aeneas has not been not wholly convinced by Venus' promises and instructions; in particular he is not confident that the Carthaginians will be friendly. This is why he is so heartened (463) to find the pictures of the Trojan war, which indicate the city of a civilised people, ready to be moved to pity by suffering.

453. 'For while he was looking around at everything, in the shadow of the huge temple'; the postposition of *dum* after its verb *lustrat* is an artificiality characteristic of poetic diction. There are about 80 instances in the *Aeneid* of such a reversal of prose order.

454–6. 'while he marvelled at the city's prosperity, and the harmonious handiwork of the several artists and the work that had gone into these achievements'; for *manus* cf. *Aen.* 12.210, Prop 3.21.30, Milton, *P.R.* 4.59 'carv'd work, the hand of fam'd Artificers', and for *operumque laborem* line 507 and *Geo.* 2.155. *Inter se* (working together) is used in a condensed sense also in *Aen.* 2.454, 4.193, 8.452; *intra se* (with *miratur*, 'inwardly marvels') is read by a ninth century MS, but *secum* is Virgil's normal phrase for 'inwardly'.

456. **ex ordine**: i.e. there was a series of panels along the wall.

458. **Atridas**: Agamemnon and Menelaus. Achilles was fierce towards them (as well as towards Priam) because of his

anger against Agamemnon, which led to his withdrawal from the
fighting (Hom. *Il.* 1).

459. **quis iam locus**: the adjective *quis* is much less common
in prose than *qui*, but is preferred by Virgil, cf. 615.

461. **En Priamus**: this probably refers to the picture described
at greater length in 483-7, where Priam goes to Achilles and
beseeches him to return the body of Hector (*Il.* 24.471 f.). The
rest of this line and the next have some specific reference to
Priam: he gained glory and won sympathy by daring to approach
Achilles, and this is appreciated by the Carthaginians who have
made a picture of the scene.

461-2. 'here too there are due rewards for glory, here too
there are tears for human happenings and mortal sufferings
touch the heart'. *Sua* is in the sense of *propria* ('glory has its own
reward'); it is used freely in this sense by the poets even where it
does not refer to the subject, cf. *Aen.* 3.469. *Rerum* is an extended
objective genitive (cf. *Aen.* 2.784) helped also by phrases like
fessi rerum (178); the meaning of the word is simply 'happenings',
like 204, 229, 452. Line 462 is often detached from its context
and quoted to summarise the note of pathos in the *Aeneid*; there
is no harm in this provided that it is understood that the meaning
is 'people are sympathetic', not 'the world is full of sorrows, is a
vale of tears'.

463. The meaning is 'we need not fear — the Carthaginians
know of our sufferings and evidently are people who feel pity and
sympathy'; see note on 450 (*timorem*). *Tibi* is ethic dative; cf. 258.

464. **animum pictura pascit inani**: 'he fed his thoughts on
the lifeless picture', cf. *Geo.* 2.285.

465. **umectat**: cf. Lucr. 1.920. For *flumen* cf. our 'flood of
tears'.

466 f. For an analysis of the pictures see note on 418 f.

466. **Pergama**: the citadel of Troy, frequent for Troy itself
(cf. 651); the word also occurs in the singular *Pergamum*, but not
in hexameter poetry.

468. **hac Phryges**: 'in another direction the Trojans were in
flight': *Phryges* is Greek nominative plural with short final syllable.

469 f. The story of Rhesus' death is told in *Iliad* 10 and in
Euripides' *Rhesus*; he was a Thracian who came to help the
Trojans, and Diomedes (*Tydides*, 471) and Odysseus made a

night attack on his camp immediately after his arrival, killing him and many of his followers. There was an oracle (this is not in Homer or Euripides) that if his horses cropped the grass of Troy and drank from the river Xanthus Troy would not fall: hence the Greek attack and the removal of the horses to the Greek camp.

470. **primo ... prodita somno**: 'taken by surprise as soon as they slept'. Servius gives two explanations: either when sleep is deepest, or on their first night; both ideas are present. Henry has an excellent note on this.

473. **gustassent**: 'could have tasted', for the subjunctive implying purpose ('in order that they might not have tasted') cf. line 193 and *Geo.* 3.469.

Xanthum: one of Troy's rivers, see note on 100–1.

474 f. Virgil is following the Greek tradition that Troilus, the young son of Priam, was ambushed by Achilles when unarmed; again there was an oracle about the fate of Troy (as with Rhesus), namely that if Troilus had lived to the age of twenty, Troy would not have been taken (Plautus, *Bacch.* 953 f.); see my article in *C.Q.* 1960, 145 f., for a detailed discussion of this passage.

474. **amissis ... armis**: i.e. he is caught without his armour on, all he has is the spear (see below) which he has been using as a goad.

475. **impar congressus Achilli**: 'who was no match for Achilles when he met him in battle'; the dative with words like *congredi* (cf. *certare*) is mainly poetic, cf. 493.

476–8. 'was dragged along by his horses, and fallen backwards was entangled with the empty chariot, still grasping the reins in spite of all; his neck and hair were being dragged along the ground, and the dust was scored by his reversed spear'. For *fertur equis* cf. *Geo.* 1.514; *curru* is dative, cf. 156. *Lora tenens tamen* indicates that he is wounded, but still clings on in the hope of yet controlling his horses; the unusual diaeresis after the second foot serves to emphasise *tamen*. *Versa hasta* means that the spear, which he had been using reversed as a goad (cf. 9.609 f.), now trails on the ground; it does not refer (as some commentators think) to the spear of Achilles with which Troilus was transfixed. The final syllable of *pulvis* is lengthened in arsis (see note on 308); it may have been long in early Latin (Enn. *Ann.* 282).

479. The picture of the Trojan women beseeching the hostile

goddess Pallas and taking a robe (*peplum*) as an offering is based on Hom. *Il.* 6.297 f.

481. **tunsae**: 'beating', see note on 228.

483 f. The picture of Achilles receiving a ransom from Priam for Hector's body (*Il.* 24.502 f.) is prefixed by a reference to what had happened previously to the body (note the pluperfect tense, *raptaverat*). In Homer Achilles dragged Hector's body around Patroclus' tomb: Virgil follows a later Greek version (Eur. *Andr.* 107 f.) which emphasises even more the cruelty of Achilles.

488. Aeneas' recognition of himself fighting against the Greek leaders (cf. *Il.* 20.332 f.) relates the pictures to the story, as did his personal reactions to the picture of Hector (485 f.).

489. Memnon the Aethiopian (son of Aurora — Eos — 751; his followers are called Eastern, *Eoas*) belongs to the post-Iliad period of the Trojan war, after the death of Hector.

490 f. Penthesilea, queen of the Amazons, also came to Troy near the end of the war; she as well as Memnon figured largely in the cyclic epic *Aethiopis*, and their exploits are described by Quintus of Smyrna (fourth century A.D.). Penthesilea is a proto-type of Virgil's Camilla. Amazons are mentioned in Hom. *Il.* 3.189.

490. **lunatis ... peltis**: crescent-shaped shields, of the Amazons again in 11.663.

492. 'in the act of buckling her golden girdle beneath her naked breast'. *Subnectens* must refer to the action of the picture (see Mackail); Servius' explanation *subnexa habens* cannot be right.

494–656. *Dido comes to the temple, and while she is attending to the city's affairs, Aeneas' lost companions approach. Ilioneus on their behalf asks for help, which she readily grants. Aeneas then comes forth from the cloud and gratefully expresses his thanks. She is amazed to find that so famous a hero has come to her kingdom, and proclaims sacrifices and a feast. Aeneas for his part sends Achates to bring presents.*

494 f. In this very idyllic scene the characters of Aeneas and Dido are presented most sympathetically. The tributes paid to Aeneas by Ilioneus when he is unaware of his presence give a picture of a king held in admiration and affection by his men; and Dido is beautiful, altogether queenly in her attributes, and

at the same time modest and sympathetic. All the way through we see indirectly what kind of an impact each is having on the other.

The build-up of expectation for Dido's appearance has been developed long before she comes into the narrative, by Jupiter's instructions to Mercury, by Venus' telling Aeneas of her story (see note on 364), by the pictures she had had painted on Juno's temple. When she appears she is like Diana in beauty; she is intent on the welfare of her people; she is kind and generous to Ilioneus; she is filled with admiration for Aeneas; and she ends her speech to him with words which indicate to the reader the bond of sympathy, humanity, and mutual understanding likely to exist between her and Aeneas: *me quoque per multos similis fortuna labores* . . . (628). It is a happy start to a tragic tale.

494. **Dardanio Aeneae**: dative of agent (with *videntur*), cf. 440. The epithet *Dardanius* is used here because Aeneas' emotions are due to the Trojan scenes he has been gazing at.

497. **incessit**: of Juno in 46, of Venus in 405.

498 f. The simile is based (like the simile in Ap. Rh. 3.876 f.) on Hom. *Od.* 6.102 f. where Nausicaa is compared with Artemis; Aulus Gellius (9.9) records Probus' hostile criticisms of Virgil's adaptation, particularly to the effect that the comparison is much more appropriate to Nausicaa dancing among her maidens than to Dido giving instructions to her people. This is certainly true, but the Virgilian simile — as so often — aims at setting up implications, half-defined penumbrae of meaning, at substituting for Homeric clarity a density of associations which reaches forward and backwards into the narrative. Here we reach backwards towards the disguised Venus who seemed to Aeneas (329) like Diana, and forward to the simile in 4.143 f. where Aeneas is like Apollo on the ridges of Cynthus; and we see Dido not only as the composed queen of her people which the narrative presents, but also possessed of the joyful beauty and vivacity of a goddess dancing. See also note on 502, and Pöschl, *The Art of Vergil*, pp. 60 f.

498–502. Eurotas was the river on which Sparta stood (cf. 316), Cynthus a ridge in Delos (where Latona gave birth to Apollo and Diana), cf. 4.147; *Oreades* (Greek plural with short -es) are mountain nymphs. *Diana* elsewhere has a short first syllable; see note on 258.

502. 'joy thrills the silent heart of Latona'; as her mother watches, she is proud of her daughter's beauty. This line (based on Hom. *Od.* 6.106) is said to be irrelevant in Virgil's simile, but it surely conveys the effect which Dido has upon those watching her, particularly Aeneas. For *pertemptant* cf. *Aen.* 5.828, *Geo.* 3.250.

505–6. 'Then by the goddess's doors, beneath the centre of the temple's vault, escorted by warriors, and positioned high up on her throne she took her seat.' *Foribus divae* refers to the inner sanctuary of the goddess, where her statue would be; cf. *Geo.* 3.16 *in medio mihi Caesar erit templumque tenebit*. *Testudo* is an architectural term for an arch or vault. The Roman senate often met in a temple.

512. 'and had driven away to far distant shores'; for *penitus* cf. 536, *Ecl.* 1.66; *alias* means different from where Aeneas landed; for the accusative *oras* cf. 553 and see note on 2.

514–15. **coniungere . . . ardebant**: the infinitive with *ardere* is mainly poetic, cf. 581.

515. **res . . . incognita**: 'the uncertainty of the situation', i.e. they do not know what has happened or how they will be received by the Carthaginians.

516. **dissimulant**: 'they conceal their · eagerness (Page)', rather than 'they remain in hiding'.

519. **veniam**: 'favour', cf. *Aen.* 4.435, 11.101; the word does not necessarily mean pardon.

521. **maximus Ilioneus**: their 'elder statesman', who is also the spokesman to King Latinus in 7.212 f.

522–3. **condere . . . dedit**: 'has allowed to found', see note on 66.

523. **gentis frenare superbas**: he refers to the barbarians round about Dido's city (339, 4.39 f.).

524. **maria**: accusative of extent of space, cf. 67.

526. **propius**: from nearer, i.e. 'more favourably', cf. *Aen.* 8.78, Tac. *Ann.* 13.57.

527–8. **populare . . . venimus**: infinitive of purpose; cf. *Aen.* 3.4–5 *quaerere . . . agimur* (with my note, Oxford edition) and compare notes on 66, 357, 704. The greatly extended use by the poets of the infinitive was made possible partly as a revival of early Latin usage (there are fairly frequent instances in Plautus — e.g. *missa sum ludere*) which had died out in prose in favour of more cumbersome methods of expression, and partly by Greek influence.

It is a brief and economical way of expressing the relationship of two clauses (compare *ad penatis populandos*, or *penatium populandorum causa*).

529. 'Conquered people do not have such violence nor such pride in their hearts'; the sentence is not two separate clauses.

530–3. These four lines are repeated in 3.163–6. For line 530 cf. Enn. *Ann.* 23 *est locus Hesperiam quam mortales perhibebant*; for the parenthetical construction (Servius says *deest 'quam'*) cf. line 12. *Hesperia* means the Western Land, and is used frequently by Virgil of Italy.

531. **ubere**: 'fertility', cf. 3.95, and Homer's οὖθαρ ἀρούρης (*Il.* 9.141).

532. **Oenotri**: first applied to the inhabitants of S. Italy, and then by the poets to the Italians generally; Aristotle (*Pol.* 7.9.2) relates a tradition that a king of the Oenotrians called Italus gave his name to the country. Others made Italus a Sicilian, and Servius mentions a derivation from the Greek word for a calf (ἰταλός, Latin *vitulus*); cf. Aul. Gell. 11.1.1.

533. **Italiam dixisse ... gentem**: 'have called their nation Italy', a variation on the expected 'have called their land Italy'.

534. This is the first of rather more than fifty 'half-lines' in the *Aeneid*, cf. 560, 636. They are an indication of incomplete revision, not a deliberate metrical device; see my note (Oxford edition) on 5.294.

535. The setting of Orion in the autumn was associated with storms (*Aen.* 7.719, Hor. *Odes* 1.28.21, 3.27.18, *Epod.* 10.10); thus the constellation itself was regarded as hostile to sailors (cf. *Aen.* 4.52, Hor. *Epod.* 15.7 *nautis infestus Orion*), and here is used by metonymy for the storm it causes. For *adsurgens fluctu* of a storm cf. *Geo.* 2.160. It is impossible to believe (as many commentators suggest) that *adsurgens* also means the rising of the constellation. The first vowel of *Orion* varies in quantity; see note on 258.

536–8. 'and scattered us afar with its fierce south winds over waves and barriers of rock as the ocean mastered us'.

540. **hospitio ... harenae**: 'the welcome of the shore', which shipwrecked sailors have a right to expect. Servius quotes Cicero, *Pro Rosc.* 72 *quid est tam commune quam ... litus eiectis?*

543. A magnificent line, made specially memorable by the use of *sperate*, almost in the sense of *respicere* 'have a thought for',

'expect action from'; it is much extended from the fairly common poetic sense of 'expect (but not hope)' as in *Aen.* 2.658, 4.419, 11.275. For *fandi atque nefandi* 'right and wrong', cf. Cat. 64.405, Livy 10.41.3.

544 f. The tribute by Ilioneus to his (supposedly) absent leader conveys to the reader a perhaps warmer picture of Aeneas than the direct narrative references to his *pietas*; line 555 especially is an indication of the affection in which Aeneas was clearly held.

544–5. The order is *quo alter nec pietate iustior fuit nec bello et armis maior*. Others supply *nec* before *iustior* and take *pietate* with *maior*.

546. **vescitur aura**: a Lucretian phrase, cf. Lucr. 5.857.

547. **umbris**: 'land of darkness'; for this local meaning cf. *Aen.* 6.461.

548–9. 'nor would you regret taking the initiative in a contest of kindness'; *nec . . . paeniteat* is potential, rather than equivalent to *ne paeniteat* as in *Ecl.* 2.34, 10.17, where the meaning is different.

549 f. He means that they have resources in Sicily also with which they can repay kindness, in addition to what they have with them; for Acestes see note on 195.

552. 'to prepare planks in your woods and trim timber for oars'; cf. *Aen.* 4.399, 5.753.

553–4. the order is *ut Italiam, si datur . . . tendere, laeti . . . petamus. Italiam* is accusative of motion towards, see note on 2 and cf. *Aen.* 6.696.

556. **nec spes iam restat Iuli**: 'our hopes of Iulus are gone', i.e. the hope placed in him as Aeneas' heir; cf. 4.274.

561. **vultum demissa**: 'lowering her eyes'; for the middle use of *demissa* see note on 228.

562. **secludite curas**: 'cast your cares aside'; Servius says *pro 'excludite'*.

563. 'harsh necessity and the newness of my kingdom . . .'; she fears the hostile people of the neighbourhood as well as the possibility of attack from Tyre by her brother.

564. **custode**: singular for plural, common in prose with *miles, eques, hostis* and national names (*Romanus, Poenus,* etc.); cf. *Aen.* 9.380.

565. **Aeneadum**: cf. 157 — Dido takes up Ilioneus' words *rex erat Aeneas nobis* (544). For the form of the genitive see note on 3.21.

567. **obtunsa**: 'unfeeling', so as to be indifferent to what we hear about; the next line explains that they are not so far away from the civilised world (from the path of the sun, cf. *Aen.* 6.796 *extra anni solisque vias*), not so benighted, as not to hear about such great events.

569. **Saturniaque arva**: the golden age in Latium was under Saturnus' rule (*Ecl.* 4.6); Latium was said to be so-called because Saturnus hid there (*latuit*) when deposed by Jupiter (cf. *Aen.* 8.319 f.).

570. Eryx was a half-brother of Aeneas who gave his name to the well-known town and mountain in Sicily; see note on 5.24.

573. **urbem quam statuo, vestra est**: this is a very striking example of the attraction of the antecedent to the case of the relative, or perhaps it is better to say of the antecedent being treated as if taken into the relative clause (cf. 72): *quam urbem statuo, ea vestra est*. It has an archaic ring about it, cf. Ter. *Eun.* 653.

574. 'Trojans and Tyrians will be treated by me with no distinction (no discrimination)'; the phrase is very unusual, and acts as a passive for *agam de Troianis et Tyriis nullo discrimine*. The singular *agetur* emphasises the unity of the two subjects. Nonius quotes the line with *habetur*, but this is no improvement.

576. **certos**: 'reliable men'.

578. 'if by chance he has been cast ashore and is wandering in any woods or towns'; for the elliptical condition ('in the hope that') cf. 181.

579. **animum arrecti**: 'their hearts excited'; *animum* is retained accusative, see note on 228.

580. **erumpere**: 'burst out of', unusual in this transitive sense, cf. the commoner *evadere* (5.689), *exire* (5.438).

584. i.e. Orontes (113 f.).

587. **purgat**: supply *se*, 'dispersed', cf. Lucr. 4.341.

588. **restitit**: 'stood there'; Virgil conveys a statuesque picture of Aeneas as the cloud cleared away.

589. **os umerosque**: accusative of respect, as in 579.

589 f. 'for his mother herself had breathed upon her son and given him beautiful flowing locks and the radiant glow of youth and a happy brightness in his eyes.' The passage is based on *Od.* 6.229 f. (= *Od.* 23.156 f.) where Athena beautifies Odysseus.

592 f. The Homeric simile (*Od.* 6.232 f.) compares the beauti-

fication of Odysseus with the overlaying of silver with gold, a single vivid image; Virgil — as is his way — elaborates by adding marble to Homer's picture, and giving a new image of decorated ivory; cf. *Aen.* 12.67 f., and generally 10.134 f.

593. **Pariusve lapis**: marble, cf. Hor. *Odes* 1.19.6, *Aen.* 3.126, 6.471.

597. **sola**: it is the first friendly welcome he has received from a foreign people.

598. **reliquias Danaum**: cf. 30.

599. **exhaustis**: most MSS have *exhaustos*, but *exhaurire casus* is the more Virgilian usage, cf. 4.14, 10.57.

omnium: this form occurs only here in Virgil, and such an elision in the fifth foot is very striking; it occurs otherwise only with the word *Ilium* (e.g. 6.64).

600. **urbe domo socias**: 'give us a share in your city, your home'.

601-2. 'is not in our power, nor in the power of any of the Trojan people anywhere'. The phrase *quidquid ... gentis* takes the place of a genitive after *opis*, equivalent to *nec totius gentis Troianae*. The neuter pronoun followed by a genitive is a favourite turn with Catullus (e.g. 3.2 *quantum est hominum venustiorum*).

603-5. 'May the gods (if there are any powers who have thought for the good, if there is any justice anywhere) and your own inner knowledge that you have done right bring you worthy rewards.' That this is the correct way of taking the phrases is shown by *Aen.* 9.252 f.: *quae vobis, quae digna, viri, pro laudibus istis | praemia posse rear solvi? pulcherrima primum | di moresque dabunt vestri.* Many commentators take *mens ... recti* as a second subject of *usquam est*, but this is impossible with the reading *iustitiae* and very difficult with *iustitia*. I have preferred the reading of the rest of the MSS (*iustitiae*) against *iustitia* (first hand in *M*) partly because the genitive following the neuter pronoun chimes well with 601-2 *quidquid ... gentis*, and partly because the turn *iustitia est aliquid* (cf. Ov. *Met.* 6.542-3 *si numina divum sunt aliquid*, Prop. 4.7.1 *sunt aliquid manes*) does not seem Virgilian. For *si qua* in the sense 'as surely as there are' Page (whose note on this passage is first rate) compares *Aen.* 3.433 f.

605 f. The extravagant compliments are based on Hom. *Od.* 6.154 f.

607–8. 'as long as shadows move on the mountain slopes, as long as the heavens feed the stars'; for the first phrase cf. Hor. *Odes* 3.6.41–2 *sol ubi montium | mutaret umbras*, and for *convexa* cf. 310. The second phrase is from Lucr. 1.231 (cf. 5.525) *unde aether sidera pascit*; cf. Sen. *N.Q.* 7.20.2.

609. This line occurs in *Ecl.* 5.78 (Daphnis will be famous as long as fishes swim and bees feed on thyme).

610. There is an irony in these closing words; it is the call of Italy in Book 4 which leads to Dido's desertion and death.

611. **Ilionea**: this *-ĕă* accusative ending is a transliteration of the Homeric form.

613. **primo aspectu**: 'at the first sight of him'. This is the same sense as if *primo* were an adverb.

616. **immanibus applicat oris**: 'drives you to these savage shores'; *applicare navem* is the technical term for bringing in a ship to land.

617. **Dardanio Anchisae**: the spondee in the fifth foot, with hiatus, gives a rhythmic effect that is very unusual in Latin (in Homer hiatus and spondaic fifth feet are frequent): it is used in the *Aeneid* five times, always with names; cf. 3.74, 7.631, 9.647, 11.31.

618. **Simoentis**: one of Troy's rivers, see note on 100–1. Servius tells us that goddesses and nymphs gave birth by the banks of rivers or in woods.

619. The story is that the Greek Teucer, brother of Ajax, on his return from the Trojan war to Salamis, was forced to leave his home; he founded a new Salamis in Cyprus (Hor. *Odes* 1.7.21 f.). There seems no source before Virgil for his having gone to Sidon to get help from Dido's father Belus who was waging a successful war in Cyprus.

Sidona: Greek accusative, motion towards.

623 f. Dido heard of the Trojan war from Teucer who told her both about the Greeks (Pelasgi) and their enemies the Trojans; he had praised the latter highly, and bearing the same name as they did (*Teucri*) wanted it to be thought that he was descended from the same ancestry (as indeed he was, through his mother Hesione).

625. **ipse hostis**: probably Teucer himself, rather than the Greeks generally.

630. A famous line of which the meaning is 'I am not unacquainted with suffering and I am learning how to help the

unhappy (now that I am in a position to do so).' Some argue,
following Servius, that *non* goes with the whole line: 'I am not, as
someone inexperienced, learning . . . (I don't have to learn)', but
this seems wholly unlikely.

632. **indicit honorem**: 'proclaimed sacrifices' in honour of
the safety of Aeneas.

634-5. 'a hundred bristling backs of great boars', i.e. 'a
hundred great bristly-backed boars'.

636. **dii**: all the MSS have *dei*, but Aulus Gellius (9.14.8) read
dii and explained it as a genitive of *dies*, quoting various parallel
(*acii*, *specii*, etc.); the meaning thus is 'the day's joyful gifts', in
apposition to the previous lines. If *dei* is read, the reference is to
Bacchus and the joy of wine (cf. 734 *laetitiae Bacchus dator*). This
is attractive, but it seems to me that the co-ordination with the
previous lines, if this were an extra item, would be harsh. The
choice of reading here is very difficult to make, especially as the
half-line may indicate that Virgil had not completed what he
wanted to say, but the balance inclines towards *dii*.

639. Supply *sunt*; cf. 703 and 4.131. The *vestes* are coverlets
for the couches (*Geo.* 2.464), and we are reminded of Cat. 64, of
which line 637 is a reminiscence (Cat. 64.46).

640. **ingens argentum**: 'a vast quantity of silver', rather than
'massive pieces of silver', cf. phrases like *ingens pecunia* (Cicero).

caelataque in auro: these embossed decorations would be on
golden plate; the phrase does not refer to inlaid gold on the silver
plate just mentioned.

641-2. 'a long series of exploits extending through the lives of
their many heroes from the distant beginning of their race'.

645. **ferat**: jussive subjunctive in parataxis, cf. *Aen.* 4.289.

646. **cari**: 'loving', an unusual active use of the word; cf. *Aen.*
11.215.

stat: 'was always, lay always' (Conway), who explains that it
is a slightly stronger form of assertion than *est* and compares
Lucr. 2.181 *tanta stat praedita culpa.*

648. **pallam**: a long robe, here decorated with golden
embroidery (Lucr. 5.1428), and therefore stiff.

649. **velamen**: the veil is bordered with yellow acanthus, a
common type of floral design. The stylised leaf of the acanthus
was used as part of the decoration of Corinthian capitals.

650. Helen's epithet 'Argive' is from Homer (*Il.* 2.161); *Mycenis* is used in a general sense to mean the realm of Greece — specifically Helen was from Sparta where she was the wife of Menelaus; cf. *Aen.* 2.577-8 (of Helen) *scilicet haec Spartam incolumis patriasque Mycenas | aspiciet?*

651. Pergama is Troy (466); the unlawful marriage is with Paris. For the lengthening of the last syllable of *peteret* see note on 308; for the polysyllabic ending with a Greek word cf. (e.g.) *elephanto* (3.464), *cyparissi* (3.680), *hyacinthi* (11.69).

652. **matris Ledae**: Helen was the daughter of Leda by Jupiter in the guise of a swan; cf. *Aen.* 7.364.

653. Ilione, the eldest of Priam's daughters, is not mentioned in Homer. According to a later legend she became the wife of Polymnestor of Thrace.

655. **bacatum**: 'of pearls', a very rare word from *baca*, a berry or a thing shaped like a berry, quite often a pearl.

duplicem ... coronam: this seems to be a crown encircled by two bands of gold and gems (cf. *Aen.* 5.251).

657-94. *Venus intervenes by instructing Cupid to disguise himself as Ascanius and make Dido fall in love with Aeneas. She spirits Ascanius away.*

657f. The scheming intervention of Venus is Hellenistic in tone, based on the trickery devised by Hera and Athena in Apollonius Rhodius 3.6f., where they persuade Aphrodite to cause her son Eros to shoot his love-arrows at Medea. The tone of the passage in Apollonius is mocking and the behaviour of the goddesses frivolous and cruel. Virgil has modified and dignified his picture of the Goddess of Love (for Venus was much more than a Roman Aphrodite), but elements of cruelty remain, and Venus shows an irresponsible pleasure in what to her is the subtle use of her great power. Here she is no longer *alma Venus, Venus Genetrix,* great mother of Aeneas and Rome, but a toned-down version of "laughter-loving Aphrodite" (cf. 8.370f.), a personification of the tyranny of love which led Virgil to exclaim (4.412) *improbe Amor, quid non mortalia pectora cogis!* Venus' motivation, apart from her desire to exercise her special power, is here very weak; Dido is already showing hospitality to Aeneas, and the upshot of the goddess's schemes is to delay Aeneas and nearly cause the abandonment of his mission. As far as Dido is concerned, Venus shows the ruthless recklessness for her human enemies which is seen so often among the gods and goddesses of Ovid's *Metamorphoses*. The divine machinery of the *Aeneid* generally suggests the care of providence for humans (albeit very imperfectly understood), but here and there come flashes of primitive cruelty and wanton exercise of power.

657–60. 'But the Cytherean goddess turned over in her mind fresh devices and fresh plans, to make Cupid change his appearance and aspect and come instead of sweet Ascanius, and fire the queen to passion with his gifts and instil the flames of love into her innermost being.' Notice the use of the adjective *novus* to introduce not merely a change in the narrative events, but a change of mood from the idyllic first meeting of Dido and Aeneas to the sombre and threatening undertones of disaster; cf. 5.603 f., the transition from the happy celebration of the games to the firing of the Trojan ships. Venus is called *Cytherea* from her island (680); *faciem* and *ora* are retained accusatives (see note on 228); *furentem* is proleptic.

661. **timet**: cf. Juno's taunt to Venus in 4.96 f. that she is frightened and therefore suspicious of Carthage.

ambiguam ... bilinguis: *ambiguam* is 'untrustworthy', (*esse ambigua fide*, Livy 6.2.3), and *bilinguis* is 'double-tongued', 'treacherous', as several times in Plautus. The two phrases combine to suggest the proverbial bad faith of Carthage, *Punica fides*.

662. **urit atrox Iuno**: 'the image of cruel Juno chafes her'.

663. Cupid is frequently depicted in art with wings (cf. Prop. 2.12.5); the compound *aliger* does not occur before Virgil.

664–5. Cupid symbolises the power of Venus; pictures of him breaking or trampling on the thunderbolt occur on coins. The thunderbolt is called *tela Typhoëa* because Jupiter used it against the giant Typhoeus (Typhon), burning him to ashes (Aesch. *P.V.* 358 f.). I have punctuated so that *solus* goes with *qui*, as Servius recommends: in this way the *qui* clause comes in more neatly, and *mea magna potentia* is much better without *solus*.

667. **frater**: Ovid (*Her.* 7) twice makes play with the relationship of the half-brothers Aeneas and Cupid.

667–8. **ut ... iactetur**: indirect question, 'you know how he is storm-tossed'; the plural *nota* (these are things known to you) is much less normal than *notum*, and influenced by Greek.

668. **iactetur**: for the lengthening of the final syllable in arsis see note on 308. All the major MSS, except the first hand of *F*, have *iacteturque*, which heals the metre but makes no sense.

671–2. **vereor ... hospitia**: 'I fear the outcome of this hospitality inspired by Juno; she will not be inactive at such a crucial time.' Venus presumably is afraid that Carthaginian friendliness will turn out to be a plot to destroy the Trojans. It was Jupiter, not Juno, who made Dido welcome the Trojans, but Venus naturally assumes that Juno as patron goddess of Carthage is active. The metaphorical use of *cardo* (hinge, hence critical time, turning point) does not occur before Virgil: Statius imitates it with *fatorum in cardine summo* (*Theb.* 10.853). Cf. Sir Winston Churchill's 'The Hinge of Fate'.

673. Conway well remarks on the military metaphors and the 'cruel play on the literal and metaphorical meaning of *flamma*' characteristic of Venus, 'whose affection, even for her son, never knows where to stop and does more harm than good'.

674. **ne quo se numine mutet**: 'so that she may not change her mind because of any divine influence', i.e. that of Juno.

675. **mecum teneatur**: 'be kept on my side', continuing the military metaphor of 673.

679. **pelago ... Troiae**: 'which have survived from the sea and the flames of Troy'; the nouns are probably ablative, rather than dative as after *superesse*.

680 f. Notice the hissing of the *s*'s, as Venus gleefully unfolds her plot.

680–1. **super ... Idalium**: *super* is used because Venus' sacred groves would be in high inaccessible places; Cythera, the island off S. Greece, gave Venus one of her most frequent epithets (657); Idalium — also Idalia, 693 — was in Cyprus.

683. **noctem non amplius unam**: this paratactic construction (one night, not more) is quite common in prose.

684. **falle**: a very strange use, 'impersonate' or 'counterfeit' his appearance, cf. *mentiri* in *Ecl.* 4.42.

pueri puer: a repetition common in Greek, cf. *Aen.* 3.329, 4.83, 5.569, 10.600.

685–8. The build-up of subordinate clauses (*ut, cum ... , cum*) is very unusual in Virgil, and here deliberately used to lead up to the climax in 688.

686. **laticemque Lyaeum**: high-flown poetic diction for wine;
Lyaeus (cf. *Aen.* 4.58) is the Greek equivalent for Liber (Bacchus
the 'releaser' of cares). It is here used as an adjective, see Conway
ad loc. and cf. *Aen.* 4.552.

688. **fallasque veneno**: 'poison her unobserved', picking up
the idea of *occultum*, cf. *Aen.* 7.350. *Venenum* is said to be derived
originally from *Venus* ('love-charm'); for this use cf. Prop. 2.12.19.

692. **inrigat**: the metaphor is from channels of water refreshing the land; cf. Lucr. 4.907-8 *somnus per membra quietem / inriget*,
and for the same verb with a different construction cf. *Aen.* 3.511.

693-4. 'where soft marjoram breathes its fragrance over him
and wraps him round with its blossoms and sweet shade'. Cf.
Cat. 61.6-7 (addressing Hymenaeus) *cinge tempora floribus / suave
olentis amaraci*; the flower was connected with love and is appropriate for Venus (Lucr. 4.1179).

695-756. *Cupid disguised as Ascanius arrives, and the banquet begins.
Dido is capitivated by his charm. After a song by the minstrel, she asks
Aeneas to tell the story of his seven-years' wanderings.*

695 f. The joyful mood of the banquet ·has undertones of
impending disaster as Virgil takes the reader beyond the narrative
(712, 718, 749) and enables him to appreciate the tragic irony of
Dido's happy words of welcome (731 f.). The reader is invited, as
all through Book 4, to consider the interrelation of divine and
human causation, the tension between the myth of Cupid and
the psychology of Dido. It would be a great mistake to think of
Dido as powerless to resist the divine plan; a set of circumstances
encompass her which she can accept or resist. The circumstances
which have arisen are not her responsibility, but her reaction to
them is. At each point in the narrative the decision is hers.

697 f. 'When he got there the queen had already taken her
position amidst the gorgeous tapestries, placing herself in the
centre, on a golden couch.' *Aulaeis* refers to the curtains or
draperies decorating the hall (Hor. *Odes* 3.29.15); the ablative
is used very loosely, as a sort of ablative of attendant circumstances. *Sponda* is a couch on which banqueters reclined, and
as hostess Dido has her couch in the centre. *Aurea* (ablative)
is scanned as a spondee by synizesis (slurring) of the *e*, cf.
726.

700. 'and they all take their places on couches with purple coverlets'; *discumbitur* is impersonal passive.

701 f. The description of the banquet is based on Hom. *Od.* 1.136 f. with considerable elaboration; cf. also *Geo.* 4.376 f.

701. **Cererem**: 'bread', see note on 177.

702. **tonsisque ... villis**: 'bring serviettes of smooth nap', (literally 'shorn'); the same words occur in *Geo.* 4.377.

703. Supply *sunt*, as in 705; cf. 639.

703–4. 'whose task it was to prepare in due order the long feast, and to honour the household gods with blazing fires'. The fifty servants *intus* ('in the kitchen') are contrasted with the two hundred waiters (705); the reading *longam* is discussed as an alternative to *longo* (read by all the MSS) by Aulus Gellius (4.1.15), and the grammarian Charisius cites it. *Flammis adolere penatis* is a good example of elevated poetic style to avoid the common-place ('keep a good fire going').

704. **cura ... struere**: the use of the infinitive following a noun is frequent in the poets; cf. *Aen.* 2.10 (with Page's note) and see note on 527–8.

710. 'the radiant face of the god and his dissembling words'; *flagrantis*, as Servius says, because he was a god; *simulata* means 'spoken as if by Ascanius'.

711. These are the presents brought from the Trojan ships; see 648–9.

712. This is the first of many anticipatory comments in Virgil's own person on the narrative of Dido's fate — 'unhappy Dido, doomed to disaster'; cf. 718–19, 749, 4.68, 169f. In 4.450, 529, 596 the epithet *infelix* has ceased to be anticipatory, and has become actual.

713. **expleri mentem nequit**: 'cannot satisfy her heart', a middle use of *expleri* with a retained accusative; see note on 228, and cf. *Aen.* 8.265.

ardescitque tuendo: cf. Cat. 64.91 f. (of Ariadne falling in love with Theseus), a poem which Virgil several times recalls in memorable passages of Book 4, e.g. 305, 316, 657–8.

716. **falsi ... genitoris**: 'of the deluded father'.

717. The sentence ending after the second foot is unusual, and throws great weight on the sinister verb *petit*.

717–19. 'her gaze and all her thoughts were rivetted upon

him; now and then she held him on her lap; poor Dido, she did not know that an all-powerful god sat there'. The emphasis on *deus* at the sentence-ending at a bucolic diaeresis is very powerful.

719–20. **memor ... Acidaliae**: 'mindful (of the instructions) of his Acidalian mother'. This epithet of Venus is said by Servius to come from a spring in Boeotia where the Graces, attendants of Venus, used to bathe.

720. **abolere Sychaeum**: 'efface the memory of Sychaeus'; cf. line 343.

721–2. 'tries to capture with living love her long-slumbering affection and oblivious heart'; for Dido love was a thing of the past, epitomised in her memory of Sychaeus.

723. Cf. 216.

724. **vina coronant**: the same phrase in *Aen.* 7.147, cf. also *Geo.* 2.528 *cratera coronant*. In *Aen.* 3.525–6 there is the phrase *cratera corona induit*, which suggests that Virgil has altered the meaning of Homer's κρητῆρας ἐπεστέψαντο ποτοῖο (e.g. *Od.* 1.148) from 'filling to the brim' to literally crowning with leaves or flowers.

725. **fit strepitus tectis**: 'a clamour arises in the hall'. This is the reading of the best MSS; others have *it*, a reading known to Servius. With *it*, *tectis* would be dative: 'to the roof', cf. *Aen.* 5.451 *it clamor caelo*. But the parallel with 730 seems decisive.

vocemque ... volutant: 'and they send their words echoing', cf. *Aen.* 5.149, 10.98.

726. 'lamps hang from the golden panelled ceilings'; cf. Lucr. 5.295 f. *Laquearia* means panelled ceilings rather than chains hanging from the ceilings, as Conway holds. For the scansion of *aureis* cf. 698.

727. **funalia**: torches of waxed rope (*funis*).

729. **quam**: supply *implere*; cf. *Aen.* 9.300.

729–30. **omnes a Belo**: if this means (as it probably does) 'everyone from the time of Belus' or 'everyone descended from Belus', then Belus cannot be Dido's father (621), but must be the early founder of the Tyrian dynasty (cf. Carthaginian names like Hanni*bal*, Hasdru*bal*). But it is possible that it means 'all the guests in turn after Belus'; cf. Plaut. *Most.* 347, *Pers.* 771.

731. One of Jupiter's epithets was *Hospitalis*; Alcinous when entertaining Odysseus (*Od.* 7.179 f.) pours a libation to Zeus. For *nam* see note on 65.

732 f. The tragic irony in Dido's prayer (*laetum, meminisse minores, bona Iuno*) is very powerful.

735. **coetum ... celebrate faventes**: 'attend our gathering with good will', cf. for *coetum* Cat. 64.33, for *celebrate faventes Aen.* 8.173.

736. **in mensam ... honorem**: 'she poured in libation an offering of the wine on to the table', cf. *Aen.* 8.279. For *laticum* cf. 686 (singular), *Geo.* 3.509 (plural).

737. **libato**: ablative absolute of one word, cf. *auspicato, impetrato.*

summo ... ore: 'put it just lightly to her lips'; for *tenus* cf. *Aen.* 2.553.

738. **increpitans**: normally rendered 'with a challenge', though the word elsewhere always has a connotation of blame. Henry's note on the passage leads him to the conclusion that as the word must mean blame, and as Bitias has done nothing blameworthy, Dido must be blaming the wine. It seems perhaps more likely that as Bitias politely waits for her to drink it down, she hands it on impatiently (cf. *Aen.* 3.454, *Geo.* 4.138), jestingly rebuking him for thinking she would drink it (Servius says: *et verecundiam reginae ostendit, et morem Romanum; nam apud maiores nostros feminae non utebantur vino, nisi sacrorum causa certis diebus*).

738–9. 'He promptly drained the foaming bowl and soaked himself in its brimming gold'; the vigorous language brings a note of comedy to relieve the undertone of impending tragedy.

739. **auro**: Henry neatly comments 'The expression *auro* ... seems sufficiently strange to us, to whom the expression *glass* ... does not ... seem in the least degree strange.'

740–1. The minstrel sings at the banquet, as Demodocus sings three times at Alcinous' banquet (*Od.* 8). The mythical giant Atlas was vaguely connected with physical philosophy, and as his mountain was in Africa he is a suitable tutor for Iopas.

742 f. The subject of Iopas' song is partly based on Ap. Rh. 1.496 f., where Orpheus sings of heaven and earth, stars and moon, rivers and mountains, and is reminiscent of Silenus' song in *Ecl.* 6; but above all it recalls *Geo.* 2.477 f. (phrases and two whole lines are the same), a passage in which Virgil expresses his wish to be like Lucretius and understand the nature of things.

742. **solisque labores**: i.e. eclipses (*lunaeque labores* in *Geo.* 2.478).

744. This line is repeated in *Aen.* 3.516. Arcturus (the Bear-Watcher) is a bright star near the Great Bear; Hyades are the 'rainers', as Virgil indicates with his epithet *pluvias* (see note on 267–8) — they rose at the time of the spring rains. The twin Triones are Ursa Major and Ursa Minor — the seven stars of Ursa Major (the Plough) gave the word *septentriones* for 'north'.

746. **mora ... obstet**: i.e. what stops them from ending sooner in the winter.

747. **ingeminant plausu**: 'applaud again and again', Virgil uses *ingeminare* both transitively and intransitively.

749. **longumque bibebat amorem**: 'drank deep draughts of love', deep and therefore lasting, cf. *Aen.* 3.487.

751. The reference is to Memnon, see note on 489; Dido is thinking of all the questions she can.

752. Aeneas had met both Diomedes (97) and Achilles (*Il.* 20.160 f.) in single combat.

755–6. 'for it is now the seventh summer that carries you in your wanderings over all the lands and seas'. Dido shows that she knows already (from Teucer) how long it is since Troy fell. The words *septima ... aestas* are also used by Beroe a year later in 5.626, which suggests that the ritual number seven was in Virgil's mind, and that he had not revised the *Aeneid* for chronological inconsistencies.

AENEID 2

Introductory note

Few if any of the stories of antiquity have captured the imagination more than the tale of the wooden horse and the fall of Troy. For the Greeks it was a tale of triumph in which the tragedy of the victims might sometimes overshadow the joy of the conquerors (as in Euripides); for Virgil it was a tale of doom and disaster which was the prelude to a new dawn — 'Ilion falling, Rome arising'. *Aeneid* 2 is in itself almost wholly tragic and dark, with only rare flashes of hope; but within the whole poem the darkness is seen as the night which preceded the dawn of Roman civilization. There is a symmetrical balance of position with Book 8, the book of Aeneas at the site of Rome.

The similarity of *Aeneid* 2 to Greek tragedy has often been discussed; probably Virgil knew Sophocles' tragedies (now lost) called *Sinon* and *Laocoon*, and there are echoes from the *Troades* and the *Hecuba* of Euripides. Certain formal resemblances to Greek tragedy can be observed; for example the account of Laocoon's death reminds us of a messenger's speech; invocations and reflections by the poet (e.g. 241–2, 402) are reminiscent of a chorus; Creusa appears at the end as *dea ex machina*. But this aspect of the book should not be exaggerated: Virgil had no intention of grafting a piece in tragic form on to the epic narrative. The main resemblance is not really formal, but consists partly of the unity and completeness of the plot within the book, and partly of the intensity of tragic pathos. The contrast with the discursive narrative of diverse events in the far less intense atmosphere of *Aeneid* 3 is very marked indeed.

The book is made up of three episodes of roughly equal length: the story of the wooden horse (1–249); the sack of the city and the death of Priam (250–558); the fortunes of Aeneas and his family (559–804). Of these the middle section is the most intense; the first sets the scene for the disaster in vigorous and vivid description, and the last shows how the general catastrophe affected the one family upon whose escape the fortunes of Rome depended.

In this book Aeneas appears as a brave and impetuous warrior, determined to do all that courage can and when, in spite of courage, all is lost, to court death in battle, to make the heroic gesture. Gradually he has to learn that this is not enough; that the responsibilities which he bears go beyond the satisfaction of his personal honour. At the first sight of the burning of Troy he rushes madly to battle: *arma amens capio; nec sat rationis in armis ... furor iraque mentem praecipitat, pulchrumque mori succurrit in armis ... moriamur et in media arma ruamus.* Like wolves he and his followers go into battle; he invokes the ashes of Troy to witness that he made no effort to save his own life, that he exposed himself to every danger. Later he is restrained by Venus from killing Helen, and reminded of his responsibilities towards his own family; when his

father refuses to go Aeneas again falls into despair and is on the
point of rushing out to seek death. Again a divine intervention is
necessary to prevent him. Finally at the loss of Creusa he plunges
into the burning city regardless of his personal safety, and is
restrained only by the supernatural vision of his wife. Only at
the end of the book, when the prophecy of Hector's ghost is
reiterated by Creusa, does Aeneas begin to comprehend that not
only Troy but the whole heroic age must be left behind, and a
new way learned. The vision of Creusa is the prelude to the long
lessons of the years of wanderings and battles in Latium, as the
divine plan is increasingly revealed. As she speaks her last words
to him the jagged confusions of human emotions in this time of
total disaster are soothed and softened by the prospect of long
years and other destinies. What seems so terrible in an immediate
and personal context as to destroy the individual utterly is now
seen in the wider context of history, as a part of the life of nations.
For Aeneas the solution must not be to throw himself into the
flames which are consuming the past and the present, but to build
a life for the future out of the ruins.

   1–56. *Aeneas begins his story, and tells of the discovery of the wooden
horse on the beach and of the different opinions among the Trojans about
the best thing to do. Laocoon vehemently urges its destruction.*

   1 f. Aeneas begins his story to Dido in words heavy with sorrow
and tragic memory — the scars of suffering are by no means
healed. But for the first quarter of the book there is nothing tragic;
the account is fast moving and factual, but with an undercurrent
of impending doom, *fata Troiana*. The narrative begins immediately, without preamble, with the story of the horse, and in a
passage of intense irony Aeneas describes the joy of the Trojans
when they think that the Greeks have at last gone away. Some
however are suspicious about the horse, and the speech of Laocoon
has a desperate urgency, with diction and sound-imagery of an
unusually exaggerated kind; the tension is released as Aeneas'
closing reflexion takes us for a moment away from the events he is
describing to the unchangeable sequel in history: *Troiaque nunc
staret, Priamique arx alta maneres.*

   1. **intentique ora tenebant**: 'in rapt attention kept their
gaze still', cf. *Aen.* 7.250, 8.520; Servius says '*aut ora intuebantur*

loquentis, aut immobiles vultus habebant', of which the second is probably correct. Another possibility is the meaning 'kept quiet', cf. *Geo.* 4.483, but this adds less to the rest of the line.

2. **toro**: the couch on which he was reclining at the banquet.

3 f. Notice how these lines are filled with expressions of sorrow: *infandum . . . dolorem, lamentabile* (a most sonorous word), *miserrima, quis . . . temperet a lacrimis.* So Odysseus (*Od.* 9.12 f.) begins his story to Alcinous with emphasis on the sufferings which he is asked to recall.

4–5. **ut . . . eruerint**: 'how they overthrew', indirect question dependent on the notion of 'telling' in *renovare dolorem*.

5–6. 'dreadful things which I saw myself, and in which I was myself greatly involved'.

7. The Myrmidons were Achilles' special soldiers, and the Dolopians, also from Thessaly, were specially associated with Achilles' son Pyrrhus. Ulysses (Odysseus) is a particularly hateful character from the Trojan point of view, unscrupulous and cruel (44, 261); Sinon purposely speaks about him (90, 125, 164) in Trojan terms. See W. B. Stanford's fascinating book *The Ulysses Theme.* For the genitive form *Ulixi*, always used by Virgil, cf. 90, 436, 3.273, 613, 691 and note on 1.30 *Achilli*.

9. **praecipitat**: intransitive, 'is speeding from the sky', i.e. has passed its mid course. *Cadentia* means that in the night sky one constellation after another is seen to set, or perhaps is used more loosely of the stars growing pale at first dawn (cf. *Aen.* 8.59). Notice the lilting rhythm with no strong caesura to follow the trochee in the third foot, and the rhyme of *-dent-*.

10. **amor . . . cognoscere**: poetic use of the infinitive, see note on 1.704.

12. **refugit**: perfect, 'has recoiled'.

15 f. For a brilliant account of the Trojan Horse in art and literature see R. G. Austin, *J.R.S.* 1959, pp. 16–25, summarised in his edition of Book 2, pages 34–6. It is mentioned three times in the *Odyssey* as a familiar story, and figured in cyclic epic (*Ilias Parva* and *Iliupersis*). It was a frequent subject in Roman drama (Livius Andronicus and Naevius both wrote an *Equus Troianus*), and it can be seen from an amusing passage in Plautus (*Bacch.* 925 f., 987 f.) how very well known it was.

15. **instar montis**: 'the size of a mountain'; the word *instar*

(here in apposition to *equum*) is a neuter noun, meaning 'equivalent (weight)', and its most common usage is with the genitive, meaning 'as big as', 'like'; cf. Cic. *Att.* 10.4.1 (*epistola*) *quae voluminis instar erat*, and *Aen.* 3.637, 7.707.

divina Palladis arte: the horse was Ulysses' idea, and Epeos (264) made it with the help of the goddess Athena (Hom. *Od.* 8.493 τὸν Ἐπειὸς ἐποίησεν σὺν Ἀθήνῃ; cf. Eur. *Tro.* 10).

16. **aedificant . . . intexunt**: metaphors used in ship-building; *costas* means the 'ribs' of the structure.

abiete: the *i* is treated as a consonant, making the word a dactyl, cf. *ariete* (492), *parietibus* (442). The material of which the horse is made (pine here, cf. 258) is later said by Sinon to be maple (112); this may be taken as a sign either of lack of revision or of lack of special interest in carpentry. The word *robur*, when used of the horse in 186, 230, 260, has the general sense of 'wood' rather than its special meaning 'oak'.

17. 'they pretend that it is a votive offering for their return; that is the story spread around'. *Votum* is a noun rather than (as Servius suggests) a verb.

18. **delecta . . . corpora**: 'selecting picked men'. *Corpora virum* is a periphrasis for *viri* with the idea, as Conington says, of so many bodies filling up the space.

19. **caeco lateri**: 'into its dark side', in prose *in caecum latus*. The dative of motion towards is common in Virgil especially with compound verbs; see Page ad loc., line 85 and cf. 9.729 *incluserit urbi*.

20. **uterum**: its womb, cf. 38, 52, *alvus* in 51, and *feta armis* in 238. The metaphor was traditional, cf. Eur. *Tro.* 11, Enn. *Scen.* 76–7 *gravidus armatis equus, | qui suo partu ardua perdat Pergama*.

21. **in conspectu**: 'in sight of Troy'; Tenedos was a few miles off the coast.

22. **dives opum**: the same phrase in *Aen.* 1.14.

23. 'now just a curve of coastline, and a treacherous landfall for ships'; it is often said that this line is a comment by Virgil, not in the person of Aeneas, but when *nos* follows so closely this is inconceivable. Aeneas refers to the deterioration of the famous harbour during the war, and his words help to explain why the Trojans so readily assumed that the Greeks had sailed away.

25. 'we thought — gone, sailed on the wind for Mycenae';

observe the staccato effect of the omission of *sumus* (cf. 651) and
eos.

26. This is a very memorable line, simple in diction, slow,
monotonous with dissyllables, with patterned alliteration of *s* and
l — it is like a long deep sigh of relief.

29–30. These lines express the thoughts in the minds of the
Trojans as they visit the Greek camp. *Tendebat* means 'had his
tent', (understand *tentoria*), a normal military phrase; cf. *Aen.*
8.605. Servius says *classibus* refers to the cavalry, and Mackail
follows him; but no reader would take it in this way unless prevented from understanding it to mean 'fleet' by something in the
context. Here a mention of the Greek fleet, so prominent a feature
of the Trojan landscape for ten years, is extremely appropriate.

31. 'Some gaze in amazement at the fatal gift to the maiden
goddess Minerva'; Hyginus (*Fab.* 108) says the inscription on
the horse was *Danai Minervae dono dant*.

33. **hortatur**: for the infinitive after *hortari* cf. 74 and see note
on 1.357 (*suadere*).

34. **sive dolo**: Servius tells a story that Thymoetes' wife and
son were put to death by Priam; hence Thymoetes had a motive
for treachery.

35. **Capys**: he was one of those who came with Aeneas, cf.
1.183, 10.145; he gave his name to Capua.

36 f. In Hom. *Od.* 8.507 f. the Trojans debate whether to break
the horse open, throw it from a cliff, or accept it.

37. **subiectisve**: our MSS all have -*que*, but Servius reports
that some early MSS had -*ve*. There are many instances (see
Austin's note for references) where -*que* is used when -*ve* would
seem more natural; on the other hand -*ve* and -*que* are constantly
confused in the MSS, and in this instance -*que* seems to me
unacceptable, even allowing that the first *aut* clause links two
methods of destruction as opposed to the idea in the second *aut*
clause (investigation).

38. 'or to pierce and explore the hollow recesses of its belly'.

41 f. Laocoon figures in the epic cycle (*Iliupersis*), and there
was a tragedy by Sophocles called *Laocoon*. He was a son of
Priam and priest of Apollo (see note on 201). In the general
tradition of the fall of Troy his part was subordinate to that of
Cassandra, and it seems certain that it is an innovation by Virgil

to make him the central character. For further and full discussion see Austin's edition of Book 2, pp. 44-5, and 94-9.

44. The attention is compelled by the alliteration of *d*, leading to the summary: 'is this all you've learned about Ulysses?' Laocoon does not actually know that Ulysses was the originator of the idea of the horse, but he is quite sure that plots and trickery of all descriptions are likely to come from that source.

45 f. Laocoon makes two precise suggestions: the first (which is correct) is that the horse contains Greek warriors, the second is that it is a kind of scaling ladder by which the walls can be breached. If neither of these is correct, he says, there is some (other) trick behind it.

48. error: 'deception', cf. Livy 22.1.3.

49. timeo Danaos et dona ferentis: from the time of Donatus this phrase has become a proverbial expression with its meaning slightly twisted. Laocoon here says: 'I fear the Greeks even when they are making offerings', that is to say religious offerings to Minerva as a goddess of Troy.

51. feri: of a horse at 5.818, of a tame stag in 7.489.

curvam compagibus: a favourite Virgilian ablative, where *curvis compagibus* would be more normal; cf. 208, 765 and Mackail's Appendix A in his edition.

53. The assonance of this line, intended to convey the reverberation caused by the quivering spear, is most remarkable, mainly because of the trochaic caesurae and the rhyme of *-ere, -ae*.

54 f. 'and if the fates of the gods and their intentions had not been against us, he would have prevailed on us to despoil with steel the Greek hiding place, and Troy would now be standing, and lofty citadel of Priam you would yet survive'. For *mens deum* cf. 170, *Geo.* 4.220, Ov. *Met.* 15.137: some take the phrase to refer to the Trojans' minds (cf. *Ecl.* 1.16), but this gives an unbalanced sentence. For *impulerat* (the indicative used vividly in a past unfulfilled condition) cf. *Geo.* 2.133, Hor. *Odes* 2.17.28. For *staret* some MSS have *stares*, but the change from third person narrative to second-person apostrophe in the parallel clauses is very effective.

57-199. *A group of Trojan shepherds bring in the Greek Sinon, who has allowed himself to be captured in order to persuade the Trojans to take*

the wooden horse into the city. He tells his story of deceit, pretending that
he was about to be put to death by Greeks, but made his escape and is now
throwing himself on the Trojans' mercy. The Trojans pity him and
release his fetters; Sinon completes his story, telling them that the horse is a
religious offering in atonement for the stolen Palladium, and that if they
take it into Troy the defeat of the Greeks is certain.

The story of Sinon, like that of Laocoon, occurs in the epic
cycle (not in Homer), and there was a tragedy by Sophocles
called *Sinon*. Virgil's version is probably the first from a Trojan
point of view. There are marked similarities with the Achaemenides episode in 3.588 f.; see Mackail's edition, Appendix B.
Sinon (a parallel to Tarquin in treachery) is among the Trojan
pictures which Lucrece sees in Shakespeare's *Rape of Lucrece*
(1501 f.).

> 'At last she sees a wretched image bound,
> That piteous looks to Phrygian shepherds lent . . .'

Two points stand out in Virgil's brilliant treatment of this
episode; first the contrast between the guile and cold deception
of Sinon and the warm hearts of the Trojans who are moved to
pity; and secondly the masterly rhetoric which Sinon commands in
all its moods, despair, subtlety, humility, anger, appeals to pity.
Austin in his commentary summarises Sinon's speech with the
words: "Cicero would have enjoyed reading it, and would have
recognised its quality'.

57. **manus**: retained accusative, see note on 210.

59. **Dardanidae**: noun (cf. 72) in apposition with *pastores*.

60. **hoc ipsum**: i.e. to be brought to the king, so that he could
tell his lying story.

61. **animi**: 'in heart', 'in courage', genitive of 'sphere in
which', (not locative); see my note on 5.202 *furens animi* (Oxford
edition).

62. 'either to weave his web of lies or to meet certain death';
the first alternative is if he succeeded in getting himself taken to
the king, the second is if the shepherds decided to kill him as soon
as they found him.

65–6. 'Now listen to the treachery of the Greeks, and from one
act of crime comprehend it all'; with *omnis* understand *insidias*
(rather than *Danaos*). This is in direct reply to Dido's request

(1.754) *dic . . . insidias Danaum*; Aeneas now says he will give one
example for all, the last one. For the half-line see note on 1.534;
the others in this book are 233, 346, 468, 614, 623, 640, 720, 767,
787.

68. **circumspexit**: Virgil (unlike Catullus) rarely has a
spondee in the fifth foot (35 instances altogether — mostly with
Greek words — compared with 30 in the four hundred lines of
Catullus 64); here it has a most marked aesthetic effect, conveying
the slow hopelessness of Sinon's gaze. For further metrical
references see my note on 5.320 (Oxford edition).

73. 'At his words of anguish our feelings changed, and all
menacing gestures ceased'; the contrast of Trojan friendliness
with Greek ruthlessness is very marked. Donatus says 'bonitatem
Troianorum vult Aeneas ostendere', Taubmann 'tribuit poeta
ubique pietatem simplicitatemque animi Troianis'.

74. **cretus**: sc. *sit*, passive participle of *cresco* with active
meaning; cf. *Aen.* 3.608, 4.191.

75. **quidve ferat**: 'what information he is bringing'; cf. *Aen.*
10.150.

memoret quae sit fiducia capto: 'let him say what he relies
on as a captive'; Sinon has indicated that he has no place now
among the Greeks, so the Trojans ask him to say what grounds he
has for thinking they will wish to receive him: 'What is the
prisoner's case, what has he to say for himself?' (Henry, quoting
Tac. *Ann.* 3.11). This seems the best interpretation of a difficult
passage; another of Servius' suggestions is 'let him remember
what a captive must depend on', i.e. telling the truth, but this
seems impossible for *memoret*.

76. This line (the same as 3.612) is not in the chief MSS, is not
appropriate here with *inquit* following, and should therefore be
omitted.

77. **fuerit quodcumque**: 'come what may'.

79-80. 'and if Fortune has made Sinon unhappy, she shall not
also — tyrant though she may be — make him false and untruth-
ful'. For *improba* cf. 356, *Aen.* 4.412 *improbe Amor.*

81-2. **aliquod . . . nomen**: 'any mention of the name', cf.
Aen. 1.181 *Anthea si quem* ('any sign of Antheus') and Ov. *Met.*
9.8, 15.497.

82. **Belidae . . . Palamedis**: the story first occurs in cyclic

epic (*Cypria*), and Euripides wrote a tragedy called *Palamedes*;
cf. also Eur. *Orest.* 432 f., and Cic. *De Off.* 3.97–8. Ulysses, angry
because Palamedes had uncovered the trick by which he had
tried to avoid going to Troy, forged a letter in which Palamedes
promised to betray the Greeks, and hid gold in his tent. Palamedes was put to death. The suggestion that Palamedes 'forbad
the war' (84) may be added by Virgil to make Sinon's speech
more persuasive. *Belides* is derived from Belus, father of Danaus
and Aegyptus, not the same as Dido's ancestor (1.621, 729);
Virgil lengthens the *i* of the patronymic as if it were from Beleus
(cf. 104).

83. **falsa sub proditione**: 'under a false accusation of
betrayal', (so Servius), a curiously compressed phrase; Conington
thinks it means 'under a false information', but as the story concerned betrayal of the Greeks we would expect that idea here.

84. The alliteration of *in-* and the elisions are emphatic in the
highest degree.

85. **cassum lumine**: 'deprived of the light', cf. Lucr. 5.719,
Aen. 11.104.

86. The main clause begins here: 'it was to him that my father
sent me as a companion and a relative by blood'; *et* rather
unusually links *comitem* which is predicative and *propinquum* which
is attributive.

87. Compare what Achaemenides says in 3.614–15.

88. **regno incolumis**. Palamedes was one of the *reges*.

90. **pellacis**: the word is not found elsewhere before the
fourth century; the very rare noun *pellacia* occurs in Lucr. 2.559
(= 5.1004) *placidi pellacia ponti*. The verb *pellicere* ('entice') is fairly
common. Some MSS have *fallacis*, which seems like a gloss or an
easier reading substituted.

91. **superis concessit ab oris**: 'departed from the shores of
life', a phrase in high epic style, in keeping with the rhetorical
eloquence which Sinon commands.

94. **fors si qua tulisset**: 'if any chance brought it about';
cf. line 34, 11.345. *Tulisset* is reported future perfect; cf. 136, 189,
756.

97. **mali labes**: 'slip towards disaster'; Servius says *ruinam
significat, a 'lapsu'*, and Justin (17.1.5) imitates the passage and
takes it in this way: *haec prima mali labes, hoc initium impendentis*

ruinae fuit. Cf. also Lucr. 2.1145 *dabunt labem putrisque ruinas.* In *Aen.* 6.746, the only other place where Virgil uses the word *labes*, it has its other meaning, 'stain', which is not inconceivable here.

98. **terrere**: historic infinitive, frequent in Virgil, cf. 132, 169, 685, here used for repeated action (cf. *Aen.* 4.422).

99. **in vulgum**: the masculine is much rarer than the neuter form; cf. Lucr. 2.921.

ambiguas: 'double-edged'.

quaerere conscius arma: 'he sought assistance for his conspiracy against me'; *conscius* is literally 'as a conspirator', 'with deliberate intent'. *Arma* is vague, anything he could use for his purpose, suspicion, hostility: Servius says *arma sunt instrumenta cuiuslibet rei.*

100. **enim**: an archaic usage meaning 'indeed', cf. line 164 and 6.317.

Calchante ministro: the sentence is broken off, left unfinished by aposiopesis. Calchas was the chief seer of the Greeks, cf. Hom. *Il.* 1.68 f.

101. **sed . . . autem**: a colloquialism, only found elsewhere in comedy, helping to convey the change of tone as he comes to the end of his speech.

103. 'and it's enough to hear that name, then exact now the overdue punishment'; *iamdudum* with the imperative is an elliptical way of combining past and future (take it now, you should have long ago), cf. Sen. *Ep. Mor.* 84.14 *relinque ista iamdudum*, Ov. *Met.* 11.482.

104. **Ithacus**: with some contempt, describing Ulysses without mentioning his name; cf. 122.

Atridae: the sons of Atreus, Agamemnon and Menelaus, cf. 415, 500 and *Aen.* 1.458.

105. **ardemus scitari**: for the infinitive cf. 316 and *Aen.* 1.515, 4.281.

108. 'Sinon begins with casual simplicity, almost as if he were telling a bedtime story' (Austin). Austin's detailed comments on the rhetorical trickery of Sinon's speeches are vivid and penetrating.

110. **fecissentque utinam**: 'if only they had done it', cf. *Aen.* 3.615.

112. **contextus acernis**: see note on 16.

114. **scitantem**: Servius says *id est scitaturum*, 'to consult';

M^2 and some other MSS have the supine *scitatum*, but *scitantem* seems acceptable as an extension of phrases like *mittere auxilium orantes*. Eurypylus is mentioned in Hom. *Il.* 2.736.

116. The reference is to the sacrifice of Iphigenia at Aulis; cf. Lucr. 1.84 f.

118–19. **animaque litandum Argolica**: 'favour must be won with a Greek life'; *litare* is a ritual word, meaning to obtain favour by sacrificing. Notice the emphatic position of *Argolica*.

121. **cui fata parent**: '(as they wondered) for whom they were to prepare death, who it was that Apollo demanded'; the indirect question is loosely linked to the previous sentence, cf. *Aen.* 12.718 f. This is the interpretation which Servius gives (*cui praeparent mortem*) and the deliberative question fits well with the gerundives of 118: 'you must sacrifice — whom then are we to sacrifice?' For *fata parare* cf. 132. Others take *fata* as nominative 'for whom the fates are preparing' but the absence of an object is very strange. Others again accept the conjecture *paret*, making Apollo the subject.

123–4. **quae ... flagitat**: 'he demands to know what these indications of the divine will mean'; cf. *Aen.* 3.359 f.

124–5. 'And now many of them were beginning to prophesy for me the cruel crime of that schemer, and silently were foreseeing the future'. *Canere* is in the sense of foretelling by prophecy; *taciti* means, as Austin points out, that Sinon's friends brooded over what they saw coming to him; perhaps it also implies that they did not speak out or take action.

126. **tectus**: 'shut up in his tent', cf. *Aen.* 7.600.

129. **composito**: 'in accordance with the agreement' (*ex pacto*, Servius); cf. *composita hora*, at the agreed hour.

rupit vocem: 'broke into words', broke silence; cf. *Aen.* 3.246, 4.553, 11.377. The phrase is based on the Greek ῥῆξαι φωνήν.

131. **tulere**: 'accepted', in the sense of *aequo animo tulerunt*.

132. **parari**: historic infinitive, see note on 98.

133. **salsae fruges**: 'salted corn' (*mola salsa*), frequent in sacrificial offerings; cf. *Aen.* 12.173.

136. 'I lay hidden waiting for them to set sail, if only they would'; in *dum darent* the subject expresses his purpose in waiting, cf. *Aen.* 1.5. The conditional clause is of the special type — often with *forte* — where the if clause is not the protasis to the expressed

main clause, and conveys an idea of purpose or hope; cf. *Aen.* 1.181, 578 and especially 2.756. *Dedissent* is reported future perfect, cf. 94; the thought in his mind is 'if only they will go'.

137 f. Sinon comes to his peroration in the well-known oratorical style, with an appeal for pity (*miseratio*).

139. 'from whom perhaps they will even exact a penalty for my escape'; *quos* and *poenas* are accusatives after *reposcere* (cf. *Aen.* 7.606); *fors* is adverbial, probably archaic, equivalent to *forsit, forsitan*, cf. 5.232, and for *fors et* 11.50.

141. **quod**: as in *quod si*, literally 'with regard to which', cf. *Aen.* 6.363.

142–3. 'by any faith which anywhere still remains uncorrupted among men'; the whole clause acts as object to the preposition *per*, cf. *Aen.* 6.459.

145. **ultro**: the commonest meaning of this word is 'first, of one's own accord' (59, 193, 279, 372); here the shade of meaning is 'beyond what might be expected' (*Aen.* 5.55), 'into the bargain' (Austin). See Page's excellent note ad loc.

148. 'whoever you are, from now forget the Greeks you have lost'.

151. **quae ... belli**: 'what is its religious purpose, or what kind of military machine is it?' These are the two possible meanings of the horse which were debated by the Trojans before Sinon came. For the long first syllable of *religio* cf. 188, 365, 715, and *Aen.* 1.30 (*reliquias*).

154. **aeterni ignes**: i.e. the heavenly bodies.

160–1. The apostrophe to Troy, rather than the Trojans, adds to the rhetorical effect — *magnificentius*, says Servius.

163–4. 'But indeed from the time when the godless son of Tydeus along with Ulysses, the deviser of sin . . .' *Ex quo* is picked up by *ex illo* after an unusually long series of subordinate clauses. For *sed enim* cf. *Aen.* 1.19, 6.28 and note on 100. Diomedes, son of Tydeus, is called *impius* with reference to this particular crime, but perhaps also (as Servius says) because he had fought against gods (Hom. *Il.* 5.330 f.); for the hostile attitude to Ulysses see note on 7, and particularly 125 and 6.529 *hortator scelerum*.

166. **Palladium**: the story of the sacred image of the maiden goddess Pallas Athena, on which the safety of Troy depended (*fatale*), goes back to cyclic epic (it is not in Homer). According to

one version it was a false Palladium which the Greeks stole, and the real one was brought from Troy to Rome by Aeneas; according to another Aeneas recovered it from Diomedes after the fall of Troy. For a full account see Austin's note on 163.

168. **ausi**: understand *sunt*; the parallelism with *corripuere* prevents possible ambiguity in this long sentence.

169. **fluere . . . referri**: historic infinitives, cf. 98; for the last part of the line cf. *Geo.* 1.200.

170. **deae mens**: the monosyllabic ending is unusual and emphatic; see note on 1.105, and cf. 250, 355.

171. **ea signa**: 'signs of it', i.e. her hostility, a frequent Latin idiom, cf. *Aen.* 7.595 *has poenas = harum rerum poenas*.

Tritonia: a frequent epithet of Pallas (615, cf. 226), apparently from an obscure lake Tritonis in Africa near which she was said to have been born or first alighted on earth after her birth (Lucan 9.354).

172. **vix positum . . . arsere**: *vix positum est cum arsere*, one of the types of parataxis of which Virgil was fond, cf. 692, 3.90.

174–5. The meaning is that apart from the miraculous behaviour of the image (flashing eyes, salt sweat), an apparition of Pallas herself was three times seen.

178–9. 'unless they seek new omens in Argos, and bring back the deity (which they have now taken away with them over the sea in their curved ships)'. Lines 177–8 are what Calchas said; line 179 is Sinon's comment. Conington's version of 179 (the divine favour which they originally brought away with them from Greece) has been followed by some, but is improbable.

180. **et nunc quod**: a rather loose and colloquial opening to a sentence, 'as to the fact that', found sometimes in Cicero's letters, and cf. Lucr. 4.885, Cat. 83.4. Translate 'The reason why they have gone . . . is because they are preparing. . .'.

181. **pelagoque remenso**: 'when they have travelled back again over the sea'; cf. *Aen.* 5.25 *remetior astra*, and for the passive sense 3.143.

185. **hanc tamen**: slightly disjointed, still referring to the horse, the *hanc effigiem* of the previous sentence. The connexion seems to be: 'they have made this horse to expiate their crime, but Calchas said it had to be of enormous size, so that it could not be taken into Troy'.

186. **caeloque**: dative of motion towards, cf. 688, 6.178.

188. **antiqua sub religione**: so that it could not take the place of the Palladium (183), and save Troy from destruction.

189. **violasset**: reported future perfect, cf. 94.

190. **in ipsum**: on Calchas himself.

193-4. 'Then Asia would herself in mighty warfare come to the walls of Pelops, and that fate awaited our descendants'; cf. *Aen.* 11.286. Pelops (who gave his name to the Peloponnese) was grandfather of Agamemnon. The prophecy came true when the Trojan-Romans conquered Greece; cf. 1.283 f., 6.836 f.

195. Cf. Shakespeare, *Rape of Lucrece*, 1548 f. 'Look, look, how listening Priam wets his eyes, / To see those borrow'd tears that Sinon sheds . . .'

196. **coacti**: 'forced', cf. Ov. *Met.* 6.628, Juv. 13.133 *vexare oculos umore coacto*.

197. Diomedes and Achilles are linked also in 1.752; Achilles came from Pthia in Thessaly, near Larissa.

198. The 'thousand ships' (cf. 9.148) goes back to Aesch. *Agam.* 45. The actual number in Homer's catalogue has been counted as 1186, 'but', Austin asks, 'could Helen's face have launched 1186 ships?'

199-249. *At this point a terrible portent occurs: twin serpents from the sea seize Laocoon and his two sons and kill them. The Trojans regard this as a final indication that the horse must not be harmed, and amidst scenes of rejoicing they take it inside Troy.*

The story of the death of Laocoon is told in a passage of great immediacy and power, and has always been one of the best known parts of the *Aeneid*. The description of the snakes is vivid and terrifying, and effects of rhythm and sound are used throughout with the utmost skill to reinforce the meaning of the words; but perhaps the main impact is the remorseless inevitability of doom. We are reminded of a messenger's speech in Greek tragedy (e.g. Eur. *Hipp.* 1210 f.), when events are described which are too full of horror to be presented on the stage.

The passage was used by Lessing (*Laocoon*, 1766), as a basis for his famous discussion of the difference between the techniques of poetry and the fine arts. The marble group of Laocoon and his two sons (now in the Vatican), dating probably from the second half of the first century B.C., was regarded by Pliny (*Nat. Hist.* 36.37) as surpassing all other works of painting or sculpture; it is possible that Virgil knew it, or knew a painting from which it derived. For a full appreciation of the passage, and a discussion of the source-material and the variations in the Laocoon legend, see R. G. Austin, *J.R.S.* 1959, p. 20 and his note (with full bibliography) on *Aen.* 2.199–227.

199–200. 'Then another thing happened to shake the unhappy Trojans, much more significant and much more terrifying, confusing our blind wits'; the alliteration is marked, and the unusual position of *magis* is very emphatic.

201. Laocoon in the general tradition was a priest of Apollo: see note on 41 f. and 199 f. Servius explains that the priest of Neptune had been killed and Laocoon was appointed to his duties. The metonymy *ductus sorte* (=*factus sorte ducta*) is not uncommon; cf. Cic. *Rep.* 1.51.

202. The altars are presumably on the shore, cf. *Aen.* 3.21.

203. The snakes come from the direction of Tenedos because that is the direction from which the Greek fleet is to come (cf. 21 f.). Henry draws attention to the parallels between the serpents and the fleet, from their red crests corresponding with the flame signal (256) to their reception by Athena corresponding with her part in Troy's destruction (615).

203–4. Notice how the separation of *angues* from its adjective *gemini* by a series of descriptive phrases gives tension to the sentence.

205. **incumbunt pelago**: 'breast the sea'; *pelago* is dative, cf. *Aen.* 1.84.

206. **iubaeque**: the crests on their heads give a dragon-like effect to the serpents; Pliny (*N.H.* 11.122) firmly says *draconum cristas qui viderit, non reperitur*, and Livy (43.13.4) mentions such a thing as a prodigy. Page quotes Milton, *P.L.* 7.496 f. (of the serpent) 'with brazen Eyes / and hairie Mane terrific'.

208. **sinuatque ... terga**: 'arches its enormous length in coils'; *sinuo* is always transitive, cf. *Geo.* 3.192 and Ov. *Met.* 3.42.

209–11. The alliteration, especially of *s*, is very powerful, and the description is brought to an end with a patterned line of gruesome finality. For other snake descriptions in Virgil cf. 379 f., 471 f., *Geo.* 2.153 f., 3.425 f., *Aen.* 5.84 f., 273 f.

210. 'their gleaming eyes shot with blood and fire'; *oculos* is retained accusative (here after a verb with a middle meaning), cf. 57, 219, 221, 273, 275, 393, 511, 629, 721 and note on 1.228 *oculos suffusa*. *Suffecti* is rare in this sense, cf. Val. Fl. 2.105 *maculis suffecta genas*.

212–13. Notice how after the lingering descriptive passage the two staccato short sentences convey the rapidity of the events. For *agmine* cf. *Aen.* 5.90, *Geo.* 3.423, and note on 782.

217. The unusual pause after the fifth foot, and the double monosyllable at the line ending, compel the attention for the statuesque description of the next two lines.

218–19. **collo squamea circum terga dati**: 'entwining their scaly bodies round his neck'; for the tmesis of *circumdati* cf. 792, for its construction cf. 510, and for the middle use cf. *cingitur* in 511.

221. **perfusus ... vittas**: retained accusative with a passive meaning in the verb, see note on 210.

223. **qualis mugitus, fugit cum**: 'like the bellowing when a bull has escaped ...'; the full construction would be *tales clamores tollit qualis est mugitus. . . .* The comparison, apart from its main point of resemblance (cries of agony), conveys with intense irony that Laocoon is now in the situation of the sacrificial victim (202).

224. **incertam**: 'ill-aimed'.

225. **at**: the particle of transition conveys that the struggle is over, and leaves the death of Laocoon unnarrated.

226. **saevaeque ... Tritonidis**: i.e. Athena, see note on 171. For *saeva* cf. 1.479, the picture of the Trojan women supplicating the hostile Athena.

231. **tergo**: poetic dative of motion towards after the compound *intorserit*, 'hurled at', cf. 236, 240. *Intorserit* (like *laeserit*) is causal subjunctive.

232. With *sedes* understand *divae* (i.e. *Minervae*); the word *simulacrum* is here applied to the horse (cf. 172, of the Palladium).

234. **muros ... moenia**: *muros* are the city walls which they breach by the gate, and *moenia* the buildings within.

235 f. For descriptions of the entry of the horse cf. Eur. *Tro.* 511 f., *Hec.* 905 f., Plaut. *Bacch.* 933 f. Notice the very short clauses, with eight main verbs in six lines, to convey the relentless movement of the action.

235. **accingunt**: intransitive, used reflexively; cf. *Aen.* 1.104.

235-7. 'and put rollers under its feet and secure hemp ropes tightly on its neck'; *lapsus rotarum* (literally 'the glidings of wheels') is a very ornate phrase, cf. *remigium alarum* (1.301).

238. **feta armis**: for the metaphor see note on 20.

241 f. Aeneas' invocation is based on Enn. *Scen.* 92 f. *o pater, o patria: o Priami domus. . . .*

242. **Dardanidum**: for the form of the genitive see note on 3.21.

245. Observe how the finality of this line is achieved by slow spondees, alliteration of *s*, use of the powerful word *monstrum*, and juxtaposition of the conflicting religious terms *infelix* and *sacrata*.

246-7. Once again, and for the last time, Cassandra prophesies disaster, and once again is not believed. *Fatis . . . futuris* is dative of purpose, a condensed turn for *fatis futuris canendis; credita* agrees with *ora*, not *Cassandra*.

248. **esset**: for *futurus esset*; the subjunctive is causal after *miseri quibus* (cf. 231).

250-67. *Night falls; the Trojans sleep. The Greek fleet leaves Tenedos, and Sinon receiving a fire signal from them opens the horse. The Greeks hidden in it come out, kill the Trojan sentries, and open the gates of Troy to their companions.*

After the slow-moving and reflective final lines describing the entry of the horse within the walls of Troy, the narrative now becomes very rapid. The whole of the book so far has been concerned with whether or not the Trojans will bring the horse into their city; now that thay have done so, the immediate disastrous consequences are compressed into just a few lines.

250. 'Meanwhile the heavens revolved and night sped up from the Ocean'; the first phrase is from Ennius, *Ann.* 211, the second from Hom. *Od.* 5.294 ὀρώρει δ' οὐρανόθεν νύξ: the Homeric rhythm is also imitated.

252. **Myrmidonumque**: see note on 7; here the word is used generally for the Greeks.

255. 'in the friendly silence of the quiet moon', i.e. in the still of night advantageous for their purpose. Some commentators have argued that *tacita* means 'not visible', as *luna silens* is used of the night before the new moon (cf. Cato *De Agr.* 29); but the

descriptive impact of the phrase is like Catullus' *quam sidera multa, cum tacet nox* (7.7; cf. *Geo.* 1.247), or Coleridge's 'quietly shining to the quiet moon'. It is evident in line 340 that the moon is shining; for further references see Austin's note ad loc.

256 f. The tradition of the fire-signal varied; according to some versions Sinon sent a signal to Agamemnon, and in 6.517 Helen gives a signal to the Greeks (to show them the way after landing). Virgil's version here is appropriate and vivid for a narrative centred on Troy — the reader pictures himself in Troy, not in the Greek ships.

257. **extulerat**: the tense is strange and has led some editors to think that the construction is *ibat cum extulerat*, 'they were proceeding after Agamemnon had given the sign', an unacceptably weak sense. *Extulerat* like *laxat* is in the inverted *cum* clause: 'they were proceeding when suddenly Agamemnon had given the signal and Sinon is releasing the Greeks. . .'.

iniquis: i.e. to Troy, cf. 54.

260. **se ... promunt**: 'get themselves out'; the word is not used reflexively before Virgil. Austin says 'the Greeks cheerfully decant themselves from the Horse's depths'.

261 f. The men in the horse are in groups of three, each containing one of the leading Greek generals — Ulysses, Neoptolemus, Menelaus. Thessandrus was a son of Polynices, Sthenelus a close friend of Diomedes, Acamas a son of Theseus, Thoas a Homeric hero (*Il.* 2.638 f.), Machaon a surgeon, Epeos — as Virgil tells us (cf. Hom. *Od.* 8.493) — the maker of the horse which Ulysses had planned.

263. **Pelidesque Neoptolemus**: Neoptolemus (Pyrrhus) was the son of Achilles, and grandson of Peleus; his prominent part in the story is told in lines 469 f.

primusque Machaon: *primus* is strange, but presumably means 'chieftain', cf. *Il.* 11.506; it does not mean that he was first to come out (being mentioned seventh), nor that he was a leading surgeon.

266–7. Notice how the fourth foot coincidence in 266 prepares for the even more decisive coincidence (diaeresis before and after a dactyl) of 267; see note on 1.7.

268–97. *The ghost of Hector appears to Aeneas, and tells him that he must escape from Troy, taking with him Troy's sacred emblems and the Penates.*

268 f. Here for the first time in the book Aeneas himself comes into his story. The passage is one of the most dramatic in the *Aeneid*, with its contrast between the happy sleep of Aeneas, freed at last from anxiety because he believes that the Greeks have gone, and the terse statements of disaster which he receives from Hector's ghost. The reversal of events is total: Aeneas believes that the long ordeal is over; Hector tells him that there is no chance whatever of Troy's survival. The themes of the *Aeneid* are briefly set out; the imminent destruction of Troy, the impossibility of its defence; the responsibility of Aeneas for rescuing from the ashes the gods of his city and founding a new home for them. Thus that he should escape when so many died is seen to be a divine requirement, a duty to be accepted, not an act of cowardice. In the course of the book he still shows signs of courting the noble death, and still feels impelled to defend himself for having escaped with his life (431 f.), but Hector's words mark the first stage in the transformation of Aeneas from a Trojan warrior to an instrument of history.

The dream vision is a favourite Virgilian technique for the amalgamation of past, present, and future; it is often used (like prophecies) to emphasise the connexion of the divine plan with the human action. This is among the most memorable because it also contains psychological elements of the dream-world (like Dido's dream in 4.465 f.); the confusion of Aeneas and his inability to recall past events, the lonely sad apparition of Hector, combine to produce an effect of a secondary world outside the real one. For other prophetic dreams and visions cf. that of the Penates in 3.147 f., of Mercury in 4.265 f., 556 f., of Anchises in 5.722 f., of Tiberinus in 8.31 f.

271. Cf. Lucr. 1.125 f. (Ennius' vision of Homer) *spèciem lacrimas effundere salsas | coepisse*; Enn. *Ann.* 6 *visus Homerus adesse poeta*.

272. 'as he was in days gone by when dragged behind the chariot'; cf. Hom. *Il.* 22.396 f., Enn. *Scen.* 101. Austin points out that Dido must have thought of the picture of Hector on the walls of her temple to Juno (1.483). For the ghost still showing the wounds of life cf. *Aen.* 1.353 f. (Sychaeus), 6.494 f. (Deiphobus), and Tac. *Ann.* 1.65 (Quintilius Varus). The tradition of the dragging of Hector's body round the walls is post-Homeric; see note on 1.483 f.

273. **traiectus lora**: 'pierced with thongs'. The accusative *lora* is a remarkable instance of a retained accusative (see note on 210) with a passive verb (*traicere lora per pedes*, so *traiectus lora per pedes*) where there is no middle idea (as in 275) nor any idea of accusative of respect (as in 221). The nearest parallel in Virgil is *Ecl*. 3.106 (*flores*) *inscripti nomina regum*.

274–5. 'Ah me, what a sight! How different indeed from that other Hector who came back wearing the trophies of Achilles, or after hurling Trojan firebrands on the Greek ships.' Servius tells us that the first phrase is from Ennius (*Ann*. 7). Compare Ov. *Met*. 6.273 and Milton, *P.L.* 1.84–5 'But O how fall'n! how chang'd / From him, who in the happy Realms of Light. . . .' Achilles lent his armour to Patroclus, and Hector captured it when he killed Patroclus (*Il*. 17.194 f.). The Trojan attack on the Greek ships which they almost set on fire is described in *Il*. 15; also *Il*. 22.374.

275. **redit**: the present tense is used very vividly to indicate Aeneas' remembrance of the earlier event side by side with the present vision.

exuvias indutus: retained accusative after the middle use of *indutus* ('having put on'); cf. 393, 721–2 and note on 210.

Achilli: for the form of the genitive cf. 7 and note on 1.30. Contrast line 476 (*Achillis*).

277–8. 'with matted beard, hair clotted with blood, and those wounds, those many wounds he received around the walls of his native city'. Cf. Hom. *Il*. 22.367 f.

281 f. Aeneas' words have the inconsequential nature of a dream: in reality he knew only too well the manner of Hector's death. In his dream he remembers only that Hector has recently been absent from the Trojan ranks, and in phrases of intense pathos asks him why. Macrobius (*Sat*. 6.2.18) quotes a passage from Ennius (*Scen*. 72 f.) *o lux Troiae, germane Hector, | quid ita cum tuo lacerato corpore | miser es, aut qui te sic respectantibus | tractavere nobis?*

283. **exspectate**: vocative, agreeing with *Hector*; the sense is somewhat predicative, cf. *Aen*. 12.947.

ut: with *aspicimus*, equivalent to 'how gladly', cf. *Aen*. 8.154 f.

287. **moratur**: 'heed', cf. *Aen*. 5.400.

289 f. Hector's speech justifies the flight of Aeneas from Troy,

which in certain traditions had been regarded as a coward's way out. He begins by giving precise instructions — Aeneas is to escape; and he follows with the reasons. First, Troy cannot be saved, all that could be done has been done; secondly, Aeneas has a destiny to fulfil in taking Troy's gods to a new home over the sea. Servius' comments stress that Hector shows Aeneas' flight to be *utile, necessarium* and *honestum*.

290. **alto a culmine**: 'from its topmost heights', the Greek κατ᾽ ἄκρης (*Il.* 13.772); cf. 603.

293. **penatis**: cf. *Aen.* 1.6 *inferretque deos Latio*, with the note there, and 3.148 f.

295. 'for them seek a city, which in the end you shall establish, a mighty city, when you have wandered over the ocean's width'; cf. *Aen.* 3.159 f. *Magna* belongs rather to the relative clause than to the main clause.

296–7. These are the *sacra* of 293; Vesta, the goddess of the hearth, is very closely linked with the Penates, cf. 5.744, 9.258 f. For the undying fire on her altar at Rome cf. Ov. *Fast.* 6.297.

298–317. *Aeneas awakes, climbs to the roof of his father's house, sees the scenes of destruction all around him and wildly prepares to rush to the battle.*

298. **diverso . . . luctu**: 'the city was a turmoil of grief everywhere'; Virgil is very fond of *misceri* to describe confusion, cf. 329, 487, 1.124, 12.445.

299–300. 'although the house of my father Anchises was in a remote part, set back and screened by trees'.

301. **ingruit**: 'advanced upon us', cf. *Aen.* 8.535.

303. **ascensu supero**: 'climbed on to', cf. *Aen.* 6.676.

304 f. The main point of the comparison in this brilliant simile is that Aeneas and the shepherd both helplessly watch and listen from a height while destruction is caused all round. The Homeric simile on which it is based (*Il.* 4.452 f.) compares a battle-scene with two rivers meeting, while a shepherd listens from the mountains; Virgil has taken the detail of the shepherd from Homer and made it central in his picture. For the comparison with both fire and flood cf. *Aen.* 12.521 f. and for flood cf. also 496 f., Hor. *Odes* 3.29.33 f., 4.14.25 f., Spenser, *F.Q.* 2.11.18.

307. **inscius**: 'bewildered', almost 'helpless'; it was a situation which he had not known before.

309. **fides**: 'the proof', cf. *Aen.* 3.375; or perhaps with bitter sarcasm 'the trustworthiness of the Greeks', i.e. their perfidy.

310. The Trojan Deiphobus, who had married Helen after the death of Paris, appears to Aeneas in the underworld (6.494 f.).

311. **Volcano**: the name of the fire-god is used by metonymy for fire, cf. Ceres, Bacchus, etc.

312. **Ucalegon**: a well-known example of metonymy for *domus Ucalegonis* (cf. Hor. *Sat.* 1.5.71–2); Horace (*Ep.* 1.18.84) alludes to this passage, and so does Juvenal (3.199). Ucalegon was one of Priam's friends (Hom. *Il.* 3.148).

Sigea ... relucent: Sigeum was a promontory near Troy, cf. *Aen.* 7.294. The phrase is imitated by Dryden, *Annus Mirabilis* 231 (of the Fire of London): 'A key of fire ran all along the shore, / And lighten'd all the river with the blaze.'

314 f. In these lines Aeneas shows the typical characteristics of the Homeric hero courting a brave death: thoughts of valour drive out *ratio*, and he is a victim of *furor* and *ira*. This wild and impetuous attitude is one he has to try to learn to conquer as he leaves the Homeric world and journeys towards a different way of life; but his success in conquering it is intermittent and imperfect.

315. **glomerare manum bello**: 'to mass together a group for fighting'. *Glomerare* is a favourite word with Virgil; for this sense cf. 9.792.

317. 'my thoughts were of the glory of death in battle'; *pulchrum (esse) mori in armis* is the subject of *succurrit* (=*subit*). For the thought cf. Hor. *Odes* 3.2.13 *dulce et decorum est pro patria mori*.

318–69. *Panthus, priest of Apollo, arrives at Anchises' house and tells him that the city is lost. With a few companions Aeneas goes into battle.*

318. **Panthus**: the word is contracted from Panthoos in the Greek style and has a long *u* in the nominative and in Virgil's vocative form *Panthu* (322). Servius tells the story of how Panthus, the son of Othryas, had been captured from Delphi, brought to Troy, and made priest of Apollo by Priam. He is mentioned in Hom. *Il.* 3.146.

319. **arcis Phoebique**: i.e. of the temple of Apollo on the citadel.

320–1. The verb *trahit* applies strictly only to the third of its objects; to the first two supply from it a verb like *portat*. *Sacra* are the emblems of which Hector had spoken; *deos* refers to images of the gods, especially of the Penates; cf. 293.

320. **parvumque nepotem**: we hear no more of Panthus' little grandchild. Austin's comment is excellent: 'he is a pathetic prolepsis, as it were, of Iulus'.

321. **limina**: i.e. Anchises' house, which Aeneas is just leaving.

322. **quo ... loco**: 'Where is the decisive battle?' For the meaning of *res summa* cf. Livy 23.49.8 *ibi rem summam agi cernentes*. Others take *quo ... loco* to be metaphorical — 'in what condition', (so Austin, comparing *Aen.* 9.723, Hor. *Epist.* 1.12.25); others again take *res summa* as equivalent to *respublica* ('how is our country?'), but this is very unlikely. Aeneas eagerly and rapidly asks which way to go to join the last stand; the slow and hopeless reply of Panthus is in very strong contrast.

quam ... arcem: 'what strongpoint are we holding'; *arx* is used in its widest sense, referring not specifically to the citadel, but to any point which could be held; *prendimus* is probably perfect, literally 'have we taken?'

324. The movement of the line reflects Panthus' hopelessness; the slow spondee filling the first foot, the sonorous adjective of inevitability *ineluctabile* (not found before Virgil, cf. *Aen.* 8.334), and the assonance of long *e*, combine to produce a memorable opening to Panthus' speech comparable with the splendid lines of Homer (*Il.* 6.448 f.) ἔσσεται ἧμαρ .... Macrobius (*Sat.* 5.1.9) quotes this passage as an example of *copiosissime dicere*, and continues *quis fons quis torrens quod mare tot fluctibus quot hic verbis inundavit*?

325. **fuimus**: 'have been', i.e. are no more; the perfect tense conveys that all is over. Cf. *Aen.* 7.413 *sed fortuna fuit*, Prop. 2.8.10 *altaque Troia fuit*. Dryden imitates the construction in *All for Love* (5.1.75 f.): 'O horror, horror! / Egypt has been; our latest hour is come!'

326-7. **omnia ... Argos transtulit**: 'has handed over everything we had to Argos', cf. Hor. *Odes* 3.29.51 (*Fortuna*) *transmutat incertos honores*. *Argos* is accusative plural of motion towards.

327-8. Notice the alliteration of pairs of words, adding to the emphasis which the words themselves have.

329. **incendia miscet**: 'hurls firebrands all around'; for *miscere* cf. 298.

330. insultans: 'mocking us'; the emphatic position of this word conveys the irony of the Trojans now suffering at the hands of the prisoner they had treated kindly.

bipatentibus: 'double' gates (cf. Enn. *Ann.* 61, *Aen.* 10.5), emphasising that both halves are flung wide open.

332. angusta viarum: cf. *strata viarum* (1.422, where see note), and line 725.

333. 'a steel line of flashing blades unsheathed stands ready to slaughter us'; for *acies* cf. *Aen.* 6.291. The ablative of description *mucrone corusco* acts almost as a compound adjective with *acies*; see Mackail's edition of the *Aeneid*, Appendix A.

336. numine divum: Panthus as the priest of Apollo expresses the will of all the gods, and Aeneas hearing that they intend the destruction of Troy rushes madly out to sell his life dearly (353–4).

337. Erinys: the Greek Fury (573, 7.447), the personification of the force leading to destruction.

341. adglomerant: the word is transitive, and *se* is to be supplied from 339, cf. *Aen.* 1.440.

Coroebus, son of Mygdon king of Phrygia, is first mentioned in Eur. *Rhes.* 539; Virgil has given him the part of Othryoneus in Homer *Il.* 13.363 f. who came late (*illis . . . diebus*) to Troy to help the Trojans in the hope of marrying Cassandra (246).

344. gener: 'would-be son-in-law', cf. *Ecl.* 8.18.

346. audierit: causal subjunctive. The incomplete line conveys most poignantly a sense of frustration and pathos, and would have been very difficult to complete effectively in revision, but it cannot be regarded as a deliberate device; see note on 1.534.

347. audere in proelia: a very unusual phrase, cf. Stat. *Th.* 1.439. Gronovius' conjecture *ardere* is attractive.

348. super: adverbial; his speech is intended to add to their existing enthusiasm, cf. 355 *furor additus*; compare *Aen.* 10.556, 11.685. With *his* supply *dictis*.

349–50. si vobis . . . sequi: 'if your enthusiasm to put all to the hazard is resolved to follow me'. Some MSS have *audentem* — 'if your enthusiasm is resolved to follow me as I put all to the hazard'. Neither is wholly satisfactory and the passage might well have been revised; the emendations carry little conviction.

351–2. excessere . . . di: cf. Tac. *Hist.* 5.13 (the siege of

Jerusalem) *audita maior humana vox, excedere deos*. See Austin ad loc. for the *evocatio deorum* at the destruction of a city.

353. **moriamur ... ruamus**: a famous example of the grammarians' hysteron proteron. Page rightly points out the inadequacy of this explanation; see also my note on *Aen.* 5.316 (Oxford edition). The more important verb is put first, and the impact of the sentence is 'Let us die, and let us do so by rushing into battle'. Notice the absence of strong caesurae, and the assonance of *a* and *r*.

354. The gnomic line (*sententia*) is of a kind not very common in Virgil, but frequent in Lucan and the Silver Age; cf. Stat. *Th.* 10.493 *est ubi dat vires nimius timor*.

355 f. Wolf similes occur several times in Homer; there are three others in the *Aeneid*, two of them applied to Turnus (9.59 f. 9.565 f., 11.809 f.). The effect here is to reinforce the concept of *furor*, and to suggest the wild and violent anger of the Trojans in this moment of the final destruction of their city.

355. **lupi ceu**: the unusual word order and line ending suggest the Homeric λύκοι ὡς.

356. **improba**: 'irresistible', cf. 80 with note, and 9.62.

359–60. **mediaeque ... iter**: 'the road through the centre of the city', possessive genitive, cf. *Aen.* 9.391 f.

360. **cava**: 'enfolding', cf. *Aen.* 1.516, 6.866.

363. The simplicity and finality of this line makes it one of the most memorable of the whole poem — 'in one sad night consum'd and throwen down' (Spenser, *F.Q.* 3.9.39). Austin compares Livy 1.29.6.

364. **inertia**: 'unmoving', i.e. lifeless, rather than 'helpless'.

365. **religiosa**: for the long first syllable see note on 151.

367. **quondam**: 'sometimes', cf. 416, 7.378.

369. **pavor**: for the lengthening of the final syllable (which in this case was long in early Latin) in arsis cf. 411, 563 and see note on 1.308.

Notice the rhythm of the paragraph ending (cf. 267), and for the phraseology cf. Tac. *Hist.* 3.28 *omni imagine mortium*.

370–401. *The Greek Androgeos mistakes the Trojans for Greeks; he and his followers are killed and the Trojans disguise themselves in Greek armour.*

371. **Androgeos**: the name of a Greek not otherwise known;

it was also the name of Minos' son (6.20). Notice the long final syllable (the Greek Attic second declension) and the Greek genitive *Androgeo* (392).

374. **rapiunt ... feruntque**: cf. the Greek phrase for plundering, ἄγειν καὶ φέρειν.

377. **sensit ... delapsus**: *sentio* with a participle (instead of accusative and infinitive) is an unparalleled imitation of the normal Greek construction after such verbs; Austin quotes Milton, *P.L.* 9.792 'and knew not eating death'. Instances such as *Geo.*2.510 *gaudent perfusi sanguine fratrum* (cited by commentators) are quite normal Latin.

379 f. The simile is an elaborate reworking of Hom. *Il.* 3.32 f. where Paris draws back from the battle like a man who has seen a snake. Virgil has characteristically varied and decorated his original, especially in adding a description of the snake (381).

379. **aspris**: a very rare syncope for *asperis*, cf. the common cases of *periclum*, *repostus*, etc.

380–1. Notice the sound-effects: the slowness of *nitens* ('treading on it') followed by the very rapid dactyls with trochaic caesurae, and the rhyme in the descriptive line which after the action of 380 focusses on the picture of the snake (for which cf. *Geo.* 3.421). *Attollentem iras* combines the ideas of rousing up its anger and lifting its angry head.

381. **colla**: Greek accusative of respect, see note on 1.320.

382. **abibat**: 'was trying to escape'. Servius says 'bene imperfecto usus est, non enim *abiit*'.

383. **densis ... armis**: 'and we surround him with our massed weapons'; *circumfundimur* is middle, or reflexive, cf. 401.

385. **aspirat**: 'smiles on'; the metaphor is from a favouring breeze, cf. *Aen.* 9.525, Ov. *Met.* 1.3.

390. The staccato phrasing (for *utrum dolus sit an virtus*) is in keeping with the rest of Coroebus' rapid words.

391. For postponed *deinde* cf. *Aen.* 1.195; compare *tum* in 5.382.

392. **Androgeo**: genitive, see note on 371.

clipeique ... decorum: 'the handsome device of his shield', i.e. his shield with its handsome device. *Insigne* is used as a noun, cf. *Aen.* 7.657 *insigne paternum*, Livy 29.25.11.

393. **induitur**: middle, see note on 275. Servius explains that the shield is 'put on' by inserting the hand through the straps; cf. 672.

394. **ipse**: the word is somewhat redundant, but the view reported by Servius that the passage should be punctuated so that *ipse = Aeneas* is quite impossible.

396. **haud numine nostro**: 'protected by gods not our own'; almost 'under false colours'.

398. **Orco**: for the dative cf. 85 and 5.691–2 *morti | . . . demitte.*

400–1. The concept of Greeks rushing back again into the wooden horse is most unconvincing; it is rare for Virgil to indulge in hyperbolical conceits of the kind beloved by many Silver Age writers.

402–52. *Coroebus sees Cassandra being dragged away into captivity and tries to save her; in the fighting which follows many of Aeneas' companions are killed. Aeneas with two friends finds himself near Priam's palace which is on the point of capture.*

402 f. This passage affords under close analysis an example of a relatively unrevised section of the poem; it contains some exceptionally fine writing and some imperfections that would doubtless have undergone revision. The pathos of the picture of Cassandra and the devotion of Coroebus (403–8) is superbly done, and so is the sad account of the deaths of Aeneas' comrades, especially Rhipeus and Panthus, followed by Aeneas' magnificent outburst of emotion (424–34). The linking passages are less successful: line 409 is repetitive of 383; the recognition of the disguised Trojans (413 f., 422 f.) is somewhat unclear in narration; the simile (416 f.) is of a conventional kind, made memorable only by its superb word-music. Lines 434–6 add detail which is less relevant than is usually the case; 436 is awkwardly expressed; the sentence in 438–41 is syntactically clumsy; the use of *has* in 450 is strange. The contrast with the high polish of the previous parts of this book serves to emphasize the extraordinary skill and uniform perfection which Virgil achieved in the workmanship of his fully revised work. This does not of course imply that the relatively unrevised parts of the poem (among which the second half of Book 2 is clearly to be counted) are inferior in their high poetic qualities; they do however lack the touch here and there which would have brought them up to the level of finish which the *Georgics* have and most of the *Aeneid* has — the quality of never nodding (*aequalitas*) which Quintilian praises (10.1.86).

402. 'Alas, nobody may put any trust in the gods when they are hostile', i.e. the gods have decided on the destruction of Troy, and so the success of Aeneas and his followers cannot last.

403 f. For the story of how Ajax son of Oileus violated the temple of Athena (226) by dragging off her priestess Cassandra see note on 1.41.

405–6. **lumina frustra, lumina**: for the use of repetition to achieve pathos (perhaps a specially Alexandrian feature of style) cf. *Aen.* 6.495–6 *lacerum crudeliter ora, | ora manusque ambas*, *Aen.* 10.821–2 *at vero ut vultum vidit morientis et ora, | ora modis Anchisiades pallentia miris*, *Aen.* 12.546–7 *domus alta sub Ida, | Lyrnesi domus alta, solo Laurente sepulcrum*. Austin quotes Milton, *Lycidas* 'But O the heavy change now thou art gone, | now thou art gone, and never must return'.

410. **delubri**: i.e. of Athena's temple.

411. **obruimur**: for the lengthening of the final syllable in arsis before the caesura see note on 369.

412. 'from (because of) the appearance of our armour and the confusion caused by our Greek plumes'.

413. 'Then the Greeks shouting in frustration and angry at the maiden's rescue . . .'; we may assume from this the initial success of Coroebus in rescuing Cassandra. For *gemitu* cf. *Aen.* 3.664; for *ereptae virginis* (objective genitive) cf. Livy 37.51.6 *ira provinciae ereptae*.

414–15. Ajax son of Oileus is here referred to; see note on 403 f. The mention of the Atridae, Menelaus and Agamemnon, is significant because Cassandra became Agamemnon's slave-girl. For *Dolopes* see note on 7.

416 f. The simile of winds meeting is based on Hom. *Il.* 9.4 f.; the passage is also reminiscent of the storm description in *Aen.* 1.82 f.

416. **rupto . . . turbine**: 'when a whirlwind breaks', cf. *Geo.* 3.428.

418–19. The alliteration of *s* is very heavy, and the post-ponement of the subject (Nereus) — cf. *Aen.* 7.464 f. — adds to the elaborate effect. Here the lesser sea-god has the attribute of Neptune's trident.

422. **primi**: this is difficult (because the Trojans have already been attacked, 413 f.), and has given rise to suggested trans-

positions (420–3 to follow 412) and even to acceptance of *P*'s reading *Priami*. It is best to take it to mean that these men were the first to be able to explain the confusion.

mentitaque tela: 'quae nos Graecos esse mentiebantur' (Servius).

423. **ora ... signant**: 'they observe that our speech sounds different'; the epic convention in Virgil as in Homer (a necessary one) is that the Trojans and the Greeks speak the same language, but in a situation like this the more realistic idea of different languages is an easily acceptable inconsistency. For *signant = discernunt* cf. perhaps *Aen.* 5.317.

424. **ilicet**: 'instantly', cf. 758.

425. Athena is often called *armipotens*; cf. *Aen.* 11.483.

428. **dis aliter visum**: this is a Stoic formula, here used very elliptically — you might have thought he would therefore have been spared, but the gods willed otherwise; cf. Sen. *Ep. Mor.* 98.4–5 where the good Stoic is urged to say when disaster befalls *dis aliter visum est*, or better still *di melius*. For Virgil the Stoic formula left the problem unanswered.

429 f. The pathos builds up in this little cameo; the apostrophe to Panthus emphasises it, and the claims he had on the favour of heaven; the alliteration of *p* and the present participle (bringing the actuality of the scene to the reader) add to the effect. Cf. *Aen.* 9.327–8. Thus the emotional pitch is raised in readiness for Aeneas' outburst as he invokes his burning city, again emphasised and made memorable by alliteration (of *c, m, v, f, m*), especially in the strange phrase *flamma extrema meorum* ('the final fire that engulfed my people'). The word *occasus* (several times used by Cicero in this sense, cf. also *Aen.* 1.238) carries powerful emotional overtones.

433. **vitavisse vices Danaum**: for the omission of the subject *me* cf. *Aen.* 6.352. *Vices Danaum* should be taken together 'hazards from the Greeks', vicissitudes of battle; it is a powerful and unexpected phrase made easier by the preceding *tela*. It is most unlikely that *Danaum* should be taken with *manu*, as in the punctuation of Mynors, Hirtzel and others.

436. **et**: the meaning, awkwardly expressed, is that Iphitus was disabled by old age and Pelias also disabled, by a wound from Ulysses.

438 f. This is a jerky sentence with *sic* breaking the run of the syntax; the passage from 434–51 lacks its *ultima manus* (see note on 402 f.).

439. **nulli**: rare in the plural, cf. *Geo.* 2.10.

441. **obsessumque ... limen**: 'the entrance to the palace besieged by a tortoise formation'; *testudo* refers probably to the cover of shields held over the head rather than the siege-engine later developed and given this name; cf. *Aen.* 9.505.

442 f. The arrangement of the scenes of battle is chiastic: the Greeks attack the gates (441), and others climb the walls (442–4); the Trojans defend the walls (445–9) and the gates (449–50).

442. **parietibus**: the first syllable is lengthened by the treatment of the following *i* as a *j*; see note on 16.

443. **ad tela**: most MSS have *ac tela*, but *ad* was preferred by Servius ('id est, contra tela'), and *clipeosque ac tela* are an odd pair for *sinistris*.

445. **tota**: most MSS have *tecta*, but this would be a feeble adjective for *culmina*.

448. **decora alta**: cf. *Aen.* 1.429. Some MSS have *illa* (cf. 503), but *alta* is better with *devolvunt*; cf. also Stat. *Th.* 5.424.

451. **instaurati animi**: 'my courage revived'; the following infinitives are after the idea of desire (*rursus ardebam*) conveyed by the phrase.

453–505. Aeneas gets on to the roof of Priam's palace by means of a back entrance, and joins in dislodging a tower on to the besiegers. But they still come on, and Pyrrhus breaches the gates; the Greeks pour into the palace and massacre the Trojans.

453–505. Here the narrative moves to a high pitch of horror, preparatory to the climax in the death of Priam. Domestic touches are interwoven in the military narrative (455 f., 483 f., 489 f., 501 f.), and the picture of Pyrrhus in his insolent power is drawn in the most compelling colours (469 f., 479 f., especially 491 f. *instat vi patria Pyrrhus*, 499 f. *furentem caede Neoptolemum*). By arranging his narrative so that Aeneas climbs to the roof to join the defenders Virgil is able to make Aeneas' eye-witness narrative of the horror within (of which he was a helpless spectator) particularly graphic and detailed.

453–5. 'There was an entrance, a hidden gate and a through

passage linking the parts of Priam's palace together, a remote doorway in the rear. . .'. For *usus* Servius says *verbum iuris* (i.e. right-of-way); Currie compares (*G. and R.* 1959, p. 165) 'Crooked Usage', a street in Chelsea. For the doorway in the rear cf. Hom. *Od.* 22.126 f., Hor. *Epist.* 1.5.31 *atria servantem postico falle clientem.* Evidently Hector and Andromache lived in a part of Priam's palace, and Andromache could make her way privately from the women's quarters by this postern gate and passage from Hector's part into Priam's.

457. **ad soceros**: 'to her parents-in-law', i.e. Priam and Hecuba; cf. Ov. *Met.* 3.132 *soceri tibi Marsque Venusque.*

Astyanacta: Greek accusative. The farewell scene between Hector and his wife and son in Hom. *Il.* 6.402 f. is well-known; Hector called his son Scamandrius, but everyone else called him Astyanax, prince of the city; cf. *Aen.* 3.482 f. Virgil does not refer to his fate at the sack of Troy (he was hurled from the walls to his death), but the reader's knowledge of it adds to the pathos of this passage.

458. **evado**: the transition is rather abrupt; Servius says rightly *hac evado*, i.e. Aeneas gets to the roof by means of the back entrance and an inner stairway.

460 f. Notice the long separation of the accusative *turrim* from its verbs *adgressi, convellimus, impulimusque*; it is interesting that Servius found it necessary to tell his readers 'et est ordo: turrim convellimus'.

461. **videri**: supply *solita est*; the tower was a regularly used observation point.

463-4. **qua . . . dabant**: 'where the top stories offered joints that would give way'; i.e. at the point where the tower joined the walls from which it rose. Cf. Juv. 10.105 f.

465. Notice the imitative rhythm: the dactylic feet, the elision at the caesura, the absence of any further masculine caesura, the trochaic breaks in fourth and fifth foot (cf. 380). The effect continues in the following dactylic line, and the 'run-on' verb *incidit*.

469. Pyrrhus (also called Neoptolemus, cf. 263) was the son of Achilles; his name means in Greek 'red-haired', and the following line, with its description of light and glitter, hints at the etymology. The end of his story is mentioned in *Aen.* 3.295 f.

470. exsultat: 'prances'; Virgil's choice of word perhaps causes an association with the form of dance known as the Pyrrhic (Eur. *Andr.* 1135 f., Plato *Laws* 815a, Pliny *N.H.* 7.204).

telis . . . aëna: 'fiery in his flashing bronze armour'; cf. Hom. *Il.* 13.341, and cf. Tennyson's phrases in *The Princess* (5.39) 'sheathing splendours and the golden scale / of harness, issued in the sun'.

471 f. Virgil's simile is based essentially on the idea of shimmering light — note the emphatic position of *in lucem* — coming from the scales of the snake with its old slough (*exuviae*) cast off, but he has added to it the notion of the sinister danger which Pyrrhus presents; observe the Homeric phrase *mala gramina pastus* (βεβρωκὼς κακὰ φάρμακ', *Il.* 22.94) and the description of the snake's fangs (475). Perhaps too we may connect the renewed snake (*novus*) with the renewal of Achilles in Neoptolemus (which in Greek means 'new war'). Spenser imitates the simile (*F.Q.* 4.3.23):

> So fresh he seemed and so fierce in sight;
> Like as a Snake, whom wearie winters teene
> Hath worne to nought, now feeling sommers might,
> Casts off his ragged skin and freshly doth him dight.

Lines 473 and 475 are from *Geo.* 3.437 and 439; line 474 from *Geo.* 3.426; for other snake descriptions see on 209–11, and for an excellent account of snake imagery in Book 2 see B. M. W. Knox, *A.J.P.* 1950, pp. 379 f.

471. **mala gramina pastus**: 'that has fed on evil plants'; for the accusative cf. *Geo.* 3.314, 4.181.

476–7. Periphas is an obscure name taken from Homer (*Il.* 5.842); Automedon, the charioteer of Achilles, now armour-bearer to his son, is frequently referred to. Pyrrhus was born to Achilles and Deidamia while Achilles was in the island of Scyros — hence *Scyria pubes*.

481–2. The previous lines had described Pyrrhus' general assault on the gates, as he tried to break through them with an axe and to tear the posts from their sockets (which is achieved in 492–3); now specifically we hear that he made a hole in the gates by knocking out one of the planks, making a wide gaping (*lato ore*) opening in them.

483-4. The rhythm of line 483 is haunting, with its absence of main caesura in third or fourth foot (cf. 12.619): the repetition *apparet, apparent* at the beginning of both lines and both sentences draws the attention arrestingly to this repugnant military profanation of the domestic scene.

485. **armatosque vident**: this is generally taken to mean 'they (the Greeks) see armed men', i.e. the Trojans inside on guard (449, 492); but the imagery of the previous lines requires that the subject of *vident* should be the Trojans inside, Priam and those around him.

486 f. Servius says this passage is based on the destruction of Alba Longa (i.e. in Ennius: cf. also Livy 1.29).

486-7. **gemitu ... miscetur**: 'is in an uproar of groans and pitiful confusion'; for *miscetur* see note on 298.

487-8. **penitusque ... ululant**: 'and throughout their length and breadth the echoing halls are shrill with the cries of women'; *cavae* ('hollow') helps to produce the effect of the noise, cf. 53. For *ululant* cf. *Aen.* 4.667 f., a similar passage describing the scene in Dido's palace when her death was discovered.

488. **aurea**: notice the contrast between the beauty of the stars in the heavens and the horror of the earthly scene.

491. **vi patria**: cf. *Aen.* 3.326 *stirpis Achilleae fastus*; Pyrrhus has the violence and arrogance of his father Achilles.

492. **ariete**: for the scansion see note on 16.

493. **emoti ... postes**: 'the gates, wrenched from their sockets, fall flat'; see Page's note ad loc. for a full account of how these *postes* (part of the gates) were attached by pivots to the *limen* and to the lintel.

494. **rumpunt**: 'force', cf. *Aen.* 10.372 f. *ferro rumpenda per hostis | est via*.

496 f. The simile is based on Hom. *Il.* 5.87 f.; see also note on 304 f. The idea of *reckless* destruction is made dominant by the repetition in the narrative (*furentem*, 499) of *furens* in the simile (498).

498. **cumulo**: cf. *Aen.* 1.105.

499-501. The repetition (*vidi ipse ... vidi*) strengthens the pathos and the antithesis between the attackers (Pyrrhus, Menelaus, Agamemnon) and the victims (Hecuba, Priam); cf. Enn. *Scen.* 94 f. (referred to on 241 f.) *vidi ego te adstantem ope barbarica....*

501. **centumque nurus**: i.e. fifty daughters and fifty

daughters-in-law (503; cf. *Il.* 6.243 f., 24.495 f. for Priam's fifty sons). *Nurus* is frequent in Ovid to mean young women generally, e.g. *Met.* 3.529.

504. **barbarico . . . auro**: i.e. Eastern gold, cf. *Aen.* 8.685 and the passage from Ennius quoted on 499–501.

506–58. *Aeneas tells the story of the death of Priam. The old king had put on his armour and was on his way to meet death at the hands of the enemy when Hecuba prevailed on him to seek sanctuary with her and her daughters at the altar. One of his sons, Polites, had been wounded by Pyrrhus and came running, pursued by Pyrrhus, to the altar, where he fell dead before his father's eyes. Priam's angry outburst is answered by a sword-thrust, and the old king of Troy lies dead.*

506 f. Here the contrast between the violent insolence of the young invader Pyrrhus and the helpless old king and his family is intense and horrifying. The pathos of the domestic scene between Priam and Hecuba is followed by the appearance of Pyrrhus exulting in bloodshed (*ardens insequitur*); the outraged protest of Priam is answered in coldly insolent and sarcastic phrases and Pyrrhus' arrogant *nunc morere* is promptly and heartlessly fulfilled. The passage ends by transferring the perspective from the immediate and particularised bloodshed to the long vista of history, where Priam is no longer a brave helpless old man but the symbol of Troy's dead past, the nameless headless corpse who once had been king of Asia's proudest city.

For discussion of the various versions from which Virgil has built his picture of Priam's death see note on 554 f.

506. After the finality of the previous line, in which the hopelessness of total disaster is conveyed, Aeneas resumes to tell the story of Priam's death with a line of poignant simplicity, quite without the elaboration of sorrow with which he introduced his story at the beginning of the book.

509 f. 'he vainly put on those shoulders unsteady with age the armour which in his late years had long been unused, and he fastened round him the sword which he could no longer manage, and moved towards the thick of the enemy to meet death'.

511. **cingitur**: used in a middle sense, see notes on 218–19 and 275, and cf. *Aen.* 4.493.

513 f. The altar to Zeus Herceus (Hom. *Il.* 24.306, Eur. *Tro.*

483, Sen. *Ag.* 448), in the centre of the open courtyard, is here given a Roman aspect by the mention of the Penates.

516. For the simile cf. Eur. *Andr.* 1140 f. *Praecipites* is elliptical — 'driven headlong'.

520. **aut**: this usage, found often in Plautus, merely introduces another question not necessarily alternative to the first; cf. 595 and *Geo.* 4.324.

521-2. Probably Hecuba means that the situation does not permit of armed resistance (*defensoribus = telis*) and would not even if Hector were alive; possibly however Servius is right in thinking that the second sentence is left incomplete with an ellipse of words like *Troiam servare posset*.

526. Polites, Priam's son, is mentioned several times in Homer, e.g. *Il.* 2.791.

528. **vacua atria**: Polites runs across a part of the palace not yet filled by men fighting.

529. **infesto vulnere**: 'with weapon poised to kill'; cf. *Aen.* 7.533 for *vulnus* in the sense of *telum vulniferum*.

530. Notice the vehement rhythm of the two pyrrhic verbs *tenet, premit*, the second causing a conflict of accent with ictus in the fifth foot. The paratactic construction is typically Virgilian: 'is on the point of catching him as he presses close upon him with his spear'. For *iam iamque* cf. *Aen.* 12.754.

536 f. For the *pietas* of the gods cf. *Aen.* 4.382, 5.688 f.

538-9. 'who made me see my son's death with my own eyes'; *coram* is adverbial. For *facere* with the infinitive cf. Enn. *Ann.* 452 and Lucr. 3.301.

540. **satum quo te mentiris**: 'whose son you lyingly claim to be', because you show none of his better qualities. Homer tells in *Iliad* 24 the story of how Priam visited Achilles in his tent to plead for the return of Hector's body; Achilles granted the request and Priam returned safely back to Troy.

541-2. **iura ... erubuit**: 'he had respect for the rights of a suppliant's trust'; the use of *erubesco* with a direct object (= *erubescendo servavit*) is very striking; cf. Prop. 3.14.20 *fratres erubuisse deos* and compare *palleo* in Hor. *Odes* 3.27.27 f. *pontum mediasque fraudes | palluit audax*.

544. **fatus**: supply *est*, as with *repulsum* in the next line; the effect is rapid and staccato.

544. **sine ictu**: without power to penetrate.

546. **summo ... umbone**: 'from the surface of the shield's boss'; the very end of the spear just pierces the outside of the shield sufficiently to hang there by its point.

547–8. 'So then you shall report this and go to tell the tale to my father Pelides', i.e. in the underworld; for *Pelides* see note on 263.

549. Pyrrhus refers ironically to lines 540–1. *Memento* is sarcastic: 'be sure you don't forget to tell him that Neoptolemus disgraces his father's name'.

550. **trementem**: 'non formidine sed aetate' (Servius).

552–3. **coruscum ... ensem**: emphasis is put on the flash of the sword through the division of adjective and noun by the two verbs; cf. 470 f.

553. **lateri**: *in latus*; the dative with *abdere* (the ablative is much more usual) depicts the moment of striking.

capulo tenus: for the preposition *tenus* following the ablative which it governs (its normal construction) cf. *hactenus, quatenus,* and *Aen.* 3.427.

554 f. The tradition of the murder of Priam by Pyrrhus is not mentioned in Homer when Odysseus tells Achilles of his son's exploits (*Od.* 11.505 f.). It was in cyclic epic, and occurs in Euripides (*Hec.* 23 f., *Tro.* 16 f., 481 f.) and vases depict Pyrrhus killing Priam at the altars. The different version, according to which Pyrrhus killed him at Achilles' tomb on the shore, is referred to in 557; Servius quotes Pacuvius for this version, and suggests that Virgil uses it to allude to the death of Pompey, murdered on the shore of Egypt (Lucan 8.667 f.). Certainly no Roman could read lines 557–8 without thinking of Pompey; and equally certainly Virgil has achieved by his strange conflation of two contrasting versions an astonishing effect of lasting desolation succeeding the immediate horror of destruction.

554–5. Some modern editors punctuate after *Priami*, so that *fatorum* goes with *sorte*, but this is very abrupt, and *sorte* can stand by itself meaning 'by the decree of fate', cf. *Aen.* 10.501.

556–7. **tot ... Asiae**: 'once the proud ruler of Asia, proud indeed with all those countless peoples and lands'; cf. 363 and Spenser *F.Q.* 3.9.39 'and of all Asie bore the soveraigne crowne'. *Regnatorem* is perhaps best taken in apposition to *illum*

(Priam), though it is possible to take it with *Pergama*.

557–8. The final picture is one of awful desolation; as his city burns to ashes the proud ruler becomes a mutilated nameless corpse. Cf. Shelley's *Ozymandias*: 'Nothing beside remains. Round the decay / of that colossal wreck, boundless and bare / the lone and level sands stretch far away'.

559–66. *The death of Priam makes Aeneas think of his own family; he looks round for support, but is alone.*

559–66. This short passage marks the transition from the middle section of the book (the destruction of Troy culminating in the death of Priam) to the final section which is concerned with Aeneas' own family. The tale of public disaster changes to the tale of private concern.

559. **tum primum**: the shock of realisation which comes to Aeneas now for the first time is that the disaster not only affects him in a military capacity, but also involves the safety and lives of his family, his father Anchises (the same age as Priam), his wife Creusa, and their little son Iulus.

562–3. 'there came to my mind the thought of Creusa left alone, my house plundered, the fate of little Iulus'.

562. For the different forms of the legend about Aeneas' wife (whose name was Eurydice in the earlier versions) see note on 730 f.

563. **domus**: the final syllable is lengthened in arsis, see note on 369.

564. 'I turned my head and looked round to see what support was at hand', i.e. on the walls, helping the defence. He finds none — they have all jumped off or been engulfed in the flames.

567–87. *Aeneas catches sight of Helen hiding at the temple of Vesta; fury blazes up in him and he thinks of avenging his burning city by killing her.*

567 f. This passage (567–87 and the transitional line 588) is not given by the major manuscripts of Virgil and survives because it is quoted in Servius' commentary. Servius says that it was a passage written by Virgil but removed by the editors of the *Aeneid*, Varius and Tucca. Its authenticity has long been disputed, but it is highly likely that the passage is Virgilian (see Austin's

commentary pp. 217 f.) and it is equally clear that Virgil was
not satisfied with it (which may well have been apparent,
perhaps through indications in the margins of the manuscript,
to the editors who deleted it). There are difficulties in the
language (especially 584 f.) and the account of Helen's fear (571 f.)
contradicts the story of how she was in league with the Greeks in
6.515 f.

What is particularly interesting is that Virgil's concept of the
character of Aeneas, of the frenzied despair to which he had
given way, was such that he could present his hero thus. Even in
the second half of the poem, after Aeneas has learned much about
how to restrain impetuous emotions, we often find him (especially
in Book 10 and at the end of 12) yielding to moods of violence.
It is possible that Virgil deleted the passage because he could not
on second thoughts allow his hero to speak of killing a woman;
but his first thoughts had allowed it, and should remind us that
the efforts of Aeneas in the poem to control violence in himself
and others meet with only very imperfect success. Aeneas is a
man of violence who tries hard to learn a better way.

567–9. **super unus eram cum ... aspicio**: 'I was the only
one left when suddenly I saw'; *super eram* is separated by tmesis,
cf. *Ecl.* 6.6. The transition is a little abrupt, the sense being 'I had
just realised I was alone when . . .'

569. **Tyndarida**: Greek accusative, 'daughter of Tyndareus',
i.e. Helen.

570. **erranti**: sc. *mihi* — presumably Aeneas is looking for the
best way of getting through to Anchises' house.

573. **communis Erinys**: a fine phrase: Helen is the personification of destruction (Aesch. *Agam.* 689 f., 749) both for Greece
and Troy. Lucàn imitates the phrase in 10.59 (of Cleopatra)
Latii feralis Erinys. On the possible contradiction with the passage
in Book 6 where Helen seems to be on good terms with the
Greeks see on 567 f. For *Erinys* see note on 337.

575–6. **subit ira ... ulcisci**: for the poetic use of the infinitive
cf. *Aen.* 9.757 and see note on 1.704.

576. **sceleratas sumere poenas**: a much disputed phrase,
but it probably should be understood in the sense which it
naturally bears, namely 'to exact a punishment wicked to
inflict'. It would be a strange Virgilian experiment in language

if we had to extract the meaning 'punishment for her crime'; 'criminal punishment' means something quite different from 'punishment for crime'. Aeneas as he tells his story realises now that to have killed a woman at an altar would have been *sceleratum*. But he goes on to describe (585–6) how his blind anger had made the deed seem at the time a praiseworthy act.

577. **Spartam ... Mycenas**: Sparta was the home of her husband Menelaus, Mycenae is a generalised term for Greece (cf. 1.650).

579. **patris**: the MSS of Servius read *patres*, which requires the sense of *parentes* (cf. 457), but the rhythm of the line is against this.

natosque: Helen had a daughter Hermione and (according to some) a son Nicostratus — but the phrase may be very general.

581–2. The future perfects in the rhetorical questions convey the idea 'all this has been so, and shall I do nothing about it?'; cf. *Aen.* 4.591.

584–7. The text here is uncertain in the highest degree, clearly because the passage was unfinished.

584. **nec habet**: this is an emendation for *habet haec*, which can hardly stand because of *tamen*; cf. Eur. *Orest.* 1133 (Pylades on the idea of murdering Helen) δυσκλεὴς ἂν ἦν φόνος, and *Aen.* 11.790 f. See Austin's discussion of the difficulties in his notes ad loc. and his article in *C.Q.* 1961, 185 f.

585. **nefas**: the abstract word is used meaning *nefariam feminam*, like *coniugium* for *coniugem* in 579; cf. Stat. *Th.* 7.514.

merentis: accusative plural with *poenas* rather than genitive singular; see note on 576. It is a very strange phrase and *merenti*, read by one MS, may be right.

587. **ultricis flammae**: 'the fire of vengeance'; *flammae* is a late correction of the senseless *famam* or *famae* of the MSS. It gives a strange phrase and an unparalleled genitive after *explesse*, and it must be said that the text here cannot be established with anything approaching certainty.

588–623. *Venus appears to Aeneas and rebukes him, telling him to think instead of the safety of his family. She reveals to him the giant shapes of gods and goddesses working the destruction of Troy.*

588 f. The supernatural vision which Venus allows Aeneas to see is one of the finest passages in the poem, and gives the fullest

scope for Virgil's imaginative and pictorial powers. All through the *Aeneid* Virgil is fascinated by the possibilities of describing poetically the visual aspect of an imagined world beyond human sight, and this is perhaps the most brilliant, most majestic and most awe-inspiring of all his 'gleams of a remoter world'.

588. iactabam: 'I was wildly saying', cf. *Aen.* 1.102.

589 f. Observe how the inverted *cum* clause, which itself compels the attention upon sudden action, is given special power by the postponement of the subject *alma parens* to the very end.

591. confessa deam: 'revealing her divinity'; cf. the description of Venus in 1.405 *et vera incessu patuit dea*, and for the abstract meaning of *deam* cf. Ov. *Met.* 12.601 *fassusque deum*. Mackail quotes Dryden's 'assumes the god'.

591–2. qualisque . . . solet: 'in appearance and stature the same as she is when the gods see her'; except when disguised as mortals the gods were thought of as larger than humans.

594–5. Venus uses phrases (*indomitae irae, quid furis*) which relate Aeneas' wild and violent reactions towards Helen to the forces of passion and frenzy which he so often encounters in others throughout the poem.

595. quonam . . . recessit: 'wherever has your love for us gone?' By *nostri* Venus means the family.

597. superet coniunxne: for postponed *-ne*, which is rare, cf. Hor. *Epist.* 2.2.65; for *superare* meaning survive cf. 643.

598. quos omnis: governed by *circum* in the next line.

599–600. 'if my care were not preventing it, the flames would already have taken them off and the enemy sword drunk their blood'; the condition is made more vivid by the use of primary tenses as in 6.292 f. For *tulerint = abstulerint* cf. 555; for *haurire* in this sense cf. *Aen.* 10.314.

601 f. The construction is: it is not the beauty of Helen, nor the wickedness of Paris, *but* the merciless gods who are responsible for the destruction. For the thought cf. Hom. *Il.* 3.164.

601. tibi: 'I tell you', ethic dative, cf. *Aen.* 1.258.

Tyndaridis . . . Lacaenae: Helen of Sparta, see note on 569, and cf. *Aen.* 6.511.

602. culpatusve: 'wicked', a usage of the word not found before Virgil; cf. Stat. *Ach.* 1.23 (Paris) *culpatum relegebat iter.*

divum ... divum: Venus' indignation finds expression in the repetition of the responsible agents, Juno in particular with Jupiter acquiescing.

604–6. 'Look — for I will remove all the cloud which now veils your vision and dims your mortal sight, misty and dark all around you.' The idea is based on Hom. *Il.* 5.127 where Athena speaks in similar tones to Diomedes; Virgil has elaborated it into a majestic and preternatural vision of giant powers at work.

610. **Neptunus**: here in his capacity as Poseidon the Earth-shaker (*'Ενοσίχθων*); his hostility was due to his having been cheated by Laomedon of his promised reward when he and Apollo had built the walls of Troy (hence *Neptunia Troia*, 625); cf. *Aen.* 5.810–11.

612. **Juno**: her hostility to Troy (which dogs the Trojan exiles throughout) was explained at the beginning of the poem (see note on 1.1 f.); it was due to her love for Carthage (which the Trojan-Romans would destroy), her anger at the judgment of Paris against her, and the favour of Jupiter for the Trojan Ganymede.

Scaeas: the most famous gates of Troy, said to be so called because they were on the west, i.e. the left hand side (*σκαιός*) looking north; cf. *Aen.* 3.351. Thus they faced the Greek camp.

615. **Tritonia ... Pallas**: see note on 171. As the chief goddess of the Greeks she is naturally to be found in the forefront of the destruction of Troy, in spite of having a temple on the citadel there (165 f.).

616. **nimbo ... saeva**: 'flashing out from a storm-cloud, a terrifying figure with her Gorgon-shield'; against the back-drop of darkness appears the terrible radiance of Athena. Servius took *nimbus* to mean the divine halo which surrounds goddesses, but Henry demolished this unnatural meaning for *nimbus*. Servius also mentions the reading *limbus* ('radiant with her bordered robe', cf. *Aen.* 4.137); but this metonymy is most unnatural. It is possible to take *saeva* as ablative, but this gives less good balance. Athena's shield bore the head of the Gorgon Medusa, decapitated by Perseus; cf. *Aen.* 8.437–8.

619. **eripe ... fugam**: Servius paraphrases *eripe* with *accelera*, *raptim fac*. Venus here echoes Hector's instructions in 289, where see note.

622–3. 'There appear before me terrible shapes, and the mighty

powers of divinities hostile to Troy': the half-line (see note on
1.534), with its sonorous assonance, is majestic and awe-inspiring.

624–633. *Aeneas now realises that Troy's hour of destruction has
come, like the final fall of a tree beneath the woodman's axe. He makes
his way home.*

626 f. The simile is based on Hom. *Il.* 4.482 f. (cf. Ap. Rh.
4.1682 f.). It is admirably imitated by Spenser, *F.Q.* 1.8.22

> as an aged tree,
> High growing on the top of rocky clift,
> Whose hartstrings with keene steele nigh hewen be,
> The mightie trunck halfe rent, with ragged rift
> Doth roll adowne the rocks, and fall with fearefull drift.

The points of comparison in Virgil's simile are (i) the ash, like
Troy, is old; (ii) like Troy it is mighty; (iii) like Troy it has
resisted for some time. The effect of the simile is tremendous: it
marks the actual moment of Troy's destruction and it gives a
certain distance and inevitability to the events which until now
Aeneas could not accept. He has felt till now that he ought to
have been able to prevent the chopping down of the tree of Troy:
now he sees it as a *fait accompli*.

626. **ac veluti**: 'and it was as when', cf. *Aen.* 4.402 f., 6.707 f.,
for this elliptical way of introducing a simile.

627–9. 'when it has been hacked at with the steel of blow after
blow of the axes and the farmers eagerly vie with each other to
bring it down; it looks like falling all the time and as its leafy
boughs shiver, and its lofty top is shaken, it sways to and fro'.
Notice the personification (not unusual with trees and frequent
in the *Georgics*) of *coma* and *vertex*, *vulneribus* and *congemuit*. *Comam*
is retained accusative, see note on 210.

630. **supremum**: adverbial accusative, cf. 693, 3.68.

631. **traxitque ... ruinam**: 'torn away from the hill top
crashed to the ground all its length', cf. Cat. 64.105 f., Ov. *Met.*
8.776. For *trahere ruinam* cf. 465–6, 8.192. There is no need to feel
difficulty over *avulsa* applied to a tree cut down: the image is of
a great mass torn out of its surroundings.

632. Notice the sudden quiet tone after the finality of Troy's
fall, emphasised by the alliteration of *d*. Much has been written

about the uncertainty of Aeneas' movements in this passage—most readers will have assumed that before now he had come down from the roof. This line would fit well after 566, and it is quite clear that 567–631 had not been finally dovetailed into the sequence of the narrative.

deo: some MSS read *dea*, but Servius and Macrobius support *deo*; the concept of divinity may be masculine even when applied to a goddess, as with the Greek θεός.

634–670. *Aeneas reaches home, but Anchises refuses to leave. Aeneas in despair prepares to court death again by rushing out against the Greeks.*

634 f. The first appearance of Anchises in the poem shows a helpless old man whose useful years are long past (647); as yet he knows nothing of the future destiny of his son, and the transformation in him when the divine intention is revealed by the signs from heaven is very remarkable indeed. From the useless old man he is transfigured into the intrepid companion and counsellor of Aeneas; he plays a very dominant role in *Aeneid* 3 (see note on 3.1 f.). Aeneas' filial devotion to him is shown very plainly in this passage (cf. *primum . . . primum*, 636, and lines 657–8).

At this setback to his plans for escape Aeneas lapses again into the wild frenzy and despair which have already been so marked a feature of his character in this book. He longs for death (655); he is ready to make the ultimate heroic gesture of throwing his life away (668–70). He has not yet recognised that his destiny imposes upon him the obligation of survival.

637. **abnegat . . . producere**: for the construction cf. *Geo.* 3.456, *Aen.* 4.428.

638. **integer aevi**: genitive of respect, see note on 1.14 and compare 5.73 *aevi maturus*. Cf. Enn. *Scen.* 414 *deos aevi integros*.

640. **agitate fugam**: Servius is probably right in saying that the meaning is 'consider'; others take it as equivalent to *agite* ('take flight').

642–3. 'it is enough and more than enough that I have seen one destruction and survived my city when it was captured'; Anchises refers to the sack of Troy by Hercules when Laomedon cheated him of the promise of his famous horses; cf. *Aen.* 8.290 f.

Excidia is a poetic plural, which accounts for the rare use of *una* in the plural.

644. 'Speak to me your last words as I now am, as I now am composed as if in death, and depart'; Anchises adopts an attitude as if already dead and asks for the final valediction customary at death (cf. *Aen.* 9.483 f.).

645. **ipse manu mortem inveniam**: 'I myself will find death by my own acts'; i.e. by rushing upon the enemy. Some MSS have *manum morti*, 'a hand to kill me', but the wide meaning of the ablative *manu* to reinforce *ipse* is very much in Virgil's style; cf. 3.372, 5.499.

646. **facilis iactura sepulcri**: this is, as it is meant to be, a very startling sentiment in view of the importance attached in the ancient world to burial. Anchises minimises a situation which Aeneas could not possibly accept: he tries to convince his son that when the last farewells have been duly spoken all will be well.

648. **divum . . . rex**: a reminiscence of Ennius, cf. *Aen.* 1.65.

649. The story was that Anchises boasted of Venus' love for him, for which Jupiter resolved to punish him with a thunderbolt; Venus however diverted it so that he was scorched but not killed.

651. **effusi lacrimis**: a bold and exciting phrase; instead of 'we shed floods of tears' Virgil says 'we were flooded in tears', i.e. we dissolved into tears; the *ne* clause depends on the idea of fear or prayer in this phrase.

coniunxque Creusa: *-que* means 'both'; the nouns are all in partial apposition to *nos*.

653. **fatoque urgenti incumbere**: 'add his weight to the burden of our fate', cf. Livy 3.16.5.

654. **inceptoque . . . isdem**: 'he stayed firm in his intention and in the palace where he was', a slight zeugma.

655. Notice the fierce alliteration of *r* in this frenzied decision of Aeneas.

660. **hoc**: the neuter singular has a long syllable (though the vowel is short) because of its origin *hod-ce*; cf. 664, 703.

663. Observe the rare variation in metrical treatment within the same line of *pătris, pătrem*; cf. Hor. *Odes* 1.32.11.

664. **hoc erat . . . quod**: 'was this why', literally 'that you are saving me was (for) this, was it, that I should see. . . . ?' *Hoc* is the

predicate to the *quod* clause, and is explained by the *ut* clause. For the idiomatic use of *erat* cf. *Aen.* 7.128.

669. **sinite ... revisam**: the jussive subjunctive is used in parataxis with *sino*, which in prose takes the accusative and infinitive; cf. *Aen.* 5.163, 717.

670. **numquam**: rather colloquial, cf. *Ecl.* 3.49 *numquam hodie effugies*.

671–729. *As Creusa begs Aeneas not to leave them, a tongue of fire suddenly plays around Iulus' head. Anchises asks for confirmation of the omen, and following thunder on the left a shooting star is seen. Anchises now declares himself ready to leave and Aeneas sets forth carrying his father on his shoulders and leading his little son by the hand; Creusa follows behind.*

671 f. The transformation of Anchises from dejection to joy after the divine signs is total and immediate (see note on 634 f.); similarly Aeneas is transformed from the frenzied warrior to the man of destiny. The transformation is symbolised in the last four lines of the passage: previously he had known no fear as he felt in his despair that he had nothing to lose, but now — as he tries to lead his family and his people out to safety — every breeze and every sound terrifies him.

The tableau of departure — Anchises on Aeneas' shoulder, little Iulus holding his hand, Creusa following behind — was already well-known in art long before Virgil, and after him continued to be illustrated constantly in sculpture, painting, illuminated manuscripts and on coins (see Austin's note on 708 for some references).

676. **expertus**: 'from what you know of the situation'.

678. **quondam**: anticipatory, 'I who was once your wife (but shall soon be your widow)'.

681 f. **manus ... parentum**: 'in between the embracing arms and faces of his grief-stricken parents'. The phrase is very precisely pictorial: Creusa on her knees is holding Iulus out towards Aeneas (674), who puts out his arms to take him.

682–3. 'a thin tongue of flame was to be seen, radiating its light from the very top of Iulus' head'; the omen is reminiscent of the story of the flames surrounding the head of the infant Servius Tullius, marking him out as destined for kingship (Livy

1.39.1); compare also the flames on Lavinia's head in *Aen.* 7.71 f.
Servius draws attention to the meaning of *apex* as part of the
headdress of a priest (e.g. *Aen.* 8.664) but for the meaning 'tongue
of flame' cf. Ov. *Fast.* 6.636, and see K. Quinn, *Virgil's Aeneid*,
pp. 388–9.

685 f. The historic infinitives (cf. 98) convey rapid action;
excutere means that they tried to extinguish the flames by shaking
out Ascanius' hair.

687. Anchises is often seen in Book 3 as the man especially able
to interpret divine signs; he was said to have received this gift
from Venus, cf. Enn. *Ann.* 18+9.

690. **hoc tantum**: 'just this', parenthetical, cf. 79.

pietate: notice the key word of the poem here used as the
basis for Anchises' claim for divine help.

691. 'give us an augury now, father, and confirm this omen';
the MSS read *auxilium* but Probus (on *Ecl.* 6.31) read *augurium*
a Sendrvius' explanation of the rest of the line shows that he read
it. Anchises means that he has taken the flame as an omen sent
spontaneously (*oblativum*); another one sent in response to prayer
(*impetrativum*) will confirm the divine intention. For *deinde* (next,
immediately in the future) cf. *Aen.* 4.561.

693. **laevum**: adverbial accusative, cf. 630; for the left as
favourable in Roman augury cf. *Aen.* 9.631 and Cic. *Div.* 2.82.
In Greek augury the right was favourable.

694. **stella facem ducens**: 'a star leaving a trail of light',
i.e. a shooting star; compare the simile of a shooting star in *Aen.*
5.527 f., and cf. *Geo.* 1.365 f., Lucr. 2.206 f. *nocturnasque faces caeli
sublime volantis ! nonne vides longos flammarum ducere tractus*?

696–7. **claram ... signantemque vias**: 'brilliant and leaving the trace of its path'; the parallel with *Aen.* 5.526 *signavitque
viam flammis* suggests that this is the meaning here, rather than (as
Servius and others say) 'pointing out the way' (cf. Ap. Rh.
4.294 f.). For Mt. Ida in the Troad cf. 801.

697–8. 'after that its path still shone out in a long trail, and all
the place for miles around was smoky with sulphur-fumes', i.e.
after the star had disappeared (*tum*) the signs of its passage
remained.

699. **se tollit ad auras**: the picture is of the hitherto dejected
Anchises rising to his full height and flinging his arms high in joy.

703. **vestroque in numine**: 'under your protection', cf. 396 and 9.247.

707. **cervici imponere nostrae**: 'put yourself on my shoulders'; *imponere* is the passive imperative with a middle sense, and *cervici* the common poetic use of the dative for *in cervicem*.

711. **longe servet**: 'follow at a distance'. This part of Aeneas' plan leads to disaster; Servius attempts to save Aeneas from blame by explaining *longe* as *valde*, but this is impossible.

712. **animis advertite vestris**: notice the variation on the prose phrase *animadvertere; animis* is dative, cf. 707.

713. **egressis**: for the dative cf. *Aen.* 1.102.

714. **desertae**: it is very difficult here to choose between various possibilities: (i) the temple is derelict (because of the war, or its replacement by another, or some other cause); (ii) Ceres was worshipped in remote places, as the rustic deity of earth; (iii) the temple was in commemoration of Proserpina, Ceres' lost daughter. The last would fit best with the cypress, the tree of mourning.

717. Now that Anchises has been persuaded to leave, Aeneas' thoughts turn to Hector's instructions (293).

721-2. **umeros ... insternor**: retained accusative after a passive verb with a middle sense; see note on 275. *Super* is adverbial, and *veste et pelle* hendiadys — 'with the covering of a skin'.

725. **pone**: cf. *Geo.* 4.487 *pone sequens*. The word has an archaic flavour.

opaca locorum: 'the darkness of the way', cf. 332.

727. **ex agmine**: Housman's *exagmine* (= *examine*) here and in 7.703 is accepted by Mackail and Mynors, but Virgil does not elsewhere use *examen* of people.

730-95. *Just as they are reaching safety the noise of the enemy is heard, and in the confusion Creusa is lost. Aeneas retraces his steps, wildly shouting his wife's name; then there appears to him a supernatural phantom of her, and she bids him depart on his destined journey, leaving her in the care of the goddess Cybele.*

730 f. This tremendous passage shows signs of incomplete finish: (half-lines, 767, 787; lines repeated elsewhere, 774-5, 792-4; perhaps the inconsistency of 781-2 with *Aen.* 3.7 (where

see note). It may serve as a reminder that what Virgil did not achieve in the *Aeneid* because of his premature death is insignificant compared with what he did.

The tension between Aeneas' personal grief and the necessity for him to accept the will of heaven for Troy has been a dominant aspect of this book. Here it reaches its superb climax as his wild sorrow and reckless despair is countered by the serene appearance of Creusa's phantom, telling him that these things do not happen unless the gods will it so — *non haec sine numine divum eveniunt.*

Virgil has used the conflicting versions of the tradition for his own purposes; in some sources Aeneas' wife was called Eurydice, and it was only later that Priam's daughter Creusa was cast in this role. Again in early sources Aeneas' wife accompanied him into exile: Virgil needed the version which could bring the story of the burning of Troy to this terrifying and yet comforting finale. The story of the loss of another Eurydice, which he had told in *Georgics* 4, adds to the poignancy and pathos here, and brings into relief the happier ending. For a full discussion of the sources see Austin's note on 795.

731. **evasisse**: 'got through', cf. *Aen.* 12.907.

731-2. **creber . . . pedum sonitus**: 'the sound of many feet'; notice the imitative rhythm of the dactyls, and the elliptical construction of *ad auris (veniens) adesse.*

735. **male . . . amicum**: *inimicum*, cf. 23, *Geo.* 1.105 *male pinguis harenae.*

736. **avia**: 'by-ways'; the adjective *avius* is used in the neuter plural as a noun, cf. *Aen.* 9.58.

738 f. 'alas, the tragedy of it, my wife Creusa — was it by fate that she was taken from me and stopped? Or did she lose the way or tired out pause for rest? I cannot tell — but I never saw her again.' The disjunctive style is used very appropriately for Aeneas' confused emotions in the face of this disaster for which he was primarily responsible. There has been doubt among the commentators about how to take 738-9, but the balancing positions of *-ne* make it clear that Aeneas asks (i) was it by fate that she was snatched off and stopped coming with us or (ii) was it due to her own frailty, in losing her way or giving up through weariness?

738. **misero**: dative after *erepta* with *mihi* understood.

739. **lassa**: Austin has an excellent note on the deliberate use here of this 'more homely' alternative to *fessus*. *M* has *lapsa*, which Mynors accepts.

740. We are irresistibly reminded here of the end of the story of Eurydice in *Geo.* 4.500 f.

744. **fefellit**: 'was missing, to the despair of. . . .'; this is a very intense use of the word, combining the ideas of her absence having been unnoticed till then and of her deceiving the hopes of her friends who were expecting her; cf. *Aen.* 4.17.

745. The line is made memorable by its two striking elisions, the second hypermetric (cf. *Aen.* 1.332).

750. **stat . . . renovare**: 'my firm purpose is to risk again . . .'; cf. *Aen.* 12.678.

752. **portae**: the city gate by which he had got out, cf. 730.

754. **lumine lustro**: 'scan them with intent gaze', cf. *Aen.* 8.153 *totum lustrabat lumine corpus*.

756. A poignant and unforgettable line — 'if only, if only she has gone there'. For the *si forte* type of condition cf. 136; *tulisset* is reported future perfect after the historic present *refero* (I went home thinking 'if only I shall find she has gone there').

761 f. The sanctuary of Juno is evidently on the citadel; Austin calls attention to the irony of the place for helpless suppliants being used as a dumping-ground for loot.

762 f. **Phoenix**: tutor of Achilles, leader of the embassy to him in Hom. *Il.* 9.

771 f. The final scene of Aeneas' search is introduced with a slowing of movement, emphasised by the rhyme of *quaerenti* and *ruenti*, and the assonance of *i* and *o*. The words *ipsius umbra Creusae* are quoted by St. Augustine (*Conf.* 1.13) when he speaks of the fascination Virgil exercised upon him in his boyhood.

772. **infelix**: as Servius says, *mihi non sibi*.

772-3. The words *simulacrum, umbra, nota maior imago* most impressively build up a picture of a supernatural apparition (cf. 591 and Ov. *Fast.* 2.503 — of the ghost of Romulus — *pulcher et humano maior*).

774-5. Both these lines occur elsewhere, 774 in 3.48, 775 in 3.153, 8.35. It is perhaps better to supply *visa* to govern the infinitives in 775 rather than (as most do) to regard them as historic.

774. **steteruntque**: notice the short *e* of *-erunt*, used very rarely by Virgil (cf. 3.681, 10.334); he greatly prefers the perfect ending *-ēre*.

777–8. **non haec ... eveniunt**: this is the lesson of the book which Aeneas has been (understandably) so slow to learn.

779. **fas**: 'the laws of heaven', i.e. fate, cf. *Aen.* 6.438, *Geo.* 1.269. Supply *sinit* rather than *est. Ille* is formulaic, cf. *Aen.* 7.558.

780. The elliptical construction — supply *obeunda sunt* to *exsilia* — gives an impression of oracular style.

781 f. This is the first indication to Aeneas of the site of the new settlement which Hector's ghost had prophesied (294–5).

Hesperia means the western land, and was commonly applied to Italy (1.530).

781–2. 'Where the Lydian Tiber flows with smooth sweep through the fertile fields of the people'; the point of *virum* is that Aeneas' destined home is already peopled by the Italians who will contribute so much to the future race of Rome. The river Tiber is called *Lydius* because much of its course was through the land of the Etruscans (*Geo.* 1.499), a people thought to have originated in Lydia in Asia Minor (*Aen.* 8.479, Herod. 1.94).

782. **leni fluit agmine**: from Ennius (*Ann.* 173).

783. **regia coniunx**: i.e. Lavinia; notice that Aeneas does not conceal this part of the prophesy from Dido.

784. **Creusae**: objective genitive, 'tears for .. ', cf. *Aen.* 1.462.

785. **Myrmidonum ... Dolopumve**: see note on line 7.

786. **servitum**: supine, rare in elevated poetry, and adding a domestic touch here to Creusa's words to her husband.

787. **Dardanis**: 'a woman of Dardanus' line'; Dardanus was the founder of the dynasty of Priam, Creusa's father.

788. **magna deum genetrix**: Cybele, whose main seat of worship was in the Troad (3.111, 6.784, 9.80 f.).

789. **nati ... amorem**: 'cherish your love for our son'; these final words are the only touch of pathos in Creusa's serene explanation of what has happened to her.

790–1. These phrases, emphasised by the heavy alliteration of *d* and *t*, are again reminiscent of Eurydice in *Geo.* 4 (499 f.); cf. 740.

792 f. 'Three times then I tried to put my arms round her neck;

three times the phantom vainly clasped escaped my grasp, like the light winds and very like a winged dream.' These three lines are translated from Hom. *Od.* 11.206 f., and occur again in *Aen.* 6.700 f., where Aeneas tries to embrace the ghost of his father Anchises.

795. **sic demum**: 'and so it was that at last . . .'; the tale of tragedy is over.

796–804. *Aeneas returns to the rest of his family and finds their number augmented by other refugees. The morning star rises and as dawn breaks Aeneas sets off for the mountains.*

798. **collectam exsilio pubem**: 'a band assembled for exile'; *exsilio* is dative of purpose, cf. *Aen.* 1.22. There is much bitterness in these words: *pubes collecta* would normally have some different purpose than exile — the truth is revealed in the appositional phrase, *miserabile vulgus*.

799–800. **parati in quascumque**: there is an ellipse after *parati* of a verb like *proficisci*.

800. **deducere**: the technical phrase for founding a colony.

801 f. Observe the symbolism of the new dawn after Troy's dark night of disaster; notice too that Lucifer, the morning star, is the planet Venus. Varro records a tradition that Venus guided her son to Latium by means of her star; cf. 1.382.

803–4. Once again, for the last time, Aeneas stresses that there was no hope left of staying in Troy; so he yields to fate and departs carrying his father to the mountains.

AENEID 3

Introductory note

After the intense tragedy of the second book, Book 3 provides a relaxation of tension, a diminution of emotional involvement on the part of the reader. Its function is in many ways comparable with that of the fifth book, to provide a breathing space between two books of great dramatic power. Most of this book is written in an objective style; there is, for example, only one simile, and only in the passage concerning Andromache does Virgil aim at the pathos elsewhere so characteristic of him. The movement is diffuse and expansive, rather than concentrated and intense. Emotionally in this book we rest; intellectually, however, our interest is maintained in the unfolding of the major themes of the poem.

The story of the wanderings of Aeneas clearly offers a possibility of a Virgilian Odyssey. In a number of places Virgil does indeed attempt to recapture the other-worldly atmosphere of strange adventures which were so familiar to him from *Odyssey* 9–12: the episode of the Harpies is partly based on *Odyssey* 12 (see note on 209 f.); Aeneas comes in sight of Scylla and Charybdis (see note on 420 f.); and above all the encounter with the Cyclops (see note on 617) is reminiscent of *Odyssey* 9. The fantastic world of Homeric folktale had indeed cast its spell over Virgil. But essentially the voyage of Aeneas is different from that of Odysseus; it is set in the real world of the Roman Mediterranean, and the many episodes are given coherence by the progressive revelation to Aeneas of the goal which he is seeking. Through oracles from Apollo or his prophets Aeneas gradually learns more and more of his future city and its destiny.

Virgil's arrangement of his material for the seven-year journey is very carefully worked out, with variation of length and interest in the different stages, and a comparison with the account of Dionysius of Halicarnassus shows the ways in which he has avoided the danger of a dull catalogue of land-falls and departures (for a full account of this see the introduction to my Oxford edition). The journey may best be divided into three groups of three: in the Aegean (Thrace, Delos, Crete); in Greece (Strophades, Actium, Buthrotum); in Italy and Sicily (Castrum Minervae, Etna, voyage round Sicily). The variety of mood and intention in these stages is very considerable: Thrace is grim, terrifying; Delos heartening and exciting; Crete plague-ridden and disastrous; the Strophades weird and frightening; Actium wholly Roman and aetiological; Buthrotum prophetic; Castrum Minervae (the first landing in Italy) at once hopeful and full of foreboding over future wars; Etna and Polyphemus grandiose, rhetorical, baroque; and lastly the passage round Sicily provides a quiet rounding-off conclusion to the voyage.

Three especial themes in the book should be emphasised. The first is the sense of toil and weariness as the Trojan exiles wander from place to place over the unending seas; the suffering and endurance called for seems almost intolerable, and is an indispensable prelude to explain the weakness and weariness of Aeneas which lead him to stay with Dido when he should be pressing onwards towards Italy. The second is the progressive revelation to the Trojans, mainly through Apollo, of their destiny and future glory, expressed in proud patriotic terms (97 f., 158 f., 462). The third is the part played by Anchises in guiding and advising his son, especially in religious matters, towards the understanding and achievement of his mission. Aeneas learns from his father many of the things which he must teach his son, and his son's sons, so that the city of Rome will be founded aright on the moral and religious principles which the gods ordain for the future capital of the world. Aeneas must leave the heroic world of Troy and enter the world of Rome's imperial destiny; he must leave the dead past and enter the unborn future.

1–12. *After the destruction of Troy Aeneas and his companions build a fleet, and at the beginning of summer set sail for unknown lands.*

1 f. The short opening paragraph links the new narrative with what went before by means of a brief backward glance (as at the beginning of Book 5). There is very strong emphasis in these lines — as indeed throughout the book — on the divine background to the human action (2 *visum superis*; 5 *auguriis divum*; 7 *quo fata ferant*; 9 *dare fatis vela*; 12 *cum . . . penatibus et magnis dis*). The mention of Anchises' instructions in line 9 prepares the way for the important part to be played in this book by Aeneas' father in helping and advising his son (102 f., 263 f., 472 f., 610 f.); the honour in which he is held reflects the importance of the father-son relationship in Roman family life. Aeneas always received from Anchises the help and guidance which he himself was to give to Iulus.

1. **res Asiae**: 'the kingdom of Asia', cf. *Aen.* 8.471 *res Troiae*. Priam is called *regnatorem Asiae* in 2.557.

2. **immeritam**: a final protest against the divine decision (*visum superis*) to destroy Troy.

3. **humo fumat**: 'was a flattened smoking ruin'; notice the change in tense: Troy had fallen and was still smoking as Aeneas began to prepare for departure.

Neptunia Troia: see note on 2.610.

4. **diversa exsilia**: 'a far-off place of exile' (so Servius) rather than 'different places of exile'; cf. 2.780 *longa tibi exsilia*.

desertas ... terras: 'empty lands', in contrast with the flourishing civilisation which they formerly knew.

4–5. **quaerere ... agimur**: for the final use of the infinitive cf. 682–3 and note on 1.527–8.

5–6. **sub ipsa Antandro**: 'just by Antandros', a town in the Troad on the other side of Mt. Ida from Troy.

6. **molimur**: 'toil at building', cf. 132.

7. **incerti**: throughout the early part of Book 3 the Trojans are ignorant of the whereabouts of their destined city, in spite of Creusa's prophecy in 2.781 f. where Hesperia and the Tiber were named. This is one of a number of minor inconsistencies which Book 3 contains; see the Intro. to my Oxford edition of Book 3, pp. 19 f.

sistere: 'to stop' (=*consistere*), cf. *Geo*. 1.479.

8–10. 'Scarcely had early summer begun — and father Anchises was urging us to entrust our ships to the fates — when I set sail. . . .'; line 9 is slightly parenthetical. The burning of Troy was traditionally placed in the late winter or early spring.

11. **fuit**: 'once stood', (was and is not); cf. *Aen*. 2.325.

12. This line is a reminiscence of Ennius (*Ann*. 201 *dono, ducite, doque volentibus cum magnis dis*). The unusual rhythm of the trochaic caesura in the third foot without a main caesura in the fourth, the spondaic fifth foot, and the monosyllabic ending all echo Virgil's source and would remind the Roman readers at this important point in the narrative of their first national hexameter poet. The line ending is used again in *Aen*. 8.679 in the picture on Aeneas' shield of Augustus leading the Italians to battle.

penatibus et magnis dis: cf. 2.293 f. (Hector's instructions to Aeneas to take the *penates* with him). It is uncertain whether the *magni di* were the *penates* (as Varro says) or different deities; it seems best to regard the phrase as broadening the meaning of *penates* by associating them with the public cult and such allied deities as Vesta and the Lares.

13–18. *Aeneas sails to Thrace, and begins to build a city there.*

13 f. Aeneas' visit to Thrace was well established in the legend (Livy 1.1.4); Virgil has added to it from poetic sources the story of Polydorus and its macabre sequel.

13. **terra procul ... colitur**: 'there lies at a distance a land. . . .'; *procul* does not necessarily imply a very great distance. *Colitur* is used in a general sense, 'is inhabited', 'is known of', 'exists', cf. 73.

Mavortia: Thrace had very strong associations with Ares and Mars, cf. line 35, *Geo.* 4.462 *Rhesi Mavortia tellus*.

14. **Thraces arant**: for the parenthetical syntax, quite common in Virgil, cf. *Aen.* 1.12; for the final short syllable of the Greek nominative plural *Thraces* cf. *Cyclopes* (644).

regnata Lycurgo: the intransitive verb *regnare* is here used in the passive as if it were transitive on the analogy of *regere*; cf. *Aen.* 6.793. *Lycurgo* is dative of the agent, cf. 275. Lycurgus resisted the introduction of the worship of Dionysus into Thrace.

15. **hospitium**: 'place of friendship', cf. 61.

17. **fatis ingressus iniquis**: this anticipates the narrative, and prepares the reader for the grim sequel.

18. The people of this new town are to be called Aeneadae; Virgil is not specific about the name of the town itself, perhaps because the legend varied (there was a town called Aenus at the mouth of the Hebrus, associated with Polydorus — Pliny, *Nat. Hist.* 4.43, and also a town Aeneia in Chalcidice said to have been founded by Aeneas). For the aetiological association of place-names with the Aeneas legend cf. Pergamum (133), Chaonia (335) and note on 1.267–8 (Iulus and Ilium).

19–68. *As Aeneas tears up some myrtle and cornel shoots in order to wreathe the altars, drops of blood come from the broken stems. Then a cry is heard from beneath the earth, and the voice of Polydorus tells Aeneas that the shoots have grown from the spears which transfixed him when he was murdered after being sent to Thrace. Aeneas calls a council, and the Trojans decide to leave; funeral rites for Polydorus are prepared.*

19 f. The grim and weird story of Polydorus and the drops of blood trickling from the myrtle shoots is not found before Virgil; no trace exists in the very varied tradition about him of this sequel to his death. Moreover there is no reason to think that Polydorus played any part in the Aeneas legend before Virgil,

although as we have seen (see note on 13 f.) Aeneas' visit to Thrace was part of the normal tradition.

The introduction of the supernatural sequel to Polydorus' death may of course be due to some lost source of Virgil, but it seems more likely that it was Virgil's own invention, based upon such folklore as the spear thrown by Romulus on to the Palatine, which took root and grew into a tree, or the stories of Dryads or Hamadryads, the nymphs who lived in trees and were sometimes physically identified with them, so that an injury to the tree caused them injury; cf. Ap. Rh. 2.476 f., Ov. *Met.* 8.738 f., and Shelley's lines on the Woodman '. . . killing the tall treen / the soul of whom, by Nature's gentle law, / was each a Wood-nymph.' Virgil's story was imitated by Dante (*Inf.* 13) and Spenser (*F.Q.* 1.2.30 f.):

> And thinking of those braunches greene to frame
> A girlond for her dainty forehead fit
> He pluckt a bough; out of whose rift there came
> Small drops of gory bloud, that trickled downe the same.

> Therewith a piteous yelling voyce was heard,
> Crying, O spare with guilty hands to teare
> My tender sides in this rough rynd embard,
> But fly, ah fly far hence away. . . .

It remains to ask why Virgil has introduced into the Aeneas legend this altered version of the story of Polydorus. It is intended to make us feel that the long voyage which ends in the foundation of Rome begins in tragedy, horror, and despair. It is an episode of primitive folklore, and in it Aeneas receives his first omen of the voyage, a grim and unhappy one. It serves to emphasise the atmosphere of gloom and sorrow in which Aeneas, still a 'ghost of Troy' rather than yet 'father of Rome', sets out from his destroyed homeland. See C. S. Lewis, *A Preface to Paradise Lost*, chap. vi.

19. **Dionaeae**: Venus has this epithet (cf. *Ecl.* 9.47) as daughter of Dione, child of Oceanus and Tethys.

19–20. **divisque . . . operum**: 'and to the gods who give their favour to new undertakings'; Servius specifies Jupiter, Apollo and Bacchus. For *auspicibus* cf. *Aen.* 4.45; here of course the hoped-for favour was not forthcoming.

21. **caelicolum**: archaic form of the genitive plural of the first declension, cf. 1.565 *Aeneadum* and line 550 *Graiugenum*.

22–3. **quo ... myrtus**: 'on the top of which grew cornel shrubs and a bristling thicket of myrtle-shoots'; for the omission of the verb to be in a descriptive passage cf. 216 f., 533 f., 618 f. Myrtle and cornel were used for making spears, cf. *Geo.* 2.447–8; the word *hastile* is here used of the spiky growth of the tree, but with a forward reference to its real meaning ('spear'), cf. 46. *Horrida* is frequent in this sense of 'bristling', cf. *Aen.* 10.178, 11.601–2, and Milton's 'horrid arms', 'horrent arms'.

24. **silvam**: 'undergrowth', cf. *Geo.* 1.76, 152.

25. **tegerem ut**: the conjunction is preceded by its verb only in poetry; cf. 473 for a striking instance.

27–8. 'For when the first sapling was torn out of the ground, its roots severed, there came oozing from it drops of black blood. . .' The antecedent for *quae* (*arbori*) is taken into the relative clause; cf. 94. The dative *huic* (prose would have *ab hac*) is a poetic extension of the dative of the thing concerned in an action; *mihi* in the next line is a much more normal example of this construction.

30. **gelidusque ... sanguis**: 'and my blood curdles, frozen with fear'; cf. 259, *Aen.* 10.452.

31. **lentum**: 'tough', 'springy', cf. *Geo.* 4.34.

31–2. **convellere ... insequor**: for the extended poetic use of the infinitive see note on 4–5. The analogy is with verbs like *instare, pergere*; there is no other instance of the infinitive with *insequi*.

34. **Nymphas**: i.e. Hamadryads, see note on 19 f.

35. **Gradivumque patrem**: this is a name of Mars (line 13); cf. *Aen.* 10.542.

Geticis: the Getae lived in Thrace, cf. *Geo.* 3.462.

36. 'that they would duly give a favourable issue to what I had seen, and lighten the omen'. The construction is an indirect petition after the idea of *orans* which is present in *venerabar*. Aeneas realises that what he has just witnessed is clearly an omen, and apparently a bad one, and he prays that it may be changed to good.

39. **lacrimabilis**: probably 'piteous' rather than 'tearful'; cf. *Aen.* 7.604 *lacrimabile bellum*.

40. **vox reddita**: 'an answering cry', cf. *Aen.* 7.95.

42. **pias**: Aeneas' own epithet, here with reference to religious obligations and common nationality.

42-3. 'I am no stranger to you, for Troy gave me birth; and this welling blood is not coming from wood.' For the use of *aut* with the negative carried forward to its clause cf. 162. Only the words *externum* and *de stipite* are affected by the negative.

45. **Polydorus**: the details of the story are told in 49 f.; for Virgil's sources see note on 19 f.

45-6. 'Here was I transfixed, here an iron crop of weapons covered me over, and grew up with pointed shafts', i.e. the volley of spears which pinned him to the ground took root and grew into myrtle and cornel shoots. The metaphor of *ferrea seges* is one of which Virgil was fond; cf. 7.526, 12.663.

47. **mentem ... pressus**: 'overwhelmed in mind'; for the retained accusative *mentem* cf. 65, 81, 428, and note on 1.228.

48. This line is found also at 2.774; for the form *stetĕrunt* see note there.

49-57. The insertion of this narrative of past events to explain the present is perfectly natural when we remember that Aeneas is recounting the story to Dido — what he did not know at the time he now does know, so that he can tell the complete story. The transition back to the main narrative (56-7) by means of the exclamation against the corrupting power of gold would have special significance for Dido, as Pygmalion had murdered her husband Sychaeus for gold.

49 f. This part of the story of Polydorus (who was Priam's youngest son) is quite closely modelled on Euripides' *Hecuba* (10 f., 716 f., 781-2).

61. **Threicio regi**: Polymestor, who had married Iliona, one of Priam's daughters.

55-6. Notice the staccato effect of the short phrases which conclude the narrative about Polymestor.

55. **fas omne abrumpit**: 'broke all his sacred obligations', i.e. those of kinship as well as hospitality and good faith.

56-7. **quid ... fames!**: for the phraseology cf. *Aen.* 4.412 *improbe Amor, quid non mortalia pectora cogis*! Pliny (*Nat. Hist.* 33.6) refers to Virgil's phrase in a passage decrying luxury.

57. **sacra**: 'accursed'. The phrase *sacer esto* occurs in the Twelve

Tables, and probably by Virgil's time this meaning had an archaic flavour; cf. *Geo.* 3.566.

58–9. Aeneas' language here has something of the formality of the Roman senate; he is most anxious to follow the correct procedure in the face of this crisis.

60–1. The infinitives are in apposition to *idem animus (est)*; the variation (active, passive, active) is unusual.

61. **pollutum hospitium**: 'this place where friendship had been desecrated': see line 15 and cf. *Aen.* 7.467 *polluta pace*.

dare classibus Austros: 'to give the fleet its winds', a personification of the impatient fleet.

62. **instauramus**: 'we renew'; in a sense Polydorus was already buried (lines 22, 41), but the appropriate rites had not been performed.

63. **tumulo**: 'on the mound', the one referred to in line 22.

stant manibus arae: 'altars are set up in honour of his shade'; cf. line 305 (Hector) and 5.48 (Anchises), and Bailey, *Religion in Virgil*, pp. 259 f., 290 f.

65. **crinem ... solutae**: for the retained accusative see note on 47.

66. For the offerings given cf. *Aen.* 5.77 f.; the spirit was supposed to partake of them. For *cymbia* ('cups') cf. *Aen.* 5.267; Servius says they were boat-shaped (*cumba*).

67–8. **animamque ... condimus**: 'we lay his spirit to rest in its tomb'. Previously it has been restless and disturbed; now it receives due burial and peace; cf. *Aen.* 6.152.

68. To call on the ghost of the dead man for the last time was a regular procedure at Roman funerals; cf. *Aen.* 2.644, 6.231, 506.

69–83. *The Trojans sail to Delos, the sacred island of Apollo, and are hospitably received by Anius.*

69 f. The visit to Delos occurs also in Dionysius' version (1.50) of Aeneas' wanderings. It was a very suitable episode for Virgil to include, partly because of its attractive literary associations (75–6), but mainly because Delos above all places offered the setting for prophecy and revelation of the goal of the Trojan voyage, the theme which provides a unifying motif throughout this book.

This second episode of Aeneas' voyage gives a strong contrast

in mood with the sorrow and gloom of the opening movement of
the book; after four preliminary lines describing the departure it
continues with an attractive picture of the famous island and
concludes with calm and serene phrases describing the arrival at
the harbour and the meeting with Anius, an old friend of Anchises.

70. **lenis crepitans**: for the adjective used adverbially with a
present participle (not a prose usage) cf. *Aen.* 5.764. *Crepitans*
('rustling') is unusual and colourful in this context.

Auster: Delos is south of Thrace; the geographical direction
of winds is not to be pressed in the poets (Servius says 'auster
autem quivis ventus').

73-4. 'There is a sacred land lying in the midst of sea, dearly
loved by the mother of the Nereids'. For *colitur* cf. 13; the mother
of the Nereids (sea-nymphs) was Doris, wife of Nereus.

74. The rhythm of this line (which also occurs in *Ciris* 474) is
Greek, and contains several features which are rare in Latin:
there is a hiatus after *matri* and another after *Neptuno*, the fifth
foot is spondaic and it is preceded by a spondaic fourth foot, a
very unusual rhythm. See note on 1.617.

Neptuno Aegaeo: the epithet refers primarily to the Aegean
sea in which Delos is situated, but also suggests Aegae, the place
of Poseidon's palace in Homer (*Il.* 13.21 f.).

75-6. 'it used to float around from coast to coast until the
Archer God in due gratitude fixed it firmly to lofty Myconos and
Gyarus'. Apollo is called *pius* because he fulfilled his obligations
to the island that had sheltered his mother Latona (Leto) from
Juno's wrath when she gave birth to him and Diana. Throughout
antiquity Delos was regarded as one of the main seats of Apollo;
cf. Hom. *Od.* 6.162 f., Hor. *Odes* 3.4.60 f., *Aen.* 4.144. The arrival
of Aeneas at Delos is the subject of one of Claude Lorrain's
classical landscapes (in the National Gallery); Keats has a fine
description of Apollo's island in *Hyperion*, Book III, beginning:

> Chief isle of the embowered Cyclades,
> Rejoice, O Delos, with thine olives green
> And poplars, and lawn-shading palms, and beech,
> In which the Zephyr breathes the loudest song,
> And hazels thick, dark-stemm'd beneath the shade;
> Apollo is once more the golden theme.

75. **arquitenens**: this compound adjective (cf. 544 *Palladis armisonae*) has a Homeric ring (ἀργυρότοξος, κλυτότοξος, τοξοφόρος); it is found in Latin as early as Naevius.

76. **errantem**: compare the floating island of Aeolia (Hom. *Od.* 10.1 f.), and the stories of the Planctae and Symplegades ('wandering', 'clashing' rocks). The legend that Delos was once a floating island is found first in Pindar (quoted in Strabo 10.485); cf. also Callimachus (*Hymn. Del.* 35 f.), Prop. 4.6.27 f., Ov. *Met.* 6.333-4, and Spenser *F.Q.* 2.12.13.

Mycono e celsa Gyaroque: these two islands, adjacent to Delos, are coupled in Stat. *Th.* 3.438, an imitation of this passage.

77. **dedit**: 'granted'; for the poetic use with the infinitive, see note on 1.66.

contemnere ventos: because when it floated, it was at the mercy of the winds; cf. Pliny's description (*Ep.* 8.20.6 f.) of the little floating islands on Lake Vadimon.

78. **fessos**: a key word in this book; notice how early in the wanderings it is used. The Trojans are weary exiles, struggling onwards, from the first stages of their pilgrimage.

80 f. Like the Roman kings, Anius combined the offices of *rex* and *sacerdos*; cf. Ov. *Met.* 13.632 f. According to Servius (on *Aen.* 8.158) Anchises had visited Anius before the Trojan war.

81. **tempora**: retained accusative, see note on 47.

lauro: Apollo's tree (91); cf. Ov. *Met.* 1.452 f.

84-120. *At Delos Aeneas prays to Apollo for guidance, and receives an oracular response bidding the Trojans to seek out their 'ancient mother'. Anchises interprets this as the island of Crete, and they prepare to set out.*

84 f. In Thrace, the first stage of his journey, Aeneas received an omen and a supernatural revelation to tell him that he was not to make his home there. Now at the oracle of Apollo in Delos he receives the first positive indication during his voyage of where his goal is. The oracle is delivered by the god himself (line 99), not through an intermediary priestess; the special guidance given by Apollo to the Trojan exiles is thus stressed.

The directions of Apollo (which are misinterpreted by Anchises — see note on 94-8) are concluded with a brief statement of the glorious future awaiting the house of Aeneas, a prophecy reiterated by the Penates (158 f.). Such prophecies form a bright pattern

within the *Aeneid* which is in interplay with the darker tones of
toil and suffering. Compare especially Jupiter's speech in *Aen.*
1.257 f., the oracle to Latinus (7.96 f.), the speech of Tiberinus
(8.36 f.), and Jupiter's final speech in 12.830 f. The same prophetic
effect is achieved by the vision of Roman heroes in 6.756 f., and
the description of Aeneas' shield (8.625 f.).

85. propriam: 'to be our own', i.e. lasting, permanent; cf.
167 and *mansuram* in the following line.

Thymbraee: this epithet of Apollo (cf. *Geo.* 4.323) derives
from Thymbra in the Troad, where Apollo had a well-known
temple.

86–7. 'keep safe Troy's other citadel, the remnant left by the
Greeks and cruel Achilles.' *Pergama* was the citadel of Troy — the
real one has been destroyed and Aeneas and his followers are
now symbolically the only 'citadel' left; cf. 8.37, and the Greek
proverb 'Men, not walls, make a city'. (Thuc. 7.77.7).

87. reliquias ... Achilli: cf. *Aen.* 1.30, and Spenser *F.Q.*
3.9.41, 'and with a remnant did to sea repaire'.

88. sequimur: the indicative is sometimes used vividly instead
of the subjunctive in what is equivalent to a deliberative question;
cf. 367.

89. augurium: an omen as an indication of the divine will;
cf. *Aen.* 2.691.

90. The paratactic construction — *vix ea fatus eram (cum)* (or *et*)
tremere omnia visa sunt — and the dactylic movement help to
convey the immediacy of the response.

91. liminaque laurusque: the lengthening in arsis of the
first -*que* is in imitation of Homeric lengthening of τε; all the
16 instances of this in Virgil are before a double consonant
except this one and *Aen.* 12.363. See also note on 1.308.

92. mons: Mount Cynthus, cf. *Aen.* 4.147.

cortina: cf. *Aen.* 6.347. The word means a rounded vessel, and
in an oracular shrine it was placed on the sacred tripod. The
word *mugire* is associated with supernatural happenings in 4.490,
6.256.

94–8. The riddling oracle is taken by Anchises to refer to
Crete, the homeland of the Trojan king Teucer; in fact Italy is
meant, the original home of Dardanus (see note on 167–8).

94–5. Notice the heavy alliteration of *d*, giving an archaic impressiveness for the beginning of the oracle, and the emphatic effect of putting the relative clause first (with the antecedent *tellus* taken into it; cf. 27) and resuming it with *eadem*.

94. **duri**: the word stresses the qualities of toughness and endurance which the Trojan exiles, and later the Roman nation, were called upon to display in adverse circumstances.

95. **ubere laeto**: 'in her loving bosom'. Both words have a double meaning, applicable to *mater* and *tellus*. *Uber* means the mother's breast or the earth's fertility; *laetus* can mean the mother's joy or the fruitfulness of the land.

96. **antiquam ... matrem**: personification of the 'mother' country is natural and frequent in all literature; cf. *Geo.* 2.173–4, *Aen.* 7.762, and Mother Earth in the story of Brutus and the Tarquins, or Deucalion and Pyrrha.

97–8. These lines are based on Hom. *Il.* 20.307–8 where Poseidon prophesies that Aeneas will rule the Trojans, and his sons's sons and those who come thereafter; Virgil has widened the area of rule to the whole world.

102 f. Notice that it is to Anchises that the interpretation of the oracle is left; see note on 1 f.

102. **volvens monimenta**: 'pondering the traditions'; the meaning of *monimenta* (information which they left) is defined on 107.

104. Crete was Jupiter's island because he was born and brought up there by the nymphs (*Geo.* 4.149 f.). See also on 111 f.

105. **mons Idaeus**: Mt. Ida in Crete gave its name to Mt. Ida in the Troad (112).

ubi: the conjunction is postponed (cf. 25), and the verb *est* omitted.

106. For Crete's hundred cities cf. Hom. *Il.* 2.649, Hor. *Odes* 3.27.33 f.; *uberrima regna* picks up *ubere laeto* in 95.

107. **maximus ... pater**: 'first ancestor'; *maximus* is used in the sense of *maximus natu*.

108. **Teucrus**: the Latin form is much more commonly *Teucer*. Anchises, having missed the clue in *Dardanidae duri* is following the version of the legend according to which Teucer had arrived in Troy from Crete before Dardanus came from Italy (Apollod. 3.12.1). As it turns out however (167 f.) the correct version is the one which gave priority to Dardanus.

Rhoeteas: Rhoeteum was a promontory near Troy, cf. *Aen.* 6.505.

109–10. Virgil is closely following Homer's lines about Dardanus founding Troy (*Il.* 20.216 f.).

110. **steterant**: 'had come into existence'.

111 f. 'From here came the mother who dwells on Mt. Cybelus, and the cymbals of the Corybants and our grove of Ida; from here came the custom of obedient silence at the rites, and yoked lions bowed their necks beneath the chariot of the queen'. The goddess here described is Cybele or Cybebe, the *Magna Mater*, the Berecynthian mother (*Aen.* 6.784 f.) whose rites were introduced into Rome from Phrygia at the end of the third century B.C. She is invoked by Aeneas in *Aen.* 7.139, 10.252; she had taken Creusa into her care on the last night of Troy (2.788 f.); it is at her prayer that Jupiter turns the Trojans ships into nymphs (9.82 f.). Cf. Catullus' brilliant description of her worship (poem 63), and Lucr. 2.600 f., Ov. *Fast.* 4.179 f. Her cult in Phrygia was influenced by the cult of Rhea in Crete, and the clashing of cymbals in her worship by the Corybantes was linked with the legend of the Curetes in Dicte drowning the cries of the infant Jupiter (Lucr. 2.633 f.) when Saturn was hunting for him.

111. **cultrix Cybeli**: for *cultrix* cf. *Geo.* 1.14. Some MSS read *Cybele*, the goddess's name, but this leaves *cultrix* without construction.

112. **nemus**: the last syllable is lengthened in arsis, see note on 2.369.

fida silentia sacris: this associates Cybele with Demeter, another personification of the concept of the Mother goddess, whose initiation ceremonies at Eleusis were never to be divulged; cf. Hor. *Odes* 3.2.25 f.

113. The lions which draw the chariot of Cybele (Cat. 63.76 f., *Aen.* 10.253) probably symbolise her power over untamed nature.

114. Notice how the postposition of *qua* puts emphasis on the words which precede it, an emphasis strengthened by the alliteration of *d*.

115. **Cnosia regna**: the kingdom of Cnossos, chief town of King Minos' Crete.

116. **modo Iuppiter adsit**: 'only let Jupiter be favourable', the paratactic equivalent of *dummodo*, 'provided that'.

118. **meritos ... honores**: 'the offerings called for', 'deserved' by the occasion. For *honores* cf. 264, 547.

119. Neptune and Apollo were the gods with whom the description of the Delos episode began (74 f.); the due sacrifices to them conclude the Trojan visit to the island.

120. The black victim is for the potentially hostile deity, the white one for the potentially propitious (*felix*).

121–34. *The Trojans sail from Delos to Crete, where they land and begin to build a town called Pergamum.*

121 f. The visit to Crete does not occur in other extant versions of the Aeneas legend. By including Crete Virgil has been able to enrich his story with all the associations between Crete and Troy mentioned by Anchises (104 f.), and especially to give a setting for a new prophecy of the future glory of Rome and the Trojans (154 f.).

122. **Idomenēa**: this is the Homeric form of the Greek accusative, cf. *Aen.* 1.611 (*Ilionea*). Idomeneus of Crete was one of the main Greek chieftains in the war against Troy (Hom. *Il.* 13.210 f.). Servius tells the story of how on his return from Troy Idomeneus was caught in a storm, and vowed that if he were saved he would sacrifice the first thing he saw on landing. This was his son; when he fulfilled his vow a pestilence came on the land, and he was driven out. He went to the land of the Sallentini in Calabria and founded a state there (line 400); cf. also *Aen.* 11.264–5. Mozart's *Idomeneo* is based on this story.

123. **hoste vacare domum**: 'here was a home for us unoccupied by the enemy', or possibly 'his palace was empty of our enemy'.

astare: 'were standing ready', cf. *Aen.* 2.303.

124. **Ortygiae**: a name of Delos, meaning 'Quail-island'; various stories survive in explanation of the name, for instance that Latona's sister, Asteria, was turned into a quail to avoid the love of Jupiter.

125 f. These islands of the Cyclades are all close to Delos, to the south.

125. **bacchatamque iugis Naxon**: 'Naxos that holds Bacchic revel on its mountains'; *bacchata* is generally explained as passive in meaning ('revelled upon', cf. *Geo.* 2.487), but this makes *iugis* very awkward; an active meaning such as that given in the

translation is normal of persons (*Aen.* 4.301), and here the personification of the island is quite natural.

126. **niveamque Paron**: the white marble of Paros was famous, (*Geo.* 3.34, *Aen.* 1.593).

127. **Cycladăs**: notice the short final vowel of the Greek declension; cf. *tripodas* (360), *lebetas* (466), *Hyadas* (516), *Cyclopas* (647), and compare note on 14.

legimus freta: 'thread the straits' (Fairclough); cf. 706.

concita: 'made rough by'; Servius rightly explains that the sea is naturally more disturbed near land. Cf. Tac. *Agr.* 10.6, and for the rough waters around the Cyclades cf. Hor. *Odes* 1.14.19 f., Livy 36.43.1. A few inferior MSS read *consita*, 'planted with', 'strewn with'.

128. **nauticus . . . clamor**: 'the shouts of the sailors', doubtless including the calling of the time by the bo'sun (*celeuma*), but conveying also the general hubbub of the happy crew (*socii*).

129. **Cretam . . . petamus**: perhaps the actual words of the sailors, in *oratio recta*, rather than indirect command.

131. **Curetum**: see note on 111.

132. **optatae**: 'longed for', cf. 509, not here 'chosen'.

molior: cf. line 6 and *Aen.* 1.424.

133. **Pergameam**: adjective agreeing with *urbem*, understood from the previous line. Cf. 349 f. for calling new places by old names. Velleius and Pliny mention a town Pergamum in Crete.

134. **hortor amare**: poetic use of the infinitive of indirect command, as also in 144, 608–9. See note on 4–5.

amare focos: 'to cherish their homes'; *focos* has something of the sense of *penates*.

arcemque attollere tectis: 'to raise the citadel high with buildings', cf. *Aen.* 2.185 f.

135–91. *As the Trojans busy themselves with building their new home in Crete, a pestilence suddenly attacks them. Anchises suggests that they should return to Delos to consult the oracle again, but a vision of the Penatès appears to Aeneas at night, telling him that it is in Hesperia, now called Italia, that he is to found his destined city. Anchises recognises his error in interpreting the oracle of Apollo, and the Trojans leave Crete.*

135 f. Notice the sudden change of mood, from confidence to disaster (contrast 69 f.). The alternation of hope and gloom is

characteristic of this book, as the Trojans struggle on towards their goal (as indeed it is characteristic of the whole *Aeneid*; cf. especially the last sections of Book 6 and Book 12). The mood changes again at 147 f., where the heartening prophecy of the Penates is described in a passage of remarkable visual impact. Dreams and visions play a major part in the pattern of the *Aeneid*, emphasising the connection of the divine plan with the human action, often occurring at moments when Aeneas is near despair or disaster; see notes on 84 f. and 2.268 f.

135. **Iamque fere . . . cum**: the first two words indicate a description of the present situation (*subductae sunt, operata est, dabam*), and prepare us for an alteration to it, which is given in the inverted *cum* clause; cf. *Aen.* 5.327 f.

136. **operata**: 'were occupied with', cf. Liv. 4.60.2; the word probably includes an idea of the religious ceremonies involved, cf. *Geo.* 1.339.

137–9. 'when suddenly the expanse of the air was infected and upon our bodies there came a corrupting pestilence, pitiable to see; upon the trees and the crops too it came, a pestilence and a season of death'. The build-up of the words in this sentence cannot be rendered in English without repetition; new points are added in the Latin as the sentence unfolds about its single main verb. For the phraseology cf. *Geo.* 3.478 f., Lucr. 6.1090 f.

139. **letifer annus**: *letifer* is a poetic word (cf. Cat. 64.394); for *annus* = 'season' cf. *Aen.* 6.311.

140. 'Men gave up the sweet breath of life'; the subject of *linquebant* is unexpressed as in 106, 110. The unexpected use of *linquere* is a variation on phrases like *linquebant lumina vitae* (Lucr. 5.989). Notice the very heavy assonance of *-ebant*.

141. **sterilis**: a clear example of the proleptic use of an adjective; 'burnt them so that they became barren'.

exurere: historic infinitive, cf. 666–7.

Sirius: the Dog-star, associated commonly with heat and fever, cf. *Geo.* 2.353, *Aen.* 10.273.

142. **victum . . . negabat**: 'the diseased crop gave no sustenance', cf. *Geo.* 1.149.

143 f. This passage is similar to the situation in Hom. *Il.* 1.59 f., where Achilles urges the Greeks to consult the priests in order to find out the cause of Apollo's anger, shown in the plague he has sent.

143. **oraclum**: syncope for *oraculum*, which is unmanageable in hexameters; cf. *periclis* (711).

143-4. **remenso . . . mari**: 'sailing back again', cf. *Aen.* 2.181.

145 f. The indirect questions are dependent on the idea of 'asking' conveyed in the previous lines; cf. *Aen.* 2.651 f.

145. **fessis . . . ferat**: the alliteration of *f*, and the vivid phrase *fessae res*, add to the intensity of the prayer.

148 f. For the significance of this vision see note on 135 f. It comes to Aeneas in sleep (151), the natural light sleep when visions can be seen, not the deep sleep (*sopor*, 173) in which unreal dreams and figments of the imagination occur.

148. 'The sacred images of the gods, the Phrygian Penates'; *effigies* means the actual images which Aeneas is carrying with him (cf. *Aen.* 2.293): the Penates appear to him in the form in which he knows them. *Effigies . . . Phrygiique Penates* is a hendiadys, cf. *Aen.* 1.54, 61.

151. **in somnis**: a frequent poetic plural, cf. *Aen.* 4.560.

151-2. 'very clear in bright light, where the full moon came pouring in through the open windows'. The meaning of *insertas* is much disputed. I incline to accept one of the suggestions of Servius — 'unshuttered' — as making the best sense; the word would then be a Virgilian coinage making a negative adjective from the participle of *sero*. Other suggestions are 'latticed' (also Servius, perhaps rightly), 'inset' (an uninteresting epithet, to say the least), and 'translucent' (hardly possible from the Latin).

153. This line occurs also in 2.775 and 8.35; it is best to understand the infinitives as dependent on *visi* rather than as historic infinitives.

154-5. Apollo takes the initiative (*ultro*) without waiting for Aeneas to return to Delos (*Ortygia*). Observe the rhetorical case of the tense usage, much more vivid than 'what he would have told you'.

156-9. Notice how the antithesis of *tua nos* (155) is continued in these lines, and resumed in the subject *idem*. Impressiveness is sought by very simple devices of diction. For the prophecy of Roman greatness see note on 84 f., and cf. especially *Aen.* 1.278 f.

159-60. The alliteration here is very marked indeed, first of *m* and then of *l*, reinforced by the -*ng*-, -*gn*-, -*nqu*- sounds. This, along with the repetition of *magnus*, continues the feeling of impressiveness secured by obvious art. The phraseology is reminiscent of Hector s words in 2.294–5 *his moenia quaere | magna*. . . .

161–2. 'It was not these shores which Delian Apollo urged you to seek, nor did he bid you make your settlement in Crete'. For *non* continued by *aut* cf. 42–3. Observe the interwoven order; *Delius Apollo* is the subject of both clauses, though the adjective is in one clause and the noun in the other.

162. **Cretae**: the locative of *Creta* is very rare indeed.

163–6. These lines occur in exactly the same form in 1.530–3, where see notes.

167–8. The three clauses are all without a main verb; the effect is an oracular brevity.

167–8. One of the most frequent epithets of the Trojans is *Dardanidae*. One Latin version of the story was that the brothers Iasius and Dardanus set out from Italy to make a settlement abroad, and Dardanus went to Troy and Iasius to Samothrace. But in another version (*Aen.* 7.207 f.) Dardanus is said to have gone both to Samothrace and Troy. For Dardanus and Teucer as founders of Troy see note on 108; cf. also 8.134 *Dardanus Iliacae primus pater urbis et auctor*.

170. **Corythum**: Corythus and Electra were the parents of Iasius and Dardanus (Dardanus, however, was born of Electra by Jupiter). The city bearing Corythus' name was identified with Cortona, north of Trasimene; cf. *Aen.* 7.209.

171. **Ausonias**: this very common word meaning Italian is cognate with *Aurunci*, a people of central Italy.

Dictaea: Dicte was the mountain in Crete where Jupiter was born (cf. 104).

173. **nec sopor illud erat**: 'nor was that an empty dream'; Virgil is following the distinction made in Hom. *Od.* 19.547 between ὄναρ and ὕπαρ (see note on 148 f.). Cf. also *Aen.* 8.42, 10.642.

175. Cf. Enn. *Ann.* 418 *tunc timido manat ex omni corpore sudor*.

176 f. Sacrifices are made after a supernatural vision also at 5.743 f., 8.68 f.

177–8. **munera ... focis**: 'I offer pure sacrifice at the hearths'; for *libare* cf. 303, 354. *Intemerata* (not found before Virgil) means that there is no violation of the required ritual.

180–1. 'He recognised that our people were of double ancestry, of twofold parentage, and that he had been deceived by a new mistake about ancient lands'; both Dardanus and Teucer were *parentes*.

182. **Iliacis ... fatis**: 'hard-pressed by Trojan destiny'. The same phrase is used by the shade of Anchises to Aeneas in 5.725. The ill-fortune of Troy was proverbial, cf. 6.62. The word *exercite* suggests Stoic terminology; in some ways (but not all) Aeneas is like a Stoic undergoing his testing time.

183. **Cassandra**: cf. 2.246 f., 10.67 f.; it was fated that because she had spurned Apollo her prophecies should be disbelieved.

184. The subject (*Cassandram*) of the infinitive *portendere* is omitted; cf. 144, 146, 472. *Portendere* reports the imperfect indicative; cf. *Aen*. 1.619.

186. Notice the strong rhetorical emphasis on the word *Hesperiae*, repeated from the previous line in the same position of the line; cf. 253–4.

187. **crederet ... moveret**: past potential subjunctives: 'who would have believed. . . ?'

190. **paucisque relictis**: thus Virgil accounts for the existing town of Pergamum in Crete.

191. **cava trabe**: the metonymy of *trabs* for *navis* (cf. *Aen*. 4.566) is common from Ennius onwards.

   currimus aequor: accusative of extent of space, cf. *Aen*. 1.67.

192–208. *The Trojans endure a great storm at sea for three days and nights, and on the fourth day reach the Strophades.*

192–5. These lines, which are modelled on Hom. *Od*. 12.403–6 (= 14.301–4), are almost exactly repeated in *Aen*. 5.8–11.

194. **caeruleus ... imber**: 'a black storm-cloud'; for *caeruleus* of dark colour cf. 64.

195. **et inhorruit ... tenebris**: 'and the waves grew rough under its dark onset'. For *inhorruit* cf. Pacuvius *ap*. Cic. *De Div*. 1.24 *inhorrescit mare, tenebrae conduplicantur*, and *Geo*. 1.314, *Aen*. 10.711; compare also Cat. 64.269, and line 285 of this book where (as here) a dactylic rhythm is used for the surge of the sea.

199. **abstulit**: 'took from us', 'hid', cf. *Aen*. 1.88.

   ingeminant ... ignes: 'the clouds are rent, and the lightning redoubles its fury'; cf. Ov. *Fast*. 2.495.

200. The violence of being 'hurled off course' is reflected by the harsh alliteration of *c*; *caecis* means 'unseen, dangerous', cf. 706.

201–2. Notice the interlaced order with *ipse* in one clause and *Palinurus* in the next; cf. 161–2.

201. negat discernere: the reflexive subject of the infinitive is omitted, cf. 603 and *Geo.* 2.234; the phrase is equivalent to *negat se posse discernere*.

202. nec: *negare* is sometimes followed by a redundantly negative co-ordinating word; cf. Cic. *Acad.* 2.79.

meminisse: a rather unexpected word, apparently meaning 'recognize, keep reckoning of'; in the darkness he has no navigational aid from the sky, or from landmarks.

Palinurus: the chief helmsman of the Trojans (cf. 513); his story is told at the end of Book 5, and in 6.347 f.

203. tris adeo . . . soles: 'for three long days'; *adeo* intensifies *tris*, cf. *Aen.* 7.629.

incertos . . . caligine: 'obscured in black darkness'; *incertos* means there was *nihil certum*, both literally and metaphorically.

205–6. 'Only on the fourth day did we at long last see land rising up, revealing mountains far off and curling smoke'; for *aperire* cf. 275.

207. vela cadunt: 'down come the sails', i.e. the yard-arm to which the sails were attached is taken down (cf. 549) so that they can bring the ships into land by rowing.

208. The same line occurs in 4.583; cf. also line 290, Enn. *Ann.* 384, Spenser, *F.Q.* 2.12.10 'with his stiffe oares did brush the sea so strong'. For *caerula* (the neuter of the adjective used as a noun) cf. 315, 434.

209–77. *The Trojans land on the Strophades, kill some cattle for a meal, and are at once attacked by the Harpies, half-human monsters who pollute their food. Aeneas and his men drive them off, and Celaeno, oldest of the Harpies, in a hostile prophecy proclaims that the Trojans will not found their city until hunger has made them eat their tables. They set sail and after passing Ithaca land at Leucate.*

209 f. The episode of the Harpies is partly based on Apollonius (2.178 f., esp. 262 f.), the tale of how the two sons of Boreas drove the Harpies away from Phineus; there are also some marked points of similarity with the theft of the cattle of the Sun-God by Odysseus' companions (Hom. *Od.* 12.260 f.).

This episode and the episode of Achaemenides (588 f.) are the

two major mythological adventure stories which Virgil includes
in the wanderings of Aeneas; there is also the brief account of
Scylla and Charybdis (554 f.). They serve to give variety and add
an element of mystery and fantasy to the national and quasi-
historical atmosphere of most of the voyage. In tone and mood
they do not harmonize with the rest of this book; they are
Odyssean rather than Roman; and yet like a touch of baroque
on an unadorned building they give a irrational pleasure. They
are handled differently: the Achaemenides story is elaborated
into a piece of grandiose and hyperbolic writing, but the story of
Harpies depends on the rapid and direct narrative of strange and
unreal events. A link with the main theme is achieved by Celaeno's
prophecy about the tables, a very old feature of the legend which
Virgil was the first to attribute to the Harpies (see note on 256 f.).
The main effect of this passage is to bring the reader away from
the mood of hope which the previous episode has encouraged
into an atmosphere of hostility, gloom and disaster; we see the
Trojans again as exiles wandering in a wilderness of sea, very far
from their promised home.

209. **Strophadum**: these are small islands to the west of the
Peloponnese; they did not figure in the Aeneas legend before
Virgil.

210-11. 'They are islands set in the wide Ionian sea, called by
their Greek name Strophades'. *Stant* is used in its geographical
sense, cf. *Aen.* 8.233 and our 'London stands on the Thames'.
Virgil here refers to the derivation of Strophades from the Greek
στρέφεσθαι ('turn'), because in one version of the story the sons
of Boreas were here turned back by the goddess Iris from their
pursuit of the Harpies (Ap. Rh. 2.296 f.).

211. **īnsŭlăe Ionio**: a remarkable instance of the shortening
of a diphthong in hiatus after the Greek style; cf. *Geo.* 1.437, 4.461,
Aen. 5.261.

Ionio in magno: the Ionian sea was the southern part of the
Adriatic; *Ionium* is used as a noun (*mare* being understood), cf.
'the Atlantic'.

211-12. **dira Celaeno Harpyiaeque**: in Homer the Harpies
are personifications of storm-winds ('Snatchers', from ἁρπάζειν),
cf. *Od.* 1.241, 14.371, 20.61-78. Their names (Swiftfoot, Whirlwind, Swiftwing — Hom. *Il.* 16.150, Hes. *Theog.* 267) are

appropriate for storm-winds, and so is Celaeno (κελαινός, 'dark'),
a name which is not found before Virgil. They are represented
as birds with the faces of women, and are often associated with
the Sirens and with the Furies (cf. 252). The concept of Harpies
as foul and disgusting creatures came later, and was especially
associated with the story of how Zeus sent them to torment
Phineus by snatching his food from him and polluting what
remained (Ap. Rh. 2.178f.). When the Argonauts passed his
home in Bithynia he appealed to them for help, and the sons of
Boreas (Calais and Zetes) drove the Harpies away and would
have killed them had not Iris intervened, promising that they
would never torment Phineus again. There is a full description
of the Snatchers in William Morris, *The Life and Death of Jason*,
5.229 f.; cf. also Dante, *Inf.* 13.10 f.; Milton, *P.L.* 2.596 f. ('harpy-
footed Furies'), *P.R.* 2.401 f., 'Both Table and Provision vanished
quite / with sound of Harpies' wings and Talons heard'. In *The
Tempest* (3.3) Ariel enters 'like a harpy; claps his wings upon the
table; and, with a quaint device, the banquet vanishes'.

212. **Harpyiae**: the word scans as three long syllables, the
middle syllable being the Greek diphthong υι.

214–15. 'There never arose from the waters of Styx any more
horrid abomination than these, nor any more savage plague
sent by the angry gods'. *Monstrum* indicates a supernatural horror
(cf. 658, 4.181, 8.198); *ira deum* is explanatory of *pestis*. The
Harpies have a place at the entrance to the underworld in
6.289.

217–18. The perpetual hunger of the Harpies gives special
point to Celaeno's prophecy in 256 about the Trojans eating
their tables because of *dira fames*.

218. For the incomplete line, see note on 1.534; the others in
this book are 316, 340, 470, 527, 640, 661.

220. This is reminiscent of the forbidden cattle of the Sun-God
in Hom. *Od.* 12.261 f., 353 f.

220. **laeta**: 'sleek': Servius says *pinguia*.

221. **caprigenum**: a striking adjective of an archaic type;
Macrobius (*Sat.* 6.5.14) cites instances from Pacuvius and Accius,
and there is an instance in Cicero's verse (*caprigeni pecoris custos*).

223. **in partem praedamque**: 'to share the spoil', a good
example of hendiadys, cf. *Aen.* 1.54.

224. For *-que . . . -que* ('both . . . and') cf. 91. The couches are
'built up' of turf, leaves, etc.; cf. *Aen.* 11.66. *Epulari* is very rare
with the ablative ('feast on', like *vesci*); cf. *Geo.* 2.537.

226. **clangoribus:** a strange and vivid word applied to the
noise of their wings; Day Lewis well renders 'hoarse vibration of
wing-beats'. Servius cannot be right in applying it to their cries
because of *tum vox* in 228.

228. **tum vox . . . odorem:** cf. Lucr. 3.581. Notice the omission of *est* or *fit*; the whole phrase has a strange rhythm.

229 f. **rursum . . . rursum:** this archaic form of *rursus* occurs
in Virgil only here and once in the *Georgics*.

230. This verse occurs at *Aen.* 1.311, where *clausam* is grammatical, as here it is not. Probably some early scribe or reader of
Virgil remembered it and inserted it here in his copy.

231. Notice the emphasis on the religious associations of the
banquet; cf. 222 f.

232. **ex diverso caeli:** 'from a different quarter of the sky'.
The neuter of *diversus* is used as a noun, cf. *Aen.* 2.716, and see
note on 1.422.

234–5. Notice the variation of construction with *edico:* first
the jussive subjunctive in parataxis (cf. 456 f.), and then the
accusative with the gerundive.

236. **iussi:** supply *sunt*, cf. 561.

236–7. **tectos . . . latentia:** both epithets are predicative:
'they put their swords out of sight and hide their shields from view'.

239. Misenus has been posted as a look-out and now gives the
alarm on his trumpet; the story of his death is told in *Aen.* 6.162 f.

240. **nova:** 'strange', 'weird'.

241. **obscenas:** a very strong word, cf. 262, 367, *Aen.* 4.455.

pelagi: the parentage of the Harpies varied considerably in
legend; Servius recounts a version which made them children of
Sea and Earth.

242–3. The invulnerability of the Harpies (*accipiunt* = feel) is
not mentioned elsewhere; compare, however, the brazen feathers
of the Stymphalian birds (Hercules' sixth labour).

244. **semesam:** = *semiesam*, cf. *semustum* (578).

245–6. These lines have a very vivid visual impact; notice too
how the spondaic rhythm slows the movement for the grim
prophecy.

245. **praecelsa**: a very rare variant for *excelsus*. Virgil is fond of the intensifying *prae*; cf. *praepinguis* (698), *praedives, praedurus, praedulcis, praevalidus*.

Celaeno: see note on 211-12, and cf. Spenser, *Faerie Queene* 2.7.23 where Celaeno is a bird of ill-omen at the entrance to Mammon's cave:

> Whiles sad Celeno, sitting on a clift,
> A song of bale and bitter sorrow sings . . .

246. **infelix vates**: 'prophetess of doom', cf. *Faerie Queene* 2.12.36, 'The hellish Harpies, prophets of sad destiny'.

rumpitque . . . vocem: 'and breaks out with this cry'. This unusual poetic sense of *rumpere* is first found in Virgil; see note on *Aen.* 2.129.

247-8. 'War as well, is it? You are ready to wage war, are you, in return for the slaughter of our cattle and the killing of our heifers?' *Pro* is used ironically; some recompense would be expected, instead of one wrong heaped on another.

248. **Laomedontiadae**: the epithet has implications of treachery (cf. *Geo.* 1.502, *Aen.* 4.542); the early Trojan king Laomedon cheated the gods of the promised reward for building the walls of Troy (Hor. *Odes* 3.3.21 f.).

252. **Furiarum ego maxima**: the Harpies are commonly identified with the Furies; the phrase *Furiarum maxima* is used in *Aen.* 6.605 of the Fury, who is engaged in the harpy-like activity of preventing the damned from reaching the food spread out before them.

254. The repetition of *Italiam* helps to build up the tension in this line of mocking irony before the resolution of tension in *sed non.* . . .

255. **datam**: even Celaeno must admit that the city is promised; cf. 501.

256 f. 'until terrible hunger and the wrong you have done in trying to kill us compel you to gnaw at your tables, and chew them up in your mouths.'

The prophecy is fulfilled in *Aen.* 7.109 f., when the Trojans immediately after landing in Italy make a meal of *poma agrestia* laid out on thin platters of bread (*Cereale solum*). The meal is insufficient, so they eat the platters too, and Iulus cries '*Heus etiam mensas consumimus*', upon which Aeneas recognizes the omen and recalls the prophecy, wrongly attributing it to Anchises. Virgil was the first to attribute it to Celaeno, and it is indeed suited to the strange and fabulous world of the ever-famished Harpies; for the sources of the story see note on 7.107 f.

256. **nostraeque iniuria caedis**: for the genitive of definition ('wrong consisting of . . .') cf. *Aen.* 1.27 and line 604. The word *caedes* is here used with rhetorical exaggeration of the unsuccessful attempt to slaughter the Harpies.

257. **ambesas**: 'eaten round', 'gnawed round the edge', a very rare word; cf. *Aen.* 5.752.

259–60. Cf. line 30; *gelidus* here as there is predicative. *Deriguit* means 'curdled', like *coit* in 30. The word is nowhere else used in this sense.

260–1. There is a quite marked zeugma here; the sense is *non iam armis petere salutem sed exposcendo pacem*.

262. **sint**: subjunctive as part of the *iubent* construction.

263. Notice how Anchises takes the initiative; see note on 1 f.

passis: *pandere* does not occur elsewhere in Virgil with *palmas*; his usual phrase is *tendere palmas*.

264. **meritosque . . . honores**: 'proclaims due sacrifices', cf. 118. *Indicere* is a formal and solemn word, cf. *Aen.* 1.632.

266. **placidi**: 'graciously', cf. *Aen.* 4.578.

pios: the keyword of the poem, see note on 42 and cf. *Aen.* 1.526.

267. **excussosque . . . rudentis**: 'to free and let out the sheets'. The previous phrase refers to the mooring-rope; this phrase refers to the ropes attached to the lower corners of the sails, which would be paid out according to the angle required with the wind.

269. Virgil imitates Hom. *Od.* 11.10 τὴν δ' ἄνεμός τε κυβερνήτης τ' ἴθυνε, using -*que* . . . -*que* (see note on 91) and the Greek trochaic caesura in the third foot without a strong caesura in the fourth foot, an unusual Latin rhythm which here gives an effect of speed.

270. **nemorosa Zacynthos**: Homer's ὑλήεσσα Ζάκυνθος (*Od.* 9.24), hence the licence of the short *a* before the double consonant *z*.

270–1. The first three names are from Homer *Od.* 9.24, all

places near Ithaca. Neritos surely derives from Homer's Mt. Neriton on Ithaca (*Od.* 9.22, *Il.* 2.632), but clearly Virgil thinks of it as an island.

272. **Laertia regna**: *Laertius* is an adjective from Laertes, Odysseus' father.

273. Notice the vehemence of this line, reinforced by the spondaic movement with two heavy elisions. The Virgilian Ulysses (*dirus Ulixes, scelerum inventor*) is an unpleasant character, very different from the Homeric Odysseus; see note on 2.7.

Ulixi: for the genitive form see note on 2.7.

274 f. In the tradition of Aeneas' voyage as given by Dionysius (1.50.3–4) the Trojans stopped and built temples at Zacynthus, Leucas, and Actium. Virgil, wishing to avoid sameness of episodes, brings them past Zacynthus and then combines Leucas and Actium into a single stage without reconciling the geographical facts. Leucate, with its well-known temple to Apollo was a notoriously dangerous promontory on the southern tip of the island of Leucas; Actium, some thirty or forty miles further north, also had a temple to Apollo recently restored by Augustus in honour of his victory (Suet. *Aug.* 18, *Aen.* 8.704). Cf. *Aen.* 8.677 where Leucate is mentioned as the scene of the battle of Actium, and for further geographical discussion see R. B. Lloyd, *A.J.Ph.*, 1954, pp. 292 f.

275. **nautis**: dative of agent, cf. 14.

aperitur: 'is revealed to view', cf. 205–6.

Apollo: the name of the god stands for his temple, a common metonymy; cf. 552.

276. **parvae . . . urbi**: i.e. the little town which Augustus had recently enlarged into Nicopolis; for elaboration of this kind of effect cf. Aeneas' visit (8.337 f.) to Evander's simple dwelling on the site of Rome.

278–93. *The Trojans make offerings and celebrate games at Actium; Aeneas dedicates a shield to Apollo, and they sail on again to Buthrotum.*

278 f. Actium, like Zacynthus and Leucas, was one of the places in this area which figured in the Aeneas legend (Dion. 1.50.4). Virgil has put special emphasis on Actium by transferring there the games associated in the legend with Zacynthus, thus linking the past with the present by giving a prototype for Augustus'

great Actian games (see note on 280). This aetiological intention is the more noticeable because this is the only one of the episodes on the way to Italy which does not contain prophecy or some other indication of progression towards the ultimate goal; it stands out as an Augustan episode in the midst of Aeneas' voyage.

278. **insperata**: because they have been sailing through Greek seas and have just passed the most dangerous area of all, the islands around Ithaca (282–3).

279. 'we perform the rituals of purification to Jupiter, and make the altars blaze with our offerings': *lustramur* is here middle ('we purify ourselves'), see note on 405.

280. **Actia**: the poetic form of *Actiacus*, the adjective of Actium, the name of the promontory off which Augustus defeated Antony and Cleopatra in 31 B.C. The temple to Apollo was restored and enlarged, and Augustus instituted at Nicopolis, the site of his camp, a large-scale festival called the Actian games. They were modelled on the great Greek festivals, and the extended account in *Aeneid* 5 of the anniversary games for Anchises is clearly associated with the revived interest in this type of athletic competition which Augustus stimulated; see the Intro. to my *Aeneid* 5 (Oxford), pp. x f.

281. **exercent patrias ... palaestras**: 'engage in their traditional wrestling-bouts'; for *exercere* cf. *Aen.* 4.87.

282. **evasisse**: 'to have avoided'; the transitive use is quite common in poetry, cf. *Geo.* 4.485, *Aen.* 5.689.

284. 'Meanwhile the sun rolls on through the great circle of the year', an ornate poetic expression for the passage of time as winter comes on (285). The accusative *annum* is governed by the preposition in the verb.

286. **aere cavo clipeum**: 'a shield of curved bronze', i.e. made concave by beating, cf. *Aen.* 10.784.

gestamen: 'accoutrement', that which is carried, cf. *Aen.* 7.246.

Abantis: Servius suggests that Abas was one of the Greek party whose armour the Trojans captured during the sack of the city (*Aen.* 2.389 f.). The dedication of enemy spoils suggests the trophies which Augustus dedicated after his victory at Actium.

287. **rem carmine signo**: 'I commemorate the event with a verse', i.e. an inscription, cf. *Ecl.* 5.42.

288. In Latin inscriptions the verb *dat* or *dedicat* is frequently abbreviated or omitted. The phrase here is rather elliptical, as *de* depends on some understood verb like *erepta*. Notice the irony of the inscription with *victoribus* where *victis* would be expected.

291. **aërias Phaeacum ... arces**: 'the cloud-capped towers of the Phaeacians', a mysterious and haunting phrase. The fairyland of the Phaeacians, ruled by King Alcinous, was the last of all the places visited by Odysseus; by the time of Apollonius (4.991 f.) it was definitely localised at Corcyra.

abscondimus: 'we lose from view', a most remarkable use of the word, imitated by Seneca (*Ep. Mor.* 70.2) and Claudian (*R.P.* 3.140). Servius says it was a nautical technical term.

292. **legimus**: 'skirt', cf. 706.

portu: dative, cf. 541, 692.

293. **Chaonio**: the name of a part of Epirus (cf. 334–5) where Buthrotum was a town on the coast.

294–355. *At Buthrotum the Trojans hear that Helenus, son of Priam, is ruling over part of Pyrrhus' kingdom and is married to Andromache. Aeneas meets Andromache as she is making offerings at the empty tomb of Hector. She tells the story of her misfortunes since the fall of Troy, and Helenus approaches and welcomes the Trojans hospitably.*

294 f. The visit of the Trojans to Buthrotum was well established in the tradition of the legend, but the introduction of Andromache seems to be a Virgilian innovation. She figured, of course, very largely in other stories which would be familiar to Virgil especially perhaps from Euripides' *Andromache* and *Troades*, and Virgil's introduction of her here raises the level of emotional intensity in a book which otherwise has little of the sensitive pathos which we so frequently find elsewhere in the *Aeneid*.

This long episode is constructed in three scenes: the arrival, the prophecy of Helenus, and the departure. The long central prophecy (see note on 374 f.) is slow-moving and factual, combining reminiscence of literary sources with emphasis on religious ritual, and making little demand on the emotions. It is framed by the two scenes about Andromache, both of them full of pathos and sympathy which become particularly marked in the final scene (488–91). Only here in the whole book do we see the Trojans in contact with human society (except for the very brief

mention of Anius and the meeting with the castaway Achaemenides).

294. **occupat auris**: 'strikes our ears', 'comes on our startled
ears', a vivid use of the word.

295. **Priamiden Helenum**: the Trojan Helenus, one of the
sons of Priam, appears a number of times in the *Iliad*; he is the
best of augurs (*Il.* 6.76). Cf. Ov. *Met.* 15.436 f. for his prophecy
to Aeneas of Rome's greatness.

296. **coniugio**: 'the bride', abstract for concrete, cf. *Aen.*
2.579.

296. **Aeacidae Pyrrhi**: Pyrrhus or Neoptolemus, son of
Achilles, was the great-grandson of Aeacus. The story about
Pyrrhus and Helenus (see Servius' note on 2.166) was as follows.
At the fall of Troy Helenus and Andromache became captives of
Pyrrhus. Helenus with his prophetic powers foresaw that the sea
voyage for the Greeks would be fraught with calamity, and urged
Pyrrhus to return home by land. This he did, accompanied by
Helenus and Andromache; and when he died (see note on 332)
he left to Helenus in gratitude a share of his kingdom, and
Andromache for wife.

297. 'and that Andromache had passed to a husband of her
own race again', i.e. a Trojan (she originally came from Thebe
in Asia Minor, but the reference here is to her having been married
to Hector).

298. **miro ... amore**: the strong phrase suggests the overwhelming longing of the exile to meet his old friend.

299. **compellare**: for the infinitive dependent on the noun
amor cf. *Aen.* 2.10 and line 670 (*potestas*).

300 f. 'I set out from the harbour, leaving behind me the ships
on the shore, as it chanced just at a time when Andromache was
making her libation to the dead, a libation of ritual feasts and
gifts of sorrow, in front of the city in a grove by the stream which
the exiles pretended was Simois. She was calling Hector's ghost
to visit his tomb, a cenotaph of green turf where she had consecrated twin altars, there to shed her tears'.

The construction of the sentence is elaborate, with a gradual
build-up of phrases before the verb and then the subject, and then
very late in the sentence the key word *Hectoreum*.

301 f. The pouring of libations and the offering of food at

inferiae for the dead was normal; cf. 66 and *Aen.* 5.77 f. For the invocation of the dead cf. *Aen.* 5.98, 6.506.

301. **sollemnis**: 'ritual', 'regularly performed'.

302. **falsi Simoentis**: i.e. this river was called Simois after the real Simois in Troy (cf. *Aen.* 1.100).

303. **libabat**: cf. 177–8.

304. **viridi quem caespite**: the impact of this part of the sentence is given by the individual phrases taken in their order; the effect is achieved by a certain loosening of the syntax. The tomb was of green turf, it was a cenotaph, Andromache had dedicated twin altars there.

305. **causam lacrimis**: the tomb with its altars 'causes' Andromache's tears because here her sorrow has its focal point.

306–7. **Troia circum arma**: probably 'Trojan warriors accompanying me' (as they were, 347) rather than 'the Trojan armour I was wearing'.

307. **magnis . . . monstris**: 'a marvel so incredible', it seems supernatural, unreal, to Andromache. The poetic plural *monstra* is of the type where the plural adds impressiveness, as *templa, sceptra*, etc.

309. **labitur**: 'she falls', i.e. faints, cf. *Aen.* 11.818.

longo . . . tempore: the ablative is probably by analogy with the common *longo post tempore*.

310–12. Andromache can hardly believe that Aeneas is really present in person — she half believes he is a phantom, come in response to her invocations at Hector's tomb — why then has he come and not Hector?

313–14. 'Hardly could I make this brief reply to her distraught words, in my confusion stammering these broken phrases'; *hiscere* occurs only here in Virgil, cf. *hiare* in the same sense in *Aen.* 6.493.

317. **deiectam coniuge tanto**: 'bereaved of your noble husband'; the use of *deiectus* is similar to that in *spe deiectus*, etc. Notice the slow spondees here.

319. **Pyrrhin**: for *Pyrrhine*, cf. *Aen.* 6.779, 12.797.

conubia servas: an extension of such phrases as *promissum servare, amicitiam servare*, cf. *Aen.* 2.789.

321 f. Andromache contrasts her fate with that of Priam's daughter Polyxena, who was sacrificed on the tomb of Achilles;

cf. Eur. *Hec.* 218 f., Ov. *Met.* 13.439 f. For the form of the sentence cf. *Aen.* 1.94 f., 5.623 f.

323. **sortitus**: the Greeks drew lots for their prisoners after the fall of Troy (Eur. *Tro.* 235 f.).

324. **heri**: *herus* (*erus*) is a common word in comedy, but it is very rare indeed in epic and the high style; Andromache's use of the everyday word emphasises her anger and contempt.

327. **servitio enixae**: 'bringing forth a child in slavery', cf. Eur. *Andr.* 24 f. The child was Molossus, ancestor of the Molossian kings of Epirus.

328. **Ledaeam Hermionen**: Hermione was the daughter of Helen and Menelaus of Sparta, Helen the daughter of Leda (*Aen.* 1.652). We hear in Homer (*Od.* 4.3 f.) of the arrangements for the marriage of Hermione and Pyrrhus; in Euripides' *Andromache* she is married to him, but leaves him for Orestes.

329. 'handed me over into the possession of Helenus, a slave to a slave'; for the repetition in the Greek style cf. *Aen.* 1.684, 5.569. The co-ordinating -*que* is not necessary grammatically, and so adds fuller emphasis; cf. *Aen.* 5.447, 12.289.

transmisit habendam: the phrase is scornful, suggesting the transfer of property.

331. **coniugis**: Orestes' intended bride, cf. *Aen.* 2.344 (*gener*).

scelerum furiis agitatus: 'hounded by the madness of his crimes', cf. *Aen.* 4.471. The story of how Orestes killed his mother Clytemnestra to avenge his father and of his subsequent madness induced by the Furies was a very well-known one in Roman drama and art; see Austin on *Aen.* 4.469 f.

332. **excipit**: 'caught', a usage common in hunting terminology, cf. *Ecl.* 3.18.

Pyrrhus was killed in Apollo's temple at Delphi (Eur. *Or.* 1653 f.), and Servius explains *patrias* by referring to a tradition that Pyrrhus had set up an altar to his father Achilles in this temple. Thus Pyrrhus in a sense suffers what he had inflicted on Polites and Priam (*Aen.* 2.526 f., esp. 663).

333. **reddita cessit**: 'was duly bequeathed and passed'; the compound *re-* in *reddere* does not always mean 'back', but may indicate 'appropriately', cf. *Aen.* 4.392, 5.386.

334–5. 'who called the plains by the name Chaonian, and the whole area Chaonia after Chaon of Troy'. The etymological association (see note on 18) seems to be Virgil's own; Chaon is not heard of elsewhere, and the general tradition about the Chaonians was that they were so called before the Trojan war.

336. 'and set this our Pergama and this Ilian citadel upon their hills'; for the re-use of Trojan names in Epirus cf. 302, 349 f.

337–8. Notice the emphasis on divine motivation; although Andromache does not know, she puts her questions so as to lead to the answer of Roman destiny.

339. **superatne**: 'is he still alive?'; cf. *Aen.* 2.567. 643.

340. This is the only half-line in the *Aeneid* where the sense is incomplete. It is very difficult to see what was in Virgil's mind when he wrote these four words; all we can say is that he began some thought which he could not bring into the form in which he wanted it, and he left it there and went on.

341. **tamen**: the force of this is very obscure, and in view of the uncertainty of the intended meaning of the previous line must remain so.

amissae cura parentis: i.e. Creusa. Virgil does not tell us how Andromache knew that Creusa had been lost.

343. This line is repeated in 12.440. Creusa, Aeneas' wife, was a sister of Hector.

348. **multum lacrimas**: *P* has *lacrimans*, and Servius knew the reading, but pointed out that we need *lacrimas* as the object of *fundit*. The adverbial use of *multum* is common enough (*Aen.* 6.481, 11.49), but its use here is strange. It is very likely that in revision Virgil would have recast this line.

349–51. Helenus has called his town by the names of his old home-town: it is a little Troy, with a citadel called Pergama — a copy of mighty Pergama —, with a dried-up river called Xanthus, very different from the whirling Xanthus of Troy (Hom. *Il.* 20.73), and with a Scaean gate, called after the west gate of Troy (*Aen.* 2.612).

349. **simulataque magnis**: literally 'made like the mighty Pergama', cf. Ov. *Met.* 13.721, Cic. *Ad Att.* 9.8.2.

353 f. The king receives the Trojans in the colonnades around the *aula*, in the centre of which is the altar.

354. **aulai**: this archaic disyllabic form of the genitive ending is found in Ennius, is used very frequently by Lucretius (169

times), but occurs only four times in Virgil (*Aen.* 6.747, 7.464, 9.26) and not at all in Ovid or Silver Age epic.

354. **libabant pocula Bacchi**: 'they poured in libation the juice of wine'; for the metonymy of *Bacchus* for *vinum* cf. *Aen.* 1.215.

356–73. *Aeneas consults Helenus about his voyage and Celaeno's threat. Helenus takes him to the temple and begins his prophecy.*

359. **Troiugena**: 'Trojan-born', cf. *Aen.* 8.117, 12.626 and compare *Graiugena* (550).

360. **tripoda ac Clarii laurus**: *tripoda ac* is Mackail's emendation for *tripodas*, which gives a harsh asyndeton. Others read *tripodas Clarii et*, found in some late MSS. The priestesses of Apollo's shrine at Delphi gave their prophecies from their position on the sacred tripod, their hair crowned with laurel; cf. 81, 92 and Lucr. 1.739. Apollo's epithet *Clarius* is from his worship at Claros near Colophon.

360–1. Here Aeneas refers to various methods of divination, first astrology, and then augury from the cries or flight of birds; cf. *Aen.* 10.175 f. Astrology was much discussed by the Romans, but is rarely mentioned in the *Aeneid*, never at length. For signs from birds cf. *Ecl.* 9.14 f., *Aen.* 1.393 f., 12.244 f. The word *praepes* is a strange one; as a technical term in augury it indicated 'high', and 'propitious', but it came to be used in a much wider sense in poetry, simply meaning 'winged', 'flying'.

362–3. 'for all the divine signs have spoken to me of my journey in favourable terms'. The reference is to the various signs and oracles which Aeneas has already received, such as the prophecies by Apollo and the Penates, and the signs given to Anchises in Book 2. For the strange phrase *omnis religio* cf. *Aen.* 12.182 and *fas omne* (5.800).

364. **repostas**: 'remote', syncope for *repositas*, cf. *Aen.* 1.26.

367. **vito**: for the indicative in a deliberative question cf. 88.

368. **possim**: potential, *sequens* having the sense of *si sequar*.

369. **hic**: 'at this', cf. *Aen.* 2.699, 735.

370. **vittasque resolvit**: the garlands were removed before the oracular trance, so that the hair fell loose and no hindrance might prevent the abandonment of the person to the gods; cf. *Aen.* 6.48.

372. **multo suspensum numine**: 'tensely anxious in the manifold presence of deity', cf. *Aen.* 2.114, 729.

374–462. *Helenus makes his prophecy, telling the Trojans that they still have far to go; they will know that they have reached the site of their city by the sign of the white sow. There is no need to fear Celaeno's threat. They must beware of the eastern coast of Italy, and after sacrificing in the prescribed manner must sail on round Sicily, thus avoiding Scylla and Charybdis. Above all they must make constant prayer and sacrifice to Juno. They must then land at Cumae to consult the Sibyl; she will tell them of the wars to be fought in Italy.*

374 f. Just as the visit to Buthrotum forms a centre-piece for the events of Book 3, so the long speech of Helenus is the central feature of this visit. It is by far the longest piece of prophecy about the voyage of Aeneas; it may be compared with Circe's prophecy to Odysseus in Hom. *Od.* 12.37–141, and with that of Phineus in Ap. Rh. 2.311 f.

The speech is delivered in oracular style, that is to say it is admonitory, emphatic, directly didactic; its effects are not subtle or sophisticated, and the level of emotional tension is not high. It contrasts very markedly in this with the passages about Andromache which precede and follow it. There are lines with very obvious rhetorical effects, especially those involving repetition (383, 412, 433 f.), and alliteration is frequent (375–6, 424–8 455–9). The metrical movement does not have Virgil's usual variety of cadence and is in some way reminiscent of his predecessors. For fuller discussion see my Oxford edition ad loc.

Virgil is able to choose which events of the voyage Helenus should reveal by telling us (377 f.) that Juno permits him to reveal only part of the future (cf. Ap. Rh. 2.311 f.). Thus he omits mention of Polyphemus, the death of Anchises, the storm which drives the Trojans to Carthage, the visit to Carthage, the return visit to Sicily with the burning of the ships and the death of Palinurus, the visit to the underworld. Helenus' speech is very largely concerned with divine signs, propitiation of deities, consultation of oracles. In three places Helenus dwells on his theme at some length: the method of sacrificing, Scylla and Charybdis, the Sibylline oracle. The first and third of these have direct reference to contemporary Roman religion, the second is

inspired by Circe's prophecy in Homer. We see Virgil here, as
often elsewhere, interweaving reminiscence of Homer with Roman
aetiology.

374–5. **maioribus . . . auspiciis**: a technical term of religion,
cf. Cic. *De Rep.* 2.26.

375. **fides**: 'proof', cf. *Aen.* 2.309.

375–6. 'thus does the king of the gods apportion the fates and
turn the wheel of change, this is the sequence of the cycle of events';
notice how oracular impressiveness is built up by the accumulation of phrases of similar meaning. For *volvit* cf. *Aen.* 1.22, for
vertitur Aen. 2.250.

375. **deum rex**: the monosyllabic ending, reminiscent of
Ennius, contributes to an archaic effect, cf. line 12 and *Aen.* 1.65.

377–8. **hospita lustres aequora**: 'traverse the oceans that
will receive you'. *Hospita* is neuter plural as though from *hospitus*
('receiving', 'welcoming'), an adjective of *hospes* whose existence
is suggested by the feminine singular *hospita* (539).

381. **rere propinquam**: Italy was in fact near, but not the
part of it to which Aeneas had to sail. For *rere = reris* cf. *Aen.*
7.437.

383. 'a long pathless path with long coastlines lies between
you and Italy'; for *dividit* cf. *Aen.* 12.44 f. The line has a very
oracular ring about it, with the oxymoron of *via invia* and the
obvious device in the repetition of *longus*, and it is emphasised by
the assonance of *i*, the rhyme at the caesura and line-ending, and
the coincidence of words with feet in the second half.

384–7. **ante . . . quam . . . possis**: cf. 255 f. for *ante . . . quam*
with the subjunctive of futurity.

384. **Trinacria . . . in unda**: Sicily was called Trinacria
(cf. 429, 554) because of its triangular shape with its three
promontories; the supposed derivation was τρεῖς ἄκραι. The
Homeric form of the word was Thrinacia ('trident island').

lentandus remus: 'you must bend the oar'; the verb, which
is rare and poetic, refers to the 'give' of an oar in the water due
to its slight pliancy, cf. Cat. 64.183. There is also an overtone of
struggle and effort involved.

385. **salis Ausonii**: the meaning is the sea to the south-west
of Italy, commonly called the Tyrrhenian sea; the epithet is used
to link with Ausonia as Aeneas' promised land (378).

386. The nominatives in this line require some verb to be supplied from *lustrandum*, e.g. *adeunda sunt*.

infernique lacus: cf. 441 f. with note.

Aeaeaeque insula Circae: after leaving Cumae and calling at Caieta Aeneas passed the island of the enchantress Circe (*Aen.* 7.10 f.), half-way between Cumae and the mouth of the Tiber. Circe's island Aeaea in Homer is in the East (*Od.* 12.3–4); later tradition placed her in the West (Hes. *Theog.* 1011 f., Ap. Rh. 3.311 f.), but she always had strong associations with the Black Sea area and the magic of Colchis. See note on *Aen.* 7.10–11.

388. **signa**: 'signs', i.e. indications by which they will know they have reached the correct place (cf. *Aen.* 1.443).

tu . . . teneto: the phrase is reminiscent of Homeric formulae (σὺ δ' ἐνὶ φρεσὶ βάλλεο σ σιν, σὺ δὲ σύνθεο θυμῶ). Notice the conglomeration of *t*'s, and the formal ring of this form of the imperative, suitable for the didactic style (Virgil has it often in the *Georgics*).

389 f. The legend of the portent of the sow is found (with considerable variations) in the Aeneas saga from an early stage; cf. Lycophr. 1255 f., and my Oxford edition ad loc. for full discussion. The prophecy is repeated by Tiberinus (8.43 f.), and its fulfilment described in 8.81 f. Helenus refers the portent to the site of Aeneas' new city (presumably Lavinium); Tiberinus adds that it indicates the foundation of Alba in thirty years' time.

It is possible that there is a connexion between this Trojan legend and the Latin word *troia* (French *truie*) meaning a sow (though *troia* is not found before the eighth century). This would give an etymological association comparable with that of the *lusus Troiae* (where *Troia* is perhaps connected with an Etruscan word meaning 'maze-like movements'; see note on *Aen.* 5.545 f.).

389. **secreti**: 'remote', emphasising the idea of distance and also contrasting the later fame of the Tiber with its present obscurity, cf. *Aen.* 5.83.

390. Notice the monosyllabic ending (see note on 375); here the effect is, as Page says, one of 'archaic simplicity and rudeness'. The line is marked by strong assonance of *i*.

litoreis: *litus* is not commonly used of a river bank; cf. *Ecl.* 5.83.

391. 'delivered of a litter of thirty young'; for *enixa* cf. 327, for *caput* (compare our 'head' of cattle) cf. *Aen.* 5.61 f.

392. **albi ... nati**: a parenthetical insertion into the sentence (understand *erunt*), typical of Virgil's fondness for parataxis; cf. 14.

394 f. This refers to Celaeno's prophecy (see note on 256 f.), which was the immediate cause of Aeneas' inquiries (365 f.).

394. **nec ... horresce**: *nec* is commonly used in verse, and sometimes in prose, for *neve* (*Geo.* 2.96).

396. After his introductory statements about the length of the voyage, and the sign of arrival, Helenus begins to outline the events of the voyage.

397. 'which is the nearest shore bathed by the tide of our sea'; it is less than a hundred miles from this point in Epirus to the heel of Italy.

398. **malis ... Grais**: dative of agent. The epithet *malis* is natural in the mouth of a Trojan after the sack of Troy. Virgil allows himself some degree of anachronism in describing the part of the world known in his times as *Magna Graecia*, which the Greeks did not colonise till long after the fall of Troy.

399. **Narycii ... Locri**: Narycium (*Geo.* 2.438) was a town of the Locri who lived near Euboea. The story went that they were shipwrecked on their return from Troy with Ajax son of Oileus (*Aen.* 1.40 f.), and some made their way to Southern Italy.

400. **Sallentinos ... campos**: in Calabria, the part of Italy nearest to Epirus.

milite: 'soldiery', 'soldiers', a frequent use of the collective singular.

401. **Lyctius Idomeneus**: Lyctos was a town in the east of Crete (*Ecl.* 5.72); for Idomeneus see note on 122. The last syllable of his name is a diphthong, as in Greek.

401–2. Petelia lay on the coast between the Sallentini and the Locri; the name is presumably connected with the old Latin word *petilus*, 'thin', 'small', so that *parva* is an etymological epithet (see note on 693). Philoctetes, who came from Meliboea in Thessaly, was said in one version of the legend about him to have fled from his home to Southern Italy where he founded Petelia and Crimissa (Lycophr. 911 f.).

402. **subnixa**: 'resting on', cf. *Aen.* 1.506; the word here includes the nuance of 'defended by'.

403 f. Helenus here indicates by implication rather than direct

instruction that the Trojans will land in Italy when they first sight it, and after paying their vows will move on to Sicily (cf. 521–50).

403. quin: the use of *quin(= quin etiam)* adds an extra point with strong emphasis.

steterint: 'are anchored', a nautical use of the verb, cf. 277.

405. It was a Roman custom to cover the head during sacrifice; the Greeks did not do so (cf. Lucr. 5.1198 f., Ov. *Fast.* 3.363). Virgil is very fond of this sort of aetiological reference to the origins of customs familiar in his time; cf. 443 and *Aen.* 5.596 f. (*lusus Troiae*), and see note on 18.

velare: imperative passive, used in a middle sense, cf. 279, 509, 545.

406–7. The veiled head prevented the sight of ill-omen, as the formula *favete lingua* prevented the hearing of ill-omen.

411. angusti . . . Pelori: 'the headlands of the narrow strait of Pelorus begin to show space between them'. This is a very remarkable use of *rarescere*; the nearest parallel seems to be Tac. *Germ.* 30 *colles paulatim rarescunt* (the hills gradually thin out, become less frequent). Pelorus was the promontory at the north-east tip of Sicily, cf. 687; evidently here it gives its name to the Straits of Messina.

412. laeva . . . laeva: the repetition is in the emphatic style of an oracle (cf. 383), and the line is also made to sound impressive by the pattern of alliteration of *l* and *t*.

413. dextrum . . . litus: as soon as the Trojans come west of the toe of Italy they must strike leftwards across to Sicily in spite of the long detour round the island; they must not follow Italy round to the right, which would involve the passage of the Straits of Messina.

414 f. The Romans believed — rightly — that Sicily was once joined to Italy; cf. Pliny *N.H.* 2.204, Ov. *Met.* 15.290. The name Rhegium is connected with ῥηγνύναι ('break off').

415. 'such great changes can be brought about by the long process of time past'; in the context the phrase does not mean that things gradually change, but that in the long process of the ages major changes occur (in this case, suddenly).

416–17. 'when the two countries were one unbroken stretch, the sea came mightily in the midst'. Most editors punctuate so that the *cum* phrase goes with what precedes; I have followed Mackail's punctuation, which gives a more forceful and more idiomatically Latin order. For *protinus* ('straight on') cf. *Ecl.* 1.13, *Aen.* 10.340.

418–19. 'and separated the lands and cities from each other by a coast-line, and flowed between them in a narrow tide-way.' For *interluere* cf. *Aen.* 7.717, and in general cf. Lucretius' description of the Straits of Messina (1.720–1).

420 f. Scylla, the monster with six necks, and Charybdis, the whirlpool, are described in Hom. *Od.* 12.73 f., 222 f. Virgil recalls some Homeric features, but his Scylla is different (see note on 424 f.). By Virgil's time Scylla and Charybdis were traditionally situated in the Straits of Messina (Ap. Rh. 4.789 f., Lucr. 1.722); the Italian promontory still preserves the name Scilla. Ovid (*Met.* 13.900 f.) tells the story of how Scylla, because of the enmity of Circe, was transformed first into a monster and then into a rock; in *Met.* 13.730 f., he closely follows this passage in Virgil. Spenser (*F.Q.* 2.12.3–8) uses Scylla and Charybdis allegorically in his Rocke of Vile Reproch and Gulfe of Greedinesse.

420. **implacata**: a very rare word, an alternative form for *implacabilis*, found only here and in Ov. *Met.* 8.845.

421–3. 'and three times with the deep whirlpool of her abyss does she suck down the mighty billows of the sea into a fathomless depth, and each time she hurls them up again to the heavens and lashes the stars with the spray'. Virgil is following Homer *Od.* 12.105–6 and 235 f. The meaning of *ter* is that Charybdis produces this effect three times in quick succession each day at a particular point in the tide; she probably was thought of as being able to influence the tide, so as to go into action whenever a ship drew near. In mythology she was a *femina voracissima*, born of Neptune and Earth, who stole the cattle of Hercules and was struck by Jupiter's thunderbolt and hurled into the sea. In her new home she preserved her old characteristics.

421. **barathri**: 'abyss' of land or sea, often used of the under-world (Lucr. 3.966, *Aen.* 8.245). Virgil's phraseology here is very similar to Cat. 68.107 f. *tanto te absorbens vertice amoris / aestus in abruptum detulerat barathrum.*

422. **in abruptum**: the neuter of the participle is used as a noun; cf. *Aen.* 12.687 and Milton, *P.L.* 2.408 f. 'Upborne with indefatigable wings / over the vast abrupt'.

423. **verberat**: cf. *Aen*. 5.377 and Shakespeare, *Othello* 2.1.12 'The chidden billow seems to pelt the clouds'. The hyperbole is emphasised by the rhythm, with words coinciding with feet in the second half of the line.

424 f. In Homer (*Od*. 12.85 f.) Scylla is described as a monster with twelve feet and six necks, hidden in a cave to her middle, and hanging out her necks to fish for dolphins and sea-dogs. She has a voice like a new-born hound; this seems to be the origin of the later version, which Virgil follows, that she had wolves or dogs below the waist. Her name was connected etymologically with σκύλλειν ('tear', 'rend') and σκύλαξ ('a young hound'). Cf. *Ecl*. 6.75, Lucr. 5.892, Ov. *Met*. 13.730 f., 14.63 f.; in *Aen*. 6.286 *Scyllae biformes* are among the monsters at the entrance of Hell. Spenser's Errour (*F.Q*. 1.1.13–15) is based on Scylla, and so is Milton's description of Sin (*P.L*. 2.650 f.). 'About her middle round / a cry of Hell Hounds never ceasing barkd / with wide Cerberean mouths full loud, and rung / a hideous Peal. . . .'

424–8. The assonance and alliteration in the description of Scylla is very marked indeed, so that the exaggerated sound effects fit the gruesome monster.

425. **ora exsertantem**: cf. Hom. *Od*. 12.94, 251 f. Notice how Virgil has exaggerated Homer's picture by making Scylla drag the ships on to the rocks after seizing her prey. *Exsertare* (the frequentative form of *exserere*: 'always darting out') is a very rare word.

426 f. 'Her upper part is of human shape: she is a fair-bosomed maiden down to the waist, but below she is a sea-monster of horrible appearance, with a belly of wolves ending in the tails of dolphins'.

427. **pube tenus**: the preposition *tenus* follows its noun and takes the genitive or (more commonly) the ablative; cf. 1.737, 2.553.

428. **commissa**: the passive participle is used in a middle sense (literally 'joining the tails of dolphins on to a belly of wolves'); see note on 47. For the word cf. Ov. *Met*. 12.472 f. (of a Centaur) *latus eruit hasta / qua vir equo commissus erat*.

429–30. Pachynus (or Pachynum) is the south-eastern promontory of Sicily; cf. 699. For *Trinacrii* see note on 384; *meta* is a metaphor from the turning point in a stadium. Observe the emphasis thrown on *longos* by the postposition of *et*, and the very spondaic movement.

432. **caeruleis . . . saxa**: Scylla's dogs (see note on 424 f.) are the colour of the sea, cf. *Aen.* 5.819; for the rocks cf. *Aen.* 1.200 f.

433 f. The emphasis which Helenus achieves here is extreme, first by means of the use of his own name, then by repetition (*si, unum, iterum, Iunoni*).

435. **proque omnibus unum**: 'and one thing to outweigh all the rest', a much stronger way of saying *ante omnia*.

437. Notice the great emphasis on propitiating the hostility of Juno; see intro. to Book 1, and compare *Aen.* 8.60 f.

438. **cane vota libens**: 'gladly chant prayers', cf. 546 f.

439. **supera**: 'win over', cf. *Aen.* 8.61.

440. **finis Italos mittere**: 'you will be sent to the shores of Italy'; the passive form 'you will be sent' rather than 'you will come' puts emphasis on the divine guidance.

441 f. The events here prophesied are fulfilled at the beginning of Book 6. The lakes near Cumae are the Lucrine and Avernian lakes, which in Virgil's time were joined (*Geo.* 2.161 f.); the latter of course was the one particularly associated with the underworld.

443. **insanam vatem**: the Sibyl of Cumae, Apollo's priestess. Her frenzy is described in *Aen.* 6.46 f., 77 f. The collection of her oracles known as the Sibylline books played a very considerable part in Roman religion (cf. *Ecl.* 4); during Augustus' reign they were transferred to the temple of Apollo on the Palatine.

rupe sub ima: 'deep in a rocky cave', cf. *Aen.* 6.42 f.

444. **foliisque . . . mandat**: 'and writes down marks and words on leaves', cf. *Geo.* 3.158. Servius quotes Varro to the effect that the Sibyl wrote on palm leaves.

446. **digerit in numerum**: 'she arranges in order', i.e. she writes a phrase or two on a particular leaf, and for the consecutive understanding of her prophecies it is essential that the leaves should be in order.

450 f. Cf. Shakespeare, *Titus Andr.* 4.1.104 f. 'The angry northern wind / will blow these sands like Sibyl's leaves abroad, / and where's your lesson then?'

452. 'Men depart without receiving advice, and hate the abode of the Sibyl'; for the vague subject cf. 110. The meaning of

inconsultus is very unusual; it generally means either 'without being consulted' or 'not having taken counsel, rash'.

453–6. 'Here do not let any thoughts of the loss of time have such weight with you . . . as to prevent you from approaching the priestess'. *Morae dispendia* is an unusual phrase, literally 'the expenditure of delay'.

455. **sinus implere secundos**: 'make your canvas billow before the wind'; *secundus* is transferred from its common association with *ventus* to the sails affected by a favouring wind.

456–7. **poscas . . . canat**: *canat* is jussive subjunctive in parataxis with *poscas*; cf. Aeneas' actual words to the Sibyl (*Aen.* 6.76) *ipsa canas oro*.

458 f. In *Aen.* 6.83 f. the Sibyl briefly prophesies the events in Italy, and Anchises (*Aen.* 6.890 f.) gives details; line 459 is repeated in the third person in 6.892.

459. **fugiasque ferasque**: indirect deliberative questions.

462. 'Onwards then and make Troy mighty by your deeds, and raise her to the skies'. *Ingentem factis* is proleptic, and very emphatic because at the moment of Helenus' words Troy was a ruin, and the Trojans a small band of exiles.

463–505. *Helenus bestows presents upon the Trojans, and gives his last instructions. Andromache adds her gifts to Ascanius in memory of Astyanax. Aeneas bids them farewell and promises eternal friendship between their two cities.*

464. **gravia ac secto elephanto**: I now accept with some uncertainty Schaper's emendation for *gravia sectoque elephanto* given by all the MSS and by Servius. The MSS reading involves the lengthening of the short final vowel of *gravia*, and although this can be paralleled in Ennius (e.g. *Ann.* 147) there is no certain instance in Virgil (except for final *-que*). The corruption can be accounted for by the insertion of *-que* to eliminate the hiatus, and the consequent dropping of *ac*.

464. **secto elephanto**: for the hiatus in this position cf. 1.617; for the polysyllabic ending see note on 1.651.

466. **Dodonaeosque lebetas**: bronze cauldrons were hung from branches in the famous shrine of Jupiter at Dodona. Dodona was not far from Buthrotum, and some forms of the legend connected Helenus with Dodona.

467. 'a breast-plate interwoven with chain and triple-meshed in gold', i.e. a coat of mail; cf. *Aen.* 5.259 f.

468. 'a superb helmet with flowing plumes set at its apex', literally 'the apex (*conum*) and flowing plumes of a superb helmet'. Attention is concentrated on the plume in its setting rather than on the whole helmet, and something of the logic of the sentence is sacrificed.

469. **arma Neoptolemi**: i.e. Helenus had been bequeathed these possessions by Neoptolemus, see note on 296.

sunt ... parenti: these are special gifts of honour for Anchises; for *sua* cf. *Aen.* 1.461.

470. The half-line, which is of a stop-gap nature, suggests that this is an unrevised passage, an impression which is strengthened by the absence of subtlety in the rhythm of 465-7 and the fact that 467 occurs in *Aen.* 5.259 in very similar form.

duces: 'pilots' to guide the fleet.

471. 'he makes up the complement of oarsmen, and also fits out the crew with equipment', i.e. to replace the men lost or left behind in Crete. Cf. Livy 26.39.7, *Aen.* 8.80.

472 f. Notice how Anchises plays the leading part in organising; see note on 1 f.

473. **ferenti**: 'following', cf. *Aen.* 4.430.

475. **Anchisa**: the normal Latin vocative of such Greek words is in long -*e*, but the influence of vocatives such as *Aenea* led to some variation.

dignate: 'thought worthy of'; *dignari* is used passively several times in Cicero.

476. **cura deum**: 'beloved of the gods', cf. *Aen.* 10.132.

bis ... ruinis: see note on *Aen.* 2.642-3.

477. **ecce tibi**: 'look'; *tibi* is ethic dative, cf. *Aen.* 5.419. Helenus points in the direction of Italy, across the short sea-passage.

hanc arripe velis: 'make for it under full sail'; *arripere* has here a strong element of its cognate word *rapidus*, cf. *Aen.* 9.13, 10.298.

478. Helenus repeats the warning he has given earlier (381 f.).

praeterlabare: jussive subjunctive in parataxis with *necesse est*, quite a common construction (cf. 234-5, 456-7). The accusative *hanc* is governed by the preposition in the verb; cf. 688 and *Aen.* 6.874.

479. The very heavy alliteration of *p* gives an oracular emphasis to the line.

pandit: 'reveals' (in his oracular response through Helenus); cf. 252.

480. **nati pietate**: the often stressed quality of Aeneas is here given special emphasis by the most unusual rhythm of a heavy stop in the fifth foot.

481. **provehor**: 'go on' speaking, cf. Cic. *Dom.* 32.

482 f. It was of Hector that Andromache spoke when she met Aeneas (310 f.); it is of their son Astyanax that she speaks now as she says goodbye.

483. **picturatas**: a rare word, not found before Virgil, nor often afterwards (cf. Stat. *Th.* 6.58).

subtemine: this word, sometimes spelled *subtegmine*, refers to the golden thread which is either woven into the yarn to make the picture, or embroidered on it.

484. **nec cedit honore**: 'nor does she fall short in honouring the guests'. With *cedit* understand the dative *Heleno* — Helenus had paid due honour to his departing guests by his gifts and his speech, and Andromache does likewise. Some MSS read the dative *honori*, and Servius preferred this.

486. The alliteration of *m* and the assonance of final *-um*, *-em* are very marked, reflecting the controlled sadness of her words.

489. 'for you are the only picture I have left now of my Astyanax'; for Andromache's son Astyanax see note on 2.457.

super: the adverb is used adjectivally, almost equivalent to *superstes* or *quae superest*.

490–1. 'he had the same look in his eyes, the same gestures, the same expression as you have, and he would now have been the same age as you, growing up to manhood'; cf. Hom. *Od.* 4.149 f. (Telemachus' resemblance to Odysseus).

493 f. We are reminded of Aeneas' words at Carthage, *O fortunati quorum iam moenia surgunt* (*Aen.* 1.437).

494. **sua**: the word is used non-reflexively (cf. 469), and its reference to the second person makes the statement very general. Page well says, 'The speaker places those he is addressing among a class of men, viz. those whose toils are over. Every man has his destiny (*fortuna sua*) to work out, and, until it is worked out, he cannot rest.'

495. Aeneas recalls Creusa's words to him in 2.780 *longa tibi exsilia et vastum maris aequor arandum*.

496. For the 'ever-receding' land of Italy cf. *Aen.* 5.629 *Italiam sequimur fugientem*, 6.61.

497. **effigiem Xanthi Troiamque**: for the new settlement with the old names cf. 349–51.

498-9. **melioribus ... Grais**: 'under better auspices, I trust, and less likely to be exposed to the Greeks'; *fuerit* is perfect subjunctive expressing a wish with *opto*.

500. **Thybrim ... Thybridis**: Virgil prefers the Greek form *Thybris* to the Latin *Tiberis*. Aeneas knows of the Tiber as his goal from Creusa's prophecy in *Aen.* 2.782.

502 f. 'then one day we will make these cities of kinsmen, these neighbouring peoples of ours, Hesperia and Epirus (each of us have the same Dardanus as our first founder, the same fortunes) — we will make both our peoples into one Troy in spirit; this is a prospect for which our descendants must strive'. The sentence is complicated, particularly in the reiteration of the object (*cognatas urbes populosque propinquos*) by *utramque*, which stands for *utrosque*, assimilated to *Troiam*.

503. **Epiro Hesperiam**: *Hesperiam* is in apposition to *populosque*: 'neighbouring peoples, Hesperia to Epirus'. Servius and some MSS read *Hesperia*, in which case both *Epiro* and *Hesperia* would be local ablative.

506-47. *After leaving Buthrotum the Trojans sail to Acroceraunia. Here they spend the night; they set off early next day and sight Italy. They land at Castrum Minervae, and Anchises interprets the sight of four white horses as an omen both of peace and of war. They make offerings to Juno and re-embark.*

506 f. The Trojans now sail north past the Ceraunian mountains towards Acroceraunia, the point for the shortest sea-passage to Italy; cf. *Geo.* 1.332, Hor. *Odes* 1.3.20. Virgil has not adopted the general tradition (Dion. Hal. 1.51.2) that the Trojans crossed from Onchesmus, a place considerably south of Acroceraunia, because the name was connected with a version of the tradition according to which Anchises died there.

After the slow-moving account of the stay at Buthrotum the narrative speed changes, and events follow one another rapidly.

There is a feeling of urgency now that the Trojans have come at last into the part of the world which is to be their home.

506. **vicina Ceraunia iuxta**: the disyllabic preposition is postponed, as often in poetry, cf. 75.

507. **iter Italiam**: the accusative of motion towards without a preposition is used here after the verbal notion in the noun *iter*; cf. *Aen.* 6.542.

508. **sol ruit**: an unusual phrase, meaning not necessarily 'the sun set', but 'the sun sped on its course'; cf. *Aen.* 10.256 f.

509. **sternimur**: middle in sense, 'we throw ourselves down', cf. *Geo.* 4.432.

gremio: cf. Lucr. 1.251 *in gremium matris terrai*, *Aen.* 5.31.

510. **sortiti remos**: 'after we had allotted the order of rowing', cf. Ap. Rh. 1.358, 395, Prop. 3.21.12. The reference is to the allocation of places at the oars for the next day's rowing; it is done in advance so that a quick start can be made.

511. **fessos ... artus**: 'slumber flows through our weary limbs'. The metaphor is from channels of water refreshing the land; it is not only the dampness of sleep but its diffusing power which is pictured metaphorically. Cf. *Aen.* 5.857, and (with a different construction of *inrigare*) *Aen.* 1.691 f.

512 f. 'Not yet was Night, drawn by the Hours, reaching the mid-point of her circuit (when) Palinurus rose...'. The juxtaposition of these two clauses without subordination is characteristic of Virgil's paratactic style, cf. 358.

512. **Nox Horis acta**: Night is drawn in her chariot (cf. *Aen.* 5.721) across the sky by the Hours. The personified Hours play a large part in Greek literature; in Homer they guard the gates of heaven and roll back the clouds (*Il.* 5.749 f., 8.393 f.), and they occur very frequently in Pindar and afterwards as personifications of the seasons. They figure less prominently in Latin literature, generally as personifications of the divisions of day or night, as here; cf. Ov. *Fast.* 1.125, *Met.* 2.26, 118. Compare Milton, *P.L.* 6.2 f. 'Morn, / wak't by the circling Hours, with rosie hand / unbarrd the gates of Light.'

513–14. 'tests for all the winds, and tries to feel the breeze blowing in his ears', i.e. he turns his head so as to feel (or hear) the direction of the wind as it blows into one ear or the other — a much more reliable method than wetting a finger and holding it up.

515 f. Compare the description of Odysseus watching the stars as he guides his raft (Hom. *Od.* 5.271 f.).

516. This line is repeated from *Aen.* 1.744, where see note.

517. **circumspicit**: 'looks round and sees', because Orion, unlike the other constellations mentioned, is in the southern part of the sky. Orion the hunter is 'armed with gold' because his belt and sword are formed by two lines of stars.

Oriona: Greek accusative, cf. *cratera* (525). For the spondaic fifth foot cf. 549 and see note on 2.68.

518. 'when he saw that all the signs were favourable in the cloudless sky'; i.e. no sign of bad weather, no *stellis acies obtunsa* (*Geo.* 1.395). The use of *constare* is like the common use in the phrase *ratio constat*.

520. **velorum ... alas**: compare *volare* in 124, and *Aen.* 1.224 *mare velivolum*.

521. **rubescebat**: the word is not found before Virgil; cf. *Aen.* 7.25.

stellis ... fugatis: cf. Hor. *Odes* 3.21.24 *dum rediens fugat astra Phoebus*, *Aen.* 5.42, and the beginning of FitzGerald's Omar Khayyam: 'Awake, for Morning in the Bowl of Night / has flung the Stone that puts the Stars to flight'.

522. **humilem**: land sighted far off, even when hilly, appears as a smudge on the horizon. The words *obscurus* and *humilis* here are purely visual, but perhaps they may also suggest the contrast of the humble present with the glorious future.

523–4. The threefold repetition of the word *Italiam* gives the dramatic emphasis required, with a suggestion also of the word passing from lip to lip. The heavy pause in line 523 after the elision of the run-on word gives rhythmical emphasis to reinforce the emphasis of diction.

525. **cratera**: Greek accusative, cf. 517.

525–6. **corona induit**: i.e. a crown of leaves or the like is put around the wine-cup; see note on 1.724, and cf. Tib. 2.5.98.

528. **potentes**: the genitive with *potens* is common in Livy and the poets, cf. *Aen.* 1.80.

530. **crebrescunt**: 'freshen', cf. *Aen.* 5.764.

531. This is the site of Castrum Minervae in Calabria, where the temple was a well-known landmark (Strabo 6.281).

532. **vela legunt**: 'furl the sails', cf. *Geo.* 1.373. The Trojans

now begin to row, the normal method of approaching or leaving harbour. Although they know that this is not the part of Italy where they are to stay, they land to perform the rites Helenus had instructed them to pay (403 f.).

533–5. 'There is a harbour shaped like a bow curving away from the waves which the East winds drive; the rocky breakwaters foam with salt spray but the harbour itself is safe behind them'. For the use of *ab* cf. 570. Notice the alliteration of *s*, imitative of the sea; cf. *Aen.* 5.866.

535–6. 'the tower-like cliffs extend their arms to form two walls, and the temple shelters back from the shore'. For the 'arms' cf. Ov. *Met.* 11.229 f.; for *gemino muro* cf. *Aen.* 1.162 f. The word *refugitque* adds a little touch of personification.

537. **primum omen**: on arrival in Italy the Trojans would naturally be looking for anything which could be interpreted as an omen, and the first feature to present itself is the sign of the four horses. Compare the sign of the horse's head revealed to the Carthaginian settlers (*Aen.* 1.442 f.). The four white horses suggest a Roman triumphal procession; cf. Livy 5.23.5, Prop. 4.1.32, Ov. *A.A.* 1.214.

539. **terra hospita**: 'land of our sojourn', see note on 377–8.

540. **armantur ... armenta minantur**: the assonance is extremely marked, and coupled with the threefold repetition of *bellum* makes Anchises' speech sound formal and oracular. There seems to be an etymological connexion intended between *armari* and *armenta* (see note on 693); for *armenta* of horses cf. *Geo.* 3.129, *Aen.* 11.494.

541. **olim**: 'sometimes', an archaic use surviving in poetry, cf. *Aen.* 5.125.

543. 'there is hope of peace too'; i.e. as well as expectation of war first. This symbolises the whole concept of the Roman mission: first war against the proud, then civilisation for the subdued peoples.

544. **Palladis armisonae**: Minerva, to whose temple they have come, is here given her Greek name and an epithet associating her with her martial aspects (cf. *Aen.* 11.483). The adjective *armisonus* seems to have been coined by Virgil; for other striking compound adjectives (which Virgil uses sparingly) cf. 75, 221, 553, and for further discussion see my note ad loc. (Oxford edition).

545 f. The Trojans now obey the instructions given by Helenus (403 f.); for *capita velamur* see note on 405, and on 1.228.

545. **ante aras**: these are not the altars of the temple, but those which Aeneas has set up on the shore (cf. 404).

546-7. 'and in accordance with the instructions upon which Helenus had especially insisted we duly offer sacrifice, as we had been bidden, to Juno of Argos.' The causal ablative *praeceptis* is in a loose syntactical relationship to the sentence. Juno is here called *Argiva* (cf. 1.24) to stress her association with the Greeks in whose territory the Trojans have temporarily landed. For *adolere* cf. *Ecl.* 8.65, Ov. *Met.* 8.740.

548-87. *The Trojans sail across the bay of Tarentum, escape Scylla and Charybdis, and approach the Sicilian coast near Mt. Etna. They pass a night of fear in the shadow of the volcano.*

548 f. After the rapid narrative of the previous section Virgil now changes the movement again, as he comes to a part of the poem which is concerned with descriptions of terror and power on the grand scale. The first indication of this is the mention of Etna far off (554); then Scylla and Charybdis are described in the high rhetorical style before the full-scale portrayal of the mighty volcano (571 f.). The mood is thus established for the grandiose rhetoric of the story of Polyphemus.

549. 'we turn the ends of the sail-covered yards towards the sea'. The yard (*antemna*) was the name of the crosspiece fixed across the mast to which the sail was attached; sometimes it would consist of two pieces joined at the centre, and therefore the plural *antemnae* is commonly used. *Cornua* was the technical term for the two ends of the yard, cf. *Aen.* 5.832, Ov. *Met.* 11.482-3. The meaning is that the sailors of each ship hoist and adjust the yard with the attached sail; it would have been lowered when the sails were furled (532).

The rhythm of this line is very unusual indeed; it has no caesura at all except that made by elision in the third foot, and consequently ictus and accent coincide throughout. The fifth foot is spondaic, which is rare in Virgil and generally occurs when a Greek word is involved; see note on 2.68. The rhyme of *velatarum* ... *antemnarum* is also very striking. There does not seem to be any correspondence of the rhythm with the sense; it appears that Virgil has used a line of unusual sound-effects simply for variety.

550. **Graiugenum**: genitive, see note on 21; for the formation of the word cf. *Troiugena*, 359.

551 f. Aeneas is now sailing across the Gulf of Tarentum from the 'heel' to the 'toe' of Italy; Lacinium is the promontory on the far side of the gulf, and Caulon (Caulonia) and Scylaceum are further on, in reverse order. There is a certain amount of anachronism in the use of these names; see note on 398.

551. **Herculei ... Tarenti**: there were many different accounts of the foundation of Tarentum, as Virgil's *si vera est fama* suggests. One of the famous towns in this area (Heraclea) bore Hercules' name, and he was particularly associated with the nearby town of Croton (Ov. *Met.* 15.12 f.). In the legend he returned to Greece by this route after killing the cattle of Geryon in Spain.

552. **diva Lacinia**: 'the Lacinian goddess', i.e. the temple of the Lacinian goddess, Juno; for the metonymy cf. 275. This temple of Juno at Lacinium was very famous; cf. Cic. *De Div.* 1.48, Livy 24.3.3. According to Dionysius (1.51.3) Aeneas landed here and sacrificed to Juno; Virgil has avoided undue repetition of landings and departures by placing the sacrifices to Juno at the previous landing at Castrum Minervae.

553. **navifragum**: a much rarer variant of *naufragus*.

554. **e fluctu**: dependent on the idea of *apparere* in the verb *cernitur*.

Trinacria ... Aetna: *Trinacrius* is an epithet of Sicily, cf. 384; Etna is described in 571 f., where see notes.

555. 'the mighty groaning of the sea as it dashed against the rocks'; the two phrases form a single complex image. For *gemitus* with inanimate subjects cf. 577, *Aen.* 5.806.

556. **fractasque ... voces**: 'and the voice of the breakers reverberating on the shore'. This is a very unusual use of *voces*, more so than in English (cf. Wordsworth's 'Two voices are there; one is of the sea ...', and Psalm 93.3 'The floods have lifted up their voice'). Two considerations have led Virgil towards this vivid phrase; the first that a much easier personification of the sea has already been made with the word *gemitus*, and the second that musical instruments, particularly the bugle, have

a 'voice' in Latin (*Aen.* 7.519, Ov. *Met.* 1.338). The meaning of
fractae (cf. *Geo.* 4.72) is generally taken as 'intermittent', but it is
perhaps better to refer it to the pulsating or reverberating effect
of a noise low in pitch. There is probably also a suggestion of the
idea of 'breaking' waves; cf. *Aen.* 1.161, 10.291. I have tried to
convey these two converging streams of meaning in my translation by rendering *fractae* twice.

557. 'the waters seethe and the sand swirls in the surge'; cf.
Hom. *Od.* 12.240 f. (Charybdis) and for *exsultant Aen.* 7.464.

558–9. Cf. Helenus' words in 420 f.

560. **eripite**: the omission of the object (*nos*) is natural in
excited speech.

561 f. Palinurus' ship takes the lead in the dangerous situation,
as in *Aen.* 5.833 f.

561–2. **rudentem ... proram**: 'groaning prow'. For the
verb cf. *Aen.* 7.16, 8.248; it is not normally applied to inanimate
subjects, but cf. the personifications in 555–6 and 566.

563. **cohors**: 'company'; the word is mainly poetic in this
wide sense, cf. *Aen.* 10.328, 11.500.

564 f. Compare the rhetorical and hyperbolical description
of storm waves in *Aen.* 1.106 f., Ov. *Tr.* 1.2.19 f., and Shakespeare,
Othello, 2.1.190 f.

> And let the labouring bark climb hills of seas
> Olympus-high, and duck again as low
> As hell's from heaven.

564. **curvato gurgite**: 'on the arching billow', cf. Hom. *Od.*
11.244, *Geo.* 4.361.

idem: the reiteration of the subject by means of this word
seems to hold them for a moment on the summit of the wave.

565. **manis imos**: *manes* here means 'the abode of the shades',
cf. *Geo.* 1.243, *Aen.* 4.387.

desedimus: 'instantaneous' perfect (from *desidere*); cf. *Aen* 1.84.

566. **clamorem**: this word, like *gemitus* (555), *voces* (556),
rudens (561) is rarely applied to inanimate things. It makes us
think of the monster Charybdis as well as of the whirlpool.

567. **elisam**: 'forced out', an unexpected use of the word,
perhaps with the overtone of the 'shattered' wave (Lucan
9.339). We might say 'the splintered spray'.

rorantia: the hyperbole has disturbed some commentators, but it is surely wholly in keeping with the rest of the superbly exaggerated picture of Charybdis' whirlpool. Page well quotes *Othello* 2.1.13 f.

> The wind-shak'd surge, with high and monstrous mane,
> Seems to cast water on the burning bear
> And quench the guards of the ever-fixed pole.

568. **ventus cum sole reliquit**: 'the sun set and the wind forsook us'; a change of wind often occurs at dawn or sunset.

569. **Cyclopum**: see note on 617. By Virgil's time they had long been localised in the area of Mt. Etna; cf. Eur. *Cycl.* 20 f., Callim. *Hymn.* 3.46 f., *Aen.* 8.416 f. The volcanic rocks in the sea off Mt. Etna are today called Scogli dei Ciclopi.

570–1. 'There is a harbour away from the reach of the winds, undisturbed and spacious in itself, but close to it Etna thunders in terrifying eruptions'. Compare Homer's description of the harbour on the island near the land of the Cyclopes (*Od.* 9.136 f.). For *ruinae* ('falling material') cf. *Aen.* 1.129, Hor. *Odes* 3.3.8.

571 f. In his description of Etna Virgil writes in the grand style of hyperbole. There has so far been little of this kind of writing in *Aeneid* 3; here Virgil has led up to the heightened style by lines 564–9, and now he lays on his colours very thickly. For this he was criticised by Favorinus (Aul. Gell. 17.10), who compares Pindar's description (*Pyth.* 1.21 f.) to the disadvantage of Virgil, mainly because he found the powerful effect at which Virgil aims altogether over-powering.

Lucretius discusses the eruption of Etna in 6.639 f. (cf. also 1.722 f.); he was imitated by the author of the didactic poem called *Aetna*. Pliny's accounts of the eruption of Vesuvius (*Ep.* 6.16 and 20) may be compared, though they are more detailed and specific. There are some vividly descriptive passages in Arnold's *Empedocles on Etna*, Act II, and Spenser has a fine simile referring to the dragon with which the Red Cross Knight fought (*F.Q.* 1.11.44):

> As burning Aetna from his boyling stew
> Doth belch out flames, and rockes in peeces broke,
> And ragged ribs of mountaines molten new,
> Enwrapt in coleblacke clouds and filthy smoke,
> That all the land with stench, and heaven with horror choke.

572 f. The two *interdum* clauses are particularised descriptions
of the general picture in line 571: the first of them describes the
more visual aspects of flame and smoke, and the second the active
features of an eruption.

572. **atram . . . nubem**: 'shoots a burst of cloudy blackness
up to the heavens'. The transitive use of *prorumpere* is very rare,
and not precisely paralleled. It is based on the passive used in the
sense of the intransitive active, e.g. Lucr. 6.436, *Aen.* 1.246, 7.459.
passage Cf. *rumpere* in 246.

574. **globos flammarum**: cf. *Geo.* 1.472 f. *undantem ruptis
fornacibus Aetnam, | flammarumque globos liquefactaque volvere saxa*, a
passage which Virgil echoes again in 576, 580.

575 f. 'sometimes it belches forth and hurls high rocks torn
from the living body of the mountain, and with a groan brings up
balls of molten rock to the surface, bubbling up and boiling from
its very foundations'. The phrase *avulsaque viscera* is explanatory
of *scopulos*, a kind of hendiadys; for the metaphorical use of
viscera cf. Ov. *Met.* 1.138 and compare Milton, *P.L.* 1.233 f.
'thundring Etna, whose combustible / and fuelled entrails thence
conceiving fire / sublim'd with mineral fury, aid the winds. . . .'
For *eructans* cf. *Aen.* 6.297 and Milton, *P.L.* 1.670 f. 'There stood
a Hill not far, whose griesly top / belchd fire and rouling smoke'.
For *glomerare* cf. *Aen.* 2.315, 4.155, 6.311. Notice the pattern of
alliteration and assonance in these powerfully descriptive lines:
initial *e*, the *-ac-* sounds in *liquefactaque saxa*, initial *g*. |

578 f. Enceladus was one of the Giants who rebelled against
Jupiter (*Aen.* 4.179, Hor. *Odes* 3.4.56). His fate was to be struck
down by Jupiter's thunderbolt, and according to the most common
version of the legend he was buried under Mt. Inarime, and it
was Typhoeus (Typhon) who was buried under Etna. In Virgil's
version the punishments are reversed; cf. also *Aen.* 9.716.

578. **semustum**: for this spelling (*semi, ustum*) cf. 244.

580. **ruptis . . . caminis**: 'as its furnaces burst open'; the
meaning is that the furnaces of Etna cannot contain the flames of
the thunderbolt which are issuing from Enceladus' burning body;
cf. *Aen.* 1.44.

581. **mutet latus**: 'changes position'.

intremere omnem: the rhythm here is most unusual, with
the marked conflict of accent and ictus in the fifth foot; clearly

Virgil intends by this dislocation of the rhythm to reflect the violence of the earthquake. Note also the powerful alliteration of *m* in this line and the next.

582. **caelum subtexere fumo**: 'veils the sky with smoke'; the metaphor is weaving something beneath an object overhead, hence concealing it; cf. Lucr. 5.466, 6.482.

583. **noctem illam**: 'all through that night'; observe how the alliteration of *m* continues through this slow menacing spondaic line.

immania monstra: 'terrifying horrors'; the word *monstra* has an aura of the supernatural, cf. 26, 307.

585–6. **nec lucidus aethra siderea polus**: 'nor were the heavens bright with starry radiance'; *aethra* is a rare and vivid word which Servius well defines as *splendor aetheris*. Cf. Enn. *Ann.* 435, Lucr. 6.467, *Aen.* 12.247.

587. **nox intempesta**: 'timeless night', the dead of night when time seems to stand still. The phrase is used by Ennius (*Ann.* 102, 167) and Lucretius (5.986); cf. also *Geo.* 1.247, *Aen.* 12.846. Notice how the fear and dread of the passage is finalised in this spondaic line with most subtle alliteration of *n*, *m*, *t*.

588–654. *The Trojans meet an emaciated castaway, who appeals to them for help. He tells them that he is Achaemenides, left behind on the island by Ulysses after his encounter with the Cyclops Polyphemus.*

588 f. The episode about Achaemenides and Polyphemus did not figure in the Aeneas legend, and indeed Achaemenides is not heard of before Virgil; it seems very probable that Virgil invented this part of his story. Its purpose is to introduce a reworking of Homer's story about the Cyclops; Odyssean touches have already occurred in this book with the Harpies (partly based on an Odyssean episode, see note on 209 f.), Phaeacia (291), Circe (386), Scylla and Charybdis (420 f.). But this is a far more sustained and direct attempt to bring Aeneas into the world of Homer.

There are many indications that Virgil was not satisfied with the episode; there are signs of imperfect finish (621, 640, 661, 669, 684 f.), and the marked similarities between Achaemenides and Sinon (*Aen.* 2.57 f.) suggest that when Virgil was writing the second book he used this passage as a quarry, intending to recast or remove it later on; see Mackail's edition, Appendix B. We may conjecture that as the *Aeneid* progressed Aeneas became to Virgil a less legendary figure, more Roman, more historical, less Odyssean.

But while Virgil may have felt uncertain whether the episode was a proper part of the fabric of the poem, we may still admire it as a stitched-on piece of brilliant colours. It is a passage of rhetorical and grandiose writing, detached from the immediate world of human experience, and capable of being handled in sonorous and grandiloquent hyperbole. This was the kind of writing which the Silver Age loved; Virgil uses it far less often, but we should beware of thinking that it was alien to him. The boxing match in *Aeneid* 5 is another such episode. Ovid was evidently much impressed by the story of Achaemenides, and tells it at length in a recast version (*Met.* 14.160 f.).

588. **primo ... Eoo**: 'with the first appearance of the morning star'. The adjective *Eous* (eastern) is here used as a noun; cf. *Geo.* 1.288, *Aen.* 11.4.

590–1. 'in the last stages of exhaustion and emaciation, the extraordinary figure of a man unknown to us, most pitiable in aspect. . . .' *Nova* suggests that the Trojans had seen nothing like this degree of wretchedness before; the strangeness of the picture is emphasised by the abstract turn of the subject (*forma viri procedit* instead of *vir procedit*). Compare the castaway Ben Gunn in *Treasure Island*: 'unlike any man that I had ever seen . . . yet a man it was'.

593. **respicimus**: 'we stared at him'; for this meaning of fixing the eyes upon something cf. *Aen.* 2.615, 7.454. The very brief sentence helps to convey the drama of the events.

593–5. 'His squalor was terrible to see, his beard unkempt, his clothing held together with briars; yet in all else he was a Greek, and had in days gone by been sent to Troy in the service of his country.' The descriptive passage is given impetus by the omission of the main verbs.

594. **at cetera Graius**: the expression here is elliptical; the thought is that in some respects he was unidentifiable (because of his wretched plight), but in others — which Virgil does not specify — he could be recognised as Greek. After the ten years siege the Trojans could recognise a Greek when they saw one even

thus changed. *Cetera* is the Greek accusative of respect; cf. *Aen.* 4.558, 9.656.

595. This line seems to anticipate the narrative rather strangely, but if we remember that Aeneas is telling the story to Dido such an anticipation is acceptable.

600. **spirabile lumen**: 'the light of life which we breathe', a strange and haunting innovation, based on the normal use of *spirabilis* applied to the air; cf. Ov. *Met.* 14.175 (of Achaemenides) *lumen vitale*, and for an analogous image *Geo.* 2.340 *cum primae lucem pecudes hausere.*

601. **tollite me**: 'take me on board', cf. *Aen.* 6.370.

quascumque ... terras: accusative of motion towards, cf. 254. For *quascumque* ('any at all') cf. 654 and 682.

602-3. Compare Sinon's words in *Aen.* 2.77 f.

602. **sciŏ**: only with *scio* (*Ecl.* 8.43) and *nescio* (fairly often) does Virgil scan as short the final *-o* of a verb. In the Silver Age this scansion became much more common. In a few disyllabic words (other than verbs) the short final *-o* is normal (iambic shortening); e.g. *duo* (623), *ego, modo, cito.*

me ... unum: 'that I am one of the men from the Greek fleet'.

603. **fateor ... petiisse**: for the omission of the reflexive subject of the infinitive cf. 201.

605. **spargite me in fluctus**: the phrase is elliptical for *dilacerate meum corpus et spargite*; cf. the fuller expression in *Aen.* 4.600 f.

606. **pereo, hominum**: there is hiatus between these two words; a special effect is achieved here as the natural pause after *pereo* is accentuated while he stays for a moment on the grim word, and emphasis is put on *hominum*, the key word of his speech.

607-8. 'He spoke, and clasping our knees, grovelling at our knees, he clung to us.' The phrases express Achaemenides' intense emotion; they contrast with the calmness of the following lines as the Trojans reassure him. *Volutans* is unusual in this intransitive usage; cf. Ov. *Am.* 3.6.45.

608-9. Again we are reminded of the story of Sinon (*Aen.* 2.74 f.).

608. **quo sanguine cretus**: 'of what parentage he comes'; for the past participle of *crescere* (= *natus*) cf. *Aen.* 2.74, 4.191.

609. **deinde**: to be taken with *hortamur fateri*: for the post-position of *deinde* cf. *Aen*. 1.195.

610f. Compare Priam's reception of Sinon, *Aen*. 2.146f. Notice how Anchises (not Aeneas) takes the initiative; see note on 1 f.

611. **praesenti pignore**: 'with a ready sign of friendship', i.e. the offering of his hand.

613f. Achaemenides' first words immediately take us into the world of Homer's *Odyssey* with the mention of Odysseus' home Ithaca and then of Odysseus (Ulysses) himself. Achaemenides begins quietly and formally with information about himself; then the parenthesis of 615 leads into the heightened tone and sustained hyperbole of the description of Polyphemus.

613. **infelicis**: an unexpected epithet (echoed in 691); Servius wanted it to mean 'accursed', but the word in Virgil when applied to humans always has a strong suggestion of sympathy. It is perhaps an echo of κάμμορος, used a number of times by Homer of Odysseus, and it puts the emphasis on the toils which Odysseus endured.

614. **Achaemenides**: nothing is known of him before Virgil; see note on 588 f.

614–15. 'and because my father Adamastus was poor — and if only such poverty had remained my lot in life — I went away to Troy'. Cf. Sinon's words in *Aen*. 2.87. By *fortuna* he means his humble lot as son of a poor man, infinitely preferable to his present plight.

616. **crudelia limina**: by saying 'cruel entrance' rather than 'cruel cave' or the like Virgil reminds us of the part of Homer's story which Achaemenides does not tell, how Odysseus and his companions got out past the blinded Cyclops waiting at the entrance to the cave by clinging under the sheep as they went out to graze.

617. The strong assonance of *o* begins the series of striking sound effects in this powerful descriptive passage.

Cyclopis: the Cyclopes in Homer (*Od*. 9.106f.) were a race of savage one-eyed giants, shepherds by occupation (cf. 657). Chief among them was Polyphemus, who is often (as here) simply called Cyclops. Virgil's version here follows Homer, with no reference to post-Homeric features like the forging of thunderbolts in their cave (*Aen*. 8.418f.), or the half-pathetic amorous Polyphemus who loved Galatea (*Theoc*. 11, Ov. *Met*. 13.749f.).

For the history of the Polyphemus legend, and other stories analogous to it, see Frazer's Loeb edition of Apollodorus, Appendix 13, and D. L. Page, *The Homeric Odyssey*, chap. 1; one of the best known is the story of the great black giant in the third voyage of Sindbad the Sailor.

618. The very marked sense pause after the second-foot trochee is most unusual and striking, and is reinforced by the alliteration of *d*, the absence of a main verb, and the very unusual syntax.

domus ... cruentis: the ablatives of description have a most abrupt impact because the words are not of the qualitative kind normally used in this construction; the syntax produces an effect of violence and strangeness which is appropriate to the subject-matter.

619. This is another remarkable line, composed very largely of descriptive adjectives, with the verb again unexpressed, and marked assonance of initial *i* and *a*.

621. 'not easy to look upon, nor would anyone dare to speak to him'; Macrobius (*Sat.* 6.1.55) quotes a line from Accius as Virgil's source: *quem neque tueri contra nec adfari queas.*

622. This self-contained line is the climax of the description; its finality is emphasised by the unusual degree of correspondence of ictus and accent in the middle of the line.

623f. Virgil here follows Homer quite closely (*Od.* 9.289f.), except that in Homer it is not until the second night that Odysseus blinds Polyphemus, by which time he has eaten six of his men.

623. **vidi egomet ... cum**: 'with my own eyes I watched while . . .', a much less common construction than *vidi frangentem*. Notice how the suspense is built up in this sentence as clause follows clause before the verb *frangeret*.

625. **natarent**: cf. Cic. *Phil.* 2.105 *natabant pavimenta vino, Geo.* 1.372.

627. Notice the alliteration of *t* and *d* in this gruesome line, which is an elaboration of Hom. *Od.* 9.292 f.

630. **simul**: = *simul ac*, cf. *Ecl.* 4.26 f., *Geo.* 4.232 f.

631-2. 'he laid his lolling head down to sleep, stretched out on the floor of the cave in all his mighty bulk'; cf. Hom. *Od.* 9.372 and *Aen.* 6.422 f.

632-3. Virgil here is virtually translating Hom. *Od.* 9.373-4;

cf. also Ov. *Met.* 14.211 f. where also the word *frusta* ('fragments') is used.

634. **sortitique vices**: 'drawing lots for our parts'; cf. 376 and Hom. *Od.* 9.331.

635 f. Homer (*Od.* 9.375–94) has a much longer description of the blinding of Polyphemus. Great emphasis is put on Virgil's favourite word *ingens* by its position at the end of its clause and the beginning of the line.

636. **quod ... latebat**: 'his only eye, deep-set in his savage brow'; for *latere* in this sense cf. Cic. *N.D.* 2.143.

637. **Argolici clipei**: the 'Greek shield' was the large round type commonly used by the Greeks (and by the Romans), said to have been invented by the sons of Abas of Argos; cf. 286.

Phoebeae lampadis instar: 'like the lamp of Phoebus', i.e. the sun (cf. Ov. *Met.* 13.853); compare *Aen.* 4.6. For *instar* cf. *Aen.* 2.15.

640. **rumpite**: a much stronger word than the normal *solvite*, expressing urgency (cf. 667). The incomplete lines here and at 661 are among indications that the passage was not finally revised; see note on 588 f.

641 f. **qualis quantusque ... centum alii**: 'there are a hundred others of like appearance and size as Polyphemus. . . .' For *qualis quantusque* cf. *Aen.* 2.591 f.

642. **lanigeras**: for the colourful compound adjective cf. Enn. *Sat.* 66, *Geo.* 3.287. The description of the pastoral way of life of the Cyclopes strongly recalls Homer (cf. *Od.* 9.187 f., 237 f.).

644. **Cyclōpĕs**: this is the Greek form of the nominative plural with a short final syllable; cf. the accusative *Cyclopas* (647), and see note on 127. This line has a trochaic caesura in the third foot without a strong caesura in the fourth, a rhythm used by Virgil only rarely and for special effect; see note on 269. Here it emphasises the powerful words *infandi Cyclopes*.

645–7. 'The horns of the moon are now filling with light for the third time while I have been dragging out my days', or more idiomatically 'since I first began to drag out. . .'. For this rare use of *cum* (=*cum interea*) cf. *Aen.* 5.627 f., 10.665, Prop. 2.20.21 f.

647. **lustra**: 'dens', cf. *Geo.* 2.471, *Aen.* 4.151.

647–8. 'looking out for the monstrous Cyclopes from a rock'; he is hiding in the woods and from time to time climbs to a point of vantage to look for a ship and observe his enemies.

647. **Cȳclōpăs**: the first syllable here is left short (contrast 644 and the other instances of the word in this book); for the Greek accusative see note on 127.

649–50. 'The trees afford me a wretched existence on berries and stony cornels, and the vegetation keeps me alive on the roots I pull up.' *Cornum* (*Geo.* 2.34) is a sort of wild plum; this is Henry's comment on the cornel tree: 'Its oblong, red, shining berries, consisting of little more than a mere membrane carrying a large and hard stone, are sold in the streets of the Italian towns. "Bad enough food for a hungry man!" said I to myself, as I spat out some I had bought in Bassano, and tasted for the sake of Achaemenides.'

652–3. 'To these ships, whatever they might be, I gave myself'. *Addicere* is a legal word, 'to make over'; *addictus* means a bondsman. *Fuisset* is a reported future perfect; *addixi* contains a meaning like *vovi me in potestate futurum*.

655–91. *The blinded Polyphemus and his fellow Cyclopes appear. Taking Achaemenides with them the Trojans set sail with all speed, and as the wind is from the north they succeed in avoiding Scylla and Charybdis and they sail southwards along the coast of Sicily.*

655 f. For Polyphemus see note on 617; for the whole episode see note on 588 f.

655–8. In this passage Virgil very deliberately and obviously makes the sound and movement of the lines match the sense. It is appropriate for a description of the giant Polyphemus that the effects should be heavy and immediately apparent (cf. 424–8), not subtle and haunting as so often elsewhere in Virgil. Alliteration of *m* is noticeable from the beginning, developing into a marked assonance of *-um* and *-em* sounds; there is rhyme at the line endings of 656–7 (see Austin's note on *Aen.* 4.55); the elisions of 657 (over the caesura) and 658 (the first three words all elided) are very noticeable, in the latter case with spondaic movement, asyndeton and accumulation of adjectives (cf. *Aen.* 4.181 for a less exaggerated effect). We are reminded of Pope's well-known lines (*Essay on Criticism*, 370–1):

> When Ajax strives some rock's vast weight to throw,
> The line too labours, and the words move slow.

659. 'A lopped pine-trunk guides his hand and supports him
as he goes'; cf. Hom. *Od.* 9.319, Milton, *P.L.* 1.292 f. MSS
authority is stronger for *manu* than *manum*, but Quintilian supports
the latter, and to take *regit et vestigia firmat* together gives a weak
repetition of verbs and an awkward rhythm.

660–1. There is a touch of pathos here, reinforced by the
similar sound of *sola* and *solamen*; cf. Hom. *Od.* 9.447 f.

661. This incomplete line is filled in some MSS with *de collo
fistula pendet*, but where some of the primary MSS omit there is
immediately a strong case for exclusion.

663. **lăvit**: archaic third conjugation form; cf. *Geo.* 3.221, 359,
Aen. 10.727 and contrast *Aen.* 6.219, 12.722.

inde: 'from it' (i.e. the water); we should say 'he bathed his
eye in it'.

666 f. The description of flight is reminiscent of the escape of
Odysseus (*Od.* 9.471 f.). The dactylic rhythm and the use of
historic infinitives help to convey speed.

669. Notice the absence of the subject of *sensit*: Polyphemus
is so much in our minds that when the narrative returns to him
it is not necessary to mention him again.

vocis: this is strange in view of *taciti* (667), and may be a further
indication that this passage was unrevised. It cannot mean the
sound of the oars, as Servius suggests, and it seems best to take it
to refer to the shouting of time by the bo'sun. The contradiction
with *taciti* is not insuperable; they keep quiet until they are
confident that they are out of range.

670. **dextra adfectare potestas**: 'chance of clutching at us
with his hand'; for *potestas* with the infinitive cf. *Aen.* 7.591 and
compare line 299. *Adfectare* is strangely used, perhaps by extension
of phrases like *adfectare imperium*; he has no chance of 'aiming at'
the ship with a grab.

671. **potis**: a word with rather an archaic flavour (*potis est* =
potest) used only three times in Virgil.

fluctus aequare sequendo: probably this means that
Polyphemus could not keep up with the speed of the ships which
the waves, whipped up by the wind, gave them (cf. *Aen.* 10.248);
the other possibility is that Polyphemus was getting out of his
depth.

672 f. Polyphemus' cry, and the appearance of the other

Cyclopes, is based on Hom. *Od.* 9.395 f.; Virgil has greatly extended the 'pathetic fallacy' of the reaction of personified Nature.

673. **penitusque**: 'deep within', i.e. far inland.

674. **immugiit**: not found before Virgil, cf. *Aen.* 11.38. For *mugire* of the earth cf. *Aen.* 4.490, 6.256 and compare line 92. Cf. Milton, *P.L.* 2.788–9 'Hell trembl'd at the hideous Name, and sigh'd / from all her Caves, and back resounded "Death!"'

677–81. This is one of the most striking pieces of visual imagery in Virgil; every word is telling as he builds up the massive and eerie picture of these giant figures thronging the shore. The simile (679 f.) is the only one in Book 3.

677. **nequiquam**: 'frustrated', because Aeneas' ships are out of range.

lumine torvo: 'each with a single glaring eye'; they are all one-eyed, like Polyphemus.

679–81. **quales cum ... constiterunt**: 'like oaks standing there'; for this method of introducing a simile cf. *Aen.* 8.622.

679. **vertice celso**: 'with their high tops' (cf. *Aen.* 9.679 f.) rather than 'on a high mountain-peak'.

680. **aeriae**: a very poetic word; cf. line 291 and Tennyson's 'the aerial poplar'.

coniferae: again a colourful word, which is not found elsewhere till the third century.

681. **constitĕrunt**: for the scansion see note on 2.774; the perfect of *consistere* is similar in meaning to the present of *stare*.

Iovis ... Dianae: Jupiter had a famous oak grove at Dodona, and Diana the huntress was naturally associated with woods, and in her person as Hecate of the underworld is connected with cypresses, the trees of death.

682. **quocumque**: 'in any direction' (cf. 601, 654) i.e. whichever way the wind will blow them fastest. They get a south wind, which drives them towards Scylla and Charybdis, but all is well when it suddenly changes to north (687).

682. **rudentis excutere**: see note on 267; for the infinitive see note on 4–5.

684–6. I have discussed the difficulties of these three lines fully in my Oxford edition; I do not think that any interpretation or emendation of them (see Mynors's *app. crit.*) produces a sentence which would have satisfied Virgil. They represent jottings of metrical phrases which would have been shaped later into a final version. As they stand in the MSS and as I have printed them the best meaning that can be extracted is 'On the other hand the instructions of Helenus bid them not to hold their course between Scylla and Charybdis (a way which on both sides is only a hairsbreadth from death)'. *Ni* is equivalent to *ne*; *teneant* is strangely third person where we would expect *teneamus*. For *leti discrimine parvo* cf. *Aen.* 9.143, 10.511.

687. For the narrow straits of Pelorus cf. 411.

688. **vivo . . . saxo**: 'of natural rock', cf. *Aen.* 1.167.

689. In this line and in the last section of the book Virgil makes great use of the poetic possibilities of proper names of places (as Milton often does). The places mentioned here are on the east coast of Sicily, in the order in which they would be reached going southwards.

Megarosque sinus: i.e. the bay of Megara Hyblaea. The normal adjective is *Megaricus*; cf. 280, 401.

690-1. **relegens errata retrorsus litora**: 'skirting again in the opposite direction the coasts of his previous wanderings', i.e. with Odysseus when he came north from the land of the Lotus Eaters. For the passive use of the intransitive verb *errare* cf. *Aen.* 2.295.

692-718. *The Trojans continue to sail round Sicily, finally reaching Drepanum where Anchises dies. From there, Aeneas tells Dido, they were driven by a storm to Carthage; and so he ends the tale of his wanderings.*

692 f. In this final section of the book Virgil brings us away from the fabulous world of the Cyclopes back to the real world of the voyage of Rome's first founder. He does it by a kind of catalogue, consisting of very short descriptions of some of the most famous places of Sicily; it is reminiscent of Hellenistic descriptions of places, origins and etymologies such as we find, for example, in Apollonius. It ends the book with a sort of diminuendo.

692-4. 'There lies an island fronting a Sicilian bay, over against wave-beaten Plemyrium; the ancients called it Ortygia'. Virgil is describing the bay of Syracuse; Plemyrium is the headland at the south, and Ortygia is an island on the north side of the bay.

692. **praetenta**: literally 'spread in front of'; *sinu* is dative, cf. 292. Compare *Aen.* 6.60 *praetentaque Syrtibus arva*.

693. **undosum**: a very clear instance of an etymological adjective, 'translating' the Greek word Plemyrium (πλημυρίς, the tide). See note on 1.267-8, and cf. 698, 703.

694. **Ortygiam**: this was also a name of Delos (line 124). The name here is probably due to the association with Diana, who was born on Delos and connected with the Arethusa story (see next note).

694 f. The river Alpheus in South Greece (Elis) passes underground a number of times in its course; hence the story about its underwater passage from Greece to Sicily. The legend was that the river-god Alpheus pursued the nymph Arethusa, and Diana changed her into a fountain; whereupon Alpheus followed her under the sea, and united his waters with hers in Ortygia. Cf. *Ecl.* 10.1 f., Shelley's *Arethusa*, and Milton, *Arcades*, 28 f.

> Of famous Arcady ye are, and sprung
> Of that renowned flood, so often sung,
> Divine Alpheus, who by secret sluse
> Stole under Seas to meet his Arethuse.

695. The rhythm of the line ending is harsh and unusual; cf. *Aen.* 5.731 with my note there (Oxford edition) for full discussion.

696. **ore ... tuo**: cf. *Aen.* 1.245; the construction is ablative of means ('by way of').

698. **exsupero**: 'I sail past', an unusual sense; the singular after the plural *veneramur* is a little harsh, as is the number of heavy consonants in the line.

stagnantis Helori: another etymological adjective (see note on 693); ἕλος is the Greek word for marsh.

699. **hinc**: 'after that', a variant on *inde* (697).

Pachyni: the south-eastern tip of Sicily, cf. 429.

700. **radimus**: 'skirt', a metaphor from grazing the turning-point in a race; cf. *Aen.* 5.170, 7.10.

numquam concessa moveri: 'not allowed ever to be disturbed'; the construction here is analogous to Virgil's quite frequent use of *dare* with the infinitive (cf. 77), though it is more striking in this passive form.

701. Camerina: about fifty miles west of Pachynus, on the south coast of Sicily. Servius tells the story that when the near-by marsh (which was also called Camerina) was causing a pestilence, the inhabitants of the town consulted the oracle to ask whether they should drain the marsh, and were told not to do so in a response which became a Greek proverb: 'Don't move Camerina; it is better not moved.' They ignored the oracle and drained the marsh, with the result that the town was sacked by enemy forces who approached over the land where the marsh had been.

701–2. The town of Gela took its name from the river Gelas; the long *a* in its scansion is unusual and perhaps helped by the following *fl-*. *Immanis* should be taken with *fluvii*, referring to the terrible winter torrent of the river.

703 f. Servius here comments on the anachronism of the description of all these places, and finds special fault with it because it is put in the mouth of Aeneas.

703. arduus ... Acragas: *arduus* (steep, Greek ἄκρος) is a clear etymological epithet; see note on 693. This famous and important town, which the Romans called Agrigentum, was about halfway along the southern coast of Sicily.

704. magnanimum: this is the only adjective with which Virgil employs the old genitive form in *-um* (cf. *Geo.* 4.476, *Aen.* 6.307), except perhaps *omnigenum* in *Aen.* 8.698.

generator equorum: a number of Pindar's odes honour victors in the chariot-race who came from Agrigentum; Pliny (*N.H.* 8.155) tells of the tombs of horses there.

quondam: 'once'; the anachronism here, in the mouth of Aeneas, seems very harsh, but the meaning 'one day (destined to be)' is wholly inappropriate.

705. palmosa Selinus: Selinus (on the south west coast) is a third declension word with long *-us* (genitive *Selinuntis*). *Palmosa* is generally taken to mean 'famous for its palm-trees', but it is more likely to mean 'conferring the victor's palm', because the plant σέλινον (selinon), a kind of parsley, which figured on the coins of Selinus, was one of the plants used for the victor's crown, especially at the Isthmian games. Thus we have another etymological epithet (see note on 693).

706. Lilybaeum: the western extremity of the south coast of Sicily. Virgil emphasises the forbidding nature of the place, cruel with its hidden rocks, to prepare for the harsh blow of fate described in the following lines.

707. Observe the very unusual rhythm of this remarkable line, with a trochaic caesura in the third foot and no caesura in the fourth; cf. *Aen.* 5.781, 12.619.

Drepani inlaetabilis ora: Drepanum is on the west coast of Sicily, not far from Eryx; its shore is *inlaetabilis* (a rare word) because of the death of Anchises.

708 f. The place of Anchises' death varied very considerably in different versions of the legend: Servius says 'bene hic subtrahitur, ne parum decoro amori intersit', and certainly Virgil could not have conceived Book 4 in its present form, with Aeneas staying with Dido forgetful of fate, if Anchises had still been alive. Moreover, by placing the death of Anchises at this stage, Virgil has motivated the second visit to Sicily (in Book 5), which seems to have been original in his version, and is able to give a narrative of the religious ceremonies and games on the anniversary of Anchises' death in the part of the poem where there is proper room for them.

708–10. The tension is held all through this sentence: first *hic* reiterating *hinc*, then the clause in apposition to the subject, the sigh of *heu*, the object of the verb followed by a pause caused by an unusually placed elision, a phrase in apposition to the object, and then at last the verb and the reiterated object.

710. **pater optime**: the apostrophe here is much more than a rhetorical or metrical device (contrast 696); the expectation of emotion has already been built up, and so the apostrophe may be used to reinforce it, cf. *Aen.* 4.408 f.

711. **erepte**: this use of the vocative of the past participle is a favourite with Virgil; cf. *Aen.* 2.283.

714–15. Virgil uses his favourite threefold repetition (*hic . . . haec . . . hinc*) to close the speech; cf. 408–9.

714. **meta**: 'the end'; the word means the turning-point at either end of a race-course (cf. 429), and hence can mean the finish of a race as well as the turning-points during the race; cf. *Aen.* 10.472, 12.546. Aeneas omits mention of the storm which drove him to Carthage after leaving Sicily because it has already been described to Dido (*Aen.* 1.535 f.), and he pays her the compli-

ment of implying that now they have reached Carthage their trials are over.

716–18. The phrases *intentis omnibus* and *conticuit tandem* remind us of the start of his story at the beginning of Book 2.

717. **fata renarrabat divum**: 'recited the destiny sent by heaven', cf. *Aen.* 2.54. The force of *re-* is not that he told the story for the second time, but that he went through (this time in words) the events again.

718. Notice the pattern of alliteration, *c*, *q*, and *f*. Page comments on the contrast of the momentary stillness and repose here both with the adventures just told and with the opening words of Book 4.

AENEID 4

Introductory Note

The story of Dido's tragedy has always been the best known part of the *Aeneid* (Ov. *Trist.* 2.533 f., cf. *Her.* 7; Macrob. *Sat.* 5.17.4 f.). It was a favoured theme in twelfth century French romances; in Chaucer's *House of Fame* it has twice as much space as the rest of the *Aeneid*; Marlowe's *Dido, Queen of Carthage* is among the most familiar dramas on the subject, and the operas of Purcell and Berlioz are well known. It has been said that Dido is the only character created by a Roman poet to pass into world literature. Far more often than not Dido has been sympathetically portrayed.

Virgil's source material for the legend of Dido was very varied. There are traces in the Greek historian Timaeus (third century B.C.) of the story of her flight to Libya, and she figured (as did Aeneas) in Naevius' *Bellum Punicum* (late third century).The prose writers of the Aeneas legend, such as Virgil's contemporaries Livy and Dionysius, naturally make no mention of a visit by Aeneas to Dido, because the chronology would not permit of it: Carthage was not founded until several centuries after the time of Aeneas. What is certain is that Virgil's detailed treatment of Aeneas' visit to Dido in Carthage is very largely original.

Certain heroines in literature were available as models for

Virgil, but here again we find that his treatment of Dido is profoundly different from any of his sources. The gentle Nausicaa in Homer (*Od.* 6) has nothing in common with the tormented Dido; Dido is closer in situation to the Homeric witches, Circe and Calypso, both of whom are obstacles to Odysseus on his homeward voyage. But they are supernatural figures who do not arouse our pity — as Dido most certainly does. Apollonius Rhodius' Medea in *Arg.* 3 presented Virgil with certain ideas (see note on 1 f., 166 f., 474 f., 522–9) and with the concept of describing love in an epic poem in the tone of elegy or lyric; but Apollonius' Medea is a young girl, excited, confused, uncertain, while Dido is a mature queen well aware of the issues involved. Finally the Ariadne of Catullus 64, deserted by Theseus, had a marked effect on Virgil's poetry, especially in passages of pathos (see note on 296 f., 657–8), but the sadness and loneliness of Ariadne is something quite different from the tragic sublimity of Dido.

Indeed the word tragic is wholly appropriate for Dido in this book. We know much less about Aeneas' feelings here — only a touch now and then to tell of the love he must sacrifice (see note on 279 f.); it is Dido who holds the stage and in many ways she resembles the tragic figures of Greek drama (see note on 296 f., 450 f., 630 f. and K. Quinn, *Latin Explorations*, pp. 29 f.) more than her predecessors in epic or epyllion. She falls indeed from prosperity and success to utter disaster; the contrast between the capable, beautiful and wholly admirable queen in Book I and the terrifying personification of hatred and vengeance which she becomes in the second half of Book 4 is truly the stuff of the great Greek tragedies (one thinks especially of Euripides' Phaedra or Medea).

The essential basis of the tragedy is that Dido gives up everything for her personal love for Aeneas; she allows the width of her abilities and excellencies and interests to narrow to this one object, so that when she finds it is unattainable she has left herself with nothing. Carthage has come to a halt (86 f.) and Anna is right when she says in the last scene (682–3) that Dido has brought to destruction not only herself but all the people of Carthage. Dido has burnt all her bridges and her pride can know no retreat; she utterly fails to understand Aeneas' arguments about his duty (see note on 331 f.), because in her eyes personal considerations override everything else. She has allowed herself to be drawn into a position from which she can find no way back; she has allowed herself to become enmeshed in a net of circumstances. Whether she could have resisted successfully had she tried we do not know; all we know is what happened when she yielded.

The element of pathos in the first half of the book as Dido allows herself to be swept on is very great; and in the second half it persists, intermingled with a feeling of horror and terror as she becomes no longer a queen, no longer a woman, but a stylised and archetypal fury of vengeance (see note on 362 f., 584 f.). The tragedy is that she should have been driven — or should have driven herself — to a point where her human qualities are entirely submerged in a sweeping torrent of frenzy, hatred and despair. Near the end of the book, in her final speech, both these aspects (pathos and hatred) are present; lines 651–8 show us the generous queen brought piteously to tragic disaster, the unhappy woman for whom St. Augustine and many since shed tears. But in her very last words (659–62) we see again her frantic desire for vengeance — she cannot now have it in life, but in death she must and will. This is the Dido whose anger still burns in the underworld when Aeneas meets her, and who is no more moved by his words than if she were flint or Marpesian rock (6.471). What has brought her to destruction and turned her heart to flint? Her own faults, folly, pride? Or the force of uncontrollable events, the pressure of hostile circumstances too powerful to resist? Or both?

1–55. *Dido is consumed with love for Aeneas, and tells her sister Anna that had she not firmly resolved after Sychaeus' death not to marry again she might have yielded. Anna in reply enumerates the advantages of marriage with Aeneas, and Dido is persuaded.*

1 f. The opening section of the book concentrates completely on Dido and her love for Aeneas. During the Trojan story of Books 2 and 3 the reader has hardly been conscious of the listening Dido, but now the theme of the end of Book 1 is resumed and kept in the foreground. The note is one of foreboding; imagery of fire, illness, wounding, frenzy, madness is constant throughout this section and the next (*saucia, vulnus, carpitur igni,*

male sana, flammavit, furentem, flamma, vulnus, uritur, furens, demens,
pestis and finally (101) *ardet amaxns Dido traitque per ossa furorem*).

There are some reminiscences of Catullus' Ariadne (Cat. 64),
and many of Apollonius' Medea (*Argonautica* 3), and Virgil's
intimate portrayal of the lover's anguished heart owes much to
both. But his Dido is of a different dimension from either of these;
we have seen her in Book 1 as a proud queen, a woman of outstanding abilities and achievements, so that her agony, uncertainty, and final despair is far more tragic.

The part played by Anna is structurally not unlike that of
Medea's sister Chalciope in Apollonius, though the differences
are great, especially in that Medea does not tell Chalciope of her
true emotions. We may also compare the nurse or confidante in
Greek tragedy; Anna's persuasive speech, full of rhetorical devices
to lead Dido to the course Anna knows she wants to take, is somewhat similar to that of the nurse to Phaedra in Euripides'
Hippolytus, 433 f. Its persuasive intention is wholly and immediately successful, so that Dido who had sworn that the earth
should swallow her up before she violated *pudor* (27) now can
accept that her duty towards Carthage's future as well as her
personal inclinations justify her in violating it (55).

1. **At regina**: the beginning of the book focusses on Dido,
and these two words recur at decisive moments in the book,
i.e. 296 and 504.

saucia cura: the imagery of love's wound (cf. *vulnus*, line 2)
is frequent throughout this section (cf. especially the simile in
69 f.); *cura* in this sense of the anxious suffering of the lover is
frequent in poetry, cf. 394, *Aen.* 6.444, and *Cat.* 64.250 *multiplices
animo volvebat saucia curas*; this is the first of many reminiscences
of Catullus' Ariadne.

2. **vulnus alit venis**: 'nourishes the wound with her life-
blood'; i.e. keeps the wound unhealed, cf. 67.

caeco carpitur igni: 'is consumed by a fire she keeps hidden';
cf. Medea in Apollonius 3.296 in whose heart 'deadly love burned
secretly' (cf. also 3.286, 'Love's arrow blazed in her heart like
fire'). For *carpere* in this sense, 'destroy, consume', cf. Prop. 3.5.3
and line 32.

3 f. Notice that Dido, herself a queen, is moved by the qualities
of Aeneas as well as his personal appearance; contrast the fine

description of Medea in Ap. Rh. 3.453 f. where her memories and thoughts of her beloved Jason are entirely visual.

6. 'The next day's dawn was moving over the earth with Phoebus' torch'. Notice the interwoven order of *postera . . . Aurora*, and for the phrase *Phoebea lampas* (the sun) cf. *Aen.* 3.637.

8. **unanimam . . . sororem**: 'her loving sister'. Anna was in Naevius' version of the story, and in Virgil corresponds to some extent with Chalciope, Medea's sister in Apollonius; see note on 1 f.

male sana: 'barely sane', cf. *Aen.* 2.23.

9. **quae . . . terrent**: 'oh, the dreams which frighten my distracted heart'; a translation of Medea's words in Ap. Rh. 3.636. Servius knew a reading *terret*, in which case *insomnia* would mean sleeplessness, but the parallel with Apollonius is decisive, and cf. *Aen.* 6.896.

10. **quis**: like *quae* in the previous line and *quam* in the next, this is exclamatory (= *qualis*); cf. 47 and *Aen.* 6.771.

sedibus hospes: cf. Cat. 64.176.

11. 'what distinction he has in his looks, what courage and martial prowess'; cf. *Aen.* 3.490. Austin supports the view that *armis* means 'shoulders' (from *armus*, cf. 11.644, 12.433), but in an ambiguity of this kind the reader naturally takes the more normal meaning (cf. 1.545) unless the context prevents it. Servius has a good remark on this line: 'et bene virtutis commemoratione excusat supra dictam pulchritudinis laudem.'

12. Dido indeed knows that he is of divine descent; cf. *Aen.* 1.617.

13. **degeneres**: probably 'degenerate' (with reference to *genus* in the previous line) rather than 'not of divine birth'. The fearlessness of Aeneas has appeared from his narrative in Books 2 and 3, to which Dido refers in the following phrases.

17. **deceptam morte fefellit**: 'cheated and deceived me by his death', i.e. frustrated my hopes of long-lasting happiness; the word *deceptus* is frequent on tombstones, for *fefellit* cf. *Aen.* 2.744. The death of Dido's husband Sychaeus at the hands of her brother Pygmalion was briefly described in *Aen.* 1.343 f.

18. **thalami taedaeque**: 'the bridal chamber and marriage torch', frequent synonyms for marriage, cf. 339, 550.

19. **forsan potui**: 'perhaps I could have. . . .' The indicative

of *possum* is normal to express past potential sentences. In prose, however, the subjunctive would be used after *forsan*.

culpae: here Dido herself recognizes that to break her oath of loyalty to Sychaeus would be a fault or a sin; later (172) Virgil's narrative tells us the same. The word (like the Greek hamartia) does not *necessarily* carry strong moral condemnation; the extent to which it does must be determined from the context.

21. **sparsos ... penatis**: 'the bespattering of my household gods with blood shed by my brother'; cf. Cat. 64.181.

22–3. **animumque labantem impulit**: 'moved my wavering heart'; *labantem* is consequential upon *inflexit sensus*, and need not be taken predicatively.

24. **optem ... dehiscat**: 'I would wish that the earth should gape open'; the paratactic subjunctive with *optare* is quite common.

25. **adigat**: cf. *Aen.* 6.594; *abigat* is read by *F* and some modern editors (cf. *Aen.* 11.261).

26. **Erebo**: this (local ablative) is the reading of the majority of the good MSS against the rather easier *Erebi* of others; for *Erebus* (the underworld) cf. 510.

27. **pudor**: here 'conscience' (cf. 55); she had promised Sychaeus' ashes (552) that she would be loyal to his memory by not marrying again. In Rome the goddess Pudicitia was worshipped only by *matronae univirae*, and *univira* is frequent on tombstones.

28–29. Notice the emphatic metrical features (reinforcing the balancing *ille ... ille*): the run-on word *abstulit* with assonance (*amores abstulit*), and the strong alliteration of *s*.

30. **sinum**: her bosom, cf. Ap. Rh. 3.804.

32. 'will you waste away in loneliness and grief all through your youth?'; for *carpere* (future passive) cf. line 2; by *iuventa* Anna means that Dido is still of marriageable age.

33. **Veneris nec**: *nec* is postponed, cf. 124.

35–8. Notice the antithesis between *aegram* and *placitone*: Anna says 'I grant that no would-be husbands have moved you in your desolation up to now, but surely you won't resist a love which you want?'.

36. **non Libyae ... Tyro**: 'not in Libya, nor before that in Tyre'; the cases are unusual, *Libyae* being locative when one would expect *Libya*, and *Tyro* ablative of place where instead of

the locative *Tyri*. Servius' alternative — 'suitors of Libya or Tyre' — is less likely.

Iarbas: an African king, cf. 196 f. According to one version of the legend (Justin 18.6) Dido committed suicide to escape marriage with him.

38. placitone ... amori: 'a pleasing love' (cf. Ov. *Am.* 2.4.18); for the dative see note on 1.475.

39. Dido herself (*Aen.* 1.563–4) had told the Trojans about her need to defend her kingdom against local attack. Anna knows the kind of argument that will sway her.

40–1. The Gaetulae and Numidae were peoples to the south and west of Carthage; Syrtis was the name of the famous quick-sands with their hinterland to the south-east (cf. *Aen.* 1.111).

41. infreni: 'riding without bridles' (cf. *Aen.* 10.750), doubt-less also containing the metaphorical meaning of 'wild'.

42. hinc deserta siti regio: 'on this side is an area deserted because of drought', i.e. to the south and south-east, where the Barcaei lived their nomadic life. Barca was the name of the family to which Hasdrubal and Hannibal belonged.

43–4. Anna refers to the danger of attack from Dido's brother Pygmalion from whom she had fled; cf. line 325.

44. For the half-line see note on 1.534; others in this book are 361, 400, 503, 516.

45. Iunone secunda: Anna mentions Juno as the chief goddess of Carthage (1.15), and also as goddess of marriage (line 166).

49. 'with what mighty achievements will Punic glory soar'. Notice the irony of the suggestion that Carthage will grow great by assimilating Rome.

50. sacrisque litatis: 'when favourable sacrifices have been obtained'; see note on 2.118–9, and Prop. 4.1.24.

52. aquosus Orion: the setting of Orion in the autumn was associated with storms; see note on 1.535.

53. 'while the ships are still damaged, and the weather is impossible'; cf. *Geo.* 1.211.

54. incensum: a few MSS have *impenso* ('with great love', cf. Lucr. 5.964) and both readings were known to Servius, but *impensus* in this sense does not occur elsewhere in Virgil, and *amore* fits better with *incensum*; Anna heaps fuel on the fire, she does not light the fire.

55. **solvitque pudorem**: 'broke the bonds of conscience'; notice how easily Dido is persuaded to reject her oath to Sychaeus (24 f.). In Glover's words 'To resolve to win the love of Aeneas is no wrong thought or action, but to attempt it against her conscience is the first step towards shame.'

56–89. *Dido makes sacrifices to win the gods' favour. In her frenzied state she is like a deer shot by a hunter's arrow; she cannot ever forget her love, and the building of her city is neglected.*

56 f. The picture of Dido's frenzied love, given in the opening lines of the book, is now even more vividly painted. Her propitiatory sacrifices are fully described and the situation seems hopeful, but first in a personal intervention into the narrative (65–7), and then in a memorable simile Virgil presents again the undertones of impending tragedy. We return to the narrative, and Dido's frenzy is reflected in the emotional distraction of her behaviour; this was in part evident to those present (she stops in mid-sentence, she hangs on his lips) but the reader is also taken behind the scenes and sees her alone, unhappy, trying to console herself by memory and imagination. Finally, her utter pre-occupation with her love, to the exclusion of all else, is explicitly stated.

56. **pacem**: 'divine approval', cf. *Geo.* 4.535, *Aen.* 3.370.

57. **bidentis**: sheep in their second year have two prominent teeth; Henry's note on the subject is well worth reading.

58. These three deities, Ceres, Apollo, Bacchus, are invoked probably as being especially concerned with the foundation of cities. Ceres is called *legifera* because the discovery of corn was associated with the beginnings of settled life, cf. *Geo.* 1.7 f., Ov. *Met.* 5.343 *prima dedit leges*. For *Lyaeus* cf. *Aen.* 1.686.

59. **Iunoni**: see note on 45.

60 f. For the detailed description of sacrifices (a frequent feature in the *Aeneid*) cf. especially *Aen.* 6.243 f.

61. **fundit**: supply as object *pateram* from the previous line, in the sense of *vinum de patera*.

62. **ante ora deum**: i.e. in front of the images of the gods.

spatiatur: a solemn ritual word; cf. *incessit* of Dido leading her procession in *Aen.* 1.497.

63. **instauratque**: 'renews' i.e. 'inaugurates afresh', cf. line 145 and *Aen.* 3.62.

64. **pectoribus**: for the lengthening in arsis of the final syllable see Austin ad loc. and cf. lines 146 and 222.

65. The poet intervenes in his narrative to comment on it; cf. lines 169 f., 412 and especially *Aen.* 10.501 f. *nescia mens hominum. . . .* The implication here is that the priests imagine that the sacred rites which they prescribe and interpret will ensure Dido's happiness, unaware as they are of the destructive nature of Dido's frenzied love (*furentem*), unaware that her 'wound' is not being cured.

66. **est**: contracted form for *edit*, cf. *Aen.* 5.683. This phrase and the next are reminiscent of the first two lines of the book; no change has been effected by the sacrifices.

mollis: accusative plural, cf. Cat. 45.16 *mollibus in medullis*.

68. **infelix**: cf. *Aen.* 1.712, 749 and in this book lines 450, 529, 596; the undertone of impending tragedy is made more and more clear.

69 f. This wonderful simile well illustrates how Virgil can use traditional epic machinery of Homer in a new way. The actual point of comparison is in the wounded deer rushing wildly about; the additional details in the simile relate to the themes of the story and point forward as well as backwards, indirectly anticipating the events and involving the reader in a half-knowledge of the future as well as a recollection of the past. Dido, the hunted and helpless victim, has been caught *incauta*; this is a word of grim association, often suggesting resultant disaster (*Aen.* 3.332, 10.812). The arrow of love has not yet caused death, but will do so and cannot be dislodged (73). And finally the hunting shepherd is unaware of having shot his victim, as Aeneas is unaware of the disastrous effect of the love he has caused. As Austin points out, the contrast between the emphatic run-on word *nescius* and the following *illa* adds to the unconscious cruelty. See further Otis, *Virgil*, pp. 72 f., Pöschl, *The Art of Vergil*, pp. 80 f.

70. **nemora inter Cresia**: archery is particularly associated with Crete, cf. *Aen.* 5.306. For Mt. Dicte (73) in Crete cf. *Aen.* 3.171.

73. Notice the pattern of alliteration at the close of the simile: *haer-, l, l, har-*.

75. **Sidonias**: Virgil uses *Tyrius* and *Sidonius* interchangeably to refer to Dido's original home in Tyre.

paratam: notice the significance of this word — Dido can show Aeneas that she has already done what he yet has to do; cf. *Aen.* 1.437 *o fortunati quorum iam moenia surgunt.*

77. **eadem**: a repetition of the banquet at which some days earlier Aeneas had recounted his story.

78–9. **audire ... exposcit**: poetic infinitive, cf. *Aen.* 9.193 and see note on 1.527–8.

79. **pendetque ... ab ore**: cf. Ariadne in Cat. 64.69 f.

80–1. The sun has long since set; now the dim moon in turn sets, and the constellations one after another. The last phrase is repeated from *Aen.* 2.9 where see note.

82. **stratisque relictis**: the reference (as Servius saw) is to the couch on which Aeneas had reclined at the banquet (Ov. *Met.* 5.34).

83. **absens absentem**: the Greek type of repetition is very emphatic, cf. *Aen.* 1.684, 10.600.

84. Dido recalls in imagination the events of the day (cf. Ap. Rh. 3.453 f.), hearing and seeing Aeneas, holding Ascanius in her lap; the words *absens absentem* extend to this line too.

85. 'if thus she could solace a love beyond words'; *fallere* literally is 'deceive', i.e. seem to satisfy. For the Greek form of the conditional sentence ('in the hope that') see note on 1.181–2.

86 f. This passage is vitally important as indicating quite specifically that Dido has now abdicated the queenly responsibilities which she had been performing so admirably before Aeneas came (1.423 f., 507 f.). Notice how the slow spondaic movement reflects the lack of activity.

88–9. 'all building stops and the mighty threatening walls and the structures that tower sky-high are idle'; the metrical effects are noticeable here, with the elision of *opera* after the third foot, the pause in the fifth foot, and the assonance of *aequataque machina. Minae* probably is general ('threatening walls', cf. *Aen.* 1.162), but it might more specifically mean (as Servius says) 'pinnacles of the walls'. *Machina*, as Servius saw and as is shown by a passage in Val. Fl. 6.383, means 'structure', not 'machinery' (cranes, scaffolding, or the like); the former meaning is an extension of the Lucretian phrase *machina mundi*, while the latter would be inappropriate with the verbs *pendent interrupta.* Virgil uses the word elsewhere only of the Trojan horse (2.46 etc.).

90–128. *In Olympus the goddesses Juno and Venus converse about the mortal scene. Juno, hoping to prevent the establishment of the Trojan race in Italy, proposes an alliance between Trojans and Carthaginians. Venus agrees if Jupiter can be persuaded (as she knows he cannot), and Juno plans that Dido and Aeneas shall seek shelter from a storm in the same cave, and that here she will join them in marriage.*

90 f. The ruthless and malicious scheming of the goddesses is here shown at its most blatant. Juno's desire is clear — to frustrate the foundation of Rome by keeping Aeneas at Carthage, and to this end she uses on Venus all her powers of irony and persuasion. Venus' intentions are much less clear; presumably she is confident, in the light of what Jupiter had foretold of the future (1.257 f.) that Juno's plans will be frustrated, so that it gives her pleasure to appear to support them, and thus score over her divine adversary. As for Dido — neither goddess sees her as more than an instrument in the pursuit of their own policies. The portrayal of the goddesses here owes something to the beginning of Apollonius 3, where Hera and Athena go to Aphrodite for help in their schemes; and we are reminded of Venus' intervention in *Aen.* 1.657 f., where see note.

90. **peste**: the word has been used already (in an anticipatory context) of Dido's love, *Aen.* 1.712; cf. its use by Catullus in his prayer to be released from the cruel disease of his love for Lesbia, 76.20.

92. **Saturnia**: Juno, daughter of Saturnus, cf. 1.23.

93–5. 'Glittering indeed is the glory and piled high the booty which you come back with, you and your boy, mighty and memorable is your majesty indeed, if one woman is brought low by the trickery of two gods.' Juno's opening phrases are sarcastic in the highest degree, with the ironical adjective placed first (cf. 6.523), the military metaphor applied to a goddess whose battles were not real ones, the derogatory *tuque puerque tuus* (Cupid), and the rhetorical antithesis of two against one, gods against a mortal woman. *Numen* is in loose apposition to *tuque puerque tuus*, cf. Ov. *Met.* 4.452, and for *memorabile numen* Ov. *Met.* 4.416–17. The reading *nomen*, found in some late MSS, is very attractive; cf. *Aen.* 2.583.

96 f. Cf. *Aen.* 1.661 f., for Venus' fear of Carthage.

98. 'But what will be the end of it, or what do you now hope to get with all this opposition?' With *quo* ('whither') understand some verb like *tendis* ('what is your object'); *certamine tanto* is ablative of means.

99–100. **quin ... exercemus?**: 'Why don't we rather work out... ?'; this use of *quin* is from colloquial speech, cf. 547. *Exercere* is extended from its normal use in phrases like *odium exercere, amores exercere.*

101. Cf. *Aen.* 1.675; Juno says that Venus' plan for Dido to fall in love with Aeneas is more than fulfilled — she is on fire with frenzied passion; for *trahere* cf. Ov. *Met.* 4.675.

102–3. 'So let us rule this people together, with equal authority'; cf. *Aen.* 7.256–7. Juno then proceeds to forms of words which make concessions: *servire, permittere.* For Juno to propose that the Carthaginians should be a dowry for the hated leader of the Trojans rightly arouses Venus' suspicions; in 12.819f. Juno is only reconciled to the Trojans on the condition that in their intermarriage with the Italians they shall be the recessive partner.

105. **simulata mente**: 'with pretended purpose', i.e. as if she were really interested in a union between the Trojans and Carthaginians, whereas in fact her only purpose is to keep the Trojans from settling in Italy (*Aen.* 1.19f.).

locutam: for the omission of the pronoun *eam* see note on 383.

106. 'so that she might divert the kingdom of Italy to Libyan shores'. *Quo* introduces a final clause (= *ut eo modo*); *oras* is accusative of motion towards.

109. **si modo ... fortuna sequatur**: 'provided that success will follow ...', but, as she goes on to say, she has doubts.

110. **sed ... feror, si**: 'but I am tossed in doubt because of the fates, uncertain whether....'; *fatis* is causal ablative dependent on the phrase *incerta feror* (= *fatis distrahor*). The next two lines depend on *si* (= *num*), and all three clauses refer to the same option: 'whether he wishes one city, or *approves* mingling or treaties'. Venus in fact knows very well that he does not.

115–16. Notice the matter-of-fact prosaic diction; Juno speaks of how to deal with an item on the agenda.

119. **Titan**: the sun, child of the Titan Hyperion, cf. *Aen.* 6.725.

radiisque retexerit orbem: 'reveals the world with his rays' cf. *Aen.* 5.65, the same phrase, 9.461.

121. **alae**: the groups of horsemen (132), excitedly active (*trepidant*) in closing in on the wild animals with a cordon (*indagine*).

124. The postponed *et* seems to link the two unsuspecting subjects more closely.

126. This line, characteristic of Juno's power as *pronuba*, is repeated from *Aen.* 1.73, where see notes.

127. **hic hymenaeus erit**: 'this shall be their wedding'; this Greek word is elsewhere plural in Virgil, but cf. Cat. 66.11.

127–8. 'The Cytherean goddess did not oppose her request, but nodded agreement and smiled at having seen through her trickery'. For Venus' epithet *Cytherea* cf. *Aen.* 1.257; her smile here reminds us of Homer's 'laughter-loving Aphrodite', and especially of her malicious pleasure in herself tricking people (cf. Hor. *Odes* 3.27.67 *perfidum ridens Venus*). *Dolis . . . repertis* might mean 'at the trickery Juno had devised', but the words refer better to Venus' perception of Juno's deceit (105).

129–172. *Dido and her Carthaginians, accompanied by Aeneas and the Trojans, ride out for the hunt. In the midst of the joyful scene Juno sends a storm, and Dido and Aeneas shelter in the same cave. The powers of Nature seem to perform the ritual of a wedding ceremony, and Dido now considers herself to be married to Aeneas.*

129f. In this passage the contrast between joy and gloom is total. The hunt is described in the most radiant and brilliant colours; it is full of movement, excitement and splendour. The beauty of Dido's appearance is fully described (137f.), while Aeneas for his part is no less majestic than Apollo (143f.). The young Ascanius enjoys every moment of the chase.

The fulfilment of Juno's plans is introduced in menacing lines (160f.), with sinister repetition of the words of her speech to Venus (161, 165). The primeval and elemental forces of Nature and the supernatural enact a ceremony which corresponds in a daemonic way to the real events of a marriage. Dido is deluded by these cosmic manifestations, and the poet interrupts his narrative to reflect on the inevitable sequence of events now set in train.

130. **iubare exorto**: 'when the sun's rays appeared'; for the singular use of *iubar* cf. Ov. *Met.* 7.663 *iubar aureus extulerat Sol.*

131. The omission of the verb 'to be' is striking here; cf. *Aen.* 1.639, 3.618. Possibly a verb may be supplied by zeugma from *ruunt* or *it*; in this case cf. Hor. *Epist.* 1.6.58. *Retia rara* are wide-meshed nets, *plagae* are smaller nets; cf. Hor. *Epod.* 2.32 f.

132. **Massyli**: an African people to the west of Carthage, cf. 483, *Aen.* 6.60.

132. **odora canum vis**: literally 'the keen-scented power of dogs', i.e. keen-scented strong dogs. The type of phrase is Homeric (cf. *Il.* 11.690, 23.720) and is found in Lucretius with *canum* (4.681, 6.1222); it is particularly remarkable here because of the archaic type of monosyllabic ending (cf. *Aen.* 1.65 and Austin's full note on this passage) and the innovated meaning of *odorus*.

135. Notice the strong alliteration and assonance (*s*, *f*, *man-*) to add emphasis to the fine colourful picture.

137. 'wearing a Sidonian cloak with embroidered border'; *chlamydem* is a retained accusative with the passive verb used in a middle sense, see note on 1.228 and cf. 216–17, 493, 509, 518, 589–90, 644, 659.

138. **crines nodantur in aurum**: 'her hair was fastened with (on to) a golden clasp'; for a similar three-fold repetition of 'golden' in a descriptive passage cf. *Aen.* 7.278–9, 8.659–71, 11.774–6.

142. **agmina iungit**: 'joins his troop with hers', cf. *Aen.* 2.267.

143 f. The comparison of Aeneas with Apollo is primarily concerned with beauty and majesty; secondly with hunting and archery; and thirdly is reminiscent of the comparison of Dido with Diana in 1.498 f., with which there are several similarities (*exercet . . . choros, per iuga Cynthi, mille secutae, pharetram fert umero, gradiens*). In Apollonius Jason is compared with Apollo (1.307 f.).

143. **hibernam Lyciam**: 'Lycia in winter'; Servius tells us that Apollo was said to give oracles during the winter months in southern Asia Minor at Patara in Lycia (through which a river called Xanthus flowed, not to be confused with Troy's Xanthus), and during the summer in Delos, where he was born (see note on 3.75–6); cf. Hor. *Odes* 3.4.60 f.

146. **Cretesquē Dryopesque**: notice the lengthening in arsis of the first -*que*; see note on 3.91. This and the quadrisyllabic

ending give a Greek touch to the metre, to correspond with the Greek names. The peoples mentioned come from widely separated parts; the Dryopes from North Greece and the Agathyrsi from Scythia.

147. **Cynthi**: the highest hill of Delos, cf. *Aen.* 1.498.

148. **premit crinem fingens**: 'shapes and secures his locks', cf. *Aen.* 6.80.

149–50. Aeneas is compared with Apollo first in the composure and majesty of his movements (*haud segnior ibat*), and second in his beauty (*tantum decus*).

152. **deiectae**: 'dislodged', frightened by the hunters.

154. **transmittunt**: 'cross', cf. Cic. *Fin.* 5.87, Lucr. 2.330, *Aen.* 6.313; the subject of this clause as of the next is *cervi*.

155. **glomerant**: 'mass', cf. *Aen.* 1.500, 2.315.

158. **pecora inter inertia**: 'in among all these timid creatures', cf. *Aen.* 9.730. The hunt is depicted on the Low Ham mosaic (see *J.R.S.* 1946, p. 142).

160. Observe how the movement changes from the joyful hunting scene by means of the slow rhythm of spondees and the menacing alliteration of *m*. For *misceri*, suggesting disturbance, see note on 1.124. Notice too how closely the following lines correspond with Juno's speech (lines 120 f.), especially the crucial line 165 (=124). This passage is imitated by Spenser, *F.Q.* 1.1.6–7.

163. **Dardaniusque nepos Veneris**: i.e. Ascanius, Venus' Trojan grandson.

166 f. The marriage in a cave is reminiscent of the marriage of Jason and Medea in Ap. Rh. 4.1130 f., but the difference is profound. In Apollonius the occasion is a happy one, a real marriage; in Virgil the elemental powers of nature and supernatural divinities conspire to produce a parody of a wedding, a hallucination by which the unhappy Dido is deceived. *Dant signum* refers generally to the inauguration of the ceremony, here performed by Mother Earth, the oldest of divinities, and Juno in her special capacity as goddess of marriage. The 'lightning flashes' (*fulsere ignes*) seem to Dido to be the wedding torches; the ether 'witnesses' the marriage, and the nymphs sing the wedding song. Milton (*P.L.* 9.782 f., cf. also 1000 f.), put the imagery of this passage to a different use:

> 'Earth felt the wound, and Nature from her seate
> Sighing through all her Works gave signs of woe,
> That all was lost'.

169 f. Notice how Virgil here intervenes in his narrative, partly to anticipate the results of the action (169–70), partly to reveal its effect on Dido (esp. 172).

170. Supply *iam* to the first clause: Dido is no longer affected by appearances or reputation, nor does she any longer think of a hidden love.

172. 'She calls it marriage, and under this name she cloaks her sin'; for *praetexere* cf. 500, for *culpa* cf. 19. For Dido's belief that it was marriage cf. lines 316, 324, 496; for Aeneas' denial cf. lines 338–9.

173–218. *The terrifying figure of Rumour is described; she spreads abroad in malicious terms the story of the love of Dido and Aeneas. Finally she goes to King Iarbas, Dido's suitor; angered beyond measure he asks Jupiter if he is aware of so disgraceful a situation, or whether his worship is vain.*

173 f. The personification of Rumour occurs as early as Homer (*Od.* 24.413 f.; cf. Hesiod, *Works* 761 f. where she is a goddess); the detail of Virgil's picture incorporates some memorable phrases from Homer's personified Strife (*Il.* 4.442–3; see note on 176–7), but is very greatly enlarged and elaborated. The style of description is grandiose and rhetorical, in some ways baroque, and it has met with disapproval from many commentators. But this is a style of writing which Virgil enjoyed (cf. for example Polyphemus in Book 3 and the boxing match in Book 5 — and, rather differently, Atlas in this book, 246 f.); and it is used here to vary the pathos and intensity of the developing human tragedy by transporting the reader to a world of imagination, to a dimension of non-human imagery.

Among the imitations of this passage mention should be made of Ovid, *Met.* 12.41 f.; Chaucer, *House of Fame*, 3.266 f.; Pope, *Temple of Fame*, 258 f.:

> When on the goddess first I cast my sight,
> Scarce seem'd her stature of a cubit's height;
> But swell'd to larger size, the more I gazed,
> Till to the roof her towering front she raised . . .

Such was her form, as ancient bards have told,
Wings raise her arms, and wings her feet infold;
A thousand busy tongues the goddess hears,
And thousand open eyes, and thousand listening ears.

175. **mobilitate viget**: 'she thrives on speed'; other creatures
weaken the faster they go, but Rumour gets stronger. For the
phrases cf. Lucr. 6.340 f. (of a thunderbolt).

176–7. This is a close imitation of Hom. *Il.* 4.442–3, where
personified Strife is described, small at first but then her head
reaches the heavens while she walks on the earth; Virgil has
added the notion of Rumour being timid at first while she is small.

177. This line is repeated in *Aen.* 10.767; Pease has a long note
on hyperbole, and quotes Ben Jonson 'As her brow the clouds
invade / Her feet do strike the ground'.

178. **ira inritata deorum**: 'provoked by her anger against
the gods', because they exterminated her children, the Giants
and the Titans (Ap. Rh. 2.39 f., Hor. *Odes* 3.4.73 f.).

179. Coeus (*Geo.* 1.279) was a Titan and Enceladus (*Aen.*
3.578) a Giant; both were destroyed by Jupiter. Mother Earth
then bore one last child, Fama, to be their sister and take
vengeance on gods and men with her evil tongue.

181. **monstrum horrendum ingens**: a reminiscence of the
description of the Cyclops in 3.658.

181–3. 'for every feather on her body there is a watchful eye
beneath (astonishing to tell) — and she has as many tongues, too,
as many shouting mouths, as many pricked-up ears'. Compare the
hundred-eyed monster Argus, whose eyes became the rings on the
tail of Juno's peacock.

184. **caeli medio terraeque**: 'between earth and sky', cf.
Ov. *Met.* 12.39 f., and for the construction *Aen.* 9.230.

185. **stridens**: notice the effect of the 'run-on' spondaic
word filling the first foot, a rare rhythm (cf. 190 and 562). Very
strong emphasis is thus put on the descriptive participle. *Stridens*
is similarly placed in *Aen.* 9.419, 12.859 (referring to an arrow).

186. **custos**: 'watching', so as to miss nothing.

188. 'as persistent a messenger of what is false and distorted as
of the truth', cf. *facta atque infecta canebat* (190).

191 f. The accusative and infinitive reports Rumour's story;

it is not wholly untrue in itself, but it is phrased in malicious terms, calculated to anger Iarbas.

191. **cretum**: 'born of', cf. *Aen.* 2.74.

193. 'now they enjoy the winter, all its length, in dalliance together'; for *quam longa* cf. *Aen.* 8.86, for *hiemem fovere* (a striking phrase, literally 'keep the winter warm') cf. *Geo.* 4.43 and compare Val. Fl. 2.371. Some take *hiemem* as accusative of duration of time, with *fovere inter se* meaning 'enjoy each other's company' (cf. *Aen.* 1.718), but this seems less likely.

194. **regnorum immemores**: this is indeed true of both of them (cf. 86 f., 225).

195. **virum diffundit in ora**: 'spread abroad on to men's lips', i.e. caused them to pass on the rumours.

196. **Iarban**: see note on 36; Austin well comments how Virgil has drawn a subtle picture of primitive mentality in this fierce barbarian despot. Iarbas plays a large part in Marlowe's *Dido, Queen of Carthage*.

198. Iarbas is the son of Jupiter Hammon (or Ammon); this was the epithet of Jupiter in Africa, presumably indicating that an original local god Hammon was identified by the Romans with their Jupiter. For his famous African oracle (in the land of the Garamantes) cf. Lucan 9.511 f.; for the Garamantes cf. also *Aen.* 6.794. The name of Iarbas' mother, the nymph ravished by Jupiter, is not known. *Satus* ('son of') is mainly poetic, cf. *Aen.* 2.540, 5.424.

201. **excubias divum aeternas**: 'as the ever-lasting sentinel of the gods', in apposition to *vigilem ignem*.

201-2. It seems best to supply *erat* to the clauses, cf. 131; it is however possible to regard the nouns as accusative after some verbal notion taken by zeugma from *sacraverat*.

203. **animi**: 'in mind', genitive not locative; cf. 300, 529 and see note on 2.61.

204. **media inter numina divum**: 'surrounded by the encompassing divinity of the gods', a strong phrase; cf. *Aen.* 1.447.

206. **nunc**: because Iarbas had introduced the worship which had not existed before.

Maurusia: 'Moorish', a general word for African, not here specific for Mauretania (cf. Hor. *Odes* 2.6.3-4).

207. **Lenaeum libat honorem**: 'pours in libation offerings
of wine'; cf. *Aen.* 1.736, and for *Lenaeus* (god of the wine-press)
cf. *Geo.* 2.4.

209–10. Notice the emphasis on the first word in each clause —
'is it in vain? . . . are the lightnings aimless? . . . are the noises
purposeless?'

211 f. Notice the build-up of irony and disgust — first *femina*
(he expects to dictate to women), then *nostris in finibus* (*my* land),
errans (she was a homeless exile), *exiguam* (a tiny city, nothing like
mine), *pretio* (I sold her the site — notice the alliteration of *p* here),
litus arandum (I gave her a barren bit of sand to plough), *loci
leges* (and conditions of tenure). Iarbas performed all these acts
of charity for a helpless exile, and what happens? *Conubia nostra
reppulit*: 'she has rejected my offer of marriage'.

212. For the foundation of Carthage cf. *Aen.* 1.365 f., and
compare Marlowe, *Dido, Queen of Carthage*, 4.2.12–13, 'Where,
straying in our borders up and down, / She crav'd a hide of
ground to build a town'.

214. **dominum**: here contemptuous, 'as lord and master',
because she seems to Iarbas to be in a wholly dependent
position.

215 f. This powerful expression of contempt for the Trojans
may be compared especially with Numanus the Rutulian's
speech in 9.598 f., particularly 617 f. where they are taunted with
being Phrygian women, not Phrygian men; and with Turnus'
words in 12.97 f., where he refers to Aeneas as *semivir Phryx*, with
crimped hair dripping with myrrh. For the taunt that Aeneas is
another Paris (abducting another Helen) cf. *Aen.* 7.321, 363,
9.138 f. The quadrisyllabic ending *comitatu* (see note on 1.651)
reinforces the unRoman tone of the line.

216–17. 'his chin and oiled locks tied up with a Maeonian
bonnet'; there is extremely heavy alliteration of *m*. *Maeonius*
(cf. 8.499) means Phrygian or Lydian, *mitra* was a foreign type of
headdress worn especially by women (Cat. 64.63, Juv. 3.66 —
cf. *Aen.* 9.616). *Mentum crinemque subnexus* is an example of the
retained accusative construction (cf. 137), *subnexus* having a middle
force. The major MSS read *subnixus* ('supporting'), but *subnexus*
is a more appropriate word (cf. *Geo.* 3.167, *Aen.* 10.138) and the
palaeographical confusion is a very easy one.

218. **quippe**: highly sarcastic (=*scilicet*), cf. *Aen.* 1.39.

The alliteration of *f* is startling in the extreme; it is generally avoided by the poets (cf. Quint. 12.10.29 for unfavourable comments about the sound of *f*), and here it gives a violent scorn to Iarbas' closing words.

219–237. *Jupiter tells Mercury to convey a message to Aeneas, reminding him of his destiny, and ordering him to sail away from Carthage.*

219 f. The intervention of Jupiter is reminiscent of that of Zeus in Hom. *Od.* 5.28 f., where he sends Hermes to order Calypso to let Odysseus go; but the difference is very marked. The message from Jupiter is to Aeneas personally, stating powerfully the reasons why he must leave; it is an action directed at the conscience of Aeneas. Aeneas must remember his divine mission, and he then is in a position to act accordingly — it is not necessary to release him (as it is with Odysseus) from a situation with which he cannot cope. We are justified to some extent in rationalising the action of Jupiter and Mercury as the promptings of Aeneas' conscience; the vision of Mercury speaks to him as an inner voice, persuading him towards what he knows is the right course. But if we accept this psychological undertone to the narrative we must not lose sight of the terms in which Virgil presents it — the king of the gods gives his instructions, his messenger flies through the breezes, finds Aeneas, speaks to him and vanishes again back beyond the clouds. The supernatural — however much we rationalise it — is presented in the most powerful visual pictures.

222. Mercury is Jupiter's personal messenger, as in 1.297; cf. Hermes in Hom. *Od.* 5.28 f.

adloquitur: the final syllable is lengthened in arsis, see note on 1.308 and cf. line 64.

225. **exspectat**: 'delays', a very unusual usage in the sense of *moratur, deterit tempus* (Servius). Housman conjectured *Hesperiam,* but the ablative *Karthagine* requires a verb; in any case the innovated shade of meaning is perfectly acceptable.

fatisque datas: the theme of the city granted by fate runs through the *Aeneid,* cf. for example 1.258, 3.255, 11.112.

227 f. 'It was not such a man as this that his beautiful mother promised us, therefore twice rescuing him from Greek warfare;

but that he would be one who would rule Italy teeming with empire and clamorous with war, who would produce a people of the noble blood of Teucer, and bring all the world beneath the sway of laws.' This is one of the finest expressions in the poem of the Roman mission; first to conquer in war, and then to bring laws and civilisation. Compare Jupiter's speech in 1.263 f., Anchises' in 6.847 f., Jupiter's in 12.838 f.; for the fulfilment under Augustus cf. *Geo.* 4.561 f., *victorque volentis | per populos dat iura.*

228. bis: once from Diomedes (Hom. *Il.* 5.311 f.) and once from burning Troy (*Aen.* 2.589 f.).

vindicat: for the present tense (she is his rescuer), cf. 549 and *Aen.* 8.141, 9.266.

230. Teucri: for Teucer, ancestor of the Trojans, see note on 1.38.

232. nulla: 'not at all', literally 'no glory', an idiomatic expression, cf. *Aen.* 6.405.

233. 'and he does not shoulder the task for his own fame'; *super* is used (as Servius says) in the sense of *pro*, like the Greek ὑπέρ.

234. pater: we would say in English 'does he grudge his son Ascanius. . . ?'; for the destiny of Ascanius cf. *Aen.* 1.267 f.

235. Notice the hiatus at the caesura; cf. *Aen.* 1.16, and see Austin's full discussion in his note on this line.

236. prolem Ausoniam: his offspring will be Italian (cf. 3.171) as well as Trojan (230), because of the fusion of the races; cf. 6.756–7.

Lavinia . . . arva: for *Lavinius*, the adjective of Lavinium, Aeneas' first settlement in Italy, cf. 1.2.

237. 'Let him sail — this is the long and short of it, let this be my message'. The other possible meaning — 'be my messenger of this decree' — seems less natural.

238–278. *Mercury puts on his winged sandals, takes his wand, and flies down to earth, alighting first on Mt. Atlas. When he reaches Carthage he finds Aeneas busy with the enlargement of Carthage, and angrily delivers Jupiter's message, telling him to think of his destiny and that of Ascanius in Italy. The message delivered, Mercury disappears into thin air.*

238 f. The account of Mercury's journey is very vividly descriptive, and plays the same sort of function in the variety of

narrative tone as the description of Rumour (see note on 173 f.).
Colour and shape from another world is painted for us on Virgil's
canvas. Mercury himself is depicted in words as he was so often
in visual art, with his golden winged sandals, his wand; this
passage is reminiscent of Homer (*Od.* 5.44 f.) and so is the end of
the description when Mercury swoops down like a bird wheeling
around the rock-pools on the shore.

Into the description of Mercury is inset a strange and memorable picture of Atlas, at once a mountain and a giant. The passage
is ornate, baroque, even in some sense grotesque; it has come in
for harsh criticism from most commentators, mainly on the ground
that a poet should know whether he is describing a mountain or
a man. The ambiguity is subtle: in 246–7 with *apicem* and *latera*
and *duri* (hard or enduring) and *vertice* there is nothing inappropriate for a mountain, which is what the reader is expecting to be
described; yet all the words could apply to a man. With *caput*
in 249 we see the mountain changing, with *umeros, mento senis,
horrida barba* it has indeed changed. Those who have seen the
giant profile of Idris in the changing shadows of Cader Idris will
respond to what Virgil is trying to do here.

239. **talaria**: these are the famous winged sandals, or perhaps
more precisely anklets (line 259), of Mercury (Hermes); cf. Hom.
Od. 5.44 f. (= *Il.* 24.340 f.), a passage which Virgil closely
follows here. Statius (*Th.* 1.303 f.) has a variation on the Virgilian
theme; Milton's description of Raphael's flight (*P.L.* 5.266 f.)
ends 'Like Maia's son he stood, / and shook his Plumes, that
Heav'nly fragrance filld / the circuit wide'.

242. **virgam**: 'his wand', i.e. the *caduceus* ($\dot{\rho}\dot{\alpha}\beta\delta o\varsigma$); for Hermes
as $\psi\upsilon\chi o\pi o\mu\pi\acute{o}\varsigma$, guide of the dead, cf. Hom. *Od.* 24.1 f. where he
conducts the souls of the suitors down to the underworld.

244. The first phrase is from Homer (Hermes puts to sleep
or awakens anyone he wishes); the second, which is not, elaborates
adimitque, and means 'unseals the eyes in death', so that the ghosts
can see. For *resignare* cf. Hor. *Epist.* 1.7.9; Conington compares
Statius' use (*Th.* 3.129) of *signare* (sealing the eyes of the dead).
In Roman ritual the eyes were closed by relatives at death (*Aen.*
9.487) and opened again on the pyre (Pliny, *N.H.* 11.150).

245. **illa fretus agit ventos**: 'using this he drives the winds';
the image appears to be that of a charioteer with a whip.

tranat: 'flies through' cf. Lucr. 4.177, *Aen*. 10.265, and compare *Aen*. 6.16.

247. **Atlantis**: for the mixed picture of man and mountain see note on 238 f., and compare Ov. *Met*. 4.657 f.; for Atlas cf. also lines 481–2 and *Aen*. 1.741, 6.796 f. The Titan Atlas was condemned to support the heavens on his shoulders; he was identified with Mt. Atlas in N. Africa.

248–51. 'whose pine-covered head, for ever veiled in dark clouds, is assailed by wind and rain alike; a mantle of snow conceals his shoulders; then streams rush down from the old man's chin, and his bristling beard is stiff with ice'.

250. **tum**: used in enumerations to mean the next thing one notices, cf. *Aen*. 1.164.

251. **praecipitant**: used intransitively, cf. line 565 and *Aen*. 2.9.

252. **paribus nitens ... alis**: 'poised on balanced wings'; for *nitens* cf. Ov. *Pont*. 2.7.27, for *paribus alis* cf. *Aen*. 5.657.

Cyllenius: Mercury was born on Mt. Cyllene in Arcadia (*Aen*. 8.139).

254. **avi similis**: again the detail is taken from Homer (*Od*. 5.51 f., where Hermes is like the cormorant speeding low over the waves in quest of fish).

257. **litus harenosum ad Libyae**: the major MSS have *ao*(*P*) and *at*(*M*) for *ad*, but there are no grounds for omitting it as some editors do. For the position of the preposition cf. line 671, *Aen*. 6.58 *corpus in Aeacidae*, 7.234, 9.643.

258. A frigid line, with learned Alexandrian allusiveness; Maia, Mercury's mother, was the daughter of Atlas.

259. **alatis ... plantis**: cf. Shakespeare, *King John*, 4.2.174 'Be Mercury, set feathers to thy heels', and Keats, *Endymion*, 4.331 'foot-feather'd Mercury'.

magalia: 'huts', a Carthaginian word (1.421).

260. **fundantem ... novantem**: 'establishing fortifications and building new dwelling places'; the rhyme reinforces the emphasis on Aeneas' activities, which should be taking place in Italy on his own behalf, not in Carthage on Dido's.

261. **atque**: 'yes, and ...', a further reason for Mercury's displeasure — Aeneas is not only acting as Dido's architect (in Conington's phrase), but his dress and accoutrements are in

luxurious eastern style. Thoughts of Mark Antony and Cleopatra may have entered the mind of the Roman reader.

iaspide: a Greek word denoting the precious stone jasper; it scans *ĭāspide*. It is probably the hilt of the sword rather than the scabbard that is bestarred with jasper.

262. **laena**: a thick outer cloak which would look particularly splendid in bright colours (Juv. 3.283).

263-4. **dives ... fecerat**: 'a gift which rich Dido had made', i.e. a rich gift, as befitted a rich giver. *Munera* is poetic plural, adding impressiveness.

264. **telas discreverat**: 'had interwoven the texture'; *discreverat* is literally 'separated'.

265. **invadit**: 'he attacks him', a powerful word rarely used of speech, cf. Tac. *Ann.* 6.4.

tu nunc: notice the anger of the monosyllables before anything specific is said — you of all people, now of all times.

266. **uxorius**: 'under a wife's sway', very contemptuous, cf. Hor. *Odes* 1.2.19-20.

267. **oblite**: Virgil is very fond of attracting the predicate into the vocative, cf. *Aen.* 2.283.

268. **ipse deum tibi me**: notice the juxtaposition of the three pronouns representing the three actors in this drama, Jupiter himself, you, me. *Deum* is archaic genitive for *deorum*, as often.

270f. Much of Mercury's speech is repeated from Jupiter's; this is a very frequent feature of Homeric epic, but much rarer in Virgil. Here it is employed to bring home to the reader by reiteration the gravity of Aeneas' negligence.

271. **Libycis teris otia terris**: Mercury rewords the second half of line 235 by substituting *Libycis . . . terris* for *inimica in gente* (which Aeneas would not have understood and might have disputed), and intensifying *moratur* into *teris otia*. Notice the resultant disappearance of Jupiter's hiatus, and the introduction of the assonance of *ter*.

273. This line (an interpolation suggested by 233) is not in the major MSS, and should be omitted.

274. **spes heredis Iuli**: 'the hopes placed in your heir Iulus'; the genitive is probably objective (cf. 1.556, 6.364) rather than subjective ('the hopes Iulus has'). To call Aeneas' son Ascanius and Iulus in the same line emphasises the second name — and

draws the reader's attention to his destiny as the founder of the
Julian line (see note on 1.267–8).

278. 'and vanished from sight far away into thin air'; a fine
line on which Austin comments (with regard to the elision of
tenuem) 'the syllable vanishes, just as the god does'. The line is
repeated in 9.658 (of Apollo).

279–95. *Aeneas is aghast and immediately decides to leave. He is now
faced with the bitter prospect of trying to explain to Dido as best he can
why he must leave the land and the woman he loves.*

279 f. In this brief passage, for the first time in the book, our
attention is turned upon the feelings of Aeneas; so far Dido has
occupied the stage. There is no wavering about his decision, no
question in his mind of how he should react to this conflict
between duty and love; he decides instantly and overwhelmingly
for duty. It is only after the decision that we see into his mind and
emotions as he tries to decide how best to explain to Dido that his
love for her (see note on 291) must yield to his duty. He is a
lonely figure amidst his rejoicing Trojans, and there is great
irony and pathos in the description of his desperate efforts to
decide how to approach her, for in the upshot she is totally
unable to understand his motivation, and in his attempted
explanation (333 f.) there is nothing either *mollis* (293) or *dexter*
(294).

279. Notice the very marked assonance of initial *a*, (picked
up at the beginning of each of the next three lines, and continued in the three after that) which seems to reinforce the
powerful imagery and diction used to describe Aeneas' aghast
amazement.

281–2. These lines clearly express the conflict of love and duty
in Aeneas, and his immediate recognition of guilt and decision
for duty: Dido's country is *dulcis*, but he has received his mandate
from heaven, and so is on fire to go, *ardet abire*. For *ardet* with the
infinitive (a mainly poetical use) cf. *Aen.* 1.515.

283. Notice how the deliberative questions involve the reader
in Aeneas' dilemma; cf. *Aen.* 9.399.

ambire: 'approach', 'try to win over', *blanditiis circumvenire*
(Servius); cf. *Aen.* 7.333, Hor. *Odes* 1.35.5.

285–6. 'and he shoots his swift thoughts one way and another,

rapidly directing them towards all kinds of aspects, turning them
through all possibilities'; these lines, which are repeated in 8.20–1,
are based on Homer's διάνδιχα μερμήριξεν (e.g. *Il.* 1.189).
Tennyson has 'this way and that dividing the swift mind.' The
next line too is Homeric, e.g. *Il.* 2.5.

288. **Mnesthea**: Greek accusative. These men are captains of
Aeneas' ships, cf. 5.116f., 1.510, 1.611.

289. **aptent**: this and the following verbs are jussive subjunctives, reporting Aeneas' orders which in direct speech would
be imperatives.

290. **arma**: 'tackle', a nautical technical term (compare 299),
cf. *Aen.* 5.15, 6.353. Servius and others take it to mean 'weapons',
in case of a Carthaginian attack — but it seems unlikely that
Aeneas is thinking along such lines.

rebus … novandis: 'for the change of plan'.

291. **optima Dido**: notice that the phrase is in oratio obliqua,
reporting the words of Aeneas. It refers to the respect and gratitude which Aeneas feels towards Dido for her queenly qualities
and gracious reception of the Trojans, while *tantos … amores* in
the next line defines their relationship more personally. That
Aeneas was in love with Dido is made very clear by Virgil (cf.
also 221, 332, and especially 395); but he has now decided
irrevocably to sacrifice his love for his mission.

293–4. 'he would look for a way of approaching her and try
to find the kindest occasion for telling her, the right method for
the purpose.' For the phraseology cf. Dido's words to Anna in
423.

295. **laeti**: the contrast between the enthusiastic Trojans,
joyful to be on their way again, and the unhappy plight of
Aeneas is very poignant.

296–330. *Dido senses that Aeneas is preparing to leave; she becomes
distraught like a Bacchanal, and then appeals to him in a speech of despair,
reproach, and intense pathos.*

296 f. The series of three speeches of which this is the first
relates the story of Dido and Aeneas closely to a Greek tragedy;
we are reminded for example of the conflict of wills between
Medea and Jason in Euripides' *Medea* (446 f.), and the simile
of 301 f. brings the action into relationship with the tragic event

of Euripides' *Bacchae*. There are other important literary sources too: the Medea of Apollonius (e.g. 4.355 f.) and the Ariadne of Catullus 64. The influence of Catullus is especially marked in the pathos of the speech (see notes on 316, 327 f.) but Dido's tragic plight is at a higher level of intensity. The pathos is deepened by the enormous contrast between her present helplessness and her past greatness and dignity; and the tragedy is the more terrible because of its inevitability. We know that her pleas, however moving, cannot possibly win Aeneas over because he is not free to be won.

296. **At regina**: see note on line 1.

297. Dido sensed Aeneas' plans before he came to tell her (*praesensit*, felt a 'presentiment') and first of anyone caught wind of the intended departure (one might have expected one of her subjects to see the preparations beginning, and rush to tell her — but Rumour gets there first). For *excipere* cf. Livy 2.4.5; for the general idea cf. the imitations in Ov. *Met.* 4.68, Val. Fl. 8.410 f.

298. **omnia tuta timens**: 'anxious even when all seemed safe', not — with Henry — 'because everything seemed too quiet'; cf. Ov. *Met.* 7.47. Dido's conscience makes her uneasy (see Austin's notes on 297 and 298).

eadem impia Fama: 'it was that same evil Rumour . . .'; *eadem* refers back to 173 f., *impia* to 174. Some take *eadem* as accusative plural, but this is unnatural.

301 f. The simile, in which Dido is compared with a Bacchante (*Thyias*) wildly revelling on Mt. Cithaeron in Boeotia in honour of the god Bacchus, is of the utmost importance in the development of Dido's frenzy; it marks the point at which she begins to lose control of her actions, becomes 'possessed'. The nature of her frenzy has been stressed often indeed in this book (see note on 1 f.) and the words *furenti* (298), *saevit inops animi, incensa* (300) reinforce what we know already. But the Bacchic simile goes much further, suggesting wholly uncontrolled behaviour and potential destruction; Virgil uses such a simile again to describe Amata (7.385 f.) after she has been maddened by the fiend Allecto; (cf. also 10.41). The imagery (which is very closely-packed) recalls Euripides' *Bacchae*, where the action takes place near Mt. Cithaeron; the feeling of impending tragedy is thus strengthened.

301. **commotis ... sacris**: 'by the brandishing of the sacred emblems'; cf. Hor. *Odes* 1.18.11 f.

302. **Thyias**: the epithet derives from θύειν, 'to rage'; the -yi- is a diphthong, and the word scans as a trochee.

302 f. 'when the biennial rites arouse her as the Bacchic cry is heard, and Cithaeron calls her at night with its noise'. For *trieterica*, every three years by Roman inclusive reckoning, every two years by ours, cf. Ov. *Rem.* 593, *Met.* 6.587. *Audito ... Baccho* means when the Bacchic cry (*euhoe Bacche*, 7.389) was heard, rather than when the god Bacchus was heard.

304. **ultro**: 'first', i.e. before he could speak to her.

305. The use of *perfide* is the first of a number of reminiscences of Ariadne's speech to Theseus in Cat. 64.132 f. Notice the anger with which Dido begins, reflected in the hissing *s*'s as well as in the diction of the opening words; but her anger quickly gives way to entreaty.

306. For the omission of the reflexive subject (of *posse*) cf. *Aen.* 2.432–3.

307. **data dextera**: 'the pledge given', an indefinite phrase, which probably in the context with *amor* refers to the 'marriage' in the cave.

308. **moritura**: the word is ambiguous — Aeneas doubtless takes it with reference to the danger from Dido's rejected suitors (cf. 323, 325 f.) but the reader suspects another implication.

309. **hiberno ... sidere**: 'in the season of winter'; the metonymy of *sidus* for *tempestas* is common in certain contexts, cf. *Geo.* 1.1.

moliris ... classem: 'are you busied with your fleet'; the verb is a favourite with Virgil, cf. 233 and *Aen.* 3.6.

311 f. Dido says that Aeneas would not even set out for Troy (if it still existed) in such conditions; how then can he think of leaving for an unknown destination?

314 f. Dido turns from the logic of the preceding lines to an appeal to pure pity; the simple words *mene fugis*? (do you want so much to get away from me?) convey strong pathos, which is continued by the broken word order normal with a prayer (cf. *Aen.* 12.56), the jerky hexameter ending of the pronouns *tuam te*, and the long build-up of clauses before the main verb *miserere*.

316. A very clear imitation of Catullus' Ariadne (64.141) *sed*

conubia laeta, sed optatos hymenaeos, the more noticeable because of the Greek type of rhythm with no main caesura and a quadrisyllabic ending. The nouns are synonyms, and *inceptos* means, as often, 'entered upon'; there is no implication, as some commentators suggest, that Dido thinks the wedding is incomplete.

318. **domus labentis**: 'a house destined for disaster'; Dido turns the emphasis from herself to her dynasty (cf. *Aen.* 12.59), hoping in this way to add an extra point to her argument, a point which she elaborates at length in the next lines.

320. **te propter**: 'because of *you*'; the postposition of *propter* is not common and here causes strong emphasis on *te*.

Dido refers to the hostility of local tribes whose rulers she had rejected as suitors (36); presumably they accepted this when her plea was loyalty to the dead Sychaeus, but not when they were rejected in favour of a living Trojan.

321. **infensi Tyrii**: 'my Tyrians hate me', referring to her Carthaginian subjects. This is a new touch, not previously referred to, and it adds greatly here to Dido's plea of loneliness (cf. Eur. *Med.* 506 f.); she had said nothing to Aeneas about the disapproval of her people while things went well between them.

322-3. 'my honour is lost and my one-time reputation, my only hope of reaching the stars'. For *pudor* see note on 27; she has been disloyal to Sychaeus, has not kept faith with him, and this as she now looks back could have been the one great achievement of her life. Compare Odysseus' words to his faithful Penelope (*Od.* 19.108) where he says that her reputation has reached the broad heavens; and Shakespeare, *Richard II*, 1.1.177 f. 'The purest treasure mortal times afford / is spotless reputation; that away, / men are but gilded loam or painted clay.'

323. **cui**: 'to what' rather than 'to whom', cf. *Aen.* 2.678.

hospes: 'visitor'; this is what she called him in line 10, now it is all she can call the man who she had thought was her husband. Servius tells us that Virgil's voice showed great emotion when he read these lines to Augustus.

325. **quid moror?**: 'why should I keep on?', i.e. 'what have I got to look forward to?'. She lists the unacceptable alternatives, leaving the implied answer, 'only death'.

325-6. For Pygmalion cf. 44, for Iarbas cf. 36.

327 f. 'At least if I had taken in my arms a child by you before

you left, if a darling little Aeneas were playing in my palace, whose looks would remind me of you in spite of everything, then I would not indeed feel so utterly cheated and forlorn'. This is an appeal which, in Page's words, 'would move a stone'; it does move Aeneas, but it cannot change his resolution (331–2). Nowhere else in the *Aeneid* (or in epic) is such immediacy of feeling presented in this way. *Parvulus* is the only example of a diminutive adjective in the *Aeneid*; epic requires a type of diction which precludes the homely and intimate. We are reminded irresistibly of the diminutives of the private poetry of Catullus, and especially of Cat. 61.209 f., *Torquatus volo parvulus.* . . . The fame of this astonishingly unepic phrase is testified by Juvenal (5.138) in a passage of characteristic cynicism.

Notice the use made of the particles *saltem* (a spondaic word filling the first foot, see note on 185) and *tamen* (cf. 396). Notice too the 'more than pluperfect' of the unfulfilled condition (*suscepta fuisset*). For *capta = decepta* cf. *Aen.* 1.673, 2.196; for *deserta* cf. Ariadne in *Cat.* 64.57.

331–61. *Aeneas because of Jupiter's commands keeps his love hidden and replies coldly and formally. He ends by telling Dido of Mercury's appearance to him with instructions from heaven; he is therefore leaving her for Italy not of his own free will.*

331 f. Page (ad loc.), in oft-quoted words, says 'Not all Virgil's art can make the figure of Aeneas here appear other than despicable'; he adds a cross-reference to his introduction where he says 'To an appeal which would move a stone Aeneas replies with the cold and formal rhetoric of an attorney'. The second of these statements is largely true; the first is not. Virgil has taken the utmost care to convey the reasons why Aeneas' reply is cold; it is (331–2) because he knows he must not yield and therefore he smothers his love and his emotions. He endeavours to use logical and persuasive arguments to put his case (Servius points out some of the rhetorical devices, reminiscent of a *controversia*), honestly believing that Dido will see that he has no option. The tragedy is that neither of the lovers can understand the other's point of view — when all is said between them they are further apart than they were before. When Aeneas makes his final statement about Mercury he seems to be certain that Dido will see that he must

obey; but she sees nothing except her own terrible predicament. Everything to her is personal between herself and Aeneas — she accepts no other considerations, indeed understands none. Aeneas' speech to her is indeed 'cold and formal', but Virgil has shown us very clearly that this is not because he feels no emotions but because he has decided that he must control them. Many readers of this speech would have wished it otherwise; but as it stands it is in full accord with Aeneas' acceptance of the almost intolerably heavy burden of duty. For further discussion see Austin's excellent note ad loc.

332. 'and with a great effort kept his love hidden in his heart'; for *curam* see note on line 1. Virgil has immediately given the reason why Aeneas' reply cannot be gentle: because of his divine instructions he does not meet her eyes and he stifles the anguish (cf. *Aen.* 1.209) which his love for Dido causes him. Notice how the phrases are coupled by the rhyme at the line-endings. These two lines must be kept firmly in mind as we read the deliberately cold and unemotional words which follow.

333. **pauca**: the speech is not in fact particularly short, but it contains little out of all that might have been said had Aeneas felt free to say it.

ego te: 'the two persons concerned face each other syntactically, as it were' (Austin).

335-6. 'and I shall never regret the memory of Elissa, as long as I have memory of myself and life rules these limbs'. The statement seems cold to the modern reader, but from a Stoic point of view (which Aeneas as man of God should accept) it is rebellious, it shows failure to subdue personal wishes; Aeneas from this point of view should indeed have regretted the memory of his lapse from duty.

335. **Elissae**: this is Dido's original Phoenician name (see note on 1.340), used again in line 610 and *Aen.* 5.3 (always in the genitive; the name *Dido* is not used in the oblique cases). It does not seem that there is any difference other than metrical preference in the use of the two names.

337. **pro re pauca loquar**: 'I will speak briefly for my case'; these are very cold and formal words, as in a law-court, deliberately chosen to prevent emotion getting the better of him.

337-9. Both these statements are true (he did not intend to go away secretly, nor did he propose marriage — Dido's interpretation of the cave scene was entirely her own); but their plain and brutal truth is not likely to comfort Dido. Notice the insistent spondees of 339.

337–8. **abscondere . . . speravi**: for the present infinitive with *spero* cf. *Aen.* 5.18 and compare 425–6, *Aen.* 11.503.

343. **colerem**: 'I would be looking after'; Aeneas' behaviour in Book 2 justifies this claim — he was reluctant to accept the divine instructions that he should leave Troy. By *Priami tecta alta manerent* Aeneas does not mean that he could have saved it from the Greeks, but that he would have rebuilt it and it would be existing now, still called Priam's palace though Priam was dead.

344. 'and I would myself (*manu*) have founded a re-born Pergama for the conquered'; after the Greek destruction he would have rebuilt Troy if he had been free to do so. Some early versions of the legend said that he did stay in Troy, and did restore it.

345. **Gryneus Apollo**: there was a wood sacred to Apollo at Grynium in Lydia; we have not previously heard of a prophecy associated with Grynium, nor of these *Lyciae sortes* (for Apollo's oracle in Lycia see note on 143); it was the Penates in Crete (3.166) who, interpreting Apollo's previous oracle at Delos, first revealed to Aeneas the name Italy. It is probable therefore that Aeneas refers to this oracle, giving Apollo two of his familiar epithets without meaning that the oracle was given in these places; less likely is the possibility that messages reached Aeneas from these places before he left the Troad.

347. **hic amor, haec patria est**: 'this is my love, this is my homeland'; the attraction of gender is normal. Aeneas is not free to yield to personal feelings of love (307); Italy has to be his love.

348. **Phoenissam**: a Phoenician (from Tyre); cf. *Aen.* 1.670, 714.

349–50. **quae . . . invidia**: 'why begrudge. . . ?'; for the infinitive after a noun see note on 1.704.

351 f. This is another fact from the past (cf. 345) of which we have not previously heard — it is referred to again in 6.695 f. Mackail points out the psychological insight with which Virgil portrays Aeneas here; he remembers things pointing in the same direction as Mercury's instructions though they had little impact on him at the time.

353. **turbida**: 'agitated', cf. *Aen.* 6.694 *quam metui . . .* and 695 *tua tristis imago*.

354 f. A verb like *movet* has to be supplied from the sense of the previous line. Aeneas here restates the message he received from Mercury (274 f.).

354. **capitisque iniuria cari**: 'the wrong being done to one so dear'; the genitive is objective. For the use of *caput* cf. 613, Hor. *Odes* 1.24.2.

355. **fatalibus arvis**: 'fated fields', his by destiny; cf. *Aen.* 5.82.

356 f. This is the fact which Aeneas feels sure must convince Dido. Notice the way it is built up: *nunc etiam* (there is something else which has just happened); *interpres divum Iove missus ab ipso* (what could be more conclusive?); *testor utrumque caput* (and I swear that it did happen); *mandata* (specific instructions, no option is given, no question of trying to interpret the meaning); *ipse* (I saw him personally); *manifesto in lumine* (in clear light, it was no vague dream); *intrantem muros* (he didn't suddenly appear, I watched him coming in); *vocemque his auribus hausi* (and I heard his words with my own ears). After this Aeneas feels no further arguments are needed, and he concludes simply — 'so don't prolong our agony; I am forced to go.' How little it all meant to Dido is shown by her mockery of these words (377 f.).

357. **utrumque caput**: his own and Dido's (cf. Ov. *Her.* 3.107, Ap. Rh. 3.151).

359. **hausi**: an unusual usage, cf. *Aen.* 6.559, 12.26, Livy 27.51.1. The metaphor is the same as with *bibere* (Hor. *Odes* 2. 13.32).

360–1. 'Stop making us both emotional by your pleas; I go to Italy not of my own free will'. Pease quotes Rand's excellent phrases: 'These last words resume in brief compass the elements of the tragedy that confronts Aeneas: *Italiam* — his mission; *non sponte* — his love; *sequor* — his resolution'. It is hard to imagine how Virgil would have completed this half-line — 'four words thus left rugged and abrupt' (Page).

362–92. *Dido in reply assails her lover with angry hatred and scorn; she rejects his arguments utterly and calls down curses upon him. Finally she prays for vengeance and the knowledge of vengeance.*

362 f. Charles James Fox, quoted by Henry, said of this passage 'on the whole, perhaps the finest thing in all poetry'. Dido's speech has something in common with the words of Medea in Euripides (*Med.* 465 f.) and in Apollonius (4.355 f.) but Virgil has used the resources of Latin rhetoric and hexameter technique to make it into something quite different.

The contrast with Dido's previous speech is very marked. There she had pleaded with Aeneas in words of intense pathos; here she has given up all hope of prevailing upon him, and with this realisation she changes into an archetypal symbol of hatred and revenge. Communication with her as an ordinary human being is no longer possible; what she has suffered has changed her into a kind of fury of vengeance. We feel the inevitability of that kind of frenzied progression towards disaster which is so familiar in Greek tragedy. This speech is highly rhetorical, frighteningly remote from the give-and-take of human behaviour; the frustration of hopes and pride has led to an elaborately formalised and grandiose concentration of all the hatred of her outraged heart.

362. **aversa tuetur**: 'she had been watching him without looking at him' — a very striking paradox where the literal meaning ('askance') merges with the metaphorical meaning: she rejects his every word. Similarly her ghost rejects him (*aversa*) in *Aen.* 6.469.

363. **totumque pererrat**: 'scanning him up and down'; there is no parallel for this use of *pererrare* with a personal object. Aeneas does not seem human to Dido any more.

364. **luminibus tacitis**: 'with expressionless eyes', cf. Ov. *Am.* 2.5.17 *non oculi tacuere tui* ('your eyes spoke to me').

365 f. Dido's opening words are a rhetorical commonplace — she has nothing personal to say to Aeneas now, and she has recourse to a formally elaborate imprecation. Invective based on parentage goes back to Homer (*Il.* 16.33 f.); cf. also Eur. *Bacc.* 987 f., Cat. 60.1 f., 64.154 f., and the many parallels given by Pease (ad loc.). Here there is special point in the reversal of what Dido had earlier said, in her very first words to Aeneas (1.615 f.), where she had asked if he was in very truth the one who was born of Venus to Anchises (*tune ille Aeneas . . .*); compare also her words to Anna in line 12. Now she denies it all, she has been duped by treachery (*perfide*, repeated from 305).

367. 'and Hyrcanian tigresses gave you suck'; Hyrcania was an area near the Caucasus Mts. and the Caspian Sea. Cf. Shakespeare, *3 Henry 6*, 1.4.154–5. 'But you are more inhuman, more inexorable, / O ten times more, than tigers of Hyrcania'.

admorunt: contracted for *admoverunt*.

368. 'For why should I pretend, or for what more crucial moment hold myself back?' Notice the staccato rhetorical questions in this line and the next three. The vivid indicative is used for the deliberative subjunctive (cf. 534 and *Aen.* 3.88). Dido feels that she has been finally rejected, and there is therefore no reason why she should not speak her true feelings; the possibility of pleading is gone.

369 f. The tricolon with anaphora of *num* is in the highest rhetorical style, and the distancing of her words by the use of the third person is a cold and formal indication of the distance that now separates the lovers.

371. **quae quibus anteferam?**: 'what shall I say first, what second?' (literally 'what shall I prefer to what?'). This rhetorical question could come from a Ciceronian speech — Servius gives it the rhetorical tag 'amphibolia' and explains that it suggests that *omnia et paria et magna sunt*.

372. **nec Saturnius**: the diaeresis after the second foot gives a most unusual rhythm (cf. 385); the epithet (which is frequent for Juno) is not used elsewhere in Virgil for Jupiter.

373 f. 'He was shipwrecked on my shore, destitute, and I took him in. . .'. Notice the alliteration of *e*, the asyndeton, and the unusual pause in the fifth foot.

375 f. As the fires of frenzy burn hotter in Dido her words become more disjointed: to *amissam classem* we must supply from *a morte reduxi* some verb like *servavi*, and the tricolon introduced by repeated *nunc* has no verb for the first two nouns.

376. **heu furiis incensa feror**: 'oh I am whirled by the furies on winds of fire'; cf. *Aen.* 12.946.

376 f. Dido now mocks Aeneas' words (345, 346, 356–7), and the slight variation (*horrida iussa* for *mandata*) increases the sarcasm by the use of an adjective in which she does not believe.

379 f. As Dido's overwhelming anger and scorn get the better of her, the metre becomes agitated and violent through the almost total conflict of accent and ictus in this and the following four

lines. The sarcastic word *scilicet* and the hissing of *s*'s are pointers
for the bitterness of her words about the gods; both *labor* and
sollicitat are ironical as applied to the gods, and her statement
immediately associates her with Epicurean ideas; the word
quietus is used by Lucretius of the Epicurean deities (e.g. 6.73).
Dido is not prepared to believe that anyone should sacrifice his
personal life to requirements supposed to be imposed by the gods.
It is a conflict between belief in a man-centred universe and belief
in a divinely controlled world.

381. **i, sequere**: the rhetorical device (often *i nunc*) is called
permissio. The first phrase of this line echoes 361, the second 350.

382 f. 'I hope, indeed I hope, if the righteous deities have any
power, that you will drain the cup of punishment on rocks in mid-
ocean, and often call on the name of Dido'. The word-order, with
the wide separation of *mediis . . . scopulis* seems to emphasise the
hoped-for isolation of her shipwrecked lover, far from human aid.
The parenthesis bitterly recalls Aeneas' promise to Dido in 1.603 f.,
and the use of the epithet *pius* against Aeneas is full of irony.
Dido's use of her own name adds pathos; cf. 308, 596 and
Catullus' frequent use of his own name in his lyrics.

383. **hausurum**: for the omission of the pronoun (*te*) cf. 105,
493.

384 f. At the middle of this line the conflict of accent and ictus
changes to coincidence, which continues at the beginning of the
next two lines: the effect is to convey a kind of deliberateness
(emphasised by sonorous alliteration of *m* and *n*), as Dido
collects herself for her final measured curse. In two places the
coincidence is very marked — the fourth foot of this line consisting
of a single spondee (for full discussion of this see my note on *Aen.*
5.116, Oxford edition); and the second foot of the next line
consisting of a single dactyl.

The diction contains elements of ambiguity and foreboding.
In *atris ignibus* the primary meaning is the murky torches of the
Furies (cf. 7.456); Dido, like Medea in Ap. Rh. 4.386, will be a
fiend of vengeance. But there is also (as Servius saw) a hint at the
flames of her funeral pyre (cf. lines 661–2). Similarly the reference
to her death may suggest, though she does not say so, that it will
be the means of her vengeance. Finally the vagueness of *umbra*
makes her threat more wide-ranging; her soul will be in the

underworld (387), but visions, phantoms, memories of her will always and everywhere haunt Aeneas.

385. **anima seduxerit artus**: 'has severed body from soul', an unusual phrase (called hypallage by Servius because *animam artubus* would be more normal).

387. **haec ... imos**: 'the report of it will reach me deep in the underworld'; for the local meaning of *manes*, 'place of the shades', cf. *Geo.* 1.243. Dido's blood-curdling speech concludes with the expression of her distraught desire for vengeance and also for the knowledge that she has achieved it.

388. **medium ... sermonem**: cf. line 277; the meaning is not that the speech is unfinished but that no opportunity is given for reply.

389. 'leaving him frightened, deeply uncertain, rehearsing many answers'; notice the rhyme of *-antem*, indicating the dinning insistence in Aeneas' mind.

393-415. Aeneas, in spite of his longing to comfort Dido, returns to the fleet. The Trojans make their preparations for departure. Dido in her misery determines to make one further appeal to Aeneas through her sister Anna.

393. **pius Aeneas**: some commentators have here failed to understand the significance Virgil has put into the use of the epithet. Page, for example, says (intro. p. xix) 'Virgil .. begins the next paragraph quite placidly *at pius Aeneas*... ! How the man who wrote the lines placed in Dido's mouth could immediately afterwards speak of 'the good Aeneas etc.' is one of the puzzles of literature'. But the only possible defence for Aeneas' actions is his *pietas*; in any other capacity than as man of destiny he should have stayed — *pietas* is why he must leave, and Virgil wants us to remember this. It may be that many (presumably including Page) would wish that *pietas* had not prevailed, but it is utterly wrong to object to being told that it has done so.

We might translate 'But Aeneas, because of duty....' For further discussion see Austin's excellent note ad loc.

395. **magnoque ... amore**: 'shaken to the heart by his great love'; the nature of the conflict in Aeneas is once more powerfully emphasised. For the construction of *animum* see note on 137, and cf. *Aen.* 3.47 *mentem formidine pressus*.

396. **iussa tamen divum**: the Stoic, in times of personal sorrow, consoled himself with the formula *dis aliter visum* (the will of the gods was otherwise). This is what Aeneas has to do.

397. Once again, as in 294–5, Virgil stresses the joy of the Trojans in contrast to the sorrow of Aeneas.

398. **natat uncta carina**: 'the vessel shiny with pitch goes afloat'; the use of the singular here gives a sudden picture of one of the many ships as it is launched. For *natat* cf. Cat. 4.3, *Aen.* 8.93.

399 f. 'and they bring oars with leaves still on and unshaped logs from the woods in their eagerness to depart'; i.e. the branches for oars and the logs — for general repairs during the voyage — are brought on board untrimmed; for the phrases cf. *Aen.* 1.552.

401. **cernas**: 'you could have seen them'; for the second person, and for the use of the vivid present, cf. *Aen.* 8.691.

402 f. The simile is very typically Virgilian, reminiscent of the poet of the *Georgics* (cf. especially *Geo.* 1.185–6); compare the bee similes in *Aen.* 1.430 f., 6.707 f., 12.587 f. Apart from one example in Apollonius (4.1452 f., where ants are mentioned briefly along with flies) this is the only simile in Greek or Latin epic concerned with ants. The main point of comparison, of course, is hustle and busy movement, but there is an important subsidiary point, namely smallness and distance. We are invited to see the Trojans as Dido saw them from her palace, tiny, far-off, remote from her now.

402. **ac velut**: for the elliptical way of introducing a simile ('and it was as when') cf. *Aen.* 2.626, 6.707.

404. **it ... agmen**: from Ennius, who according to Servius applied the phrase to elephants. Virgil gives a most attractive mock-grandeur to the world of the ants; notice the spondaic movement of this line and the next two, conveying the mighty effort involved.

405. **grandia**: a splendid touch — compare the description of the mouse from a mouse's point of view in *Geo.* 1.181–2.

406. **cogunt**: 'marshal', a military term, cf. Tac. *Hist.* 2.68 *agminis coactores*; this kind of personification is frequent with the bees in *Geo.* 4 (e.g. 67 f., 82 f.).

408. 'What were your feelings, Dido, then, when you saw all this?' The apostrophe here is enormously effective; the personal involvement of the poet with Dido's tragic plight is such that his

direct address to her seems natural and real rather than rhetorical; compare *Aen.* 3.710.

409. **fervĕre**: notice the third conjugation form (cf. 567), fairly frequent in the poets but rather remarkable here after *fervet* (407). Compare also *fulgĕre* (*Aen.* 6.826), *stridĕre* (*Geo.* 4.556).

411. **misceri ... tantis clamoribus**: 'a confusion of shouting and noise'; for this use of *misceri* cf. 160.

412. 'Tyrant love, to what do you not drive mortal hearts?' Virgil follows his moving apostrophe to Dido with a different kind of subjective intrusion into the narrative, a reflexion on what has happened to his characters (cf. 3.56-7). The line is based on Ap. Rh. 4.445 (cf. 3.297) when Medea purposes to kill her brother so that she can escape with her lover, and the poet reflects on the cruelty of love. Virgil's epithet *improbus* implies excess (cf. *Aen.* 2.80 and see Austin on 4.386). Dido is like the slave of an all-powerful tyrant, under a compulsion which she cannot or will not resist.

415. **frustra moritura**: 'and go to her death in vain', i.e. she has resolved to die if she finds no way of keeping Aeneas, so she must first try every way to keep him.

416-49. *Dido begs Anna to make a further appeal to Aeneas, asking him to wait for favourable weather before he departs; she asks just for time to accustom herself to her sorrow. But Aeneas is resolute, like an oak tree buffeted by the gales but not overthrown.*

416 f. Dido's last plea, made through Anna, makes the pathos of her situation even more apparent as she relents from the implacable anger of her last speech; and the dilemma of Aeneas is once again presented with intense insight. The simile of the oak tree is preceded by phrases of tension — *nullis ille movetur fletibus ... aut voces ullas tractabilis audit ... fata obstant ... placidasque viri deus obstruit auris*. The pressure on the oak tree is violent — *Alpini Boreae nunc hinc nunc flatibus illinc eruere inter se certant ... it stridor ... consternunt terram frondes ... concusso stipite*; and so with Aeneas — *tunditur ... persentit curas*. The final unforgettable line — *mens immota manet, lacrimae volvuntur inanes* summarises the conflict and its upshot more poignantly than Aeneas' own summary *Italiam non sponte sequor* (361), but to exactly the same effect.

416. **vides ... circum**: 'you see the bustle going on around

all along the shore'; *properari* is impersonal passive, *circum* is an adverb. Some editors punctuate so that *circum* goes with the next line; this is highly improbable, as is well argued by Henry.

419. **si potui**: 'if I was able'; the surface meaning is (*si* = *siquidem*) 'as surely as I was able': Anna understands Dido to mean that she had expected it, and will endure it. But *si* may also be taken ironically: 'if I could have expected it (but I could not), then — as is not the case — I shall be able also to bear it'; cf. Hor. *Odes* 3.5.31 f.

419. **sperare**: 'expect', as in 292, *Aen.* 11.275.

420–1. 'But perform for me, Anna, in my misery, this one favour'. The dislocation of rhythm at the line ending (see Austin ad loc.) expresses something of Dido's agitation.

421 f. Servius reports from Varro a version of the tradition according to which it was Anna with whom Aeneas fell in love: the suggestion here of a close relationship between them may be a trace of that version.

422. **colere**: the historic infinitive is here used for repeated or continuous action, cf. *Aen.* 2.98, 11.822.

423. **noras**: notice the past tense (*noveras*); in spite of the new appeal she is to make, Dido subconsciously puts Aeneas in the past. The phraseology of the line is reminiscent of 293 where Aeneas has to approach Dido as best he can; now the situation is reversed.

424. These are measured and chilling words: Aeneas has changed from *coniunx* to *hospes* (323) and now to *hostis*; he has conquered and in the pride of his victory can only be addressed in suppliant tones. Dido torments herself with words she had never thought to utter to anyone.

425 f. Dido begins rhetorically (Quint. 9.2.39 calls this figure *aversio*) by enumerating acts which would have justified Aeneas in refusing to hear her, acts of which she is innocent: she was not an ally of the Greeks when they gathered at Aulis in N. Greece (Hom. *Il.* 2.303) to sail against Troy; nor has she committed sacrilege against the grave of Anchises. The second of these statements is strange: Servius relates a vague story about a tradition that Diomedes did in fact profane Anchises' grave, and it has been suggested that Dido recalls in a confused way Aeneas' words of 351–3; but it seems best to regard it as a thought which

Dido wildly throws out as she seeks for imaginary and heinous crimes which she has not committed.

425–6. exscindere . . . iuravi: for the construction see note on 337–8.

428. negat . . . demittere: for the infinitive with *negare* in the sense of 'refuse' cf. *Geo.* 2.215–16, 3.207–8, and compare *Aen.* 2.637. For *demittere* cf. Livy 34.50.2.

432. The irony of *pulchro* (cf. 266) is reinforced by its position before the word introducing its clause (*ut*); notice the alliteration of *r* and *q* in the last two words.

433–4. 'I want just time, a respite and a breathing-space for my madness, till my fate can teach my vanquished heart how to grieve'. By *tempus inane* she means that the time would be useless to her for any other purpose than gradually to heal her wound; there was nothing she could do with it, it was mere time.

435. veniam: 'favour', as often, cf. *Aen.* 1.519.

436. 'and when he has granted it to me, I will pay it back with interest when I die'. The last phrase is purposely ambiguous, indeed obscure: Anna presumably understands it to be a vague reference to some intended benevolence (perhaps she will take back her threat of haunting him), but the reader (prepared for Dido's tragic intention, 415) visualises Dido paying back Aeneas' loan of time at the price of her death. This will be her gift in return for his: cf. *Ecl.* 8.59 f., *praeceps aerii specula de montis in undas | deferar; extremum hoc munus morientis habeto*. For *dederit* (so the best MSS) Servius read *dederis*, which destroys the ambiguity in the next phrase. *Cumulatam* is a financial metaphor, 'with interest' (Livy 2.23.6, Cic. *Phil.* 14.30); for *remittam* in this sense cf. *Aen.* 11.359.

438. fertque refertque: 'took and took again', cf. *Aen.* 12.866.

439. tractabilis: 'sympathetically', literally 'able to be dealt with', cf. line 53 and Suet. *Aug.* 65 *Agrippam nihilo tractabiliorem*.

440. 'The fates stand in the way, and the god blocks his kindly mortal ears'. The juxtaposition of *viri* and *deus* expresses in little the essence of the matter: personally as a man he would have listened, but as an instrument of destiny he cannot. For the sense of *placidas* cf. *Aen.* 7.194, 11.251, Ov. *Pont.* 1.2.127, Stat. *Th.* 5.732. Others take it proleptically — 'so that they were unmoved, tranquil', but this is inappropriate for *placidas* and far less significant in the context. See Pearce in *C.R.* 1968, p. 13.

441 f. The simile, which is developed at unusual length, gives a magnificent image of resolution which is assailed but not overthrown: the tree is fully grown, strong, deeply rooted, and though it creaks in the gales and its trunk is shaken so that its leaves fall, it remains firmly fixed in its place. Virgil has very greatly developed his sources (Hom. *Il.* 12.131 f., 16.765 f.; cf. also Cat. 64.105 f.); he has applied to mental strength what is generally an image of physical strength. Dryden imitates the passage (*Annus Mirabilis* 61) 'All bare, like some old Oak which tempests beat, / He stands, and sees below his scatter'd leaves'.

441. **ac velut ... cum**: 'and just as when ...'; this time *ac* has its own clause introduced by *haud secus* (447) — contrast 402.

annoso validam ... robore: 'mighty with the strength of years', cf. *Aen.* 6.282, 10.766.

442. **Alpini Boreae**: the localisation in N. Italy suggests Virgil's personal experience.

445 f. 'but itself, it holds firmly to its rocks, reaching as far with its roots towards Tartarus as it does with its topmost branches towards the breezes of heaven'; *ipsa* contrasts the immovable tree with its falling leaves. The words *quantum ... tendit* are repeated from *Geo.* 2.291-2.

449. 'his purpose remains unmoved, the tears fall in vain'. Whose tears? Servius says those of Aeneas (so Augustine, *C.D.* 9.4), maintaining that this phrase corresponds with the falling leaves of the tree (an unlikely reason), but adds that others think they are Dido's and Anna's too. The fact is that Virgil has not said whose tears; by not specifying he widens the area of sorrow, generalises this particular conflict into the universal conflict of pity with duty. For *lacrimae inanes* cf. *Aen.* 10.465; for the Stoic attitude (not unfeeling but resolute) cf. Sen. *Dial.* 1.2.2, *Ep. Mor.* 9.3.

450-73. *Dido now resolves on death, and is confirmed in her resolution by terrible portents and the memory of ancient prophecies. She has nightmare dreams of Aeneas pursuing her, and of her utter desolation; she is like Pentheus or Orestes hounded by the Furies.*

450 f. The narrative now becomes laden with death. Dido is encompassed with ghastly and supernatural horrors — portents of which she does not speak even to Anna, supernatural voices in the dead of night, dinning memories of ancient prophecies, nightmares of terror and desolation. The theme of Greek tragedy — *deus quos vult perdere dementat prius* — is powerfully predominant and given absolutely explicit statement in the double simile (469 f.) where Dido is compared with Pentheus and Orestes, two of the most famous tragic heroes of the Greek stage.

450. **fatis exterrita**: 'distraught by doom' — she now sees no way out from the fate she has settled for herself.

451. **caeli convexa**: 'the vaults of heaven', cf. *Aen.* 6.241, Cic. *Arat.* 314 *convexum caeli*.

453. **turicremis**: 'incense-burning', a vivid compound adjective, cf. Lucr. 2.353; see note on 3.544.

454. **latices . . . sacros**: 'holy water'; Servius thought that *latices* was the same as *vina* in the next line. This is possible, but it seems more likely that Virgil is describing two different aspects of the portent.

455. **obscenum**: 'loathsome', one of the very strongest words available; cf. *Aen.* 3.241, and especially *Geo.* 1.470 where the word occurs in the list of horrible omens and portents at Julius Caesar's death.

457 f. For the marble shrine dedicated to Sychaeus cf. Ov. *Her.* 7.99 f.; for the custom cf. Cic. *Verr.* 2.4.4 and Servius' note on *Aen.* 6.152.

460 f. 'From the shrine she thought she heard sounds, the words of her husband calling her'; notice the eerie alliteration of *v*.

462 f. 'and the lonely owl often moaning on roof-tops with its ill-boding song, prolonging its drawn-out hooting into a wail'; the assonance of the long vowels imitates the uncanny sound. For the ill-omened owl cf. *Aen.* 12.862 f., Ov. *Ibis* 223–4, *Met.* 5.549 f., and for more examples Pease's monumental note ad loc. Compare Shakespeare, *Macbeth* 2.2.4–5 'It was the owl that shriek'd, the fatal bellman, / which gives the stern'st goodnight'; and for *queri* Gray's *Elegy* 10 'The moping owl does to the moon complain'.

464. **priorum**: 'of olden days'; Dido recalls far-off prophecies which she had ignored at the time. The reading in some MSS, *piorum*, known to Servius, is much inferior.

465. The clash of word accent with ictus in this line conveys agitation; in each of the first four feet the word accent is on the second syllable of a dactyl.

465 f. Dido's dream is a reflexion of her state of mind (cf. Medea's dream in Ap. Rh. 3.616 f.); this is rare in dream descriptions, which generally are used for prophecy or revelation (see note on 2.268 f.). There is an other-worldly terror about her dream — she is being pursued, she is all alone on an endless road, she cannot find any friends (cf. 320). In this respect it resembles Ilia's dream in Ennius (*Ann.* 39 f.); the nearest parallel in the *Aeneid* is 12.908 f.

466. **ferus**: Aeneas as proud enemy (424) becomes in Dido's dream a hunter pursuing a terrified quarry.

469 f. The doubled simile illustrates Dido's frenzy, and relates her very specifically with the heroes of Greek tragedies: first she is compared with the demented Pentheus (King of Thebes) of Euripides' *Bacchae*, driven to tragic madness by Dionysus so that he sees two suns in the sky, two cities of Thebes (Eur. *Bacch.* 918–19); and secondly with Orestes, son of Agamemnon, as portrayed in Aeschylus' *Eumenides*, when after having killed his mother Clytemnestra to avenge her murder of his father he is pursued by the ghost of his mother and the Furies. There were many Roman tragedies on these subjects, by Accius, Pacuvius and others.

469. **Eumenidum**: the Greek euphemism ('kindly ones') for the Furies; cf. *Aen.* 6.250, 280, 375. They do not normally figure in the Pentheus legend, being replaced by the avenging Bacchic women, but Pease refers to a Pompeian wall painting of Pentheus with Furies in the background. The phrase *ultrices Dirae* (473) refers also to them; cf. 610, 8.701, 12.845, 869.

469. **agmina**: cf. *Aen.* 6.572 of the Fury Tisiphone, *vocat agmina saeva sororum*.

471. **scaenis agitatus**: 'hounded on the stage'; notice that the comparison is not merely with the story of a Greek tragedy, but with its actual performance on the stage. Page oddly maintains that 'the introduction of the word *scaenis* is an error; it suggests unreality'. But it is a master-stroke designed to associate Dido's tragic plight with that of the heroes of Greek tragedy, not merely with the legends about them, but with the presentation

of these legends as tragedy. There is no more 'unreality' about Greek tragedy than there is about Virgil's *Aeneid*.

472. Torches and snakes are the emblems of the avenging Furies which Clytemnestra here carries (cf. Allecto in *Aen.* 7.346, 456.).

474–503. *Dido takes the decision to commit suicide, and deceives Anna into assisting her plans by pretending that she has found magic means of freeing herself from her love. A pyre is to be built to burn the relics of Aeneas. Anna, not suspecting the real purpose of the pyre, performs Dido's orders.*

474 f. The recourse of Dido to magic identifies her more closely with Medea, especially the Medea of Apollonius (see notes on 484–5, 489 f.). Her reluctance to be driven to this expedient (493) reinforces the feeling of foreboding and horror which develops through this episode and the next. The Roman attitude to magic is well summed-up by Servius: *cum multa sacra Romani susciperent, semper magica damnarunt.* For full discussion of magic see Pease's notes on 479, 493 and Austin's note on 498.

474. **concepit furias**: 'caught the madness', cf. Cat. 64.92, Ov. *Met.* 2.640.

476. **exigit**: 'she pondered', 'went through', cf. Ov. *Met.* 10.587.

477. 'she concealed her plan with her expression, and made hope shine out on her face'; the second phrase is a very remarkable innovation, imitated by Silius (11.367). Compare the more natural use of *serenat* in *Aen.* 1.255, and for the meaning *Aen.* 1.209.

478. **gratare sorori**: there is a grim contrast with 435.

479. The use of *is* in oblique cases is generally avoided by the epic poets (see Austin ad loc.), and here the double use in the same line conveys contempt: he is not worth naming.

481. **Aethiopum**: this is a reference to the western Aethiopians (Hom. *Il.* 1.423, *Od.* 1.23–4).

482. The line (repeated in *Aen.* 6.797) is adapted from Ennius (*Ann.* 159, 339); *aptum* means 'fitted with', i.e. 'studded with'.

483. 'A priestess of Massylian race coming from there has been pointed out to me': for the Massyli, west of Carthage, see note on 132; *hinc* depends on *sacerdos* with some notion like *profecta*.

484–5. 'guardian of the precinct of the Hesperides, who both gave food to the dragon and kept safe the sacred branches on the tree, sprinkling liquid honey and sleep-bringing poppy'. The Hesperides ('daughters of the west') guarded the golden apples which Mother Earth had given to Juno when she married Jupiter; they were helped in their task by a dragon. The story has similarities with that of Medea and the Golden Fleece (guarded by a dragon, Ap. Rh. 4.127f.), and it is itself mentioned in Apollonius (4.1396f.). Difficulty has been felt from Servius onwards over the drowsy food apparently given to the sentinel dragon; it has been suggested that the honey and poppy is nothing to do with the dragon's food, but is an additional piece of magic for a different unspecified purpose, and this seems the best explanation. The alternative is that Virgil is following Apollonius' description of Medea putting the dragon to sleep by magic drugs (4.156f.) and has not properly accommodated it to his context. Mackail does not really solve it by saying 'Even a dragon had to be kept in good temper'. See further Pease's long note.

486. This is a very sleepy line, without any main caesura and with total coincidence of accent and ictus; cf. *Aen.* 5.856. Compare Shakespeare, *Othello*, 3.3.331. 'Not poppy, nor mandragora / Nor all the drowsy syrups of the world, / shall ever medicine thee to that sweet sleep / which thou ow'dst yesterday'.

487. **solvere mentes**: 'to release people's hearts' (from suffering, *duris . . . curis*), cf. 479. Hor. *Epod.* 5.71.

488. **aliis**: dative after *immittere*, supply *mentibus*.

489f. For this apparatus of magic cf. Ap. Rh. 3.532f., *Ecl.* 8.69f., 98f., Ov. *Met.* 7.199f., Tib. 1.2.43f. Pease ad loc. gives many additional references.

490. **mugire**: cf. *Aen.* 6.256.

493. **magicas . . . artis**: 'that I unwillingly arm myself with magic arts'; see note on 474f. To *invitam* supply *me*, cf. 383. For the archaic form of the infinitive *accingi* cf. *Aen.* 7.70, 8.493, 9.231, 11.242, and for the middle use of the passive see note on 137 and cf. especially 2.511.

494. **tecto interiore**: i.e. in a courtyard, cf. *Aen.* 2.512–13.

495–6. **arma viri . . . exuviasque**: cf. 507, where *arma* is specified by *ensis*, and 646; *exuviae* is a general word, no doubt including the *Iliacae vestes* of 648 (cf. 651, and *Ecl.* 8.91).

496. **impius**: the irony of the application of this epithet to *pius* Aeneas is enhanced by its position as a run-on word; in Dido's view he has broken all the ties of duty and responsibility which he owed to her. For *pietas* of love cf. Cat. 76.2, 26.

496-7. **lectumque iugalem quo perii**: 'the marriage bed which was my ruin'; cf. 648, and for Dido's belief that she was married cf. 172, 316.

497-8. 'it is my wish to rid myself of all the memories of this evil man, and the priestess shows me how'. The word *nefandus* echoes and enlarges *impius*.

500. **novis . . . sacris**: 'was using these strange rites to conceal suicide'; for *praetexere* cf. 172.

501-2. Anna was unable to understand the deep emotions and frustrated pride of her sister (as Aeneas was, cf. 6.463 f.).

502. **morte**: 'at the death', cf. 244, 436.

504-21. *Dido now proceeds to perform magic rites, aided by the priestess.*

504. **At regina**: this is the third of the sections of this book which begins thus; cf. line 1 and line 296.

505. **ingenti . . . secta**: 'towering high with logs of pine and oak.'

506. **intenditque . . . sertis**: 'both hung the place with garlands and . . .'; the construction is unusual, cf. *Aen.* 5.403. Page well compares 'hang a wall with pictures'.

507. **super**: adverbial.

508. **effigiem**: the use of effigies in magic is very frequent, cf. *Ecl.* 8.75, Hor. *Sat.* 1.8.30.

509. **crinis effusa**: retained accusative with a passive verb, see note on 137. The hair is loosened in magic, see note on 518.

510. **tonat . . . deos**: for the accusative (*tonare* being equivalent to *vocat tonanti voce*) cf. Prop. 4.1.134.

511. 'and three-fold Hecate, the three faces of the maiden Diana'. Diana in the sky is the moon, on earth the huntress, and below the earth Hecate, a goddess associated with witchcraft and horror (cf. 6.247), also called Trivia, goddess of the cross-roads which ghosts were supposed to haunt (cf. 609). She is shown in art with three faces.

512. **simulatos fontis Averni**: 'pretended to be from the fountain of Avernus', the entrance to the underworld (6.238 f.).

513 f. 'and herbs are brought, gathered by the light of the moon with bronze sickles, juicy with the milk of black poison, and the love charm too is brought, torn from the head of a colt at birth, snatched before the mother can get it.' For bronze sickles in magic (iron being taboo) cf. Ov. *Met.* 7.227. The oxymoron 'milk of black poison' is partly literal as the milk of plants can be dark, but mainly metaphorical, suggesting dark rituals, black magic. *Venenum* is cognate with *Venus* and often applied to love potions (cf. *Ecl.* 8.95, *Aen.* 7.190). The love-charm is hippomanes, a fleshy growth on baby horses supposed to have magic significance: cf. Pliny *N.H.* 8.165 (in *Geo.* 3.280, Prop. 4.5.18, Tib. 2.4.58 the word has a different sense). This meaning of *amor* is a Virgilian innovation.

517. **mola manibusque piis**: 'with holy grain and pure hands'; the ablatives are rather different in kind, and some MSS have *molam*, which is without construction. The half-line in 516 perhaps suggests an unfinished passage, but the reading *mola* may stand.

518. Magic demands the elimination of knots, cf. Ov. *Met.* 7.182–3. *Pedem* is governed by *exuta* in a middle sense ('having released'); see note on 137 and cf. *Aen.* 2.275. Pease gives references (especially from art) for 'one shoe off and one shoe on'; Servius says it is so that she may be freed, but not Aeneas.

520–1. 'then she prays to any divinity there may be, just and mindful, which cares for lovers joined in unequal alliance.' For the construction *aliquos curae* (predicative dative) *habere* cf. Cic. *Fam.* 8.8.10.

522–52. *Night falls and all the earth and its creatures enjoy sleep. But not Dido — her anguish keeps her awake and she turns over in her distracted mind all possibilities. Shall she go to the African suitors she has scorned? Or accompany the Trojans, alone or with an escort? Impossible: better to die; this is the proper atonement for her broken pledge to Sychaeus.*

522 f. The contrast between the peaceful slumber of the rest of the world and Dido's waking anguish (see next note) introduces a tormented soliloquy of mingled despair and reproach. All

possible courses of action other than suicide are unacceptable to her pride (notice *inrisa* 534); there is here a most marked contrast with Catullus' Ariadne (notice on 537). The tone of bitter irony in which she rejects these courses is powerful, and the attempt at logical reasoning full of pathos: shall she go back to her African suitors? No. Well then, *igitur* (537), go with the Trojans? They wouldn't have me. But if they did, *quid tum*? (543) — alone, or with an escort? So she brings herself to what she feels is an inevitable conclusion — *morere ut merita es*. She is too proud, too regally obdurate, to make the best of what is left to her — as she lists her possible courses she makes the worst of all of them. And the prospect of trying to restore, for her people's sake, the situation as it was before Aeneas came does not ever occur to her — she is too deeply engulfed in her tragic frenzy.

522–32. This fine passage is inspired by an equally fine one in Apollonius (3.744 f.), where a similar contrast is made between the sleeping world and the wakeful heroine. In Apollonius we see at first wakefulness at night, the sailors watching the stars, the wayfarer and the sentinel longing for repose; then sleep comes, the bereaved mother at last finds slumber, the sound of dogs barking in the city and men talking is stilled — but not on Medea came sweet sleep. Virgil has confined his picture to the stillness of the countryside (with some personification, 523) and its creatures, using his great powers of word music to convey rest and silence and to break it harshly in line 529. For further descriptions of sleeping nature see Pease's collection of passages ad loc.; compare particularly *Aen*. 8.26 f., 9.224 f.

525. **pictaeque volucres**: 'gaily-coloured birds', cf. Milton, *P.L.* 7.434 'and spread their painted wings'.

526. 'both those that live all around the limpid lakes, and those that haunt the countryside with its tangled thickets'; compare Lucr. 2.344 f. Notice the gentle alliteration of *l*.

528. This line (nearly the same as *Aen*. 9.225) is not in the best MSS and should certainly be omitted.

529 f. The movement becomes dactylic and more disturbed, with harsh alliteration of *q*, then *s*, and the *r*, *-ur-* sounds at the end of 530.

530. **solvitur in somnos**: 'relax in sleep', cf. Ov. *Met*. 7.186 and *Aen*. 5.836. Compare line 695.

532. Compare Ariadne in Cat. 64.62 *et magnis curarum fluctuat undis*.

534. **ago**: the indicative for the subjunctive of a deliberative question, cf. 368 and *Aen.* 3.88, 10.675, 12.637.

534–5. Compare Anna's words in 36 f.

536. **sim**: concessive, 'when (although) I have ...'; cf. *Aen.* 2.248.

537. **ultima**: 'most extreme', i.e. whatever they may be. Dido's pride here contrasts very sharply with Ariadne's subservience (Cat. 64.158 f.) where she is willing to be a servant to Theseus; Ovid's Dido is similarly subservient (*Her.* 7.168).

538 f. 'Shall I do it because they are thankful for my previous help and their gratitude for my past deed lives firm in their memories?' The sentence is painfully sarcastic: to appeal now to to the grudging gratitude of the Trojans is utterly unacceptable. For *quiane* cf. *quemne* in Cat. 64.180.

540. **fac velle**: 'suppose I wished it', cf. Cic. *Phil.* 2.5 *fac potuisse*.

541–2. 'Wretched one, alas, do you not know, and do you not yet feel the treachery of the race of Laomedon?'; for the perjury of Laomedon see note on 3.248.

543. **quid tum?**: the argument is — but suppose after all that the Trojans are willing to take me, should I go alone or try to persuade my Tyrians to escort me? Both ideas are impossible.

545. **inferar**: 'shall I set off after them?' — the word here does not mean attack, but hasten to join; cf. 142 and *Aen.* 1.439.

Sidonia ... revelli: cf. *Aen.* 1.360 f., where however there is no mention of difficulty in persuading the Tyrians to leave.

547. 'No, die as you have deserved, and end your sorrow with the sword'; for *quin* with the imperative cf. *Aen.* 5.635.

548. The reproach against Anna (who is not present) has some justification; Dido, though blaming herself (*ut merita es*) clutches at excuses.

549. **oneras ... obicis**: for the idiomatic present (you are the one who did it) see note on 228.

550–1. 'It was not allowed that I should in widowhood pass my life blamelessly like some wild creature without knowing such agonies of love'. This seems the best rendering of this very difficult passage: by *thalami expertem* Dido means (as Servius says) 'without marrying again after the death of Sychaeus'; and by *more ferae* she refers to life free from social and personal relationships, like a deer on the mountains (the kind of life lived by a Camilla or a Harpalyce). Page quotes Ov. *Fast.* 2.291 *vita feris similis* of the happy, primitive, innocent life of the Arcadians. Others take *more ferae* to refer to sexual promiscuity (e.g. Hor. *Sat.* 1.3.109); the meaning would then be 'It was not allowed that I should live my life out of wedlock, in the fashion of a wild creature, without incurring blame; nor that I should experience love such as that'. But this is contrary to Dido's convinced view that she was not out of wedlock. For a very good full discussion see Austin ad loc.

552. 'I have not kept the faith which I promised to the ashes of Sychaeus': this summarising line contains indeed the whole truth, as Dido well knows (cf. 15 f., 28 f.). *Sychaeo* is used as an adjective, see Page ad loc. and cf. *Aen.* 1.686; this seems preferable to accepting the reading *Sychaei* from *M* (which looks like a correction) or to understanding the Latin to mean 'I have not kept the faith to his ashes which I promised to Sychaeus'. Austin argues that the adjective would be too artificial in this context, but cf. *Aen.* 3.304.

553–83. *As Aeneas sleeps Mercury comes to him again in a vision, urging him to leave immediately for fear of attack. Aeneas immediately awakens his men, and the Trojans depart in hot haste.*

553 f. This passage, decisive as it is in the narrative, gives a relaxation of tension between the two speeches of Dido. The attention is focussed on Aeneas' obedience to his divine instructions, and for a brief while its tragic consequences are in the background.

553. **rumpebat ... questus**: cf. *Aen.* 2.129; we might say 'such were the lamentations that burst from her heart'.

555. **carpebat somnos**: a back reference to 522. Aeneas, like all nature but unlike Dido, was asleep. The phrases *iam certus eundi* and *rebus iam rite paratis* contrast the ordered purpose of Aeneas with the disordered distraction of the unhappy Dido. Critics are anxious to defend (or attack) Aeneas here on a charge of heartlessness; but the simple truth is that he has peaceful sleep because he has accepted the will of heaven.

556. **forma dei**: this is a dream, the previous appearance of Mercury had been a real visitation in daylight.

558. **omnia**: this and the following accusatives are Greek accusatives of respect, common in verse with parts of the body (see note on 1.320) and also found with *omnia, cetera, genus* (cf. 3.594, 9.650).

558. **coloremque**: for the hypermetric elision cf. 629, and see Austin ad loc. and my note on 1.332.

559. **iuventa**: some MSS have *iuventae*, but cf. *Aen*. 2.473, 9.365.

561. **deinde**: 'from now on'; cf. *Aen*. 6.756, 890.

562. **demens**: strongly emphatic by position, see note on 185.

564. **variosque ... aestus**: 'she arouses in her heart shifting tides of anger', cf. 531.

565. Mercury's alliteration is very strong as he comes to the point of his message.

566. **mare turbari trabibus**: 'the sea a turmoil of ships', i.e. Dido's ships preventing the Trojan departure. For *trabibus* cf. *Aen*. 3.191. These prophecies are vainly echoed in Dido's next speech (592 f.).

569–70. **varium ... femina**: 'a woman is always a fickle and changeable thing'; Mercury's phrase is made particularly contemptuous by the use of the neuter. The commentators collect many parallels for this *sententia*; in its context, as uttered by Mercury, it serves well to suggest to Aeneas (particularly after *certa mori*) that the present tranquillity may not last. Dryden considered this 'the sharpest satire, in the fewest words, ever made on womankind', adding that if a god had not spoken these words Virgil would not have dared to write them nor he to translate them.

571. **umbris**: 'phantom', for the plural cf. *Acn*. 5.81, 6.510.

572. **fatigat**: 'arouses', *cum clamore increpat* (Servius); cf. *Aen*. 11.714.

573. **praecipites vigilate viri**: 'At it, men, wake up', equivalent (as Mackail says) to *praecipitate et vigilate*. Mynors and others punctuate so that *praecipites* goes with what precedes ('arouses them headlong') and the speech begins *vigilate viri* — but it is effective for Aeneas to echo Mercury's word (565), and the framing of the imperatives with the two adjectives *praecipites ... citi* is forceful.

576. **ecce ... instimulat**: the elisions and conflict of accent with ictus give a breathless effect; for the infinitive after *instimulat* see note on 1.357.

576. **sancte deorum**: a Homeric turn (δῖα θεάων, used by Ennius (*sancta dearum*).

577. **quisquis es**: for the religious formula cf. *Aen.* 1.330, 9.22.

578. **placidusque**: 'graciously', cf. *Aen.* 3.266.

581. 'The same excitement seizes them all at once, they hurry and bustle', — notice the alliteration at the line ending.

582. **deseruere**: the perfect tense conveys the suddenness of departure, cf. 164, *Aen.* 1.84.

583. The same line occurs in *Aen.* 3.208, where see notes.

584–629. *From her palace Dido sees the Trojans sailing away, and bursts into a soliloquy filled with anger, self-reproach, and longing for vengeance. She calls on the sun, the gods and the furies to avenge her, first on Aeneas personally and then on all his descendants.*

584 f. This passage begins with a moving contrast between the serenity of the new dawn and the distracted and tormented emotions of the lonely queen (cf 522 f.). But pity is quickly replaced by horror. The speech she makes is a grandiloquent and formalised imprecation, arising from thwarted power, injured pride, and the uncontrollable passion for revenge. Its great impact is due to the variety of ways in which her anger and hatred is conveyed: first a useless plea for action, then a moment of self-blame followed by a violent and inhuman outburst dwelling on the horrors which she might have committed; then the recognition that she herself can do nothing, and the prayer to other powers to bring about the destruction which she cannot, the destruction first of Aeneas himself and his people, and then of his Roman descendants. Thus the particularised fury and despair of Dido turns into the generalised hostility and violence of two great peoples.

The speech is perhaps the most perfect example in the *Aeneid* of Virgil's ability to use words and metre to convey the tone and mood of an imagined situation at the highest possible point of intensity. I have endeavoured in the notes that follow to draw attention to some of the ways in which he achieves these effects.

584-5. 'And now first dawn was beginning to dapple the world with the new day's light as the goddess Aurora left the saffron bed of Tithonus'. These are calm and beautiful lines (used again in 9.459-60), describing dawn in phrases partly borrowed from Lucretius (2.144), and adding the distancing mythology of the goddess Aurora as bride of Tithonus (Hom. *Il.* 11.1, *Geo.* 1.447). Homer (e.g. *Il.* 8.1) uses the epithet κροκόπεπλος ('saffron-cloaked') of dawn; compare *lutea* in *Aen.* 7.26.

586. **e speculis**: 'from her high tower'; the remoteness of the queen and her isolation is impressed upon us; compare Amata in 12.595 f., and Ariadne in Cat. 64.126 f.

587. **aequatis . . . velis**: 'in ordered array', in formation with all their sails at the same angle; the smooth and organised departure of the Trojans contrasts with the wild disorder of Dido's thoughts and emotions.

589-90. 'three times and four times struck against her lovely breast and tore her fair hair'; for the middle use of *percussa* and *abscissa* see note on 137, and cf. 1.481, 7.503, 9.478, 11.877.

590. **pro**: the interjection, as in *pro di immortales*.

591. **inluserit**: for the use of the future perfect ('shall it be true that a stranger has mocked. . . ?') cf. *Aen.* 2.581-2, 9.785. Dido here returns again to the thought that she has been slighted and mocked; cf. 534.

592. The indefinite unstated subject helps to convey the unreality of Dido's frantic appeals — there is no audience, and the commands she gives directly in the next two lines are inaudible.

593. **diripientque**: this is the reading of the MSS. Many editors have accepted Heinsius' conjecture *deripient*, but the more violent word is more appropriate.

593-4. 'Quick, off, bring fire, get weapons, drive on the oars'. These staccato outbursts are given added vehemence by the very unusual pause after the fifth foot in 593 (echoing 590) and the intense alliteration of *t*.

596. The slow spondees and Dido's own use of the epithet *infelix* (used of her often in the narrative) convey the moment of realisation and self-reproach for her *facta impia* in breaking her oath to Sychaeus, and perhaps also, as Austin suggests, in failing in her duties to her people. Some have argued that the reference

is to the *facta impia* of Aeneas against her, but this is inappropriate
to the context and the meaning of *tangunt*.

597. 'The proper time for that was when you were offering
him a share in your power'; *cum* with the indicative stresses the
point of time (=*eo tempore quo*), cf. Tib. 1.10.8.

dextra: 'honour', the keeping of pledges, cf. 307, 314.

598 f. The omission of the antecedent (*eius*) to *quem* helps to
convey the disjointed nature of Dido's phrases. The scornful
alliteration of *p* in 598 is relaxed in 599 and then resumed in the
last word. The sarcastic use of the vague *aiunt* to introduce the
traditional qualities of Aeneas (guardian of his country's gods
and rescuer of his father) gives a cold sense of distance as she
ignores the fact that he had told her these things himself (2.707,
717).

599. **subiisse**: 'supported'; cf. *Aen.* 2.708, 12.899.

601–3. Both of these ghastly acts of vengeance which Dido
says she could have performed are from Greek mythology. The
first refers to the story of how Medea scattered on the sea the
dismembered body of her brother Apsyrtus to delay the pursuit
of her father (Cic. *Pro Lege Man.* 22); similarities between Medea
and Dido have appeared in the course of the book (especially in
Dido's use of magic; see note on 474 f.). It is interesting that
Apollonius used an alternative form of the legend which dispenses
with this act of horror.

The second reference is to the story that Atreus served up to
Thyestes the flesh of his sons (Aesch. *Agam.* 1590 f., Eur. *El.* 699 f.).
It is less likely that the reference is to Procne who killed Itys and
served him up to his father Tereus (Ov. *Met.* 6.424 f.). The horror
and barbarity of Dido's thoughts reveal the depth of tragic
madness to which she has come.

603. 'But the upshot of the battle would have been uncertain.
Let it have been!' The imaginary objection of soliloquy is answered
with violent force, with echoing alliteration of *f* (see note on 218)
and a pause after the fifth trochee (a very unusual rhythm; see
my note on *Aen.* 3.480, Oxford edition). *Fuerat* is indicative
replacing the expected past potential subjunctive; cf. *Aen.* 2.55.
Fuisset is past jussive (in a concessive sense), a rare construction;
cf. 678 for a different type of past jussive.

604–6. The long series of pluperfect subjunctives expresses

with a kind of dinning insistence Dido's preoccupation with what might have been, what she could have done, and did not. *Exstinxem* is contracted for *exstinxissem* (a much rarer contraction than *implessem* in the previous line); cf. 1.201, 5.786, 6.57, 11.118 and line 682.

604. **castra**: i.e. the encampment by their ships, cf. *Aen.* 3.519, 9.69.

606. **memet ... dedissem**: 'I would have flung myself on top of all'; compare Ap. Rh. 4.391 f. For the emphatic *memet* cf. *Aen.* 7.309.

607 f. As Dido turns from the unfulfilled past to her prayers for the future the movement slows, becoming predominantly spondaic while in measured tones she invokes the powers that can bring aid. First she calls on the all-seeing Sun (cf. Hom. *Il.* 3.277), then her special goddess Juno, goddess of Carthage and of marriage, enemy of Aeneas; then the witch of the underworld, Medea's patron goddess Hecate (see note on 511), then the avenging furies (see note on 469, and cf. Cat. 64.192 f.), and finally all gods, whoever they may be, sympathetic to her at her death (cf. 520–1).

608. 'and you Juno, mediator and witness of my suffering'; the word *interpres* suggests that Juno had, as *pronuba*, been personally involved in Dido's love.

609. **ululata**: 'whose name is shrieked'; for the passive use cf. Stat. *Th.* 3.238 and compare *Aen.* 3.14; see further Austin ad loc. The association of Hecate with crossroads is reflected in her name Trivia (e.g. *Aen.* 6.13.)

610. **Elissae**: see note on 335.

611. **meritumque ... numen**: 'turn towards my wrongs the divine power which I must deserve'; for *malis* cf. 169. Others take the meaning to be turn against evil-doers (or evil behaviour) the divine power they deserve (cf. Hor. *Epod.* 5.54).

613. **caput**: for this contemptuous use cf. 640.

terris adnare: 'sail in to land', cf. *Aen.* 1.538.

614. **hic terminus haeret**: 'and if this outcome is firm-fixed', cf. Lucr. 1.77. Some punctuate so that this is the main clause, but it is better as another subordinate clause in asyndeton; for *at* ('yet') in the main clause after a *si* clause cf. *Aen.* 6.406, *Geo.* 4.241.

615 f. These curses upon Aeneas (modelled in a general sense on Hom. *Od.* 9.532 f., Polyphemus' curse on Odysseus) in one way or another all came true. He was harassed in warfare by Turnus and his Rutulians; he left the Trojan camp and the embrace of Iulus to seek help from Evander; he saw the death of many of his men (notably Pallas); he accepted peace terms more favourable to the Italians than the Trojans (12.834 f.); and he did not rule his people for long (three years), but (according to one version of the legend) was drowned in the Numicus or (according to another) killed in battle and his body not recovered. These are the lines which confronted Charles I when he consulted the *sortes Vergilianae*; see Austin ad loc.

616. **finibus extorris**: 'exiled from his land', a rather exaggerated reference to Aeneas' departure from the Trojan camp site to seek help from Evander (*Aeneid* 8). Others take it to refer to his exile from Troy, but this was already a fact.

619. **optata**: a stock epithet, 'the lovely light'; cf. *Aen.* 6.363 *caeli iucundum lumen*.

622 f. From her specific curse upon Aeneas Dido turns to the longer vista of history and undying hatred through the generations.

623. **exercete odiis**: 'harass with your hatred'; cf. *Aen.* 5.779, 6.739.

624. **munera**: the strong irony of this word is emphasised by the heavy sense-pause after it; Dido wants as a gift to her ashes not a tribute of affection, but a promise of never-ending hatred.

sunto: the legalistic imperative, rare in verse, adds a feeling of solemn formality (cf. *Aen.* 6.153).

625 f. 'Arise, some avenger from my bones, to pursue the Trojan settlers with fire and sword, now, one day, whenever strength offers. I call on shore to fight with shore, wave with sea, weapons with weapons; let the peoples fight, themselves and their children's children'. Dido's last appeal begins with hissing *s*'s, and the powerfully effective syntactical device of the third person *aliquis* as subject to the second person verb; then she asks her Carthaginians to use against her enemies that fire and steel which she herself might have used (604 f.), but did not. The appeal to the Carthaginians is general, extending through all future time; but the specific *aliquis ultor* must have brought to Roman minds the thought of Hannibal.

629. **nepotesque**: this is a most astonishing instance of hypermetric -*que* (see note on 558); the elision has to be made not only over a full stop, but at the end of a speech. In a sense indeed the elision cannot be made at all; the never-ending hatred of Dido is reflected in the unended rhythm of her final words.

630–62. *Dido sends Barce to fetch Anna for the pretended magic rites, and meanwhile climbs the pyre and prepares to kill herself. In her last words she speaks of her life's achievement and once more prays for vengeance on Aeneas.*

630 f. In these last scenes Dido is again seen as a tragic heroine, reminding us in the manner of her death of Ajax in Sophocles, and in her final speech of Euripides' *Alcestis* (175 f.). Her last words are divided into two parts at line 659; in the first part Dido is once again the great queen of Carthage, as she bids farewell to her life and reviews its achievements; in the second she is again the fury of vengeance. At the moment of her death the beginning and the end of her tragedy are put before us in brief; under pressures which she could not resist she has moved from prosperity to disaster, from an admirable and enviable personality to one consumed and destroyed by hate.

633. 'for the black ash of the pyre encompassed her own nurse in her one-time home'; i.e. in Tyre. Whether Virgil found this detail in the legend we do not know; but it is appropriate that Sychaeus' old nurse should perform Dido's last errand, as she plans to expiate the wrong she had done to his memory. For the use of *suus* cf. *Aen.* 1.461; for *habebat* cf. perhaps *Aen.* 1.556, 6.362.

635. **dic . . . properet**: jussive subjunctive in parataxis, cf. *Aen.* 5.550–1; for the purificatory ritual cf. 6.229–30.

638. **Iovi Stygio**: i.e. Pluto, cf. Hom. *Il.* 9.457; compare *Iuno inferna* (Proserpina) in *Aen.* 6.138.

640. 'and to commit to the flames the pyre of the Trojan wretch': Dido's proclaimed intention to light the pyre that has been built (504 f.), with the possessions and effigy of Aeneas on it (507 f.), continues to the last moment her pretence of magic rites directed against Aeneas. For *caput* cf. 613 and 11.399.

641. 'So she spoke. The other hastened her step with an old woman's eagerness'. Notice the momentary relief in this dactylic

line, describing the agitated speed of the nurse as she bustles to obey her instructions.

celerabat: some MSS give *celebrabat*, but as Mackail points out this word is not used elsewhere by Virgil of a single person, 'nor could it properly be so used'.

643–4. 'rolling her blood-shot eyes, her trembling cheeks flecked with blotches of red, pale at the thought of imminent death'; the first phrase is used of Amata (7.399), the last is echoed in the description of Cleopatra in 8.709. For the retained accusative *genas* see note on 137.

645. **limina**: the word is used here of an inner section of the palace; Austin compares the use of *moenia* to mean 'buildings' of a city (as in 74).

646. **rogos**: for the poetic plural cf. *Aen.* 11.66. *P* and Servius read *gradus*, which perhaps is a correction originating from 685.

646–7. This presumably refers to a gift which Dido had earlier sought from Aeneas, as a token of affection (Sil. 8.149), not a death-weapon. Ovid elaborates the point in *Her.* 7.183 f.

648. **hic**: 'next', cf. *Aen.* 2.122.

Iliacas vestis notumque cubile: this is a reference to her preparations in 496 f., 507 f.

649. **paulum . . . morata**: 'pausing a moment in tearful thought'.

650. **incubuitque . . . dixitque**: the use of *-que . . . -que* here ('both . . . and') gives a doubled trochaic lilt and a rhyme; it seems to contribute to the finality of the line.

653 f. Dido's simple and noble statements of her life's achievements have a literary quality like the inscriptions on tombstones.

654. **magna**: the dominant meaning is the superhuman size of ghosts (cf. Creusa's ghost, 2.773 *nota maior imago*), but there is an undertone too of queenly majesty.

656. Cf. *Aen.* 1.343 f. where Venus tells how Dido's husband Sychaeus was murdered by her brother Pygmalion, and how Dido took Pygmalion's treasures and ships and men away to Carthage.

657–8. 'Happy, alas too happy, if only the Trojan ships had never touched our shores'; the phrases are strongly reminiscent of Medea's thoughts in Ap. Rh. 3.774 f., 4.32 f., and Ariadne's in Cat. 64.171–2.

659. **os impressa**: for the middle use of the verb see note on 137.

660. **sic, sic**: Servius and many others have held that as Dido speaks these words she stabs herself twice; it is less melodramatic if we take the words at their face value: 'this shall be the manner of my dying' (Austin).

661–2. 'Let the cruel Trojan's eyes drink in these flames from over the ocean, and let him take with him the ill-omen of my death.' For *haurire oculis* cf. *Aen.* 12.945–6.

663–92. *As Dido is seen to have stabbed herself wild lamentation spreads through the city. Anna rushes to the pyre and endeavours to staunch the blood, but Dido is past human aid.*

663 f. Only at the beginning and end of this scene does Virgil describe the dying queen; the greater part of the passage is taken up with the general grief of the people and the specific anguish of Anna. In this way the impact of lines 688–92 is made more striking.

663–5. Like a Greek tragedian, Virgil does not describe the death stroke (see note on 660), only the fact that it has occurred; cf. Soph. *Ajax* 828 f.

665. **sparsasque manus**: 'her hands bespattered'. Austin agrees with Henry's view that *sparsas* means 'flung wide' (Servius gives both explanations), but there seem no grounds for rejecting the more normal meaning.

666. **bacchatur**: 'rushes wildly', as Dido herself had (301).

667. For the general scene cf. the fall of Troy, *Aen.* 2.487 f. The line ends with a hiatus before a quadrisyllabic word (= 9.477); the effect is to reinforce the onomatopoeic sound of *ululatus*.

669. **ruat**: 'were falling', cf. *Aen.* 2.363 *urbs antiqua ruit*. For the comparison cf. Hom. *Il.* 22.410 f., where the lamentation for Hector is as if all Troy were falling.

670–1. 'and the raging fire was eddying all around the rooves of the houses of men and the temples of gods'; for the position of *per* cf. 257, 5.663.

672. **exanimis**: 'distraught', out of her mind in panic. Virgil uses this form and the other (*exanimus*) equally.

673. This line is repeated (of Turnus' sister) in 12.871; cf. also 11.86.

675–6. 'Was this what it was, my sister? You sought me and deceived me? This was what your pyre was for, was it (*mihi*), and the fire and the altars?' Anna now realises that she has unwittingly been the accomplice in Dido's plans for suicide. For *hoc illud* cf. *Aen.* 3.558; *mihi* is ethic dative.

677. **quid ... querar?**: cf. 371, *quae quibus anteferam*?

678–9. 'You should have called me to the same fate; the same agony and the same hour should have taken off both of us with the sword together'. The subjunctives are past jussive (= *debuisti vocare, debuit ferre*); cf. *Aen.* 3.643, 10.854, 11.162 and (with a concessive force) line 603. For *ferre = auferre* cf. *Aen.* 2.555, 600.

680. **struxi**: understand *rogum*; the omission of the object shows that Anna is thinking of nothing else.

681. **crudelis**: this is surely vocative, addressed to Dido, not nominative referring to Anna (as is often said); the second interpretation would be out of tune with the rest of Anna's words.

682–3. This is only too true; Dido's action, taken on entirely personal grounds, has repercussions upon all those towards whom she had responsibility. She has felt free to act purely as an individual; she has at the last disregarded all her obligations.

682. **exstinxti**: contracted for *exstinxisti*, see note on 606.

683–4. **date ... abluam**: 'let me wash her wound with water'; *date* is addressed to the bystanders. For the parataxis cf. *Aen.* 6.883–4.

685. **ore legam**: 'let me catch it on my lips', cf. Cic. *Verr.* 2.5.118, Ov. *Met.* 12.424–5, and Pease's many illustrative citations.

sic ... altos: 'speaking thus she had already climbed the high steps'; notice the use of the pluperfect tense. For *evadere* with the accusative in this sense cf. Livy 2.65.3, and compare *Aen.* 2.458 (*evadere ad*).

686. **semianimemque**: the *i* of *semi-* is treated as a consonant (see note on 2.16); in some compounds it is omitted, cf. *Aen.* 3.578.

689. **stridit**: 'hissed'; the word refers to the sound of air in the wound; cf. Ov. *Met.* 4.123. There is no reason to take *vulnus* as equivalent to *ensis*, as many have done, rendering *stridit* as 'grated'. The line is reminiscent of the metaphorical wound of line 67 *tacitum vivit sub pectore vulnus*.

690–1. **ter ... ter**: cf. Ap. *Rh.* 3.654–5.

692. **ingemuitque reperta**: 'and groaned when she found it'.
To *reperta* supply *luce*; some MSS have *repertam*, probably through failure to understand the ablative absolute construction.

693–705. *Because Dido's death was neither fated nor deserved Proserpina had not cut a lock of her hair to release her soul. Juno therefore sends Iris to perform the rite, and Dido's life departs into the winds.*

693 f. The final scene is quiet and tranquil after the anguish and intensity of the preceding action. Its function is similar to that of the choral ode which closes a Greek tragedy on a calm note. The action passes from the turmoil of human suffering to the inevitability and serenity of divine dispositions; and the goddess Iris, with her other-worldly beauty and colour, brings light at last to Dido's dark tragedy.

694. **Irim**: Iris is Juno's special messenger, cf. *Aen.* 5.606 f., 9.2 f.

695. 'to set free her struggling spirit from the fetters of her body'; the soul is imprisoned in the body (*Aen.* 6.734), and struggles to get away.

696–7. 'For because she was not dying by fate nor by a death she had deserved, but wretchedly before her time, set on fire by sudden frenzy. . .'. The meaning is that Dido dies only because she wished it — there was no other reason; she had not reached the end of her fated span, nor had she deserved death (e.g. by some criminal act leading to divine intervention; cf. Ov. *Fast.* 3.705 f., where the phrase *morte iacent merita* is used of such people). These lines have been subjected from Servius onwards to severe metaphysical analysis; but their impact in the context is very very clear — Dido's death is self-chosen. In *Aen.* 6.436 f. Virgil comments on the fate in the underworld of those who chose suicide — *quam vellent aethere in alto | nunc et pauperiem et duros perferre labores.*

698–9. Macrobius (*Sat.* 5.19.2) refers to the view of Cornutus that Virgil invented this ritual, but refutes it by citing Euripides (*Alc.* 73 f.) where Death plans to cut a lock of Alcestis' hair to make her sacred to the god of the underworld.

700–2. 'So Iris flew down from the sky on her saffron wings, dew-bespangled, trailing a thousand changing colours as the sun shone on her'. The supernatural beauty of the rainbow

goddess brings a calm serenity to these closing scenes; cf. *Aen.*
5.88 f., 606 f., Ov. *Met.* 11.589 f., Stat. *Th.* 10.118 f., and Ceres'
words to Iris in Shakespeare, *The Tempest* 4.1.76 f.

> Hail, many colour'd messenger, that ne'er
> Dost disobey the wife of Jupiter;
> Who with thy saffron wings upon my flowers
> Diffusest honey-drops, refreshing showers:
> And with each end of thy blue bow dost crown
> My bosky acres, and my unshrubb'd down,
> Rich scarf to my proud earth. . . .

702. **hunc**: referring to *crinem* (698).

703. **iussa**: 'as instructed', by Juno; Iris does not perform this
function on her own authority.

704–5. 'and with it all warmth left her, and her life departed
into the winds'; cf. *Aen.* 10.819–20, 11.617. The final line is gentle
and rhythmically conclusive with its fourth foot composed of a
single word (see on 1.7), and its light alliteration. Page quotes
Shakespeare, *Richard III*, 1.4.37 f.

> The envious flood
> Kept in my soul, and would not let it forth
> To seek the empty, vast and wandering air.

AENEID 5

Introductory Note

The fifth book provides a diminution of tension between the
intensity of Book 4 and the majesty of Book 6; in this respect its
structural function is not unlike that of Book 3. In order to
maintain continuity Virgil leads into his description of the games
by gradually lessening the emotional significance of the narrative,
and leads out from them again by gradually increasing it. Thus
the book starts with a last backward glance at Carthage and
continues with an impressive description of the religious ceremonies and Aeneas' filial devotion to Anchises before the games
themselves begin with the ship-race. The tension is at its lowest

for the boxing-match (see note on 362 f.), and rises again with the omen after the archery contest and the spectacular cavalcade of the *lusus Troiae* with its optimistic and patriotic impact. Thus a serene mood is established, making the intervention of Juno all the more terrifying, as she attempts again to prevent the foundation of Rome by causing the burning of the ships and the resultant despair of Aeneas. He is brought now to a point where he wonders whether to forget the fates, and is restored to confidence only by the intervention of the ghost of his father Anchises. This intervention motivates Aeneas' visit to the underworld, and the pathos of the story of Palinurus, with which the book ends, sets the tone for the mystery and awe of Book 6.

One way then in which continuity is achieved is by the subtle arrangements of mood and tension. Another is by the renewal of main themes of the poem: the religious aspect of the games is strongly stressed, and the future destiny of Rome is kept before our eyes by aetiological reference to famous Roman families (see note on 117 f.) and to the contemporary pageant of the *lusus Troiae* (see note on 545 f.). The importance of Anchises in guiding Aeneas, which had been illustrated during his lifetime in the account of the voyage (Book 3), is now further illustrated after his death; and the difficulties which beset Aeneas in fulfilling his mission are again seen to be almost overwhelming.

The description of the games themselves has as its literary source the account of the games for Patroclus in Hom. *Il.* 23, and there are frequent echoes. But in place of Homer's vivid and fast-moving narrative Virgil has substituted an elaborate and varied pattern, reducing the number of contests from eight to four, alternating the long accounts of the ship-race and the boxing with the briefer foot-race and archery, constantly changing his method of description and his way of interesting the reader in the characters and events (see Otis, *Virgil*, pp. 41 f.). I have discussed the individual events in the notes at the beginning of each; for fuller details see E. N. Gardiner, *Athletics of the Ancient World*, and the introduction to my Oxford edition of Book 5.

In addition to having a Homeric model Virgil was led to include an account of athletic games by the new popularity of festivals of the Greek type which Augustus fostered. The victory at Actium was celebrated by the inauguration of Actian games at Nicopolis in 28 B.C., and these took place subsequently every four years. Thus the description of the games represents an aspect of poetic creativity which is very characteristically Virgilian — the use of Homeric source material in such a way as to adapt it both to the more elaborately organised requirements of literary epic and to the traditions and interests of the contemporary Roman world.

1–7. *As the Trojans sail away from Carthage, they look back and see a blaze in the city; although they do not know that it comes from Dido's pyre, they feel presentiments of disaster.*

1 f. This is Virgil's transition from the tragic events of Book 4 to the resumption of the description of Aeneas' journey. It is brief and reticent and ends in slow phrases of sorrow (5–7) before Virgil tears himself away (8 f.) with lines of rapid narrative of a conventional kind which he had used before (3.192–5). The contrast in tone here is very abrupt as Virgil leaves at last a theme on which he could say no more, but on which he could never feel that enough had been said.

2. **certus**: 'resolute', cf. *Aen.* 4.554; Aeneas' decision has been taken and he cannot now be turned from his purpose.

atros Aquilone: 'darkened by the north wind', cf. Aul. Gell. 2.30.

3. **infelicis Elissae**: the adjective has frequently been applied to Dido in Books 1 and 4, and now it ends her story. It is used once more, by Aeneas to her ghost in the underworld, 6.456. For Elissa, the original Phoenician name of Dido, see note on 1.340 and 4.335.

4. **flammis**: i.e. the flames of the funeral pyre; we are reminded of Dido's last words in 4.661–2.

5. **latet**: 'is unknown to them'; the subject is the interrogative clause *quae . . . causa.*

5–7. 'but the thought of the bitter agony caused when a great love is desecrated, and the knowledge of what a woman in wild frenzy may do, led the hearts of the Trojans along paths of sad foreboding.' Notice the metrical art of these lines — the slow spondees, the alliteration of *d, f, t,* the assonance of *u* and *-um* and the coincidence of ictus and accent in the fourth foot in line 7, giving a rounding-off effect; see further the note on this passage in my Oxford edition, and compare *Aen.* 1.7, 4.705.

5. **duri magno sed**: the postposition of the conjunction throws great emphasis on to the two adjectives.

6. **polluto**: a very strong word, given added weight by the enjambement before a pause; it denotes the breaking of a sacred tie (cf. *Aen.* 3.61, 7.467), and here (note its juxtaposition with *dolores*) reflects what the Trojans now realise Dido's feelings must have been.

notumque: the neuter of the participle is used as a noun, cf. 290, *Geo.* 3.348, Livy 27.37.5, Lucan 1.70.

8–41. *When they reach the open sea, a violent storm comes upon them and Palinurus the helmsman tells Aeneas that it is impossible to hold their course for Italy, and suggests that they should run with the wind to Sicily. Aeneas agrees, and they land near the tomb of Anchises, and are welcomed by Acestes.*

8–11. These lines, modelled on Hom. *Od.* 12.403–6 (= 14.301–4) are almost exactly repeated in 3.192–5, where see notes.

10. **olli**: archaic form for *illi*, cf. *Aen.* 1.254; this is varied from 3.194 *tum mihi caeruleus* etc., which perhaps explains the singular *olli* where we would expect *ollis*, referring to the Trojans.

13. **quianam**: 'why?', an archaic word used again in *Aen.* 10.6; see *Quint.* 8.3.24 f.

14. **sic deinde**: for postponed *deinde* see note on 1.195, and cf. 321, 400.

15. **colligere arma**: 'to take in the tackle', i.e. to shorten sail (so Servius), not 'to get together their equipment', as some suggest; cf. Stat. *Th.* 7.88. For *arma* in a nautical sense cf. *Aen.* 4.290, 6.353.

16. **obliquatque ... ventum**: 'he set the sails aslant into the wind', i.e. trimmed the sheets in order to luff, that is to sail nearer to the wind, now changed from north to west (19). Compare 828 f., and Livy 26.39.19.

17–18. **auctor spondeat**: 'should pledge it with all his authority', a very emphatic phrase.

18. **hoc ... caelo**: 'in weather like this', cf. *Geo.* 1.51, *Aen.* 4.53.

sperem ... contingere: for *sperare* with the present infinitive cf. *Aen.* 4.337–8.

19 f. The wind has now changed from north to west; it is not its direction which causes the trouble, but its violence, which means they cannot make way against it and must run before it.

19. **transversa**: adverbial accusative, cf. 381, 866, 869 and *Ecl.* 3.8.

20. **in nubem ... aër**: 'the air thickens into cloud', cf. Cic. *Nat. De.* 2.101.

21-2. 'We cannot possibly battle against the storm, or make enough way against it'; for *tendere* cf. 286, and *Aen.* 1.205, 554. The infinitive with *sufficere* is rare, cf. Lucan 5.154.

23. **longe**: supply *abesse* or *esse* (*Aen.* 12.52).

24. **fraterna Erycis**: for *fraternus* (=*fratris*) cf. 630. Eryx, son of Venus and Butes, was Aeneas' half-brother; he gave his name to the well-known mountain and town in Sicily (759).

25. 'if only I remember correctly as I plot our way back by the stars I watched before', i.e. when they set out from Sicily and were driven by a storm to Carthage (3.692 f., 1.34 f.). For *servare* cf. *Aen.* 6.338; for *remetiri* (calculating one's way back) cf. *Aen.* 2.181, 3.143.

26. **pius**: see note on 1.10; here the main reference of the word is to Aeneas' position of responsibility for his men.

28-30. The order is intricate, with *tellus* postponed from its adjective *ulla* — 'could any land be more welcome to me, or one to which (*quove* =*vel ad quam*) I would rather ... than that land which. ...'

29. **demittere**: 'bring to land'; for the nautical use of *de-* cf. 57, 212. The major MSS have *dimittere*, 'dismiss', i.e. 'disembark from', cf. *Aen.* 10.366, but as no confusion is commoner in MSS than that between *de-* and *di-* it seems better to accept the technical term.

30. Acestes, the Sicilian king of Trojan lineage, is mentioned in 1.195 and 550; see note on 38. He plays an important part in the *Aeneid*, foreshadowing in legend the very close historical bonds between Sicily and Rome.

31. The last incident of his journey which Aeneas related to Dido was the death of Anchises at Drepanum (3.709 f.).

34. **advertuntur harenae**: the dative of motion towards is common in verse with compound verbs, cf. 93, 346, 434, 805.

36. **adventum sociasque rates**: 'the arrival of a friendly fleet', a good example of hendiadys, cf. *Aen.* 1.54, 61.

37 'a wild-looking figure carrying his javelins and wearing the skin of a Libyan she-bear'. This is a memorable and picturesque

line which Tacitus recalled and imitated, *Hist.* 2.88 *tergis ferarum et ingentibus telis horrentes*. For *in iaculis* cf. 550 and Ennius' phrase (*Ann.* 506) *in hastis. Horridus* conveys its basic sense of 'bristling' (cf. *Aen.* 3.23) and also its wider meaning, 'rustic' (cf. *Aen.* 7.746).

Libystidis: the adjective *Libystis* (for *Libyca*) occurs only here and in *Aen.* 8.368.

38. Servius tells the story on *Aen.* 1.550; Segesta (or Egesta) who gave her name to Acestes' town in Sicily was banished from Troy and in Sicily became the mother of Acestes (also called Egestus) by the god of the river Crimissus (near Segesta). Virgil's form *Crinisus* may be an error in the MSS or a variant of the name.

39. **veterum . . . parentum**: i.e. his Trojan mother and her ancestors — this is a common meaning of *parens*, cf. *Aen.* 9.3.

40. **gratatur reduces**: 'showed his delight at their return'; *gratari* is an archaic form of *gratulari*. The construction is accusative and infinitive (*eos reduces esse*), cf. Tac. *Ann.* 6.21.

42–71. On the next day Aeneas summons an assembly and reminds the Trojans that it is the anniversary of the death of his father Anchises. He proclaims a solemn sacrifice at the tomb, which is to be followed on the ninth day by contests in rowing, running, boxing and archery.

42 f. The detailed and colourful description of the honours paid at the tomb of Anchises gives a religious and patriotic setting to the account of the anniversary games. The games have their model in Homer (*Iliad* 23), but are also reminiscent of Roman *ludi funebres*, the games held after the funeral of important citizens (Livy 23.30.15, 28.21.10 etc.). Virgil mingles Greek and Roman traditions in the description of the religious ceremony; essentially Aeneas is celebrating the normal Roman ritual at the anniversary of a father's death (*parentatio*, see note on 59–60), but mystery and majesty is added by elements from the Greek hero-cult (*divinus*, 47, *templa*, 60, *adyti*, 84). For further discussion see Bailey, *Religion in Virgil*, pp. 291 f. Servius compares the 'deification' of Anchises here with that of Julius Caesar, but Virgil does not define the nature of Anchises' divinity very explicitly, and if there is allegory it is of a most indirect kind.

42. **primo . . . Oriente**: 'at first dawn', cf. *Aen.* 3.588. *Oriens* is a noun as in 739.

stellas ... fugarat: see note on *Aen.* 3.521. *Fugarat* is contracted for *fugaverat*; for Virgil's avoidance of the pluperfect subjunctive with *cum* see note on 1.36–7.

44. **tumulique ex aggere**: 'from a raised mound', as a Roman general would address his soldiers in camp; cf. 113.

45. Dardanus, founder of the Trojan royal line, was a son of Jupiter, cf. *Aen.* 7.219 f.

46. The passage of a year since Anchises' death is presumably to be accounted for by assuming that the Trojans stayed some months in Drepanum before spending the winter in Carthage.

47. **divini**: the word could be used of the *di parentes* in Roman religion, but may imply more than that; see note on 42 f.

51 f. 'If I were spending this day as an exile in the Gaetulian Syrtes, or caught in the Argolic sea and (held) in the city of Mycenae, yet I still would be fulfilling . . .', i.e. whether in desolate Africa or hostile Greece, whether at sea or on land. The Syrtes were the great sand-banks near Carthage, called Gaetulian by association with the Gaetuli of that area, cf. *Aen.* 4.40 and line 192. The Argolic sea could be a vague term for any part of the sea round Greece (cf. *Aen.* 3.283), but here perhaps refers to the *sinus Argolicus* near Mycenae.

52. **deprensus**: probably caught by a storm (*Geo.*4. 421) rather than caught by the Greeks; certainly it does not mean caught (surprised) by the anniversary.

urbe Mycenae: Virgil does not elsewhere use the singular form of *Mycenae*. The genitive is appositional, cf. *Aen.* 1.247.

54. **suis**: 'due' (=*propriis*); cf. *Aen.* 1.461, 3.469, and line 832.

55. **ultro**: 'actually', 'unexpectedly', cf. *Aen.* 2.145 and line 446.

ipsius et: *et* is postponed, cf. *sed* in line 5.

57. **portus ... amicos**: 'have reached land and come to a friendly haven'; the present tense *intramus* is influenced by *adsumus*.

58. **laetum ... honorem**: 'our happy tribute'; *laetus* continues the idea built up in this passage (see note on 42 f.) that the anniversary rites are to be performed not only in mourning for the dead, but also in joy for the evident concern of the gods for Anchises.

59. **poscamus ventos**: 'let us ask Anchises for favouring winds'; the point of this request at this moment seems at first obscure, but in the next line Aeneas shows how his thoughts are upon the foundation of his city at the end of his journey.

59–60. 'and may he grant me to pay these rites each year in a temple dedicated to him when my city is founded'. Virgil here looks forward to the Roman festival of the *Parentalia* described by Ovid (*Fast.* 2.543 f.) as having been instituted by Aeneas in honour of Anchises.

61–2. **boum ... capita**: 'head of cattle', cf. *Aen.* 3.391.

64 f. Two different explanations of Aeneas' meaning have been current since antiquity: 'when the ninth day brings its light', or 'if the ninth day is fine'. The first is much to be preferred; conjectures about the weather are inappropriate in epic. Further, *almus* is a permanent epithet for *dies*, cf. Hor. *Odes* 4.7.7, *Ecl.* 8.17, and its use with *lux* in *Aen.* 1.306, 3.311 etc. For the use of *si* cf. Cat. 14.17; the mode of expression may have been connected originally with superstitious fear.

64–65. **nona ... Aurora**: the solemnities at a Roman funeral lasted for nine days (Hor. *Epod.* 17.48, Apul. *Met.* 9.31).

65. **radiisque retexerit orbem**: 'reveals the world with his rays', cf. *Aen.* 4.119 (the same phrase).

66. **citae ... classis**: 'a contest for swift ships'; the genitive is regularly used of the nature of the contest, cf. Livy 10.2.15 *sollemni certamine navium*, *Geo.* 2.530, Ov. *Met.* 10.177.

67. **viribus audax**: this goes with both the following lines: Aeneas proclaims a ship-race, a foot-race, and (for those who trust in their strength) a contest in javelin throwing and archery or boxing. In fact, no javelin contest takes place, but the formula in line 68 couples javelin-throwing and archery as one type of activity, cf. *Aen.* 9.178.

69. **fidit ... committere**: this is a marked extension of the normal use of *fidere*; it has the sense here of *audere*, hence the following infinitive.

caestu: see note on 364. The spondaic line is appropriate for the announcement of the heavy-weight contest.

70. **palmae**: the palm as a prize for victory came late to Greece, not before 400 B.C.; according to Livy (10.47.3) it was introduced from Greece into the Roman world in 293 B.C.

71. **ore favete**: 'utter no ill-omened word', a religious formula tending to mean 'observe silence', cf. Hor. *Odes* 3.1.2.

72–103. *The Trojans proceed to the tomb of Anchises, where Aeneas offers libations and addresses his father's shade. Suddenly a huge snake comes forth from the tomb, tastes the offerings, and then disappears. Aeneas recognizes that this indicates the presence of Anchises' ghost at the ceremony, and the sacrifice is renewed, and followed by a ritual feast.*

72 f. For the religious significance of this passage see note on 42 f.

72. **materna . . . myrto**: the myrtle was sacred to Venus, Aeneas' mother (*Ecl.* 7.62, *Geo.* 1.28, *Aen.* 6.443); it was also sometimes associated with the dead.

73–4. Mackail points out how these lines indicate that the sports will be for all ages: Helymus, a young man, enters the foot-race, the older Acestes is in the archery contest, and the boy Ascanius leads the *lusus Troiae*. Helymus' name is associated with the Sicilian people called the Elymi.

73. **aevi maturus**: for the genitive of respect cf. *Aen.* 2.638 and note on 1.14.

75–76. The alliteration of *m* and *c* is very marked indeed, perhaps to give a tone of solemnity and archaic ritual at the beginning of the description of the ceremony.

75. **ibat**: 'set out', ingressive imperfect.

77–78. 'Here in due libation he poured on the ground two goblets of unmixed wine, two of fresh milk, two of sacrificial blood'. The spirit of the departed was supposed to partake of such libations (cf. *Aen.* 3.66 f., 301 f.); for *libare* cf. *Aen.* 1.736. The ablatives are rather extended usages of the ablative of description. For *Bacchus = vinum*, a very common metonymy, cf. *Aen.* 1.215.

80. **salve . . . iterum salvete**: 'hail . . . , again I say hail', cf. Cat. 64.23. This meaning is preferable to the suggestion (so Servius) that Aeneas had first said *salve* at the time of burial.

80–1. **recepti . . . cineres**: 'ashes recovered in vain', a difficult phrase, meaning that the rescue of Anchises from Troy (*Aen.* 6.111 *eripui his umeris medioque ex hoste recepi*) was in vain because of his death before reaching Italy (82 f. *non licuit. . . .*)

82. To this line supply *tecum quaerere* from the next clause — the postposition of *tecum* is unusual and puts emphasis on the word.

fataliaque arva: cf. *Aen.* 4.355.

83. **quicumque est**: Aeneas knows that the Tiber is his goal (2.782, 3.500), but it is still a vague and unlocated goal. Page well draws attention to the contrast of this vague phrase with the Tiber's later fame.

84 f. For the significance of the snake see note on 95; for other snake descriptions cf. lines 273 f., *Aen.* 2.203 f., 471 f., *Geo.* 2.153 f. The description here is one of exceptional colour and brilliance, without the note of fear in the other passages cited.

84. **adytis ... ab imis**: Servius comments that Virgil in treating Anchises as a god makes his tomb a kind of temple; see note on 42 f.

85. 'drew along in mighty bulk its seven undulating coils'. *Septena volumina* is a variation on *septem gyros*; the meaning is not (as Henry, followed by Page, argues) that the snake made seven circuits of the tomb, progressing in seven coils. The figure seven is probably mystic (*Aen.* 6.38), rather than a reference, as Servius says, to the seven years of Aeneas' wanderings. The distributive *septena* is equivalent to the cardinal *septem*, as often in poetry; cf. 96 *binas*, 560 *terni*.

87–8. 'blue flecks mottled its back, and a sheen of golden markings lit up its scales'; to the nominative *notae* must be supplied from *incendebat* some verb like *distinguebant*.

88–9. 'like the rainbow when it catches the sun's rays and throws a thousand changing colours on the clouds'; cf. *Aen.* 4.701, almost the same words.

90. **agmine longo**: 'with its long sweep', cf. *Aen.* 2.212, 782.

91. **levia**: 'smooth', i.e. burnished, as in 558.

serpens: this is of course the participle, not the noun.

92. **libavitque**: 'tasted', cf. *Ecl.* 5.26, *Geo.* 4.54; the shade of meaning is different from that in 77. There is the same pattern of doubled -*que* ('both . . . and') in 177, 234.

93. **successit tumulo**: 'went into the tomb', cf. *Aen.* 1.627.

94. **depasta altaria**: 'the altars he had fed off', for *depascere* used actively cf. *Geo.* 4.539.

'Because of this he resumed all the more fervently the rites he had begun in honour of his father'; for *instaurare* cf. *Aen.* 2.451, 4.63.

94–5. **incertus ... putet**: 'uncertain whether to think . . . or'; for -*ne . . . -ne* cf. 702–3.

95. **geniumne loci**: according to the pantheistic view of the old Roman religion every natural feature, hill, spring, tree, river, had its *genius*, its local god; cf. *Aen.* 7.136 and Milton, *Lycidas* 182–3 'Now Lycidas the Shepherds weep no more; / Henceforth thou art the Genius of the shore . . .'

95. **famulumne parentis**: 'or the attendant spirit of his father'; cf. Val. Fl. 3.457 f. The soul of the dead (like the *genius*) was often represented as a snake; see Conington ad loc. There is ultimately little difference between these alternative views of the snake; it represents the spirit of Anchises appearing at his own tomb.

96 f. The offerings of sheep, pigs and bullocks suggest the Roman sacrificial lustration *Suovetaurilia* (*sus, ovis, taurus*); cf. *Aen.* 11.197 f.

96. **bidentis**: sheep in their second year, see note on 4.57.

97. **terga**: accusative of respect, see note on 1.320.

99. **Acheronte remissos**: 'released from Acheron', to visit the sacrifices, cf. *Aen.* 3.303 f. Acheron was one of the rivers of the underworld (*Aen.* 6.295, Milton, *P.L.* 2.578 'Sad Acheron of sorrow, black and deep'), and was commonly used to mean the underworld itself: cf. *Aen.* 7.312.

100. **quae cuique est copia**: 'each according to his means', a 'detached' use of the relative, equivalent to *sicut cuique est copia*; cf. Plin. *Ep.* 8.8.7.

101–3. Notice the extreme simplicity of the construction of these lines with their short clauses each with its main verb; perhaps the style reflects the well-known simple ritual acts performed one after the other.

102. **ordine**: 'in their due places', suggesting ritual correctness; cf. 53, 773.

104–113. *The day of the games comes round, and the people assemble; the prizes are displayed, and the trumpet sounds for the beginning of the contests.*

104 f. Virgil's long and elaborate description of the games is modelled, with variations, on the funeral games for Patroclus described in *Iliad* 23; in turn Statius (*Thebaid* 6) and Silius (*Punica* 16) imitated Virgil. In deciding to include an account of athletic contests in the *Aeneid* Virgil had a number of motives

apart from the Homeric precedent: to relieve the emotional tension between Books 4 and 6; to concentrate attention on Anchises and the religious honours paid to him by his son (see note on 42 f.); and to serve as a prototype for current Roman customs and institutions, especially for the revival of interest in athletics fostered by Augustus.

In the description of the contests Virgil has aimed at an effect quite different from that of *Iliad* 23. Where Homer is direct and immediate in appeal, Virgil gives a more formally organised account, with a contrived balance and unity such as is appropriate for his kind of literary epic. There are many similarities of incident between Homer and Virgil, but the method and tone of the two differ completely. See further the introduction to this book.

105. **Phaethontis**: this is a name of the sun, the shining one (cf. Hom. *Il.* 11.735), not the Phaethon of mythology.

109. **circoque**: Virgil is probably thinking of a curving bank on the sea-shore, enclosing a space which could be called *circus*; cf. 289.

110 f. The successful athletes are to receive prizes of material value as well as tokens of honour like garlands. This was the case in Homer, but not in the great Greek festivals like the Olympic games. In most Roman games prizes of value were given, but at his Actian games Augustus reverted to the practice of the Olympic games.

114–50. *Four competitors enter for the ship-race, Mnestheus in the Pristis, Gyas in the Chimaera, Sergestus in the Centaurus, and Cloanthus in the Scylla. The course is out to sea, round a rock and home again. The competitors draw lots for position; the starting signal is given, and the ships get under way amidst applause.*

114 f. Virgil's ship-race corresponds with the chariot-race in Homer, both in being the first of the contests and in a number of details, especially at the turning-point. Aeneas of course had no chariots, but in any case the maritime nature of much of the first half of the *Aeneid* makes a ship-race particularly appropriate. Augustus' Actian games included a regatta, but a ship-race was not an expected part of athletic contests. No other extant ancient epic contains one.

In the introductory section to the first contest (114–50) Virgil allows himself plenty of space to set the scene. The interest is built up before the race itself by the descriptions of the competitors, the course, the waiting for the start, the excitement of the spectators.

114–15. 'For the first event four ships entered, well matched with their heavy oars, and especially chosen out of the whole fleet.' The ships are not of the same size, but they are of the same class (i.e. triremes) with an equal number of rowers. Triremes did not exist in Aeneas' time; these are contemporary Roman ships.

116 f. The competitors have all been briefly introduced to us earlier in the poem (cf. 1.222, 510, 612, 4.288). Their characters are clearly revealed in the race, and directly influence the action. Sergestus is rash and impetuous, and runs aground; Gyas is hot-tempered and foolish, and loses his chance of success through a fit of anger; Mnestheus is gallant and determined, and comes very near to victory; Cloanthus keeps going steadily and holds off the final challenge by a timely prayer to the deities of the sea.

116. **remige**: collective singular, cf. *Aen.* 4.588.

Pristim: 'Leviathan'. This is a word of vague meaning, indicating some kind of sea monster, cf. *Aen.* 10.211. There is also the form *pistrix* (*Aen.* 3.427). The ships would have figure-heads representing their names; cf. *Aen.* 10.195 f.

117 f. A considerable number of Roman families traced their origins back to the Trojans (cf. 568); Hyginus and Varro wrote works *De Familiis Troianis*. The Roman *gentes* whose ancestors figure here in the ship-race were not among the most highly distinguished; the most famous of the Memmii was the propraetor of Bithynia whom Catullus accompanied, and to whom Lucretius dedicated his poem; the best known member of the *gens Sergia* was the infamous Catiline; and we know relatively little about the Cluentii, one of whom was defended by Cicero. Servius tells us that the *gens Gegania* (of whom a number appear in the pages of Livy) was descended from Gyas; perhaps Virgil omits mention of them because the family had died out by his time.

Virgil's fondness for aetiological name associations was encouraged by the use made of them in Hellenistic poetry, but generally is directly related to the national theme of the *Aeneid*. Compare lines 568 and 718, *Aen.* 1.267 (Iulus), 6.234 (Misenus),

6.381 (Palinurus), 7.2 (Caieta), 10.145 (Capys), and the whole series in 8.337 f. and in the catalogue (7.647 f.).

117. **genus . . . Memmi**: 'from whose name comes the race of Memmius'; *Memmi* is the normal form of the genitive singular.

118. The repetition of *ingens* is reminiscent of Homer (*Il.* 16.776); cf. *Aen.* 10.842 (= 12.640). The phrase *ingenti mole* is ablative of description, 'with its mighty mass'.

118. **Chimaeram**: this fabulous tripartite dragon occurs first in Hom. *Il.* 6.179 f., a lion in front, a serpent behind, and a she-goat in the middle; cf. *Aen.* 6.288, 7.785.

119. **urbis opus**: 'the size of a city', a most remarkable phrase imitated by Ovid (*Fast.* 6.641) and Statius (*Silv.* 2.2.30 f., cf. *Th.* 6.86). For the idea cf. Cic. *Verr.* 2.5.89.

119. **triplici . . . versu**: 'with triple banks of oars', cf. Livy 33.30.5.

122. **magna**: as Centaurus is the name of a ship, it is feminine.

125. **olim**: 'at times', an archaic use (cf. *Aen.* 3.541).

126. **Cauri**: these are north-west winds bringing storms (Pliny *N.H.* 18.338); the word is sometimes spelled *Cori*.

127. **tranquillo**: 'in calm weather', ablative of time when (cf. Livy 31.23.4).

127–8. 'and rises up from the still waves as a level expanse, a favourite resort for cormorants basking in the sun'. *Campus* and *statio* are in apposition to the subject *saxum*; for *apricus* 'delighting in the sun' cf. Persius 5.179 *aprici . . . senes*.

129. **metam**: 'turning-point', see note on 3.714; presumably Aeneas has a leafy branch or young tree wedged into the flat rock to make it more easily visible.

130. **pater**: the order is unusual, and perhaps draws some attention to Aeneas' position of responsibility in making the proper arrangements.

130–1. 'so that they should know where to make the turn for home, where to come round in their long course'; cf. *Aen.* 3.430. The second phrase is a variation on the first.

132. For the drawing of lots for position cf. Hom. *Il.* 23.352 f.

133. **ductores**: 'captains'. Each ship has its captain, its helmsman (*rector*, 161), and its rowers.

134. **populea . . . fronde**: the poplar was sacred to Hercules, patron of athletes; cf. *Aen.* 8.276.

135. **umeros ... perfusa**: 'their shoulders anointed', retained accusative with a passive verb (here used in a middle
sense); cf. 269, 309, 511, 774, 869 (and also 264, 608), and note on
1.228.

136-41. Notice how the spondaic movement of the first three
lines conveys the pause and sense of waiting for action, and is
released by the rapid movement of 139-41, where dactyls
largely predominate.

136-7. **intentaque ... intenti**: 'their arms are tensed on the
oars, tensely they await the signal'; the word here is used in
two slightly different senses.

137-8. 'and the throb of nervous excitement and their eager
longing for glory clutch at their leaping hearts'. These powerfully
pictorial phrases are repeated from *Geo.* 3.105f., and are an
elaboration of Hom. *Il.* 23.370-1. *Pavor* does not mean 'fear',
but the feeling akin to trembling experienced by an athlete when
he is keyed up; *haurire* here literally means 'to drain of blood'.

139. **finibus**: 'starting-places', the *loca* of 132.

140-1. **clamor nauticus**: 'the shouts of the rowers', cf. *Aen.*
3.128.

141. **adductis ... lacertis**: 'as they bring their arms right
up to their chests', in the motion of rowing.

142. **dehiscit**: 'is split open to its depth', cf. *Aen.* 1.106, 4.24.
The long vowel of *de-* is shortened before the following vowel;
cf. *dehinc* (722), *praeeunte* (186).

143. The same verse occurs in *Aen.* 8.690. *Tridentibus* refers to
the three prongs on the prow of a ship.

144-7. 'Not with such headlong speed do chariots leap forward
over the plain in a contest for paired horses, racing away as they
come streaming out from the barriers; no, not when the charioteers
shake out the rippling reins as they give free head to their teams,
and lean right forward to use the whip.'

Virgil is influenced in his choice of simile by the fact that his
ship-race is modelled on Homer's chariot-race; there are two
images, the speed of the chariots, and the efforts of the charioteers
to get more speed. Cf. also *Geo.* 3.103f.

145. **carcere**: this is the technical term for the starting-pens
or barriers on a race course; cf. *Geo.* 1.512.

147. **iugis**: the yokes, i.e. the yoked horses, are given free rein.

148. **studiisque faventum**: 'the rival cries of supporters', cf. 450.

149–50. **vocemque ... litora**: 'the sheltered shores re-echo the noise'; the shores are *inclusa* by the foot-hills and cliffs. For *volutant* cf. *Aen.* 1.725.

150. **resultant**: 'reverberate'; cf. *Aen.* 8.305.

151–82. *Gyas gets the lead, followed by Cloanthus, with Mnestheus and Sergestus contending for third position. As they draw near the turning-point, Gyas urges his helmsman Menoetes to steer closer in; but in fear of fouling the rock he fails to do so, and Cloanthus' ship slips past on the inside. In a fury of anger Gyas throws Menoetes overboard; eventually he manages to clamber out on to the rock, while all the spectators are amused at the incident.*

151 f. The description of the race is full of incident, and all four of the competitors play important parts in it, and leave a clear impression of their individuality (see note on 116 f.).

151. **primisque ... undis**: 'and sweeps ahead over the waves right at the beginning'.

153. **pinus**: his ship of pine, cf. *Aen.* 10.206. Notice the alliteration of *p* and *t* here, indicating heaviness.

154. **aequo discrimine**: 'equidistant'.

155 **locum ... priorem**: 'strive to get forward into a leading position', i.e. to be third rather than fourth; for *superare* cf. *Aen.* 2.303.

157–8. **una ... frontibus**: 'together and prow to prow'.

162. **quo ... abis**: 'Hey! Where are you going to, so far off to the right?' The ships are making the turn in an anti-clockwise direction, i.e. to the left, as in a Roman chariot-race.

mihi: ethic dative, underlining the indignation of the speaker. Page drily says ' "Pray" and "Prithee" are accepted renderings, but a naval captain would perhaps put it otherwise'.

cursum: most MSS have *gressum*, for which there is much to be said (cf. Aul. Gell. 10.26), but it may have come in from *Aen.* 1.401 or 11.855 (non-naval contexts).

163. **litus ama**: 'hug the edge of the island', cf. Hor. *Odes* 1.25.3 f.

laeva ... cautes: 'let the oars on the left graze the rocks'; for *stringere* cf. Ov. *Am.* 3.2.12. For the parataxis *stringat sine* cf. line 717 and *Aen.* 2.669. *Palmula* is collective singular, cf. 116.

165. **pelagi . . . ad undas**: i.e. still outwards, instead of turning round the rock for home.

166. **iterum**: with *revocabat*; Servius' suggestion (adopted by Mackail) of taking it with *abis* is possible, but the broken rhythm expresses well the anxiety of Gyas.

Menoete: Greek vocative, cf. 564, 843.

168. **propiora tenentem**: 'holding a course nearer in', i.e. nearer to the turning-point; for the adjective used as a noun cf. 194.

170. **radit . . . interior**: 'grazed his way through (scraped through) inside on the left'; for *radere* cf. Ov. *Am.* 3.15.2 and *Aen.* 3.700, 7.10.

171. **tuta**: i.e. in contrast to the danger he had been in when he took the turn so fine.

172. 'Then indeed the young man blazed with furious indignation in every fibre of his being'; the headstrong Gyas is very vividly drawn, especially in contrast with his safety-first helmsman.

173. **segnem**: 'timid', 'unenterprising'; notice the emphasis given by the word order here: first the object, then a whole line in apposition to the subject before the verbal action is described.

174. **decorisque . . . salutis**: 'both of his own dignity and of his crew's safety'; *socium* is the archaic form of the genitive plural, see note on 1.4.

175. **deturbat**: 'pitches', a vivid and somewhat colloquial word, cf. *Aen.* 6.412 and Plaut. *Merc.* 116 *deturba in viam* ('kick him out').

176. **rector . . . magister**: 'helmsman' and 'pilot'; the words are practically synonymous.

subit: in the sense of *succedit*, cf. *Aen.* 6.812.

178. 'But when at long last Menoetes in his sorry state was returned to the surface from the bottom of the sea. . .'. The picture of Menoetes' helplessness is built up by the epithet *gravis*, the exaggerated *fundo imo*, the adverbs *vix tandem*, and the passive *redditus* (he could do nothing himself, he was disgorged by the sea).

180. **resedit**: 'sank down'.

181–2. Notice the similarity of participial endings, and the intricate word order. Virgil was perhaps thinking here (as he was in 357f.) of *Il.* 23.784, where all the Greeks laugh at Ajax covered in the slime in which he has slipped.

183–226. Mnestheus and Sergestus now have new hope of passing Gyas. Sergestus gets slightly ahead and Mnestheus urges his men to put forward all their efforts to avoid the disgrace of coming in last. Sergestus goes in too near to the turning-point and runs aground, breaking his oars on one side. Mnestheus leaves him behind and soon overtakes Gyas too; then he sets out after Cloanthus.

183f. Virgil now reverts to the two contestants for the third place, Sergestus in the *Centaurus* and Mnestheus in the *Pristis*. Sergestus is half a length ahead and on the inside when Mnestheus calls for a spurt; this causes Sergestus to try to hold him off by taking the turn too close in to the rocks, with disastrous consequences.

184. **Mnestheique**: Greek form of the dative; the *e* is slurred in pronunciation, cf. *Aen.* 1.41.

superare: for the infinitive dependent on a noun see note on 1.704.

185. **capit ante locum**: 'gets the lead', the adverb *ante* goes with the noun, cf. Lucr. 5.1371.

186. **ille**: for this pleonastic use of *ille* in the second of two clauses which have the same subject cf. lines 334 and 457 and see note on 1.3.

He is not a full length ahead; there is no daylight between.

praeeunte: the diphthong in *prae-* is shortened before the following vowel; cf. *Aen.* 7.524.

187. **partim ... premit**: *partim* is a form of the accusative, not the adverb. *Premit* means 'overlaps', 'is close upon', cf. *Aen.* 1.324, 467.

188. **media ... incedens nave**: 'pacing amidships', on the gang-plank.

189f. Mnestheus' speech is like that of Antilochus to his horses in Hom. *Il.* 23.402 f., where he tells them that they cannot defeat Diomedes but must beat Menelaus. Antilochus gets past Menelaus in a narrow place because Menelaus gives way; Virgil varies this by having Mnestheus get past because Sergestus rashly goes in too close.

190. **Hectorei socii**: 'my men, comrades of Hector'; the

adjective is used with the emotional intention of calling for the utmost endeavours.

192 f. These areas of sea through which Aeneas and his followers had come are in reverse chronological order. The storm at the Syrtes sandbank off Carthage is described in 1.102 f., the storm in the Ionian sea in 3.192 f.; Cape Malea (on the southern tip of the Peloponnese) was, like the Syrtes, proverbially dangerous, cf. Prop. 3.19.7–8.

192. **usi**: understand *estis*; the omission of the verb 'to be' in the second person (cf. 687) is not common.

193. **sequacibus**: 'pursuing'; cf. *Aen.* 8.432.

194. **prima**: 'victory'; for the neuter plural of the adjective used as a noun cf. 168, 335, 338.

Mnestheus: he uses his own name with some pathos in the humbling of his pride.

195. **quamquam o!**: the unfinished sentence (aposiopesis) continues the sense of pathos — the wish would have been something like *o si daretur superare* (cf. *Aen.* 11.415).

196. **hoc vincite**: 'win this victory', i.e. do not come in last. First place must go to those to whom Neptune has granted it; but not to come in last, let that be a victory. *Hoc* is cognate accusative.

197. **prohibete nefas**: 'save us from shame'; the exaggeratedly strong word *nefas* expresses Mnestheus' intense feelings.

certamine: 'effort', cf. *Aen.* 11.891.

198. The effort of the rowers as they get into their rhythm is reflected in the movement of this line, with conflict of ictus and accent in the first three feet and coincidence in the last three, each of which consists of a single word. For further discussion see my note ad loc. (Oxford edition).

aerea puppis: 'the bronze-beaked ship', cf. *Aen.* 1.35.

199. **subtrahiturque solum**: 'and the surface of the water slips from under them'; cf. Ov. *Her.* 6.67. *Solum* is not used elsewhere of the sea; it occurs of the sky in Ov. *Met.* 1.73, cf. also *Aen.* 7.111.

201. **ipse . . . casus**: 'mere chance', 'actually it was chance'.

203. **spatioque subit . . . iniquo**: 'and approached the danger area', by taking the turn dangerously close to the rocks.

204. The spondaic line, together with the unusually long word

in the second half of the line, represents rhythmically the sad end of Sergestus' hopes.

205. **murice**: 'jagged edges'. The word means the purple shell-fish with its jagged shell, and is here used of sharp rock.

206. **inlisaque prora pependit**: 'the prow, dashed against the rock, hung out of the water', cf. *Aen.* 10.303.

207. **magno clamore morantur**: 'hold her steady with loud shouts'. *Morantur* is explained by Servius as backing water, and this seems the correct sense; they try to stop the ship by reversing the oar movement, to prevent further damage. Most commentators take the sense of the phrase to be 'clamouring loudly at the delay', but this seems impossible.

208. **trudes**: 'poles', for pushing off (Tac. *Ann.* 3.46).

209. **expediunt**: 'get out', from where they were stored; cf. *Aen.* 1.178.

211. **agmine**: 'sweep', cf. 90; the word conveys the ordered progression of the series of strokes.

212. 'sets out for his shoreward course and speeds in over open water', i.e. rounds the rock and makes for home; *prona* combines its literal meaning of 'sloping downwards' — i.e. 'down'to shore from the high seas (*decurrit*) — and its metaphorical meaning of 'easy'.

213 f. The point of comparison in this remarkably pictorial simile is that Mnestheus' crew make rapid strokes at first and then speed onwards under the impetus gained, just as the dove flaps its wings furiously at the beginning of its flight, and then glides smoothly on through the sky. Cf. the comparison of the Argo with a hawk in Ap. Rh. 2.932 f.

214. **latebroso in pumice**: 'in crannied rock'; there is the same phrase in *Aen.* 12.587.

nidi: 'nestlings', cf. *Geo.* 4.17, *Aen.* 12.475.

215 f. Notice how the rhythm here corresponds with the sense: from *plausumque* to *ingentem* there is spondaic movement and alliteration of *p* and *t*; then the rhythm changes to dactyls, and there is smooth alliteration of *l* and *r*.

217. **radit iter liquidum**: 'skims her airy way'; for *liquidum* cf. 525.

celeris neque: *neque* is postponed, and *celeris* goes with *alas*.

218. **ipsa fuga**: 'speeding along on her own'; *ipsa* suggests that she has now no need of oars. Cf. Cic. *De Orat.* 1.153.

220. **alto**: 'projecting'.

222. 'taking a lesson in rowing with broken oars' (Day Lewis) which well renders the derisive humour.

224. **spoliata magistro**: 'deprived of her helmsman', cf. 176 and *Aen*. 6.353.

225. **superest**: 'is left' to overtake.

227–43. Mnestheus' final spurt to catch Cloanthus would perhaps have succeeded had not Cloanthus prayed to the gods of the sea. His prayers are heard, and he reaches harbour, the winner of the race.

228. **instigant**: 'urge on', cf. *Aen*. 11.730.

229–30. 'The leading crew think it shame not to hold on to the glory that is theirs, and the triumph already won'; *teneant* is semi-oblique (*putant indignum esse ni teneant*). For *pacisci* ('bargain') cf. *Aen*. 12.49.

231. **possunt ... videntur**: 'they can do it, because they think they can'; cf. Livy 2.64.6 *dum se putant vincere, vicere*, and Dryden, *Ann. Mir.* 190 'And seeming to be stronger makes them so'.

232. 'And perhaps Mnestheus' crew, as they came up level, would have gone on to win the prize'; it is commonly thought that this line indicates that the result might have been a dead-heat, but this implies an awkward change of subject to *utrique*. For *fors* used elliptically (=*forsitan*) cf. *Aen*. 2.139, 6.537; cf. Milton, *P.L.* 2.492 'If chance the radiant Sun. . . .'

235 f. Compare Odysseus' prayer to Athena when he was just behind Ajax in the foot-race (Hom. *Il*. 23.768 f.).

237. **voti reus**: 'in discharge of my vow'; the man whose prayer is granted is under an obligation to pay what he has promised; he is a defendant in regard to it, liable for it.

238. **porriciam**: 'cast forth', a technical term in sacrifices (Livy 29.27.5); the MSS have *proiciam*, but Macrobius (*Sat*. 3.2.2) attests this orthography in religious contexts. Cf. 776.

239 f. The description of the deities of the sea, who hear Cloanthus' prayer and give him victory, closes the long and exciting account of the race with a pictorial touch of a most attractive kind, a delightful glimpse of strange pageantry.

240. Virgil is fond of this kind of descriptive line made up of sonorous names; compare 823 f. Phorcus (an old man of the

sea) and Panopea (one of the Nereids) occur again there in the description of Neptune's retinue.

241. This line is closely modelled on Ennius *Ann.* 569 *atque manu magna Romanos inpulit amnis*; cf. Hom. *Il.* 15.694 f. and Ap. Rh. 2.598 f. (where Athena pushes the Argo through the Symplegades).

Portunus: god of harbours, identified with Palaemon (Melicertes), cf. 823 and Ov. *Fast.* 6.547.

244–85. *Aeneas distributes prizes to the crews of the three ships and their captains. When this is completed, Sergestus finally manages to bring home his disabled ship, moving slowly like a maimed snake; he duly receives his fourth prize.*

244. **satus Anchisa**: a fairly frequent phrase for Aeneas (line 424, *Aen.* 6.331). *Satus* in this sense ('begotten from') is mainly poetic.

247–8. As prizes each crew is to have three bullocks of their choice (out of the herd), some wine and a talent of silver.

optare ... ferre: for this use of the epexegetic infinitive after *dare* cf. 262, 307, 538, 572 and note on *Aen.* 1.66.

248. **magnum ... talentum**: i.e. the normal Attic talent (cf. *Aen.* 9.265).

250. **chlamydem**: a cloak of Greek type (cf. *Aen.* 4.137), here embroidered with gold.

250–1. 'round which ran a deep border of Meliboean purple with its double wavy line'. *Meliboeus* (from the town in Thessaly) is used of purple in Lucr. 2.500; for the formation of the adjective see note on 1.686. The river Maeander was proverbial for its twists and turns (Ov. *Met.* 2.246, 8.162); it is used metaphorically in Cicero (*In Pis.* 53).

252 f. Ganymede, the young and handsome son of the Trojan prince Tros was carried off from Mt. Ida by Jupiter's eagle to be cup-bearer to the gods (Hom. *Il.* 20.232 f., Theoc. 15.123 f., Ov. *Met.* 10.155 f., and note on 1.28).

254. **anhelanti similis**: i.e. so life-like that you might forget it was a picture; cf. *Aen.* 8.649 f.

254 f. This is a second picture of Ganymede on the *chlamys*. For descriptions of works of art (ecphrasis) see note on 1.418 f.

255. The eagle is Jupiter's *armiger* because it carries the

thunderbolt, cf. *Aen.* 9.563 f., Hor. *Odes* 4.4.1 f. Pliny (*Nat. Hist.* 2.146) records the belief that eagles are not struck by thunderbolts.

258. **deinde**: for the position of this word see note on 14.

virtute: 'by his prowess'.

259. 'interwoven with burnished chain and triple-meshed in gold', i.e. a coat of mail; cf. *Aen.* 3.467.

260. Demoleos is not otherwise known; for the dative cf. 845.

261. **Simoenta**: Greek accusative, cf. 634, 536. For Simois, one of Troy's rivers, cf. *Aen.* 1.100.

Ilio alto: in this line of Homeric subject-matter Virgil uses a line-ending reminiscent of Greek rhythm, with the final syllable of *Ilio* shortened in hiatus; see note on 3.211.

263. Sagaris and Phegeus were both killed by Turnus (*Aen.* 9.575, 765).

264–5. **indutus ... agebat**: 'but in days gone by Demoleos used to run wearing it, as he went in pursuit of Trojan stragglers'. *Indutus* has a middle sense, see notes on 135 and 2.275.

265. **Troas**: the Greek third declension form of the accusative plural, with short *-as*, cf. *lebetas* in the next line.

267. **cymbia**: small drinking cups, cf. *Aen.* 3.66, 9.263. *Aspera signis* means 'embossed', cf. 536.

269. **tempora**: for the retained accusative see note on 135.

taenis: 'ribbons', attached to their garlands (110). The ablative plural is here contracted (*taeniis*).

270–2. **cum ... agebat**: the imperfect is not common in an inverted *cum* clause. Here it pictorially represents the slowness and difficulty with which Sergestus got restarted: 'they were all parading with their prizes when, look, Sergestus began to bring back his ship'. Compare Cic. *Verr.* 2.2.89 and (slightly different) *Aen.* 3.301 f. Notice how this sentence is built up with descriptive dependent clauses while the main verb and the subject are held up until 272.

270. **revulsus**: 'worked himself off'; the application of this word and of *debilis* in the next line to Sergestus himself rather than his ship has a vivid effect.

273 f. For snake similes and descriptions see note on 84 f. The point of comparison here is the maimed movement, but Virgil develops the picture of the snake beyond the actual point of comparison.

273. **viae ... aggere**: 'on the causeway' rather than 'on the crown of the road'.

274. **obliquum ... transiit**: 'has run over as it came from the side'; cf. Hor. *Odes* 3.27.6 f.

274-5. **gravis ictu ... viator**: an unusual transference for *gravi ictu ... viator*, emphasised by the fifth-foot clash of word accent and ictus.

275. **saxo**: instrumental with *seminecem*, 'half-killed by a rock', rather than local 'half-dead on the road' (Henry, Page).

276 f. 'In vain as it tries to get away does it writhe its body in great curves, part of it defiant, eyes blazing, hissing head raised high; but part is crippled by the wound and holds the snake back as it tries to struggle along in knots and keeps coiling back upon itself'. The use of *dare* is a favourite Virgilian turn of diction, cf. 139, 435. For *arduus* adverbially with the participle cf. 567, 764, 838. Notice the assonance and rhyme in 278–9, and for the general picture cf. *Geo.* 3.420 f., *Aen.* 2.381 f., 475.

279. **nixantem**: frequentative form of *nitentem* ('struggling'), cf. Lucr. 3.1000, 4.506, 6.836. The less well attested variant *nexantem* (a very rare word indeed) would mean 'twining (itself)'.

282 f. This passage recalls Homer's account of how Achilles gave a prize to Eumelus who came in last in the chariot-race because of the accident which befell him (*Il.* 23.534 f.).

284. **datur**: the final syllable is lengthened in arsis; cf. 337, 521, 853, and *Aen.* 1.668.

Minervae: for Minerva as the patron of women's work cf. *Aen.* 7.805, 8.408 f.

285. **genus**: accusative of respect; cf. *Aen.* 8.114 and notes on 97, 4.558.

286–314. *Aeneas now leads the assembled company away from the shore to a grassy plain surrounded by hills, suitable for the remaining contests. He invites competitors for the foot-race, and many Trojans and Sicilians enter for it. He promises gifts for all the runners, and announces the prizes which will be awarded to the first three.*

286 f. The foot-race is modelled on *Il.* 23.740–97, but where Homer has only three competitors (Ajax, Odysseus, and Antilochus), Virgil has seven named and many unnamed runners. The main feature of the race, the fall of Nisus, is taken from *Il.*

23.773 f., where Ajax slips in the dung left by sacrificed animals, and there are other reminiscences, (see notes on 324, 325). For the incidents of the race see note on 315–19.

286. **misso**: equivalent to *dimisso* (cf. 545), meaning that the prize-giving and concluding arrangements of the ship-race have been completed.

288–9. **theatri circus**: 'the circle of a theatre'; the hills surrounding this circular plain make it a natural theatre for the games. *Theatrum* is used here in its widest sense (place for watching), not in the technical sense in which it differs from *amphitheatrum* or *circus*.

289–90. 'To this the hero moved off accompanied by many thousand people, himself in the midst of the concourse, and took his seat on a platform'. *Consessu* is best taken as ablative ('the central figure in the assemblage') rather than dative ('went to the auditorium'), because the idea of motion has already been expressed by *quo*. *Exstructo* is a neuter noun made from the participle; cf. line 6 and the use by Cicero of *suggestum* (from *suggerere*) in the sense of 'platform'.

291–2. The sentence is somewhat loosely constructed — the addition of the word *animos*, stressing the spirit required of intending contestants, means that the antecedent to be supplied for *qui* is *eorum* rather than *eos*, which the run of the sentence had led the reader to expect.

294. For the half-line see note on 1.534. The others in this book are 322, 574, 595, 653, 792, 815.

296. The construction is *Nisus insignis amore pio pueri*. Nisus is portrayed as an older man; he calls Euryalus *puer* in *Aen.* 9.217.

297 f. Diores, son of Priam, was killed by Turnus (*Aen.* 12.509). Salius and Patron, the two Greeks, presumably joined Aeneas when he was at Buthrotum (3.292 f.). Dionysius (1.51) tells us that this was so of the Acarnanian Patron.

300. The Sicilian Helymus was mentioned in 73; Panopes is not elsewhere mentioned. For the epithet *Trinacrii* (from the triangular shape of Sicily) see note on 3.384.

306. **Cnosia**: Cretan, from its chief town Cnossos. The Cretans were famed for archery, cf. *Geo.* 3.345, *Aen.* 4.70, 11.773.

307. **ferre**: 'to take away', see note on 247–8.

308. **unus**: i.e. *idem*, cf. 616.

309. **caput**: retained accusative, see note on 135.

310. **phaleris**: 'trappings'; the word is used of the decorations worn by soldiers (*Aen.* 9.458) or of the trappings which adorned horses' heads (Livy 22.52.5).

habeto: this form of the imperative has a formal and legalistic ring about it, appropriate for a proclamation (cf. 314).

311. **Amazoniam ... Threiciis**: Penthesilea and her Amazons fought for the Trojans (*Aen.* 1.490 f.), and the Thracians too were Trojan allies (*Aen.* 3.13 f.).

312–13. The shoulder-belt (or baldric) which held the quiver was studded with gold (cf. Ov. *Met.* 9.190) and fastened with a buckle (*fibula*); cf. *Aen.* 12.273 f.

315–39. *Nisus gets well ahead in the foot-race, but as he nears the finish he slips in a pool of blood. While lying on the ground he trips up Salius who was second, so that his friend Euryalus comes up from third place to win.*

315–19. 'When he had said this, they took up their positions and as the signal was heard they immediately darted forward over the course, moving away from the starting-point, sweeping forward like a cloud; as soon as they came in sight of the finish Nisus went away in front.' The old punctuation of this passage, with a full stop after *signant*, gave a most abrupt picture of the race and no very clear meaning for *simul ultima signant*. With the punctuation printed, proposed by Sandbach and discussed in full in my note ad loc. (Oxford edition) we have first a picture of the start and the massed runners, and then as they near the finish Nisus goes away in front, opening up a big gap (cf. Homer's chariot-race in *Il.* 23.373 f.). For the conjunction *simul* cf. *Aen.* 3.630 f. For *ultima signant* Sandbach suggested 'began to trample the last stretch' (cf. Ov. *Am.* 2.11.15); I prefer to take *signare* in the sense of *discernere* (cf. *Aen.* 2.422 f.), and to visualise the race as round a turning-point.

317. **nimbo similes**: the picture is not of falling rain (Henry, Page), but of the rapidly moving mass of a storm-cloud coming across the sky; cf. *Aen.* 12.450 f., 7.793 f.

318. **corpora**: 'figures' — the word is used to make us visualise the race.

320. **longo sed**: the postposition of *sed* emphasises *longo*,

already emphatic because it repeats *longe* (318) in the same position of the line.

intervallo: the spondaic ending is very unusual (see note on 2.68), and is due partly to Lucretian precedent (Lucr. 2.295, 4.187), and partly perhaps (as Page suggests) to the desire to emphasise the long distance.

323–6. 'Then just behind him, look, Diores flies along, grazing his very heels now, right up to his shoulder; if there were more of the course left, he would shoot in front and pass him. . .'.

324. **calcemque terit iam calce**: the phrase is strange, not to say anatomically impossible. The idea is based on *Il.* 23.763 f. where Odysseus, just behind, is treading in Ajax's footsteps before the dust had settled; the diction seems to be an extension of the expression *calcem terere* ('to tread on someone's heels') along the lines of phrases involving repetition like *manus manibus, pede pes*.

325. The phrase recalls Hom. *Il.* 23.765, where Ajax feels Odysseus' breath on his neck.

325–6. The present subjunctive used to express a past unfulfilled condition when the narrative is in the historic present occurs several times in Virgil; cf. *Aen.* 2.599 f., 6.292 f., 11.912 f. The effect is 'graphic', i.e. it makes the reader feel that he is present.

326. **ambiguumve relinquat**: 'or leave the issue in doubt', i.e. leave Aeneas with a dilemma, a photo-finish which he could not resolve. I have argued at length in my Oxford edition why I accept the emendation of Bentley and others for the MSS *ambiguumque*; it is much nearer to the Homeric parallels (*Il.* 23.382, 527), and no really satisfactory sense can be got from *ambiguumque*, which most modern editors accept in some sense like 'leave him behind doubtful' or 'outpace his close rival'. Recently McDevitt (*C.Q.* 1967, 313) has suggested 'and leave the result in doubt', i.e. as to whether he had passed the others as well as Helymus; this is more possible than the other renderings, but gives a rather confused picture.

327 f. The unfortunate accident at the end of the race is modelled on Hom. *Il.* 23.774 f., where Ajax slips and falls in the dung left by sacrificial animals. The subsequent disgraceful behaviour of Nisus has no parallel in Homer. It served as a model for Statius (*Th.* 6.914 f.) and Silius (16.517 f.) to go one better

and have the leader held back by his flying locks while someone else shot past to win. Such departures from seemly behaviour were censured by Chrysippus quoted in Cic. *De Off.* 3.42 where he says that just as in a race one must try one's best to win but must not trip up or pull back one's opponent, so in life it is right to want the good things but not to acquire them by foul means.

328. **levi**: 'slippery'.

331-2. **presso ... solo**: 'as he trod on the spot', or possibly 'though he pressed against the ground' (in the hope of regaining his foothold).

332. **titubata**: 'tottering'; the past participle used in an active sense, cf. *iuratus, cretus*, etc.

333. **immundoque ... sacroque**: the use of doubled *-que* ('both ... and'), along with *ipso*, gives a full-scale picture of Nisus' immersion.

336. **iacuit revolutus**: 'went head over heels and there he lay'; the tense of *iacuit* portrays the suddenness of the whole thing.

337. **Euryalus**: the last syllable is lengthened in arsis; see note on 284.

339. **tertia palma**: a delightful use of metonymy: Diores is now 'third prize', cf. 498.

340-61. *An objection is now raised by Salius. Aeneas over-rules it, but he presents Salius with a consolation prize; Nisus too is given a special prize.*

340-61. This passage is inspired by Hom. *Il.* 23.540 f., where first Antilochus and then Menelaus object to the award of the prizes after the chariot-race. Homer's account is much longer, and the indignation and subsequent magnanimity of Antilochus are superbly told. Virgil's brief description gives a lively picture of the chief persons involved in the dispute — Salius filled with excited indignation, Euryalus silent and winning sympathy, Diores vehemently opposing Salius in case he should lose his third prize, Aeneas benevolent and tactful, and finally Nisus urging with a theatrical gesture his own very doubtful claim.

340-1. 'At this Salius with loud objections appealed to the whole audience of the great stadium and to the watching fathers in the front'. *Cavea* and *consessus* are terms used of a Roman theatre or circus, cf. 288 f., *Aen.* 8.636. The phrase *ora prima patrum*

is no doubt inspired by the thought of Roman senators sitting in
the allocated front seats at the theatre or the circus (Livy 1.35.8).
The use of *implet* is colourful and unusual, extended from instances like *Aen.* 2.769, 9.480, so that it approximates here in
meaning to 'constantly assails'.

343. **lacrimaeque decorae**: 'his modest tears' — he does not
make a song and dance, which would be *indecorum*. There is also
a suggestion perhaps that his beauty (344) is enhanced.

344. **gratior et**: again the postposition of the conjunction
emphasises the word which precedes it (cf. 320).

veniens: an unexpected use, 'presenting itself'.

345. **adiuvat**: 'backs him up'.

349. Hirtzel and Mynors punctuate so that *pueri* is genitive,
but *pater Aeneas* is here addressing the runners as *pueri*; his
opening words *vestra . . . vobis* almost demand a vocative.

350. **casus**: 'misfortunes', 'bad luck'. Nisus takes him up
(354) on the more literal meaning ('fall'). By *insontis* Aeneas
means that Salius was not to blame; if he implies that Nisus was,
he could hardly have put it more mildly.

351. **tergum**: 'hide', 'skin', a common meaning, cf. 403.

352. **unguibus aureis**: for the custom of gilding the claws of
a lion-skin cf. *Aen.* 8.552 f.; for the synizesis of *aureis* (scanned as a
spondee) cf. *Aen.* 1.698.

353 f. 'Then Nisus said "If the losers get prizes like that, and
you feel sorry for people who fall, what in all fairness are you
going to award to Nisus? Why, I earned *first* prize. . . ." '

355. **laude**: 'by my merits', a common use of *laus*, cf. *Aen.*
1.461, 9.252.

355–6. The true apodosis of this past unfulfilled condition is
concealed in an ellipse: 'I earned first prize (and would have got
it) if. . .'. Cf. *Aen.* 6.358 f.

356. **tulisset**: 'snatched me away', for *abstulisset*. This use of
the word normally occurs in more important contexts (e.g. *Aen.*
2.555), so that the exaggerated diction conveys the cool audacity
of Nisus in defending his case. He seems to have convinced
Servius, who says 'bene dolum suum excusat'.

359. **Didymaonis artes**: Didymaon is not otherwise known.
This meaning of *ars* ('a work of art') is not common, but cf. Cic.
De Leg. 2.4, Hor. *Odes* 4.8.5; it is here used in the poetic plural.

360. 'taken down by the Greeks from the sacred portal of Neptune'. *Danais* is dative of agent, cf. 305, 610. We are not told how the Trojans came into possession of it — Servius suggests Helenus perhaps gave it to him, cf. *Aen.* 3.463 f. — , but the point is that this exceptionally fine shield, dedicated once to Neptune, was removed from its temple not by the Trojans but by the Greeks.

362-86. *Aeneas now announces a boxing competition. Dares comes forward, but nobody is prepared to fight him. He claims the prize.*

362 f. The boxing competition has a number of reminiscences of the shorter description in Hom. *Il.* 23.653 f., and of Ap. Rh. 2.1 f. (Amycus and Polydeuces). With the Greeks boxing was a highly skilled art practised at the great festivals, but in Roman times the use of the *caestus* had transformed it into a far more dangerous contest requiring mainly brute force and physical courage. Virgil describes the Roman type of boxing, but having little liking for it in real life he has chosen to handle the narrative on a mythological plane, in a setting of the distant days of heroes and demi-gods; the contestants (unlike those in the other events) play no further part in the *Aeneid*, and are not associated with Roman families. They are characters drawn on a large scale and in an exaggerated manner, with the alliteration and assonance of the verse often exaggerated to match (see notes on 431-2, 481).

In its length the boxing contest balances the ship-race, contrasting with the briefer accounts of the foot-race and the archery; but the method of description in the two long events is very different. The ship-race is all excitement, with multiplication of incident involving the four competitors; but in the boxing incident is at a minimum (contrast the boxing-match in Theoc. 22). The interest is concentrated on the *mise-en-scène* and on the two contestants, enormous figures of almost more than mortal strength, figures of a distant world like Lapiths fighting Centaurs, or Titans from a legendary past.

363. 'if anyone has valour and ready courage in his heart', a passage referred to by Seneca, *Ep. Mor.* 92.29.

364. **evinctis ... palmis**: the *caestus*, which Roman boxers wore on their hands, had an altogether different function from

that of the modern boxing glove. It consisted of hard leather thongs, sometimes reinforced with pieces of metal (401–5), and its object was not protection (of one's own knuckles or the other man's face) but to cause greater damage. The soft leather strips used in Homer (*Il.* 23.684) and at the Greek games were intended to protect.

364. **attollat bracchia**: compare our 'put up your fists'.

365. **pugnae**: the original meaning of this word is a fight with fists (*pugnus*).

366. **velatum ... vittisque**: 'crowned with gold and garlands'. The phrase is not a hendiadys, but refers to two separate forms of decoration, garlands and the overlaying of the horns of the bullock with gold (*Aen.* 9.627, cf. Hom. *Od.* 3.432 f.).

368–9. **effert ora**: 'thrust out his jaw', an amusingly picturesque phrase conveying the arrogant defiance of Dares.

369. **magnoque ... murmure**: 'amidst a buzz of excitement from the crowd', notice the strong alliteration of *m* here, with the *v* of *virum* picking up *vastis ... viribus* in the previous line.

370. The origin of the tradition that Paris was an outstanding boxer was generally attributed to the cyclic poets.

Paridem ... contra: the preposition follows its case, cf. 435.

372–3. 'the all-conquering Butes, a man of giant stature, who came to the games and boasted of his descent from the Bebrycian race of Amycus'; this Butes is not mentioned elsewhere. Amycus, savage king of the Bebrycian race, compelled all strangers to box with him for their lives; after many victories he was defeated by Polydeuces (Ap. Rh. 2.1 f., Theoc. 22).

376–7. 'showed his left, then his right, shot each fist out and pounded the air with punches'; cf. *Aen.* 10.892 f., 11.756. Observe how the coincidence of ictus and accent, and of words with feet, in the second half of the line helps to convey the idea of blow following blow.

379. **caestus**: see note on 364.

380. **alacris**: this archaic form of *alacer* occurs again in *Aen.* 6.685.

excedere pugna: 'were withdrawing from (a claim to) the prize', cf. *Aen.* 9.789.

384. **quo ... teneri?**: 'How long must I be kept waiting?

Quousque is separated by tmesis into its component parts; cf. 603.

387–423. *Acestes now urges Entellus, who was trained by Eryx, to oppose Dares. He protests that he is now past the prime of his youth, but none the less accepts the challenge and hurls into the ring a pair of huge gauntlets with which Eryx once fought Hercules. The spectators are all shocked and amazed; Entellus makes a taunting speech, but agrees to fight with matched gauntlets.*

387. **gravis**: 'sternly'; the adjective is used adverbially.

Entellum: known only from this passage; it was a name associated with Sicily, as we see from the city Entella.

388. **proximus ut ... consederat**: 'sitting as he was next to him'. This usage of *ut* links the clause to its main verb in a very general way, sometimes causal, sometimes temporal, sometimes local. Cf. 329, 667 and *Aen.* 7.509.

389. **frustra**: the word conveys that the glories of the past are apparently of no avail now.

391 f. 'Where now, tell us, is the divine Eryx whom you called your teacher — and all for this?' *Nequiquam* has the same sense as *frustra* in 389. Many take *nequiquam memoratus* to mean 'idly famed' (Page, Fairclough) but this is a much rarer use of the word and the rebuke is directed at Entellus not Eryx.

394 f. Entellus' words are strongly reminiscent of those of Nestor in *Il.* 23.626 f.; cf. also *Aen.* 8.560 f.

394. **gloria**: 'desire for glory', a frequent meaning of the word.

395. **sed enim**: 'but in fact', cf. *Aen.* 1.19.

396. 'my blood runs feebly, and the strength of my limbs is worn out and gone'. *Hebet* (literally, 'to be blunt') does not occur elsewhere in this sense before Val. Fl. 1.53 *ardor hebet*, 4.41 *corpus hebet somno*.

397. **fuerat**: this use of the pluperfect instead of the perfect or imperfect seems to have been a colloquialism which came into poetry while remaining rare in prose; cf. *Aen.* 10.613.

improbus: 'braggart'; the word is used of anything beyond normal bounds, see note on 2.79–80.

399 f. 'I wouldn't have needed the lure of a fine young bull to bring me here, and I don't care about prizes'; the negative applies to *pretio inductus*, and the sentence is equivalent to *venissem*

sine pretii inductu. For *moror* cf. *Aen*. 2.287, Hor. *Epist*. 1.15.16 *nam vina nihil moror illius orae*.

403. For this construction with *intendere* ('bind'), rather than the commoner *intendere terga bracchiis*, cf. 829 and *Aen*. 4.506.

404–5. 'so mighty were the seven huge ox-hides stiff with the lead and iron sewn on them'. Notice the elisions and the assonance of *-um* and *-o* in these heavy phrases. Virgil is clearly thinking of Ajax's shield of seven ox-hides, *Il*. 7.220 f.

406. **longeque recusat**: an elliptical and vivid phrase equivalent to *longe refugit recusans certamen*.

407–8. 'turns the heavy enormous folds of the gauntlets over and over'; *et pondus et volumina* is a hendiadys.

409. **senior**: 'the veteran', Entellus.

410. **caestus ... arma**: 'the gauntlets which Hercules himself wore'. *Et* is postponed; its meaning is epexegetic, i.e. *et arma* does not add a new idea, but explains *caestus*.

411. When Hercules was bringing back the cattle of Geryon (cf. *Aen*. 8.202), Eryx met and challenged him. In the resultant fight Eryx was killed.

415. **melior**: i.e. 'hotter', contrast *gelidus* in 395.

415–16. 'and jealous old age had not yet flecked both brows with white'; *aemula* means that old age is his 'rival', cf. *Aen*. 6.173.

418. **sedet**: 'is the decision of', cf. *Aen*. 2.660, 4.15.

probat ... Acestes: 'if my sponsor Acestes agrees' — Acestes is *auctor* because he urged Entellus to fight (387 f.).

419. **tibi**: 'there you are, I forego the thongs of Eryx'; *tibi* is ethic dative, here conveying scorn.

421 f. Virgil here follows Homer *Il*. 23.685 f., and Ap. Rh. 2.67 f.

421. **duplicem**: 'double-folded', a frequent Greek epithet for various forms of dress, here imitated from Ap. Rh. 2.32.

422. **membrorum artus**: 'joints of his limbs'.

lacertosque: for the hypermetric elision see note on *Aen*. 1.332; here the effect is to help to convey enormous size, along with the spondaic movement, the other elisions, and the alliteration of *m*.

423. **exuit**: 'bared', cf. *Aen*. 2.153, 4.518.

424–60. *Aeneas brings out matching pairs of gauntlets, and the fight begins. After preliminary sparring Entellus aims a mighty blow which*

misses and causes him to fall flat on the ground. He is assisted to his feet,
and in fury renews the fight, driving Dares all around the arena.

424. **extulit**: 'brought out', 'produced', cf. *Aen.* 11.73.

426. 'Immediately each took up his stance, poised on his toes';
cf. Ap. Rh. 2.90.

427. **extulit**: 'raised', cf. Ap. Rh. 2.68, Hom. *Il.* 23.686.

428. 'They held their heads high, well back out of range of
blows', i.e. not crouching, but leaning back. Greek and Roman
boxers, unlike ours, adopted a stance to guard the head, not the
head and body.

429. Again Homer and Apollonius are imitated (*Il.* 23.687,
Ap. Rh. 2.78).

pugnamque lacessunt: 'sparring for an opening', cf. *Aen.*
7.165, 11.254.

431. **membris et mole**: hendiadys, = *membrorum mole*.

431–2. Notice the strong alliteration of *t*; all through this
passage the alliteration is deliberately more marked and violent
than is usually Virgil's way; see especially 444–5.

432. **genua**: the *u* is treated as a consonant, cf. *Aen.* 12.905
(the same phrase) and *tenuia* as a dactyl (*Geo.* 1.397, 2.121);
compare the consonantal *i* in 589 (*parietibus*), 663 (*abiete*).

vastos ... artus: 'his laboured breathing shakes his huge
frame'; cf. Ap. Rh. 2.85 and *Aen.* 9.814.

433–4. **multa ... multa**: i.e. many of the punches miss, *but*
many. . . . The words are in antithesis: Heyne and Conington are
surely wrong in thinking that lines 434–6 elaborate 433 (*nequiquam*
then meaning 'without decisive effect'). For *vulnera* (= blows) cf.
Aen. 2.529, 7.533.

437–8. 'Entellus stands his ground, solid, unmoving, not changing his poised stance, just avoiding the blows with body-sway, his
eyes fixed on his opponent'. The word *nisus* well conveys the idea of
tenseness; for *exire* cf. *Aen.* 11.750 and compare *evadere* (689). Notice
the dactyls of 438, conveying the swift swaying of the body.

439. **celsam ... urbem**: probably 'assails a city towering
high with its massive walls' (cf. *Aen.* 9.711) rather than 'assails
a lofty city with siege-works'.

441. **pererrat**: 'explores'; the line occurs in almost the same
form in *Aen.* 11.766, with the same slight zeugma of *pererrare* with
aditus as well as with *locum*.

442. adsultibus: a very rare word found otherwise only once in Tacitus (*Ann.* 2.21) before the fourth century.

443. ostendit dextram: 'showed his right'; the English phrase tends to refer to a feint, but that is not so here. For the whole line cf. Ap. Rh. 2.90 f. The rhythm here imitates the meaning with its spondees, its fifth-foot pause to arouse expectation, its run-on verb to emphasise the action; this is followed by heavy alliteration, first of *v* and then of *c*. Notice too how line 446 has the same rhythmic effect as 443, and 448 echoes the run-on verb of 444.

445. celerique ... cessit: 'side-stepped swiftly, and wasn't there'.

446. ultro: 'with his own impetus'.

447. gravis graviterque: this is reminiscent of Hom. *Il.* 16.776 κεῖτο μέγας μεγαλωστί, 'mighty and mightily fallen'. The redundant *-que* adds to the emphasis of the repetition, cf. *Aen.* 3.329, 12.289.

448–9. For the simile cf. especially Cat. 64.105 f.

448. quondam: 'sometimes', cf. *Aen.* 2.367, 7.378.

448–9. aut Erymantho aut Ida: for the forest of Erymanthus (the chain of mountains in Arcadia where Hercules killed the boar) cf. Ov. *Met.* 2.499. For the forests of Ida (near Troy) cf. *Aen.* 2.696. Virgil uses the doubled geographical location in order to take advantage of the poetic suggestiveness of proper names; cf. 595.

450. studiis: 'with rival cries of support', cf. 148, 228. The ablative used without an adjective in an adverbial sense is typically Virgilian; cf. *Aen.* 12.131 and note on *Aen.* 2.51.

451. caelo: dative of motion towards (= *ad caelum*), a poetic construction here seen in its most striking form; cf. *Aen.* 11.192 (the same phrase) and *Aen.* 2.186.

454. vim suscitat ira: 'grows violent in his anger', cf. *Aen.* 12.108.

455. 'then the thought of his honour fires his strength, and his confidence in his prowess'; cf. *Aen.* 12.666–8.

456. aequore toto: 'all over the arena'; in boxing in the ancient world there was no precisely defined ring as we know it.

457. ille: Servius says 'metri causa additum est', but perhaps it adds a little to the sense ('with left and right alike').

458 f. 'thick as the hail which storm clouds send rattling on roof tops is the shower of blows. . .', cf. *Geo.* 1.449, *Aen.* 9.669 f.

460. **pulsat versatque Dareta**: 'battered Dares and sent him spinning' (Jackson Knight). *Dareta* is a third-declension form of the Greek accusative; contrast *Daren* (456).

461–84. *Aeneas intervenes and stops the fight. Dares is carried away by his friends back to the ships, and Entellus receives the ox as his prize. With a single blow he kills it as a sacrifice to Eryx, and announces his final retirement from boxing.*

463. Like a modern referee Aeneas 'stops the fight', as Achilles stopped the wrestling match in Hom. *Il.* 23.734 f.

466. **viris alias**: 'that this is strength of a different order' (Jackson Knight). The reference is to the increased strength of Entellus (454 f.) which is attributed to divine aid.

468 f. The whole of this passage is closely modelled on Hom. *Il.* 23.695 f. Notice the very slow movement, and the deliberately harsh and excessive alliteration and assonance.

469. **utroque**: 'from side to side', adverb.

471. **vocati**: his friends are summoned by the herald to collect Entellus' second prize because he cannot collect it himself (so in Homer, *Il.* 23.699).

473. **superans animis**: 'overflowing with pride', a phrase from Ennius (*Ann.* 205).

481. Day Lewis renders the movement of the verse thus: 'sprawling, quivering, lifeless, down on the ground the brute fell'. This line is a well-known example of the violent effect caused to the rhythm by ending a line with a single monosyllable, giving conflict of ictus and accent in the last two feet. The effect is intensified by the rare alliteration of *b*, and the postponement of the monosyllabic subject. We have seen that in many places in the account of the boxing match Virgil has permitted himself exaggerated effects of alliteration and assonance; here he concludes his series of pictures by painting with the whole palette.

Some examples of monosyllabic endings of an imitative kind are line 638, *Aen.* 1.105, 6.346, 10.864; others are traditional and archaic (e.g. *Aen.* 1.65).

483. **meliorem animam**: 'more acceptable victim'; Servius explains *meliorem* as less cruel, others see a sarcastic and con-

temptuous reference to Dares. But Entellus simply uses the
formula and leaves his implications ambiguous.

484. **caestus artemque repono**: 'I lay down my gloves and
my skill', cf. Hor. *Epist.* 1.1.4 f., *Odes* 3.26.3 f. Entellus announces
his retirement in the hour of victory; the slow spondees and the
simple words are most effective.

485–518. *Aeneas proclaims an archery contest, the target being a dove
secured to a mast. Hippocoon hits the mast; Mnestheus' arrow cuts the
cord; Eurytion then shoots down the bird as it flies away.*

485 f. The archery contest is modelled, often quite closely, on
Hom. *Il.* 23.850 f. In Homer there are only two competitors:
Teucer cuts the cord with his arrow, and Meriones kills the dove.
Skill with the bow figures largely in the Homeric poems, but
played no part in the great Greek games, nor in Roman *ludi*,
and Virgil's reasons for including archery here are to recall
Homer and especially to lead into the portent of Acestes' arrow
(see note on 519 f.).

486. **ponit**: so the majority of MSS (cf. 292): *P* has *dicit*.

487. **ingentique manu**: 'with his mighty hand', Homer's χειρὶ
παχείῃ; cf. 241, *Aen.* 11.556. Aeneas sets up the mast as Achilles
had done (*Il.* 23.852). Some follow Servius and render 'with a
large band of people', but this is most unnatural in the context.

de nave: i.e. the mast is removed from Serestus' ship and set
up in the ground.

488. **traiecto in fune**: probably *traiectus* refers to the rope
being passed round the mast, rather than round the bird's leg.

490. **sortem**: the singular is used to draw attention to the
method of choice, where the plural would be more usual.

492. **exit locus Hippocoontis**: *locus* means 'the lot giving
him first turn'; for *exire* cf. Hor. *Odes* 2.3.27. Hippocoon is not
otherwise known; presumably he is the brother of Nisus, son of
Hyrtacus (*Aen.* 9.406).

493. **modo . . . victor**: 'recently a prize-winner'; he was
actually second. His olive crown was not mentioned in the
account of the ship-race.

495. Eurytion is not mentioned elsewhere. Pandarus, who
broke the truce at Athena's orders and wounded Menelaus (Hom.
Il. 4.72 f.), was an outstanding archer (*Il.* 2.827, 5.95 f.).

498. **Acestes**: metonymy for *sors Acestae*, like *Mnestheus* (493) and *Eurytion* (495); cf. 339 and *Aen.* 2.201, 312.

503. **volucris ... auras**: 'cut through the winged breezes', cf. *Aen.* 6.294, 11.795.

505. 'terrified fluttered her wings in fright'; the word *timuit* is unusual with *pennis* where *tremuit* would have been normal. Slater conjectured *micuitque* (cf. *Geo.* 4.73), which Mynors accepts.

506. **plausu**: perhaps the noise of the dove's wings (Page), but much more likely the applause of the spectators (Hom. *Il.* 23.869).

507. **adducto**: 'brought to his chest', i.e. with the bowstring drawn back, cf. 141 and *Aen.* 9.632.

508. **alta**: 'the heavens', cf. *Aen.* 6.787, 9.564.

pariterque ... tetendit: 'took aim with eye and arrow together', a slight zeugma.

511. **quis**: an alternative form for *quibus*, cf. *Aen.* 1.95.

innexa pedem: for the retained accusative see note on 135, and cf. *Aen.* 6.281.

512. 'she was away in flight towards the south and the dark clouds'; *P* has *alta* for *atra*, but cf. 516. *Notos* is governed (like *nubila*) by *in*; for similar word order cf. *Aen.* 2.654, 6.416, 692.

514. **tela**: 'his arrow', a poetic plural of a somewhat striking kind, cf. *Aen.* 7.497, 10.731.

in vota: Pandarus had met his death at the hands of Diomedes.

517–18. Cf. *Geo.* 3.547; for this vague meaning of *astra* ('sky') cf. 838.

519–44. *Acestes, left with no target to aim at, shoots his arrow high into the air. It catches fire, and disappears like a shooting star. Aeneas recognises this as a good omen and awards Acestes first prize.*

519f. In this sequel to the last contest of the games Virgil raises the level of significance of the events he has been describing, and emphasises the divine background to the action of the *Aeneid*. During the account of the games the tension of the poem has been relaxed; by concluding the archery with a miraculous portent Virgil restores the high epic tone so as to lead into the patriotic account of the *lusus Troiae* and the eventful narrative which follows.

519. 'Now only Acestes was left, with the prize lost' (i.e. already won by Eurytion). For *superare = superesse* cf. 713.

520. **telum contorsit**: 'sent his arrow whirring', a more vivid phrase than with the reading *contendit* given by some MSS.

521. 'displaying both his veteran skill and his sounding bow'; for *pater* in apposition to the subject cf. 130, 424. Its second syllable is lengthened in arsis; see note on 284.

522-3. 'and destined to be of great portent'.

523-4. 'the great outcome proved it so in later days, when awe-inspiring prophets sang of the late-fulfilled omens'. There has been much debate about what is portended here; the most generally accepted explanation is that we have a reference to the comet of 44 B.C. and the deification of Caesar. But in its context the portent should be directly connected with Acestes; certainly Aeneas thinks so and says so. It seems best therefore to regard the star as portending the future greatness of Acestes, in particular the foundation and fame of his city Segesta (see note on 718), possibly with some forward reference to the part Segesta played in the First Punic War, when it immediately made common cause with Rome. I have discussed the question more fully in my note ad loc. in my Oxford edition.

524. **terrifici**: the word is poetic and rather rare. It does not imply, as some have thought, that the omen is interpreted as a bad one; there is no suggestion of that in anything which follows. It must be taken to refer to the natural feeling of dread and awe associated with supernatural happenings (cf. 529).

525. **liquidis**: 'thin', cf. *Aen.* 6.202, 7.699.

526. **signavitque viam flammis**: 'left the trace of its path in fire', not 'pointed out the way'; cf. *Aen.* 2.697.

527. **refixa**: 'unloosed', cf. Hor. *Epod.* 17.5. The stars are thought of as 'fixed' in the sky (Pliny, *Nat. Hist.* 2.28), so that shooting stars are *refixa*.

528. Compare Lucr. 2.206 f., *Geo.* 1.365 f., *Aen.* 2.693 f. For the rhythm of the line cf. *Aen.* 2.9, 4.81.

530-1. **nec ... omen abnuit**: i.e. Aeneas accepted it as an omen, and acted accordingly, regarding it as favourable. Compare Anchises in *Aen.* 2.699 f., and Tolumnius' words in 12.260.

533 f. 'for the great king of Olympus, by giving auspices such as we have seen, intended that you should be especially distinguished in the winning of honours'. The phrase *exsortem ducere honores* is a most unusual one, including a number of implications.

The basic meaning of *exsors* is 'not drawn for by lot', i.e. especially set aside (cf. *Aen*. 8.552); when applied to persons it normally means 'not sharing in', e.g. *Aen*. 6.428. Virgil combines the two meanings in this line; Acestes was excluded by lot from sharing in the contest, and this is seen to be a mark of distinction.

536. **cratera impressum signis**: 'an embossed bowl', cf. 267. *Cratera* is Greek accusative, cf. 261, 839.

537. **in magno munere**: 'as a great gift'. The unusual use of *in* adds impressiveness, cf. *Aen*. 8.273.

Cisseus: in Virgil's version (cf. *Aen*. 7.320, 10.705) this Thracian king was father of Hecuba.

538. **sui**: objective genitive of *se* depending on *monimentum*, rather than genitive of *suus* agreeing with *amoris*. This line is almost exactly repeated at 572.

541. **praelato invidit honori**: 'grudge him his preferred position'; *praelato* agrees with *honori* — it is unnatural to regard it as a second dative (of the person) after *invidit*. *Invidere* often takes an accusative of the thing grudged (*Aen*. 8.509), but the dative is not uncommon, e.g. Cic. *De Leg. Agr*. 2.103 *qui honori inviderunt meo*.

542. **quamvis ... deiecit**: the indicative with *quamvis* (by analogy with *quamquam*) is quite common in verse, though Virgil has it only here and in *Ecl*. 3.84.

543. **donis**: ablative of respect with *proximus* (= *ordine donorum*) rather than, as Servius says, dative equivalent to *ad dona*.

545–603. *The final event is an equestrian display by the Trojan boys. They process in three companies, young Priam leading one, Atys another, and Iulus the third, and they give a brilliant display of intricate manoeuvres and mock battle. This is the ceremony which Iulus introduced to Alba Longa, and it was handed on to Rome and called the lusus Troiae.*

545 f. The *lusus Troiae* brings the games to an end with the rounding-off effect of a closing ceremony, and at the same time links the events of the remote past with Virgil's own days. We hear of these equestrian manoeuvres in the time of Sulla; they were revived by Julius Caesar, and established under Augustus as a regular institution, performed by boys of noble birth (Suet. *Aug*. 43).

It seems most unlikely that the *lusus Troiae* was originally connected with Troy. The achaire verbs *amptruare, redamptruare* suggest a noun *troia* meaning 'movement', 'dancing', and the Etruscan word *Truia* found on a vase depicting horsemen and a labyrinth points in the same direction. When the legend of Rome's Trojan origins became widespread, the *lusus Troiae* could easily be associated with Troy.

The whole description of the ceremony is written with a verve which clearly reflects Virgil's enjoyment of such visual pageantry; and it is painted in the bright and joyful colours appropriate to the hopes that were placed in the promise and achievement of the younger generation, whether of Aeneas' day or Virgil's own.

545. **nondum certamine misso**: 'before the archery contest was duly concluded' (see note on 286). Servius finds difficulty with the tenses because the archery was already concluded, but the reference probably is to some final announcement or ceremony.

547. **Epytiden**: Periphas, son of Epytus, occurs in Hom. *Il.* 17.324.

548–9. **puerile . . . agmen**: Latin uses the adjective where we would say 'column of boys'.

550–1. **ducat avo turmas**: 'tell (Ascanius) to bring on the procession in his grandfather's honour'; *ducat* is jussive subjunctive in parataxis with *dic*, of *Aen.* 4.635 and line 163. For the dative *avo* cf. 603.

554–5. **quos . . . mirata fremit**: 'murmurs its admiration for them'; the accusative is after *mirata*, not as Servius says after *fremit*.

556. 'Each has his hair bound in ceremonial style with a trimmed garland'. Later (673) Ascanius takes off his helmet, so we must assume that at some stage these garlands were taken off and helmets put on. *Tonsa* is generally taken to mean that the leaves were clipped to a uniform length; it is possible however that the meaning is simply a garland of 'cut' leaves.

557. **praefixa**: 'tipped', as in *Aen.* 10.479, 12.489.

558. **levis**: 'polished', 'burnished', as in 91.

558 f. 'High on their chests and passing round their necks are pliant circlets of twisted gold'. The MSS vary (as often) between *it* and *et*, but the latter would give an intolerable construction here.

560 f. There are thirty-six boys plus three leaders (thirteen to each group). For *terni* as a variation on *tres* cf. 85. Each group is in two files of six, and each is accompanied by its trainer.

560. **vagantur**: 'weave their way', a colourful word for the wheeling movements of the ride-past.

562. **agmine partito**: 'in divided column', i.e. double file (*bis seni*).

paribusque magistris: 'each alike with its trainer'. *Paribus* suggests that the groups have their trainers stationed in corresponding positions (presumably at the side). Some argue that *magistri* are the same as *ductores*, but cf. 669.

563 f. This sentence and the next are somewhat loosely constructed: *una acies iuvenum* (*est*) *ducit quam* . . . is equivalent to *primam aciem iuvenum ducit*; *alter Atys* is very condensed for *alter ductor est Atys*, i.e. *secundam aciem ducit Atys*. Other marks of incompleteness are the repetition of 572 from 538 and the unfinished line 574.

564. The death of Polites, son of Priam, is told in *Aen.* 2.526 f. It was a common custom to name children after their grandfathers (cf. *Aen.* 12.348). For the Greek form of the vocative cf. 166.

565–70. This passage contains a number of different types of repetition: there is the threefold repetition of *albus*, a favourite turn of Virgilian diction; the repetition of the names Atys and (rather differently) Iulus; and the type common in Greek *pueroque puer* (cf. *Aen.* 1.684, 3.329).

566. **bicolor**: here 'dappled', cf. *Aen.* 8.276.

566–7. 'showing white pasterns and a white forehead held high'. *Vestigia* occurs in poetry with the meaning 'foot', cf. Cat. 64.162; here *vestigia pedis* is equivalent to *pedes*, cf. *Aen.* 7.689 f. *Primus pes* refers to the front of the foot, not to the forefoot; cf. Cat. 2.3, Prop. 2.26.11.

568. Compare the association of the sea-captains with Roman families (lines 116–23). Augustus' mother was a member of the *gens Atia*; hence there is special point in the friendship of these two boys, founders of the *gens Iulia* and the *gens Atia*.

570. Notice how the spondees slow the movement to give emphasis and dignity.

571. **candida**: the word is nearly synonymous with *pulchra*, with the additional idea of radiance, cf. *Aen.* 8.138, 608.

572. This line is an almost exact repetition of 538; see note on 563 f. We hear of gifts from Dido also on two later occasions, at points in the story where the tension is high, 9.266, 11.72 f.

575. **pavidos**: 'nervous', cf. 138.

577-8. 'After they had joyfully ridden round in front of the whole throng before the gaze of their families. . .'. For the zeugma cf. 340-1; for *lustrare* ('traverse') cf. 611.

578-9. The signal was evidently given first with a shout, and then with the crack of a whip, like the spoken words 'On your marks, get set' before the starter's gun is fired.

580 f. The boys are riding in a long double column down the centre, and at the word of command the right hand rider of each pair wheeled right and the left hand rider wheeled left (*discurrere pares*). The following two phrases explai. the same movement: each of the groups breaks up its column. formation (*agmina terni solvere*) as the files turn away from each other (*diductis choris*). Then at another word of command (*vocati*), they wheel about to face each other and charge. The *ductores* presumably remain in the centre of the field so that at the end of the charge the columns could be reformed as before.

583 f. 'Then they enter upon other movements and counter-movements, keeping corresponding positions, and they weave their circling patterns in and out, and wage phantom battles in their panoply'. In the previous sentence Virgil's account of the first manoeuvre was detailed and precise; now he describes the subsequent movements of the pageant in much more general terms, in order to convey the mood and colour of kaleidoscopic pattern. *Adversi spatiis* suggests that one half of the arena was a mirrored reflexion of the other. *Alternosque orbibus orbis impediunt* looks forward to the Labyrinth simile; cf. also *Aen.* 12.743.

585. **pugnaeque cient simulacra**: cf. Lucr. 2.41 (=324), and line 674.

588 f. Virgil uses two similes to illustrate his description of the *lusus Troiae*; the Labyrinth expresses the idea of complicated figures, and the dolphins convey the picture of swift and joyful movement.

588-91. 'It was like the Labyrinth in lofty Crete long ago, of which the story tells that it had a weaving path between blind walls and a bewildering riddle of a thousand ways, where the insoluble and irretraceable maze would break the tokens of the trail'. The Labyrinth at Cnossos was said to have been built by Daedalus for King Minos; the Athenians had to pay human sacrifice to the Minotaur which lived in the Labyrinth until Theseus killed it and returned out of the maze by means of the thread which Ariadne gave him. The story is told in Cat. 64 and in Ov. *Met.* 8.152 f. Scenes from it are portrayed on the doors of Apollo's temple in *Aen.* 6.20 f. The pattern of the Labyrinth is strongly associated with dancing movements (Hom. *Il.* 18.590 f., Plut. *Thes.* 21).

589. **ancipitemque**: the polysyllabic ending, relatively rare in Virgil, rhythmically conveys a strangeness appropriate to the description of the maze.

590–1. **qua ... frangeret**: 'so that ... in it'. *Qua* is local, and the subjunctive *frangeret* final. The reading *falleret* in *M* probably originates from a gloss to explain the very difficult meaning.

591. This line is very closely modelled on Cat. 64.114–15 *ne labyrintheis e flexibus egredientem / tecti frustraretur inobservabilis error.* Both Virgil's adjectives, which are not found earlier, are elaborations of Catullus' *inobservabilis*; and the unusual rhythm of the line is very similar, with its total absence of strong caesurae and consequent total coincidence of ictus and accent (cf. 856). This conveys a strange feeling of monotony and sameness, and the long words help to convey an unforgettable impression of being lost in an interminable maze.

592–3. **vestigia ... impediunt**: 'weave a pattern of galloping movement', cf. 585 and Lucr. 1.240.

594. **delphinum similes**: *similis* with the genitive occurs only here in Virgil, no doubt to avoid the dative plural of the Greek form *delphis* (which Virgil always uses in preference to *delphinus*). For the simile cf. Ap. Rh. 4.933 f., and compare *Aen.*8.67 3 f., Ov. *Met.* 3.683 f.

595. **Carpathium Libycumque secant**: the Carpathian sea is around the island Carpathos, between Crete and Rhodes. For the geographical location in a simile cf. 448–9.

luduntque per undas: though these words are quite unobjectionable in themselves, they are omitted in two of the primary MSS and must be regarded as an interpolated completion of an unfinished line.

596. 'the tradition of this equestrian display and these mock battles'. Cf. *Aen.* 3.408. For the *lusus Troiae* at Rome see note on 545 f.

597. Ascanius founded Alba Longa from Lavinium after the death of Aeneas, cf. *Aen.* 1.271.

598. **rettulit**: 'revived'.

600. **porro**: 'afterwards', 'in succession', a rather archaic use of the word, cf. the somewhat similar use in *Aen.* 6.711.

601. **honorem**: 'celebration', i.e. here 'tradition', cf. 58, 94.

602. **Troiaque nunc pueri**: 'the boys are now called Troy', rather an awkward phrase meaning that the performance is called Troy (we find the phrase *Troiam ludere* several times in Suetonius).

603. **hac ... tenus**: 'thus far', i.e. this was the conclusion of the games. For the tmesis of *hactenus* cf. *Aen.* 6.62 and compare line 384.

604–63. *While the games are being celebrated, Juno sends Iris down from heaven in order to incite the Trojan women to burn their ships. They are gathered on the shore weeping over Anchises' death and their endless wanderings; Iris takes on the appearance of Beroe and urges them to set fire to the ships so that they cannot wander any more. Pyrgo tells them that this is not Beroe, but a goddess; Iris reveals her divinity and driven on now by frenzy they set the ships ablaze.*

604 f. The episode of the burning of the ships figured early in the legend, but was generally localised in Italy. By placing it in Sicily Virgil stresses the association of Sicily with the early destiny of Rome (the foundation of Segesta now becoming the direct result of the loss of part of the fleet); and he also shows us Aeneas' fortunes and personal courage at their lowest ebb (687 f., 700 f.) at a time very shortly before the divine revelations of Book 6 give him the final certainty and strength to carry out his mission.

604. 'At this point for the first time Fortune changed and altered her allegiance'. *Primum* presumably means for the first time in Sicily; Fortune had been favourable at the landing and at the games.

606. This line occurs again in *Aen.* 9.2; cf. also 4.694 f., and note on 4.700–2. The entry here of Juno into the narrative makes explicit the general statement in 604 about the change of fortune, and in a moment alters the gay colours with which the games had ended into the sombre hues of forthcoming disaster for the Trojans.

607. **ventosque aspirat eunti**: 'breathes favouring winds upon her as she goes', cf. *Aen.* 4.223.

608. **movens**: 'plotting', cf. *Aen.* 3.34, 10.890.

necdum ... dolorem: cf. *Aen.* 1.25 f. and Hor. *Odes* 3.3.30 f. for Juno's long-standing anger against the Trojans. *Saturata* is used in a middle sense, see note on 135.

609. For Iris journeying to earth on the rainbow cf. Ov. *Met.* 11.589 f., 14.838.

per mille coloribus arcum: the preposition is separated from its noun by the ablative of description acting as a compound adjective (= *multicolor*).

611. **litora lustrat**: 'passes along the shore', cf. 578.

613 f. The women have not been present at the games; they did not attend *ludi funebres* in Rome, and Suetonius (*Aug.* 44) relates that Augustus excluded women from watching athletic competitions.

613–15. The movement of these lines is very slow indeed with their heavy spondees and clash of ictus and accent; the very striking repetition of *flebant ... flentes* in the same position in the line adds greatly to the effect.

613. **Troades**: notice the Greek scansion of the final short syllable; cf. *Aen.* 1.468.

acta: 'sea-shore', a transliteration of the Greek word which is not common in Latin.

615–16. The construction is accusative and infinitive of exclamation; cf. *Aen.* 1.97 f.

620. **fit Beroe**: Iris chooses the form of Beroe because the latter was away ill (650 f.), and because she was a woman of standing with the Trojans. Beroe is not otherwise known; a Doryclus, son of Priam, is mentioned in *Il.* 11.489, but it is difficult to see how he would be associated with Tmarus, a mountain in Epirus.

621. 'who had been of noble birth and in days gone by had had sons and a famous name'; i.e. when Troy still stood. *Fuissent* is subjunctive because it expresses the thought in Iris' mind, the reason why she chose the form of Beroe.

622. **Dardanidum**: archaic form of *Dardanidarum*, cf. *Aeneadum* (1.565 etc.).

625. **te**: the use of the singular (rather than *vos*) emphasises the collective fortune of the *gens Troiana*.

626. **septima ... aestas**: there is here an inconsistency with *Aen.* 1.755–6 where Dido used the same phrase; since then a

winter has intervened. Probably in revision Virgil would have altered one place or the other.

vertitur: 'is passing', rather than 'is waning'.

627 f. **cum ... ferimur**: 'while all the time we have been driven ...', an unusual construction (more often introduced by *cum interea*); cf. *Aen.* 3.645 f., 10.665.

627–8. All four nouns are the object of *emensae* ('travelling through'). Servius interprets *sidera* as storms or climes; perhaps the second is better.

629. **Italiam ... fugientem**: 'an ever-receding Italy', cf. *Aen.* 3.496, 6.61.

630. **Erycis ... fraterni**: see note on 24.

631. **muros iacere**: 'found our city-walls'. The verb *iacere* is common with words like *fundamenta*, but not normal with *muros*; cf. however Prop. 2.34.64.

civibus: i.e. we shall then be citizens, not roaming exiles.

632. **rapti ... penates**: cf. *Aen.* 1.378, 2.293, 717, 3.148 f.

633. **Troiae**: predicative; 'shall no walls ever again be called walls of Troy'?

634. **Hectoreos**: the adjective has an emotional effect, see on 190: Jackson Knight renders it 'to remind me of Hector'. For the use of the old names in the new city cf. 756 and especially *Aen.* 3.349 f.; for these rivers of Troy cf. 261, 803.

636. **Cassandrae**: the fate of Cassandra, who was gifted with prophecy but never believed, is told in *Aen.* 2.403 f.

638. **agi res**: the monosyllabic ending gives a most abrupt and emphatic ending; see on 481. Notice too the staccato short sentences, three in succession without a verb expressed.

639. **nec ... prodigiis**: understand *esto*; *tantis ... prodigiis* is ablative of attendant circumstances, 'in the face of. . . .'.

640. **animumque**: 'will', 'intent'; for the idea cf. *Aen.* 1.150.

641. **infensum**: 'deadly', 'destructive', cf. *Geo.* 4.330., *Aen.* 9.793.

642 f. 'and from where she stood, raising her right hand high, with all her might she brandished it and threw'. The emphasis on *iacit* is compelling because of the heavy pause after a first foot in which word accent conflicts with ictus; cf. *Aen.* 10.336, 12.730.

646. **vobis**: 'I tell you', ethic dative, cf. 162.

Rhoeteia: an epithet meaning Trojan, from the promontory Rhoeteum near Troy, cf. *Aen.* 3.108.

648 f. **qui ... eunti**: these are indirect questions after *notate*. *Spiritus* is 'proud bearing', cf. Cic. *De Leg. Agr.* 2.93 *regio spiritu*.

651 f. **aegram ... munere**: 'sick and fretting because she was the only one not present at so important a ceremony'. The subjunctive represents the thought in Beroe's mind. *Tali ... munere* refers to the funeral ceremonies and the lamentations of the women (613 f.).

654 f. 'But the matrons at first were uncertain, and gazed with angry eyes on the ships as they wavered between their wretched love for the land they had reached and the kingdoms which called them with the voice of fate'. *Spectare* is historic infinitive, cf. 685 f. The word *miserum* indicates the sadness of their folly. For the causal ablative *fatis* cf. *Aen.* 10.109.

657–8. Cf. *Aen.* 9.14–15, almost identical lines about Iris, and see note on 4.700–2. Mercury (4.276 f.) and Apollo (9.656 f.) take their departure from the mortal scene by sudden disappearance, but Iris has her own path along the rainbow (see note on 609).

657. **paribus ... alis**: 'on balanced wings', cf. *Aen.* 4.252.

658. **secuit ... arcum**: 'cut a rainbow', i.e. made a rainbow by cutting through the air (cf. *Geo.* 1.406, *Aen.* 6.899).

660 f. The meaning is that some snatch fire from the hearths (of the Trojan encampment, cf. 668–9), while others despoil the four altars to Neptune (639–40).

661. **frondem**: common in the singular meaning 'foliage'.

662. **furit**: note the emphasis on the verb as it begins the sentence with strong conflict of ictus and accent; it picks up *furore* (659), and emphasises that the Trojan women (like Dido and Turnus) are victims of this madness which afflicts those who oppose the divine plan.

immissis ... habenis: literally 'with the reins let loose', i.e. in full career, with unbridled frenzy, cf. Lucr. 5.787, *Aen.* 6.1.

663. **transtra per**: for *per* following its noun cf. *Geo.* 3.276, *Aen.* 4.671. This usage is generally confined to cases like this one where other nouns governed by *per* follow it.

663. **pictas abiete puppis**: 'painted ships of pine'. *Abiete* is ablative of description dependent on the noun *puppis*, an

extended use of the ablative of which Virgil is fond, cf. 77–8, 609. For its scansion (as a dactyl) cf. 432.

664–99. *The news reaches the Trojans. Ascanius immediately rides off and brings the women to a realization of their crime. But the Trojans cannot put out the flames, and Aeneas prays to Jupiter either to send help or to bring final destruction upon them. Jupiter hears his prayer; the flames are quenched by a thunderstorm, and all the ships saved except four.*

664. **cuneosque theatri**: these are the tiers, the wedge-shaped blocks of seats in a Roman theatre or circus; the phrase is here applied to the natural 'theatre' used for the games.

666. **respiciunt ... volitare favillam**: 'look back and see ash eddying up'; the accusative and infinitive is used as if after *vident*.

667 f. 'And first of them all Ascanius, just as he was as he gaily led his galloping troop, straight away set off in hot haste towards the confusion in the camp'. For *ut* cf. 388; the total effect is that of the phrase *sicut erat*.

669. **castra**: the encampment by the ships, cf. 660.

exanimes: 'breathless', cf. *Aen.* 4.672.

670 f. Notice the excited and staccato rhythm of the speech, where the mid-line pauses contribute greatly to the effect.

670. **novus**: 'strange', beyond belief; cf. *Aen.* 3.591.

673. **inanem**: 'empty', conveying the clang of the helmet (Ov. *Fast.* 4.209), rather than 'sham' or 'useless'.

674. **qua ... indutus**: 'clad in which', cf. *Aen.* 10.775 and contrast the other construction of *induere* (e.g. *exuvias indutus, Aen.* 2.275). For the rest of the line cf. 585.

677. **sicubi**: 'any they could find', literally 'if there were any anywhere' (*si, alicubi*).

678. **piget ... lucisque**: 'they are ashamed of their deed and of the light of day', i.e. they want to hide in the darkness because of their shame.

681. **posuere**: equivalent to *deposuere*, cf. 286.

681–2. **vivit ... fumum**: 'the caulking was still alive, belching out a slow smoke'; the pictorial effect is enhanced by the comparatively unusual juxtaposition of noun and adjective with like endings, cf. 845.

683. **est**: 'eats at', 'devours', cf. *Aen.* 4.66 and line 752.

pestis: i.e. the deadly fire, cf. *Aen.* 9.540.

685. **pius**: here the adjective has special reference to Aeneas' responsibility for his men and his mission, and particular force as Aeneas appeals to the *pietas* of Jupiter.

abscindere: historic infinitive, cf. 655.

687. For the form of the prayer cf. *Aen.* 2.689 f. Aeneas' brief phrases are direct and urgent: this latest disaster, so soon after the short period of relaxation from toil, leaves him broken and weary in heart.

exosus: active, cf. *Aen.* 11.436, 12.517, 818. For the omission of *es* cf. 192.

688. **pietas antiqua**: 'your loving-kindness of old', cf. *Aen.* 2.536 f., 4.382.

689. **da ... classi**: 'grant that the fleet may escape the flames'; for *evadere* cf. *Aen.* 3.282.

691 f. 'If not, then do in your own person what is left to do — cast me down to destruction with your death-dealing thunderbolt if so I deserve, and overwhelm me here with your right hand'. I follow Servius in taking *quod superest* adverbially, with *me* or *nos* supplied as the object of the sentence. For the thought cf. *Aen.* 12.643 *id rebus defuit unum*. There is another, perhaps less likely, interpretation according to which *quod superest* is the object. equivalent to *reliquias Troiae*, 'the remnants of Troy'. Cf. 796.

694 f. Notice the imitative alliteration of *t* and *r*, and later of *s*; compare the description of the storm in *Geo.* 1.322 f.

694. **sine more**: 'in wild fury', literally 'without restraint', cf. *Aen.* 7.377, 8.635.

695. **ardua terrarum**: 'the high places of the land'; for Virgil's fondness for the neuter of the adjective followed by a partitive genitive see note on 1.422, and cf. especially *Aen.* 8.221.

696. 'a downpour violent with torrential rain and deepest black on the misty south winds'; cf. *Geo.* 3.196, 278.

697. **super**: 'on top' (i.e. the decks were awash) rather than from above' or 'to overflowing'.

700–45. *Aeneas in despair wonders whether to abandon his fated mission altogether. Nautes advises him to leave behind some of his company in Sicily, and take the rest onwards to Italy. As Aeneas is pondering this advice there appears to him in the night a vision of his father Anchises, who tells him to accept Nautes' advice; but before establishing his city in Italy he is to visit the underworld to meet his father and hear his destiny.*

700 f. In this passage we see very clearly the tension between Aeneas' duty towards his divine mission and the human weaknesses of character with which he has to struggle. He is aware that he is the chosen instrument of the will of the gods, but sometimes it seems that the task is almost too great for the frailty of a mortal man to achieve. At this stage in the poem his strength to continue is at its lowest ebb; and it is at this point that the vision of his father promises the inspiring revelations of Roman destiny which are given to Aeneas in the underworld (6.756 f.). Thereafter Aeneas' strength and determination to fulfil his mission are no longer in doubt.

702–3. For *-ne . . . -ne* in an indirect question (here an indirect deliberative question) cf. 95. The jingling similarity of rhythm in the second halves of these two lines perhaps reproduces the insistent dinning of the problem in Aeneas' thoughts.

703. **oblitus fatorum**: see note on 700 f.

704–5. 'whom above all Tritonian Pallas had taught, whom she had made renowned for great knowledge of her lore'. Varro tells us that the Nautii were priests of Pallas because Nautes was supposed to have bought back the Palladium (*Aen.* 2.166) to Italy. For *Tritonia* as Pallas' epithet see note on *Aen.* 2.171.

706–7. 'She it was who gave him replies about what the great anger of the gods was portending or what the march of the fates demanded'. These two lines are parenthetical and the subject of the main sentence (Nautes) is picked up by *isque* as if it were a new sentence (cf. *Aen.* 6.684, 9.549). *Haec* is Pallas; *quae* does not go with *responsa* but introduces the indirect question.

709 f. Notice the slow oracular style of Nautes' speech. There is a marked absence of mid-line pauses; the first four lines are all end-stopped and self-contained sentences which give a noticeable hortatory effect. Nautes' lack of emotion or excitement throws into clearer relief the anxiety of Aeneas, on whom rests the ultimate responsibility. The first two lines are *sententiae* expressing Stoic ideas; notice the contrast between *fata* (destiny which we all must follow) and *fortuna* (a set of circumstances which we may fight against, and overcome by endurance).

713. The word order is *huic trade (eos) qui amissis navibus superant*; *superant* means 'are left over', cf. 519.

716. **quidquid**: for the use of the neuter applied to people cf. *Aen.* 1.601, Hor. *Epod.* 5.1.

717. The word order again is complicated; the normal order would be *sine (ut) fessi moenia his terris habeant.* For the jussive subjunctive in parataxis with the imperative *sine* cf. 163.

718. **permisso nomine**: 'if the name be allowed', by Acestes, or by Aeneas.

Acestam: the town was called Egesta by the Greeks, Segesta by the Romans; for etymological associations of this kind see note on 117 f. For the association of Trojans with Sicily cf. Thuc. 6.2.3, Cic. *Verr.* 2.4.72.

720. 'then indeed is he racked in mind with every kind of torment'; far from being comforted by Nautes Aeneas is made even more anxious, but at this point when his responsibilities press so heavily he receives through Anchises Jupiter's assurance (726 f.).

721. **bigis**: Night (like Phoebus, line 739) drives across the sky in her chariot, and the stars follow in her train; cf. Enn. *Scen.* 112–13 (*sacra Nox*) *quae cava caeli | signitenentibus conficis bigis,* Tib. 2.1.87 f., and Milton, *Comus* 553–4 'The drowsy frighted steeds | That draw the litter of close-curtain'd sleep'.

722. **facies**: the actual shade of Anchises is in Elysium (735). This is an apparition or vision sent by Jupiter; see note on 2.268 f. (the apparition of Hector).

725. **Iliacis exercite fatis**: 'hard-pressed by Trojan destiny'; the same phrase occurs in *Aen.* 3.182. Its Stoic ring chimes in with Nautes' opening words (709–10).

728. **pulcherrima**: the placing of the adjective belonging to the antecedent (*consiliis*) in the relative clause is a common Latin usage, cf. *Aen.* 3.546.

729. **fortissima corda**: 'bravest hearts', cf. *Aen.* 2.348–9.

730. **aspera cultu**: 'rough in its way of life', cf. *Aen.* 1.263 f., 9.603 f.

731. **Ditis**: Virgil generally calls the king of the underworld Dis, but never uses the nominative; the sole occurrence of the name Pluton is where the nominative is needed (*Aen.* 7.327). The rhythm of the line ending here is most striking; cf. *Geo.* 2.153 and my note on this passage (Oxford edition).

732. **Averna**: sometimes the lake with its fabled entrance to the underworld (*Aen.* 3.442), sometimes the underworld itself (*Aen.* 7.91); here probably the latter. Virgil sometimes uses the neuter plural form, sometimes the masculine *Avernus* (813); cf. *Tartara* (734) and *Tartarus* (*Aen.* 6.577).

733. **congressus ... meos**: 'seek a meeting with me'. The word is common in prose but very rare indeed in poetry, except in its military meaning; Virgil has probably used the poetic plural here to avoid prosiness.

namque: the connexion of thought is that Aeneas would not be permitted to visit Tartarus (*Aen.* 6.563). The postposition of the colourless word to the end of the line is unusual.

734. **tristes umbrae**: in apposition to *Tartara*, *umbrae* being used in its local sense ('grim region of darkness').

734-5. Tartarus and Elysium are described in *Aen.* 6.548 f., 637 f.

735. **colo. huc**: there is hiatus between these two words, cf. *Aen.* 1.16.

Sibylla: the priestess of Apollo, cf. *Aen.* 3.441 f., 6.10 f.

736. **multo ... sanguine**: 'when you have paid rich sacrifice', ablative of price. The sacrifices are described in *Aen.* 6.243 f.

737. This promise is fulfilled when Anchises describes the pageant of Roman heroes waiting to be born, *Aen.* 6.756 f.

738. 'dewy Night is sweeping round past the mid-point of her course', i.e. her chariot has passed the mid-point of her orbit through the sky, cf. 721, 835.

739. **saevus**: because the dawn banishes ghosts. Cf. the Ghost in *Hamlet* (1.5.58 f.). 'But soft! Methinks I scent the morning air; / Brief let me be'. Compare *Geo.* 1.250.

741. Compare Hom. *Od.* 11.210, where Odysseus begs the phantom of his mother to stay. Notice the broken urgency of this line and the next, accentuated by the omission of the reflexive with *proripis* and the large number of short words.

deinde: apparently equivalent to *posthac*, in the context implying 'so soon'; cf. 9.781 (=*posthac*).

743 f. Sacrifices are made after supernatural appearances at *Aen.* 3.176 f., 8.542 f. Notice how the agitated excitement of Aeneas is calmed by the ritual performance of these religious ceremonies, described in the appropriate sonorous and formulary diction.

744. Vesta, goddess of the hearth, was closely associated with the Lar (more often plural, Lares) and Penates; cf. *Aen.* 8.542 f., 9.258 f.

745. **farre pio**: this is the *mola salsa* used in sacrifices, cf. *Aen.* 2.133, 4.517. For *pius* cf. also *Aen.* 4.637 *pia tege tempora vitta*; in these contexts it means 'required by religion'.

plena ... acerra: cf. Hor. *Odes* 3.8.2 f. *acerra turis | plena*.

746–78. *Aeneas follows out the new plan, and a city is founded under Acestes' rule for those staying behind; a temple is dedicated to Venus at Eryx, and Anchises' tomb has a priest and a sanctuary appointed for it. After nine days of celebration in honour of the new city the Trojans say their farewells to those staying behind; sacrifices are made, and they sail for Italy.*

746. **accersit**: alternative spelling for *arcessit*.

748. 'the plan which now was firmly settled in his mind', cf. Cic. *Ad Att.* 8.11.1 *constitit consilium*, and *Aen.* 2.750 (*stat*).

750. **transcribunt**: 'enrol', a technical term (according to Servius) like the much commoner *adscribere*.

752. **ambesa**: literally 'eaten round', (*Aen.* 3.257) hence here 'charred'.

753. **rudentisque**: for the hypermetric *-que* cf. 422.

754. **sed ... virtus**: 'but their valour in war never sleeps'; cf. Lucr. 1.72 (of Epicurus) *ergo vivida vis animi pervicit, Aen.* 11.386.

756–7. **hoc ... iubet**: 'this he bids be their Ilium, these lands their Troy'; see note on 634. The town is to be called Acesta; these are presumably the names of parts of it. Others take the meaning to be that Acesta is now to be metaphorically their Ilium and their Troy — this seems less likely in view of 633 f.

758. **indicitque forum**: 'proclaims an assembly', cf. *comitia indicere* (Livy). Notice the very Roman terminology here, as in 750, 755.

759 f. This temple of Venus on Mt. Eryx (see note on 24) was a very famous one in Greek and Roman times, cf. Thuc. 6.46.3, Tac. *Ann.* 4.43.5. There was a temple of Venus Erycina at Rome near the Colline Gate.

760. **Idaliae**: Idalium in Cyprus was one of Venus' most favoured abodes (*Aen.* 1.681) and as such is linked with Eryx in Theoc. 15.100 f.

760–1. Compare Andromache's sacrifices at Hector's cenotaph, *Aen.* 3.300 f. For the significance of this worship see on 42 f.; the deification of Anchises is implied rather than stated.

761. For the formation of the adjective cf. *stirpis Achilleae* (*Aen.* 3.326), *Cytherea* (line 800). For the spondaic ending (commoner with a Greek word than otherwise) see note on 2.68.

762. Aeneas had decreed for Anchises a religious ceremony of nine days with games on the ninth (64); this further period of nine days is to celebrate the foundation of the city.

764. **creber et aspirans**: 'and blowing steadily'; for the adverbial use of *creber* cf. 278 and *Aen.* 3.70.

765. **procurva**: an extremely rare word not found elsewhere in classical Latin except for *Geo.* 2.421.

766. **noctemque diemque morantur**: probably 'they delay a night and a day' rather than 'they prolong night and day' by trying to make them last longer.

768. **nomen**: 'the very mention of it'; *P* has *numen* ('its power') which many editors accept, but *nomen* gives a better balance with *facies*, and more force to the sentence.

770 f. Aeneas is now completely in control of the situation again, consoling rather than consoled (708), calmly making all the necessary arrangements.

772. Eryx was the guardian deity of the place, cf. 24.

Tempestatibus agnam: cf. *Aen.* 3.120, Hor. *Epod.* 10.24. There was a temple to the *Tempestates* near the Porta Camena.

773. **ex ordine**: 'duly', cf. 102 and *Aen.* 7.139.

774–8. Almost the whole of this passage is made up of phrases and lines which occur elsewhere; cf. *Geo.* 3.21, lines 237–8, *Aen.* 3.130, 290. The familiar phrases give a calm ritualistic ending to this section of the poem. For the construction of *caput* see note on 135; for *tonsae* cf. 556; *procul* here is 'apart', away from the rest.

779–826. *Meanwhile Venus complains to Neptune of Juno's hostility to the Trojans, and asks for his promise that the Trojans will safely cross the sea to Italy. Neptune gives his promise, but says that one life must be lost so that the others shall be safe. The seas are calmed as Neptune rides over them, attended by his retinue.*

779 f. At this critical moment of the narrative of the human events, as Aeneas sets out on the last stage of his long journey,

the scene moves on to the divine plane so that the events which follow are seen to be part of a larger context. The speech of Venus reflects her angry resentment against Juno, and expresses vividly and emotionally the insistent theme of Juno's disregard of the Fates, of Jupiter, of Neptune himself (792). Compare *Aen.* 1.229 f., 10.18 f.

781. Notice the emphatic position of *Iunonis*, the word which comes immediately to Venus' lips: we might translate 'Juno, with her fierce anger and implacable heart, forces me...'. The rhythm of the line is unusual; the absence of strong caesura in third and fourth foot gives coincidence of ictus and accent in the middle of the line which sharply contrasts with the conflict in the first two feet; compare *Aen.* 2.483, 12.619, both memorable lines.

neque exsaturabile: equivalent to *et inexsaturabile*; cf. Prop. 2.28.52, Ov. *Met.* 1.110. The word *exsaturabilis* does not occur elsewhere except for one instance in Statius (*Th.* 1.214); see note on 591.

783. **pietas nec**: the postposition of *nec* emphasises *pietas*, which refers both generally to Aeneas' quality (*Aen.* 1.10, 253) and specifically to his due worship of Juno (*Aen.* 3.547).

784. **infracta**: 'broken', cf. *Aen.* 7.332, 9.499, 10.731, 12.1. The adjective *infractus* = 'unbroken' occurs only in late Latin.

quiescit: cf. the ironical words of Juno in *Aen.* 7.297 f. *at credo mea numina tandem | fessa iacent, odiis aut exsaturata quievi*.

785 f. 'It is not enough that in her accursed acts of hatred she has devoured their city from the heart of Phrygia's people'. The language is very harsh, perhaps partly in imitation of Homer (*Il.* 4.34 f., where Zeus supposes that Hera will not be satisfied until she has eaten Priam and his children raw), but it is also appropriate to Venus' anger against Juno. Some of the most powerful language in the *Aeneid* issues from the mutual hatred of these two goddesses; cf. *Aen.* 10.16–95.

786 f. 'nor that she has dragged the remnants of Troy through the utmost retribution'. The image is perhaps that of dragging captives off in chains, or even dragging a dead body (like Hector's) behind a chariot to satisfy the desire for vengeance. For *traxe* (syncope for *traxisse*, a mark of archaising style) cf. Lucr. 3.650, 5.1159 and *Aen.* 4.606, 682.

787. **reliquias**: cf. *Aen.* 1.30, 598, 3.87.

cineres ... peremptae: 'the ashes and bones of the dead city'; Henry well points out that the suggestion of savagery against a dead body conveys the height of barbarism.

788. **sciat ipsa**: 'be it hers to know' (Fairclough); i.e. it is completely inexplicable to all right-minded people. The words which Venus uses here recall Virgil's question (*Aen.* 1.11) *tantaene animis caelestibus irae?*

789 f. Venus refers to the storm, aroused by Aeolus at Juno's instigation, with which the adventures of the Trojans begin in the *Aeneid* (1.84 f.). Compare *molem* (790) with 1.134; *maria omnia caelo miscuit* with 1.133 f.; *Aeoliis procellis* with 1.65 f.; *in regnis hoc ausa tuis* with 1.138–9.

791. **nequiquam**: in vain because Neptune's intervention saved the Trojans.

793. **per scelus**: notice the emphatic position, in front of *ecce etiam* which would naturally begin a sentence. The phrase colours the whole sentence, but syntactically is to be linked with *actis* (drove them on a path of crime), cf. 786 and Hor. *Odes* 1.3.26.

794–5. The object to be supplied for *subegit* is *Aenean*. Venus' phrases are deliberately exaggerated — four ships (not the fleet) were lost, and Sicily was by now not wholly unknown.

796. **quod superest**: adverbial, 'for the rest', 'henceforward'; cf. 691 and *Aen.* 9.157, 11.15. As in 691, so here it could be equivalent to *reliquias* as object to *liceat* ('let what remains sail safely ...'), but the balance of probability is against it.

796–7. **dare ... tibi**: 'commit their sails to you over the waves in safety' rather than 'sail in safety over the waves through your help' which — while idiomatic for *dare vela* (*Aen.* 3.191) — gives an impossible construction for *tibi*.

797. **Laurentem**: the *ager Laurens* evidently extended from the Tiber to Ardea (*Aen.* 7.650); the noun Laurentum was the name either of this region or of an ancient town within it, perhaps identical with Lavinium.

799. **Saturnius**: this epithet is normally applied to Juno (606); in using it of Neptune (who was of course also a child of Saturnus) Virgil is perhaps recalling the line of similar rhythm in *Aen.* 4.372.

800 f. The tone and movement of Neptune's speech contrast most markedly with the emotional excitement of Venus. It is calm

and slow and reassuring; and the sentence beginning at 804 is unusually long and complex (almost rambling) compared with Virgil's normal style. It is the speech of a revered old counsellor.

800. **Cytherea**: for this epithet of Venus born from the sea (*unde genus ducis*) near Cythera cf. *Aen.* 1.257.

801–2. The storm aroused by Aeolus at the instigation of Juno (1.81 f.) was calmed by Neptune; and we may assume that he was also responsible for the calming of the storms in 3.192 f., 5.10 f.

803. **Xanthum Simoentaque**: the rivers of Troy, cf. 634.

805. **exanimata**: 'breathless', 'panic-stricken', cf. *exanimes* (669).

806. **daret**: supply *et cum*. The phrases which follow are closely imitated from Hom. *Il.* 21.218 f.

808. **Pelidae**: the meeting of Aeneas and Achilles, son of Peleus, is described in *Il.* 20.158 f., and the rescue of Aeneas in *Il.* 20.318 f. For the dative after *congressus* cf. *Aen.* 1.475.

810. **nube cava**: 'enfolding cloud', cf. *Aen.* 1.516, Hom. *Il.* 20.444.

811. Neptune and Apollo helped to build the walls of Troy, but were cheated of the agreed reward by Laomedon; cf. *Aen.* 4.542.

813. Notice the slow spondees to give due impressiveness to his promise. For *portus Averni* (Cumae) cf. *Aen.* 6.2, and *Geo.* 2.161 f.

814–15. Palinurus (840 f.) is to be the scapegoat for the successful completion of the voyage; the repetition of *unus* stresses the point. For *quaerere* (= 'look for in vain', 'miss') cf. *Aen.* 1.217, Prop. 1.17.18.

817 f. The picture of Neptune driving over the waves in his chariot, attended by his retinue of creatures and deities of the sea, is painted in the most brilliant colours. It is based on Homer's memorable description of Poseidon's journey in *Il.* 13.23 f., and it has points of similarity with Virgil's earlier description of Neptune in *Aen.* 1.142 f.; but it has a more sustained pictorial imagery than either of these passages.

817–18. 'Father Neptune yoked his horses in their golden harness, then put the bit in their foaming mouths as they chafed to be away, and let all the reins run out free through his hands'. The word *feris* conveys the high-spiritedness of the horses, cf. *Aen.* 4.135.

821. **vasto**: 'savage', 'threatening', rather than 'vast'.

822. 'Then there come the manifold figures of his company';
for the absence of a main verb cf. *Aen.* 1.639 f., 3.618 f., 4.131.
It has been suggested that this description of Neptune's retinue is
based on a piece of sculpture by Scopas in the circus of Flaminius
(Pliny, *Nat. Hist.* 36.26); at all events the passage has a most
marked visual impact (cf. lines 240–1 and *Geo.* 4.334 f.).

cete: 'sea-monsters'; a Greek neuter plural, cf. *Tempe* (*Geo.*
2.469).

823 f. For these deities of the sea, compare Spenser, *F.Q.*
4.11.11 f., and Milton, *Comus* 867 f. Glaucus was a fisherman who
became a sea-god (Ov. *Met.* 13.896 f.); Palaemon, also called
Melicertes, son of Ino, is identified with Portunus (241), cf. Ov.
Met. 4.416 f.; Triton was a son of Neptune whose skill at trumpet-
ing with a sea-shell Misenus vainly tried to emulate (*Aen.*
6.171 f.). Compare the final lines of Wordsworth's sonnet 'The
world is too much with us. . . .'

> So might I, standing on this pleasant lea,
> Have glimpses that would make me less forlorn:
> Have sight of Proteus rising from the sea
> Or hear old Triton blow his wreathéd horn.

For the plural *Tritones* cf. Stat. *Ach.* 1.55. Phorcus was an old
man of the sea (Hom. *Od.* 13.96); Thetis, the mother of Achilles,
was the most famous of the Nereids; Melite and Panopea were
also Nereids; the nymphs in line 826 are taken from Hom. *Il.*
18.39–40. The metrical pattern of this line of Greek names is also
Greek (cf. *Geo.* 1.437, 4.336).

827–71. *The Trojans proceed on their voyage, Palinurus leading.
During the night the god Sleep comes to Palinurus, disguised as Phorbas,
and urges him to rest from his vigil. Palinurus refuses, and Sleep casts
him into the sea. When the loss of the helmsman is discovered; Aeneas takes
over the control of the ship and in deep sorrow speaks his farewell to
Palinurus.*

827 f. The story of Palinurus with which the book ends leads
into the atmosphere of Book 6; the liquid notes of pathos which
are so marked a feature of the *Aeneid* are heard here at their
clearest. As often in the poem, sorrow is to be endured at the

moment of success. The sequel to Palinurus' death is told in *Aen.* 6.337 f. (where see notes).

The origin of the legend of Palinurus, the helmsman who gave his name to Cape Palinurus in S. Italy, is a typical aetiological story to account for the foundation of a town (cf. *Aen.* 6.378 f., and Servius' note). It seems likely that the legend can be traced back to Timaeus in the third century, and it probably came to Virgil through Varro; cf. also Dionysius 1.53.2.

The factual material of the legend has been transformed into poetry by the adaptation of a number of Homeric passages: the story of Elpenor in *Od.* 11, the death of Phrontis in *Od.* 3.278 f., the god Sleep in *Il.* 14.231 f. Fired by these sources Virgil's imagination worked on the prosaic material of the legend so as to produce an episode of haunting beauty and pathos.

827. **suspensam**: 'anxious'; cf. *Aen.* 4.9.

828. **pertemptant**: 'came over', 'pervaded', a poetic use of the word, cf. *Aen.* 1.502.

829. **attolli malos**: the masts could be taken down when the ships were not being sailed (cf. 487).

intendi bracchia velis: 'the yard-arms to be hung with their sails'; for *intendere* cf. 403. *Bracchia* in the sense of *antemnae* is no common; cf. Val. Fl. 1.126.

830 f. Notice the emphasis on the regularity and precision of the manoeuvre given by the words *una*, *pariter*, *una*. The serene description of ordered progress heightens the pathos of the subsequent disaster.

830. **fecere pedem**: 'set the sheets', i.e. fastened the ropes at the bottom of the sail to make the desired angle with the wind; cf. Cat. 4.21.

830–2. 'and together they let out their sails now to the left, now to the right; in unison they turn their lofty yard-arms now this way, now that'. *Cornua* is the technical term for the ends of the yard-arms (cf. *Aen.* 3.549), here being adjusted for tacking.

832. **sua**: 'its own', i.e. favourable, cf. 54.

833 f. Notice how the attention is concentrated on Palinurus before the fresh start in the narrative at 835.

834. **ad hunc ... contendere**: 'direct their course towards him', i.e. set their course by him.

835 f. The new scene is set in peacefully descriptive verses, with

alliteration of *m* and assonance of long vowel sounds. See note on 721 for Night's chariot; *meta* is here the half-way mark of her course through the sky, see note on 129.

838. **Somnus**: Homer tells in *Il.* 14.231 f. how the god Sleep charmed the eyes of Zeus at Hera's request. There are fine descriptions of Somnus and his home in Ov. *Met.* 11.592 f., Stat. *Th.* 10.84 f.; cf. also Stat. *Silv.* 5.4 (where see Frère's introductory note in the Budé edition for a discussion of ancient concepts of the god and representations of him in art).

839. 'sundered the dusky air and parted the darkness'; the diction of this line conveys a strange other-worldly effect of midnight powers at work.

840 f. Here Virgil's art in giving emphasis by rhythmical and other means to an emotional part of the narrative can be very clearly seen. Line 840 is balanced with an effective simplicity by means of the repetition of *te . . . tibi* and the similar endings of *petens* and *portans*; there is very marked alliteration of *p* and *t*, and the insistent beat of the rhythm on the two dactylic words *somnia tristia* which fill the fourth and fifth feet is made all the more marked because they have similar grammatical endings. Finally *insonti* (the key word for the pathos of the whole passage) is given great emphasis by its position in the sentence (last word), by its position in the line (first word before a heavy pause), and by its spondaic slowness after the dactylic movement of the previous line.

For the use of the vocative to add to the feeling of personal involvement cf. *Aen.* 4.408.

840. **somnia tristia**: a vague phrase of foreboding, where *somnia* does not mean specifically 'dreams' but rather 'the sleep that brings doom', cf. 854 f.

841. **deus consedit**: 'alighted in his divine power'; *deus* has some predicative force, the subject still being *Somnus*, cf. *Aen.* 1.412, 692.

842. **Phorbanti similis**: compare Allecto in *Aen.* 7.406 f., where she appears in disguise to Turnus, and, like Somnus, first tries persuasion and then uses her divine power.

loquelas: this is not a common word, and is employed here, as Page well says, to suggest the 'soft insinuating words he uses'; cf. Lucr. 1.39, 5.231.

843. **Iaside**: for Iasius, son of Jupiter, a founder of the Trojan race, cf. *Aen.* 3.168. The Greek vocative form ends in long -*e*, cf. *Aen.* 1.97.

844. **aequatae**: 'steadily', 'evenly', as opposed to gusty or veering winds.

845. **fessosque ... labori**: 'steal your weary eyes from their vigil'. The metaphor is a vivid one, imitated in Stat. *Silv.* 4.4.29. For the dative used with words meaning 'take away from' (*demere, eripere*, etc.) cf. 260, 726, *Aen.* 7.282–3. The juxtaposition of words with similar endings (*fessos, oculos*) is generally avoided by Virgil, and can therefore achieve a certain effect when used; cf. 682, *Aen.* 6.269–70, 469, 638–9.

847. **vix attollens ... lumina**: 'hardly lifting his eyes', (because so intent on steering) rather than 'barely able to lift his eyes' (because of the power of the god).

848. **mene**: very emphatic — 'do you ask me of all men?' (Jackson Knight). Others may be tricked by the smiling face of the sea (cf. Lucr. 2.557 f., 5.1002 f.), but not so the helmsman of long experience.

849. **ignorare**: 'act as if I did not know', i.e. forget what I know.

monstro: 'demon'; the word in this usage conveys the idea of a vast and supernatural agent of evil. It is used of the wooden horse (*Aen.* 2.245), of the Harpies (3.214), of Polyphemus (3.658), of Fama (4.181), of Cacus (8.198).

850. **Aenean credam**: the pathos of this episode is greatly increased by the stress laid on Palinurus' loyalty as a helmsman, his sense of duty to the trust placed in him; cf. his words in the underworld to Aeneas (6.351 f.).

quid enim?: it is perhaps best to take these words as parenthetical — 'for what then?'; cf. Hor. *Sat.* 1.1.7, 2.3.132. Others prefer to regard them as postponed from the beginning of the sentence 'for how could I entrust. . . . ?'

851. **et caelo**: sc. *fallaci*, 'to the uncertainties of wind and weather'. Most MSS have *caeli* (a noun for *sereni*) but the first hand of *P* and Servius read *caelo. Serenum* then is a noun, cf. *Geo.* 1.393, Lucan 1.530, and compare *tranquillum* in line 127. The objection to the reading *caeli* is that *et* is then left without meaning.

totiens ... sereni: 'when I have been so often cheated by the false promise of bright weather'.

853. **amittebat**: for the lengthened final syllable see note on
284. Notice the assonance of *dabat, amittebat, tenebat*, emphasising
the steady monotonous determination of Palinurus.

854 f. 'Then behold, the god shook over both his temples a
branch dripping with the dew of Lethe, made sleepy with the
power of Styx, and as he gradually yielded closed his swimming
eyes.' These lovely lines were remembered and imitated by
Valerius Flaccus (8.84) and by Silius (10.354 f.). For Lethe, the
river of forgetfulness, see note on 6.705. For the rhythm of line
856, where there is no strong caesura at all, cf. 591 and *Aen.*
4.486.

857. **primos**: the word conveys the idea of the gradual
penetration of the body by sleep until finally the innermost being
is subdued.

858. **et**: in the sense of inverted *cum*, cf. *Aen.* 2.692.

858. **super incumbens**: 'looming over him', cf. 325 and *Geo.*
2.377.

858–9. Palinurus even in sleep does not relax his hold, so that
the helm and a part of the ship are torn away with him; cf. *Aen.*
6.349 f.

861. **ales**: Sleep is often depicted in literature and art as
winged; see note on 838 and cf. Prop. 1.3.45, Stat. *Th.*
10.137 f.

863. **interrita**: 'without alarm', a slight personification of the
fleet.

864 f. 'And now the fleet voyaging on was approaching the
cliffs of the Sirens, in former days perilous and white with the
bones of many victims — at this time the rocks were re-echoing
with roaring afar in the ceaseless surf, — when father Aeneas
saw. . . .' The reference is to the legend that the Sirens killed
themselves after Odysseus had got safely past them; when Aeneas
reaches the rocks the enchanting voices are past history (*quondam*)
and now (*tum*) only the harsh booming of the sea against the lonely
rocks is to be heard.

864. **Sirenum**: the story is told in Hom. *Od.* 12.39 f. The
Alexandrians had established geographical locations for Homer's
stories, and the Sirens were placed in the islands called Sirenusae
near Capreae.

866. **rauca**: perhaps adverbial with *sonabant* rather than

agreeing with *saxa*, cf. *Aen.* 9.125. Notice the alliteration of *s*, imitative of the seething surf.

867. **fluitantem:** 'drifting'; *ratem* is supplied from the following clause.

869. **animum concussus:** 'sick at heart'; for the construction see note on 135.

870–1. It is a most effective piece of irony that Aeneas in his last farewell to Palinurus attributes his death to the very thing which he had so resolutely refused to do (848 f.). The sequel to the story is told in *Aen.* 6.337 f.

AENEID 6

Introductory note

The sixth book is the focal point of the *Aeneid*; much of what has gone before is resumed in it, and it provides the new impetus for the second half of the poem. In itself it offers some of Virgil's greatest poetry, and his deepest thought.

There are three particular aspects of the book which may be distinguished: firstly it provides Virgil with a setting for the exposition of his religious thought; secondly the final section of the book is the most outstanding patriotic expression of the whole poem; and thirdly the events in the underworld are a personal experience for Aeneas, with a profound effect upon his character and resolution.

The structure of the book is tripartite: first the preparations for the descent (1–263); secondly the journey through the underworld to Elysium (264–678); thirdly (679–fin.) the meeting with Anchises and the revelation first of the nature of life beyond the grave and then of the greatness of Rome's future history.

1. *Preparation* (1–263).

In the long preliminaries to the actual descent to the underworld Virgil builds up a picture of religious ceremonies, of mystery and awe appropriate for the supernatural experiences in the rest of the book. The mysterious Labyrinth on the doors of Apollo's temple, the prophetic frenzy of the Sibyl, the ritual prayers and

formal request of Aeneas and the frightening oracular replies of
the Sibyl lead to the two themes of the last part of this section,
the death and funeral of Misenus and the discovery of the golden
bough. The sudden unnecessary death of Misenus introduces a
motif of the frailty of human life, and serves to emphasise still
further the supernatural mystery of the experience Aeneas is
about to undergo. Aeneas will visit the halls of Pluto, and return
again; but one act of folly has blotted out Misenus' life for ever.
This theme is interwoven structurally with the search for the
golden bough, strange talisman of life and death, symbolising
light in darkness, survival in destruction.

2. *The journey* (264–678).

For the background to Aeneas' experience Virgil has drawn
on the rich heritage of Greco–Roman mythology and folklore;
the eleventh book of Homer's *Odyssey* is several times recalled, and
there are elements from Pindar and doubtless from many Orphic
catabaseis of the kind which is parodied in Aristophanes' *Frogs*,
and especially there are Orphic ideas from the myths of Plato, those
of the *Phaedo*, the *Phaedrus*, the *Gorgias* and *Republic* 10. (Fuller information on these sources is given in the appropriate places in
the commentary; see also my article in *Greece and Rome*, 1964, pp.
48 f., and the introductions to the editions of Butler and Fletcher.)

Using this background of the traditional machinery of Hell,
the rivers, the ferryman, the dog, the place of everlasting sinners,
Virgil describes the meeting of Aeneas with three of the ghosts of
his past, Palinurus, Dido, Deiphobus. Palinurus had been swept
overboard by the god Sleep near the very end of the journey,
and Aeneas feels remorse and guilt that he was not able to save
his faithful helmsman. When he encounters Dido he speaks to her
in tones of sorrow and self-blame. To Deiphobus he expresses his
feelings of guilt at not having been able to find his body. In a
sense Aeneas travels again through the sorrows and regrets of his
past life (Palinurus and Dido have played very large parts in the
poem, and Deiphobus recalls all the suffering of Book 2). He looks
backwards with sorrow and self-reproach; but he is taught that
the past cannot now be altered, that no amount of brooding over
what might have been can change the facts. This is made
especially clear to him by Dido — as he had rejected her in life,

now in death she rejects him. The hard lesson that Aeneas has to learn about the past is summarised when Deiphobus leaves him for the last time and tells him that he must go forward: *i, decus, i, nostrum; melioribus utere fatis* (546).

3. *The revelation* (679-fin.).

As the middle section of the book was concerned with the sorrow and gloom of the past, so now the last section is concerned with the hope and glory of the future. After learning something of sin and virtue from his vision of Tartarus and his first sight of Elysium, Aeneas now meets his father and learns how the good are rewarded after death (see note on 703 f.). Anchises' first words are of joy that Aeneas' devotion to his mission has overcome the trials of the journey — *venisti tandem, tuaque exspectata parenti / vicit iter durum pietas?* (687–8). He wants to show him his future *quo magis Italia mecum laetere reperta* (718). And half-way through the pageant of Roman heroes, after the description of Augustus, Anchises breaks off to ask his son whether there is any more doubt: *et dubitamus adhuc virtutem extendere factis, aut metus Ausonia prohibet consistere terra?* (806–7). When the pageant is finished it has fired Aeneas with love for the glory to come: *incenditque animum famae venientis amore* (889). From the sorrowful encounters with ghosts of his past Aeneas moves forward to fulfil the destiny of his new nation. He leaves behind the history of Troy in order to start the history of Rome.

1–41. *The Trojans arrive in Italy at Cumae; Aeneas goes to consult the Sibyl at Apollo's temple. He gazes in admiration at the pictures on the temple doors, and is called into the temple by the Sibyl.*

1 f. The final arrival of the Trojans in Italy after their seven-years' wanderings is marked by excited activity, briefly described, and by Aeneas' immediate departure to consult the Sibyl in accordance with instructions given him by Helenus (3.441 f.) and Anchises (5.722 f.). The narrative is then suspended for a description of the pictures on the doors of Apollo's temple (an ecphrasis, see note on 1.418 f.). The subject-matter (Daedalus, the Minotaur, the Labyrinth) has links with the narrative in various ways, of which the most important is the symbolism of the Labyrinth for the maze-like journey of Aeneas through the underworld. The

Labyrinth suggests the mysterious paths of the hidden world which
Aeneas must trace; it is a frequent visual symbol of death. It may
also suggest the idea of the exclusion of all but those selected to
enter; for a very full discussion see W. F. J. Knight, *Cumaean
Gates*, Oxford, 1936. Other possible links between the ecphrasis
and the narrative are the father-son relationship of Daedalus and
Icarus compared with that of Aeneas and Ascanius, and the
similarity of the complex of rooms and corridors in a Minoan
palace with Aeneas' underworld journey (see Mackail, Appendix
C, where he argues for a tradition of a Minoan settlement at
Cumae). Above all the ecphrasis takes us back into the shadowy
distances of ancient mythology and folk-lore, and thus helps to
establish the atmosphere of awe and mystery which Virgil seeks.

1–2. These linking lines, referring to Aeneas' last farewell to his
helmsman Palinurus and his arrival on the shores of Italy, were
regarded by some scholars in antiquity as part of Book 5; but the
opening phrase, *sic fatur*, is taken from the beginning of Hom.
Il. 7 and *Od.* 13, and beyond reasonable doubt Virgil wished Book
6 to begin thus.

1. **classique ... habenas**: the metaphor from horses is
common, cf. Lucr. 5.787, *Geo.* 2.364, *Aen.* 1.63, 5.662.

2. Cumae, ten miles west of Naples, was a famous and flourishing city during the first millenium B.C.; it was the first Greek
colony in Italy and was founded by settlers from Chalcis (line 17)
in Euboea (Livy 8.22.5) at a very early date (though long after
the time of Aeneas of course), probably about 750 B.C. The area
was well-known to Virgil, who lived much of his life in this part
of Italy. Augustus restored the temples and the Sibyl's worship at
Cumae (after the completion of the major military works in this area,
Geo. 2.161 f.), but within a generation or two Cumae fell into decline.

3. **obvertunt ... proras**: it was normal to beach ships with
the prow seawards, doubtless in readiness for quick launching.

4. **ancora fundabat**: 'the anchors began to secure'; the
imperfect expresses the continued activity of the sailors all along
the shore as a variation from the instantaneous pictures conveyed
by the present tenses.

6 f. For the kindling of fire from flint cf. *Aen.* 1.174 f.; for the
notion of its being 'concealed' in flint cf. *Geo.* 1.135.

7–8. 'Some plunder the woods, tangled home of wild creatures';

tecta is in apposition to *silvas* (cf. 179). For *rapere* in this sense cf. *Aen.* 2.374. They are seeking timber for fuel, water and meat for food.

9. **pius**: Aeneas' epithet here refers primarily to his religious duties and the fulfilment of his mission to his father (cf. 403).

9–10. **arces . . . secreta**: the ruins of the temple of Apollo are still to be seen on the acropolis of Cumae; the cave of the Sibyl, some little way off (*procul*), cut into the west edge of the cliff, has been discovered and excavated in recent times, and may now be seen in all its eerie grandeur.

10. **Sibyllae**: the priestess of Apollo, see note on 3.443. Sibylla was a type-name for such oracular priestesses; this particular Sibyl was called Deiphobe (36).

11–12. 'into whom the prophetic god of Delos breathes his mighty purpose and will'; for Apollo of Delos see note on 3.75–6.

13. **Triviae**: Diana is naturally associated with her brother Apollo: for her epithet as goddess of the cross-roads, identifying her with Hecate, cf. 35, 69 and note on *Aen.* 4.511.

14f. Servius tells the story of how Daedalus helped Pasiphäe, wife of Minos, king of Crete, to satisfy her love for the bull (lines 24f.), a love which Venus, angered, had implanted in her. As a result of this the hybrid monster called the Minotaur was born to her; it was kept in a labyrinth built by Daedalus, and fed on human sacrifices. After Daedalus had helped Theseus solve the maze (28f.), he was imprisoned but escaped by making himself wings and flying north to Cumae (or in other versions Sardinia or Sicily); cf. Ov. *Met.* 8.183f., Hor. *Odes* 1.3.34–5.

15. **praepetibus**: 'swift', see note on 3.360–1.

16. **insuetum per iter**: 'by a novel route', i.e. by flying.

enavit: the verb is used of sailing or flying as well as swimming; cf. Enn. *Ann.* 21, Lucr. 3.591, *Aen.* 4.245 and lines 134, 369, 671.

17. **Chalcidica**: see note on 2.

19. **remigium alarum**: 'the oarage of his wings', i.e. the wings on which he had 'rowed' through the air; for the metaphor see note on 1.301.

20. **in foribus**: for the ecphrasis see note on 1 f.

Androgeo: Greek genitive as in 2.392. Androgeos, a son of Minos, was killed by the Athenians, and as recompense Minos demanded the payment of seven youths and seven maidens each year as a sacrifice to the Minotaur; cf. Cat. 64.76f.

20–2. pendere poenas: 'to pay as recompense', *poenas* is in apposition to *septena ... corpora*.

21. Cecropidae: Cecrops was a legendary king of Athens, cf. *Cat.* 64.79.

23. respondet Cnosia tellus: i.e. the pictures of Crete 'balance' the pictures of Athens. Cnossos was the chief town of Crete, cf. *Aen.* 3.115.

24 f. For the story see note on 14 f.

24. suppostaque: contracted for *suppositaque*, cf. 59 *repostas* and *Aen.* 1.26.

27. 'here is the famous toil, the insoluble maze, of the palace'; the reference is to the Labyrinth, see note on 5.588–91 and cf. *Cat.* 64.115.

28. reginae: the story switches from Pasiphae to her daughter Ariadne, whose love for Theseus is here referred to; he killed the Minotaur and found his way out of the maze by the thread which Ariadne at Daedalus' instigation gave him, cf. *Cat.* 64.113.

sed enim: 'but indeed', cf. *Aen.* 1.19.

31. sineret ... haberes: 'You, Icarus, would have had a large part if grief had permitted it'; *sineret* is conditional (supply *si*), and the condition past unfulfilled, cf. 34–35. Daedalus' son Icarus flew too near the sun on the wings his father had made for him and fastened on with wax, so that the wax melted and he fell into the sea and was drowned.

33. protinus: 'one after the other', cf. *Geo.* 4.1.

omnia: scanned as a trochee by synizesis, or with consonantal *i*, cf. *Aen.* 7.237 and notes on 1.41, 2.16.

36. Deiphobe Glauci: Deiphobe, daughter of Glaucus, is the name of the Sibyl (see note on 10).

37. 'The moment does not call for sight-seeing on your part'; the reading *poscunt* offered by some MSS is much inferior.

39. praestiterit: perfect subjunctive, expressing a potential idea, 'it would be better'.

bidentis: sheep in their second year, cf. *Aen.* 4.57.

42–76. *The Sibyl in her cave goes into a prophetic trance and calls on Aeneas to make his prayer to Apollo. He does so, asking to be allowed to enter into the kingdom granted to him by fate, and promising a temple and a festival to the god and a special shrine for the Sibyl.*

42 f. The prayer of Aeneas is closely linked with the special worship paid to Apollo (patron god of Actium, cf. *Aen.* 8.704, 720 f.) by Augustus, and looks forward aetiologically to the marble temple built for Apollo on the Palatine in 28 B.C. and the transference to it of the Sibylline books.

42. 'The side of the cliff of Cumae is hollowed out into a huge cave'; for the cave of the Sibyl see note on 9–10; for the Euboean colonisation of Cumae cf. line 2.

43. **aditus . . . ostia**: these are slits or windows leading out from the cave laterally.

47. **non . . . unus**: i.e. the colour and expression of her face is transformed; cf. Lucan 5.165 f. for an elaborate description of prophetic frenzy.

49–50. 'and she was bigger to look upon, and her voice of no mortal sound'; the infinitive is epexegetic (cf. Hor. *Odes* 4.2.59 *niveus videri*), and the accusative *mortale* adverbial, cf. *Aen.* 1.328, *Geo.* 3.149. Other examples in this book are 201, 288, 401, 467, 481. For the idea cf. *Aen.* 2.773.

50. **quando**: 'since'; the postposition of the conjunction to fourth place is very unusual; cf. *Aen.* 10.366.

52. **enim**: there is an ellipse of meaning: 'are you slow? Hurry then, for. . . .'

53. **attonitae**: 'awe-struck'; the temple is personified as if it were affected like a human at the god's presence.

56. **semper miserate**: 'you who have always felt pity for . . .'; Virgil is fond of the vocative of the past participle (cf. 83, 125).

57 f. Paris (renowned for his archery) with Apollo's help killed Achilles (grandson of Aeacus) by shooting him in the heel, the only part of him not invulnerable; cf. Hom. *Il.* 22.359 f., Ov. *Met.* 12.580 f.

57. **derexti**: contracted perfect, see note on 4.604–6.

tela manusque: 'the weapons and the aim'.

58. **corpus in Aeacidae**: for the position of the preposition see note on 4.257.

obeuntia: 'bordering', cf. *Aen.* 10.483.

59. **repostas**: 'remote', contracted for *repositas*, cf. 24.

60. The references are to Carthage, cf. *Aen.* 1.111, 4.132; *praetenta* is 'fringing', cf. *Aen.* 3.692.

61. fugientis ... oras: cf. *Aen.* 5.629.

62. hac ... tenus: 'thus far', cf. *Aen.* 5.603.

Troiana ... fortuna: the implication is that it has been unfavourable right up to this moment.

fuerit: 'let it have followed' (and follow no longer), perfect subjunctive of a wish.

64. dique deaeque omnes: Juno especially, and Pallas, and Neptune were deities whose plans and wishes were hindered by Troy's prosperity (cf. 2.610 f.).

66–7. non indebita ... fatis: a frequent theme of the *Aeneid*, cf. *Aen.* 1.382, 7.120.

67. considere Teucros: accusative and infinitive after *da*, cf. 697 and see note on 1.66.

69 f. These promises relate to subsequent events in Roman history; the festal days for Phoebus predict the *Ludi Apollinares*, founded during the Second Punic war, while the marble temple refers to the new temple built in honour of Apollo by Augustus on the Palatine (cf. Suet. *Aug.* 29, Hor. *Odes* 1.31). The references to the Sibyl's oracular responses (see note on 3.443) are also especially relevant to Augustus' temple to Apollo, as the Sibylline books and the priests in charge of them (*lectos ... viros*) were transferred to it (Suet. *Aug.* 31). Servius ad loc. tells the story of the origin of the books in the reign of Tarquinius Superbus; see also Page ad loc.

74. Aeneas' request is in fulfilment of Helenus' instructions (3.441 f.).

76. ipsa canas oro: 'I beg you to sing them yourself'; the paratactic jussive subjunctive is a reminiscence of Helenus (3.456–7 *poscas* / *ipsa canat*).

77–97. The Sibyl gives her prophetic reply, indicating the trials which still await Aeneas, but urging him to continue on in spite of all.

77 f. The Sibyl's reply foretells in allusive terms the events of the second half of the poem. There will be fighting against Turnus, the new Achilles, because of his claim to Lavinia, the bride promised to Aeneas by Latinus; Juno's hostility will continue; but help will come from a Greek city, i.e. Pallanteum (see note on 97). The leading theme is the parallelism between the war just fought against the Greeks, and the new war: the rivers of Troy are equated with the Italian rivers, the Rutuli with the Greeks, and particularly Turnus with Achilles. This parallel, several times stressed in the second half (see note on 89) reaches its fulfilment in Book 12, where the final single combat between Aeneas and Turnus is a re-enactment of the combat of Hector and Achilles, this time with the opposite result.

77. **Phoebi ... patiens**: 'able to endure', cf. *Aen.* 9.607, 10.610.

immanis: 'wildly', adverbial; cf. *Aen.* 7.510.

78. **si ... possit**: 'if thus she might'; for the form of the condition see note on 1.181–2. The perfect tense *excussisse*, as Fletcher well points out, conveys 'be rid of' rather than 'get rid of.'

79–80. 'All the more he wearied her foaming mouth, taming her wild heart and moulding her to his will by his pressure'; the image is from taming a horse (cf. *excussisse*). *Fatigare* means to try to break down opposition through constant pressure, wearing out the victim; cf. *Aen.* 1.316, 5.253.

84. **terrae**: genitive (not locative) like *pelagi*, (sea-dangers and land-dangers).

Lavini: Lavinium was the first settlement of Aeneas in Italy, cf. *Aen.* 1.258 (where see note on the scansion of the word).

86. **sed non ... volent**: 'but they will not also wish that they had come', i.e. they will wish that they had not come.

88 f. Simois and Xanthus were rivers of Troy (cf. *Aen.* 1.100–1, 1.473), here equated with the Tiber and the Numicus, as the Greek camp is equated with that of the new enemy, Turnus and his Rutulians.

89. **alius ... Achilles**: i.e. Turnus, who is often compared with the Greeks in the second half of the poem, cf. *Aen.* 7.371 f., 9.138 f., 742. Turnus was born of the nymph Venilia, Achilles of the sea-goddess Thetis.

90. **addita**: 'to harass them'; Macrobius says *infesta*, quoting Lucilius *si mihi non praetor siet additus atque agitet me*. The word simply means 'present in addition', and derives its hostile meaning from the context. For Juno's opposition see note on 1.1 f.

91. **cum**: equivalent to *cum interea*, 'while all the time you will be praying for help to every possible Italian tribe. . .'.

93–4. The first foreign bride was Helen, this one will be Lavinia.

94. For the half-line see note on 1.534; the only other in this book is 835.

96. **qua**: 'along the road on which. . .'. The MSS almost all have *quam* which may well be right (cf. *Aen.* 5.710, and Shakespeare, 3 Henry 6. 3.3.16–17 'Yield not thy neck to fortune's yoke'), but Seneca (*Ep. Mor.* 82.18) has *qua*, and on the whole the paradox with the reading *quam* seems awkward. The words *tua te* have better force with the reading *qua*.

97. **Graia . . . ab urbe**: a reference to Evander's help (cf. *Aen.* 8.51 f.).

98–155. *Aeneas in reply says that he is aware of the magnitude of his task; he asks to be allowed to visit his father in the underworld. The Sibyl describes the formidable nature of the journey, and states two prerequisites: the acquisition of the golden bough and the expiation of pollution incurred by the death of one of Aeneas' companions.*

98 f. In this passage Virgil continues to develop the mood of awe and mystery preparatory to the descent to the underworld in three ways: firstly by emphasising the superhuman qualities required for a journey undertaken by only very few mortals (Orpheus, Pollux, Theseus, Hercules); secondly by introducing the mysterious talisman of the golden bough with its strange and magical associations; and thirdly by describing the unexpected disaster to Misenus and the need to expiate the pollution (see note on 156 f.).

99. **ambages**: 'riddling responses', cf. Tac. *Ann.* 12.63.

remugit: 'boomed forth'; the word suggests the re-echoing and supernatural effect of the cave, cf. *Aen.* 3.92.

100–1. 'So violently did Apollo shake the reins as she raged, turning the goads in her heart'; the metaphor from horse-driving (79–80) is continued, cf. *Aen.* 5.147, 9.718. *Ea* has the sense of *talia* (= *tali modo*).

103–5. 'No aspect of toil, maiden, can rise before me as something new or unexpected; I have anticipated everything and considered it in advance silently in my heart'. These are Stoic terms, cf. Sen. *Ep. Mor.* 76.33 f., where Virgil's lines are quoted to illustrate the Stoic attitude, and Cic. *De Off.* 1.81 f.

104. **mi**: *mihi*, cf. 123; these are the only two places in Virgil where the form (archaic and colloquial) occurs.

107. **Acheronte refuso**: 'where Acheron comes welling up', from the underworld (*Aen.* 5.99) into Lake Avernus (here called *palus*).

109. **contingat**: 'let it be permitted me', subjunctive of wish.

110 f. Aeneas refers to his rescue of Anchises from Troy (*Aen.* 2.707 f.), and their subsequent voyage together in quest of Italy (Book 3, *passim*).

115. **quin**: 'indeed', adding a new point like *quin etiam*, cf. *Aen.* 1.279.

116. **mandata dabat**: especially in *Aen.* 5.722 f.

118. **Hecate**: Diana as goddess of the underworld (Trivia, line 13); cf. 247, 564 and note on 4.511.

Avernis: i.e. the woods around Lake Avernus, see note on 126.

119. The story of Orpheus' descent to the underworld to rescue his wife Eurydice, and how he lost her by looking back, is told in *Geo.* 4.467 f. The monsters of Hell were charmed by his music (120); for *fides canorae* ('tuneful strings') cf. Hor. *Odes* 1.12.11 (again with reference to Orpheus).

120. **Threicia**: Orpheus came from Thrace, cf. 645, Ap. Rh. 1.23 f.

121. When the mortal Castor died, his twin brother, the immortal Pollux, was allowed to die in his stead for six months each year (or on alternate days, Hom. *Od.* 11.303).

122-3. Theseus and Hercules (Alcides) are linked again in Charon's account of mortal visitors to Hell (392-3). Theseus (with Pirithous) attempted to carry off Proserpina (397) and was sentenced to eternal punishment, chained to a seat (618); one of Hercules' labours was to bring back the dog Cerberus (395). According to another version of the legend he also rescued Theseus; see note on 617-18.

122. **quid Thesea magnum**: the punctuation I have adopted means that the sentence takes a slight shift after the *si* clauses; this is far more natural than taking the *si* clauses with what precedes. It is also more natural to take *magnum* with *Thesea* rather than punctuate with a comma after *Thesea* so that *magnum* would go with *Alciden*.

Thesea: Greek accusative, cf. 393, 585.

123. **et mi ... summo**: 'my ancestry too goes back to Jupiter' (through Venus).

125. **sate sanguine**: 'born of the blood', a mainly poetic phrase, cf. line 331 and *Aen.* 8.36.

126. **Anchisiade**: Greek vocative with long *e*, cf. 348 and *Aen.* 1.97.

Averno: 'by way of Avernus' rather than 'to Avernus', because in this context Avernus is more likely to mean the lake itself than the underworld. Some MSS have *Averni* ('the descent of Avernus', cf. Plin. *Nat. Hist.* 16.110 *descensus speluncae*), which may be right.

127. Cf. Spenser, *F.Q.* 2.3.41:

> But easie is the way, and passage plaine
> To pleasures pallace; it may soone be spide,
> And day and night her dores to all stand open wide.

atri ... Ditis: Dis (Pluto) is black as befits the darkness of Hades; cf. Ov. *Met.* 4.438 *nigri Ditis*.

128–9. Cf. Milton, *P.L.* 3.18–21:

> I sung of Chaos and Eternal Night,
> Taught by the heav'nly Muse to venture down
> The dark descent, and up to reascend,
> Though hard and rare. . . .

132. **Cocytus**: one of the rivers of hell, the river of lamentation (323, *Geo.* 3.38).

134. **bis**: instead of the normal once, cf. Hor. *Odes* 1.28.16 *et calcanda semel via leti*, Hom. *Od.* 12.21–2.

innare: for the poetic infinitive cf. *Aen.* 2.10; for the word in the sense of sailing cf. 369 and note on 16.

136–7. 'Hidden in a shady tree is a golden bough, its leaves and its pliant stem all golden'. Virgil's sources for the golden bough are not known: it is a mysterious talisman whose significance in folk-lore cannot be defined with precision. Sir James Frazer in his great work on comparative anthropology and folk-lore to which he gave the title *The Golden Bough* associates it with tree-magic, and particularly with the mistletoe, with which Virgil compares it in a simile (205 f.). It is a symbol of mystery, a kind of light in darkness, a kind of life in death. See R. A. Brooks, *A.J.Ph.* 1953, pp. 260 f., and C.P. Segal, *Arion* 1965, pp. 517 f. and 1966, pp 34 f.

138. **Iunoni infernae**: Juno of the underworld is Proserpina
(142); cf. *Aen.* 4.638 where Stygian Jupiter is Pluto.

140–1. 'But it is not permitted to enter the hidden places of
earth till a man has plucked the golden-tressed growth from the
tree'. *Quis* stands for *aliquis* (*M* has *qui*, which involves an awkward
conflation of a temporal and a relative clause, equivalent in sense
to 'except to the man who. . .'). For the lovely compound adjective
auricomus, not found before Virgil, cf. Lucr. 6.152 *lauricomus* and
see note on 3.544; cf. also Norden ad loc.

142–3. **suum ... instituit**: 'has laid it down that it should
be brought to her as her own special offering'; cf. line 632.

149. At first the reader perhaps thinks, wrongly, of Palinurus;
but this idea is dispelled by the phrase *heu nescis*, and we realise
that another death has occurred at the moment of the voyage's
completion. See note on 156 f.

tibi: 'I must tell you', ethic dative.

150. **funere**: 'dead body', cf. 510, *Aen.* 9.491.

152. **sedibus ... suis**: 'first duly place him in his resting-
place', cf. 328 and (for *suus*) 233.

153. **nigras**: appropriate, of course, for the underworld, cf.
243, 249.

sunto: this form of the imperative is legalistic and impressive,
cf. *Aen.* 4.624.

156–82. *Aeneas finds that the dead body referred to is that of Misenus,
killed when he foolishly challenged Triton to a contest on the trumpet.
He sets about organising funeral rites for Misenus.*

156 f. The episode of Misenus has similarities with that of
Palinurus (see note on 149); both die near the very end of the
voyage, both are modelled to some extent on Homer's Elpenor
(*Od.* 11.51 f.), and both have their names perpetuated in geographical place-names (see note on 234–5). But they play different
roles in the development of the story, and there is no reason to
believe (as some commentators have) that Virgil would have
eliminated one of the two stories in revision (see my Oxford
edition of Book 5, Intro. pp. xxvii f.).

The main function played by the episode of Misenus in the
structure of the narrative is to act as an indication of the nature
of mortality. Aeneas, by his special qualities, is to be allowed to

transcend the normal conditions, but for Misenus there is no return from the underworld. In a sense he represents a sacrifice for the success of the mission (as Palinurus certainly does); but more especially his unexpected fate conveys the feeling of the imminence of death in life, and the very elaborate description of the funeral rites (212 f.) reinforces this feeling.

156. **lumina**: retained accusative with a passive verb, cf. 281, 470 and see note on *Aen*. 1.228.

160–1. 'They conversed much together with different suggestions, wondering what dead comrade. . .'. *Serebant* (from *serere*, 'join') is connected etymologically (Varro, *L.L.* 6.64) with *sermo*; the indirect question is loosely attached to the main sentence.

162. **atque**: 'and suddenly', cf. *Ecl*. 7.7, *Aen*. 1.227, 10.219.

illi: Fletcher rightly finds this very unnatural, there being no change of subject; he conjectures *illic*.

164. **Misenum Aeoliden**: perhaps son of the Trojan Aeolus (*Aen*. 12.542), but more likely son of the god of the winds (*Aen*. 1.52 f.). Misenus was mentioned as a trumpeter in *Aen*. 3.239.

165. **ciere**: for the epexegetic infinitive after *praestantior* cf. *Ecl*. 5.1–2.

166. **Hectora circum**: 'in Hector's retinue'; *Hectora* is a Greek accusative governed by the postponed preposition *circum*.

168. **illum**: the death of Hector at the hands of Achilles was one of the scenes depicted on Dido's temple to Juno (1.483 f.).

170. **non inferiora secutus**: 'following no lesser cause', cf. *Aen*. 11.291.

171. **personat aequora**: 'made the ocean resound', cf. 418.

concha: the sea-shell was the sea-god Triton's own special bugle (*Aen*. 10.209, Ov. *Met*. 1.333 f.), so that Misenus' folly is highly provocative.

172. **demens**: notice the emphasis given by the pause after an initial spondee, cf. 590, *Aen*. 4.185, 562.

173–4. 'in jealousy Triton caught him, if it is right to believe it, and drowned the mortal in the foaming wave amidst the rocks'. For *excipere* cf. *Aen*. 3.332, 11.517; for *si credere dignum est* applied to a myth cf. *Geo*. 3.391.

177. **aramque sepulcri**: 'the altar of a tomb', i.e. a pyre, as a sacrifice to the powers of death, cf. *Aen*. 3.63.

178. **caelo**: dative of motion towards (=*ad caelum*), cf. *Aen.* 2.186, 5.451.

179 f. This passage is closely based on Ennius *Ann.* 187–91 (cf. also Hom. *Il.* 23.114 f.):

> Incedunt arbusta per alta, securibus caedunt:
> percellunt magnas quercus, exciditur ilex,
> fraxinus frangitur atque abies consternitur alta,
> pinus proceras pervortunt; omne sonabat
> arbustum fremitu silvai frondosai.

183–211. *Aeneas is guided to the golden bough by two doves; he picks it and takes it to the Sibyl.*

186. **forte**: Servius draws attention to the stop-gap nature of the word; *R* has *voce*, but that seems to be a scribal improvement. The correlation with *forte* in 190 gives a heavy stress to the apparent coincidence, which Aeneas realises to be in fact a divine sign.

187. **si**: introducing a wish, cf. *Aen.* 8.560.

190. The dove is Venus' sacred bird (193, 197), cf. Ov. *Met.* 13.673–4.

195. **pinguem**: 'fertile', able to produce so rich a bough.

197. **vestigia pressit**: 'stopped', cf. 331, 389 and *Aen.* 2.378.

199. **prodire**: historic infinitive, cf. 256, 491–2, 557.

200. **acie**: 'with their gaze', cf. *Aen.* 12.558.

201. **fauces . . . Averni**: 'the jaws of evil-smelling Avernus'; the reference is to the sulphurous exhalations of this volcanic area, cf. 240–1, and (for *fauces*) also 273. Compare Spenser, *F.Q.* 1.5.31.

202. **liquidumque per aëra**: 'through the yielding air', cf. *Aen.* 5.217, 525.

203. **sedibus optatis**: i.e. the place Aeneas was longing to find.

gemina: 'of twin nature' (=*biformis*), i.e. with leafy boughs and a golden bough, as explained in the next line; cf. Ov. *Met.* 2.630. *R* has *geminae* (the two doves) which is much weaker in the context.

204. 'from which the sheen of gold shone out with its contrasting colour through the green branches'; for *discolor* cf. Ov. *Tr.* 5.5.8, for *aura* cf. Lucr. 4.252. Spenser imitates the use of *discolor*

in *F.Q.* 3.11.47 (of Iris) 'when her discolourd bow she spreds through heaven bright'.

205 f. 'Just like the mistletoe which often in the woods in the cold of winter puts out new leaves, nourished by a tree not its own, entwining the smooth trunk with its yellow growth'; see note on 136–7.

209. **sic ... vento**: 'such was the foil tinkling in the gentle breeze'; *brattea* is thin metal, cf. Lucr. 4.727. The verb in this phrase is not relevant to the mistletoe comparison, only to the description of the bough.

211. **cunctantem**: this has seemed to many a contradiction with 147–8, but in fact refers quite appropriately to the natural resistance of a plant with pliant stem (137) to being picked off; for a not dissimilar usage cf. *Geo.* 2.236, and *Aen.* 5.856 ('slowly yielding').

212–35. *The funeral rites for Misenus are performed.*

212 f. Virgil gives a long description of the funeral rites (cf. Pallas' funeral, *Aen.* 11.59 f.); he is in any case fond of describing religious rites, being a poet interested in antiquity and tradition, and here the additional purpose is served of building up the mood for the entrance to the underworld (as also in the following episode, the preparatory sacrifices). The description is based on Patroclus' funeral (Hom. *Il.* 23.163 f.), but it also contains Roman elements such as the averted faces, the *dapes*, the *lustratio* and the *novissima verba* (cf. *Aen.* 11.97 f.). See Fletcher ad loc. and Bailey, *Religion in Virgil*, pp. 287 f.

213. A mournful and sonorous line; notice the pause after the first foot spondee, and the rhyme of the verbs.

214. **pinguem**: 'rich' perhaps in the sense of resinous (Lucr. 5.296), in which case the word goes more closely with *taedis* than with *robore secto*. But it may simply mean that the huge pyre is amply provided with pine and oak; it is unlikely that *pinguem* goes with *taedis* and *ingentem* with *robore secto*.

215. **atris**: probably from the cypresses (216), cf. *Aen.* 3.64. The cypress with its dark foliage was the tree of death, cf. Hor. *Odes* 2.14.22 f.

220. **defleta**: 'lamented', cf. *Aen.* 11.59, Lucr. 3.907.

221. The reference is probably to the tradition of purple shrouds for the burial of great men (cf. *Aen.* 11.72, Livy 34.7.2–3)

rather than to well-known purple garments which Misenus had worn in life (for which perhaps cf. *Aen.* 11.195).

223-4. subiectam ... facem: 'with faces averted held the torch applied beneath according to the ancestral tradition'; cf. Lucr. 6.1285.

225. dapes: sacrificial offerings of food.

fuso ... olivo: 'bowls of flowing olive oil'; notice the Greek nominative *crateres* with short final syllable, cf. 289.

226. Cf. Hom. *Il.* 23.250 f., a passage which Virgil has very much in mind; see note on 212 f.

228. 'and Corynaeus collected the bones and placed them in a bronze urn'; *lecta* is equivalent to *collecta*, cf. Ov. *Her.* 10.150.

229. circumtulit: 'circled'; a strange use of the word, apparently a traditional technical term in religion; Servius quotes Plautus *pro larvato te circumferam.*

230. felicis: fertile, as opposed to the wild olive (oleaster), cf. *Aen.* 7.751.

232-3. 'placed on top a tomb and the hero's own equipment, his oar and his trumpet'; above the burnt out pyre Aeneas has a tomb constructed, adorned with Misenus' oar (for the seven-years' voyage, cf. also Hom. *Od.* 12.15) and his special emblem, the trumpet (cf. 164 f.). For the use of *suus = proprius* cf. *Aen.* 1.461. That *arma* does not here mean weapons is shown by 217 and Hom. *Od.* 12.13; the armour was placed on the pyre which was burnt and is now covered up by the mound. For *arma*, 'equipment', cf. *Aen.* 1.177.

234-5. It has indeed kept its name through the centuries; at the present day Punta di Miseno is a very prominent land-mark in the Cumae area, with its remarkable flat top; for the aetiology see note on 5.117 f. and cf. 381.

236-63. *The preparatory sacrifices are made, and Aeneas and the Sibyl enter the underworld together.*

238. scrupea: a rare word, used by Ennius, meaning 'jagged', made up of small pointed stones.

239. volantes: 'birds', cf. line 728 and Lucr. 2.1083; the participle is used as a noun. For the general description cf. Ap. Rh. 4.601 f., Lucr. 6.740 f., and note on 201.

242. This line is omitted by most of the major MSS, and is undoubtedly spurious, a gloss added by some learned scribe. It makes the derivation of Avernus from the Greek negative prefix ἀ- and ὄρνις (bird).

243. **terga**: Greek accusative of respect, cf. 495–6 and *Aen.* 5.97.

244. **fronti**: 'on to their heads', = *in frontem*; for this ritual cf. *Aen.* 4.61.

245–6. For the plucking and burning of hairs from a sacrificial victim cf. Hom. *Od.* 3.446.

247. **caeloque Ereboque potentem**: 'powerful both in the upper world and in Erebus'; for Hecate see note on 118. *Caelum* is used several times in this book (e.g. 719) to mean the upper world; for Erebus cf. *Aen.* 4.26.

249 f. The mother of the Furies (see note on 280) is Night (cf. *Aen.* 7.331, 12.860) and her sister is Earth; for the black lamb cf. Hom. *Od.* 11.32, *Il.* 3.103, and for the barren cow Hom. *Od.* 11.30.

252. **Stygio regi**: Pluto (*Iuppiter Stygius* in 4.638).

253. **solida ... viscera**: 'whole carcasses'.

254. **super**: the last syllable is lengthened in arsis, cf. 768 and see note on 1.668. The MSS here (as there) have added *-que* to 'heal' the metre.

255. **lumina**: some MSS have *limina*, but the point here is the time (dawn; cf. Ap. Rh. 3.1223–4), not the place (east) as is the case in Cat. 64.271 *vagi sub limina solis*.

256. **mugire**: historic infinitive, cf. 199; for supernatural happenings of this kind cf. *Aen.* 3.90 f., 4.490 f.

257. For the dogs associated with Hecate cf. Ap. Rh. 3.1217 (Jason's invocation of Hecate, which Virgil clearly has in mind here).

258. **procul ... profani**: a religious formula excluding the uninitiated, cf. Hor. *Odes* 3.1.1 f.

262. **antro se immisit aperto**: 'rushed forward into the open cave'; *se immisit* is a strong phrase, often used in a military context, cf. Livy 9.4.10.

263. **aequat**: 'kept pace with', cf. *Aen.* 3.671.

264–94. *The poet invokes the gods of the underworld to permit him to tell of the journey. At the entrance Aeneas and the Sibyl are confronted by various horrible shapes of personified forms of suffering, and a host of monstrous and unnatural creatures of mythology.*

264 f. Virgil had many possible sources for personifications such as those presented here (273–81), e.g. Hesiod *Theog.* 211 f., Lucr. 3.59 f., Cic. *Nat. De.* 3.44; but we do not know of any previous writer who described them as being at the entrance to the underworld. On the other hand the monsters (285–9) are mostly associated with Hell, and are placed there e.g. in Aristophanes' *Frogs* (143, 278). Several of them are connected with Hercules, personifying an archaic barbarity of which he purged the world (cf. his encounter with Cacus, 8.184 f.). The choice of the personifications is based partly on traditional folklore, but with special contemporary overtones (e.g. Discordia), and perhaps special reference to Aeneas himself (*ultrices Curae*). In particular there are echoes of Lucretius throughout (3.59 f., 4.732, 5.22 f., 5.890 f.) as Virgil describes the horrors and fears from which Lucretius strove so hard to free men's minds. Virgil gives a kind of medieval iconography of Hell, but avoids the grosser and more ghastly features possible in such a description (see Butler's *Aeneid 6*, note on 285–9). Compare the different list in Spenser's imitation of this passage (*F.Q.* 2.7.21–3).

264–7. The new invocation draws special attention to the importance of the events about to be described (cf. *Aen.* 7.37 f.); it is addressed not to the Muses but to the mysterious primordial deities of the underworld.

265. Chaos (cf. *Aen.* 4.510) was the parent of Night and Erebus; Phlegethon is the burning river of the underworld (cf. 551), Pyriphlegethon in Homer (*Od.* 10.513).

266. **sit numine vestro**: 'let it be permitted by your divine power'; understand *fas* from the previous clause, rather than taking *sit* in the sense of *liceat*.

268 f. Observe the slow spondaic movement of these famous lines, and the juxtaposition of nouns and adjectives (a feature of normal usage generally avoided by Virgil, and thus available for special effect, cf. 638 f., Norden's Appendix IV, and see note on 5.845).

270 f. 'like people walking through the woods in the grudging light of a dim moon, when Jupiter has hidden the heavens in shadow and black night has taken the colour away from the world'.

Page quotes Milton, *P.L.* 1.63 'no light, but rather darkness visible'.

273. 'In front of the porch itself, in the very jaws of Orcus....'; Virgil visualised the end of the cave as a narrow passage (*fauces*) leading to a porch or forecourt outside the actual entrance to the palace of Dis. Orcus was a Latin deity identified with Pluto (Dis); the word is often used, as here, to mean the underworld (cf. *Aen.* 4.242).

274. **ultrices ... Curae**: 'the stings of guilty conscience' (so Servius); cf. *Juv.* 13.192 f.

275. **Morbi tristisque Senectus**: the same words in *Geo.* 3.67; cf. Sen. *Ep. Mor.* 108.28 where the Virgil passage is quoted to illustrate the statement *senectus enim insanabilis morbus est*.

276. Virgil has in mind Lucr. 3.65 f. *turpis enim ferme contemptus et acris egestas ... videntur ... quasi iam leti portas cunctarier ante*. *Malesuada* is a very rare word (Plaut. *Most.* 213); Virgil may be thinking of Hom. *Od.* 17.286 f.

278. **consanguineus Leti Sopor**: in Homer (*Il.* 14.231) Sleep is the brother of death.

278–9. **mala mentis Gaudia**: again Virgil is probably thinking of the Lucretius passage (3.59 f.) where *avarities* and *honorum caeca cupido* are the evil qualities which lead to misery. Seneca (*Ep. Mor.* 59.3) interprets *gaudia* as *voluptates*.

280. For the Eumenides cf. 250, 375, *Aen.* 4.469. Notice the alliteration of *d* in the last two words; Virgil gives to the hated Discordia (with all its connexions with civil war) the characteristic snaky hair of the Furies. For personified Discordia cf. *Aen.* 8.702, Ennius quoted in Hor. *Sat.* 1.4.60, and Homer's personified Eris (Strife), (*Il.* 20.48).

ferreique: the word scans as a spondee by synizesis; cf. line 412 and *Aen.* 1.698.

281. **crinem**: retained accusative, see note on 156.

282. **in medio**: this may mean, as Servius suggests, in the middle of the porch, but it is more likely that we are now in the courtyard inside the gates, as Virgil gradually phases out the notion of a palace and prepares to describe the large scale geography of Hell.

283–4. The elm has vain dreams clinging like bats beneath its boughs; these are the *falsa insomnia* of the ivory gate (896) waiting to attend and mislead sleeping mortals in the upper world. This is presumably a piece of ancient folklore (*vulgo . . . ferunt*) which Virgil has transformed into a pictorial tableau of remarkable visual impact.

283. **vulgo**: better with *ferunt* (a common tradition) than with *tenere* ('clinging everywhere', cf. *Aen.* 3.643).

285 f. 'And in addition many monstrous shapes of different wild creatures have their dens at the doors, Centaurs and bipartite Scyllas. . .'. See note on 264 f. and cf. Milton's description (*P.L.* 2.622 f.):

> 'A Universe of death, which God by curse
> Created evil, for evil only good,
> Where all life dies, death lives, and nature breeds,
> Perverse, all monstrous, all prodigious things,
> Abominable, inutterable, and worse
> Than Fables yet have feignd, or fear conceiv'd,
> Gorgons and Hydras, and Chimeras dire.'

286. **Centauri . . . Scyllaeque**: the Centaurs, composite figures of a human and a horse, occur in a more cheerful context in *Aen.* 7.675; for Scylla, a maiden above and sea-monster below (*biformis*, cf. 25) see notes on 3.420 f., 424 f. Centaurs and Scyllas (as well as Chimaeras) are mentioned by Lucretius (5.890 f., cf. 4.732) as creatures which cannot have existed. Scylla is pluralised (like Triton, 5.824); this is helped by confusion with the other Scylla (*Ecl.* 6.74–5).

287. **Briareus . . . belua Lernae**: Briareus was a hundred-armed giant also called Aegaeon (*Aen.* 10.565). The beast of Lerna (a place in Argos) was the hydra killed by Hercules (*Aen.* 8.300); cf. Lucr. 5.26.

288. For the Chimaera, a tripartite dragon, cf. Lucr. 5.905 and see note on 5.118; cf. also *Aen.* 7.785 where Turnus has a firebreathing Chimaera as the emblem on his helmet.

289. **Gorgones**: Greek nominative plural with short -*es*, cf. 225; the most famous Gorgon was Medusa (see note on 2.616). Hercules was confronted by her phantom on his descent to Hell.

Harpyiaeque: see note on 3.211–12.

forma tricorporis umbrae: i.e. Geryon, cf. 7.662, 8.202, Lucr. 5.28. It was one of Hercules' labours to deal with him.

291. **aciem**: 'blade', 'edge', cf. *Aen.* 2.333.

292-4. 'and if his wise companion had not warned him that they were unsubstantial bodiless creatures flitting about in the unreal semblance of shape, he would have rushed at them. . . .' The present subjunctives are used to make the past unfulfilled condition more vivid and immediate, cf. *Aen.* 2.599 f., 5.325 f.

295-336. *At the river Styx waits the ferryman Charon, a figure of horrid squalor. The shades flock to the river, and Charon ferries across those who have been buried, leaving the others to wait for a hundred years.*

295 f. The ferryman Charon is perhaps the best-known of all Pluto's people; he is a 'demon' of folk-story, often portrayed (as Charun) on Etruscan tombs. In literature he has become less terrifying; he is a grumpy and rather humorous character in Aristophanes' *Frogs* (180 f.), and Virgil's presentation of him is to some extent mock-heroic (see note on 385 f.), affording a contrast with the pathos of the other elements in the story.

295. **Acherontis**: Acheron was one of the rivers of the under-world (cf. line 107, *Aen.* 5.99, Hom. *Od.* 10.513 f.); it is here identified with Styx (154, 385), traditionally the river which the unburied may not cross.

296-7. 'Here a whirlpool thick with mud and of unfathomed abyss boils up and belches all its sand out into Cocytus'; for Cocytus see note on 132.

298 f. 'The grim ferryman who guards these waters and rivers is Charon, of horrible unkempt appearance with a mass of tangled white hair on his chin'. *Portitor* is strictly 'harbour-master' (*portus*), but as this harbour-master was also the ferryman the traditional rendering may stand. Notice the interwoven order at the beginning and the jingling rhyme of *has . . . aquas*. For Charon cf. *Geo.* 4.502 and note on 295 f.

300. **stant lumina flamma**: 'his eyes are fixed and fiery', literally 'are fixed with flame', cf. *Aen.* 12.407 f. *iam pulvere caelum stare vident*, and Hom. *Il.* 13.474. The reading *flammae*, whether genitive singular or nominative plural, would give very strange Latin.

303. **ferruginea**: 'rust-coloured', dull red, cf. Lucr. 4.76, *Geo.* 1.467, and Mackail ad loc. In 410 the boat is *caeruleus* ('greyish'); both words suggest a dusky colour.

304. 'aged now, but a god's old age is fresh and green'; for *crudus* cf. ὠμογέρων in Hom. *Il.* 23.791. The phrase is imitated in Tac. *Agr.* 29 *adfluebat omnis iuventus et quibus cruda ac viridis senectus*.

305 f. Compare Homer's description of the ghosts, *Od.* 11.36 f.

306–8. These three lines are repeated from *Geo.* 4.475–7. For the form *magnanimum* see note on 3.704.

309 f. The main point of the simile (for which cf. Hom. *Il.* 3.2 f., 6.146, Ap. Rh. 4.216 f., *Geo.* 4.473 f.) is the large number of ghosts (*quam multa . . . quam multae*); a second point of similarity is the fluttering of the ghosts like leaves and birds; a third is that for the ghosts, as for the leaves and the migrating birds, the summer of their lives is past. Milton imitates Virgil in *P.L.* 1.302 f. 'Thick as Autumnal Leaves that strow the Brooks / in Vallombrosa. . .'.

311. **annus**: 'season', cf. Hor. *Odes* 3.23.8.

313–14. These famous lines are especially memorable because the pathos of the thought is reinforced by a slow spondaic movement with most subtle assonance (notice especially *-an-*, and *-or-* at the close); for the thought cf. Milton, *P.L.* 2.606–7 'And wish and struggle, as they pass, to reach / the tempting stream . . .'.

313. **orantes primi transmittere**: this construction is a Grecism (= *ut primi transirent*, Servius), cf. *Aen.* 9.231.

transmittere cursum: 'to make the crossing', cf. *Aen.* 4.154; here however the accusative is cognate.

317. **enim**: 'indeed', cf. 28.

324. 'by whose divinity the gods fear to swear and break their oath'; an oath by Styx was the most binding of all possible oaths, cf. Hom. *Il.* 15.37. *Numen* is cognate accusative, cf. 351.

325. **inhumataque**: the tradition that the unburied would not find rest is common throughout Greek and Latin literature, cf. Hom. *Il.* 23.70 f., *Od.* 11.71 f.

327–8. The construction is *non datur Charoni transportare eos trans ripas. . . .*

330. **revisunt**: i.e. they had been forced to wait some distance away, and then at last could come back; the spondees and elisions in this line contribute to the sonorous effect of the Sibyl's final sentence.

333. **mortis honore**: 'death's tribute', i.e. burial, cf. *Aen.* 10.493.

334. Leucaspis is not heard of elsewhere; the sinking of the ship of Orontes and his Lycians was described in *Aen.* 1.113 f.

337-83. *Aeneas meets the ghost of his helmsman Palinurus and hears the story of his death. Palinurus begs for burial, or to be taken across the Styx although unburied, but the Sibyl replies that this is impossible. She consoles him by telling him that the cape where he died will bear his name for ever.*

337 f. For the story of Palinurus see note on 5.827 f. There are certain inconsistencies between the account here and that in Book 5, for instance that the sea there was calm while here it is stormy, and that *Libyco cursu* (338) is a strange phrase for the last stage of the journey between Sicily and Italy (even allowing that the Trojans had come from Carthage before that). It is probable that Virgil would have made the necessary minor changes in revision. For fuller discussion see the Intro. to my Oxford edition of *Aeneid* 5, pp. xxv f.

The factual material of the legend of Palinurus probably came to Virgil through Varro, and he has conflated it with Homer's story of the unburied Elpenor, whose ghost is the first to appear to Odysseus in *Od.* 11. Virgil has added a pathos typical of his method of writing; the account of the death of Palinurus at the end of Book 5 is one of the most moving passages in the *Aeneid*, and here we see the sequel, the undeserved suffering of the faithful helmsman, and the deep sorrow of Aeneas at the irrevocable loss of his comrade, a scapegoat required by destiny for the safe arrival in Italy. It is the first of the events of the past which Aeneas must live through again in his passage through the underworld, and then leave behind for ever (see Otis, *Virgil*, pp. 290 f.).

337. **sese . . . agebat**: 'was moving', cf. *Aen.* 8.465, 9.696.

338. **Libyco . . . cursu**: 'on the journey from Libya', cf. 5.833 f. The phrase is strange in view of the long stop in Sicily during the voyage from Carthage to Italy.

339. 'had fallen from the ship, flung forth in mid-ocean'. The ablative after *effusus* draws attention to his plight after his fall rather than to his fall itself.

345. There is no reference to this promise earlier in the *Aeneid*.

345-6. **finisque . . . Ausonios**: accusative of motion towards, cf. *Aen.* 1.2-3.

346. The unusual monosyllabic ending expresses excitement and indignation; see note on 5.481.

347. **cortina**: the cauldron of the oracular tripod, hence the oracle, cf. *Aen.* 3.92.

348. **nec ... mersit**: i.e. I was not drowned, but did in fact reach Italy.

349 f. 'for the rudder was in fact ripped away by some mighty force (the rudder which I was holding firmly as its appointed guardian, directing the course of the ship), and as I went headlong I dragged it with me'. The connexion of thought is perhaps simply 'for the truth is as follows', or possibly (as Servius says) 'for I had the rudder which saved me from drowning'. For *praecipitans* intransitively used cf. *Aen.* 2.9.

351. **maria aspera iuro**: 'I swear by the rough seas', cf. 324.

352-4. 'that I did not feel any fear so much for myself as in case your ship, stripped of its steering-gear, deprived of its helmsman, might sink in those great surging billows'. For *capere timorem* cf. Livy 33.27.10; for the omission of the subject of the infinitive (*me*) cf. *Aen.* 2.432-3, 4.305-6. *Excussa magistro* is an innovation equivalent to *unde excussus erat magister* (*Aen.* 1.115).

355. **tris**: accusative plural (*tres*) cf. *Aen.* 3.203.

356. **vix**: i.e. the Italian coast was still far off. Virgil is here recalling the passage from Homer (*Od.* 5.392 f.) where Odysseus reaches the coast of Phaeacia by swimming after his raft was destroyed; cf. also note on 360.

359. The unfulfilled condition depends on an ellipse: 'was reaching safety (and would have reached it) had not' ..., cf. *Aen.* 5.355 f., 8.522 f.

360. 'trying to grab with clutching fingers the jagged top of a high cliff', cf. Hom. *Od.* 5.428 f. and for this use of *mons* cf. *Aen.* 12.687.

361. **praedamque ... putasset**: 'and foolishly thought that I was booty worth having'.

363. **quod**: 'therefore', cf. *Aen.* 2.141.

364. **per spes ... Iuli**: cf. *Aen.* 4.274.

365-7. **aut tu ... aut tu**: notice the emphasis on the appeal to Aeneas personally in both cases (either to bury his body or take him over the Styx although unburied).

366. portusque require Velinos: notice the co-ordination, where in English we would say 'by returning to the harbour of Velia'; see note on 2.353 and Page on 6.361. Virgil was criticised in ancient times for this anachronism, as Velia (just north of Punta di Palinuro in Lucania) was not founded till long after Palinurus' day (Aul. Gell. 10.16).

369. innare: 'journey over', see note on 16.

371. saltem: with the whole sentence; if Palinurus could not share in the successful conclusion of the Trojan mission, at least he should find peace in death.

374. severum: 'grim', cf. *Geo.* 3.37 f. *Furias amnemque severum / Cocyti metuet.*

379 f. Servius says this is based on history; when the people of Lucania were suffering from a plague the oracle told them to placate the ghost of Palinurus, and so they consecrated a grove and a tomb to him.

379. piabunt: 'appease', cf. Hor. *Ep.* 2.1.143.

381. It is still called Punta di Palinuro; for the aetiology see note on 234–5.

383. cognomine terrae: 'in the name of the land', in the fact that the land would bear his name. The major MSS all read *terrae*; Servius read *terra* and explained *cognomine* as ablative of *cognominis* ('bearing the same name'), and many modern editors accept this. But Virgil nowhere else uses such an ablative form (for *cognomini*), although Ovid does (e.g. *Met.* 15.743); and it really seems that the testimony of the MSS should prevail.

384–416. *Aeneas and the Sibyl are challenged by Charon; the Sibyl shows the golden bough and Charon ferries them across the Styx to the further shore.*

384 f. In the encounter with Charon (see note on 295 f.) the epic tone is lowered to afford relief between the emotional tension of the encounters with Palinurus and with Dido. Charon's challenge (388 f.) is blustering and bombastic (390–1), and he proceeds in a tone of indignation and complaint to inform the newcomers that he was made to suffer for it when he failed on previous occasions to keep the rules, adding (395–7) some gratuitous information about those occasions. The Sibyl replies coolly and sarcastically, urging Charon to keep calm (399) and ironically building up her description of Cerberus (400–1); she grandiloquently draws attention to Aeneas' qualities and mission (403–4), and pauses for her words to take effect. They have no effect, so peremptorily she tells him to take a look at the golden bough which she carries, and he is promptly deflated (*nec plura his*, 408). The scene ends with the half-comic picture of the mighty figure of Aeneas among the weightless ghosts, very nearly sinking the ship.

385. **iam inde**: 'from where he was', cf. *iam istinc*, 389.

392. **nec . . . sum laetatus**: Charon 'got no joy' from breaking the rules and according to Servius was chained up for a year as a punishment.

Alciden: Hercules went down to the underworld to bring back the dog Cerberus (*Tartareum . . . custodem* 395 f., cf. 400 f., and see note on 122–3).

393. **Thesea Pirithoumque**: they tried to steal Proserpina (*dominam Ditis* 397, cf. 402 and see note on 122–3).

394. **essent**: the subjunctive is sometimes used in poetry after *quamquam* by analogy with the use after *quamvis*; cf. Ov. *Met.* 14.465.

398. **Amphrysia**: this epithet of Apollo, whose priestess the Sibyl was, derives from his period of servitude to Admetus in Thessaly on the banks of the river Amphrysus (*Geo.* 3.2). Servius is justified in his comment *longe petitum epitheton*.

402. **patrui**: Proserpina was daughter of Jupiter by Ceres; Pluto was Jupiter's brother.

servet . . . limen: 'look after the home', cf. *Aen.* 7.52, 8.412.

403. **pietate . . . et armis**: cf. *Aen.* 1.10, 545.

405. **nulla**: 'not at all', cf. *Aen.* 4.232 and Cat. 8.14.

406. **at**: introducing the main clause after a conditional clause, as in *Aen.* 4.615, *Geo.* 4.241. Notice the staccato narrative as the Sibyl produces her credentials (the subjunctive *agnoscas* is mockingly deferential) and Charon instantly yields.

407. **corda**: Charon's heart, poetic plural as often, cf. 49, 80.

408. **nec plura his**: sc. *dicta sunt*; no more was said on either side.

409. **fatalis virgae**: 'the fateful bough'; the golden bough is *fatalis* because only those whom fate favours may have it (cf. 147). We do not know on what occasion Charon had last seen it,

possibly when Orpheus descended to bring back Eurydice (obviously Hercules and Theseus had not had it).

411. **iuga**: 'benches', a very rare use of the word in this sense, an imitation of the Greek ζυγά.

412. **deturbat**: 'pushes out of the way', cf. *Aen.* 5.175.

laxatque foros: 'and clears the gangways'.

alveo: 'in his hollow boat', cf. Prop. 3.7.16. The word is scanned as a spondee by synizesis, cf. 280 and *Aen.* 7.33.

413-14. 'the boat of skins groaned at the weight and took in a quantity of water through the seams'; *sutilis* is 'sewn', i.e. stitched together; *rimosa* ('chinky') means that the seams gaped apart. The boat was adequate for ghosts, but was put under most severe strain by a living warrior. Compare Hom. *Il.* 5.838 f., where Athena mounts Diomedes' chariot and the axle groans at the weight.

417-25. *Cerberus guards the far bank of the Styx; the Sibyl throws a sop to him, and together with Aeneas enters the region of the untimely dead.*

417 f. The dog of the underworld is mentioned in Homer (*Il.* 8.366 f., *Od.* 11.623 f.), but not by name — he is first named in Hesiod (*Theog.* 311), and thereafter is a favourite figure in poetic descriptions of Hell, with three or more heads and snakes for hair (cf. Hor. *Odes* 2.13.33 f., 3.11.17 f., Spenser *F.Q.* 1.5.34). Virgil does not dwell on frightening or repulsive aspects of Cerberus; like Charon he is part of the traditional machinery of Hell, stylized and unreal compared with the personal reality of the ghosts of Palinurus, Dido and Deiphobus.

417-18. 'the massive shape of Cerberus makes these realms re-echo with his barking from all three throats'. For *personare* cf. 171; *trifaux* does not occur elsewhere.

420. 'a morsel made sleepy with honey and drugged meal'; the phrase 'a sop to Cerberus' is based on this line. Compare generally the drugging of the dragon in Ap. Rh. 4.149 f.

421. **fame**: the final *e* is long, a survival of a fifth declension form, cf. Lucr. 3.732.

422-3. 'and promptly relaxed his mighty frame as he sank down on the ground and lay stretched out in all his bulk, covering the whole cave'. The tone is mock-heroic and humorous; Disney would have done it justice.

424. **sepulto**: 'buried in sleep', cf. *Aen.* 2.265.

425. **evadit**: 'got away from', cf. *Aen.* 3.282.

425. **inremeabilis**: 'that permits no return', cf. *Aen.* 5.591 (of the Labyrinth).

426–93. The Sibyl and Aeneas now reach Limbo, the region of the untimely dead. Here are the souls of infants, the unjustly condemned, suicides and those who died from unhappy love. Here they meet the shade of Dido; Aeneas speaks to her in tones of deep affection and remorse, but she turns from him without a word.

426 f. The area of Hades where the untimely dead are gathered was traditional, and Virgil uses it chiefly as a setting for the ghosts of Dido and Deiphobus. He does not define how long the ghosts remain here (one traditional version was that they stayed for the rest of their natural life, but the impression in Virgil is one of static permanence), nor endeavour to reconcile this feature of the traditional topography of Hades with the metaphysical speech of Anchises (724 f.). For a discussion of these inconsistencies see Norden's edition, pp. 11 f.; but it is more profitable to consider what Virgil has achieved poetically by his Limbo than to dwell on eschatological inconsistencies.

The first three classes (infants, the unjustly condemned, suicides) are briefly described without any specific references, and serve to build up the atmosphere of sorrow and bewilderment which becomes powerfully predominant at the appearance of Dido's ghost. In the Mourning Fields we meet first a series of traditional heroines who make no especial emotional impact (see note on 445 f.), a crowd scene preparatory to the appearance of the most tragic figure of the whole *Aeneid*. Aeneas attempts to explain his conduct, and his reasons for sacrificing his personal feelings of love for her, just as he had in Book 4 (see notes on 460, 463) — but this time *he* is pleading while *she* is not listening. Echoes of Book 4 in his speech (456, 463, 466) increase the feeling of tragic irony, and when Dido finally rejects him he is still looking back, tormented with guilt and remorse, to the sorrows of the past, not yet turning (as at the end of his experiences in the underworld he learns he must) to a new future. He has to learn the hard lesson that he has caused Dido's death, that her ghost is implacably hostile to him, and that there is nothing he can now do about what has happened except to leave the past behind.

426. 'Straight away sounds could be heard, and a great
noise of wailing'; the postponed *et* emphasises the imitative alliteration of the words beginning with *v*.

427. **in limine primo**: many editors punctuate so that this
goes with what follows and refers to the threshold of life (cf. Lucr.
3.681, Lucan 2.106, Sil. 13.548), but in this topographical picture
in limine primo (at the entrance to Limbo) balances *hos iuxta* (430).

428. **exsortis**: 'without having had a share in', equivalent to
expertes (Servius), cf. Livy 23.10.3.

430. **damnati ... mortis**: 'condemned to death'; the genitive
is similar to the prose phrase *damnari capitis*, cf. also Hor. *Odes*
2.14.19.

431. **sine sorte**: a reference to the Roman practice of appointing the jury by lot; they were presided over by a *quaesitor* (432)
and would constitute a *consilium* (433).

432. **Minos**: he is a judge of the underworld in Homer (*Od.*
11.568 f.); cf. Plato *Gorg.* 524a, Hor. *Odes* 4.7.21–22.

433. **consilium**: 'jury'; some MSS have *concilium* ('a gathering
of the dead'), but the legal technical term is appropriate here.

435. **peperere**: perfect of *pario*, 'produced' death for themselves, i.e. committed suicide, a variant for *mortem sibi consciscere*.

436–7. 'How they would now wish, in the upper world high
above, to endure both poverty and hard suffering'. Virgil's
comment recalls Achilles' statement in the underworld (Hom.
Od. 11.488 f.); 'I would prefer to be a serf on earth serving a poor
master rather than to be king of all the dead'. It runs counter to
the contemporary Stoic attitude to suicide as an honourable
escape from an intolerable position (Hor. *Odes* 1.12.35–6).

436. **aethere in alto**: compare the use of *caelum* for the upper
world as viewed from the underworld (719) and cf. *ad superos*
(481).

438. **tristique ... unda**: the major MSS read *tristisque ...
undae*, which is accepted by modern editors; but the ablative
(supported by Servius) gives a far more Virgilian ring, and it is
hard to think that *palus undae* is possible Latin (*palus aquae* would
be). Cf. *Geo.* 4.479 and Hor. *Odes* 2.14.8–9 *Geryonen Tityonque
tristi / compescit unda*.

438–9. The second phrase repeats and emphasizes the first —
the hateful waters hem them in, yes, Styx with its ninefold winding

imprisons them; the lines are repeated almost exactly from *Geo.* 4.479–80. Cf. Milton, *P.L.* 2.434 f.: 'our prison strong, this huge convex of Fire, / outrageous to devour, immures us round / ninefold, and gates of burning Adamant / Barrd over us prohibit all egress'.

440. fusi: 'extending', an unusual use of the word, cf. Lucan 4.670.

441. Lugentes Campi: 'the Mourning Fields'; we do not know from what source Virgil derived this name, or whether it is original with him. The personification of *campi* makes it remarkable and memorable; Fletcher compares the Wailing Wall.

443. myrtea: sacred to Venus, goddess of love, cf. *Aen.* 5.72.

445 f. This crowd scene of seven heroines irrelevant to the action of the *Aeneid* serves to focus the attention very sharply on the one who is not irrelevant — *inter quas Phoenissa*. . . . The scene is based on the long procession of heroines in Hom. *Od.* 11.225 f.; cf. especially 11.321, 326. Phaedra's love for her step-son Hippolytus is well-known from Euripides and Seneca; Procris (concealed and jealously watching her husband Cephalus) was accidentally killed by him (Ov. *Met.* 7.694 f.); Eriphyle, bribed by a necklace, induced her husband Amphiaraus to join the Argive war against the Thebans in which he was killed, and his son Alcmaeon killed her in vengeance; Evadne, the wife of Capaneus, killed herself on his pyre; for Pasiphae's passion for the bull (which caused Minos to cast her into prison, where she died) cf. lines 25 f.; Laodamia, the wife of Protesilaus, the first Greek to be killed at Troy (Cat. 68.73 f., Ov. *Her.* 13), chose to accompany him back to the underworld after he had been permitted to visit her for a brief time; Caeneus was the maiden Caenis, changed by Neptune into a male and after death reverting to her original sex (Ov. *Met.* 12.172 f.).

453–4. 'like the moon which a man sees or thinks he sees rising up through the clouds at the month's beginning', i.e. faint because (i) a crescent moon (ii) in a cloudy sky. For *aut videt aut vidisse putat* cf. Ap. Rh. 4.1479–80 and Milton, *P.L.* 1.783–4.

455. Notice the reiteration at this last moment of Aeneas' love for Dido, cf. *Aen.* 4.395.

456. infelix Dido: so Virgil has often called her, and so she called herself at the end (4.596).

verus mihi nuntius: cf. the beginning of Book 5 for the
forebodings of the Trojans when they saw flames in Carthage.

460. For the sense cf. *Aen.* 4.361 *Italiam non sponte sequor.* The
form of the line is very similar indeed to Cat. 66.39 where the
lock of hair, snipped from Queen Berenice's head, says *invita o
regina tuo de vertice cessi.* It is astonishing that Virgil has transferred
a line from a mock-heroic, indeed comic, context to this passage
of intense emotional pathos. I do not find it satisfying to see in
this, as many commentators do, a supreme example of Virgil's
skill to do the near impossible successfully; I prefer to regard the
line as a wholly unconscious reminiscence.

462. **senta situ**: 'rough with neglect', i.e. 'ragged and
forlorn' (Page); *sentus* is a very rare word indeed (cf. Ter. *Eun.*
236, Ov. *Met.* 4.436) meaning 'uncared for', and *situs* conveys
absence of activity, a feeling of mould and decay (cf. *Geo.* 1.72).
Compare Milton, *P.L.* 1.180–1 'Seest thou yon dreary Plain,
forlorn and wild, / the seat of desolation . . . ?'.

463. **imperiis . . . suis**: cf. *Aen.* 4.237, 356 f.

466. **quem fugis?**: an echo, the irony of which the reader
easily catches, of Dido's *mene fugis* (*Aen.* 4.314); as Aeneas had
turned from Dido, Dido now turns from Aeneas.

extremum . . . hoc est: 'this is the last word which fate
allows me to speak to you'; notice the broken rhythm caused by
the elision of the monosyllable *te* and by the two monosyllables
in the sixth foot.

467–8. 'With these words Aeneas tried to soothe her fiery
grim-eyed anger, shedding tears'. *Torva tuentem* would apply
naturally to Dido herself, but is very striking with *animum*,
deliberately reminiscent perhaps of this kind of phrase in Greek
tragedy (Soph. *Ajax* 955, Aesch. *Choeph.* 854). For the adverbial
accusative cf. Lucr. 5.33 *acerba tuens* (= *Aen.* 9.794). *Lacrimasque
ciebat* might mean 'sought to arouse her tears', but cf. *Aen.* 3.344.

469 f. Dido's silence is modelled on that of Ajax in Hom. *Od.*
11.563 f., on which Longinus (9.2) comments that the silence is
more sublime than any words.

470. **vultum . . . movetur**: retained accusative, see note on
156.

471. Notice the irony again by comparison with *Aen.* 4.366–7
where Dido reviled Aeneas as being born from no natural mother,

but from the Caucasus mountains. For the simile cf. Eur. *Med.*
27 f.

Marpesia cautes: i.e. marble; Marpessos was a mountain
in Paros, famous for its marble, cf. *Aen.* 1.593.

474. 'answers her sorrow and requites her love'; for Sychaeus
cf. *Aen.* 1.343 f. By strict logic Sychaeus has no place here in the
Lugentes Campi; but logic is over-ridden by the poetic intention
to show that Dido no longer needs Aeneas, indeed has resumed her
deep devotion to her previous husband (4.457 f., 552, 656).

477–93. *Next they approach the final area of Limbo, home of the
renowned in war. Here they meet the ghosts of various Argive warriors,
and then of Trojan friends who welcome Aeneas with joy; finally the shades
of the Greek warriors run from Aeneas in panic.*

477 f. The ghosts in this last section of Limbo constitute a
crowd scene preparatory to the meeting with Deiphobus (494 f.).
The first group, the Argives, are described objectively, but the
other two (Trojans and then Greeks) are both brought into
emotional relationship with Aeneas through their joy and their
panic respectively; thus the way is prepared for Aeneas' deeply
emotional meeting with Deiphobus.

477. **molitur**: 'he presses along', cf. *Aen.* 10.477.

478. **ultima**: i.e. the furthest fields of this particular area
(Limbo).

479–80. These are three of the seven Argive leaders against
Thebes.

481. **ad superos**: 'in the world above', cf. 568, 680.

481. **caduci**: 'fallen', an unusual use of the word which
generally means 'destined to fall', and is normally applied to
inanimate things; cf. however Lucr. 5.1363, *Geo.* 1.368 (fallen
leaves), and *Aen.* 10.622 (a warrior destined to die).

483 f. The list of names is taken from Homer (*Il.* 17.216) and
the rhythm (with no main caesura in third or fourth foot, and a
polysyllabic ending) is also Greek. The three sons of Antenor are
given in Hom. *Il.* 11.59 f. as Polybus, Agenor, and Acamas.

484. Ceres' priest, Polyboetes, is not heard of elsewhere.

485. **Idaeumque**: Priam's charioteer, cf. Hom. *Il.* 24.325.

489 f. The contrast of the panic-striken Greeks with the
delighted Trojans is highly effective, underlined by the use of

historic infinitives and the alliteration of *v* and *t*. Compare generally Hom. *Od.* 11.605 f., where the ghosts are terrified of Hercules.

492. 'as when they ran for their ships in days gone by'; a reference to Trojan successes in the Trojan War which compelled the Greeks to retreat to the beach where their ships were anchored (e.g. Hom. *Il.* 15.320 f.).

492-3. 'some raised a cry, but only a little one; the noise they tried to produce mocked their wide-open mouths'; the ghosts can only squeak (cf. Hom. *Od.* 24.5), however loudly they try to shout.

494–547. *Aeneas meets the ghost of his comrade-in-arms, Deiphobus, still bearing the marks of the cruel wounds inflicted upon him. In grief and remorse Aeneas asks what happened, explaining that he was not able to find Deiphobus' body for burial. Deiphobus replies that Helen, his wife, had betrayed him to the vengeance of Menelaus and Odysseus; in his turn he asks Aeneas for his story. The Sibyl interrupts to hasten Aeneas on and Deiphobus retires to his place among the shades, wishing Aeneas better fortune for his future.*

494 f. Aeneas' meeting with Deiphobus is modelled in a general way upon that of Odysseus with the ghost of Agamemnon (Hom. *Od.* 11.387 f.), but Virgil has intensified the emotional mood by the sense of guilt which Aeneas feels for not having been able to pay the final rites to Deiphobus' dead body. This is the last of the three ghosts of his past encountered by Aeneas in the underworld; Deiphobus has not played a large part in the poem as Dido and Palinurus had, but he was mentioned in Book 2 in the account of Troy's last night (2.310), and his fate exemplifies the fate of all those comrades of Aeneas who did not survive the sack of Troy. Aeneas cannot tear himself away from conversation with his old friend, and after the Sibyl's intervention it is Deiphobus who ends the meeting, urging Aeneas to march on to the future. This is the point at which Aeneas is finally brought to realise that the past is dead.

495. **ora**: accusative of respect, like *manus, tempora, naris*; cf. 243 and see note on 1.320.

495-6. **ora . . . ora**: for this type of repetition, a method of increasing pathos, see note on *Aen.* 2.405-6.

496–7. 'and his temples disfigured, his ears ripped off, his nostrils torn with a shameful wound'; *inhonesto* implies moral condemnation (= *turpis*). For the idea of ghosts retaining their wounds cf. 450, *Aen*. 2.272 f.

499. **supplicia**: 'punishment', i.e. the vengeance taken on him by the Greeks for marrying Helen after the death of Paris in the last year of the war.

502. **cui . . . licuit?**: 'who had such power over you?'; cf. Lucan 9.1025.

502–3. **suprema nocte**: 'on that last night' (of Troy's existence), cf. 513.

503. **caede Pelasgum**: 'slaughter of the Greeks'; for the word Pelasgi cf. *Aen*. 1.624.

505. **tumulum . . . inanem**: a cenotaph, cf. *Aen*. 3.300 f. (Andromache's cenotaph for Hector, where she too calls on the *manes* of the dead man). For the three-fold invocation cf. Hom. *Od*. 9.65.

505. **Rhoeteo litore**: i.e. the shore near Troy, cf. 3.108.

507. **nomen et arma**: i.e. an inscription, and a dedication of armour, not of course Deiphobus' own.

507. **te amice**: shortening in hiatus is extremely unusual; see note on 3.211. It does not occur elsewhere in the *Aeneid* with a monosyllable; cf. *Ecl*. 2.65, 8.108.

509. **tibi . . . relictum**: 'left undone by you', dative of agent.

510. **funeris**: 'corpse', cf. 150.

511. **Lacaenae**: Helen, the woman of Sparta, cf. *Aen*. 2.601, and see note on 499.

512. **monimenta**: 'memorials of her'; bitterly sarcastic.

513–14. **ut . . . egerimus**: 'how we passed', perfect subjunctive (of *agere*) in an indirect question.

513. **falsa inter gaudia**: cf. *Aen*. 2.239 for the joy of the Trojans as they took in the wooden horse.

515. **fatalis**: 'sent by fate', cf. *Aen*. 2.237 *scandit fatalis machina muros*. *Saltu* gives a more exaggerated picture than *scandit*; it is a reminiscence of Ennius (*Scen*. 76–77) *nam maximo saltu superabit gravidus armatis equus, | qui suo partu ardua perdat Pergama*.

venit: the indicative is used after *cum* in its purely temporal sense, *eo tempore quo*, cf. 564.

516. For the imagery of the wooden horse pregnant with soldiers cf. *Aen.* 2.20, 243; this again goes back to Ennius, quoted on the previous line.

517 f. 'she was leading the Trojan women, feigning a religious dance, as they celebrated Bacchic rites all around the city'. This account of Helen's activity on the last night, as she contrives by the feigned celebration to give torch signals to the Greek fleet, is somewhat at variance with Aeneas' meeting with her as she hid in panic in Vesta's temple (2.567 f.). Doubtless the reason for this is the use of different sources and the incomplete state of revision of that part of *Aeneid* 2 (where see notes).

517. **euhantis orgia**: *euhare* (or *euare*) is to shout the Bacchic cry (cf. Cat. 64.391, *Aen.* 7.389), and here it is followed by an extended kind of cognate accusative (cf. 644).

521. **infelix ... thalamus**: Deiphobus was now married to Helen, see note on 499.

523. **egregia**: bitterly ironical, cf. *Aen.* 4.93.

524. **et ... ensem**: 'she had even removed my trusty sword from beside my head', i.e. before removing the armour from the rest of the house and calling in her former husband Menelaus (sarcastically called *amans* in line 526). For *capiti* cf. Tac. *Hist.* 2.49 (*pugionem*) *capiti subdidit*.

528. **quid moror?**: 'Why prolong the story?', cf. *Aen.* 2.102.

529. **Aeolides**: i.e. Ulysses, a reference to the version of his ancestry which made him the child of Anticleia not by Laertes, but illegitimately by the infamous Sisyphus, son of Aeolus; cf. Ov. *Met.* 13.31 f. For the especial hostility of the Trojans to Ulysses see note on 2.7 and cf. 2.164.

530. **instaurate**: 'renew' (e.g. *Aen.* 5.94), here in the sense of 'repay'.

531–2. As Conington points out, Virgil here has given to the indirect question the word order of a direct question: *qui te casus, age fare, attulerunt?*

533–4. **fatigat ut ... adires**: 'is dogging you so that you came....': the imperfect denotes a past effect of the present situation.

535 f. Fletcher well points out the contrast of this description of bright sunlight with the 'sad sunless dwellings' of the underworld; cf. *Aen.* 7.26.

537. 'and perhaps they would have spent all the allotted time talking thus', i.e. all the time allotted to Aeneas in the underworld, probably thought of as a single day. For *fors* (= *forsitan*) cf. 2.139; for *traherent* (= *traxissent*, past potential) cf. 31, 34.

540. For the parting of the ways cf. Plato, *Gorg.* 524a.

542. **Elysium**: 'to Elysium'; for the accusative of motion towards after a verbal noun (*iter*) cf. *Aen.* 3.507.

543. **exercet poenas**: 'brings into effect the punishment', (cf. *Aen.* 4.100, Tac. *Ann.* 1.44) by sending them on to Tartarus, the lowest part of Hell.

545. **explebo numerum**: 'I will fill up the number' (i.e. resume my allotted place); cf. Sen. *Phaedr.* 1153.

546. 'Onwards, glory of our race, onwards; and enjoy better fate'. Deiphobus' words mark a crucial turning-point in the development of the sixth book; Aeneas' encounters with his past are now over, and his thoughts must turn to the future.

548–627. Next they see Tartarus, the place of the worst sinners, guarded by the Fury Tisiphone. The Sibyl tells Aeneas that he may not enter; she describes to him the sinners and their punishments.

548f. The description of the damned in Tartarus is firmly based on Greek tradition: the tortures of Tityos, Tantalus (see note on 601f.) and Sisyphus are described in Homer (*Od.* 11.576f.), and the existence of Tartarus as a place of punishment for great sinners is an essential part of the underworld in Platonic myth (*Phaed.* 113e, *Gorg.* 526b). The visual impact of Virgil's passage is very great, and he may have based his writing partly on visual art, such as the painting by Polygnotus (Paus. 10.28f.).

Interspersed with the individual sinners are categories of sin (608f., 621f.). This again is in the Greek tradition (Plato, *Phaed.* 113e, Aristoph. *Frogs* 146f.), but Virgil has given his categories a special Roman relevance (see notes on 608f., 621f.).

The selection of the traditional sinners departs often from the orthodox. Salmoneus (585f.) is by no means a well-known figure; and the punishments allotted to several of the famous sinners differ from the usual version (see notes on 601f., 616–17, 617–18). Many commentators have seen in this a mark of incomplete revision by Virgil, as it may well be; but in scenes of this kind considerable variation may well be expected, and a

rhetorical and grandiose impact is more significant than antiquarian accuracy.

551. **Phlegethon**: the burning river, cf. 265.

552. **adamante**: a Greek word (e.g. Hes. *Theog.* 161) meaning
the hardest kind of substance; cf. Milton, *P.L.* 2.645-6, 'And
thrice threefold the Gates; three folds were Brass, / Three Iron,
three of Adamantine Rock, / Impenetrable, impal'd with circling
fire, / Yet unconsum'd.'

555. **Tisiphone**: one of the three Furies, cf. *Aen.* 10.761. The
word in Greek means 'voice of vengeance', cf. *ultrix* in 570.

557. **exaudiri**: historic infinitive, cf. *Aen.* 4.460.

558. **stridor . . . catenae**: the second phrase explains the
first. Notice the alliteration of *r*.

559. **strepitumque . . . hausit**: 'and, terrified, listened agog
to the noise'; for *hausit* cf. *Aen.* 4.359. Some MSS have *strepituque*
. . . haesit 'terrified by the noise, froze in his tracks' (cf. *Aen.* 3.597).
There is little to choose between the readings.

561. **plangor ad auras**: 'lamentation rising to the breezes';
this is the reading of the majority of MSS, and there is not much
to be said for the alternative *clangor ad auris* ('din reaching my
ears').

563. 'it is not permitted for any innocent person to set foot
on this threshold of crime'; for *insistere* with the accusative cf.
Geo. 3.164.

564. **Hecate**: see note on 118.

565. **deum poenas**: 'the punishment inflicted by the gods',
subjective genitive.

566. **Cnosius . . . Rhadamanthus**: like his brother Minos
(432) the judge Rhadamanthus was from Crete (see note on 23);
he is a judge of the dead in Plato *Gorg.* 523e.

567f. 'and he cross-examines them, hears their stories of
falsehood, and compels them to admit those sins whose atonements any of them in the world above, rejoicing in his pointless
deceit, had postponed till the late hour of death'. The phrase
commissa piacula is condensed: 'atonements incurred' for sins
committed.

571. **insultans**: 'leaping upon them', a vivid and terrifying
picture; for Tisiphone's whip and snakes cf. *Geo.* 4.482, Stat. *Th.*
1.112f., Val. Fl. 7.149.

572. **agmina saeva sororum**: i.e. Allecto and Megaera. For *agmina* cf. *Aen.* 4.469.

573. **horrisono**: a rare compound adjective, cf. *Aen.* 9.55; compare Milton, *P.L.* 2.879 f. 'On a sudden open flie / With impetuous recoil and jarring sound / Th' infernal dores, and on thir hinges grate / Harsh Thunder'.

574. **custodia**: abstract for concrete (*custos*, cf. *Aen.* 9.166), referring to Tisiphone. The connexion of thought is: 'You see Tisiphone? — the Hydra is worse'.

576. The Hydra, with its fifty (or sometimes a hundred) heads, is one of the species of the Lernean Hydra killed by Hercules (line 287, *Aen.* 7.658).

577–9. 'Then Tartarus itself stretches open and extends sheer beneath the shades twice as far as is the upward gaze at the sky towards heavenly Olympus'. Cf. Hom. *Il.* 8.16, Lucr. 4.416–17, and Milton, *P.L.* 1.73 f. 'As far remov'd from God and light of Heav'n / as from the Center thrice to th' utmost Pole'. *Caeli* is objective genitive after *suspectus*.

580. The Titans, sons of Mother Earth, rebelled against Jupiter and were destroyed; cf. *Geo.* 1.278 f. and see note on 4.178.

582. The two sons of Aloeus were Otus and Ephialtes; they piled Ossa on Pelion and Mt. Olympus on top of both in order to reach heaven and attack Jupiter, cf. Hom. *Od.* 11.305 f., *Geo.* 1.280 f.

582–3. **immania . . . corpora**: in apposition to *Aloidas*.

585 f. The story of Salmoneus and his punishment in Tartarus is a much less well-known one than the others mentioned in this section; cf. Manil. 5.91 f. *Salmonea* is Greek accusative, cf. 122, and *lampada* in 587, *Ixiona* in 601. *Dantem poenas dum . . .* means 'paying the penalty (incurred) while . . .', a strange ellipsis, but cf. Cicero's translation of Simonides (*Tusc.* 1.101) *Dic, hospes, Spartae nos te hic vidisse iacentes, / dum sanctis patriae legibus obsequimur.* There is a good deal to be said for a full stop after *poenas* and Havet's transposition of 586 and 587.

588. **mediaeque . . . urbem**: the city (called Salmone) in the middle of the region called Elis, which was specially associated with Jupiter Olympius.

590. **demens**: for the emphatic effect of a spondee filling the first foot cf. 172.

591. Salmoneus imitated thunder by driving horses over a bridge of bronze (Manil. 5.92).

593-4. **non ille ... lumina**: 'not torches he, nor flames of smoky pine', cf. 587. For the use of *ille* cf. *Aen.* 1.3, 5.457.

595. **Tityon**: the punishment of Tityos who assaulted the goddess Latona is told in Hom. *Od.* 11.576 f.; cf. also Lucr. 3.984 f., Hor. *Odes* 3.4.77 f.

596. **cernere erat**: 'it was possible to see', a common construction of the verb 'to be' in Greek, apparently mainly colloquial in Latin.

598. **immortale**: this aspect of the story is stressed in the passage in Lucretius (3.984 f.), and is reminiscent of the Prometheus legend (Hes. *Theog.* 523).

599. **rimaturque epulis habitatque**: 'both gropes for its feast and lives permanently. . . .'; for *rimari* cf. *Geo.* 1.384, for *-que . . . -que* cf. line 556.

601 f. 'Why should I mention the Lapiths, Ixion and Pirithous, above whom a black rock looms, ever about to totter and most like to fall?' The punishment of the tottering rock and the forbidden food (603 f.) is of course normally associated with Tantalus (hence our word 'tantalise'). Ixion (who assaulted Juno) is generally stretched out on a wheel (616–17) and Pirithous (see note on 122–3) confined in chains (Hor. *Odes* 3.4.79–80); they were two of the Lapiths, a Thessalian people best known for their battle against the Centaurs. The discrepancy with the normal legends has led to emendation of the text, with the postulation of a lacuna in which Tantalus was mentioned and the reading of *quo* (with *R*) for *quos*, or to the transposition of 616–20 after 601 (cf. Val. Fl. 2.192 f., Stat. *Th.* 1.712 f.). But it seems more likely that Virgil has varied the legends or accepted some unusual version.

602. **cadentique**: the hypermetric elision helps to convey the overhang of the rock; see note on *Aen.* 1.332.

603. **adsimilis**: cf. *Aen.* 5.254 *anhelanti similis*, 12.754 *similisque tenenti*.

603-4. 'On high festive couches golden posts shine resplendent, and before his gaze banquets of regal luxury are displayed'. *Genialis torus* would normally be associated with marriage, but here is used in a very general sense (cf. *Geo.* 1.302).

605. **regificos**: a very rare word meaning 'regal'; for the formation cf. *magnificus*.

Furiarum maxima: 'the oldest of the Furies', a vague phrase not intended to be identified. It was used of the Harpy Celaeno in *Aen.* 3.252, and Servius sees here a reference to *Fames*.

608 f. This list of types of sinners is partly based on Greek tradition but is also related to Roman ideas (cf. the corresponding list of the blessed in Elysium, 660 f.). The ties of family life are emphasised in 608–9; the legal obligation of a *patronus* towards his *cliens* (one of the items of the Twelve Tables) in 609, the expectation of the unselfish use of riches (cf. *Geo.* 2.507, Hor. *Odes* 2.2) in 610–11; then the relationship with Roman history becomes closer with the reference to adultery in 612 (no doubt Augustus' moral reforms which culminated in the *Leges Iuliae* of 18 B.C. were already in the air), to civil war in 612–13 and to the arming of run-away slaves by Sextus Pompey (Hor. *Epod.* 9.9–10) in 613.

610. **repertis**: 'gained', cf. 718.

613. **impia**: a normal term for civil war, cf. *Aen.* 1.294, *Geo.* 1.511.

615. **aut quae ... mersit**: 'or the shape of punishment, the fortune which has overwhelmed them'. For *forma* cf. 626; the indicative is unusual in an indirect question, instances like 779 being rather easier; cf. Prop. 3.5.27 f.

616–17. The punishment of for ever rolling a stone up a hill and seeing it come bounding back was traditional for Sisyphus. To be stretched out on a wheel is normally Ixion's fate, but unless we accept a transposition of lines or a lacuna (see note on 601 f.) we must regard the wheel as here assigned to some other sinner than Ixion.

617–18. Virgil has here departed from the normal legend, which was that Theseus, punished for attempting to carry off Proserpina (see note on 122, where the normal version is implied), was rescued by Hercules from the chair to which he was fixed. The passage is discussed by Hyginus in Aul. Gell. 10.16 as an error by Virgil. Servius' comment is 'frequenter variant fabulas poetae'.

618. Phlegyas, ancestor of the Lapiths, was punished for setting fire to Apollo's temple at Delphi.

621 f. After the mythological figures of 616–20 Virgil returns

to generalised crimes with possible application to the contemporary Roman world; various allegorical interpretations have been suggested from Servius' time onwards (621–2 Curio, Caesar's tribune, cf. Lucan 4.824; 622 Mark Antony) but Virgil is not in any way specific. Lines 621–2 are said by Macrobius to have been adapted by Virgil from a work of his friend Varius.

625–6. **non . . . vox**: repeated from *Geo.* 2.43–4, and based on Homer, *Il.* 2.488 f., Ennius *Ann.* 561–2.

628–36. *Aeneas and the Sibyl turn away from Tartarus and enter Elysium.*

629. **carpe viam**: 'hasten along the way', cf. *Geo.* 3.347 and *corripere* in 634.

630–1. **Cyclopum . . . portas**: this is the entrance to Elysium, impassable to the living except with the talisman of the golden bough. It was constructed (*educta*, cf. *Aen.* 2.461, 12.674) by Vulcan and his Cyclopes in their forges (cf. *Aen.* 8.418 f.).

632. 'where they bid us to place our appointed offerings', i.e. the bough. This is more natural than to take *praecepta* as the subject of *iubent* — 'where our instructions bid us. . .'.

633. **per opaca viarum**: 'through the darkness of the paths'; for the use of the neuter plural of the adjective as a noun see note on 1.422 and cf. *Aen.* 2.725.

637–78. *The Sibyl and Aeneas reach the Groves of the Blessed in Elysium, where idyllic scenes meet their eyes. They are directed to Anchises.*

637 f. The description of Elysium is partly based on Homer (*Od.* 4.561 f.), but there are also strong Orphic elements indicated by the presence of Orpheus himself and his disciple Musaeus, recalling passages in Pindar (e.g. *Ol.* 2.61 f.) and Plato (e.g. *Phaed.* 114b). As in the description of Tartarus the mention of specific individuals is varied with the enumeration of categories of people (660 f.); the contrast between the gloom of Homer's underworld, to which all save those of divine descent must go, and the bright light of Virgil's Elysium, open to all whose virtue in life qualifies them, is very great indeed. Virgil has used all his skill in diction and metre to build up a picture of peace and serenity, contrasting very markedly with the gloom and sorrow of Aeneas' journey up to now.

637. **perfecto ... divae**: 'when the offering to the goddess had been duly made', i.e. the golden bough to Proserpina.

638–9. Notice the juxtaposition of nouns and adjectives with similar endings, see note on 268 f.

640. 'An atmosphere that is more bounteous and of brilliant radiance clothes these plains'; *et* links *largior* with the ablative of description (equivalent to a compound adjective) *lumine purpureo*. Virgil is recalling Homer's description of Olympus (*Od.* 6.44 f.); cf. also Lucr. 3.18 f. For *vestit* cf. Lucr. 2.148.

642 f. Cf. Milton, *P.L.* 2.528 f. (the fallen angels):

> Part on the Plain, or in the Air sublime
> Upon the wing, or in swift race contend,
> As at th' Olympian Games or Pythian fields;
> Part curb thir fierie steeds, or shun the Goal
> With rapid wheels, or fronted Brigads form.

643. This line elaborates the wrestling (*palaestra*) of the previous line.

644. **pedibus ... choreas**: 'beat out the dances with their feet'; notice the imitative alliteration. *Choreas* is an extended cognate accusative (cf. 517); the *e* is generally long (*Aen.* 9.615, 10.224) but cf. Tib. 1.3.59. Compare Milton, *P.L.* 2.546 f.:

> Others more mild,
> Retreated in a silent valley, sing
> With notes Angelical to many a Harp ...

645. The Thracian priest, Orpheus (see notes on 119, 120) is here in Elysium not only as the patron of music, but also as the legendary founder of the Orphic religious beliefs expounded by Anchises (724 f.).

646–7. 'plays as accompaniment to the rhythm the seven distinct notes, plucking them now with his fingers, now with his ivory plectrum'. The ancient lyre had seven strings and Orpheus plays his lyre to accompany (*obloquitur*, cf. Lucr. 4.981) the songs.

648. **Teucri**: an early ancestor of the Trojans, like Dardanus (650); cf. 500 and see notes on 1.38, 3.167–8.

649. **nati melioribus annis**: cf. Cat. 64.22.

650. Ilus was grandfather of Priam and Assaracus of Anchises (Hom. *Il.* 20.232 f.).

651. **inanis**: 'phantom' (269), rather than 'empty' (1.476).

653. **currum**: contracted for *curruum*.

657. **paeana**: a song of joy originally in honour of Apollo: the Greek loan word has the Greek form of the accusative; cf. *Aen*. 10.738.

658. **lauris**: the reading of *G*, preferable to the *lauri* of most MSS, cf. *Geo*. 3.334.

658–9. 'from which source the mighty river Eridanus flows up through the forest to the world above'. Eridanus is the river Padus (Po); cf. *Geo*. 1.482, 4.366 f.

660 f. This generalised list is parallel to those in Tartarus (612 f., 621 f.); it indicates the chief point of difference between Virgil's Elysium and Homer's (*Od*. 4.563 f.), in that here the entrance is open not only to those of divine descent but to all those whose merits qualify them.

660. **manus ... passi**: a rather striking example of *constructio ad sensum*, *manus* being equivalent to *viri*.

662. **vates**: here 'poets', under the patronage of Apollo, cf. 669.

663–4. 'or those who enriched life by finding new ways of living it, and those who made people remember them by their service'. These are very wide categories indeed, making Elysium potentially open to all mankind; cf. Aug. *Civ. Dei* 21.27. For *excolere* cf. Cic. *Tusc*. 1.62, *Rep*. 6.18; for *artes* (not 'skills' or 'arts' but the good way of life) cf. the common use of *bonae artes*, and Hor. *Odes* 4.15.12 *veteres ... artes* ('the traditional way of life'). *Aliquos* has much stronger MSS support than the variant *alios*.

667. **Musaeum**: like Orpheus, a legendary poet and musician, cf. Plato *Apol*. 41a, *Rep*. 363c.

667–8. **medium ... habet**: 'for a dense crowd had him in their midst', i.e. he was easily identifiable as someone of importance.

670. **illius ergo**: 'for him'; the archaic preposition *ergo* (like *causa*) takes the genitive and follows its noun, cf. Lucr. 3.78.

671. **tranavimus**: see note on 16.

674. **riparumque toros**: 'river banks to recline on', cf. *Aen*. 5.388. In general cf. Spenser, *F.Q.* 4.10.24.

679–702. *Aeneas meets Anchises, who is surveying the unborn ghosts of his Roman descendants. Father and son welcome each other.*

679 f. Here Aeneas' journey through the underworld ends. He has travelled through the sorrows of his past in order to learn

from Anchises of his future. As father and son face each other, Anchises rejoices in the triumph of *pietas*; Aeneas however is still bewildered and lonely, indeed in need of the full confidence and pride in his mission which his father is soon to give him.

680. These are the ghosts waiting by the river of Lethe for rebirth, cf. 703 f., 748 f.

681. **studio recolens**: 'eagerly surveying them', for *studio* cf. *Aen.* 5.450, 12.131.

683. **moresque manusque**: 'and their characters and feats'.

685. **alacris**: archaic form of *alacer*, cf. *Aen.* 5.380.

687–8. 'and has your devotion to duty, awaited by your father, overcome the hard toil of the journey?' This phrase summarises the first half of the *Aeneid*; it has indeed been *iter durum* and it has indeed been *pietas* that has prevailed.

689. 'to hear your familiar voice and make reply', cf. *Aen.* 1.409.

691. **nec . . . fefellit**: 'nor has my anxious hope misled me'.

692–3. 'Over what lands and what mighty seas have you travelled to reach my welcoming arms'; cf. Cat. 101.1. For the postponement of *per* (which governs *terras* as well as *aequora*) cf. *Aen.* 5.512.

694. Anchises' fears about Aeneas' stay in Carthage with Dido were indeed justified: this was the hardest part of the journey for his *pietas* to overcome.

695. The ghost of Anchises appeared to Aeneas in sleep while he was in Carthage (4.351 f.) and after the burning of the ships in Sicily (5.722 f.).

696. **limina**: accusative of motion towards, cf. *Aen.* 1.553.

697. Aeneas says that his fleet is on the Tyrrhenian Sea (west of Italy) to explain that his voyage to Hesperia is complete.

698. **teque . . . nostro**: these are almost the same words (with *amplexu* for *aspectu*) which Aeneas had used to Dido's ghost (465).

700–2. These lines are repeated from *Aen.* 2.792–4 (see notes there), where they are used of Creusa's ghost. The loneliness of Aeneas is very strongly stressed in this passage.

703–51. *Aeneas sees a great concourse of ghosts at the river Lethe, and asks Anchises what this means. Anchises explains that they are waiting for rebirth, and gives an account of the soul's relationship with the body, and what happens to it after death.*

703 f. The famous account of the purification and transmigration of souls is presented in diction which often recalls Lucretius but offers a view of life after death directly opposed to the Epicurean view of the destruction of the soul at death. Anchises' speech is based largely on Orphic and Pythagorean ideas of purification and rebirth, especially as expressed by Plato (*Rep.* 10.614 f., *Phaed.* 113 f., *Phaedr.* 248 f., *Gorg.* 493 f.). Roman Stoicism had much in common with these Greek doctrines, and phraseology that is especially Stoic is sometimes used (*spiritus intus*, *igneus vigor*; we are reminded of the Stoic passage in *Geo.* 4.219 f.).

The speech serves, as has often been pointed out, as a convenient piece of 'machinery' to introduce the pageant of Roman heroes waiting to be reborn; but its significance is far wider than that. It expresses a picture of hope after death, of virtue rewarded; it offers something of an explanation for the unexplained suffering of this life. With its emphasis on how the soul is defiled and tainted by the body (its tomb or prison) it reverses the Homeric attitude, and it brings Aeneas away from the heroic world to the spiritual climate of Virgil's own times.

For further discussion see Bailey, *Religion in Virgil*, pp. 275 f., Guthrie, *Orpheus and Greek Religion*, pp. 157 f., Otis, *Virgil*, pp. 300 f.

705. Lethe is the river of forgetfulness (Plato, *Rep.* 621a); Virgil indicates the meaning of the Greek word with *oblivia* (715) and *immemores* in 750. Cf. Milton, *P.L.* 2.582 f.

> 'Far off from these a slow and silent stream,
> Lethe the River of Oblivion roules
> Her watrie Labyrinth, whereof who drinks,
> Forthwith his former state and being forgets . . .'

praenatat: 'flows past'; for *natare* cf. Enn. *Ann.* 596, Lucr. 5.488, and for the force of *prae* (=*praeter*) Hor. *Odes* 4.3.10.

707 f. For the bee simile cf. Hom. *Il.* 2.87 f., Ap. Rh. 1.879 f., and note on *Aen.* 1.430 f.

707. **ac velut**: for this way of introducing a simile ('and it was as when') cf. *Aen.* 2.626 f., 4.402 f.

711. **porro**: 'in the distance', an unusual and apparently archaic use, cf. Plaut. *Rud.* 1034; compare the somewhat similar usage in *Aen.* 5.600.

713. Anchises' explanation of the doctrine of transmigration of souls (*altera corpora*) is given more fully in 724 f.; see note on 703 f.

715. **securos latices**: 'the draught that takes away their cares'; cf. Plato *Rep.* 621a where Lethe is called Ameles, the river that removes cares.

718. 'so that you may rejoice the more with me now that you have found Italy'; so far Aeneas has had little cause for joy.

719–20. **ad caelum ... sublimis**: 'aloft to the upper world', cf. 896.

721. Aeneas' sufferings during his mission are reflected in his astonished question — how could anyone possibly want to be back in the upper world?

724 f. For Anchises' speech see note on 703 f.

724. **principio**: a Lucretian way of introducing an explanation (cf. e.g. Lucr. 5.92).

camposque liquentis: a poetic periphrasis for the sea; cf. Lucr. 6.1142, *Geo.* 3.198.

725. **Titaniaque astra**: Titan's stars are the sun and the stars, cf. *Aen.* 4.119, where the sun is called Titan. Some think that the reference is to the sun alone, but the plural (though it can be paralleled, Ov. *Met.* 14.172) would be awkward.

726–7. 'and flowing through its members a mind sets the mass in motion and mingles with the mighty structure'; cf. Tennyson, *To Virgil*, 'Thou that seest Universal / Nature moved by Universal Mind'; Wordsworth, *Tintern Abbey*, 'A motion and a spirit, that impels / All thinking things, all objects of all thought, / And rolls through all things'; Pope, *Essay on Man* (1.267–8) 'All are but parts of one stupendous whole, / Whose body Nature is, and God the soul'.

728. **inde**: i.e. from the *spiritus* and *mens*, cf. *Geo.* 4.221 f.

vitaeque volantum: 'the lives of flying creatures', a poetic periphrasis (in the Lucretian style) for birds, cf. Lucr. 2.1083.

730–1. 'Those seeds have a fiery force and an origin in heaven, insofar as. . . .'; *igneus* is a Stoic term for the divine fire of the world soul, the *spiritus intus*, the *anima mundi*; cf. 747.

733. **hinc**: i.e. from the body, which causes mortal emotions far removed from things spiritual; cf. Cic. *Tusc.* 3.11, Hor. *Epist.* 1.6.12.

auras: the air of heaven.

734. The concept of the body as a prison-house (or a tomb) goes back to Orphic belief and is expressed by Plato; cf. Plato *Crat.* 400c, *Phaed.* 66b. Compare Wordsworth, *Intimations of Immortality*: 'Shades of the prison-house begin to close / Upon the growing Boy'.

735. **cum . . . reliquit**: = *eo tempore quo*, cf. 515.

737-8.. 'and it is necessary that many taints, long associated with the body, must be deeply ingrained in wondrous ways'; *penitus* goes with *inolescere*, *concreta* (cf. 746) means 'growing up with', hence 'associated with'. For *inolescere* cf. *Geo.* 2.77; *modis . . . miris* is a Lucretian phrase, see note on *Aen.* 1.354.

739. **exercentur**: 'they are disciplined', contrast the construction in 543. The lines which follow describe the three forms of discipline or purification — by air, water, and fire.

742. **infectum . . . scelus**: 'the stain of crime', the crime with which they have been stained; cf. Cic. *Att.* 1.13.3.

743 f. Many editors punctuate so that lines 743-4 are parenthetical, and *donec* in 745 depends on the verbs in 740-2. This gives a contorted sentence, and it is much preferable to take the passage in the order in which it is presented, with *donec* dependent on *tenemus*. The meaning is that those who are nearly spotless stay in Elysium until they are quite spotless and then depart for the ultimate heaven. The others pass through Elysium and then wait by the river for rebirth. Elysium, in the underworld, is the penultimate paradise — the real paradise is in heaven (cf. Plato, *Phaed.* 114c). I have argued this point in detail in *Greece and Rome*, 1964, 57 f.

743. **quisque suos patimur manes**: 'we all endure our own ghosts', i.e. are guiltily aware of the imperfections of our souls, stained and blotched with earthly sins.

746-7. 'and has left unsullied the ethereal spirit and the fire of pure air', i.e. removed the blemishes so that the soul is the pure Stoic fire which can return to God.

747. **aurai**: archaic genitive, common in Lucretius, used only four times in Virgil, cf. *Aen.* 3.354 (where see note), 7.464, 9.26.

748. Cf. Plato *Rep.* 10.615a, *Phaedr.* 248e.

rotam: the wheel of time, a phrase used in Orphic writings, said by Servius to occur in Ennius.

752–853. *Anchises points out to Aeneas the famous Romans who are waiting their turn to be born: the Alban kings, Romulus, Augustus, the Roman kings and many heroes of the Roman Republic.*

752 f. The pageant of Roman heroes is the most sustained of all the patriotic passages in the *Aeneid*: it is comparable with *Aen.* 1.257 f., 8.626 f., 12.819 f. (cf. also *Geo.* 2.149 f.). It is a list of *exempla* familiar in rhetorical writing, owing something too to visual art, to friezes and groups of statues. But Virgil has trans-figured these sources into majestic and sonorous poetry. His structural method is to interweave crowd scenes (the Alban kings, the Roman kings, the many heroes of the Republic) with descriptions where the spot-light is focussed on single individuals (Romulus, Augustus, Brutus, Caesar and Pompey); thus he has given form and shape to his emotional and intellectual presenta-tion of the character of Rome.

The description begins quietly with the distant antiquarian interest of the Alban kings, and it rises to a crescendo for Romulus, founder of Rome, great mother of men; then the crescendo swells to its loudest for Augustus, restorer of the Golden Age. The chronological sequence so far followed is thus broken, so that the second founder of Rome may follow the first. At this point the description breaks off as Anchises asks his son whether he still feels doubts or fears about his mission; Aeneas does not reply, but the reader can answer for him. There can be no further hesitation now — this is the decisive moment of the whole poem.

The next section begins with a crowd scene of Roman kings, followed by the spot-lit figure of Brutus. This is a very ambivalent passage: admiration for Brutus is muted by feelings of pathos (cf. Aug. *Civ. Dei.* 3.16), and in the *anima superba* of this early Brutus we surely feel an undertone of reference to his famous descendant, the assassin of Caesar. Virgil takes no political position, but he powerfully portrays the ambition as well as the idealism of such men — *laudumque immensa cupido*.

After another brief crowd scene the attention is focussed on Caesar and Pompey, and here again it is the tragedy of the situation that is stressed, not the rightness or wrongness of a cause. No attempt is made to blacken Pompey because of his association with the East (contrast Antony in *Aen.* 8.685 f.).

Finally we have the densest crowd scene of all, preparatory

to the famous passage outlining, with every justification, the contribution of Rome to world civilisation. It is interesting to compare the passage at the beginning of Cicero's *Tusculan Disputations* where Cicero concedes intellectual and literary dominance to the Greeks, but regards the Romans as superior in practical and ethical qualities (*mores, leges, res militaris, gravitas* etc.). These are proud claims which Anchises makes, — first to conquer in war, and then to establish a peace in which the people are ruled with mercy and given the benefits of Roman civilisation and settled ways of life (cf. *Aen.* 4.229 f.). Doubtless the Roman achievement of them was imperfect, but they constituted an ideal and a sense of calling which constantly illuminated the long centuries of the Roman Empire in the west.

755. **legere**: 'scan', cf. 34.

756. **deinde**: 'in the future', cf. 890.

760. **pura**: 'headless', with just the shaft; Servius quotes Varro to the effect that such a spear was given as a prize of valour to a young warrior for his first victory; it seems also to have been awarded for any special act of valour.

761. **proxima ... loca**: 'has allocated to him the next place in the world above', i.e. will be the first of the throng of ghosts to be reborn.

762. **Italo ... sanguine**: of Trojan descent 'mixed with Italian blood', i.e. son of the Trojan Aeneas and the Italian princess Lavinia (see note on 7.52 f.).

763. **Silvius, Albanum nomen**: i.e. the kings of Alba Longa were all called Silvius (cf. 769, Livy 1.3) as their dynasty name, here derived by Virgil (765) from the circumstances of the birth of this son of Lavinia (cf. Ov. *Fast.* 4.41 f., Livy 1.3.6). The tradition about him varied; according to Livy he was a son of Ascanius, according to Virgil and Dionysius a younger brother of Ascanius. In *Aen.* 1.267 f. Ascanius is clearly designated as the first king of Alba Longa; he cannot be mentioned here because he is already on earth, so the list starts with his successor Silvius.

763. **postuma**: 'latest-born' (Aul. Gell. 2.16.5) not 'posthumous' (Servius).

767. **proximus ... Procas**: i.e. he is standing next to Silvius, not next to be born (he was late in the order of the Alban kings, later than Capys).

768. **Numitor**: Numitor was the last Alban king, grandfather of Romulus (777). For the lengthening in arsis of the last syllable of *Numitor* cf. 254.

769. **pariter**: equally with Aeneas, rather than equally for devotion and valour.

770. Servius tells the story that the guardian of Silvius Aeneas usurped the throne from him for a long time.

regnandam: used transitively as in 793, *Aen.* 3.14.

772. **civili ... quercu**: the 'civic crown' of oak, awarded to a Roman who had saved a fellow citizen's life in war. It had been voted to Augustus as a perpetual honour in 27 B.C., and adorned the portals of his palace (Ov. *Fast.* 1.614, *Trist.* 3.1.36).

773 f. These are little towns near Rome, some of them deserted by Virgil's time; their impact on the Roman reader would be one of parochial affection. Fidena normally has a long *i* and the plural form *Fidenae*; *Collatinus* is the adjective of Collatia.

776. Cf. Milton, *P.L.* 12.140 (Michael's speech) 'Things by their names I call, though yet unnam'd.'

777. **avo**: Numitor (768), the father of Ilia, who had been deposed by his brother Amulius. His grandchildren Romulus and Remus were thrown into the Tiber, but survived and restored Numitor to his kingdom.

Mavortius: Romulus was son of Mars and Ilia; this is the archaic form of the adjective *Martius*, cf. 1.276, 3.13.

778. **Assaraci ... Ilia**: for Assaracus, a Trojan ancestor, cf. 650; Ilia is the Trojan name (cf. *Aen.* 1.274) of Rhea Silvia, the Vestal Virgin who was mother of the twins.

779–80. 'Do you see how the twin crests stand out from his head and the father of the gods himself marks him out already with his special emblem?' *Viden* is contracted for *videsne*, (note that the second syllable is short), and is followed by the indicative in parataxis, *viden ut* being equivalent to *ecce*, cf. Cat. 61.77–8, and lines 855 f. *Superum* is archaic genitive, cf. *Aen.* 1.4; others following Servius take it as accusative, so that the meaning would be that Mars marks Romulus out as a god. But *superus* in the singular in this sense is not paralleled, and the *honos* is probably Jupiter's thunderbolt rather than any emblem of Mars. The phrase *geminae ... cristae* perhaps signifies reconciliation with Remus.

782. Cf. *Aen.* 1.287 and Milton, *P.L.* 12.370–1 'and bound his Reign / With earths wide bounds, his glory with the Heav'ns'.

783. 'and being a single city shall encircle her seven citadels with a wall'; the reference is to the unity of the city of seven distinct hills.

784 f. Rome, the great mother of men (cf. *Geo.* 2.167 f.), is compared with Cybele, the Great Mother of the gods, whose special worship was at Mt. Berecynthus in the Troad (*Phrygias . . . urbes*); see note on 3.111 f., and cf. 2.788, 9.82, 10.252. The second point of comparison in the simile is the turret-like diadem of the goddess and the turreted defence walls of Rome (cf. Lucr. 2.606 f.). Compare Spenser, *Ruines of Rome* 6: 'Such as the Berecynthian Goddesse bright / in her swift charret with high turrets crownde, / proud that so manie Gods she brought to light'.

789. **Caesar**: i.e. Augustus, picked up in *hic vir hic est* ('yes, this is indeed. . .'). It is impossible to maintain that this is Julius, because he occurs later in the pageant (826 f.). Augustus is at first among the other descendants of Iulus (789–90), and then is picked out alone (791). His position next to Romulus breaks the chronology and emphasises his status as second founder of Rome (Suet. *Aug.* 7).

791. **hic vir hic est**: notice that the second *hic* is short, cf. *Aen.* 4.22.

792. **divi genus**: Julius Caesar was deified after his death, and Augustus, his adopted son, received the title *divi filius*.

792. Strong emphasis is put on *aurea* by its position at the head of the relative clause, with *qui* postponed to fourth place. The restored golden age is prophesied in *Ecl.* 4 (esp. 6 f.), and in more general terms in *Aen.* 1.286 f. For the original golden age under Saturnus cf. *Geo.* 2.538 f., *Aen.* 8.319 f., esp. 324.

794. **Garamantas**: Greek accusative with short final syllable. These were an African people (cf. *Aen.* 4.198, *Ecl.* 8.44) conquered by the Romans in 19 B.C., but this is no certain reason for dating this passage as late as that.

794. **Indos**: cf. Prop. 2.10.15, where India is mentioned with Parthia and Arabia as an area of Augustus' triumphs.

795. **iacet . . . tellus**: an elliptical and evocative phrase, *tellus* being logically equivalent to 'the land which he will rule', i.e. his empire will extend beyond the known world, beyond the path of the Zodiac.

797. This line, based on Ennius, is repeated from *Aen.* 4.482, where see notes.

798–9. 'At the prospect of his arrival even now the Caspian realms shudder because of oracular responses, and the Maeotian land too'; these are the areas of the Scythians and the Parthians, the north-eastern boundary of Rome's empire. There is possibly a reference to the recovery of the standards from the Parthians in 20 B.C.

800. **septemgemini . . . Nili**: the adjective refers to the Nile's delta, cf. Cat. 11.7; the whole line is particularly significant because of Augustus' victory over Egypt at the battle of Actium. Notice the emphasis given by alliteration of *t*.

turbant: intransitive, 'are in confusion', cf. Lucr. 2.126, Cic. *Fin.* 1.34.

801 f. The point of comparing Augustus with Hercules (Alcides) and Bacchus (Liber) is (i) they all made their influence felt over very large areas; (ii) they were all connected with civilising activities; (iii) they were all mortals destined to become gods (Hor. *Odes* 3.3.9 f.).

802. **fixerit . . . licet**: 'although he transfixed the bronze-footed stag'; this and the following two phrases refer to three of Hercules' labours, the stag of Cerynaia (Arcadia), the wild boar of Erymanthus (also Arcadia), and the hydra of Lerna in Argos.

804–5. 'nor he who victorious guides his yoked animals with reins of vine-shoots, Liber, driving his tigers from the lofty summit of Nysa'; for Bacchus' exploits see note on 801 f. Mt. Nysa (in India) is where Bacchus' worship was said to have originated (the name Nysa was subsequently used of other centres of his cult). The yoking of tigers suggests the power of civilisation over wild nature (cf. Hor. *Odes* 3.3.13 f.).

806–7. The interpolation by Anchises of this query is enormously significant: the vision of Augustus must surely dispel any lingering doubts or frailties. Some MSS have *virtute extendere vires* but cf. *Aen.* 10.468.

808 f. The description of Numa Pompilius, second king of Rome, emphasises the peaceful (*ramis . . . olivae*) and religious (*sacra ferens*) aspect of this successor to Romulus, son of Mars, the war-god. Cf. Livy 1.18 f., Ov. *Met.* 15.482 f. Numa is the embodiment of Jupiter's promise in *Aen.* 12.836–7 *morem ritusque sacrorum / adiciam.*

810–11. **primam ... fundabit**: 'will establish the little city on the basis of laws', cf. *Aen.* 4.231, Livy 1.19.1.

811. **Curibus**: Cures was a little town of the Sabine territory, said to have given the Romans their name *Quirites*, cf. *Aen.* 7.710.

812 f. The tradition about Tullus Hostilius, third king of Rome, was concentrated on military exploits (Livy 1.22, Juv. 5.57); nothing is known about why Ancus Marcius, the fourth king, should be called boastful and overfond of popularity.

816. **popularibus auris**: a common metaphor (=*favore*) in prose and verse.

817. **Tarquinios reges**: the fifth (Tarquinius Priscus) and seventh (Tarquinius Superbus) kings of Rome. Servius Tullius, the sixth king, is omitted because of the bracketing of the Tarquins; in a sense he is included in their dynasty.

animamque ... Bruti: the first consul of Rome (509 B.C.), who expelled Tarquin the Proud and 'recovered authority' for the people. The story of the rape of Lucretia (which led to the expulsion) by Sextus, son of Tarquin the Proud, is told by Shakespeare, *Rape of Lucrece*. The transference of Tarquin's epithet (*superbus*) to Brutus, his avenger, is paradoxical and thought-provoking (see note on 752 f.). The punctuation of Norden and others (based on Servius), with a comma after *superbam*, so that the epithet goes with Tarquin, gives a quite impossible word order for the next line.

818. **fascesque**: the rods symbolising authority (*Geo.* 2.495, *Aen.* 7.173), wrapped round an axe (819), which were carried by the consul's lictors in the Roman Republic.

820 f. The story of how Brutus' sons joined Tarquin in his efforts to return to Rome is told in Livy 2.5. Brutus as consul had to put them to death for their rebellion (notice the savage alliteration of *p* in 821), and Virgil reflects with compassion rather than pride on Brutus' devotion to duty.

822. **ferent**: 'will extol', as did Livy and Valerius Maximus (5.8), and doubtless many rhetorical declamations.

823. **laudumque ... cupido**: an expansion of *amor patriae* couched in unexpectedly unfavourable terms. Virgil seems to suggest that the desire to show extreme devotion to duty may be activated by unworthy motives of a too inflexible kind. Servius comments: 'non extorquere vim naturae debet amor patriae'.

824-5. The Decii (father and son) devoted themselves to death on the battlefield (Livy 8.9, 10.28); the Drusi were one of the most famous Roman families of all (Augustus' wife Livia was one of their number); Torquatus, who won his *cognomen* from having killed a giant Gaul in combat (Livy 7.10) and stripped him of his necklace (*torques*), later put his sons to death for having fought out of line (Livy 8.7); Camillus recovered Rome from the Gauls after they had taken it, according to the Roman version (Livy 5.49 f.), and regained the standards captured at the River Allia.

826 f. The identity of Caesar and Pompey (opponents in the civil war — *paribus . . . in armis*, both wearing Roman armour, cf. *Geo.* 1.489) is not specified until 830-1 by the words *socer . . . gener* (cf. Cat. 29.24); this refers to Pompey's marriage to Caesar's daughter Julia.

826. **fulgere**: for the unusual third conjugation form see on 4.409, and cf. Lucr. 5.1095.

830. **aggeribus . . . Alpinis**: Caesar invaded Italy from Gaul (i.e. past the Alps and Monaco) and across the Rubicon.

831. **adversis . . . Eois**: 'with Eastern troops to face his enemy'; Pompey had withdrawn to Greece to collect additional forces.

832. **ne . . . bella**: 'do not make such great wars habitual in your thoughts'; this is a rare variation of construction for *ne adsuescite animos bellis* (as in *Aen.* 9.201). Cf. Hor. *Sat.* 2.2.109.

833. The alliteration of *v* to help to convey the notion of violence is overpowering here. For *viscera* we would say 'heart'.

834-5. Anchises speaks to both Pompey and Caesar, but especially to Caesar, direct descendant of himself and the Olympian goddess Venus. The feeling of pathos is intensified by Anchises' personal appeal; this is the first time he has addressed the ghosts he is describing.

836 f. This section concerns the conquerors of Greece, and the references are all relevant to Aeneas' own times (*Achivis, Argos, Agamemnoniasque Mycenas, Aeaciden, Achilli, Troiae templa*); the burning of Troy will ultimately be avenged. Compare *Aen.* 1.283-5.

836-7. 'That Roman over there will triumph over Corinth and victoriously drive his chariot to the lofty Capitol'. *Corinthus* is feminine, and *triumphatus* treated transitively (cf. *Geo.* 3.33). The reference is to Mummius who celebrated a triumph for his victory over Corinth in 146 B.C. (cf. Hor. *Epist.* 2.1.193).

838. ille: Aemilius Paullus, the Roman general who defeated King Perseus of Macedonia at the battle of Pydna in 168 B.C. Perseus claimed descent from Achilles (grandson of Aeacus); cf. Prop. 4.11.39.

Mycenas: Agamemnon's capital, cf. *Aen.* 1.284.

839. Achilli: for the form of the genitive see note on 1.30.

840. The reference is to the violation of Minerva's temple in Troy by Ajax, son of Oileus; see notes on 1.41 and 2.403 f.

841. magne Cato: the elder Cato (the censor); his implacable hostility to Carthage begins the Carthaginian theme that occurs several times in the next few lines.

Cossus: one of the three Romans (see note on 855) who won the *spolia opima*; this was in 428 B.C. (Livy 4.19).

842. Gracchi genus: probably not merely the two famous brothers, but their immediate ancestors who achieved military glory in the Second Punic War and afterwards, and indeed their mother Cornelia (daughter of Scipio), proverbial model of a Roman matron.

842-3. Scipio Africanus the elder won the final battle of the Second Punic War at Zama in 202 B.C.; Scipio Africanus the younger (Aemilianus) destroyed Carthage in the Third Punic War. For *fulmina belli* cf. Cic. *Balb.* 34; Lucr. 3.1034.

844. Fabricium: the Roman general against Pyrrhus in the early third century B.C., a type of *iustitia* (the Roman Aristides) and *parsimonia* (Cic. *Tusc.* 3.56, Val. Max. 4.3.6).

Serranus was the cognomen of Regulus, famous Roman commander in the First Punic War who left his plough to become consul (like Cincinnatus); Virgil derives his cognomen from *serere* ('to sow').

845-6. 'Where do you hasten my weary gaze, you Fabii? You surely are the famous Fabius the Great, the one man who saved our state by delaying'. The *gens Fabia* was famous in early Republican times (Livy 2.48 f.), and Quintus Fabius Maximus Cunctator was the Roman general who after the disasters at Trasimene and Cannae saved the Romans from Hannibal by his delaying tactics (Livy 22 *passim*). His position of honour at the end of the pageant is due to the fact that he saved Rome from the greatest enemy in all her history; he exorcises the memory of Dido's curse *exoriare aliquis nostris ex ossibus ultor* (4.625). Virgil presents his achievement in an adapted quotation from Ennius (*Ann.* 370) *unus homo nobis cunctando restituit rem*, thus reinforcing the mood of antiquity and history, and paying tribute to his great predecessor in Roman national poetry.

847 f. The 'others' referred to are the Greeks, and their achievements in sculpture (bronze or marble), oratory, and astronomy are conceded by the Romans. When one thinks of the Roman achievement in portraiture in stone, and in oratory (the most practical of the branches of literature, in which Cicero might well be pitted against Demosthenes), it seems that Anchises does less than justice in these matters to his own people — doubtless so that the impact of what the Romans do claim may be all the greater.

847. 'others will beat out bronze so that it breathes in softer lines'; for *spirantia* cf. *Geo.* 3.34, Hor. *A.P.* 33, and Addison's lines 'Where the smooth chisel all its force has shown / And soften'd into flesh the rugged stone'.

850. **radio**: the rod used for geometry, cf. *Ecl.* 3.41.

851. 'But, Romans, never forget that government is your medium' (Day Lewis). This proud claim was amply justified by Augustus and his long line of successors.

852. **artes**: i.e. in place of the 'fine arts' the Roman will practice the art of government.

pacique imponere morem: 'to add civilisation to peace', not (with Fletcher) 'to add tradition to peace', i.e. make it customary. The reading *pacisque*, adopted by many editors, has no manuscript authority of any importance, nor does Servius support it (as used to be thought from a misreading of Servius).

For the dative after *imponere* cf. *Aen.* 2.619; for the singular *mos* in the sense of *mores* (cf. *Aen.* 1.264) or *cultus* compare *Aen.* 8.316 *quis neque mos neque cultus erat*. In these famous lines the bipartite nature of Rome's mission is clearly stated; first to establish peace by taming the proud, and secondly to offer a settled and civilised way of life in which the people are ruled with mercy.

854–92. *Anchises now mentions one more Roman hero, Marcellus, famed in the Second Punic War. Aeneas enquires about a sad figure*

*accompanying him, and is told that this is the young Marcellus, destined
to an early death.*

854 f. In this passage the *Aeneid* comes into its closest contact
with contemporary events. The death of Marcellus (see note on
861) in 23 B.C. was a deeply-felt tragedy for the Roman world;
it is very possible that Virgil himself attended the magnificent
funeral ceremonies in the Campus Martius. The tribute to him
by Anchises is filled with pathos, with Virgil's sense of sympathy
for the wastage of youthful death (as with Pallas, Lausus,
Euryalus); and its position immediately following the trumpet
notes of joyful pride in 851–3 presents the equipoise between
triumph and disaster which the *Aeneid* so constantly explores. It is
part of Virgil's special art to have given us, in Conway's words,
'this sudden gust of tragedy, when the sky at last seemed clear'.
In the corresponding position at the end of the second half of the
poem Virgil similarly mutes the long-awaited triumph of Aeneas
by concentrating our attention in the final lines of the poem not
on the victor but on the vanquished. Because of this it seems
unreasonable to suppose, as some do, that this passage was added
to Book 6 after the pageant of heroes had already been composed;
it is far more likely that these expressions of the joy and the sorrow
of Rome's history were planned together.

855–6. **aspice ut ... ingreditur**: for the parataxis see note
on 779–80.

855. **spoliis ... opimis**: the *spolia opima* ('rich spoils') were
awarded to a Roman general who killed the enemy general in
personal combat. They were first awarded to Romulus, and then
to Cossus (line 841); the third recipient was Marcellus, who
killed the general of the Insubrian Gauls (222 B.C.) and served with
distinction against Hannibal in the Second Punic War. Cf. Prop.
4.10.

858. **sistet eques**: the battle against the Gauls was mainly a
cavalry engagement (Plut. *Marcell.* 7).

859. The normal version was that the captured spoils should
be dedicated to Jupiter Feretrius; here Virgil follows a tradition
that they were dedicated to the deified Romulus (Quirinus). The
subject is discussed at length by Butler ad loc.

861. This is the Marcellus (son of Octavia, Augustus' sister)
who married Augustus' daughter Julia and was marked out as

his heir, but died at the age of 19 in 23 B.C. (cf. Prop. 3.18, Hor. *Odes* 1.12.45 f.). Servius and Donatus tell how Octavia burst into tears when Virgil read this passage to her and Augustus.

862. 'but his expression was not happy and his eyes were downcast'; *deiecto vultu* (ablative of description) depends on *lumina*.

865. **instar**: probably 'presence', in the sense of impressiveness, greatness; or possibly 'resemblance' to his ancestor. For the word see note on 2.15; it occurs very rarely indeed without an accompanying genitive.

869-71. 'The fates will only give the world a glimpse of him and will not allow him to live longer than that. You gods above, you decided that the Roman stock would be powerful beyond bounds if this gift should be hers to keep'. *Fuissent* is reported future perfect: *'nimium potens erit si dona propria fuerint'*, so *visa est superis nimium potens fore si . . . fuissent.*

872-3. 'What deep lamentation from the people will the Campus Martius send echoing up to the mighty city of Mars!' Marcellus was buried with extraordinary funeral honours (*funera*, 874) in Augustus' Mausoleum on the Campus Martius, adjacent to the Tiber; the word *Mavortis* goes with *urbem* but also defines the meaning of *campus* (for the archaic form cf. 777).

874. **praeterlabere**: the long slow word gives a solemn, pictorial effect; cf. *Geo.* 2.157 *fluminaque antiquos subterlabentia muros.*

876. **in tantum spe tollet**: 'raise so high in hope'; it is however very possible that *spe* is an archaic form of the genitive, cf. *Geo.* 1.208.

876-7. 'nor will the land of Romulus ever in the future feel so proud of any of its sons'; for *quondam* cf. Hor. *Sat.* 2.2.82, and compare the similar use of *olim* (e.g. *Aen.* 1.289).

882-3. 'Alas, unhappy boy, if only somehow you could break through harsh fate! You will be Marcellus'. With this punctuation line 882 is a wish (cf. 187) and the next three words give the identity of the youth, not yet specified but of course guessed by every Roman, so that their impact is overwhelming in their simplicity. Most editors punctuate with a comma after *rumpas*, so that *eris* is the apodosis of a condition. This affords no satisfactory sense ('if you could break through fate, you most certainly will be a Marcellus, a true Marcellus'). Page has an excellent note on the subject.

883–4. 'Let me strew lilies, radiant blossoms, with unsparing hand'; the construction is *date spargam* (cf. *Aen.* 4.683–4), and *flores* is in apposition to *lilia*. The alternative explanation ('give me lilies, let me strew radiant blossoms') gives an unnatural construction to *spargam*.

885. **accumulem**: 'load', cf. *Aen.* 5.532. Anchises, as Conington says, identifies himself with the mourners at the funeral on earth, long centuries hence.

889. 'fired his heart with love of the glory to come'; this line finely summarises the impetus given to Aeneas' resolution by the vision of his people's future.

891. **Laurentisque . . . populos**: the people in the area of King Latinus' settlement in Latium, see note on 5.797.

893–901. *There are two gates of Sleep leading out of the underworld, one of horn for true shades, and the other of ivory. Aeneas and the Sibyl leave by the ivory gate, and Aeneas rejoins his fleet and sails north to Caieta.*

893 f. The Gates of Sleep come from Homer: in *Odyssey* 19.562 f. Penelope tells of the gates of dreams, one of horn for true dreams and one of ivory for false dreams (κέρας, 'horn', being thought to be connected with 'fulfil', κραίνω; and ἐλέφας, 'ivory', with 'deceive', ἐλεφαίρομαι). This image has been adopted by Virgil to serve as a way of exit from the underworld as the cave of Avernus provided an entrance.

Many views have been expressed on why Aeneas and the Sibyl leave by the gate of false dreams. (We may leave on one side the view that the false gate must be used because the time is before midnight, and true dreams appear after midnight; it is doubtful whether this was a common belief in Virgil's day, and in any case it has no relevance to Virgil's text). On one level it is fully adequate to say that as Aeneas and the Sibyl are not *verae umbrae* they do not qualify for the horn gate; but there are other levels to be considered. Particularly we may note how this imagery concentrates the attention of the reader on dreams, so that in a sense we may regard the underworld as a dream or vision of Aeneas, personal to him (see Otis, *T.A.Ph.A.* 1959, pp. 173 f.). The book is thus a part of Aeneas' experience, a re-enactment of his past and a vision of his future; it profoundly affects his personality. Finally there is another level; possibly Virgil symbolises the uncertainty of his own religious vision, a dimly seen and groping concept, based on hope not faith, of virtue rewarded and suffering to some extent explained. This is far indeed from the gloom of Homer's ghosts, but far too from the certainty of religious conviction upon which Milton's *Paradise Lost* is based. Glover quotes 'The best in this kind are but shadows', and Fletcher 'We are such stuff as dreams are made on'.

895. **elephanto**: the quadrisyllabic ending adds to the Greek atmosphere here, see note on 1.651.

896. **ad caelum**: i.e. to our world, cf. 719. For the false dreams cf. 283–4.

897–8. **his ... dictis**: i.e. with the instructions he had been giving (890 f.).

899. **viam secat**: cf. Lucr. 5.272, *Geo.* 1.238, *Aen.* 12.368, and (somewhat differently) 5.658.

900. **Caietae**: well north of Cumae, on the way to the Tiber. The name is derived (*Aen.* 7.2) from Aeneas' nurse who died on their arrival there.

recto ... litore: 'straight along the shore', ablative of route, cf. *recto flumine* (8.57). Some editors accept *limite* from inferior MSS, to avoid the repetition with 901, but the stop-gap nature of 901 (repeated from 3.277) is sufficient explanation of this; see also note on 1.429.

Index to the Notes

Reference is given to the main note or notes on each subject, where further references will often be found. There are separate sub-headings under 'metre' and 'prosody'.

A full index of proper names is to be found in Mynors's Oxford Text, and there is a complete word-index of Virgil's works by M. N. Wetmore (New Haven, 1930).